THE
INDIAN CALENDAR

THE
INDIAN CALENDAR

WITH TABLES FOR THE CONVERSION OF HINDU AND MUHAMMADAN INTO A.D. DATES, AND VICE VERSÂ

ROBERT SEWELL
SANKARA BALKRISHNA DIKSHIT

With Tables of Eclipses Visible in India
BY

Dr. ROBERT SCHRAM

MOTILAL BANARSIDASS PUBLISHERS
PRIVATE LIMITED • DELHI

First Indian Edition: Delhi, 1995

ISBN: 81-208-1207-1

Also available at:

MOTILAL BANARSIDASS
41 U.A. Bungalow Road, Jawahar Nagar, Delhi 110 007
120 Royapettah High Road, Mylapore, Madras 600 004
16 St. Mark's Road, Bangalore 560 001
Ashok Rajpath, Patna 800 004
Chowk, Varanasi 221 001

PRINTED IN INDIA

BY JAINENDRA PRAKASH JAIN AT SHRI JAINENDRA PRESS,
A-45 NARAINA, PHASE I, NEW DELHI 110 028
AND PUBLISHED BY NARENDRA PRAKASH JAIN FOR
MOTILAL BANARSIDASS PUBLISHERS PVT. LTD.,
BUNGALOW ROAD, DELHI 110 007

FOREWORD

During the past decades considerable progress has been made in understanding and evaluating Indian astronomy and mathematics, due primarily to the researches carried out by David Pingree. In this connection his monumental *Census of the Exact Sciences in Sanskrit,* Series A. Vol. I(1970), II(1971), III(1976), IV(1981) published in Philadelphia deserves to be mentioned side by side with the "History of Mathematical Astronomy in India" in the Dictionary of Scientific Biography, Vol. XV. New York 1978, pp. 533-633, "Jyotiḥśāstra. Astral and Mathematical Literature", *A History of Indian Literature,* Vol. VI, 4, Wiesbaden 1981, and finally "Jyotiḥśāstra", Part I of *A Descriptive Catalogue of the Sanskrit and other Indian Manuscripts of the Chandra Shum Shere Collection in Bodleian Library,* Oxford 1983. Further R. Billard: *L'astronomie indienne: Investigation des textes sanscritset des données numériques,* Paris 1971, *Publications de l'Ecole Française d'Extrême-Orient* LXXXIII, and H.-G. Türstig: *Jyotisa: Das System der indischen Astrologie,* Wiesbaden 1980, *Beiträge zur Südasien-Forschung* 57 may be mentioned here, although both these latter books came under some criticism from D. Pingree.

In spite of the advanced knowledge of the system and the history of Indian astronomy and mathematics, comparatively little attention has been paid to the more practical side of astronomy, that is to say to the calendar. In particular the non-technical literature has hardly ever been taken into consideration. The wealth of information found in Buddhist sources reflecting the difficulties encountered in ancient times, when it became necessary to determine and to keep correct dates in every day life, has been almost completely neglected. Nevertheless the rules laid down for fixing the date of the *uposatha* or the beginning of the rainy season are highly interesting in many respects: Here we learn for instance that intercalary months were enforced by royal decree: Vinaya-Piṭaka: Mahāvagga: Vassūpanāyikakkhandhaka: Vin I 138, 31-36 (PTS edition). How much information can be gleaned from literature is aptly demonstrated by the very informative article by C. Vogel: "Die Jahreszeiten im Spiegel der altindischen Literatur", *Zeitschrift der Deutschen*

Morgenländischen Gesellschaft 121.1971, pp. 284-326 (with an addendum ibidem 122.1972, p. *12*).

In a way practical difficulties similar to those experienced by the early Buddhists in India are not altogether alien to the present historian when it comes to calculating dates mentioned in inscriptions or colophons of manuscripts. First of all inadequate date given in the inscriptions themselves, and different calendar systems being in use at the same time, create problems, as the discussion by D. Pingree: "A Note on the Calendars Used in Early Indian Inscriptions", *Journal of the American Oriental Society* 102.1982, pp. 355-359 shows.

Some help in solving such problems can be found in rather old publications: The pioneering articles by Hermann Jacobi (1850-1937) reprinted in his *Kleine Schriften,* Wiesbaden 1970 are still valuable today, and the publications by Robert Sewell (1845-1925) have been used by generations of epigraphists and historians. As these still important research tools have been out of print for a long time and are very hard to find, the general introduction to the Indian calendar is reprinted here as a first step. It has been supplemented by R. Sewell in two further books, which also deserve to be reissued in the course of time: *Eclipses of the Moon in India,* London 1898, and: *Indian Chronography. An Extension of the 'Indian Calendar' with Working Examples,* London 1912. Finally a series of articles by the same author, which originally appeared in *Epigraphia Indica,* has been collected as: *The Siddhāntas and the Indian Calendar Being a Continuation of 'Indian Chronography',* Calcutta 1924.

In contrast to researches on the calendar in India proper, which have been somewhat neglected since R. Sewell's days, closely related systems borrowed from India have also been described more recently. First, as an old publication, A.M.B. Irwin: *The Burmese Calendar,* London 1901 can be mentioned. The Laotian time reckoning has been described after an early attempt by L. Finot: "Recherches sur la littérature Laotienne", *Bulletin de l'Ecole Fraçaise d'Extrême-Orient* 17, 1917, pp.1-221 (on the calendar pp. 30-34) by Prince Phetsarath: "Le calendrier laotien", *Bulletin des Amis de Laos,* 4.1940, pp. 107-140, also in English as: "Tiao Maha Upahat Phetsarath: The Laotian Calendar", in: *The Kingdom of Laos,* Saigon 1959, pp. 97-125, and: S. Dupertuis: "Le calcul du calendrier laotien", Peninsule, *Etudes Interdisciplinaires sur l'Asie du Sud-Est peninsulaine,* 2/3, Paris, April 1981, pp. 25-118. For Thailand, where a rather old and probably highly interesting manuscript copied in AD 1578 under the title *Adhikamāsavinischaya* (text in Lānnā: Thai Yuan, describing Buddhist ecclesiastic chronology) and many colophons virtually untouched still await investigation, J.C. Eade: *Southeast Asian Ephemeris, Solar and Planetary Positions, AD 638-2000,* Ithaca/New York 1989 is a most helpful book. Indian influences on Indonesian chronology have been traced by J.G. de Casparis: *Indonesian Chronology,* Leiden 1978, *Handbuch der Orientalistik,* 3. Abteilung, *Indonesien, Malaysia und die Philippinen,* I. Band Geschichte, l. Lieferung, and finally the Tibetan chronology, also heavily indepted to India, has been described by D. Schuh: *Untersuchungen zur Geschichte der tibetischen Kalenderrechnung,* Wiesbaden 1973, *Verzeichnis der Orientalischen Handschriften in Deutschland,* Supplementband 16.

Oskar von Hinüber, Freiburg i. Brsg.

PREFACE.

I.

THIS Volume is designed for the use, not only of those engaged in the decypherment of Indian inscriptions and the compilation of Indian history, but also of Judicial Courts and Government Offices in India. Documents bearing dates prior to those given in any existing almanack are often produced before Courts of Justice as evidence of title; and since forgeries, many of them of great antiquity, abound, it is necessary to have at hand means for testing and verifying the authenticity of these exhibits. Within the last ten years much light has been thrown on the subject of the Indian methods of time-reckoning by the publications of Professor Jacobi, Dr. Schram, Professor Kielhorn, Dr. Fleet, Pandit Śaṅkara Bâlkṛishṇa Dîkshit, and others; but these, having appeared only in scientific periodicals, are not readily accessible to officials in India. The Government of Madras, therefore, desiring to have a summary of the subject with Tables for ready reference, requested me to undertake the work. In process of time the scheme was widened, and in its present shape it embraces the whole of British India, receiving in that capacity the recognition of the Secretary of State for India. Besides containing a full explanation of the Indian chronological system, with the necessary tables, the volume is enriched by a set of Tables of Eclipses most kindly sent to me by Dr. Robert Schram of Vienna.

In the earlier stages of my labours I had the advantage of receiving much support and assistance from Dr. J. Burgess (late Director-General of the Archæological Survey of India) to whom I desire to express my sincere thanks. After completing a large part of the calculations necessary for determining the elements of Table I., and drawing up the draft of an introductory treatise, I entered into correspondence with Mr. Śaṅkara Bâlkṛishṇa Dîkshit, with the result that, after a short interval, we agreed to complete the work as joint authors. The introductory treatise is mainly his, but I have added to it several explanatory paragraphs, amongst others those relating to astronomical phenomena.

Tables XIV. and XV. were prepared by Mr. T. Lakshmiah Naidu of Madras.

It is impossible to over-estimate the value of the work done by Dr. Schram, which renders it now for the first time easy for anyone to ascertain the incidence, in time and place, of every solar eclipse occurring in India during the past 1600 years, but while thus briefly noting his services in the cause of science, I cannot neglect this opportunity of expressing to him my gratitude for his kindness to myself.

I must also tender my warm thanks for much invaluable help to Mr. H. H. Turner, Savilian Professor of Astronomy at Oxford, to Professor Kielhorn, C.I.E., of Göttingen, and to Professor Jacobi.

The Tables have been tested and re-tested, and we believe that they may be safely relied on for accuracy. No pains have been spared to secure this object.

R. SEWELL.

II.

It was only in September, 1893, that I became acquainted with Mr. R. Sewell, after he had already made much progress in the calculations necessary for the principal articles of Table I. of this work, and had almost finished a large portion of them.

The idea then occurred to me that by inserting the *a, b, c* figures (cols. 23, 24, and 25 of Table I.) which Mr. Sewell had already worked out for the initial days of the luni-solar years, but had not proposed to print in full, and by adding some of Professor Jacobi's Tables published in the *Indian Antiquary*, not only could the exact moment of the beginning and end of all luni-solar tithis be calculated, but also the beginning and ending moments of the nakshatra, yoga, and karaṇa for any day of any year; and again, that by giving the exact moment of the Mesha saṅkrânti for each solar year the exact European equivalent for every solar date could also be determined. I therefore proceeded to work out the details for the Mesha saṅkrântis, and then framed rules and examples for the exact calculation of the required dates, for this purpose extending and modifying Professor Jacobi's Tables to suit my methods. Full explanation of the mode of calculation is given in the Text. The general scheme was originally propounded by M. Largeteau, but we have to thank Professor Jacobi for his publications which have formed the foundation on which we have built.

My calculation for the moments of Mesha saṅkrântis, of mean intercalations of months (Mr. Sewell worked out the true intercalations), and of the samvatsaras of the cycle of Jupiter were carried out by simple methods of my own. Mr. Sewell had prepared the rough draft of a treatise giving an account of the Hindu and Muhammadan systems of reckoning, and collecting much of the information now embodied in the Text. But I found it necessary to re-write this, and to add a quantity of new matter.

I am responsible for all information given in this work which is either new to European scholars, or which differs from that generally received by them. All points regarding which any difference of opinion seems possible are printed in footnotes, and not in the Text. They are not, of course, fully discussed as this is not a controversial work.

Every precaution has been taken to avoid error, but all corrections of mistakes which may have crept in, as well as all suggestions for improvement in the future, will be gladly and thankfully received.

S. BALKRISHNA DÎKSHIT.

TABLE OF CONTENTS

PART I.

The Hindu Calendar.

Years and Cycles.

PART II.

The Various Eras.

PART III.

Description and Explanation of the Tables.

PART IV.

Use of the Tables.

PART V.

The Muhammadan Calendar.

APPENDIX.

THE INDIAN CALENDAR.

PART I.

THE HINDU CALENDAR.

1. In articles 118 to 134 below are detailed the various uses to which this work may be applied. Briefly speaking our chief objects are three; firstly, to provide simple methods for converting any Indian date—luni-solar or solar—falling between the years A.D. 300 and 1900 into its equivalent date A.D., and *vice versâ*, and for finding the week-day corresponding to any such date; secondly, to enable a speedy calculation to be made for the determination of the remaining three of the five principal elements of an Indian *pañchâṅga* (calendar), viz., the *nakshatra*, *yoga*, and *karaṇa*, at any moment of any given date during the same period, whether that date be given in Indian or European style; and thirdly, to provide an easy process for the verification of Indian dates falling in the period of which we treat.

2. For securing these objects several Tables are given. Table I. is the principal Table, the others are auxiliary. They are described in Part III. below. Three separate methods are given for securing the first of the above objects, and these are detailed in Part IV.

All these three methods are simple and easy, the first two being remarkably so, and it is these which we have designed for the use of courts and offices in India. The first method (A) (*Arts.* 135, 136) is of the utmost simplicity, consisting solely in the use of an eye-table in conjunction with Table I., no calculation whatever being required. The second (B) is a method for obtaining approximate results by a very brief calculation (*Arts.* 137, 138) by the use of Tables I., III. and IX. The result by both these methods is often correct, and it is always within one or two days of the truth, the latter rarely. Standing by itself, that is, it can always, provided that the era and the original bases of calculation of the given date are known, be depended on as being within two days of the truth, and is often only one day out, while as often it is correct. When the week-day happens to be mentioned in the given date its equivalent, always under the above proviso, can be fixed correctly by either of these methods.[1] The third method (C)

[1] See Art. 126 below.

is a method by which entirely correct results may be obtained by the use of Tables I. to XI. (*Arts.* 139 to 160), and though a little more complicated is perfectly simple and easy when once studied and understood. From these results the nakshatra, yoga, and karaṇa can be easily calculated.

3. Calculation of a date may be at once begun by using Part IV. below, but the process will be more intelligible to the reader if the nature of the Indian calendar is carefully explained to him beforehand, for this is much more intricate than any other known system in use.

Elements and Definitions.

4. *The pañchâṅga.* The *pañchâṅga* (calendar), *lit.* that which has five (*pañcha*) limbs (*aṅgas*), concerns chiefly five elements of time-division, viz., the vâra, tithi, nakshatra, yoga and karaṇa.

5. *The vâra or week-day.* The natural or solar day is called a *sâvana divasa* in Hindu Astronomy. The days are named as in Europe after the sun, moon, and five principal planets, [1] and are called *vâras* (week-days), seven of which compose the week, or cycle of vâras. A vâra begins at sunrise. The week-days, with their serial numbers as used in this work and their various Sanskrit synonyms, are given in the following list. The more common names are given in italics. The list is fairly exhaustive but does not pretend to be absolutely so.

Days of the Week.

1. *Sunday.* *Âdi*, [2] *Aditya*, *Ravi*, Ahaskara, Arka, Aruṇa, Bhaṭṭâraka, Aharpati, Bhâskara, Bradhna, Bhânu etc.
2. *Monday.* *Soma*, Abja, Chandramas, Chandra, Indu, Nishpati, Kshapâkara, etc.
3. *Tuesday.* *Maṅgala*, Aṅgâraka, Bhauma, Mahîsuta, Rohitâṅga.
4. *Wednesday.* *Budha*, Baudha, Rauhiṇeya, Saumya.
5. *Thursday.* *Guru*, Âṅgirasa, Bṛihaspati, Dhishaṇa, Surâchârya, Vâchaspati, etc.
6. *Friday.* *Śukra*, Bhârgava, Bhṛigu, Daityaguru, Kâvya, Uśanas, Kavi.
7. [3] *Saturday.* *Śani*, Saurî, Manda.

Time-Divisions.

6. *The Indian time-divisions.* The subdivisions of a solar day (*sâvana divasa*) are as follow:

A prativipala (sura) is equal to 0.006 of a second.
60 prativipalas make 1 vipala (para, kâshṭha-kalâ) = 0.4 of a second.
60 vipalas do. 1 pala (vighaṭî, vinâḍî) = 24 seconds.
60 palas do. 1 ghaṭikâ (ghaṭî, daṇḍa, nâḍî, nâḍikâ) = 24 minutes.
60 ghaṭikâs do. 1 divasa (dina, vâra, vâsara) = 1 solar day.

Again

10 vipalas do. 1 prâṇa = 4 seconds.
6 prâṇas do. 1 pala = 24 seconds.

1 It seems almost certain that both systems had a common origin in Chaldœa. The first is the day of the sun, the second of the moon, the third of Mars, the fourth of Mercury, the fifth of Jupiter, the sixth of Venus, the seventh of Saturn. [R. S.]

2 The word *vâra* is to be affixed to each of these names; *Ravi* = Sun, *Ravivâra* = Sunday.

3 In the Table, for convenience of addition, Saturday is styled O.

7. *The tithi, amâvâsyâ, pûrṇimâ.* The moment of new moon, or that point of time when the longitudes of the sun and moon are equal, is called *amâvâsyâ* (lit. the "dwelling together" of the sun and moon). A *tithi* is the time occupied by the moon in increasing her distance from the sun by 12 degrees; in other words, at the exact point of time when the moon (whose apparent motion is much faster than that of the sun), moving eastwards from the sun after the amâvâsyâ, leaves the sun behind by 12 degrees, the first tithi, which is called *pratipadâ* or *pratipad*, ends; and so with the rest, the complete synodic revolution of the moon or one lunation occupying 30 tithis for the 360 degrees. Since, however, the motions of the sun and moon are always varying in speed [1] the length of a tithi constantly alters. The variations in the length of a tithi are as follow, according to Hindu calculations:

	gh.	*pa.*	*vipa.*	*h.*	*m.*	*s.*
Average or mean length	59	3	40.23	23	37	28.092
Greatest length	65	16	0	26	6	24
Least length	53	56	0	21	34	24

The moment of full moon, or that point of time when the moon is furthest from the sun,—astronomically speaking when the difference between the longitudes of the sun and moon amounts to 180 degrees—is called *pûrṇimâ.* The tithi which ends with the moment of amâvâsyâ is itself called "amâvâsyâ", and similarly the tithi which ends with the moment of full moon is called "pûrṇimâ." *(For further details see Arts. 29, 31, 32.)*

8. *The nakshatra.* The 27th part of the ecliptic is called a *nakshatra*, and therefore each nakshatra occupies $\left(\frac{360°}{27}=\right)$ 13° 20′. The time which the moon (whose motion continually varies in speed) or any other heavenly body requires to travel over the 27th part of the ecliptic is also called a nakshatra. The length of the moon's nakshatra is:

	gh.	*pa.*	*vipa.*	*h.*	*m.*	*s.*
Mean	60	42	53.4	24	17	9.36
Greatest	66	21	0	26	32	24
Least	55	56	0	22	22	24

It will be seen from this that the moon travels nearly one nakshatra daily. The daily nakshatra of the moon is given in every pañchâṅg (native almanack) and forms one of its five articles. The names of the 27 nakshatras will be found in Table VIII., column 7. *(See Arts. 38, 42.)*

9. *The yoga.* The period of time during which the joint motion in longitude, or the sum of the motions, of the sun and moon is increased by 13° 20′, is called a *yoga*, lit. "addition". Its length varies thus:

	gh.	*pa.*	*vipa.*	*h.*	*m.*	*s.*
Mean	56	29	21.75	22	35	44.7
Greatest	61	31	0	24	36	24
Least	52	12	0	20	52	48

The names of the 27 yogas will be found in Table VIII., col. 12. *(See Art. 39.)*

10. *The karaṇa.* A karaṇa is half a tithi, or the time during which the difference of the longitudes of the sun and moon is increased by 6 degrees. The names of the karaṇas are given in Table VIII., cols. 4 and 5. *(See Art. 40.)*

[1] The variation is of course really in the motions of the earth and the moon. It is caused by actual alterations in rate of rapidity of motion in consequence of the elliptical form of the orbits and the moon's actual perturbations; and by apparent irregularities of motion in consequence of the plane of the moon's orbit being at an angle to the plane of the ecliptic. [R. S.]

11. *The paksha.* The next natural division of time greater than a solar day is the *paksha* (lit. a wing [1]) or moon's fortnight. The fortnight during which the moon is waxing has several names, the commonest of which are *śukla* or *śuddha* (lit. "bright", that during which the period of the night following sunset is illuminated in consequence of the moon being above the horizon). The fortnight during which the moon is waning is called most commonly *kṛishṇa* or *bahula* or *vadya* (lit. "black", "dark", or the fortnight during which the portion of the night following sunset is dark in consequence of the moon being below the horizon). The first fortnight begins with the end of amâvâsyâ and lasts up to the end of pûrṇimâ; the second lasts from the end of pûrṇimâ to the end of amâvâsyâ. The words "pûrva" (former or first) and "apara" (latter or second) are sometimes used for śukla and kṛishṇa respectively. "Śudi" (or "sudi") is sometimes used for śukla, and "vadi" or "badi" for kṛishṇa. They are popular corruptions of the words "śuddha" and "vadya" respectively.

12. *Lunar months.* The next natural division of time is the lunation, or lunar month of two lunar fortnights, viz., the period of time between two successive new or full moons. It is called a *chândra mâsa*, or lunar month, and is the time of the moon's synodic revolution.[2]

The names of the lunar months will be found in Table II., Parts i. and ii., and Table III., col. 2, and a complete discussion on the luni-solar month system of the Hindus in Arts. 41 to 51. *(For the solar months see Arts. 22 to 24.)*

13. *Amânta and pûrṇimânta systems.* Since either the amâvâsyâ or pûrṇimâ, the new moon or the full moon, may be taken as the natural end of a lunar month, there are in use in India two schemes of such beginning and ending. By one, called the *amânta* system, a month ends with the moment of amâvâsyâ or new moon; by the other it ends with the pûrṇimâ or full moon, and this latter is called a *pûrṇimânta* month. The pûrṇimânta scheme is now in use in Northern India, and the amânta scheme in Southern India. There is epigraphical evidence to show that the pûrṇimânta scheme was also in use in at least some parts of Southern India

1 An apt title. The full moon stands as it were with the waxing half on one side and the waning half on the other. The week is an arbitrary division.

2 The "synodic revolution" of the moon is the period during which the moon completes one series of her successive phases, roughly 29½ days. The period of her exact orbital revolution is called her "sidereal revolution". The term "synodic" was given because of the sun and moon being then together in the heavens (*cf:* "*synod*"). The sidereal revolution of the moon is less by about two days than her synodic revolution in consequence of the forward movement of the earth on the ecliptic. This will be best seen by the accompanying figure, where ST is a fixed star, S the sun, E the earth, C the ecliptic, M M¹ the moon, (A) the position at one new moon, (B) the position at the next new moon. The circle M to M¹ representing the sidereal revolution, its synodic revolution is M to M¹ plus M¹ to N. [R. S.]

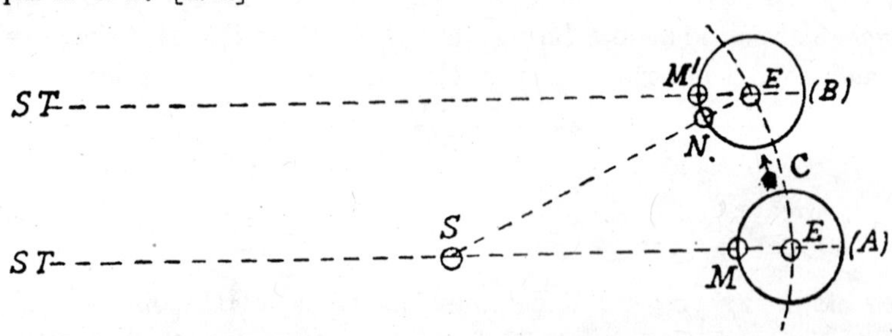

C. A. Young ("*General Astronomy*", *Edit. of* 1889, p. 528) gives the following as the length in days of the various lunations:

	d.	h.	m.	s.
Mean synodic month (new moon to new moon)	29	12	44	2.684
Sidereal month	27	7	43	11.545
Tropical month (equinox to equinox)	27	7	43	4.68
Anomalistic month (perigee to perigee) . . .	27	13	18	37.44
Nodical month (node to node)	27	5	5	35.81

up to about the beginning of the 9th century A.D.[1] The Mârvâḍis of Northern India who, originally from Mârwâr, have come to or have settled in Southern India still use their pûrṇimânta arrangement of months and fortnights; and on the other hand the Dakhanis in Northern India use the scheme of amânta fortnights and months common in their own country.

14. *Luni-solar month names.* The general rule of naming the lunar months so as to correspond with the solar year is that the amânta month in which the *Mêsha saṅkrânti* or entrance of the sun into the sign of the zodiac Mesha, or Aries, occurs in each year, is to be called *Chaitra,* and so on in succession. For the list and succession see the Tables. *(See Arts. 41—43.)*

15. *The solar year—tropical, sidereal, and anomalistic.* Next we come to the solar year, or period of the earth's orbital revolution, *i.e.,* the time during which the annual seasons complete their course. In Indian astronomy this is generally called a *varsha,* lit. "shower of rain", or "measured by a rainy season".

The period during which the earth makes one revolution round the sun with reference to the fixed stars,[2] is called a sidereal year.

The period during which the earth in its revolution round the sun passes from one equinox or tropic to the same again is called a tropical year. It marks the return of the same season to any given part of the earth's surface. It is shorter than a sidereal year because the equinoxes have a retrograde motion among the stars, which motion is called the precession of the equinoxes. Its present annual rate is about 50″.264.[3]

Again, the line of apsides has an eastward motion of about 11″.5 in a year; and the period during which the earth in its revolution round the sun comes from one end of the apsides to the same again, *i. e.,* from aphelion to aphelion, or from perihelion to perihelion, is called an anomalistic year.[4]

The length of the year varies owing to various causes, one of which is the obliquity of the ecliptic,[5] or the slightly varying relative position of the planes of the ecliptic and the equator. Leverrier gives the obliquity in A.D. 1700 as 23° 28′ 43″.22, in A.D. 1800 as 23° 27′ 55″.63, and

1 See Fleet's *Corpus Inscrip. Indic.,* vol. III., *Introduction,* p. 79 *note*; *Ind. Ant.,* XVII., p. 141 *f.*

2 Compare the note on p. 4 on the moon's motion. [R. S.]

3 This rate of annual precession is that fixed by modern European Astronomy, but since the exact occurrence of the equinoxes can never become a matter for observation, we have, in dealing with Hindu Astronomy, to be guided by Hindu calculations alone. It must therefore be borne in mind that almost all practical Hindu works *(Karaṇas)* fix the annual precession at one minute, or $\frac{1}{60}$th of a degree, while the *Sûrya-Siddhânta* fixes it as 54″ or $\frac{3}{200}$ degrees. *(see Art. 160a. given in the Addenda sheet.)*

4 The *anomaly* of a planet is its angular distance from its perihelion, or an angle contained between a line drawn from the sun to the planet, called the *radius vector,* and a line drawn from the sun to the perihelion point of its orbit. In the case in point, the earth, after completing its sidereal revolution, has not arrived quite at its perihelion because the apsidal point has shifted slightly eastwards. Hence the year occupied in travelling from the old perihelion to the new perihelion is called the anomalistic year. A planet's *true anomaly* is the actual angle as above whatever may be the variations in the planet's velocity at different periods of its orbit. Its *mean anomaly* is the angle which would be obtained were its motion between perihelion and aphelion uniform in time, and subject to no variation of velocity—in other words the angle described by a uniformly revolving radius vector. The angle between the true and mean anomalies is called the equation of the centre. *True anom. = mean anom. + equation of the centre.*

The equation of the centre is zero at perihelion and aphelion, and a maximum midway between them. In the case of the sun its greatest value is nearly 1°.55′ for the present, the sun getting alternately that amount ahead of, and behind, the position it would occupy if its motion were uniform. (C. A. Young, *General Astronomy. Edit. of* 1889, *p.* 125.)

Prof. Jacobi's, and our, *a, b, c,* (Table I., cols. 23, 24, 25) give *a.* the distance of the moon from the sun, expressed in 10,000ths of the unit of 360°; *b.* the moon's mean anomaly; *c.* the sun's mean anomaly; the two last expressed in 1000ths of the unit of 360° The respective equations of the centre are given in Tables VI. and VII. [R. S.]

5 "The ecliptic slightly and very slowly shifts its position among the stars, thus altering the latitudes of the stars and the angle between the ecliptic and equator, *i.e.,* the obliquity of the ecliptic. This obliquity is at present about 24′ less than it was 2000 years ago, and it is still decreasing about half a second a year. It is computed that this diminution will continue for about 15,000 years, reducing the obliquity to 22¼°, when it will begin to increase. The whole change, according to Lagrange, can never exceed about 1° 2′ on each side of the mean." (C. A. Young, *General Astronomy,* p. 128.)

in A.D. 1900 as 23° 17′ 08″.03. The various year-lengths for A.D. 1900, as calculated by present standard authorities, are as follow:

	d.	h.	m.	s.
Mean Sidereal solar year	365	6	9	9.29
Do. Tropical do.	365	5	48	45.37
Do. Anomalistic do.	365	6	13	48.61

16. *Kalpa. Mahâyuga. Yuga. Julian Period.* A *kalpa* is the greatest Indian division of time. It consists of 1000 *mahâyugas*. A *mahâyuga* is composed of four *yugas* of different lengths, named *Kṛita*, *Tretâ*, *Dvâpara*, and *Kaḷi*. The Kali-yuga consists of 432,000 solar years. The Dvâpara yuga is double the length of the Kali. The Tretâ-yuga is triple, and the Kṛita-yuga quadruple of the Kali. A mahâyuga therefore contains ten times the years of a Kali-yuga, viz., 4,320,000. According to Indian tradition a kalpa is one day of Brahman, the god of creation. The Kali-yuga is current at present; and from the beginning of the present kalpa up to the beginning of the present Kali-yuga 4567 times the years of a Kali-yuga have passed. The present Kali-yuga commenced, according to the *Sûrya Siddhânta*, an authoritative Sanskrit work on Hindu astronomy, at midnight on a Thursday corresponding to 17th—18th February, 3102 B. C., old style; by others it is calculated to have commenced on the following sunrise, viz., Friday, 18th February. According to the *Sûrya* and some other *Siddhântas* both the sun and moon were, with reference to their mean longitude, precisely on the beginning point of the zodiacal sign Aries, the Hindu sign Mesha, when the Kali-yuga began.

European chronologists often use for purposes of comparison the 'Julian Period' of 7980 years, beginning Tuesday 1st January, 4713 B. C. The 18th February, 3102 B. C., coincided with the 588,466th day of the Julian Period.

17. *Siddhânta year-measurement.* The length of the year according to different Hindu authorities is as follows:

Siddhântas.	Hindu reckoning.					European reckoning.			
	days.	gh.	pa.	vipa.	pra. vi.	days.	h.	mns.	sec.
The Vedâṅga Jyotisha	366	0	0	0	0	366	0	0	0
The Paitâmaha Siddhânta [1]	365	21	25	0	0	365	8	34	0
The Romaka „	365	14	48	0	0	365	5	55	12
The Pauliśa [2] „	365	15	30	0	0	365	6	12	0
The original Sûrya Siddhânta	365	15	31	30	0	365	6	12	36
The Present Sûrya, Vâsishṭha, Śâkalya-Brahma, Romaka, & Soma Siddhântas	365	15	31	31	24	365	6	12	36.56
The first Ârya Siddhânta [3] (A. D. 499).	365	15	31	15	0	365	6	12	30
The Brahma Siddhânta by Brahma-gupta (A. D. 628)	365	15	30	22	30	365	6	12	9
The second Arya Siddhânta	365	15	31	17	6	365	6	12	30.84
The Parâśara Siddhânta [4]	365	15	31	18	30	365	6	12	31.6
Râjamṛigâṅka [5] „ (A. D. 1042).	365	15	31	17	17.3	365	6	12	30.915

1 Generally speaking an astronomical Sanskrit work, called a *Siddhânta*, treats of the subject theoretically. A practical work on astronomy based on a Siddhânta is called in Sanskrit a *Karaṇa* The *Paitâmaha* and following three *Siddhântas* are not now extant, but are alluded to and described in the *Pañchasiddhântikâ*, a *Karaṇa* by Varâhamihira, composed in or about the Śaka year 427 (A.D. 505). [S. B. D.]

2 Two other *Pauliśa Siddhântas* were known to Utpala (A.D. 966), a well-known commentator of Varâhamihira. The length of the year in them was the same as that in the original Sûrya Siddhânta. [S. B. D.]

3 The duration of the year by the First Arya-Siddhânta is noted in the interesting chronogram *mukhyaḥ kâlomayamâtulaḥ.*
5 1 1 3 5 1 5 6 3
These figures are to be read from right to left; thus—365, 15, 31, 15 in Hindu notation of days, ghaṭikâs, etc. (I obtained this from Dr. Burgess.—R. S.)

4 The *Parâśara Siddhânta* is not now extant. It is described in the second *Ârya Siddhânta*. The date of this latter is not given, but in my opinion it is about A.D. 950. [S. B. D.]

5 The *Râjamṛigâṅka* is a *Karaṇa* by King Bhoja. It is dated in the Śaka year 964 expired, A.D. 1042. [S. B. D.]

It will be seen that the duration of the year in all the above works except the first three approximates closely to the anomalistic year; and is a little greater than that of the sidereal year. In some of these works theoretically the year is sidereal; in the case of some of the others it cannot be said definitely what year is meant; while in none is it to be found how the calculations were made. It may, however, be stated roughly that the Hindu year is sidereal for the last 2000 years.

18. The year as given in each of the above works must have been in use somewhere or another in India at some period; but at present, so far as our information goes, the year of only three works is in use, viz., that of the present *Sûrya Siddhânta*, the first *Ârya Siddhânta*. and the *Râjamṛigâṅka*.

The Siddhântas and other astronomical works.

19. It will not be out of place here to devote some consideration to these various astronomical works; indeed it is almost necessary to do so for a thorough comprehension of the subject.

Many other *Siddhântas* and *Karaṇas* are extant besides those mentioned in the above list. We know of at least thirty such works, and some of them are actually used at the present day in making calculations for preparing almanacks. [1] Many other similar works must, it is safe to suppose, have fallen into oblivion, and that this is so is proved by allusions found in the existing books.

Some of these works merely follow others, but some contain original matter. The Karaṇas give the length of the year, and the motions and places at a given time of the sun, moon, and planets, and their apogees and nodes, according to the standard *Siddhânta*. They often add corrections of their own, necessitated by actual observation, in order to make the calculations agree. Such a correction is termed a *bîja*. Generally, however, the length of the year is not altered, but the motions and places are corrected to meet requirements.

As before stated, each of these numerous works, and consequently the year-duration and other elements contained in them, must have been in use somewhere or another and at some period or another in India. At the present time, however, there are only three schools of astronomers known; one is called the *Saura-paksha*, consisting of followers of the present *Sûrya Siddhânta;* another is called the *Ârya-paksha*, and follows the first *Ârya Siddhânta;* and the third is called the *Brahma-paksha*, following the *Râjamṛigâṅka*, a work based on Brahmagupta's *Brahma Siddhânta*, with a certain *bîja*. The distinctive feature of each of these schools is that the length of the year accepted in all the works of that school is the same, though with respect to other elements they may possibly disagree between themselves. The name *Râjamṛigâṅka* is not now generally known, the work being superseded by others; but the year adopted by the present Brâhma-school is first found, so far as our information goes, in the *Râjamṛigâṅka*, and the three schools exist from at least A. D. 1042, the date of that work.

20. It is most important to know what *Siddhântas* or *Karaṇas* were, or are now, regarded as standard authorities, or were, or are, actually used for the calculations of pañchâṅgs (almanacks) during particular periods or in particular tracts of country, [2] for unless this is borne in mind we shall often go wrong when we attempt to convert Indian into European dates. The sketch which follows must not, however, be considered as exhaustive. The original *Sûrya-*

[1] *Karaṇas* and other practical works, containing tables based on one or other of the *Siddhântas*, are used for these calculations. [S. B. D.]

[2] The positions and motions of the sun and moon and their apogees must necessarily be fixed and known for the correct calculation of a tithi, nakshatra, yoga or karaṇa. The length of the year is also an important element, and in the samvatsara is governed by the movement of the planet Jupiter. In the present work we are concerned chiefly with these six elements, viz., the sun, moon, their apogees, the length of the year, and Jupiter. The sketch in the text is given chiefly keeping in view these elements. When one authority differs from another in any of the first five of these six elements the tithi as calculated by one will differ from that derived from another. [S. B. D.]

Siddhânta was a standard work in early times, but it was superseded by the present *Sûrya-Siddhânta* at some period not yet known, probably not later than A.D. 1000. The first *Ârya-Siddhânta,* which was composed at Kusumapura (supposed to be Paṭnâ in Bengal), came into use from A.D. 499.[1] Varâhamihira in his *Pañchasiddhântikâ* (A.D. 505) introduced a *bîja* to Jupiter's motion as given in the original *Sûrya-Siddhânta*, but did not take it into account in his rule (*see Art. 62 below*) for calculating a samvatsara. Brahmagupta composed his *Brahma-Siddhânta* in A. D. 628. He was a native of Bhillamâla (the present Bhinmâl), 40 miles to the north-west of the Abu mountains. Lalla, in his work named *Dhî-vṛiddhida*, introduced a *bîja* to three of the elements of the first *Ârya-Siddhânta*, namely, the moon, her apogee, and Jupiter, *i.e.*, three out of the six elements with which we are concerned. Lalla's place and date are not known, but there is reason to believe that he flourished about A.D. 638. The date and place of the second *Ârya-Siddhânta* are also not known, but the date would appear to have been about A.D. 950. It is alluded to by *Bhâskarâchârya* (A.D. 1150), but does not seem to have been anywhere in use for a long time. The *Râjamṛigâṅka* (A.D. 1042) follows the *Brahma-Siddhânta,*[2] but gives a correction to almost all its mean motions and places, and even to the length of the year. The three schools—Saura, Ârya and Brâhma—seem to have been established from this date if not earlier, and the *Brahma-Siddhânta* in its orginal form must have then dropped out of use. The *Karaṇa-prakâśa*, a work based on the first *Ârya-Siddhânta* as corrected by Lalla's bîja, was composed in A.D. 1092, and is considered an authority even to the present day among many Vaishṇavas of the central parts of Southern India, who are followers of the *Ârya-Siddhânta*. Bhâskarâchârya's works, the *Siddhânta Śiromaṇi* (A.D. 1150) and the *Karaṇa-Kutûhala* (A.D. 1183) are the same as the *Râjamṛigâṅka* in the matter of the calculation of a pañchâṅg. The *Vâkkya-Karaṇa*, a work of the Ârya school, seems to have been accepted as the guide for the preparation of solar pañchâṅgs in the Tamil and Malayâḷam countries of Southern India from very ancient times, and even to the present day either that or some similar work of the Ârya school is so used. A Karaṇa named *Bhâsvatî* was composed in A. D. 1099, its birthplace according to a commentator being Jagannâtha (or Purî) on the east coast. The mean places and motions given in it are from the original *Sûrya-Siddhânta* as corrected by Varâhamihira's bîja,[3] and it was an authority for a time in some parts of Northern India. Vâvilâla Kochchanna, who resided somewhere in Telingaṇa, composed a Karaṇa in 1298 A.D. He was a strict follower of the present *Sûrya-Siddhânta*, and since his day the latter Siddhânta has governed the preparation of all Telugu luni-solar calendars. The *Makaranda*, another Karaṇa, was composed at Benares in A.D. 1478, its author following the present *Sûrya-Siddhânta*, but introducing a bîja. The work is extensively used in Northern India in the present day for pañchâṅga calculations. Bengalis of the present day are followers of the Saura school, while in the western parts of Northern India and in some parts of Gujarât the Brâhma school is followed. The *Graha-lâghava*, a Karaṇa of the Saura school, was composed by Gaṇeśa Daivjña of Nandigrâma (Nândgâm), a village to the South of Bombay, in A. D. 1520. The same author also produced the *Bṛihat* and *Laghutithichintâmaṇis* in A. D. 1525, which may be considered as appendices to the *Graha-lâghava*. Gaṇeśa adopted the present *Sûrya Siddhânta* determinations for the length of

1 It is not to be understood that as soon as a standard work comes into use its predecessors go out of use from all parts of the country. There is direct evidence to show that the original *Sûrya-Siddhânta* was in use till A. D. 665, the date of the *Khaṇḍa-khâdya* of Brahmagupta, though evidently not in all parts of the country. [S. B. D.]

2 Whenever we allude simply to the "*Brahma Siddhânta*" by name, we mean the *Brahma-Siddhânta* of Brahmagupta.

3 Out of the six elements alluded to in note 1 on the last page, only Jupiter has this bîja. The present *Sûrya-Siddhânta* had undoubtedly come into use before the date of the *Bhâsvatî*. [S. B. D.]

the year and the motions and places of the sun and moon and their apogees, with a small correction for the moon's place and the sun's apogee; but he adopted from the *Ârya Siddhânta* as corrected by Lalla the figures relating to the motion and position of Jupiter.

The *Graha-lâghava* and the *Laghutithichintâmaṇi* were used, and are so at the present day, in preparing pañchâṅgs wherever the Mahrathi language was or is spoken, as well as in some parts of Gujarât, in the Kanarese Districts of the Bombay and Madras Presidencies, and in parts of Haidarâbâd, Maisûr, the Berars, and the Central Provinces. Mahratha residents in Northern India and even at Benares follow these works.

21. It may be stated briefly that in the present day the first *Ârya-Siddhânta* is the authority in the Tamil and Malayâḷam countries of Southern India;[1] the Brâhma-paksha obtains in parts of Gujarât and in Râjputâna and other western parts of Northern India; while in almost all other parts of India the present *Sûrya-Siddhânta* is the standard authority. Thus it appears that the present *Sûrya-Siddhânta* has been the prevailing authority in India for many centuries past down to the present day, and since this is so, we have chiefly followed it in this work.[2]

The bîja as given in the *Makaranda* (A. D. 1478) to be applied to the elements of the *Sûrya-Siddhânta* is generally taken into account by the later followers of the *Sûrya-Siddhânta*, but is not met with in any earlier work so far as our information goes. We have, therefore, introduced it into our tables after A.D. 1500 for all calculations which admit of it. The bîja of the *Makaranda* only applies to the moon's apogee and Jupiter, leaving the other four elements unaffected.

Further details. Contents of the Pañchâṅga.

22. *The Indian Zodiac.* The Indian Zodiac is divided, as in Europe, into 12 parts, each of which is called a *râśi* or "sign". Each sign contains 30 degrees, a degree being called an *aṁśa*. Each aṁśa is divided into 60 *kalâs* (minutes), and each kalâ into 60 *vikalâs* (seconds). This sexagesimal division of circle measurement is, it will be observed, precisely similar to that in use in Europe.[3]

23. *The Saṅkrânti.* The point of time when the sun leaves one zodiacal sign and enters another is called a *saṅkrânti.* The period between one saṅkrânti and another, or the time required for the sun to pass completely through one sign of the zodiac, is called a *saura mâsa*, or solar month. Twelve solar months make one solar year. The names of the solar months will be found in Table II., Part ii., and Table III., col. 5. A saṅkrânti on which a solar month commences takes its name from the sign-name of that month. The Mesha saṅkrânti marks the vernal equinox, the moment of the sun's passing the first point of Aries. The Karka saṅkrânti, three solar months later, is also called the *dakshinâyana* ("southward-going") *saṅkrânti;* it is the point of the summer solstice, and marks the moment when the sun turns southward. The Tulâ saṅkrânti, three solar months later, marks the autumnal equinox, or the moment of the sun's passing the first point of Libra. The Makara saṅkrânti, three solar months later still, is also called the *uttarâyana saṅkrânti* ("northward-going"). It is the other solstitial point, the point or moment when the sun turns northward. When we speak of "saṅkrântis" in this volume we refer always to the *nirayana saṅkrântis*, *i.e.*, the moments of the sun's entering the zodiacal signs, as calculated in sidereal longitude—longitude measured from the fixed point in Aries—taking no account of the annual precession of the equinoxes—(*nirayana* = "without movement", excluding the precession of the solstitial—*ayana*—points). But there is also in Hindu chronology the *sâyana saṅkrânti* (*sa-ayana* = "with

1 It is probable that the first *Ârya-Siddhânta* was the standard authority for South Indian solar reckoning from the earliest times. In Bengal the *Sûrya-Siddhânta* is the authority since about A. D. 1100, but in earlier times the first *Ârya-Siddhânta* was apparently the standard. [S. B. D.]

2 When we allude simply to the *Sûrya* or *Ârya Siddhânta*, it must be borne in mind that we mean the *Present Sûrya* and the *First Ârya-Siddhântas*.

3 See note 1, p. 2 above. [R. S.]

movement", including the movement of the *ayana* points), *i.e.*, a saṅkrânti calculated according to tropical longitude—longitude measured from the vernal equinox, the precession being taken into account. According to the present Sûrya-Siddhânta the sidereal coincided with the tropical signs in K. Y. 3600 expired, Śaka 421 expired, and the annual precession is 54". By almost all other authorities the coincidence took place in K. Y. 3623 expired, Śaka 444 expired, and the annual precession is (1') one minute. (The *Siddhânta Śiromaṇi*, however, fixes this coincidence as in K. Y. 3628). Taking either year as a base, the difference in years between it and the given year, multiplied by the total amount of annual precession, will shew the longitudinal distance by which, in the given year, the first point of the tropical (*sâyana*) sign precedes the first point of the sidereal (*nirayana*) sign. Professor Jacobi (*Epig. Ind., Vol. I, p. 422, Art. 39*) points out that a calculation should be made "whenever a date coupled with a saṅkrânti does not come out correct in all particulars. For it is possible that a *sâyana* saṅkrânti may be intended, since these saṅkrântis too are suspicious moments." We have, however, reason to believe that sâyana saṅkrântis have not been in practical use for the last 1600 years or more. Dates may be tested according to the rule given in Art. 160 (*a*).

It will be seen from cols. 8 to 13 of Table II., Part ii, that there are two distinct sets of names given to the solar months. One set is the set of zodiac-month-names ("Mesha" etc.), the other has the names of the lunar months. The zodiac-sign-names of months evidently belong to a later date than the others, since it is known that the names of the zodiacal signs themselves came into use in India later than the lunar names, "Chaitra" and the rest. [1] Before sign-names came into use the solar months must have been named after the names of the lunar months, and we find that they are so named in Bengal and in the Tamil country at the present day. [2]

24. *Length of months.* It has been already pointed out that, owing to the fact that the apparent motion of the sun and moon is not always the same, the lengths of the lunar and solar months vary. We give here the lengths of the solar months according to the *Sûrya* and *Ârya-Siddhântas*.

Serial No.	NAME OF THE MONTH.			DURATION OF EACH MONTH.													
	Sign-name.	Tamil name.	Bengâli name.	By the *Ârya-Siddhânta.*							By the *Sûrya-Siddhânta.*						
				days	gh.	pa.	days	hrs.	mn.	sec.	days	gh.	pa.	days	hrs.	mn.	sec.
1	Mesha	Śittirai (Chittirai)	Vaiśâkha	30	55	30	30	22	12	0	30	56	7	30	22	26	48
2	Vṛishabha	Vaigâśi, or Vaiyâśi	Jyeshṭha	31	24	4	31	9	37	36	31	25	13	31	10	5	12
3	Mithuna	Âni	Âshâḍha	31	36	26	31	14	34	24	31	38	41	31	15	28	24
4	Karka	Âḍi	Srâvaṇa	31	28	4	31	11	13	36	31	28	31	31	11	24	24
5	Siṁha	Âvaṇi	Bhâdrapada	31	2	5	31	0	50	0	31	1	7	31	0	26	48
6	Kanyâ	Puraṭṭâdi, or Puraṭṭâśi	Âśvina	30	27	24	30	10	57	36	30	26	29	30	10	35	36
7	Tulâ	Aippaśi, or Arppiśi, or Appiśi	Kârttika	29	54	12	29	21	40	48	29	53	36	29	21	26	24
8	Vṛiśchika	Kârttigai	Mârgaśîrsha	29	30	31	29	12	12	24	29	29	25	29	11	46	0
9	Dhanus	Mârgaḷi	Pausha	29	21	2	29	8	24	48	29	19	4	29	7	37	36
10	Makara	Tai	Mâgha	29	27	24	29	10	57	36	29	26	53	29	10	45	12
11	Kumbha	Mâśi	Phâlguna	29	48	30	29	19	24	0	29	49	13	29	19	41	12
12	Mîna	Paṅguni	Chaitra	30	20	19¼	30	8	7	42	30	21	12.52	30	8	29	0.56
				365	15	31¼	365	6	12	30	365	15	31.52	365	6	12	36.56

[1] My present opinion is that the zodiacal-sign-names, *Mesha*, etc., began to be used in India between 700 B. C. and 300 B. C., not earlier than the former or later than the latter. [S. B. D.]

[2] It will be seen that the Bengal names differ from the Tamil ones. The same solar month *Mesha*, the first of the year, is

For calculation of the length by the *Sûrya-Siddhânta* the longitude of the sun's apogee is taken as 77° 16′, which was its value in A. D. 1137, a date about the middle of our Tables. Even if its value at our extreme dates, *i.e.*, either in A. D. 300 or 1900, were taken the lengths would be altered by only one *pala* at most. By the *Ârya-Siddhânta* the sun's apogee is taken as constantly at 78°.[1]

The average (mean) length in days of solar and lunar months, and of a lunar year is as follows:

	Sûrya-Siddhânta	*Modern science*
Solar month ($\frac{1}{12}$ of a sidereal year)	30.438229707	30.438030.
Lunar month	29.530587946	29.530588.
Lunar year (12 lunations)	354.36705535	354.367056.

25. *Adhika mâsas. Calendar used.* A period of twelve lunar months falls short of the solar year by about eleven days, and the Hindus, though they use lunar months, have not disregarded this fact; but in order to bring their year as nearly as possible into accordance with the solar year and the cycle of the seasons they add a lunar month to the lunar year at certain intervals. Such a month is called an *adhika* or intercalated month. The Indian year is thus either solar or luni-solar. The Muhammadan year of the Hijra is purely lunar, consisting of twelve lunar months, and its initial date therefore recedes about eleven days in each year. In luni-solar calculations the periods used are tithis and lunar months, with intercalated and suppressed months whenever necessary. In solar reckoning solar days and solar months are alone used. In all parts of India luni-solar reckoning is used for most religious purposes, but solar reckoning is used where it is prescribed by the religious authorities. For practical civil purposes solar reckoning is used in Bengal and in the Tamil and Malayâḷam countries of the Madras Presidency; in all other parts of the country luni-solar reckoning is adopted.

26. *True and mean saṅkrântis. Śodhya.* When the sun enters one of the signs of the zodiac, as calculated by his mean motion, such an entrance is called a mean saṅkrânti; when he enters it as calculated by his apparent or true motion, such a moment is his apparent or true[2] saṅkrânti. At the present day true saṅkrântis are used for religious as well as for

called *Vaiśâkha* in Bengal and *Sittirai (Chaitra)* in the Tamil country, Vaiśâkha being the second month in the south. To avoid confusion, therefore, we use only the sign-names *(Mesha,* etc.*)* in framing our rules.

[1] The lengths of months by the *Ârya-Siddhânta* here given are somewhat different from those given by Warren. But Warren seems to have taken the longitude of the sun's apogee by the *Sûrya-Siddhânta* in calculating the duration of months by the *Ârya-Siddhânta*, which is wrong. He seems also to have taken into account the *chara.* * *(See his Kâla Saṅkalita, p.* 11, *art.* 3, *p.* 22, *explanation of Table III., line* 4; *and p.* 3 *of the Tables).* He has used the *ayanâṁśa* (the uniformly increasing arc between the point of the vernal equinox each year and the fixed point in Aries) which is required for finding the *chara* in calculating the lengths of months. The *chara* is not the same at the beginning of any given solar month for all places or for all years. Hence it is wrong to use it for general rules and tables. The inaccuracy of Warren's lengths of solar months according to the *Sûrya-Siddhânta* requires no elaborate proof, for they are practically the same as those given by him according to the *Ârya-Siddhânta*, and that this cannot be the case is self-evident to all who have any experience of the two *Siddhântas.* [S. B. D.]

* The *chara*:—"The time of rising of a heavenly body is assumed to take place six hours before it comes to the meridian. Actually this is not the case for any locality not on the equator, and the *chara* is the correction required in consequence, *i.e.*, the excess or defect from six hours of the time between rising and reaching the meridian. The name is also applied to the celestial arc described in this time."

[2] The Sanskrit word for "mean" is *madhyama*, and that for 'true' or 'apparent' is *spashṭa*. The words '*madhyama*' and '*spashṭa*' are applied to many varieties of time and space; as, for instance, *gati* (motion), *bhôga* (longtitude), *saṅkrânti*, *mâna* (measure or reckoning) and *kâla* (time). In the English Nautical Almanac the word "apparent" is used to cover almost all cases where the Sanskrit word *spashṭa* would be applied, the word 'true' being sometimes, but rarely, used. "Apparent," therefore, is the best word to use in my opinion; and we have adopted it prominently, in spite of the fact that previous writers on Hindu Astronomy have chiefly used the word "true." There is as a fact a little difference in the meaning of the phrases "apparent" and "true," but it is almost unknown to Indian Astronomy, and we have therefore used the two words as synonyms. [S. B. D.]

civil purposes. In the present position of the sun's apogee, the mean Mesha saṅkrânti takes place after the true saṅkrânti, the difference being two days and some ghaṭikâs. This difference is called the *śodhya*. It differs with different *Siddhântas*, and is not always the same even by the same authority. We have taken it as 2 d. 10 gh. 14 p. 30 vipa. by the *Sûrya-Siddhânta*, and 2 d. 8 gh. 51 p. 15 vipa. by the *Ârya-Siddhânta*. The corresponding notion in modern European Astronomy is the equation of time. The śodhya is the number of days required by the sun to catch up the equation of time at the vernal equinox.

27. It must be remembered that whenever we use the word "saṅkrânti" alone, (e.g., "the Mesha-saṅkrânti") the apparent and not the mean nirayana saṅkrânti is meant.

28. *The beginning of a solar month.* Astronomically a solar month may begin, that is a saṅkrânti may occur, at any moment of a day or night; but for practical purposes it would be inconvenient to begin the month at irregular times of the day. Suppose, for example, that a Makara-saṅkrânti occurred 6 hours 5 minutes after sunrise on a certain day, and that two written agreements were passed between two parties, one at 5 hours and another at 7 hours after sunrise. If the month Makara were considered to have commenced at the exact moment of the Makara-saṅkrânti, we should have to record that the first agreement was passed on the last day of the month Dhanus, and the second on the first day of Makara, whereas in fact both were executed on the same civil day. To avoid such confusion, the Hindus always treat the beginning of the solar month as occurring, civilly, at sunrise. Hence a variation in practice.

(1) *(a)* In Bengal, when a saṅkrânti takes place between sunrise and midnight of a civil day the solar month begins on the following day; and when it occurs after midnight the month begins on the next following, or third, day. If, for example, a saṅkrânti occurs between sunrise and midnight of a Friday, the month begins at sunrise on the next day, Saturday; but if it takes place after midnight of Friday[1] the month begins at sunrise on the following Sunday. This may be termed *the Bengal Rule*. *(b)* In Orissa the solar month of the Amli and Vilayati eras begins civilly on the same day as the saṅkrânti, whether this takes place before midnight or not. This we call *the Orissa Rule*.

(2) In Southern India there are two rules. *(a)* One is that when a saṅkrânti takes place after sunrise and before sunset the month begins on the same day, while if it takes place after sunset the month begins on the following day; if, for example, a saṅkrânti occurs on a Friday between sunrise and sunset the month begins on the same day, Friday, but if it takes place at any moment of Friday night after sunset the month begins on Saturday.[2] *(b)* By another rule, the day between sunrise and sunset being divided into five parts, if a saṅkrânti takes place within the first three of them the month begins on the same day, otherwise it begins on the following day. Suppose, for example, that a saṅkrânti occurred on a Friday, seven hours after sunrise, and that the length of that day was 12 hours and 30 minutes; then its fifth part was 2 hours 30 minutes, and three of these parts are equal to 7 hours 30 minutes. As the saṅkrânti took place within the first three parts, the month began on the same day, Friday; but if the saṅkrânti had occurred 8 hours after sunrise the month would have begun on Saturday. The latter *(b)* rule is observed in the North and South Malayâḷam country, and the former *(a)* in other parts of Southern India where the solar reckoning is used, viz., in the Tamil and Tinnevelly countries.[3] We call *a. the Tamil Rule; b. the Malabar Rule.*

[1] Remember that the week-day is counted from sunrise to sunrise.

[2] Brown's *Ephemeris* follows this rule throughout in fixing the date corresponding to 1st Mesha, and consequently his solar dates are often wrong by one day for those tracts where the 2 *b* rule is in use.

[3] I deduced the Bengal rule from a Calcutta Pañchâṅg for Śaka 1776 (A.D. 1854—55) in my posssession. Afterwards it was

29. *Pañchâṅgs.* Before proceeding we revert to the five principal articles of the pañchâṅg.

There are 30 *tithis* in a lunar month, 15 to each fortnight. The latter are generally denoted by the ordinary numerals in Sanskrit, and these are used for the fifteen tithis of each fortnight. Some tithis are, however, often called by special names. In pañchâṅgs the tithis are generally particularized by their appropriate numerals, but sometimes by letters. The Sanskrit names are here given. [1]

Tithis.	Sanskrit Names.	Vulgar Names.	Tithis.	Sanskrit Names.	Vulgar Names.
1	Pratipad, Pratipadâ, Prathamâ	Pâḍvâ, Pâdyami	9	Navamî	
2	Dvitîyâ	Bîja, Vidiya	10	Daśamî	
3	Tritîyâ	Tija, Tadiya	11	Ekâdaśî	
4	Chaturthî	Chauth, Chauthi	12	Dvâdaśî	Bâras
5	Pañchamî		13	Trayôdaśî	Teras
6	Shashṭhî	Saṭh	14	Chaturdaśî	
7	Saptamı		15	Pûrṇimâ, Paurṇimâ . Pûrṇamâsi, Pañchadaśi	Punava, Punnamî
8	Ashtamî		30	Amâvâsyâ, Darśa, Pañchadaśî	

The numeral 30 is generally applied to the *amâvâsyâ* (new moon day) in pañchâṅgs, even in Northern India where according to the pûrṇimânta system the dark fortnight is the first fortnight of the month and the month ends with the moment of full moon, the *amâvâsyâ* being really the 15th tithi.

30. That our readers may understand clearly how a Hindu pañchâṅg is prepared and what information it contains, we append an extract from an actual pañchâṅg for Saka 1816, expired, A. D. 1894—95, published at Poona in the Bombay Presidency. [2]

corroborated by information kindly sent to me from Howrah by Mr. G. A. Grierson through Dr. Fleet. It was also amply corroborated by a set of Bengal Chronological Tables for A.D. 1882, published under the authority of the Calcutta High Court, a copy of which was sent to me by Mr. Sewell. I owe the Orissa Rule to the Chronological Tables published by Girishchandra Tarkâlankar, who follows the Orissa Court Tables with regard to the Amli and Vilayati years in Orissa. Dr. J. Burgess, in a note in Mr. Kṛishṇasvâmi Naidu's "*South Indian Chronological Tables*" edited by Mr. Sewell, gives the 2 *(a)* Rule as in use in the North Malayâḷam country, but I do not know what his authority is. I ascertained from Tamil and Tinnevelly pañchâṅgs that the 2 *(a)* rule is in use there, and the fact is corroborated by Warren's *Kâla Saṅkalita*; I ascertained also from some South Malayâḷam pañchâṅgs published at Cochin and Trevandrum, and from a North Malayâḷam pañchâṅg published at Calicut, that the 2 *(b)* rule is followed there [S. B. D.]

Notwithstanding all this I have no certain guarantee that these are the *only* rules, or that they are invariably followed in the tracts mentioned. Thus I find from a Tamil solar pañchâṅg for Śaka 1815 current, published at Madras, and from a Telugu luni-solar pañchâṅg for Śaka 1109 expired, also published at Madras, in which the solar months also are given, that the rule observed is that "when a saṅkrânti occurs between sunrise and midnight the month begins on the same day, otherwise on the following day", thus differing from all the four rules given above. This varying fifth rule again is followed for all solar months of the Vilayati year as given in the above-mentioned Bengal Chronological Tables for 1882, and by its use the month regularly begins one day in advance of the Bengâli month. I find a sixth rule in some Bombay and Benares lunar pañchâṅgs, viz., that at whatever time the saṅkrânti may occur, the month begins on the next day; but this is not found in any solar pañchâṅg. The rules may be further classified as (1. *a*) *the midnight rule* (Bengal), (1. *b*) *any time rule* (Orissa), (2. *a*) *the sunset rule* (Tamil), (2. *b*) *the afternoon rule* (Malabar). The fifth rule is a variety of the midnight rule, and the sixth a variety of the any time rule. I cannot say for how many years past the rules now in use in the several provinces have been in force and effect.

An inscription at Kaṇṇaṇûr, a village 5 miles north of Srîraṅgam near Trichinopoly *(see Epigraph. Indic., vol. III., p.* 10, *date No. V., note* 3, *and p.* 8*)*, is dated Tuesday the thirteenth tithi of the bright fortnight of Śrâvaṇa in the year Prajâpati, which corresponded with the 24th day of the (solar) month Âḍi (Karka.) From other sources the year of this date is known to be A. D. 1271; and on carefully calculating I find that the day corresponds with the 21st July, and that the Karka saṅkrânti took place, by the *Ârya-Siddhânta*, on the 27th June, Saturday, shortly before midnight. From this it follows that the month Âḍi began civilly on the 28th June, and that one or the other of the two rules at present in use in Southern India was in use in Trichinopoly in A.D. 1271. [S. B. D.]

1 We cannot enumerate the vulgar or popular names which obtain in all parts of India, and it is not necessary that we should do so.

2 This is an ordinary pañchâṅg in daily use. It was prepared by myself from Gaṇeśa Daivjña's *Grahalâghava* and *Laghutithichintâmaṇi*. [S. B. D.]

Śaka 1816 expired (1817 current) (A. D. 1894) amânta Bhâdrapada, śukla-paksha. Solar months Siṁha

Tithi.	Vâra.	gh.	pa.	Nakshatra.	gh.	pa.	Yoga.	gh.	pa.	Karaṇa.	gh.	pa.	Moon's place.	Length Day. gh.	pa.	Solar date.	Muhammadan date.	Date A. D.
1	Fri.	43	59	Pûrva Phalgunî:	40	16	Siddha	31	22	Kiṁstughna	16	30	Siṁha*15	30	59	16	29	31
2	Sat.	39	47	Uttara Phalgunî:	37	57	Sâdhya	25	23	Bâlava	11	53	Kanyâ	30	57	17	30	1
3	Sun.	36	31	Hasta	36	29	Śubha	19	31	Taitila	8	9	Kanyâ	30	54	18	1	2
4	Mon.	34	23	Chitrâ	36	7	Śukla	14	50	Vaṇij	5	27	Kanyâ 6	30	52	19	2	3
5	Tues.	33	26	Svâti	36	52	Brahman	11	7	Bava	3	54	Tulâ	30	49	20	3	4
6	Wed.	33	58	Viśâkhâ	38	58	Aindra	8	24	Kaulava	3	42	Tulâ 23	30	45	21	4	5
7	Thurs.	35	29	Anurâdhâ	42	19	Vaidhṛiti	6	36	Gara	4	44	Vṛiśchi:	30	44	22	5	6
8	Fri.	38	16	Jyeshṭhâ	46	48	Vishkambha	5	49	Vishṭi	6	53	Vṛiś: 47	30	41	23	6	7
9	Sat.	42	9	Mûla	52	13	Prîti	6	2	Bâlava	10	13	Dhanus	30	38	24	7	8
10	Sun.	46	48	Pûrva Ashâḍhâ	58	11	Âyushmat	6	53	Taitila	14	28	Dhanus	30	36	25	8	9
11	Mon.	51	43	Uttara Ashâḍhâ	60	0	Saubhâgya	8	1	Vaṇij	19	16	Dha: 15	30	33	26	9	10
12	Tues.	56	44	Uttara Ashâḍhâ	4	35	Śôbhana	9	29	Bava	24	14	Makara	30	30	27	10	11
13	Wed.	60	0	Śravaṇa	10	59	Atigaṇḍa	10	58	Kaulava	29	3	Maka: 44	30	28	28	11	12
13	Thurs.	1	23	Dhanishṭhâ	16	45	Sukarman	11	54	Taitila	1	23	Kumbha	30	25	29	12	13
14	Fri.	5	18	Śatabhishaj	21	52	Dhṛiti	12	26	Vaṇij	5	18	Kumbha	30	22	30	13	14
15	Sat.	8	11	Pûrva Bhadra:	26	4	Śûla	12	7	Bava	8	11	Kum: 10	30	20	31	14	15

Amânta Bhâdrapada kṛishṇapaksha.

Tithi.	Vâra.	gh.	pa.	Nakshatra.	gh.	pa.	Yoga.	gh.	pa.	Karaṇa.	gh.	pa.	Moon's place.	Length Day. gh.	pa.	Solar date.	Muhammadan date.	Date A. D.
1	Sun.	9	59	Uttara Bhadra:	28	58	Gaṇḍa	10	45	Kaulava	9	59	Mîna	30	17	1	15	16
2	Mon.	10	30	Revatî	30	40	Vṛiddhi	8	30	Gara	10	30	Mîna 31	30	15	2	16	17
3	Tues.	9	35	Aśvinî	31	9	Dhruva	5	10	Vishṭi	9	35	Mesha	30	12	3	17	18
4	Wed.	7	26	Bharaṇî	30	27	Vyâghâta	0 54	50 52	Bâlava	7	26	Me: 45	30	10	4	18	19
5	Thurs.	4	19	Kṛittikâ	28	36	Vajra	49	43	Taitila	4	19	Vṛisha	30	7	5	19	20
6	Fri.	0 55	16 18	Rohiṇî	25	59	Siddhi	43	1	Vaṇij	0	16	Vṛi: 54	30	5	6	20	21
8	Sat.	49	55	Mṛigaśiras	22	43	Vyatipâta	35	58	Bâlava	22	45	Mithuna	30	2	7	21	22
9	Sun.	44	9	Ârdrâ	18	57	Varîyas	28	28	Taitila	16	2	Mithuna	30	0	8	22	23
10	Mon.	38	9	Punarvasu	14	55	Parigha	20	45	Vaṇij	11	9	Mithu: 1	29	57	9	23	24
11	Tues.	32	9	Pushya	10	47	Śiva	13	2	Bava	5	9	Karka:	29	55	10	24	25
12	Wed.	26	17	Aśleshâ	6	46	Siddha	5 52	24 31	Taitila	26	17	Kar: 7	29	52	11	25	26
13	Thurs.	20	45	Maghâ	3 56	4 51	Śubha	51	4	Vaṇij	20	45	Siṁha	29	49	12	26	27
14	Fri.	15	48	Uttara Phalgunî	57	25	Śukla	44	35	Śakuni	15	48	Siṁ: 14	29	47	13	27	28
30	Sat.	11	40	Hasta	55	38	Brahman	38	46	Nâga	11	40	Kanyâ	29	44	14	28	29

* Where no numbers are inserted in this column it must be understood that the moon was in the sign during the whole day.

and Kanyâ; Muhammadan months Śafar and Rabî-ul-awwal. English months August and September.

Date A. D.	OTHER PARTICULARS.
31	
1	Chandra-darśana (moon's heliacal rising). September begins.
2	Amṛita Siddhiyoga 36.29. * Haritâlikâ. Manvâdi: Varâhajayantî. Vaidhṛiti 35.10 to 44.42. Rabı-ul awwal begins.
3	Gaṇesha chaturthî.
4	Rishipañchamî.
5	Amṛita Siddhiyoga after 39. Venus enters Leo 45.44.
6	Gauryâvâhana.
7	Gaurî pûjâ. Dûrvâ ashtamî.
8	Gaurî visarjana. Aduhkha navamî.
9	
10	Padmâ Ekâdaśî. Mṛityu-yoga 60. Mercury enters Virgo 14.5.
11	Vâmana dvâdaśî.
12	Pradôsha. Sun enters Uttara Phalgunî 8.26.
13	
14	Anantachaturdaśî. Mars retrogade.
15	Proshṭhap, Pûrṇi: Sun enters Virgo 33.42.

Positions of Planets at sunrise Śukla 15th Saturday.

	Sun.	Mars.	Mercury.	Jupiter.	Venus.	Saturn.	Moon's node.
Signs.	4	0	5	2	4	6	11
Degrees.	29	10	8	12	12	3	9
Minutes.	27	26	37	25	19	48	16
Seconds.	9	2	22	7	44	43	7
Rate of daily motion. mins.	58	5	106	7	73	6	3
Rate of daily motion. secs.	30	6 *retro*	20	54	44	15	11

Ahargaṇa 34—227.

Horoscope for the above time.

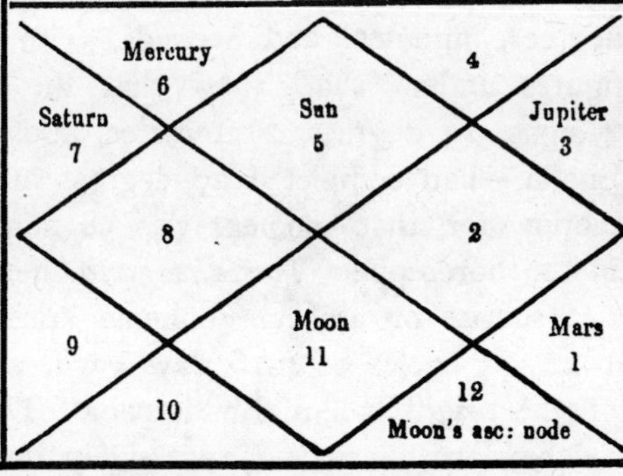

(Pûrṇimanta Âśvina krishnapaksha.)

Date A. D.	OTHER PARTICULARS.
16	Vyatipâta † from 7 to 16.32.
17	
18	Saṅkashṭî chaturthî.
19	
20	
21	Bhadrâ (Vishṭi) ends at 27.55.
22	
23	Avidhavâ navamî.
24	Heliacal rising of Mercury.
25	Indirâ ekâdaśî. Sun enters Hasta 46.37.
26	Pradôsha.
27	Śivarâtri. Mercury in Libra 29.18.
28	Pitṛi-amâvâsyâ. Vaidhṛiti 20.47 to 30.21.
29	Solar eclipse. Mṛityuyoga 55.38. Amâvâsyâ.

Positions of Planets at sunrise Amâvâsyâ, Saturday.

	Sun.	Mars.	Mercury.	Jupiter.	Venus.	Saturn.	Moon's node.
Signs.	5	0	6	2	4	6	11
Degrees.	13	9	2	13	28	5	8
Minutes.	10	13	27	49	31	17	31
Seconds.	7	30	1	4	4	7	35
Rate of daily motion. mins.	59	8	95	5	73	7	3
Rate of daily motion. secs.	1	4 *retro*	56	54	44	2	11

Ahargaṇa 34—241.

Horoscope for the above time.

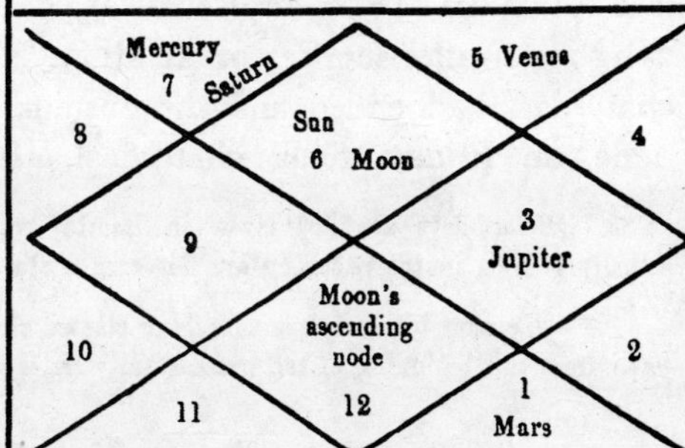

* These figures show ghatikâs and palas. † This is the name of a peculiar yoga, the declination of sun and moon being then identical.

The above extract is for the amânta month Bhâdrapada or August 31st to September 29th, 1894. The month is divided into its two fortnights. The uppermost horizontal column shews that the first tithi, "pratipadâ", was current at sunrise on Friday, and that it ended at 43 gh. 59 p. after sunrise. The moon was 12 degrees to the east of the sun at that moment, and after that the second tithi, "dvitîyâ", commenced. The nakshatra Pûrva-Phalgunî ended and Uttara-Phalgunî commenced at 40 gh. 16 p. after sunrise. The yoga Siddha ended, and Sâdhya began, at 31 gh. 22 p. after sunrise; and the karaṇa Kiṁstughna ended, and Bava began, at 16 gh. 30 p. after sunrise. The moon was in the sign Siṁha up to 15 gh. after sunrise and then entered the sign Kanyâ. The length of the day was 30 gh. 59 pa. (and consequently the length of the night was 29 gh. 1 pa.). The solar day was the 16th of Siṁha.[1] The Muhammadan day was the 29th of Śafar, and the European day was the 31st of August. This will explain the bulk of the table and the manner of using it.

Under the heading "other particulars" certain festival days, and some other information useful for religious and other purposes, are given. To the right, read vertically, are given the places of the sun and the principal planets at sunrise of the last day of each fortnight in signs degrees, minutes, and seconds, with their daily motions in minutes and seconds. Thus the figures under "sun" shew that the sun had, up to the moment in question, travelled through 4 signs, 29 degrees, 27 minutes, and 9 seconds; *i.e.*, had completed 4 signs and stood in the 5th, Siṁha,—had completed 29 degrees and stood in the 30th, and so on; and that the rate of his daily motion for that moment was 58 minutes and 30 seconds. Below are shown the same in signs in the horoscope. The *ahargaṇa*, here 34—227, means that since the epoch of the *Grahalâghava*,[2] *i.e.*, sunrise on amânta Phâlguna kṛishṇa 30th of Śaka 1441 expired, or Monday 19th March, A.D. 1520, 34 cycles of 4016 days each, and 227 days, had elapsed at sunrise on Saturday the 15th of the bright half of Bhâdrapada. The horoscope entries are almost always given in pañchâṅgs as they are considered excessively important by the Hindus.

31. *Tithis and solar days.* Solar or civil days are always named after the week-days, and where solar reckoning is in use are also counted by numbers, *e.g.*, the 1st, 2nd, etc., of a named solar month. But where solar reckoning does not prevail they bear the names and numerals of the corresponding tithis. The tithis, however, beginning as they do at any hour of the day, do not exactly coincide with solar days, and this gives rise to some little difficulty. The general rule for civil purposes, as well as for some ordinary religious purposes for which no particular time of day happens to be prescribed, is that the tithi current at sunrise of the solar day gives its name and numeral to that day, and is coupled with its week-day. Thus *Bhâdrapada śukla chaturdaśî Śukravâra* (Friday the 14th of the first or bright fortnight of Bhâdrapada) is that civil day at whose sunrise the tithi called the 14th śukla is current, and its week-day is Friday. Suppose a written agreement to have been executed between two parties, or an ordinary religious act to have been performed, at noon on that Friday at whose sunrise Bhâdrapada Sukla chaturdaśî of Saka 1816 expired was current, and which ended *(see the table)* 5 gh. 18 p., (about 2 h. 7 m.) after sunrise, or at about 8.7 a.m. Then these two acts were actually done after the chaturdaśî had ended and the pûrṇimâ was current, but they would be generally noted as having been done on Friday śukla chaturdaśî. It is, however, permissible, though such instances would be

[1] Solar days are not given in Bombay pañchâṅgs, but I have entered them here to complete the calendar. Some entries actually printed in the pañchâṅg are not very useful and are consequently omitted in the extract. [S. B. D.]

[2] The sum total of days that have elapsed since any other standard epoch is also called the *ahargana*. For instance, the *ahargaṇa* from the beginning of the present kaliyuga is in constant use. The word means "collection of days."

rare, to state the date of these actions as "Friday pûrṇimâ;" and sometimes for religious purposes the date would be expressed as "chaturdaśî yukta pûrṇimâ" (the 14th joined with the pûrṇimâ). Where, however, successive regular dating is kept up, as, for instance, in daily transactions and accounts, a civil day can only bear the name of the tithi current at its sunrise.

Some religious ceremonies are ordered to be performed on stated tithis and at fixed times of the day. For example, the worship of the god Gaṇeśa is directed to take place on the Bhâdrapada śukla chaturthî during the third part *(madhyâhna)* of the five parts of the day. A śrâddha, a ceremony in honour of the *pitṛis* (manes), must be performed during the 4th *(aparâhṇa)* of these five periods. Take the case of a Brâhmaṇa, whose father is dead, and who has to perform a śrâddha on every amâvâsyâ. In the month covered by our extract above the amâvâsyâ is current at sunrise on Saturday. It expired at 11 gh. 40 p. after sunrise on Saturday, or at about 10.40 a.m. Now the aparâhṇa period of that Saturday began, of course, later than that hour, and so the amâvâsyâ of this Bhâdrapada was current during the aparâhṇa, not of Saturday, but of the previous day, Friday. The śrâddha ordered to be performed on the amâvâsyâ must be performed, not on Saturday, but on Friday in this case. Again, suppose a member of the family to have died on this same Friday before the end of the tithi kṛishṇa chaturdaśî, and another on the same day but after the end of the tithi. A śrâddha must be performed in the family every year, according to invariable Hindu custom, on the tithi on which each person died. Therefore in the present instance the śrâddha of the first man must be performed every year on the day on which Bhâdrapada kṛishṇa chaturdaśî is current, during the aparâhṇa; while that of the second must take place on the day on which the amâvâsyâ of that month is current during the aparâhṇa, and this may be separated by a whole day from the first. Lengthy treatises have been written on this subject, laying down what should be done under all such circumstances. [1]

At the time of the performance of religious ceremonies the current tithi, vâra, and all other particulars have to be pronounced; and consequently the tithi, nakshatra, etc., so declared may differ from the tithi, etc., current at sunrise. There is a vrata (observance, vow) called *Saṅkashta-nâśana-chaturthî*, by which a man binds himself to observe a fast on every kṛishṇa chaturthî up to moonrise, which takes place about 9 p.m. on that tithi, but is allowed to break the fast afterwards. And this has of course to be done on the day on which the chaturthî is current at moonrise. From the above extract the evening of the 18th September, Tuesday, is the day of this chaturthî, for though the 3rd tithi, tṛitîyâ, of the kṛishṇa paksha was current at sunrise on Tuesday it expired at 9 gh. 35 pa. after sunrise, or about 9.50 a.m. If we suppose that this man made a grant of land at the time of breaking his fast on this occasion, we should find him dating his grant "kṛishṇa chaturthî, Tuesday," though for civil purposes the date is kṛishṇa tṛitîyâ, Tuesday.

The general rule may be given briefly that for all practical and civil purposes, as well as for some ordinary religious purposes, the tithi is connected with that week-day or solar day at whose sunrise it is current, while for other religious purposes, and sometimes, though rarely, even for practical purposes also, the tithi which is current at any particular moment of a solar day or week-day is connected with that day.

32. *Adhika and kshaya tithis.* Twelve lunar months are equal to about 354 solar days *(see Art. 24 above)*, but there are 360 tithis during that time and it is thus evident that six tithis must somehow be expunged in civil (solar) reckoning. Ordinarily a tithi begins on one day and

[1] The *Nirṇayasindhu* is one of these authorative works, and is in general use at the present time in most parts of India.

ends on the following day, that is it touches two successive civil days. It will be seen, however, from its length *(Art. 7 above)* that a tithi may sometimes begin and end within the limits of the same natural day; while sometimes on the contrary it touches three natural days, occupying the whole of one and parts of the two on each side of it.

A tithi on which the sun does not rise is expunged. It has sustained a diminution or loss *(kshaya)*, and is called a *kshaya tithi*. On the other hand, a tithi on which the sun rises twice is repeated. It has sustained an increase *(vṛiddhi)*, and is called an *ạdhika*, or added, *tithi*. Thus, for example, in the pañchâṅg extract given above (*Art. 30*) there is no sunrise during kṛishṇa saptamî (7th), and it is therefore expunged. Kṛishṇa shashṭhî (6th) was current at sunrise on Friday, for it ended 16 palas after sunrise; while kṛishṇa saptamî began 16 palas after that sunrise and ended before the next sunrise; and kṛishṇa ashtami (8th) is current at sunrise on the Saturday. The first day is therefore named civilly the (6th) shashṭhî, Friday, and the second is named (8th) ashtami, Saturday; while no day is left for the saptamî, and it has necessarily to be expunged altogether, though, strictly speaking, it was current for a large portion of that Friday. On the other hand, there are two sunrises on Bhâdrapada śukla trayôdaśî (śukla 13th), and that tithi is therefore repeated. It commenced after 56 gh. 44 pa. on Tuesday, *i.e.*, in European reckoning about 4.20 a.m. on the Wednesday morning, was current on the whole of Wednesday, and ended on Thursday at 1 gh. 23 pa. after sunrise, or about 6.33 a.m. It therefore touched the Tuesday (reckoned from sunrise to sunrise) the Wednesday and the Thursday; two natural civil days began on it; two civil days, Wednesday and Thursday, bear its numeral (13); and therefore it is said to be repeated. [1]

In the case of an expunged tithi the day on which it begins and ends is its week-day. In the case of a repeated tithi both the days at whose sunrise it is current are its week-days.

A clue for finding when a tithi is probably repeated or expunged is given in Art. 142.

Generally there are thirteen expunctions *(kshayas)* and seven repetitions *(vṛiddhis)* of tithis in twelve lunar months.

The day on which no tithi ends, or on which two tithis end, is regarded as inauspicious. In the pañchâṅg extract above *(Art. 30)* Bhâdrapada śukla trayôdaśî Wednesday, and Bhâdrapada kṛishṇa shashṭhî, Friday (on which the saptamî was expunged), were therefore inauspicious.

33. It will be seen from the above that it is an important problem with regard to the Indian mode of reckoning time to ascertain what tithi, nakshatra, yoga, or karaṇa was current at sunrise on any day, and when it began and ended. Our work solves this problem in all cases.

34. *Variation on account of longitude.* The moment of time when the distance between the sun and moon amounts to 12, or any multiple of 12, degrees, or, in other words, the moment of time when a tithi ends, is the same for all places on the earth's surface; and this also applies to nakshatras, yogas, and karaṇas. But the moment of sunrise of course varies with the locality, and therefore the ending moments of divisions of time such as tithis, when referred to sunrise, differ at different places. For instance, the tithi Bhâdrapada śukla pûrṇimâ (*see above Art. 30*) ended at Poona at 8 gh. 11 pa. after sunrise, or about 9.16 a.m. At a place where the sun rose 1 gh. earlier than it does at Poona the tithi would evidently have ended one ghaṭikâ later, or at 9 gh. 11 pa. after sunrise, or at about 9.40 a.m. On the other hand, at a place where

[1] Any assertions or definitions by previous writers on Hindu Chronology or Astronomy contrary to the above definitions and examples are certainly erroneous, and due to misapprehension. [S. B. D.]

the sun rose 1 gh. later than at Poona the tithi would have ended when 7 gh. 11 pa. had elapsed since the sunrise at that place, or at about 8.52 a.m.

35. For this reason the expunction and repetition of tithis often differs in different localities. Thus the nakshatra Pûrvâshâḍhâ (*see pañchâṅg extract Art. 30*) was 58 gh. 11 pa. [1] at Poona on Sunday, śukla 10th. At a place which is on the same parallel of latitude, but 12 degrees eastward, the sun rises 2 gh. earlier than at Poona, and there this nakshatra ended (58 gh. 11 pa. + 2 gh =) 60 gh. 11 pa. after sunrise on Sunday, that is at 11 pa. after sunrise on Monday. It therefore touches three natural days, and therefore it (Pûrvâshâḍhâ) is repeated, whereas at Poona it is Uttarâshâḍhâ which is repeated. On the other hand, the nakshatra Maghâ on Kṛishṇa 13th was 3 gh. 4 pa., and Pûrva-phalgunî was (3 gh. 4 pa. + 56 gh. [2] 51 pa. =) 59 gh. 55 pa. at Poona. At a place which has the same latitude as Poona, but is situated even at so short a distance as 1 degree to the east, the nakshatra Pûrva-phalgunî ended 60 gh. 5 pa after sunrise on Thursday, that is 5 pa. after sunrise on Friday; and therefore there will be no kshaya of that nakshatra at that place, but the following nakshatra Uttara phalgunî will be expunged there.

36. *True or apparent, and mean, time.* The sun, or more strictly the earth in its orbit, travels, not in the plane of the equator, but in that of the ecliptic, and with a motion which varies every day; the length of the day, therefore, is not always the same even on the equator. But for calculating the motions of the heavenly bodies it is evidently convenient to have a day of uniform length, and for this reason astronomers, with a view of obtaining a convenient and uniform measure of time, have had recourse to a mean solar day, the length of which is equal to the mean or average of all the apparent solar days in the year. An imaginary sun, called the *mean* sun, is conceived to move uniformly in the equator with the mean angular velocity of the true sun. The days marked by this mean sun will all be equal, and the interval between two successive risings of the mean sun on the equator is the duration of the mean solar day, viz., 24 hours or 60 ghaṭikâs. The time shown by the true sun is called true or apparent time, and the time shown by the mean sun is known as mean time. Clocks and watches, whose hands move, at least in theory, with uniform velocity, evidently give us mean time. With European astronomers "mean noon" is the moment when the mean sun is on the meridian; and the "mean time" at any instant is the hour angle of the mean sun reckoned westward from 0 h. to 24 h., mean noon being 0 h. for astronomical purposes.

Indian astronomers count the day from sunrise, to sunrise, and give, at least in theory, the ending moments of tithis in time reckoned from actual or true sunrise. The *true* or *apparent time of a place*, therefore, in regard to the Indian pañchâṅg, is the time counted from true (*i.e.*, actual) sunrise at that place. For several reasons it is convenient to take mean sunrise on the equator under any given meridian to be the mean sunrise at all places under the same meridian. The mean sunrise at any place is calculated as taking place at 0 gh. or 0 h.—roughly 6 a.m. in European civil reckoning; and the mean time of a place is the time counted from 0 gh. or 0 h.

The moment of true sunrise is of course not always the same at all places, but varies with the latitude and longitude. Even at the same place it varies with the declination of the sun, which

1 Instead of writing at full length that such and such a tithi "ends at so many ghaṭikâs after sunrise", Indian astronomers say for brevity that the tithi "is so many ghaṭikâs". The phrase is so used in the text in this sense.

2 In the case of kshayas in the pañchâṅg extract the ghaṭikâs of expunged tithis etc., are to be counted after the end of the previous tithi etc. In some pañchâṅgs the ghaṭikâs from sunrise—59 gh. 55pa. in the present instance—are given.

varies every day of the year. And at any given place, and on any given day of the year, it is not the same for all years. The calculation, therefore, of the exact moment of true sunrise at any place is very complicated—too complicated to be given in this work, [1] the aim of which is extreme simplicity and readiness of calculation, and therefore mean time at the meridian of Ujjain [2] or Lanka is used throughout what follows.

All ending moments of tithis calculated by our method C *(Arts. 139 to 160)* are in Ujjain mean time; and to convert Ujjain mean time into that of any other given place the difference of longitude in time—4 minutes (10 palas) to a degree—should be added or subtracted according as the place is east or west of Ujjain. Table XI. gives the differences of longitude in time for some of the most important places of India.

The difference between the mean and apparent (true) time of any place in India at the present day varies from *nil* (in March and October) to 26 minutes (in January and June) in the extreme southern parts of the peninsular. It is nowhere more than 65 minutes.

37. *Basis of calculation for the Tables.* All calculations made in this work in accordance with luni-solar reckoning are based on the *Sûrya-Siddhânta*, and those for solar reckoning on the *Sûrya* and *Ârya Siddhântas.* The elements of the other authorities being somewhat different, the ending moments of tithis etc., or the times of saṅkrântis as calculated by them may sometimes differ from results obtained by this work; and it must never be forgotten that, when checking the date of a document or record which lays down, for instance, that on a certain week-day there fell a certain tithi, nakshatra, or yoga, we can only be *sure* of accuracy in our results if we can ascertain the actual Siddhânta or other authority used by the author of the calendar which the drafter of the document consulted. Prof. Jacobi has given Tables for several of the principal *Siddhântas* in the *Epigraphica Indica* (*Vol. II., pp. 403 et seq.*), and these may be used whenever a doubt exists on the point.

Although all possible precautions have been taken, there, must also be a slight element of uncertainty in the results of a calculation made by our Tables owing to the difference between mean and apparent time, independently of that arising from the use of different authorities. Owing to these two defects it is necessary sometimes to be cautious. If by any calculation it is found that a certain tithi, nakshatra, yoga, or karaṇa ended nearly at the close of a solar day—as, for example, 55 ghaṭikâs after mean sunrise on a Sunday, *i.e.*, 5 ghaṭikâs before sunrise on the Monday—it is possible that it really ended shortly after true sunrise on the Monday. And, similarly, if the results shew that a certain tithi ended shortly after the commencement of a solar day,—for instance, 5 ghaṭikâs after mean sunrise on a Sunday,—it is possible that it really ended shortly before the true termination of the preceding day, Saturday.

1 Since this work was in the Press, Professor Jacobi has published in the *Epigraphia Indica* (Vol. II., pp. 487—498) a treatise with tables for the calculation of Hindu dates in true local time, to which we refer our readers.

2 Here Lanka is not Ceylon, but a place supposed to be on the equator, or in lat. 0° 0′ 0″ on the meridian of Ujjain, or longitude 75° 46′. It is of great importance to know the exact east longitude of Ujjain, since upon it depends the verification of apparent phenomena throughout India. Calculation by the different Siddhântas can be checked by the best European science if that point can be certainly determined. The great Trigonometical Survey map makes the centre of the city 75° 49′ 45″ E. long. and 23° 11′ 10″ N. lat. But this is subject to two corrections; first, a correction of 1′ 9″ to reduce the longitude to the origin of the Madras Observatory taken as 80° 17′ 21″, and secondly, a farther reduction of 2′ 30″ to reduce it to the latest value, 80° 14′ 51″, of that Observatory, total 3′ 39″. This reduces the E. long. of the centre of Ujjain city to 75° 46′ 06″. I take it therefore, that amidst conflicting authorities, the best of whom vary from 75° 43′ to 75° 51, we may for the present accept 75° 46′ as the nearest approach to the truth. The accuracy of the base, the Observatory of Madras, will before long be again tested, and whatever difference is found to exist between the new fixture and 80° 14′ 51″, that difference applied to 75° 46′ will give the correct value of the E. long. we require. [R. S.]

Five ghaṭikâs is not the exact limit, nor of course the fixed limit. The period varies from *nil* to about five ghaṭikâs, rarely more in the case of tithis, nakshatras, and karaṇas; but in the case of yogas it will sometimes reach seven ghaṭikâs.

Calculations made by our method *C* will result in the finding of a "tithi index" (*t.*), or a nakshatra or yoga-index (*n.* or *y.*), all of which will be explained further on; but it may be stated in this connection that when at any ascertained mean sunrise it is found that the resulting index is within 30 of the ending index of the tithi, (*Table VIII., col. 3*), nakshatra or karaṇa (*id. col. 8, 9, 10*), or within 50 of the ending index of a yoga (*id. col. 13*), it is possible that the result may be one day wrong, as explained above. The results arrived at by our Tables, however, may be safely relied on for all ordinary purposes.

38. *Nakshatras*. There are certain conspicuous stars or groups of stars in the moon's observed path in the heavens, and from a very remote age these have attracted attention. They are called in Sanskrit "Nakshatras". They were known to the Chaldœans and to the ancient Indian Âryas. Roughly speaking the moon makes one revolution among the stars in about 27 days, and this no doubt led to the number [1] of nakshatras being limited to 27.

The distance between the chief stars, called yôga-târâs, of the different nakshatras is not uniform. Naturally it should be 13° 20′, but, in some cases it is less than 7°, while in others it is more than 20°. It is probable that in ancient times the moon's place was fixed merely by stating that she was near a particular named nakshatra (star) on a certain night, or on a certain occasion. Afterwards it was found necessary to make regular divisions of the moon's path in her orbit, for the sake of calculating and foretelling her position; and hence the natural division of the ecliptic, consisting of twenty-seven equal parts, came into use, and each of these parts was called after a separate nakshatra (*see Art. 8*). The starry nakshatras, however, being always in view and familiar for many centuries, could not be dispensed with, and therefore a second and unequal division was resorted to. Thus two systems of nakshatras came into use. One we call the ordinary or equal-space system, the other the unequal-space system. The names of the twenty-seven stellar nakshatras are given to both sets. In the equal-space system each nakshatra has 13° 20′ of space, and when the sun, the moon, or a planet is between 0°, *i.e.*, *no* degrees, and 13° 20′ in longitude it is said to be in the first nakshatra Aśvinî, and so on. The unequal-space system is of two kinds. One is described by Garga and others, and is called here the "Garga system." According to it fifteen of the nakshatras are held to be of equal average (mean) length—*i.e.*, 13° 20′,—but six measure one and-a-half times the average—*i.e.*, 20°, and six others only half the average, viz., 6° 40′. The other system is described by Brahmagupta and others, and therefore we call it the "Brahma-Siddhânta" system. In its leading feature it is the same with Garga's system, but it differs a little from Garga's in introducing Abhijit in addition to the twenty-seven ordinary nakshatras. The moon's daily mean motion,—13 degrees, 10 minutes, 35 seconds,—is taken as the average space of a nakshatra. And as the total of the spaces thus allotted to the usual twenty-seven nakshatras, on a similar arrangement of unequal spaces, amounts to only 355 degrees, 45 minutes, 45 seconds, the remainder,—4 degrees, 14 minutes, 15 seconds,—is allotted to Abhijit, as an additional nakshatra placed between Uttara-Ashâḍhâ and Śravaṇa.

The longitude of the ending points of all the nakshatras according to these three systems

[1] The mean length of the moon's revolution among the stars is 27.32166 days (27.321674 according to the *Sûrya Siddhânta*). Its least duration is 27 days, 4 hours, and the greatest about 7 hours longer. The number of days is thus between 27 and 28, and therefore the number of nakshatras was sometimes taken as 28 by the ancient Indian Âryas. The extra nakshatra is called *Abhijit* (*See Table VIII., col. 7.*) [S. B. D.]

is given below. The entries of "½" and "1½" in subcolumn 3 mark the variation in length from the average.

The nakshatras by any of these systems, for all years between 300 and 1900 A. D., can be calculated by our Tables *(see method "C", Arts. 139 to 160)*. The indices for them, adapted to our Tables, are given in Table VIII., cols. 8, 9, 10.

The ordinary or equal-space system of nakshatras is in general use at the present day, the unequal-space systems having almost dropped out of use. They were, however, undoubtedly prevalent to a great extent in early times, and they were constantly made use of on important religious occasions. [1]

Longtitudes of the Ending-points of the Nakshatras.

Order of the Nakshatras.		System of Equal Spaces.		Systems of Unequal Spaces.						
					Garga System.			Brahma-Siddhânta System.		
1		2		3	4			4		
		Deg.	Min.		Deg.	Min.	Sec.	Deg.	Min.	Sec.
1	Aśvinî	13°	20′	....	13°	20′	0	13°	10′	35″
2	Bharaṇî	26	40	½	20	0	0	19	45	52½
3	Kṛittikâ	40	0	....	33	20	0	32	56	27½
4	Rohiṇî	53	20	1½	53	20	0	52	42	20
5	Mṛigaśiras	66	40	....	66	40	0	65	52	55
6	Ârdrâ	80	0	½	73	20	0	72	28	12½
7	Punarvasu	93	20	1½	93	20	0	92	14	5
8	Pushya	106	40	....	106	40	0	105	24	40
9	Aśleshâ	120	0	½	113	20	0	111	59	57½
10	Maghâ	133	20	....	126	40	0	125	10	32½
11	Pûrva-Phalgunî	146	40	....	140	0	0	138	21	7½
12	Uttara-Phalgunî	160	0	1½	160	0	0	158	7	0
13	Hasta	173	20	....	173	20	0	171	17	35
14	Chitrâ	186	40	....	186	40	0	184	28	10
15	Svâti	200	0	½	193	20	0	191	3	27½
16	Viśâkhâ	213	20	1½	213	20	0	210	49	20
17	Anurâdhâ	226	40	....	226	40	0	223	59	55
18	Jyeshṭhâ	240	0	½	233	20	0	230	35	12½
19	Mûla	253	20	....	246	40	0	243	45	47½
20	Pûrva-Ashâḍhâ	266	40	....	260	0	0	256	56	22½
21	Uttara-Ashâḍhâ	280	0	1½	280	0	0	276	42	15
	(Abhijit)	...		(Balance)	....			280	56	30
22	Śravaṇa	293	20	....	293	20	0	294	7	5
23	Dhanishṭhâ or Śravishṭhâ	306	40	....	306	40	0	307	17	40
24	Śatatârakâ or Śatabhishaj	320	0	½	313	20	0	313	52	57½
25	Pûrva-Bhadrapadâ	333	20	....	326	40	0	327	3	32½
26	Uttara-Bhadrapadâ	346	40	1½	346	40	0	346	49	25
27	Revatî	360	0	....	360	0	0	360	0	0

39. *Auspicious Yogas.* Besides the 27 yogas described above (*Art. 9*), and quite different from them, there are in the Indian Calendar certain conjunctions, also called *yogas*, which only occur when certain conditions, as, for instance, the conjunction of certain vâras and nakshatras, or vâras and tithis, are fulfilled. Thus, when the nakshatra Hasta falls on a Sunday there occurs

1 These systems of nakshatras are more fully described by me in relation to the "twelve-year cycle of Jupiter" in Vol. XVII. of the *Ind. Ant.*, (p. 2 ff.) [Ś. B. D.]

an *amṛita siddhiyoga*. In the pañchâṅg extract (*Art. 30*) given above there is an *amṛita siddhiyoga* on the 2nd, 5th and 18th of September. It is considered an auspicious yoga, while some yogas are inauspicious.

40. *Karaṇas.* A karaṇa being half a tithi, there are 60 karaṇas in a lunar month. There are seven karaṇas in a series of eight cycles—total 56—every month, from the second half of śukla pratipadâ (1st) up to the end of the first half of kṛishṇa chaturdaśî (14th). The other four karaṇas are respectively from the second half of kṛishṇa chaturdaśî (14th) to the end of the first half of śukla pratipadâ. [1]

Table VIII., col. 4, gives the serial numbers and names of karaṇas for the first half, and col. 5 for the second half, of each tithi.

40*a*. *Eclipses.* Eclipses of the sun and moon play an important part in inscriptions, since, according to ancient Indian ideas, the value of a royal grant was greatly enhanced by its being made on the occasion of such a phenomenon; and thus it often becomes essential that the moments of their occurrence should be accurately ascertained. The inscription mentions a date, and an eclipse as occurring on that date. Obviously we shall be greatly assisted in the determination of the genuineness of the inscription if we can find out whether such was actually the case. Up to the present the best list of eclipses procurable has been that published by Oppolzer in his "*Canon der Finsternisse*" *(Denkschriften der Kaiserl. Akademie der Wissenschaften. Vienna, Vol. LII.)*, but this concerns the whole of our globe, not merely a portion like India; the standard meridian is that of Greenwich, requiring correction for longitude; and the accompanying maps are on too small a scale to be useful except as affording an approximation from which details can be worked out. Our object is to save our readers from the necessity of working out such complicated problems. Prof. Jacobi's Tables in the *Indian Antiquary* (Vol. XVII.) and *Epigraphia Indica* (Vol. II.) afford considerable help, but do not entirely meet the requirements of the situation. Dr. Schram's contribution to this volume, and the lists prepared by him, give the dates of all eclipses in India and the amount of obscuration observable at any place. His article speaks for itself, but we think it will be well be add a few notes.

Prof. Jacobi writes *(Epig. Ind., II., p. 422)*:—"The eclipses mentioned in inscriptions are not always actually observed eclipses, but calculated ones. My reasons for this opinion are the following: Firstly, eclipses are auspicious moments, when donations, such as are usually recorded in inscriptions, are particularly meritorious. They were therefore probably selected for such occasions, and must accordingly have been calculated beforehand. No doubt they were entered in pañchâṅgs or almanacs in former times as they are now. Secondly, even larger eclipses of the sun, up to seven digits, pass unobserved by common people, and smaller ones are only visible under favourable circumstances. Thirdly, the Hindus place implicit trust in their Śâstras, and would not think it necessary to test their calculations by actual observation. The writers of inscriptions would therefore mention an eclipse if they found one predicted in their almanacs."

Our general Table will occasionally be found of use. Thus a lunar eclipse can only occur at the time of full moon *(pûrṇimâ)*, and can only be visible when the moon is above the horizon at the place of the observer; so that when the pûrṇimâ is found by our Tables to occur during most part of the daytime there can be no visible eclipse. But it is possibly visible if the pûrṇimâ is found, on any given meridian, to end within 4 ghaṭikâs after sunrise, or within 4 ghaṭikâs before sunset. A solar eclipse occurs only on an amâvâsyâ or new moon day. If

[1] According to the *Sûrya-Siddhânta* the four karaṇas are Śakuni, Nâga, Chatushpada and Kiṁstughna, but we have followed the present practice of Western India, which is supported by Varâhamihira and Brahmagupta.

the amâvâsyâ ends between sunset and sunrise it is not visible. If it ends between sunrise and sunset it may be visible, but not of course always.

41. *Lunar months and their names.* The usual modern system of naming lunar months is given above (Art. 14), and the names in use will be found in Tables II. and III. In early times, however, the months were known by another set of names, which are given below, side by side with those by which they are at present known.

	Ancient names.	Modern names.		Ancient names.	Modern names.
1.	Madhu	Chaitra	7.	Isha	Âśvina
2.	Mâdhava	Vaiśâkha	8.	Ûrja	Kârttika
3.	Śukra	Jyeshṭha	9.	Sahas	Mârgaśîrsha
4.	Śuchi	Âshâḍha	10.	Sahasya	Pausha
5.	Nabhas	Srâvaṇa	11.	Tapas	Mâgha
6.	Nabhasya	Bhâdrapada	12.	Tapasya	Phâlguna

The names "Madhu" and others evidently refer to certain seasons and may be called season-names [1] to distinguish them from "Chaitra" and those others which are derived from the nakshatras. The latter may be termed sidereal names or star-names. Season-names are now nowhere in use, but are often met with in Indian works on astronomy, and in Sanskrit literature generally.

The season-names of months are first met with in the *mantra* sections, or the *Saṁhitâs*, of both the Yâjur-Vedas, and are certainly earlier than the sidereal names which are not found in the *Saṁhitâs* of any of the Vedas, but only in some of the *Brâhmaṇas*, and even there but seldom. [2]

42. The sidereal names "Chaitra", etc., are originally derived from the names of the nakshatras. The moon in her revolution passes about twelve times completely through the twenty-seven starry nakshatras in the course of the year, and of necessity is at the full while close to some of them. The full-moon tithi *(pûrṇimâ)*, on which the moon became full when near the nakshatra Chitrâ, was called *Chaitrî;* and the lunar month which contained the *Chaitrî pûrṇimâ* was called *Chaitra* and so on.

43. But the stars or groups of stars which give their names to the months are not at equal distances from one another; and as this circumstance,—together with the phenomenon of the moon's apparent varying daily motion, and the fact that her synodic differs from her sidereal revolution—prevents the moon from becoming full year after year in the same nakshatra, it was natural that, while the twenty-seven nakshatras were allotted to the twelve months, the months themselves should be named by taking the nakshatras more or less alternately. The nakshatras thus allotted to each month are given on the next page.

44. It is clear that this practice, though it was natural in its origin and though it was ingeniously modified in later years, must often have occasioned considerable confusion; and so we find that the months gradually ceased to have their names regulated according to the conjunction of full moons and nakshatras, and were habitually named after the solar months in which they occurred. This change began to take place about 1400 B. C., the time of the

1 *Madhu* is "honey", "sweet spring". *Mâdhava*, "the sweet one". *Śukra* and *Śuchi* both mean "bright". *Nabhas*, the rainy season. *Nabhasya*, "vapoury", "rainy". *Ish* or *Isha*, "draught" or "refreshment", "fertile". *Ûrj*, "strength", "vigour". *Sahas* "strength". *Sahasya* "strong". *Tapas* "penance", "mortification", "pain", "fire". *Tapasya*, "produced by heat", "pain". All are Vedic words.

2 In my opinion the sidereal names "Chaitra" and the rest, came into use about 2000 B. C. They are certainly not later than 1500 B. C., and not earlier than 4000 B.C. [S. B D.]

Vedâṅga-jyotisha; and from the time when the zodiacal-sign-names, "Mesha" and the rest, came into use till the present day, the general rule has been that that amanta lunar month in which the Mesha saṅkrânti occurs, is called *Chaitra*, and the rest in succession.

Derivation of the Names of the Lunar Months from the Nakshatras.

Names and Grouping of the Nakshatras.	Names of the Months.
Kṛittikâ; Rohiṇî	Kârttika.
Mṛigaśiras; Ardrâ	Mârgaśirsha.
Punarvasu; Pushya	Pausha.
Aśleshâ; Maghâ	Mâgha.
Pûrva-Phalgunî; Uttara-Phalgunî; Hasta	Phâlguna.
Chitrâ; Svâti	Chaitra.
Viśâkhâ; Anurâdhâ	Vaiśâkha.
Jyeshṭhâ; Mûla	Jyeshṭha.
Pûrva-Ashâdha; Uttara-Ashâḍhâ; (Abhijit)	Âshâḍha.
(Abhijit); Śravaṇa; Dhanishṭhâ	Śrâvaṇa.
Śatatârakâ; Pûrva-Bhadrapadâ; Uttara-Bhadrapadâ	Bhâdrapada.
Revatî; Aśvinî; Bharaṇî	Aśvina.

45. *Adhika and kshaya mâsas.* It will be seen from Art. 24 that the mean length of a solar month is greater by about nine-tenths of a day than that of a lunar month, and that the true length of a solar month, according to the *Sûrya-Śiddhânta*, varies from 29 d. 7 h. 38 m. to 31 d. 15 h. 28 m. Now the moon's synodic motion, viz., her motion relative to the sun, is also irregular, and consequently all the lunar months vary in length. The variation is approximately from 29 d. 7 h. 20 m. to 29 d. 19 h. 30 m., and thus it is clear that in a lunar month there will often be no solar saṅkrânti, and occasionally, though rarely, two. This will be best understood by the following table and explanation. *(See p. 26.)*

We will suppose *(see the left side of the diagram, cols. 1, 2.)* that the sun entered the sign Mesha,—that is, that the Mesha saṅkrânti took place, and therefore the solar month Mesha commenced,—shortly before the end of an amânta lunar month, which was accordingly named "Chaitra" in conformity with the above rule (*Art. 14, or 44*); that the length of the solar month Mesha was greater than that of the following lunar month; and that the sun therefore stood in the same sign during the whole of that lunar month, entering the sign Vṛishabha shortly after the beginning of the third lunar month, which was consequently named Vaiśâkha because the Vṛishabha saṅkrânti took place, and the solar month Vṛishabha commenced, in it,—the Vṛishabha saṅkrânti being the one next following the Mesha saṅkrânti. Ordinarily there is one saṅkrânti in each lunar month, but in the present instance there was no saṅkrânti whatever in the second lunar month lying between Chaitra and Vaiśâkha.

The lunar month in which there is no saṅkrânti is called an *adhika* (added or intercalated) month; while the month which is not adhika, but is a natural month because a saṅkrânti actually occurred in it, is called *nija*, *i.e.*, true or regular month.[1] We thus have an added month between natural Chaitra and natural Vaiśâkha.

[1] Professor Kielhorn is satisfied that the terms *adhika* and *nija* are quite modern, the nomenclature usually adopted in documents and inscriptions earlier then the present century being *prathama* (first) and *dvitîyâ* (second). He alluded to this in *Ind. Ant.*, XX., p. 411. [R. S.]

The next peculiarity is that when there are two saṅkrântis in a lunar month there is a ***kshaya mâsa***, or a complete expunction of a month. Suppose, for instance, that the Vṛiśchika saṅkrânti took place shortly after the beginning of the amânta lunar month Kârttika (*see the lower half of the diagram col. 2*); that in the next lunar month the Dhanus-saṅkrânti took place

Amânta lunar months.	*Solar months; saṅkrânti to saṅkrânti.*	*Fortnights.*	*Pûrṇimânta lunar months.* [1] *By one system.*	*Pûrṇimânta lunar months.* [1] *By another system.*
1	2	3	4	5
Chaitra.		Śukla	½ Chaitra	½ Chaitra
	—Mesha saṅkrânti	Kṛishṇa	Vaiśâkha	First Vaiśâkha
Adhika Vaiśâkha	*Intercal-ated period.*	Śukla	Adhika Vaiśâkha	
		Kṛishṇa		Second Vaiśâkha
Nija Vaiśâkha	—Vṛishabha saṅkrânti	Śukla	Vaiśâkha	
		Kṛishṇa	½ Jyeshṭha	½ Jyeshṭha
(Several months are omitted here.)				
Kârttika	—Vṛiśchika saṅkrânti	Śukla	½ Kârttika	½ Kârttika
		Kṛishṇa	Mârgaśîrsha	Mârgaśîrsha
Mârgaśîrsha *(Pausha suppressed)*	—Dhanus saṅkrânti	Śukla		
		Kṛishṇa	*(Pausha suppressed)* Mâgha	*(Pausha suppressed)* Mâgha
Mâgha	—Makara saṅkrânti	Sukla		
	—Kumbha saṅkrânti	Kṛishṇa	½ Phâlguna	½ Phâlguna

shortly after it began, and the Makara-saṅkrânti shortly before it ended, so that there were two saṅkrântis in it; and that in the third month the Kumbha-saṅkrânti took place before the end of it. The lunar month in which the Kumbha-saṅkrânti occurred is naturally the month Mâgha. Thus between the natural Kârttika and the natural Mâgha there was only one lunar month instead of two, and consequently one is said to be expunged.

46. *Their names.* It will be seen that the general brief rule (*Art. 44*) for naming lunar months is altogether wanting in many respects, and therefore rules had to be framed to meet the emergency. But different rules were framed by different teachers, and so arose a difference in practice. The rule followed at present is given in the following verse.

Mînâdistho Ravir yeshâṁ âraṁbha-prathame kshaṇe | bhavet te 'bde Chândra mâsâś chaitrâdyâ dvâdaśa smṛitâḥ." ||

[1] The scheme of *pûrṇimânta* months and the rule for naming the intercalated months known to have been in use from the 12th century A.D., are followed in this diagram.

"The twelve lunar months, at whose first moment the sun stands in Mîna and the following [signs], are called Chaitra, and the others [in succession]."

According to this rule the added month in the above example (*Art. 45*) will be named Vaiśâkha, since the sun was in Mesha when it began; and in the example of the expunged month the month between the natural Kârttika and the natural Mâgha will be named Mârgaśîrsha, because the sun was in Vṛiśchika when it commenced, and Pausha will be considered as expunged.

This rule is given in a work named *Kâlatatva-vivechana*, and is attributed to the sage Vyâsa. The celebrated astronomer Bhâskarâchârya (A. D. 1150) seems to have followed the same rule,[1] and it must therefore have been in use at least as early as the 12th century A. D. As it is the general rule obtaining through most part of India in the present day we have followed it in this work.

There is another rule which is referred to in some astronomical and other works, and is attributed to the *Brahma-Siddhânta*.[2] It is as follows:

"*Meshâdisthe Savitari yo yo mâsaḥ prapûryate chândraḥ | Chaitrâdyaḥ sa jñeyaḥ pûrtid-vitve 'dhimâso 'ntyaḥ.*" ||

"That lunar month which is completed when the sun is in [the sign] Mesha etc., is to be known as Chaitra, etc. [respectively]; when there are two completions, the latter [of them] is an added month."

It will be seen from the Table given above (p. 26) that for the names of ordinary months both rules are the same, but that they differ in the case of added and suppressed months. The added month between natural Chaitra and natural Vaiśâkha, in the example in *Art. 45*, having ended when the sun was in Mesha, would be named "Chaitra" by this second rule, but "Vaiśâkha" by the first rule, because it commenced when the sun was in Mesha. Again, the month between natural Kârttika and natural Mâgha, in the example of an expunged month, having ended when the sun was in Makara, would be named "Pausha" by this second rule, and consequently Mârgaśîrsha would be expunged; while by the first rule it would be named "Mârgaśîrsha" since it commenced when the sun was in Vṛiśchika, and Pausha would be the expunged month. It will be noticed, of course, that the difference is only in name and not in the period added or suppressed.[3] Both these rules should be carefully borne in mind when studying inscriptions or records earlier than 1100 A. D.

47. *Their determination according to true and mean systems.* It must be noted with regard to the intercalation and suppression of months, that whereas at present these are regulated by the sun's and moon's apparent motion,—in other words, by the apparent length of the solar and lunar months—and though this practice has been in use at least from A. D. 1100 and was followed by Bhaskarâchârya, there is evidence to show that in earlier times they were regulated by the mean length of months. It was at the epoch of the celebrated astronomer Śrîpati,[4] or about A. D. 1040, that the change of practice took place, as evidenced by the following passage in his *Siddhânta Śekhara*, (quoted in the *Jyotisha-darpaṇa*, in A. D. 1557.)

1 See his *Siddhânta-Siromaṇi*, *madhyamâdhikâra*, *adhimâsanirṇaya*, verse 6, and his own commentary on it. [S. B. D.]

2 It is not to be found in either of the *Brahma-Siddhântas* referred to above, but there is a third Brahma-Siddhânta which I have not seen as yet. [S. B. D.]

3 In Prof. Chattre's list of added and suppressed months, in those published in Mr. Cowasjee Patells' *Chronology*, and in General Sir A. Cunningham's *Indian Eras* it is often noted that the same month is both added and suppressed. But it is clear from the above rules and definitions that this is impossible. A month cannot be both added and suppressed at the same time. The mistake arose probably from resort being made to the first rule for naming *adhika* months, and to the second for the suppressed months.

4 Thanks are due to Mr. Mahadeo Chimṇâjî Apte, B.A., L.L.B., very recently deceased, the founder of the Ânandâśrama at Poona, for his discovery of a part of Śrîpati's *Karaṇa* named the *Dhîkoṭida*, from which I got Śrîpati's date. I find that it was written in Śaka 961 expired (A.D. 1039-40). [S. B. D.]

Madhyama-Ravi-saṅkrânti-praveśa-rahito bhaved adhikaḥ
Madhyaś Chândro mâso madhyâdhika-lakshaṇam chaitat ||
Vidvâṁsas-tv-âchâryâ nirasya madhyâdhikaṁ mâsaṁ
Kuryuḥ sphuṭa-mânena hi yato 'dhikaḥ spashṭa eva syât. ||

"The lunar month which has no mean sun's entrance into a sign shall be a mean intercalated month. This is the definition of a mean added month. The learned Âchâryas should leave off [using] the mean added months, and should go by apparent reckoning, by which the added month would be apparent (true)."

It is clear, therefore, that mean intercalations were in use up to Śrîpatis time. In the *Vedâṅga Jyotisha* only the mean motions of the sun and moon are taken into account, and it may therefore be assumed that at that time the practice of regulating added and suppressed months by apparent motions was unknown. These apparent motions of the sun and moon are treated of in the astronomical *Siddhântas* at present in use, and so far as is known the present system of astronomy came into force in India not later than 400 A. D. [1] But on the other hand, the method of calculating the ahargaṇa (a most important matter), and of calculating the places of planets, given in the *Sûrya* and other *Siddhântas*, is of such a nature that it seems only natural to suppose that the system of mean intercalations obtained for many centuries after the present system of astronomy came into force, and thus we find Śrîpati's utterance quoted in an astronomical work of the 15th century. There can be no suppression of the month by the mean system, for the mean length of a solar month is longer than that of a mean lunar month, and therefore two mean saṅkrântis cannot take place in a mean lunar month.

The date of the adoption of the true (apparent) system of calculating added and suppressed months is not definitely known. Bhâskarâchârya speaks of suppressed months, and it seems from his work that mean intercalations were not known in his time (A. D. 1150.) We have therefore in our Tables given mean added months up to A. D. 1100, and true added and suppressed months for the whole period covered by our Tables. [2]

48. For students more familiar with solar reckoning we will give the rules for the intercalation and suppression of months in another form. Ordinarily one lunar month ends in each solar month. When two lunar months end in a solar month the latter of the two is said to be an *adhika* (added or intercalated) month, and by the present practice it receives the name of the following natural lunar month, but with the prefix *adhika*. Thus in the Table on p 25, two lunar months end during the solar month Mesha, the second of which is *adhika* and receives, by the present practice, the name of the following natural lunar month, Vaiśâkha. When no lunar month ends in a solar month there is a *kshaya mâsa*, or expunged or suppressed month; *i.e.*, the name of one lunar month is altogether dropped, viz., by the present practice, the one following that which would be derived from the solar month. Thus, in the Table above, no lunar month ends in the solar month Dhanus. Mârgaśîrsha is the name of the month in which the Dhanus saṅkrânti occurs; the name Pausha is therefore expunged.

The rule for naming natural lunar months, and the definition of, and rule for naming, added

1 Up to recently the date was considered to be about the 6th century A.D. Dr. Thibaut, one of the highest living authorities on Indian Astronomy, fixes it at 400 A.D. (See his edition of the *Pañcha Siddhântikâ* Introd., p. LX.). My own opinion is that it came into existence not later than the 2nd century B.C. [S. B. D.]

2 I am inclined to believe that of the two rules for naming lunar months the second was connected with the mean system of added months, and that the first came into existence with the adoption of the true system. But I am not as yet in possession of any evidence on the point. See, however, the note to Art. 51 below. [S. B. D.]

and suppressed months, may be summed up as follows. That amânta lunar month in which the Mesha saṅkrânti occurs is called Chaitra, and the rest in succession. That amânta lunar month in which there is no saṅkrânti is *adhika* and receives the name (1) of the preceding natural lunar month by the old *Brahma-Siddhânta* rule, (2) of the following natural lunar month by the present rule. When there are two saṅkrântis in one amânta lunar month, the name which would be derived from the first is dropped by the old *Brahma-Siddhânta* rule, the name which would be derived from the second is dropped by the present rule.

49. *Different results by different Siddhântas.* The use of different *Siddhântas* will sometimes create a difference in the month to be intercalated or suppressed, but only when a saṅkrânti takes place very close [1] to the end of the amâvâsyâ. Such cases will be rare. Our calculations for added and suppressed months have been made by the *Sûrya-Siddhânta*, and to assist investigation we have been at the pains to ascertain and particularize the exact moments (given in tithi-indices, and tithis and decimals) of the saṅkrântis preceding and succeeding an added or suppressed month, from which it can be readily seen if there be a probability of any divergence in results if a different *Siddhânta* be used. The Special Tables published by Professor Jacobi in the *Epigraphia Indica* (Vol., II., pp. 403 ff.) must not be relied on for calculations of added and suppressed months of *Siddhântas* other than the *Sûrya-Siddhânta*. If a different *Siddhânta* happened to have been used by the original computor of the given Hindu date, and if such date is near to or actually in an added or suppressed month according to our Table I., it is possible that the result as worked out by our Tables may be a whole month wrong. Our mean intercalations from A. D. 300 to 1100 are the same by the original *Sûrya-Siddhânta*, the present *Sûrya-Siddhânta*, and the first *Ârya-Siddhânta.*

50. *Some peculiarities.* Certain points are worth noticing in connection with our calculations of the added and suppressed months for the 1600 years from A. D. 300 to 1900 according to the *Sûrya-Siddhânta.*

(*a*) Intercalations occur generally in the 3rd, 5th, 8th, 11th, 14th, 16th and 19th years of a cycle of 19 years. (*b*) A month becomes intercalary at an interval of 19 years over a certain period, and afterwards gives way generally to one of the months preceding it, but sometimes, though rarely, to the following one. (*c*) Out of the seven intercalary months of a cycle one or two are always changed in the next succeeding cycle, so that after a number of cycles the whole are replaced by others. (*d*) During our period of 1600 years the months Mârgaśîrsha, Pausha, and Mâgha are never intercalary. (*e*) The interval between years where a suppression of the month occurs is worth noticing. In the period covered by our Tables the first suppressed month is in A.D. 404, and the intervals are thus: 19, 65, 38, 19, 19, 46, 19, 141, 122, 19, 141, 141, 65, 19, 19, 19, 19, 46, 76, 46, 141, 141, and an unfinished period of 78 years. At first sight there seems no regularity, but closer examination shews that the periods group themselves into three classes, viz., (i.) 19, 38, 76; (ii.) 141; and (iii.) 122, 65 and 46 years; the first of which consists of 19 or its multiples, the second is a constant, and the third is the difference between (ii.) and (i.) or between 141 and a multiple of 19. The unfinished period up to 1900 A.D. being 78 years, we are led by these peculiarities to suppose that there will be no suppressed month till at earliest (122 years =)

[1] It is difficult to define the exact limit, because it varies with different *Siddhântas*, and even for one *Siddhânta* it is not always the same. It is, however, generally not more than six ghaṭikâs, or about 33 of our tithi-indices *(t)*. But in the case of some *Siddhântas* as corrected with a bîja the difference may amount sometimes to as much as 20 ghaṭikâs, or 113 of our tithi-indices. It would be very rare to find any difference in true added months; but in the case of suppressed months we might expect some divergence, a month suppressed by one authority not being the same as that suppressed by another, or there being no suppression at all by the latter in some cases. Differences in mean added months would be very rare, except in the case of the *Brahma-Siddhânta*, *(See Art. 88.)*

A.D. 1944, and possibly not till (141 years =) A.D. 1963. [1] (*d*) Mâgha is only once suppressed in Saka 1398 current, Mârgaśîrsha is suppressed six times, and Pausha 18 times. No other month is suppressed.

Bhâskarâchârya lays down [2] that Kârttika, Mârgaśîrsha and Pausha only are liable to be suppressed, but this seems applicable only to the *Brahma-Siddhânta* of which Bhâskarâchârya was a follower. He further states, "there was a suppressed month in the Śaka year 974 expired, and there will be one in Śaka 1115, 1256 and 1378 all expired", and this also seems applicable to the *Brahma-Siddhânta* only. By the *Sûrya-Siddhânta* there were suppressed months in all these years except the last one, and there was an additional suppression in Śaka 1180 expired.

Gaṇeśa Daivajña, the famous author of the *Grahalâghava* (A.D. 1520), as quoted by his grandson, in his commentary on the *Siddhânta-Śiromaṇi*, says, "By the *Sûrya-Siddhânta* there will be a suppressed month in Saka 1462, 1603, 1744, 1885, 2026, 2045, 2148, 2167, 2232, 2373, 2392, 2514, 2533, 2655, 2674, 2796 and 2815, and by the *Ârya-Siddhânta* [3] there will be one in 1481, 1763, 1904, 2129, 2186, 2251 (all expired)." The first four by *Sûrya* calculations agree with our results.

51. By the *pûrṇimânta scheme.* Notwithstanding that the pûrṇimânta scheme of months is and was in use in Northern India, the amânta scheme alone is recognized in the matter of the nomenclature and intercalation of lunar months and the commencement of the luni-solar year. The following is the method adopted—first, the ordinary rule of naming a month is applied to an amânta lunar month, and then, by the pûrṇimânta scheme, the dark fortnight of it receives the name of the following month. The correspondence of amânta and pûrṇimânta fortnights for a year is shown in Table II., Part i., and it will be observed that the bright fortnights have the same name by both schemes while the dark fortnights differ by a month, and thus the pûrṇimânta scheme is always a fortnight in advance of the amânta scheme.

The saṅkrântis take place in definite amânta lunar months, thus the Makara-saṅkrânti invariably takes place in amânta Pausha, and in no other month; but when it takes place in the kṛishṇa-paksha of amânta Pausha it falls in pûrṇimânta Mâgha, because that fortnight is said to belong to Mâgha by the pûrṇimânta scheme. If, however, it takes place in the śukla paksha, the month is Pausha by both schemes. Thus the Makara-saṅkrânti, though according to the amânta scheme it can only fall in Pausha, may take place either in Pausha or Mâgha by the pûrṇimânta scheme; and so with the rest.

The following rules govern pûrṇimânta intercalations. Months are intercalated at first as if there were no pûrṇimânta scheme, and afterwards the dark fortnight preceding the intercalated month receives, as usual, the name of the month to which the following natural bright fortnight belongs, and therefore the intercalated month also receives that name. Thus, in the example given above (*Art. 45*), intercalated amânta Vaiśâkha (as named by the first rule) lies between natural amânta Chaitra and natural amânta Vaiśâkha. But by the pûrṇimanta scheme the dark half of natural amânta Chaitra acquires the name of natural Vaiśâkha; then follow the two fortnights of adhika Vaiśâkha; and after them comes the bright half of the (nija) natural pûrṇimânta

1 This relation of intervals is a distinct assistance to calculation, as it should lead us to look with suspicion on any suppression of a month which does not conform to it.

2 See the *Siddhânta-Siromaṇi*, *Madhyamâdhikâra*. Bhâskara wrote in Śaka 1072 (A.D. 1150). He did not give the names of the suppressed months.

3 I have ascertained that Gaṇeśa has adopted in his *Grahalâghava* some of the elements of the *Ârya-Siddhânta* as corrected by Lalla's bîja, and by putting to test one of the years noted I find that in these calculations also the *Ârya-Siddhânta* as corrected by Lalla's bîja was used. Gaṇeśa was a most accurate calculator, and I feel certain that his results can be depended upon. [S. B. D.]

Vaiśâkha. Thus it happens that half of natural pûrṇimânta Vaiśâkha comes before, and half after, the intercalated month. [1]

Of the four fortnights thus having the name of the same month the first two fortnights are sometimes called the "*First Vaiśâkha,*" and the last two the "*Second Vaiśâkha.*"

It will be seen from Table II., Part i., that amânta Phâlguna kṛishṇa is pûrṇimânta Chaitra kṛishṇa. The year, however, does not begin then, but on the same day as the amânta month, *i.e.*, with the new moon, or the beginning of the next bright fortnight.

Having discussed the lesser divisions of time, we now revert to the Hindu year. And, first, its beginning.

Years and Cycles.

52. *The Hindu New-year's Day.*—In Indian astronomical works the year is considered to begin, if luni-solar, invariably with amânta Chaitra Śukla 1st,—if solar with the Mesha saṅkrânti; and in almost all works *mean* Mesha saṅkrânti is taken for convenience of calculations, very few works adopting the apparent or true one. At present in Bengal and the Tamil country, where solar reckoning is in use, the year, for religious and astronomical purposes, commences with the apparent Mesha-saṅkrânti, and the civil year with the first day of the month Mesha, as determined by the practice of the country *(See above Art. 28).* But since mean Mesha-saṅkrânti is taken as the commencement of the solar year in astronomical works, it is only reasonable to suppose that the year actually began with it in practice in earlier times, and we have to consider how long ago the practice ceased.

In a *Karaṇa* named *Bhâsvatî* (A. D. 1099) the year commences with apparent Mesha saṅkrânti, and though it is dangerous to theorize from one work, we may at least quote it as shewing that the present practice was known as early as A. D. 1100. This date coinciding fairly well with Śrîpati's injunction quoted above *(Art. 47)* we think it fair to assume for the present that the practice of employing the mean Mesha saṅkrânti for fixing the beginning of the year ceased about the same time as the practice of mean intercalary months.

The luni-solar Chaitrâdi [2] year commences, for certain religious and astrological purposes, with the first moment of the first tithi of Chaitra, or Chaitra śukla pratipadâ and this, of course, may fall at any time of the day or night, since it depends on the moment of new moon. But for the religious ceremonies connected with the beginning of a samvatsara (year), the sunrise of the day on which Chaitra śukla pratipadâ is current at sunrise is taken as the first or opening day of the year. When this tithi is current at sunrise on two days, as sometimes happens, the first, and when it is not current at any sunrise (*i.e.*, when it is expunged) then the day on which it ends, is taken as the opening day. For astronomical purposes the learned take any convenient

1 Such an anomaly with regard to the pûrṇimânta scheme could not occur if the two rules were applied, one that "that pûrṇimânta month in which the Mesha saṅkrânti occurs is always called Chaitra, and so on in succession," and the other that "that pûrṇimânta month in which no saṅkrânti occurs is called an intercalated month." The rules were, I believe, in use in the sixth century A. D. *(See my remarks Ind. Ant., XX., p.* 50 *f.)* But the added month under such rules would never agree with the amânta added months. There would be from 14 to 17 months' difference in the intercalated months between the two, and much inconvenience would arise thereby. It is for this reason probably that the pûrṇimânta scheme is not recognised in naming months, and that pûrṇimânta months are named arbitrarily, as described in the first para. of Art. 51. This arbitrary rule was certainly in use in the 11th century A.D. *(See Ind. Ant., vol. VI., p.* 53, where the Makara-saṅkrânti is said to have taken place in Mâgha.*)*

After this arbitrary rule of naming the pûrṇimânta months once came into general use, it was impossible in Northern India to continue using the second, or *Brahma-Siddhânta*, rule for naming the months. For in the example in *Art.* 45 above the intercalated month would by that rule be named Chaitra, but if its preceding fortnight be a fortnight of Vaiśâkha it is obvious that the intercalated month cannot be named Chaitra. In Southern India the practice may have continued in use a little longer. [S. B. D.]

2 *Chaitrâdi*, "beginning with Chaitra"; ***Kârttikâdi***, "beginning with Kârttika; ***Meshâdi***, with Mesha; and so on.

moment,—such as mean sunrise, noon, sunset, or midnight, but generally the sunrise,—on or before Chaitra śukla pratipadâ, as their starting-point. [1] Sometimes the beginning of the mean Chaitra śukla pratipadâ is so taken.

When Chaitra is intercalary there seems to be a difference of opinion whether the year in that case is to begin with the intercalated (*adhika*) or natural (*nija*) Chaitra. For the purposes of our Table I. (cols. 19 to 25) we have taken the adhika Chaitra of the true system as the first month of the year.

But the year does not begin with Chaitra all over India. In Southern India and especially in Gujarât the years of the Vikrama era commence in the present day with Kârttika śukla pratipadâ. In some parts of Kâṭhiâvâd and Gujarât the Vikrama year commences with Âshâḍha śukla pratipadâ. [2] In a part of Ganjam and Orissa, the year begins on Bhâdrapada śukla 12th. (*See under Oṅko reckoning, Art. 64.*) The Amli year in Orissa begins on Bhâdrapada śukla 12th, the Vilâyatî year, also in general use in Orissa, begins with the Kanyâ saṅkrânti; and the Fasli year, which is luni-solar in Bengal, commences on pûrṇimânta Âśvina kṛi. 1st (viz., 4 days later than the Vilâyatî).

In the South Malayâḷam country (Travancore and Cochin), and in Tinnevelly, the solar year of the Kollam era, or Kollam ânḍu, begins with the month Chiṅgam (Siṁha), and in the North Malayâḷam tract it begins with the month Kanni (Kanyâ). In parts of the Madras Presidency the Fasli year originally commenced on the 1st of the solar month Âdi (Karka), but by Government order about A.D. 1800 it was made to begin on the 13th of July, and recently it was altered again, so that now it begins on 1st July. In parts of the Bombay Presidency the Fasli year begins when the sun enters the nakshatra Mṛigaśirsha, which takes place at present about the 5th or 6th of June.

Alberuni mentions (A.D. 1030) a year commencing with Mârgaśîrsha as having been in use in Sindh, Multân, and Kanouj, as well as at Lahore and in that neighbourhood; also a year commencing with Bhâdrapada in the vicinity of Kashmîr. [3] In the *Mahâbhârata* the names of the months are given in some places, commencing with Mârgaśîrsha. (*Anuśâsana parva adhyâyas 106 and 109*). In the *Vedâṅga Jyotisha* the year commences with Mâgha śukla pratipadâ.

53. *The Sixty-year cycle of Jupiter.* [4] In this reckoning the years are not known by numbers, but are named in succession from a list of 60 names, often known as the "Bṛihaspati samvatsara chakra," [5] the wheel or cycle of the years of Jupiter. Each of these years is called a "samvatsara." The word "samvatsara" generally means a year, but in the case of this cycle the year is not equal to a solar year. It is regulated by Jupiter's mean motion; and a Jovian year is the period during which the planet Jupiter enters one sign of the zodiac and passes completely through it

1 See *Ind. Ant.*, XIX., p. 45, second paragraph of my article on the Original *Sûrya-Siddhânta*. [S. B. D.]

2 I have myself seen a pañchâṅg which mentions this beginning of the year, and have also found some instances of the use of it in the present day I am told that at Iḍar in Gujarât the Vikrama samvat begins on Âshâḍha kṛishṇa dvitîyâ. [S. B. D.]

3 The passage, as translated by Sachau (Vol. II., p. 8 f), is as follows. "Those who use the Saka era, the astronomers, begin the year with the month Chaitra, whilst the inhabitants of Kanîr, which is conterminous with Kashmîr, begin it with the month Bhâdrapada... All the people who inhabit the country between Bardarî and Mârîgala begin the year with the month Kârttika... The people living in the country of Nîrahara, behind Mârîgala, as far as the utmost frontiers of Tâkeshar and Lohâvar, begin the year with the month Mârgaśîrsha... The people of Lanbaga, *i.e.*, Lamghân, follow their example. I have been told by the people of Multân that this system is peculiar to the people of Sindh and Kanoj, and that they used to begin the year with the new moon of Mârgaśîrsha, but that the people of Multân only a few years ago had given up this system, and had adopted the system of the people of Kashmîr, and followed their example in beginning the year with the new moon of Chaitra."

4 Articles 53 to 61 are applicable to Northern India only (*See Art.* 62)

5 The term is one not recognized in Sanskrit works. [S. B. D.]

with reference to his mean motion. The cycle commences with Prabhava. See Table I., cols. 6, 7, and Table XII.

54. The duration of a Bârhaspatya samvatsara, according to the *Sûrya-Siddhânta*, is about 361.026721 days, that is about 4.232 days less than a solar year. If, then, a samvatsara begins exactly with the solar year the following samvatsara will commence 4.232 days before the end of it. So that in each successive year the commencement of a samvatsara will be 4.232 days in advance, and a time will of course come when two samvatsaras will begin during the same solar year. For example, by the *Sûrya-Siddhânta* with the bîja, Prabhava (No. 1) was current at the beginning of the solar year Saka 1779. Vibhava (No. 2) commenced 3.3 days after the beginning of that year, that is after the Mesha saṅkrânti; and Śukla (No. 3) began 361.03 days after Vibhava, that is 364.3 days after the beginning of the year. Thus Vibhava and Śukla both began in the same solar year. Now as Prabhava was current at the beginning of Śaka 1779, and Śukla was current at the beginning of Śaka 1780, Vibhava was expunged in the regular method followed in the North. Thus the rule is that when two Bârhaspatya samvatsaras begin during one solar year the first is said to be expunged, or to have become *kshaya*; and it is clear that when a samvatsara begins within a period of about 4.232 days after a Mesha saṅkrânti it will be expunged.

By the *Sûrya Siddhânta* $85\frac{65}{211}$ solar years are equal to $86\frac{65}{211}$ Jovian years. So that one expunction is due in every period of $85\frac{65}{211}$ solar years. But since it really takes place according to the rule explained above, the interval between two expunctions is sometimes 85 and sometimes 86 years.

55. Generally speaking the samvatsara which is current at the beginning of a year is in practice coupled with all the days of that year, notwithstanding that another samvatsara may have begun during the course of the year. Indeed if there were no such practice there would be no occasion for an expunction. Epigraphical and other instances, however, have been found in which the actual samvatsara for the time is quoted with dates, notwithstanding that another samvatsara was current at the beginning of the year. [1]

56. *Variations.* As the length of the solar year and year of Jupiter differs with different *Siddhântas* it follows that the expunction of samvatsaras similarly varies.

57. Further, since a samvatsara is expunged when two samvatsaras begin in the same year, these expunctions will differ with the different kinds of year. Where luni-solar years are in use it is only natural to suppose that the rule will be made applicable to that kind of year, an expunction occurring when two samvatsaras begin in such a year; and there is evidence to show that in some places at least, such was actually the case for a time. Now the length of an ordinary luni-solar year (354 days) is less than that of a Jovian year (361 days), and therefore the beginning of two consecutive samvatsaras can only occur in those luni-solar years in which there is an intercalary month. Again, the solar year sometimes commences with the *mean* Mesha-saṅkrânti, and this again gives rise to a difference. [2]

The *Jyotisha-tattva* rule *(given below Art. 59)* gives the samvatsara current at the time of the *mean*, not of the *apparent*, Mesha-saṅkrânti, and hence all expunctions calculated thereby must be held to refer to the solar year only when it is taken to commence with the mean Mesha-saṅkrânti. [3] It is important that this should be remembered.

1 See *Ind. Ant.*, Vol. XIX., pp. 27, 33, 187.

2 These points have not yet been noticed by any European writer on Indian Astronomy. [S. B. D.]

3 As to the mean Mesha-saṅkrânti, see *Art.* 26 above.

58. *To find the current samvatsara.* The samvatsaras in our Table I., col. 7, are calculated by the *Sûrya-Siddhânta* without the bîja up to A.D. 1500, and with the bîja from A.D. 1501 to 1900; and are calculated from the *apparent* Mesha-saṅkrânti. If the samvatsara current on a particular day by some other authority is required, calculations must be made direct for that day according to that authority, and we therefore proceed to give some rules for this process.

59. *Rules for finding the Bârhaspatya samvatsara current on a particular day.* [1]

a. By the Sûrya-Siddhânta. [2] Multiply the expired Kali year by 211. Subtract 108 from the product. Divide the result by 18000. To the quotient, excluding fractions, add the numeral of the expired Kali year plus 27. Divide the sum by 60. The remainder, counting from Prabhava as 1, is the samvatsara current at the beginning of the given solar year, that is at its apparent Mesha-saṅkrânti. Subtract from 18000 the remainder previously left after dividing by 18000. Multiply the result by 361, and divide the product by 18000. Calculate for days, ghaṭikâs, and palas. Add 15 palas to the result. The result is then the number of days, etc., elapsed between the apparent Mesha-saṅkrânti and the end of the samvatsara current thereon. By this process can be found the samvatsara current on any date.

Example 1.—Wanted the samvatsara current at the beginning of Saka 233 expired and the date on which it ended. Śaka 233 expired = (Table I.) Kali 3412 expired. $\frac{3412 \times 211 - 108}{18000} = 39\frac{17824}{18000}$. $39 + 3412 + 27 = 3478$. $\frac{3478}{60} = 57\frac{58}{60}$. The remainder is 58; and we have it that No. 58 Raktâkshin *(Table XII.)* was the samvatsara current at the beginning (apparent Mesha-saṅkrânti) of the given year. Again; $18000 - 17824 = 176$. $\frac{176 \times 361}{18000} = 3$ d. 31 gh. 47.2 p. Adding 15 pa. we have 3 d. 32 gh. 2.2 pa. This shews that Raktâkshin will end and Krodhana (No. 59) begin 3 d. 32 gh. 2.2 pa. after the apparent Meska-saṅkrânti. This last, by the *Sûrya Siddhânta*, occurred on 17th March, A.D. 311, at 27 gh. 23 pa. (*see Table I., col. 13, and the Table in Art. 96*), and therefore Krodhana began on the 20th March at 59 gh. 25.2 pa., or 34.8 palas before mean sunrise on 21st March. We also know that since Krodhaṇa commences within four days after Mesha it will be expunged (*Art. 54 above.*)

b. By the Ârya Siddhânta. Multiply the expired Kali year by 22. Subtract 11 from the product. Divide the result by 1875. To the quotient excluding fractions add the expired Kali year + 27. Divide the sum by 60. The remainder, counted from Prabhava as 1, is the samvatsara current at the beginning of the given solar year. Subtract from 1875 the remainder previously left after dividing by 1875. Multiply the result by 361. Divide the product by 1875. Add 1 gh. 45 pa. to the quotient. The result gives the number of days, etc., that have elapsed between the apparent Mesha-saṅkrânti and the end of the samvatsara current thereon.

Example 2.—Required the samvatsara current at the beginning of Śaka 230 expired, and the time when it ended.

Śaka 230 expired = Kali 3409 expired. $\frac{3409 \times 22 - 11}{1875} = 39\frac{1862}{1875}$. $39 + 3409 + 27 = 3475$, which, divided by 60, gives the remainder 55. Then No. 55 Durmati *(Table XII.)* was current at the beginning of the given year. Again; $1875 - 1862 = 13$. $\frac{13 \times 361}{1875} = 2$ d. 30 gh. 10.56 pa. Adding 1 gh.

1 By all these rules the results will be correct within two ghaṭikâs where the moment of the Mesha-saṅkranti according to the authority used is known.

2 The rule for the present *Vasishṭha*, the *Sákalya Brahma*, the *Romaka*, and the *Soma Siddhântas* is exactly the same. That by the original *Súrya-Siddhánta* is also similar, but in that case the result will be incorrect by about 2 ghaṭikâs (48 minutes). For all these authorities take the time of the Mesha-saṅkrânti by the present *Súrya-Siddhánta* or by the *Árya-Siddhánta*, whichever may be available. The moment of the Mesha-saṅkrântri according to the *Súrya-Siddhánta* is given in our Table I. only for the years A.D. 1100 to 1900. The same moment for all years between A.D. 300 and 1100 can be found by the Table in Art. 96. If the *Árya-Siddhánta* saṅkrânti is used for years A.D. 300 to 1100 the result will never be incorrect by more than 2 ghaṭikâs 45 palas (1 hour and 6 minutes). The Table should be referred to.

45 pa., we get 2 d. 31 gh. 55.56 pa. Add this to the moment of the Mesha saṅkrânti as given in Table I., cols. 13—16, viz., 16th March, 308 A.D., Tuesday, at 41 gh. 40 p., and we have 19th March, Friday, 13 gh. 35.56 p. after mean sunrise as the moment when Durmati ends and Dundubhi begins. Here again, since Dundubhi commences within four days of the Mesha saṅkrânti, it will be expunged.

c. By the Sûrya-Siddhânta with the bîja (to be used for years after about 1500 A.D.). Multiply the expired Kali year by 117. Subtract 60 from the product. Divide the result by 10000. To the figures of the quotient, excluding fractions, add the number of the expired Kali year plus 27. Divide the sum by 60. And the remainder, counted from Prabhava as 1, is the samvatsara current at the beginning of the given solar year. Subtract from 10000 the remainder left after the previous division by 10000. Multiply the difference by 361, and divide the product by 10000. Add 15 pa. The result is the number of days, etc., that have elapsed between the apparent Mesha saṅkrânti and the end of the samvatsara current thereon. [1]

Example.—Required the samvatsara current at the beginning of Śaka 1436 expired, and the moment when it ends. Śaka 1436 expired = Kali 4615 expired (Table I.). $\frac{4615\times117-60}{10000} = 53\frac{9895}{10000}$ $\frac{53+4615+27}{60} = 78\frac{15}{60}$. The remainder 15 shews that Vṛisha was current at the Mesha-saṅkrânti. $\frac{(10000-9895)\ 361}{10000}$ + 15 p. = 3 d. 47 gh. 25.8 p. + 15 p. = 3 d. 47 gh. 40.8 p. Table I. gives the Mesha-saṅkrânti as March 27th, 44 gh. 25 p., Monday. 27 d. 44 gh. 25 p. + 3 d. 47 gh. 40.8 p. = 31 d. 32 gh. 5.8 p.; and this means that Vṛisha ended at 32 gh. 5.8 p. after mean sunrise at Ujjain on Friday, 31st March. At that moment Chitrabhânu begins, and since it began within four days of the Mesha-saṅkrânti, it is expunged.

d. Bṛihatsaṁhitâ and Jyotishatattva Rules. The rules given in the *Bṛihatsaṁhitâ* and the *Jyotishatattva* seem to be much in use, and therefore we give them here. The *Jyotishatattva* rule is the same as that for the *Ârya-Siddhânta* given above, except that it yields the year current at the time of mean Mesha-saṅkranti, and that it is adapted to Śaka years. The latter difference is merely nominal of course, as the moment of the beginning of a samvatsara is evidently the same by both. [2] We have slightly modified the rules, but in words only and not in sense.

The *Jyotishatattva* rule is this. Multiply the current Śaka year by 22. Add 4291. Divide the sum by 1875. To the quotient excluding fractions add the number of the current Śaka year. Divide the sum by 60. The remainder, counted from Prabhava as 1, is the samvatsara current at the beginning of the given year. Subtract the remainder left after previously dividing by 1875 from 1875. Multiply the result by 361. And divide the product by 1875. The result gives the number of days by which, according to the *Ârya-Siddhânta*, the samvatsara ends after mean Mesha-saṅkrânti. The mean [3] Mesha-saṅkranti will be obtained by adding 2d. 8 gh. 51 pa. 15 vipa. to the time given in Table I., cols. 13 to 18.

Work out by this rule the example given above under the *Ârya-Siddhânta* rule, and the result will be found to be the same by both.

The Bṛihatsaṁhitâ rule. Multiply the expired Śaka year by 44. Add 8589. Divide the sum by 3750. To the quotient, excluding fractions, add the number of the expired Śaka year

[1] In these three rules the apparent Mesha-saṅkrânti is taken. If we omit the subtraction of 108, 11, and 60, and do not add 15 p., 1 gh. 45 p., and 15 p. respectively, the result will be correct with respect to the mean Mesha-saṅkrânti.

[2] I have not seen the *Jyotishatattva* (or "*Jyotishtava*" as Warren calls it, but which seems to be a mistake), but I find the rule in the *Ratnamâlâ* of Śrîpati (A.D. 1039). It must be as old as that by the *Ârya-Siddhânta*, since both are the same. [S. B. D.]

[3] If we add 4280 instead of 4291, and add 1 gh. 45 pa. to the final result, the time so arrived at will be the period elapsed since apparent Mesha-saṅkranti. Those who interpret the *Jyotishatattva* rule in any different way have failed to grasp its proper meaning. [S. B. D.]

plus 1. Divide the sum by 60. The remainder, counted from Prabhava as 1, is the samvatsara current at the beginning of the year. Subtract from 3750 the remainder obtained after the previous division by 3750. Multiply the result by 361, and divide the product by 3750. This gives the number of days by which the samvatsara current at the beginning of the year will end after the Mesha saṅkranti. [1]

60. *List of Expunged Samvatsaras.* The following is a comparative list of expunged samvatsaras as found by different authorities, taking the year to begin at the mean Mesha saṅkrânti.

List of Expunged Samvatsaras.[2]

First Arya-Siddhânta, Bṛihat-saṁhitâ, Ratnamâlâ, Jyotis-hatattava Rules.			*Sûrya-Siddhânta* Rule without *bîja* up to 1500 A.D., and with *bîja* afterwards.			*First Arya-Siddhânta. Bṛihat-saṁhitâ, Ratnamâlâ, Jyotis-hatattava* Rules.			*Sûrya-Siddhânta* Rule without *bîja* up to 1500 A. D., and with *bîja* afterwards.		
Śaka year current.	A. D.	Expunged Samvatsara.	Śaka year current.	A. D.	Expunged Samvatsara.	Śaka year current.	A. D.	Expunged Samvatsara.	Śaka year current.	A. D.	Expunged Samvatsara.
232	309-10	57 Rudhirodgârin	234	311-12	59 Krodhana	1084	1161-62	19 Pârthiva	1087	1164-65	22 Sarvadhârin
317	394-95	23 Virodhin	319*	396-97	25 Khara	1169	1246-47	45 Virodhakṛit	1172*	1249-50	48 Ânanda
402	479-80	49 Râkshasa	404*	481-82	51 Piṅgala	1254	1331-32	11 Îśvara	1258	1335-36	15 Vṛisha
487	564-65	15 Vṛisha	490	567-68	18 Târaṇa	1340	1417-18	38 Krodhin	1343	1420-21	41 Plavaṅga
572	649-50	41 Plavaṅga	575*	652-53	44 Sâdhâraṇa	1425	1502-03	4 Pramoda	1437	1514-15	16 Chitrabhânu
658	735-36	8 Bhâva	660*	737-38	10 Dhâtṛi	1510	1587-88	30 Durmukha	1522*	1599-1600	42 Kîlaka
743	820-21	34 Śârvari	746	823-24	37 Śobhana						
828	905-06	60 Kshaya	831	908-09	3 Śukla	1595	1672-73	56 Dundubhi	1608	1685-86	9 Yuvan
913	990-91	26 Nandana	916*	993-94	29 Manmatha	1680	1757-58	22 Sarvadhârin	1693*	1770-71	35 Plava
999	1076-77	53 Siddhârthin	1002	1079-80	56 Dundubhi	1766	1843-44	49 Râkshasa	1779	1856-57	2 Vibhava

If we take the years to commence with the apparent Mesha-saṅkrânti the samvatsaras expunged by *Sûrya Siddhânta* calculation will be found in Table I., col. 7; and those by the *Ârya Siddhânta* can be found by the rule for that *Siddhânta* given in *Art. 59* above.

61. The years of Jupiter's cycle are not mentioned in very early inscriptions. They are mentioned in the *Sûrya-Siddhânta.* Dr. J. Burgess states that he has reason to think that they were first introduced about A.D. 349, and that they were certainly in use in A.D. 530. We have therefore given them throughout in Table I.

62. *The southern (luni-solar) sixty-year cycle.* The sixty-year cycle is at present in daily use in Southern India (south of the Narmadâ), but there the samvatsaras are made to correspond with the luni-solar year as well as the solar; and we therefore term it the luni-solar 60-year cycle in contradistinction to the more scientific Bârhaspatya cycle of the North.

1 It is not stated what Mesha-saṅkrânti is meant, whether mean or apparent. The rule is here given as generally interpreted by writers both Indian and European, but in this form its origin cannot be explained. I am strongly inclined to think that Varâhamihira, the author of the *Bṛihatsaṁhitâ,* meant the rule to run thus: Multiply the current Śaka year by 44. Add 8582 (or 8581 or 8583). Divide the sum by 3750. To the integers of the quotient add the given current Śaka year; (and the rest as above). The result is for the mean Mesha-saṅkranti." In this form it is the same as the *Ârya-Siddhânta* or the *Jyotishatattva* rule, and can be easily explained. (S. B. D.)

2 In this Table the *Bṛihatsaṁhitâ* rule is worked as I interpret it. But as interpreted by others the expunctions will differ, the differences being in Śaka (current) 231, the 56th; 998, the 52nd; 1339, the 37th.

By the *Sûrya Siddhânta* the years marked with an asterisk in the Śaka column of this Table differ from those given in Table I., col. 7, being in each case one earlier; the rest are the same. (S. B. D.)

There is evidence [1] to show that the cycle of Jupiter was in use in Southern India before Saka 828 (A.D. 905-6); but from that year, according to the *Ârya Siddhânta*, or from Saka 831 (A.D. 908-9) according to the *Sûrya-Siddhânta*, the expunction of the samvatsaras was altogether neglected, with the result that the 60-year cycle in the south became luni-solar from that year. At present the northern samvatsara has advanced by 12 on the southern. There is an easy rule for finding the samvatsara according to the luni-solar cycle, viz., add 11 to the current Saka year, and divide by 60; the remainder is the corresponding luni-solar cycle year. It must not be forgotten that the samvatsaras of Jupiter's and the southern cycle, are always to be taken as current years, not expired.

63. *The twelve-year cycle of Jupiter.* There is another cycle of Jupiter consisting of twelve samvatsaras named after the lunar months. It is of two kinds. In one, the samvatsara begins with the heliacal rising [2] of Jupiter and consists of about 400 solar days, one samvatsara being expunged every 12 years or so. [3] In the other, which we have named the "twelve-year cycle of Jupiter of the mean-sign system", the years are similar in length to those of the sixty-year cycle of Jupiter just described, and begin at the same moment. Both kinds, though chiefly the former, were in use in early times, and the latter is often employed in modern dates, especially in those of the Kollam era. The samvatsaras of this heliacal rising system can only be found by direct calculations according to some *Siddhânta*. The correspondence of the samvatsaras of the mean-sign system with those of the sixty-year cycle are given in Table XII. They proceed regularly.

64. *The Graha-parivṛitti and Oṅko cycles.* There are two other cycles, but they are limited to small tracts of country and would perhaps be better considered as eras. We however give them here.

The southern inhabitants of the peninsula of India (chiefly of the Madura district) use a cycle of 90 solar years which is called the *Graha-parivṛitti*. Warren has described the cycle, deriving his information from the celebrated Portuguese missionary Beschi, who lived for over forty years in Madura. The cycle consists of 90 solar years, the length of one year being 365 d. 15 gh. 31 pa. 30 vi., and the year commences with Mesha. Warren was informed by native astronomers at Madras that the cycle consisted of the sum in days of 1 revolution of the sun, 15 of Mars, 22 of Mercury, 11 of Jupiter, 5 of Venus and 29 of Saturn, though this appears to us quite meaningless. The length of this year is that ascertained by using the original *Sûrya-Siddhânta*; but from the method given by Warren for finding the beginning of the years of this cycle it appears that astronomers have tried to keep it as nearly as possible in agreement with calculations by the *Ârya-Siddhânta*, and in fact the year may be said to belong to the *Ârya-Siddhânta*. The cycle commenced with Kali 3079 current (B. C. 24) and its epoch, *i.e.*, the Graha-parivṛitti year 0 current [4] is Kali 3078 current (B. C. 25).

1 See *Corpus Inscrip. Indic.*, Vol. III., p. 80, note; *Ind. Antiq.*, *XVII.*, p. 142.

2 The heliacal rising of a superior planet is its first *visible* rising after its conjunctions with the sun, *i.e.*, when it is at a sufficient distance from the sun to be first *seen* on the horizon at its rising in the morning before sunrise, or, in the case of an inferior planet (Mercury or Venus), at its setting in the evening after sunset. For Jupiter to be visible the sun must be about 11° below the horizon. [R. S.]

3 It is fully described by me in the Indian Antiquary, vol. XVII. [S. B. D.]

4 In practice of course the word "current" cannot be applied to the year 0, but it is applied here to distinguish it from the year 0 complete or expired, which means year 1 current. We use the word "epoch" to mean the year 0 current. The epoch of an era given in a year of another era is useful for turning years of one into years of another era. Thus, by adding 3078 (the number of the Kali year corresponding to the Graha-parivṛitti cycle epoch) to a Graha-parivṛitti year, we can get the equivalent Kali year; and by subtracting the same from a Kali year we get the corresponding Graha-parivṛitti year.

To find the year of the Graha-parivṛitti cycle, add 72 to the current Kali-year, 11 to the current Saka year, or 24 or 23 to the A.D. year, viz., 24 from Mesha to December 31st, and 23 from January 1st to Mesha; divide by 90 and the remainder is the current year of the cycle.

The Oṅko[1] cycle of 59 luni-solar years is in use in part of the Ganjam district of the Madras Presidency. Its months are pûrṇimânta, but it begins the year on the 12th of Bhâdrapada-śuddha,[2] calling that day the 12th not the 1st. In other words, the year changes its numerical designation every 12th day of Bhâdrapada-śuddha. It is impossible as yet to say decidedly when the Oṅko reckoning commenced. Some records in the temple of Jagannātha at Purī (perfectly valueless from an historical point of view) show that it commenced with the reign of Subhānideva in 319 A.D., but the absurdity of this is proved by the chronicler's statement that the great Mughal invasion took place in 327 A.D. in the reign of that king's successor.[3] Some say that the reckoning commenced with the reign of Chōḍagaṅga or Chōrgaṅga, the founder of the Gāṅgavaṁśa, whose date is assigned usually to 1131-32 A.D., while Sutton in his *History of Orissa* states that it was introduced in 1580 A.D. In the zamindari tracts of Parlakimeḍi, Peddakimeḍi and Chinnakimeḍi the *Oṅko* Calendar is followed, but the people there also observe each a special style, only differing from the parent style and from one another in that they name their years after their own zamindars. A singular feature common to all these four kinds of regnal years is that, in their notation, the years whose numeral is 6, or whose numerals end with 6 or 0 (except 10), are dropped.[4] For instance, the years succeeding the 5th and 19th Oṅkos of a prince or zamindar are called the 7th and 21st Oṅkos respectively. It is difficult to account for this mode of reckoning; it may be, as the people themselves allege, that these numerals are avoided because, according to their traditions and *śâstras*, they forebode evil, or it may possibly be, as some might be inclined to suppose, that the system emanated from a desire to exaggerate the length of each reign. There is also another unique convention according to which the Oṅko years are not counted above 59, but the years succeeding 59 begin with a second series, thus "second 1", "second 2", and so on. It is also important to note that when a prince dies in the middle of an Oṅko year, his successor's 1st Oṅko which commences on his accession to the throne, does not run its full term of a year, but ends on the 11th day of Bhâdrapada-śuddha following; consequently the last regnal year of the one and the first of the other together occupy only one year, and one year is dropped in effect. To find, therefore, the English equivalent of a given Oṅko year, it will be necessary first to ascertain the style to which it relates, *i.e.*, whether it is a Jagannātha Oṅko or a Parlakimeḍi Oṅko, and so on; and secondly to value the given year by excluding the years dropped (namely, the 1st—possibly, the 6th, 16th, 20th, 26th, 30th, 36th, 40th, 46th, 50th, 56th). There are lists of Orissa princes available, but up to 1797 A.D. they would appear to be perfectly inauthentic.[5] The list from

1 Or *Aṅka*.

2 On the 11th according to some, but all the evidence tends to shew that the year begins on the 12th.

3 The real date of the Muhammadan invasion seems to be 1568 A.D. (J. A. S. B. for 1883, LII., p. 233, *note*). The invasion alluded to is evidently that of the "Yavanas", but as to these dates these temple chronicles must never be believed. [R. S.]

4 Some say that the first year is also dropped, similarly; but this appears to be the result of a misunderstanding, this year being dropped only to fit in with the system described lower down in this article. Mr. J. Beames states that "the first two years and every year that has a 6 or a 0 in it are omitted", so that the 37th Oṅko of the reign of Rāmachandra is really his 28th year, since the years 1, 2, 6, 10, 16, 20, 26, 30 and 36 are omitted. (J. A. S. B. 1883, LII., p. 234, *note*. He appears to have been misled about the first two years.

5 Sewell's *Sketch of the Dynasties of Southern India*, p. 64. *Archæological Survey of Southern India*, vol. II., p. 204.

that date forwards is reliable, and below are given the names of those after whom the later Oṅko years have been numbered, with the English dates corresponding to the commencement of the 2nd Oṅkos of their respective reigns.

Oṅko 2 of Mukundadeva	September 2, 1797.	(Bhâdrapada	śukla	12th.)
Do. Râmachandradeva . . .	September 22, 1817.	Do.		Do.
Do. Vîrakeśvaradeva . . .	September 4, 1854.	Do.		Do.
Do. Divyasiṁhadeva . . .	September 8, 1859.	Do.		Do.

PART II.

THE VARIOUS ERAS.

65. *General remarks.* Different eras have, from remote antiquity, been in use in different parts of India, having their years luni-solar or solar, commencing according to varying practice with a given month or day; and in the case of luni-solar years, having the months calculated variously according to the amânta or pûrṇimânta system of pakshas. *(Art. 12 above).* The origin of some eras is well known, but that of others has fallen into obscurity. It should never be forgotten, as explaining at once the differences of practice we observe, that when considering "Indian" science we are considering the science of a number of different tribes or nationalities, not of one empire or of the inhabitants generally of one continent.

66. If a number of persons belonging to one of these nationalities, who have been in the habit for many years of using a certain era with all its peculiarities, leave their original country and settle in another, it is natural that they should continue to use their own era, notwithstanding that another era may be in use in the country of their adoption; or perhaps, while adopting the new era, that they should apply to it the peculiarities of their own. And *vice versâ* it is only natural that the inhabitants of the country adopted should, when considering the peculiarities of the imported era, treat it from their own stand-point.

67. And thus we actually find in the pañchâṅgs of some provinces a number of other eras embodied, side by side with the era in ordinary use there, while the calendar-makers have treated them by mistake in the same or nearly the same manner as that of their own reckoning. For instance, there are extant solar pañchâṅgs of the Tamil country in which the year of the Vikrama era is represented as a solar Meshâdi year. And so again Śaka years are solar in Bengal and in the Tamil country, and luni-solar in other parts of the country. So also we sometimes find that the framers of important documents have mentioned therein the years of several eras, but have made mistakes regarding them. In such a case we might depend on the dates in the document if we knew exactly the nationality of the authors, but very often this cannot be discovered, and then it is obviously unsafe to rely on it in any sense as a guide. This point should never be lost sight of.

68. Another point to be always borne in mind is that, for the sake of convenience in calculation a year of an era is sometimes treated differently by different authors in the same province, or indeed even by the same author. Thus, Gaṇeśa Daivajña makes Śaka years begin

with Chaitra śukla pratipadâ in his *Grahalâghava* (A.D. 1520), but with mean Mesha saṅkrânti in his *Tithichintâmaṇi* (A.D. 1525.)

69. It is evident therefore that a certain kind of year, *e.g.*, the solar or luni-solar year, or a certain opening month or day, or a certain arrangement of months and fortnights and the like, cannot be strictly defined as belonging exclusively to a particular era or to a particular part of India. We can distinctly affirm that the eras whose luni-solar years are Chaitrâdi (*i.e.*, beginning with Chaitra śukla pratipadâ) are always Meshâdi (beginning with the Mesha saṅkrânti) in their corresponding solar reckoning, but beyond this it is unsafe to go.

70. *Current and expired years.* It is, we believe, now generally known what an "expired" or "current" year is, but for the benefit of the uninitiated we think it desirable to explain the matter fully. Thus; the same Śaka year (A.D. 1894) which is numbered 1817 *vartamâna*, or astronomically current, in the pañchâṅgs of the Tamil countries of the Madras Presidency, is numbered 1816 *gata* ("expired") in other parts of India. This is not so unreasonable as Europeans may imagine, for they themselves talk of the third furlong after the fourth mile on a road as "four miles three furlongs" which means three furlongs after the expiry of the fourth mile, and the same in the matter of a person's age; and so September, A.D. 1894, (Śaka 1817 current) would be styled in India "Śaka 1816 expired, September", equivalent to "September after the end of Saka 1816" or "after the end of 1893 A.D". Moreover, Indian reckoning is based on careful calculations of astronomical phenomena, and to calculate the planetary conditions of September, 1894, it is necessary first to take the planetary conditions of the end of 1893, and then add to them the data for the following nine months. That is, the end of 1893 is the basis of calculation. It is always necessary to bear this in mind because often the word *gata* is omitted in practice, and it is therefore doubtful whether the real year in which an inscription was written was the one mentioned therein, or that number decreased by one. [1]

In this work we have given the corresponding years of the Kali and Saka eras actually current, and not the expired years. This is the case with all eras, including the year of the *Vikrama* [2] era at present in use in Northern India.

71. *Description of the several eras.* In Table II., Part iii., below we give several eras, chiefly those whose epoch is known or can be fixed with certainty, and we now proceed to describe them in detail.

The Kali-Yuga.—The moment of its commencement has been already given (*Art. 16 above*). Its years are both Chaitrâdi (luni-solar) and Meshâdi (solar.) It is used both in astro-

1 See '*Calculations of Hindu dates*', by Dr. Fleet, in the *Ind. Ant.*, vols. *XVI.* to *XIX.*; and my notes on the date of a Jain *Purâṇa* in Dr. Bhândârkar's "*Report on the search for Sankrit manuscripts*" for 1883—1884 A. D., p.p. 429—30 §§ 36, 37. [S. B. D.]

2 The Vikrama era is never used by Indian astronomers. Out of 150 Vikrama dates examined by Dr. Kielhorn (*Ind. Ant.*, XIX.), there are only six which have to be taken as current years. Is it not, however, possible that all Vikrama years are really current years, but that sometimes in writings and inscriptions the authors have made them doubly current in consequence of thinking them erroneously to be expired years. There is an instance of a Śaka year made twice current in an inscription published in the *Ind. Ant.*, (vol. XX., p. 191). The year was already 1155 *current*, but the number given by the writer of the inscription is 1156, as if 1155 had been the expired year.

As a matter of fact I do not think that it is positively known whether the years of the Christian era are themselves really expired or current years. Warren, the author of the *Kálasaṅkalita* was not certain. He calls the year corresponding to the Kali year 3101 expired "A. D. 0 complete" (p. 302) or "1 current" (p. 294). Thus, by his view, the Christian year corresponding to the Kali year 3102 expired would be A. D. 1 complete or A. D. 2 current. But generally European scholars fix A. D. 1 current as corresponding to Kali 3102 expired. The current and expired years undoubtedly give rise to confusion. The years of the astronomical eras, the Kali and Śaka for instance, may, unless the contrary is proved, be assumed to be expired years, and those of the non-astronomical eras, such as the Vikrama, Gupta, and many others, may be taken as current ones. (See, however, Note 3, p. 42, below.) [S. B. D.]

nomical works and in pañchâṅgs. In the latter sometimes its expired years, sometimes current years are given, and sometimes both. It is not often used in epigraphical records. [1]

Saptarshi-Kala.—This era is in use in Kashmîr and the neighbourhood. At the time of Alberuni (1030 A.D.), it appears to have been in use also in Multân and some other parts. It is the only mode of reckoning mentioned in the *Râja-Taraṅgiṇî.* It is sometimes called the "Laukika-Kâla" and sometimes the "Śâstra-Kâla". It originated on the supposition that the seven Ṛishis (the seven bright stars of Ursa Major) move through one nakshatra (27th part of the ecliptic) in 100 years, and make one revolution in 2700 years; the era consequently consists of cycles of 2700 years. But in practice the hundreds are omitted, and as soon as the reckoning reaches 100, a fresh hundred begins from 1. Kashmirian astronomers make the era, or at least one of its cycles of 2700 years, begin with Chaitra śukla 1st of Kali 27 current. Disregarding the hundreds we must add 47 to the Saptarshi year to find the corresponding current Saka year, and 24—25 for the corresponding Christian year. The years are Chaitrâdi. Dr. F. Kielhorn finds [2] that they are mostly current years, and the months mostly pûrṇimânta.

The Vikrama era.—In the present day this era is in use in Gujarât and over almost all the north of India, except perhaps Bengal. [3] The inhabitants of these parts, when migrating to other parts of India, carry the use of the era with them. In Northern India the year is Chaitrâdi, and its months pûrṇimânta, but in Gujarât it is Kârttikâdi and its months are amânta. The settlers in the Madras Presidency from Northern India, especially the Mârvâḍis who use the Vikrama year, naturally begin the year with Chaitra śukla pratipadâ and employ the pûrṇimânta scheme of months; while immigrants from Gujarât follow their own scheme of a Kârttikâdi amânta year, but always according to the Vikrama era. In some parts of Kâṭhiâvâḍ and Gujarât the Vikrama era is Âshâḍhâdi [4] and its months amânta. The practice in the north and south leads in the present day to the Chaitrâdi pûrṇimânta Vikrama year being sometimes called the "Northern Vikrama," and the Kârttikâdi amânta Vikrama year the "Southern Vikrama."

The correspondence of these three varieties of the Vikrama era with the Saka and other eras, as well as of their months, will be found in Table II., Parts ii. and iii.

Prof. F. Kielhorn has treated of this era at considerable length in the *Ind. Antiq.*, vols. XIX. and XX., and an examination of 150 different dates from 898 to 1877 of that era has led him to the following conclusions *(ibid., XX., p. 398 ff.)*.

(1) It has been at all times the rule for those who use the Vikrama era to quote the expired years, and only exceptionally [5] the current year.

(2) The Vikrama era was Kârttikâdi from the beginning, and it is probable that the change which has gradually taken place in the direction of a more general use of the Chaitrâdi year was owing to the increasing growth and influence of the Śaka era. Whatever may be the practice in quite modern times, it seems certain that down to about the 14th century of the Vikrama era both kinds of years, the Kârttikâdi and the Chaitrâdi, were used over exactly the same tracts of country, but more frequently the Kârttikâdi.

(3) While the use of the Kârttikâdi year has been coupled with the pûrṇimânta as often as with the

1 *Corpus Inscrip. Ind., Vol. III., Introduction, p. 69, note.*

2 *Ind. Ant.*, Vol. XX., p. 149 ff.

3 In Bengâli pañchâṅgs the Vikrama Samvat, or Sambat, is given along with the Śaka year, and, like the North-Indian Vikrama Samvat, is Chaitradi pûrṇimânta.

4 See *Ind. Ant., vol. XVII., p.* 93; also note 3, p. 31, and connected Text.

5 See, however, note 2 on the previous page.

amânta scheme of months, the Chaitrâdi year is found to be more commonly joined with the pûrṇimânta scheme: but neither scheme can be exclusively connected with either the Kârttikâdi or Chaitrâdi year.

The era was called the "Mâlava" era from about A.D. 450 to 850. The earliest known date containing the word "Vikrama" is Vikrama-samvat 898 (about A.D. 840); but there the era is somewhat vaguely described as "the time called Vikrama"; and it is in a poem composed in the Vikrama year 1050 (about A.D. 992) that we hear for the first time of a king called Vikrama in connection with it. (See *Ind. Antiq.*, XX., p. 404).

At the present day the Vikrama era is sometimes called the "Vikrama-samvat", and sometimes the word "samvat" is used alone as meaning a year of that era. But we have instances in which the word "samvat" (which is obviously an abbreviation of the word *samvatsara*, or year) is used to denote the years of the Śaka, Siṁha, or Valabhi eras [1] indiscriminately.

In some native pañchâṅgs from parts of the Madras presidency and Mysore for recent years the current Vikrama dates are given in correspondence with current Śaka dates; for example, the year corresponding to A.D. 1893–94 is said to be Śaka 1816, or Vikrama 1951. (*See remarks on the Śaka era above.*)

The Christian era. This has come into use in India only since the establishment of the English rule. Its years at present are tropical solar commencing with January 1st, and are taken as current years. January corresponds at the present time with parts of the luni-solar amânta months Mârgaśîrsha and Pausha, or Pausha and Mâgha. Before the introduction of the new style, however, in 1752 A.D., it coincided with parts of amânta Pausha and Mâgha, or Mâgha and Phâlguna. The Christian months, as regards their correspondence with luni-solar and solar months, are given in Table II., Part ii.

The Śaka era.—This era is extensively used over the whole of India; and in most parts of Southern India, except in Tinnevelly and part of Malabar, it is used exclusively. In other parts it is used in addition to local eras. In all the *Karaṇas*, or practical works on astronomy it is used almost exclusively. [2] Its years are Chaitrâdi for luni-solar, and Meshâdi for solar, reckoning. Its months are pûrṇimânta in the North and amânta in Southern India. Current years are given in some pañchâṅgs, but the expired years are in use in most [3] parts of India.

The Chedi or *Kalachuri era.*—This era is not now in use. Prof. F. Kielhorn, examining the dates contained in ten inscriptions of this era from 793 to 934, [4] has come to the conclusion

[1] See *Ind. Ant.*, vol. XII., pp. 213, 293; XI., p. 242 *ff.*

[2] I have seen only two examples in which authors of *Karaṇas* have used any other era along with the Śaka. The author of the *Râma-vinoda* gives, as the starting-point for calculations, the Akbar year 35 together with the Śaka year 1512 (expired), and the author of the *Phattesâhaprakâśa* fixes as its starting-point the 48th year of "Phattesâha" coupled with the Śaka year 1626. [S. B. D.]

[3] Certain Telugu (luni-solar) and Tamil (solar) pañchâṅgs for the last few years, which I have procured, and which were printed at Madras and are clearly in use in that Presidency, as well as a Canarese pañchâṅg for A. D. 1893, (Śakâ 1816 current, 1815 expired) edited by the Palace Astronomer of H. H. the Mahârâjâ of Mysore, give the current Śaka years. But I strongly doubt whether the authors of these pañchâṅgs are themselves acquainted with the distinction between so-called current and expired years. For instance, there is a pañchâṅg annually prepared by Mr. Aṇṇa Ayyaṅgâr, a resident of Kañjnûr in the Tanjore District, which appears to be in general use in the Tamil country, and in that for the solar Meshâdi year corresponding to 1887—88 he uses the expired Śaka year, calling this 1809; while in those for two other years that I have seen the current Śaka year is used. I have conversed with several Tamil gentlemen at Poona, and learn from them that in their part of India the generality of people are acquainted only with the name of the samvatsara of the 60-year cycle, and give no numerical value to the years. Where the years are numbered, however, the expired year is in general use. I am therefore inclined to believe that the so-called current Śaka years are nowhere in use; and it becomes a question whether the so-called expired Śaka year is really an expired one. [S. B. D.]

[4] *Indian Antiquary* for August, 1888, vol. XVII., p. 215, and the *Academy* of 10th Dec., 1887, p. 394 f. I had myself calculated these same inscription-dates in March, 1887, and had, in conjunction with Dr. Fleet, arrived at nearly the same conclusions as Dr. Kielhorn's, but we did not then settle the epoch, believing that the data were not sufficiently reliable. (*Corpus. Inscrip. Indic.*, Vol. III., Introd., p. 9. [S. B. D.] See also Dr. Kielhorn's Paper read before the Oriental Congress in London. [R. S]

that the 1st day of the 1st *current* Chedi year corresponds to Aśvina śukla pratipadâ of Chaitrâdi Vikrama 306 current, (Śaka 171 current, 5th Sept., A.D. 248); that consequently its years are Âśvinâdi; that they are used as current years; that its months are pûrṇimânta; and that its epoch, *i.e.*, the beginning of Chedi year 0 current, is A. D. 247—48.

The era was used by the Kalachuri kings of Western and Central India, and it appears to have been in use in that part of India in still earlier times.

The Gupta era.—This era is also not now in use. Dr. Fleet has treated it at great length in the introduction to the *Corpus. Inscrip. Ind.* (Vol. III, "*Gupta Inscriptions*"), and again in the *Indian Antiquary* (Vol. XX., pp. 376 ff.) His examination of dates in that era from 163 to 386 leads him to conclude that its years are current and Chaitrâdi; that the months are pûrṇimânta; and that the epoch, *i.e.*, the beginning of Gupta Samvat 0 current, is Śaka 242 current (A. D. 319—20). The era was in use in Central India and Nepal, and was used by the Gupta kings.

The *Valabhi era.*—This is merely a continuation of the Gupta era with its name changed into "Valabhi." It was in use in Kâṭhiâvâḍ and the neighbourhood, and it seems to have been introduced there in about the fourth Gupta century. The beginning of the year was thrown back from Chaitra śukla 1st to the previous Kârttika śukla 1st, and therefore its epoch went back five months, and is synchronous with the current Kârttikâdi Vikrama year 376 (A.D. 318—19, Śaka 241—42 current). Its months seem to be both amânta and pûrṇimânta.

The inscriptions as yet discovered which are dated in the Gupta and Valabhi era range from the years 82 to 945 of that era.

The Bengali San.—An era named the "Bengali San" (sometimes written in English "Sen") is in use in Bengal. It is a solar year and runs with the solar Śaka year, beginning at the Mesha saṅkrânti; but the months receive lunar-month names, and the first, which corresponds with the Tamil Chaitra, or with Mesha according to the general reckoning, is here called Vaiśâkha, and so on throughout the year, their Chaitra corresponding with the Tamil Phâlguna, or with the Mîna of our Tables. We treat the years as current ones. Bengali San 1300 current corresponds with Śaka 1816 current (A.D. 1893—94.) Its epoch was Śaka 516 current, A.D. 593—94. To convert a Bengali San date into a Śaka date for purposes of our Tables, add 516 to the former year, which gives the current Śaka solar year, and adopt the comparison of months given in Table II., Part. ii., cols. 8, 9.

The Vilâyatî year.—This is another solar year in use in parts of Bengal, and chiefly in Orissa; it takes lunar-month names, and its epoch is nearly the same as that of the "Bengali San", viz., Śaka 515—16 current, A.D. 592—93, But it differs in two respects. First, it begins the year with the solar month Kanyâ which corresponds to Bengal solar Âśvina or Âssin. Secondly, the months begin on the day of the saṅkrânti instead of on the following (2nd) or 3rd day *(see Art. 28, the Orissa Rule).*

The Amli Era of Orissa—This era is thus described in Giriśa Chandra's "*Chronological Tables*" (preface, p. xvi.): "The Amli commences from the birth of Indradyumna, Râjâ of Orissa, on Bhâdrapada śukla 12th, and each month commences from the moment when the sun enters a new sign. The *Amli San* is used in business transactions and in the courts of law in Orissa." [1]

1 The Vilâyatî era, as given in some Bengal Government annual chronological Tables, and in a Bengali pañchâṅg printed in Calcutta that I have seen, is made identical with this Amli era in almost every respect, except that its months are made to commence civilly in accordance with the second variety of the midnight rule (*Art.* 28). But facts seem to be that the Vilâyatî year commences, not on lunar Bhâdrapada śukla 12th, but with the Kanyâ saṅkranti, while the Amli year does begin on lunar Bhâdrapada śukla 12th. It may be remarked that Warren writes—in A.D. 1825—(*Kálasaṅkalita, Tables p. IX.*) that the "Vilaity year is reckoned from the 1st of the krishna paksha in Chaitra", and that its numerical designation is the same with the Bengali San. [S. B. D.]

It is thus luni-solar with respect to changing its numerical designation, but solar as regards the months and days. But it seems probable that it is really luni-solar also as regards its months and days.

The Kanyâ saṅkrânti can take place on any day from about 11 days previous to lunar Bhâdrapada śukla 12th to about 18 days after it. With the difference of so many days the epoch and numerical designation of the Amli and Vilâyatî years are the same.

The Fasali year.—This is the harvest year introduced, as some say, by Akbar, originally derived from the Muhammadan year, and bearing the same number, but beginning in July. It was, in most parts of India, a solar year, but the different customs of different parts of India caused a divergence of reckoning. Its epoch is apparently A. H. 963 (A. D. 1556), when its number coincided with that of the purely lunar Muhammadan year, and from that date its years have been solar or luni-solar. Thus (A. H.) 963 + 337 (solar years) = 1300, and (A. D.) 1556 + 337 = 1893 A.D., with a part of which year Fasali 1300 coincides, while the same year is A. H. 1310. The era being purely official, and not appealing to the feelings of the people of India, the reckoning is often found to be loose and unreliable. In Madras the Fasali year originally commenced with the 1st day of the solar month Âḍi (Karka), but about the year 1800 A.D. the British Government, finding that this date then coincided with July 13th, fixed July 13th as the permanent initial date; and in A.D. 1855 altered this for convenience to July 1st, the present reckoning. In parts of Bombay the Fasali begins when the sun enters the nakshatra Mṛigaśîrsha, viz., (at present) about the 5th or 6th June. The Bengâli year and the Vilâyatî year both bear the same number as the Fasali year.

The names of months, their periods of beginning, and the serial number of days are the same as in the Hijra year, but the year changes its numerical designation on a stated solar day. Thus the year is already a solar year, as it was evidently intended to be from its name. But at the present time it is luni-solar in Bengal, and, we believe, over all North-Western India, and this gives rise to a variety, to be now described.

The luni-solar Fasali year.—This reckoning, though taking its name from a Muhammadan source, is a purely Hindu year, being luni-solar, pûrṇimânta, and Âśvinâdi. Thus the luni-solar Fasali year in Bengal and N. W. India began (pûrṇimânta Âśvina kṛishṇa pratipadâ, Śaka 1815 current =) Sept. 7th, 1882. A peculiarity about the reckoning, however, is that the months are not divided into bright and dark fortnights, but that the whole runs without distinction of pakshas, and without addition or expunction of tithis from the 1st to the end of the month, beginning with the full moon. Its epoch is the same as that of the Vilâyatî year, only that it begins with the full moon next preceding or succeeding the Kanyâ saṅkrânti, instead of on the saṅkrânti day.

In Southern India the Fasali year 1302 began on June 5th, 1892, in Bombay, and on July 1st, 1892, in Madras. It will be seen, therefore, that it is about two years and a quarter in advance of Bengal.

To convert a luni-solar Bengali or N. W. Fasali date, approximately, into a date easily workable by our Tables, treat the year as an ordinary luni-solar pûrṇimânta year; count the days after the 15th of the month as if they were days in the śukla fortnight, 15 being deducted from the given figure; add 515 to make the year correspond with the Saka year, for dates between Âśvina 1st and Chaitra 15th (= amânta Bhâdrapada kṛishṇa 1st and amânta Phâlguna kṛishṇa 30th)—and 516 between Chaitra 15th and Âśvina 1st. Thus, let Chaitra 25th 1290 be the given date. The 25th should be converted into śukla 10th; adding 516 to 1290 we have 1806, the equivalent Śaka year. The corresponding Śaka date is therefore amânta Chaitra śukla 10th,

1806 current. From this the conversion to an A. D. date can be worked by the Tables. For an exact equivalent the saṅkrânti day must be ascertained.

The Mahratta Sûr-san or Shahûr-san.—This is sometimes called the *Arabi-san.* It was extensively used during the Mahratta supremacy, and is even now sometimes found, though rarely. It is nine years behind the Fasali of the Dakhan, but in other respects is just the same; thus, its year commences when the sun enters the nakshatra Mṛigaśîrsha, in which respect it is solar, but the days and months correspond with Hijra reckoning. It only diverged from the Hijra in A.D. 1344, according to the best computation, since when it has been a solar year as described above. On May 15th, A.D. 1344, the Hijra year 745 began. But since then the Shahûr reckoning was carried on by itself as a solar year. To convert it to an A.D. year, add 599.

The Harsha-Kâla.—This era was founded by Harshavardhana of Kanauj, [1] or more properly of Thaṇeśar. At the time of Alberuni (A.D. 1030) it was in use in Mathurâ (Muttra) and Kanauj. Its epoch seems to be Śaka 529 current, A.D. 606—7. More than ten inscriptions have been discovered in Nepal [2] dated in the first and second century of this era. In all those discovered as yet the years are qualified only by the word "samvat".

The Mâgi-San.—This era is current in the District of Chittagong. It is very similar to the Bengali-san, the days and months in each being exactly alike. The Mâgi is, however, 45 years behind the Bengali year,[3] *e.g.*, Mâgi 1200 = Bengali 1245.

The Kollam era, or era of Paraśurâma.—The year of this era is known as the *Kollam âṇḍu. Kollam* (anglicé Quilon) means "western", *âṇḍu* means "a year". The era is in use in Malabar from Mangalore to Cape Comorin, and in the Tinnevelly district. The year is sidereal solar. In North Malabar it begins with the solar month Kanni (Kanyâ), and in South Malabar and Tinnevelly with the month Chiṅgam (Siṁha). In Malabar the names of the months are sign-names, though corrupted from the original Sanskṛit; but in Tinnevelly the names are chiefly those of lunar months, also corrupted from Sanskṛit, such as Śittirai or Chittirai for the Sanskṛit Chaitra, corresponding with Mesha, and so on. The sign-names as well as the lunar-month names are given in the pañchâṅgs of Tinnevelly and the Tamil country. All the names will be found in Table II., Part ii. The first Kollam âṇḍu commenced in Kali 3927 current, Śaka 748 current, A.D. 825—26, the epoch being Śaka 747—48 current, A.D. 824—25. The years of this era as used are current years, and we have treated them so in our Tables.

The era is also called the "era of Paraśurâma", and the years run in cycles of 1000. The present cycle is said to be the fourth, but in actual modern use the number has been allowed to run on over the 1000, A.D. 1894—95 being called Kollam 1070. We believe that there is no record extant of its use earlier than A.D. 825, and we have therefore, in our Table I., left the appropriate column blank for the years A.D. 300—825. If there were really three cycles ending with the year 1000, which expired A.D. 824—25, then it would follow that the Paraśurâma, or Kollam, era began in Kali 1927 current, or the year 3528 of the Julian period. [4]

The Nevâr era. This era was in use in Nepal up to A.D. 1768, when the Saka era

1 Alberuni's India, English translation by Sachau, Vol. II., p. 5.

2 *Corpus Inscrip. Indic., Vol. III., Introd., p.* 177 *ff.*

3 Giriśa Chandra's *Chronological Tables for A.D.* 1764 *to* 1900.

4 Warren *(Kálasaṅkalita, p.* 298*)* makes it commence in "the year 3537 of the Julian period, answering to the 1926th of the Kali yug". But this is wrong if, as we believe, the Kollam years are current years, and we know no reason to think them otherwise. Warren's account was based on that of Dr. Buchanan who made the 977th year of the third cycle commence in A.D. 1800. But according to the present Malabar use it is quite clear that the year commencing in 1800 A.D., was the 976th Kollam year.

was introduced. [1] Its years are Kârttikâdi, its months amânta, and its epoch (the beginning of the Nevâr year o current) is the Kârttikâdi Vikrama year 936 current, Śaka 801—2 current, A.D. 878—79. Dr. F. Kielhorn, in his *Indian Antiquary* paper on the "Epoch of the Newâr era" [2] has come to the conclusion that its years are generally given in expired years, only two out of twenty-five dates examined by him, running from the 235th to the 995th year of the era, being current ones. The era is called the "Nepâl era" in inscriptions, and in Sanskṛit manuscripts; "Nevâr" seems to be a corruption of that word. Table II., Part iii., below gives the correspondence of the years with those of other eras.

The Châlukya era. This was a short-lived era that lasted from Saka 998 (A.D. 1076) to Śaka 1084 (A.D. 1162) only. It was instituted by the Châlukya king Vikramâditya Tribhuvana Malla, and seems to have ceased after the defeat of the Eastern Châlukyas in A.D. 1162 by Vijala Kalachuri. It followed the Śaka reckoning of months and pakshas. The epoch was Śaka 998—99 current, A.D. 1075—76.

The Simha Samvat.—This era was in use in Kâṭhiâvâḍ and Gujarât. From four dates in that era of the years 32, 93, 96 and 151, discussed in the *Indian Antiquary* (Vols. XVIII. and XIX. and elsewhere), we infer that its year is luni-solar and current; the months are presumably amânta, but in one instance they seem to be pûrṇimânta, and the year is most probably Âshâḍhâdi. It is certainly neither Kârttikâdi nor Chaitrâdi. Its epoch is Śaka 1036—37 current, A.D. 1113—14.

The Lakshmaṇa Sena era.—This era is in use in Tirhut and Mithila, but always along with the Vikrama or Śaka year. The people who use it know little or nothing about it. There is a difference of opinion as to its epoch. Colebrooke (A.D. 1796) makes the first year of this era correspond with A.D. 1105; Buchanan (A.D. 1810) fixes it as A.D. 1105 or 1106; Tirhut almanacs, however, for the years between A.D. 1776 and 1880 shew that it corresponds with A.D. 1108 or 1109. Buchanan states that the year commences on the first day after the full moon of the month Âshâḍha, while Dr. Râjendra Lâl Mitra (A.D. 1878) and General Cunningham assert that it begins on the first Mâgha badi (Mâgha kṛishṇa 1st). [3] Dr. F. Kielhorn, examining six independent inscriptions dated in that era (from A.D. 1194 to 1551), concludes [4] that the year of the era is Kârttikâdi; that the months are amânta; that its first year corresponds with A.D. 1119—20, the epoch being A.D. 1118—19, Śaka 1041—42 current; and that documents and inscriptions are generally dated in the expired year. This conclusion is supported by Abul Fazal's statement in the *Akbarnâma* (Śaka 1506, A.D. 1584). Dr. Kielhorn gives, in support of his conclusion, the equation "Laksh: sam: 505 = Śaka sam: 1546" from a manuscript of the *Smṛititattvâmṛita*, and proves the correctness of his epoch by other dates than the six first given.

The Ilâhi era.—The "Târîkh-i Ilâhî," that is "the mighty or divine era," was established by the emperor Akbar. It dates from his accession, which, according to the *Tabakât-i-Akbari*, was Friday the 2nd of Rabî-uś-śânî, A.H. 963, or 14th February, [5] 1556 (O. S.), Śaka 1478 current. It was employed extensively, though not exclusively on the coins of Akbar and Jahângîr, and appears to have fallen into disuse early in the reign of Shâh-Jahân. According to Abûl Fazal, the days and months are both natural solar, without any intercalations. The names of the months and days correspond with the ancient Persian. The months have from 29 to 30 days each.

1 General Sir A. Cunningham's *Indian Eras*, p. 74.

2 *Ind. Ant.*, Vol. XVII., p. 246 ff.

3 This much information is from General Cunningham's "*Indian Eras*"

4 *Ind. Ant.*, XIX., p. 1 ff.

5 General Cunningham, in his "*Indian Eras*", gives it as 15th February; but that day was a Saturday..

There are no weeks, the whole 30 days being distinguished by different names, and in those months which have 32 days the two last are named *roz o shab* (day and night), and to distinguish one from another are called "first" and "second". [1] Here the lengths of the months are said to be "from 29 to 30 days each", but in the old Persian calendar of Yazdajird they had 30 days each, the same as amongst the Parsees of the present day. The names of the twelve months are as follow:—

1	Farwardîn	5	Mirdâd	9	Ader
2	Ardi-behisht	6	Shariûr	10	Dêi
3	Khurdâd	7	Mihir	11	Bahman
4	Tîr	8	Abân	12	Isfandarmaz

The Mahratta Râja Śaka era.—This is also called the "Râjyâbhisheka Śaka". The word "Śaka" is used here in the sense of an era. It was established by Śivaji, the founder of the Mahratta kingdom, and commenced on the day of his accession to the throne, *i.e.*, Jyeshṭha śukla trayodaśî (13th) of Śaka 1596 expired, 1597 current, the Ânanda samvatsara. The number of the year changes every Jyeshṭha śukla trayodaśî; the years are current; in other respects it is the same as the Southern luni-solar amânta Śaka years. Its epoch is Śaka 1596—97 current, A.D. 1673—74. It is not now in use.

72. *Names of Hindî and N. W. Fasali months.*—Some of the months in the North of India and Bengal are named differently from those in the Peninsula. Names which are manifestly corruptions need not be noticed, though "Bhâdûn" for Bhâdrapada is rather obscure. But "Kuar" for Âśvina, and "Âghân", or "Aghrân", for Mârgaśîrsha deserve notice. The former seems to be a corruption of Kumârî, a synonym of Kanyâ (=Virgo, the damsel), the solar sign-name. If so, it is a peculiar instance of applying a solar sign-name to a lunar month. "Âghân" (or "Aghrân") is a corrupt form of *Âgrahâyaṇa*, which is another name of Mârgaśîrsha.

PART III.

DESCRIPTION AND EXPLANATION OF THE TABLES.

73. *Table I.*—Table I. is our principal and general Table, and it forms the basis for all calculations. It will be found divided into three sections. (1) Table of concurrent years; (2) intercalated and suppressed months; (3) moments of commencement of the solar and luni-solar years. All the figures refer to mean solar time at the meridian of Ujjain. The calculations are based on the *Sûrya-Siddhânta*, without the bîja up to 1500 A.D. and with it afterwards, with the exception of cols. 13 to 17 inclusive for which the *Ârya-Siddhânta* has been used. Throughout the table the solar year is taken to commence at the moment of the apparent Mêsha saṅkrânti or first point of Aries, and the luni-solar year with amânta Chaitra śukla pratipadâ. The months are taken as amânta.

74. *Cols. 1 to 5.*—In these columns the *concurrent* years of the six principal eras are

[1] Prinsep's *Indian Antiquities, II., Useful Tables*, p. 171.

given. (As to current and expired years see Art. 70 above.) A short description of eras is given in Art. 71. The years in the first three columns are used alike as solar and luni-solar, commencing respectively with Mesha or Chaitra. (For the beginning point of the year see Art. 52 above.) The Vikrama year given in col. 3 is the Chaitrâdi Vikrama year, or, when treated as a solar year which is very rarely the case, the Meshâdi year. The Âshâḍhâdi and Kârttikâdi Vikrama years are not given, as they can be regularly calculated from the Chaitrâdi year, remembering that the number of the former year is one less than that of the Chaitrâdi year from Chaitra to Jyeshṭha or Âśvina (both inclusive), as the case may be, and the same as the Chaitrâdi year from Âshâḍha or Kârttika to the end of Phâlguna.

Cols. 4 and 5. The eras in cols. 4 and 5 are described above (Art. 71.) The double number is entered in col. 4 so that it may not be forgotten that the Kollam year is non-Chaitrâdi or non-Meshâdi, since it commences with either Kanni (Kanyâ) or Chiṅgam (Siṁha). In the case of the Christian era of course the first year entered corresponds to the Kali, Śaka or Chaitrâdi Vikrama year for about three-quarters of the latter's course, and for about the last quarter the second Christian year entered must be taken. The corresponding parts of the years of all these eras as well as of several others will be found in Table II., Parts ii. and iii.

75. *Cols. 6 and 7.*—These columns give the number and name of the current samvatsara of the sixty-year cycle. There is reason to believe that the sixty-year luni-solar cycle (in use mostly in Southern India) came into existence only from about A. D. 909; and that before that the cycle of Jupiter was in use all over India. That is to say, before A. D. 909 the samvatsaras in Southern India were the same as those of the Jupiter cycle in the North. If, however, it is found in any case that in a year previous to A.D. 908 the samvatsara given does not agree with our Tables, the rule in Art. 62 should be applied, in order to ascertain whether it was a luni-solar samvatsara.

The samvatsara given in col. 7 is that which was current at the time of the Mesha saṅkrânti of the year mentioned in cols. 1 to 3. To find the samvatsara current on any particular day of the year the rules given in Art. 59 should be applied. For other facts regarding the samvatsaras, see Arts. 53 to 63 above.

76. *Cols. 8 to 12, and 8a to 12a.* These concern the *adhika* (intercalated) and *kshaya* (suppressed) months. For full particulars see Arts. 45 to 51. By the mean system of intercalations there can be no suppressed months, and by the true system only a few. We have given the suppressed months in italics with the suffix "*Ksh*" for "kshaya." As mean added months were only in use up to A.D. 1100 (*Art. 47*) we have not given them after that year.

77. The name of the month entered in col. 8 or 8*a* is fixed according to the first rule for naming a lunar month (*Art. 46*), which is in use at the present day. Thus, the name *Âshâḍha*, in cols. 8 or 8*a*, shows that there was an intercalated month between natural Jyeshṭha and natural Âshâḍha, and by the first rule its name is "Adhika Âshâḍha", natural Âshâdha being "Nija Âshâḍha." By the second rule it might have been called Jyeshṭha, but the intercalated period is the same in either case. In the case of expunged months the word "Pausha", for instance, in col. 8 shows that in the lunar month between natural Kârttika and natural Mâgha there were two saṅkrântis; and according to the rule adopted by us that lunar month is called Mârgaśirsha, Pausha being expunged.

78. Lists of intercalary and expunged months are given by the late Prof. K. L. Chhatre in a list published in Vol. I., No. 12 (March 1851) of a Mahrâṭhi monthly magazine called *Jñânaprasâraka*, formerly published in Bombay, but now discontinued; as well as in Cowasjee

Patell's "*Chronology*", and in the late Gen. Sir A. Cunningham's "*Indian Eras*,"[1] But in none of these three works is a single word said as to how, or following what authority, the calculations were made, so that we have no guide to aid us in checking the correctness of their results.

79. An added lunar month being one in which no saṅkrânti of the sun occurs, it is evident that a saṅkrânti must fall shortly before the beginning, and another one shortly after the end, of such a month, or in other words, a solar month must begin shortly before and must end shortly after the added lunar month. It is further evident that, since such is the case, calculation made by some other *Siddhânta* may yield a different result, even though the difference in the astronomical data which form the basis of calculation is but slight. Hence we have deemed it essential, not only to make our own calculations afresh throughout, but to publish the actual resulting figures which fix the months to be added and suppressed, so that the reader may judge in each case how far it is likely that the use of a different authority would cause a difference in the months affected. Our columns fix the moment of the saṅkrânti before and the saṅkrânti after the added month, as well as the saṅkrânti after the beginning, and the saṅkrânti before the end, of the suppressed month; or in other words, determine the limits of the adhika and kshaya mâsas. The accuracy of our calculation can be easily tested by the plan shewn in Art. 90 below. (*See also Art. 88 below.*) The moments of time are expressed in two ways, viz., in lunation-parts and tithis, the former following Prof. Jacobi's system as given in *Ind. Ant.*, Vol. XVII.

80. *Lunation-parts* or, as we elsewhere call them, "tithi-indices" (or "*t*") are extensively used throughout this work and require full explanation. Shortly stated a lunation-part is $\frac{1}{10000}$th of an apparent synodic revolution of the moon (*see Note 2, Art. 12 above*). It will be well to put this more clearly. When the difference between the longitude of the sun and moon, or in other words, the eastward distance between them, is *nil*, the sun and moon are said to be in conjunction; and at that moment of time occurs (the end of) *amâvâsyâ*, or new moon. (*Arts. 7.29 above.*) Since the moon travels faster than the sun, the difference between their longitudes, or their distance from one another, daily increases during one half and decreases during the other half of the month till another conjunction takes place. The time between two conjunctions is a synodic lunar month or a lunation, during which the moon goes through all its phases. The lunation may thus be taken to represent not only time but space. We could of course have expressed parts of a lunation by time-measure, such as by hours and minutes, or ghaṭikâs and palas, or by space-measure, such as degrees, minutes, or seconds, but we prefer to express it in lunation-parts, because then the same number does for either time or space (*see Art. 89 below*). A lunation consists of 30 tithis. $\frac{1}{30}$th of a lunation consequently represents the time-duration of a tithi or the space-measurement of 12 degrees. Our lunation is divided into 10,000 parts, and about 333 lunation-parts ($\frac{1}{10000}$ths) go to one tithi, 667 to two tithis, 1000 to three and so on. Lunation-parts are therefore styled "tithi-indices", and by abbreviation simply "*t*". Further, a lunation or its parts may be taken as apparent or mean. Our tithi-, nakshatra-, and yoga-indices are apparent and not mean, except in the case of mean added months, where the index, like the whole lunation, is mean.

1 Gen. Cunningham admittedly (p. 91) follows Cowasjee Patell's "*Chronology*" in this respect, and on examination I find that the added and suppressed months in these two works (setting aside some few mistakes of their own) agree throughout with Prof. Chhatre's list, even so far as to include certain instances where the latter was incorrect. Patell's "*Chronology*" was published fifteen years after the publication of Prof. Chhatre's list, and it is not improbable that the former was a copy of the latter. It is odd that not a single word is said in Cowasjee Patell's work to shew how his calculations were made, though in those days he would have required months or even years of intricate calculation before he could arrive at his results. [S B. D.]

Our tithi-index, or "*t*", therefore shows in the case of true added months as well as elsewhere, the space-difference between the apparent, and in the case of mean intercalations between the mean, longitudes of the sun and moon, or the time required for the motions of the sun and moon to create that difference, expressed in 10,000ths of a unit, which is a circle in the case of space, and a lunation or synodic revolution of the moon in the case of time. Briefly the tithi-index "*t*" shews the position of the moon in her orbit with respect to the sun, or the time necessary for her to gain that position., *e.g.*, "0" is new moon, "5000" full moon, "10,000" or "0" new moon; "50" shews that the moon has recently (*i.e.*, by $\frac{50}{10000}$ths, or 3 hours 33 minutes—*Table X., col.* 3) passed the point or moment of conjunction (new moon); 9950 shews that she is approaching new-moon phase, which will occur in another 3 hours and 33 minutes.

81. A lunation being equal to 30 tithis, the tithi-index, which expresses the 10,000th part of a lunation, can easily be converted into tithi-notation, for the index multiplied by 30 (practically by 3), gives, with the decimal figures marked off, the required figure in tithis and decimals. Thus if the tithi-index is 9950, which is really 0.9950, it is equal to (0.9950 × 30 =) 29.850 tithis, and the meaning is that $\frac{9950}{10000}$ths of the lunation, or 29.850 tithis have expired. Conversely a figure given in tithis and decimals divided by 30 expresses the same in 10,000ths parts of a lunation.

82. The tithi-index or tithi is often required to be converted into a measure of solar time, such as hours or ghaṭikâs. Now the length of an apparent lunation, or of an apparent tithi, perpetually varies, indeed it is varying at every moment, and consequently it is practically impossible to ascertain it except by elaborate and special calculations; but the length of a mean lunation, or of a mean tithi, remains permanently unchanged. Ignoring, therefore, the difference between apparent and mean lunations, the tithi-index or tithi can be readily converted into time by our Table X., which shews the time-value of the mean lunation-part ($\frac{1}{10000}$th of the mean lunation), and of the mean tithi-part ($\frac{1}{1000}$th of the mean tithi). Thus, if $t = 50$, Table X. gives the duration as 3 hours 33 minutes; and if the tithi-part[1] is given as 0.150 we have by Table X. (2 h. 22 m. + 1 h. 11 min. =) 3 h. 33 m.

It must be understood of course that the time thus given is not very accurate, because the tithi-index (*t*) is an apparent index, while the values in Table X. are for the mean index. The same remark applies to the nakshatra (*n*) or yoga (*y*) indices, and if accuracy is desired the process of calculation must be somewhat lengthened. This is fully explained in example 1 in Art. 148 below. In the case of mean added months the value of (*t*) the tithi-index is at once absolutely accurate.

83. The saṅkrântis preceding and succeeding an added month, as given in our Table I., of course take place respectively in the lunar month preceding and succeeding that *added* month.

84. To make the general remarks in Arts. 80, 81, 82 quite clear for the intercalation of months we will take an actual example. Thus, for the Kali year 3403 the entries in cols. 9 and 11 are 9950 and 287, against the true added month Âśvina in col. 8. This shews us that the saṅkrânti preceding the true added, or Adhika, Âśvina took place when 9950 lunation-parts of the natural month Bhâdrapada (preceding Adhika Âśvina) had elapsed, or when (10,000 − 9950 =) 50 parts had to elapse before the end of Bhâdrapada, or again when 50 parts had to elapse

1 A thousandth part of a tithi is equal to 1.42 minutes, which is sufficiently minute for our purposes, but a thousandth of a lunation is equivalent to 7 hours 5 minutes, and this is too large; so that we have to take the 10000th of a lunation as our unit, which is equal to 4.25 minutes, and this suffices for all practical purposes. In this work therefore a lunation is treated of as having 10,000 parts, and a tithi 1000 parts.

before the beginning of the added month; and that the saṅkrânti succeeding true Adhika Âśvina took place when 287 parts of the natural month Nija Âśvina had elapsed, or when 287 parts had elapsed after the end of the added month Adhika Âśvina.

85. The moments of the saṅkrântis are further given in tithis and decimals in cols. 10, 12, 10*a* and 12*a*. Thus, in the above example we find that the preceding saṅkrânti took place when 29·850 tithis of the preceding month Bhâdrapada had elapsed, *i.e.*, when (30—29·850 =) 0·150 tithis had still to elapse before the end of Bhâdrapada; and that the succeeding saṅkrânti took place when 0·861 of a tithi of the succeeding month, Âśvina, had passed.

To turn these figures into time is rendered easy by Table X. We learn from it that the preceding saṅkrânti took place (50 lunation parts or 0·150 tithi parts) about 3 h. 33 m. before the beginning of Adhika Âśvina; and that the succeeding saṅkrânti took place (287 lunation parts, or ·861 tithi parts) about 20 h. 20 m. after the end of Adhika Âśvina. This time is approximate. For exact time see Arts. 82 and 90.

The tithi-indices here shew (*see Art. 88*) that there is no probability of a different month being intercalated if the calculation be made according to a different authority.

86. To constitute an expunged month we have shewn that two saṅkrântis must occur in one lunar month, one shortly after the beginning and the other shortly before the end of the month; and in cols. 9 and 10 the moment of the first saṅkrânti, and in cols. 11 and 12 that of the second saṅkrânti, is given. For example see the entries against Kali 3506 in Table I. As already stated, there can never be an expunged month by the mean system

87. In the case of an added month the moon must be waning at the time of the preceding, and waxing at the time of the succeeding saṅkrânti, and therefore the figure of the tithi-index must be approaching 10,000 at the preceding, and over 10,000, or beginning a new term of 10,000, at the succeeding, saṅkrânti. In the case of expunged months the case is reversed, and the moon must be waxing at the first, and waning at the second saṅkrânti; and therefore the tithi-index must be near the beginning of a period of 10,000 at the first, and approaching 10,000 at the second, saṅkrânti.

88. When by the *Sûrya-Siddhânta* a new moon (the end of the amâvâsyâ) takes place within about 6 ghaṭikâs, or 33 lunation-parts, of the saṅkrânti, or beginning and end of a solar month, there may be a difference in the added or suppressed month if the calculation be made according to another *Siddhânta.* Hence when, in the case of an added month, the figure in col. 9 or 9*a* is more than (10,000—33 =) 9967, or when that in col. 11 or 11*a* is less than 33; and in the case of an expunged month when the figure in col. 9 is less than 33, or when that in col. 11 is more than 9967, it is possible that calculation by another *Siddhânta* will yield a different month as intercalated or expunged; or possibly there will be no expunction of a month at all. In such cases fresh calculations should be made by Prof. Jacobi's Special Tables (*Epig. Ind., Vol. II.*) or direct from the *Siddhânta* in question. In all other cases it may be regarded as certain that our months are correct for all *Siddhântas.* The limit of 33 lunation-parts here given is generally sufficient, but it must not be forgotten that where *Siddhântas* are used with a bîja correction the difference may amount to as much as 20 ghaṭikâs, or 113 lunation-parts *(See above, note to Art. 49).*

In the case of the *Sûrya-Siddhânta* it may be noted that the added and suppressed months are the same in almost all cases, whether the bîja is applied or not.

89. We have spared no pains to secure accuracy in the calculation of the figures entered in cols. 9 to 12 and 9*a* to 12*a*, and we believe that they may be accepted as finally correct,

but it should be remembered that their time-equivalent as obtained from Table X. is only approximate for the reason given above (*Art. 82.*) Since Indian readers are more familiar with tithis than with lunation-parts, and since the expression of time in tithis may be considered desirable by some European workers, we have given the times of all the required saṅkrântis in tithis and decimals in our columns, as well as in lunation-parts; but for turning our figures into time-figures it is easier to work with lunation-parts than with tithi-parts. It may be thought by some readers that instead of recording the phenomena in lunation-parts and tithis it would have been better to have given at once the solar time corresponding to the moments of the saṅkrântis in hours and minutes. But there are several reasons which induced us, after careful consideration, to select the plan we have finally adopted. First, great labour is saved in calculation; for to fix the exact moments in solar time at least five processes must be gone through in each case, as shewn in our Example I. below (*Art. 148*) It is true that, by the single process used by us, the time-equivalents of the given lunation-parts are only approximate, but the lunation-parts and tithis are in themselves exact. Secondly, the time shewn by our figures in the case of the mean added months is the same by the Original *Sûrya*, the Present *Sûrya*, and the *Ârya-Siddhânta*, as well as by the Present *Sûrya-Siddhânta* with the bîja, whereas, if converted into solar time, all of these would vary and require separate columns. Thirdly, the notation used by us serves one important purpose. It shews in one simple figure the distance in time of the saṅkrântis from the beginning and end of the added or suppressed month, and points at a glance to the probability or otherwise of there being a difference in the added or suppressed month in the case of the use of another authority. Fourthly, there is a special convenience in our method for working out such problems as are noticed in the following articles.

90. Supposing it is desired to prove the correctness of our added and suppressed months, or to work them out independently, this can easily be done by the following method: The moment of the Mesha saṅkrânti according to the *Sûrya-Siddhânta* is given in cols. 13, 14 and 15*a* to 17*a* for all years from A.D. 1100 to 1900, and for other years it can be calculated by the aid of Table D. in *Art. 96* below. Now we wish to ascertain the moment of two consecutive new moons connected with the month in question, and we proceed thus. The interval of time between the beginning of the solar year and the beginning or end of any solar month according to the *Sûrya-Siddhânta*, is given in Table III., cols. 8 or 9; and by it we can obtain by the rules in Art. 151 below, the tithi-index for the moment of beginning and end of the required solar month, *i.e.*, the moments of the solar saṅkrântis, whose position with reference to the new moon determines the addition or suppression of the luni-solar month. The exact interval also in solar time between those respective saṅkrântis and the new moons (remembering that at new moon "*t*" = 10,000) can be calculated by the same rules. This process will at once shew whether the moon was waning or waxing at the preceding and succeeding saṅkrântis, and this of course determines the addition or suppression of the month. The above, however, applies only to the apparent or true intercalations and suppressions. For mean added months the *Śodhya* (2 d. 8 gh. 51 p. 15 vi.) must be added (*see Art. 26*) to the Mesha-saṅkrânti time according to the *Ârya-Siddhânta* (*Table I.*, col. 15), and the result will be the time of the mean Mesha saṅkrânti. For the required subsequent saṅkrântis all that is necessary is to add the proper figures of duration as given in Art. 24, which shews the mean length of solar months, and to find the "*a*" for the results so obtained by Art. 151. Then add 200 to the totals and the result will be the required tithi-indices.

91. It will of course be asked how our figures in Table I. were obtained, and what guarantee we can give for their accuracy. It is therefore desirable to explain these points. Our calcula-

tions for true intercalated and suppressed months were first made according to the method and Tables published by Prof. Jacobi *(in the Ind. Ant., Vol. XVII., pp. 145 to 181)* as corrected by the errata list printed in the same volume. We based our calculations on his Tables 1 to 10, and the method given in his example 4 on pp. 152—53,[1] but with certain differences, the necessity of which must now be explained. Prof. Jacobi's Tables 1 to 4, which give the dates of the commencement of the solar months, and the hour and minute, were based on the *Ârya-Siddhânta*, while Tables 5 to 10 followed the *Sûrya-Siddhânta*, and these two *Siddhântas* differ. In consequence several points had to be attended to. First, in Prof. Jacobi's Tables 1 to 4 the solar months are supposed to begin exactly at Ujjain mean sunset, while in fact they begin (as explained by himself at p. 147) at *or shortly after* mean sunset. This state of things is harmless as regards calculations made for the purpose for which the Professor designed and chiefly uses these Tables, but such is not the case when the task is to determine an intercalary month, where a mere fraction may make all the difference, and where the exact moment of a saṅkrânti must positively be ascertained. Secondly, the beginning of the solar year, *i.e.*, the moment of the Mesha-saṅkranti, differs when calculated according to those two *Siddhântas*, as will be seen by comparing cols. 15 to 17 with cols. 15*a* to 17*a* of our Table I., the difference being *nil* in A.D. 496 and 6 gh 23 pa. 41.4 pra. vi. in 1900 A.D. Thirdly, even if we suppose the year to begin simultaneously by both *Siddhântas*, still the collective duration of the months from the beginning of the year to the end of the required solar month is not the same,[2] as will be seen by comparing cols. 6 or 7 with cols. 8 or 9 of our Table III. We have applied all the corrections necessitated by these three differences to the figures obtained from Prof. Jacobi's Tables and have given the final results in cols. 9 and 11. We know of no independent test which can be applied to determine the accuracy of the results of our calculations for true added and suppressed months; but the first calculations were made exceedingly carefully and were checked and rechecked. They were made quite independently of any previously existing lists of added and suppressed months, and the results were afterwards compared with Prof. Chhatre's list; and whenever a difference appeared the calculations were completely re-examined. In some cases of expunged months the difference between the two lists is only nominal, but in other cases of difference it can be said with certainty that Prof. Chhatre's list is wrong. (*See note to Art. 46.*) Moreover, since the greatest possible error in the value of the tithi-index that can result by use of Prof. Jacobi's Table is 7 (*see his Table p. 164*), whenever the tithi-index for added and suppressed months obtained by our computation fell within 7 of 10,000, *i.e.*, whenever the resulting index was below 7 or over 9993, the results were again tested direct by the *Sûrya-Siddhânta.*[3]

As regards mean intercalations every figure in our cols. 9*a* to 12*a* was found correct by independent test. The months and the times of the saṅkrântis expressed in tithi-indices and tithis were calculated by the present *Sûrya-Siddhânta*, and the results are the same whether

1 For finding the initial date of the luni-solar years Prof. Jacobi's Tables I. to XI. were used, and in the course of the calculations it was necessary to introduce a few alterations, and to correct some misprints which had crept in in addition to those noted in the already published errata-list. Thus, the earliest date noted in Tables I. to IV., being A.D. 354, these Tables had to be extended backwards by adding two lines more of figures above those already given. In Table. VI., as corrected by the errata, the bîja is taken into account only from A.D. 1601, whereas we consider that it should be introduced from A.D. 1501 (*see Art.* 21). In Table VI. the century correction is given for the New (Gregorian) Style from A.D. 1600 according to the practice in the most part of Europe. I have preferred, however, to introduce the New Style into our Tables from Sept. A.D. 1752 to suit English readers, and this necessitated an alteration in the century data for two centuries. [R. S.]

2 It is the same according to Warren, but in this respect he is in error. *(See note to Art. 24.)*

3 42 calculations were thus made direct by the *Sûrya-Siddhânta* with and without the bîja, with the satisfactory result that the error in the final figure of the tithi-index originally arrived at was generally only of 1 or 2 units, while in some cases it was *nil* It was rarely 3, and only once 4. It never exceeded 4. It may therefore be fairly assumed that our results are accurate. [S.B D.]

worked by that or by the Original *Sûrya-Siddhânta*, the First *Ârya-Siddhânta*, or the Present *Sûrya-Siddhânta* with the bîja.

We think, therefore, that the list of true added and suppressed months and that of the mean added months as given by us is finally reliable.

92. *Cols. 13 to 17 or to 17a.* The solar year begins from the moment of the Mesha saṅkrânti and this is taken as *apparent and not mean.* We give the exact moment for all years from A.D. 300 to 1900 by the *Ârya-Siddhânta*, and in addition for years between A.D. 1100 and 1900 by the *Sûrya-Siddhântas* as well. (*See also Art. 96*). Every figure has been independently tested, and found correct. The week-day and day of the month A.D. as given in cols. 13 and 14 are applicable to both the *Siddhântas*, but particular attention must be paid to the footnote in Table I., annexed to A.D. 1117—18 and some other subsequent years. The entries in cols. 15 and 15*a* for Indian reckoning in ghaṭikâs and palas, and in cols. 17 and 17*a* for hours and minutes, imply that at the instant of the saṅkrânti so much time has elapsed since mean sunrise at Ujjain on the day in question. Ujjain mean sunrise is generally assumed to be 6.0 a.m.

93. The alteration of week-day and day of the month alluded to in the footnote mentioned in the last paragraph (Table I., A.D. 1117—18) is due to the difference resulting from calculations made by the two *Siddhântas*, the day fixed by the *Sûrya-Siddhânta* being sometimes one later than that found by the *Ârya-Siddhânta.* It must be remembered, however, that the day in question runs from sunrise to sunrise, and therefore a moment of time fixed as falling between midnight and sunrise belongs to the preceding day in Indian reckoning, though to the succeeding day by European nomenclature. For example, the Mesha saṅkrânti in Śaka 1039 expired (A.D. 1117) took place, according to the *Ârya-Siddhânta* on Friday 23rd March at 58 gh. 1p. after Ujjain mean sunrise (23 h. 12 m. after sunrise on Friday, or 5.12 a.m. on Saturday morning, 24th); while by the *Sûrya-Siddhânta* it fell on Saturday 24th at 0 gh. 51 pa. (=0 h. 20 m. after sunrise or 6.20 a.m.). This only happens of course when the saṅkrânti according to the *Ârya-Siddhânta* falls nearly at the end of a day, or near mean sunrise.

94. In calculating the instant of the apparent Mesha-saṅkrântis, we have taken the śodhya at 2 d. 8 gh. 51 pa. 15 vipa. according to the *Ârya-Siddhânta*, and 2 d. 10 gh. 14 pa. 30 vipa. according to the *Sûrya-Siddhânta.* (*See Art. 26.*)

95. The figure given in brackets after the day and month in cols. 13 and 19 is the number of that day in the English common year, reckoning from January 1st. For instance, 75 against 16th March shows that 16th March is the 75th day from January 1st inclusive. This figure is called the "date indicator", or shortly (*d*), in the methods of computation "B" and "C" given below (*Part IV.*), and is intended as a guide with reference to Table IX., in which the collective duration of days is given in the English common year.

96. The fixture of the moments of the 1600 Mesha-saṅkrântis noted in this volume will be found advantageous for many purposes, but we have designed it chiefly to facilitate the conversion of solar dates as they are used in Bengal and Southern India. [1] We have not given the moments of Mesha-saṅkrântis according to the *Sûrya-Siddhânta* prior to A.D. 1100, so that the *Ârya-Siddhânta* computation must be used for dates earlier than that, even those occurring in Bengal. There is little danger in so doing, since the difference between the times of the Mesha-saṅkrântis according to the two *Siddhântas* during that period is very slight, being *nil* in A.D. 496, and only increasing to 1 h. 6 m. at the most in 1100 A.D. It is, however, advisable to give a correction Table so as to ensure accuracy, and consequently we append the Table which follows, by which the difference for any year lying between A.D. 496 and 1100 A.D. can be found. It is

[1] See Art. 21, and the first footnote appended to it.

used in the following manner. First find the interval in years between the given year and A.D. 496. Then take the difference given for that number of years in the Table, and subtract or add it to the moment of the Mesha-saṅkrânti fixed by us in Table I. by the *Ârya-Siddhânta*, according as the given year is prior or subsequent to A.D. 496. The quotient gives the moment of the Mesha-saṅkrânti by the *Sûrya-Siddhânta*.

TABLE

Shewing the difference between the moments of the Mesha-sankrânti as calculated by the Present Sûrya and the first Ârya-Siddhântas; the difference in A.D. 496 (Śaka 496 current) being o.

No. of years.	Difference Expressed in			No. of years.	Difference Expressed in			No. of years.	Difference Expressed in		
	gh.	pa.	minutes.		gh.	pa.	minutes.		gh.	pa.	minutes.
1	0	0.3	0.1	10	0	2.7	1.1	100	0	27.3	10.9
2	0	0.5	0.2	20	0	5.5	2.2	200	0	54.6	21.9
3	0	0.8	0.3	30	0	8.2	3.3	300	1	22.0	32.8
4	0	1.1	0.4	40	0	10.9	4.4	400	1	49.3	43.7
5	0	1.4	0.5	50	0	13.7	5.5	500	2	16.6	54.7
6	0	1.6	0.7	60	0	16.4	6.6	600	2	44.0	65.6
7	0	1.9	0.8	70	0	19.1	7.7	700	3	11.3	76.5
8	0	2.2	0.9	80	0	21.9	8.7	800	3	38.6	87.5
9	0	2.5	1.0	90	0	24.6	9.8	900	4	6.0	98.4

Example. Find the time of the Mesha saṅkrânti by the *Sûrya-Siddhânta* in A.D. 1000. The difference for (1000—496 =) 504 years is (2 gh. 16.6 pa. + 1.1 pa. =) 2 gh. 17.7 pa. Adding this to Friday, 22nd March, 42gh. 5pa., *i.e.*, the time fixed by the *Ârya-Siddhânta* (*Table I., cols. 14, 15*), we have 44 gh. 22.7 pa. from sunrise on that Friday as the actual time by the *Sûrya-Siddhânta*.

97. *Cols. 19 to 25.* The entries in these columns enable us to convert and verify Indian luni-solar dates. They were first calculated, as already stated, according to the Tables published by Prof. Jacobi in the *Indian Antiquary* [1] (Vol. XVII.). The calculations were not only most carefully made, but every figure was found to be correct by independent test. As now finally issued, however, the figures are those obtained from calculations direct from the *Sûrya-Siddhânta*, specally made by Mr. S. Bâlkṛishṇa Dîkshit. The articles *a, b, c,* in cols. 23 to 25 are very important as they form the basis for all calculations of dates demanding an exact result. Their meaning is fully described below (*Art. 102.*).

The meaning of the phrase "moon's age" *(heading of cols. 21, 22)* in the Nautical Almanack is the mean time in *days* elapsed since the moon's conjunction with the sun (*amâvâsyâ*, new noon). For our purposes the moon's age is its age in lunation-parts and tithis, and these have been fully explained above.

98. The week-day and day of the month A.D. given in cols. 19 and 20 shew the civil day on which Chaitra śukla pratipadâ of each year, as an apparent tithi, ends. [2] The figures given in cols. 21 to 25 relate to Ujjain mean sunrise on that day.

1 See note 1 to *Art.* 91.

2 We have seen before *(Arts. 45 etc. above)* how months and tithis are sometimes added or expunged. Now in case of Chaitra śukla pratpadâ being current at sunrise on two successive days, as sometimes happens, the first of these civil days, *i.e.*, the day *previous* to that given by us, is taken as the first day of the Indian luni-solar year *(see Art. 52)*. This does not, however, create any confusion in our method C since the quantities given in cols. 23 to 25 are correct for the day and time for which they are given; while as for our methods A and B, the day noted by us is more convenient.

99 When an intercalary Chaitra occurs by the true system *(Arts. 45 etc. above)* it must be remembered that the entries in cols. 19 to 25 are for the śukla-pratipadâ of the *intercalated,* not the *true,* Chaitra.

100. The first tithi of the year (Chaitra śukla pratipadâ) in Table I., cols. 19 to 25, is taken as an apparent, not mean, tithi, which practice conforms to that of the ordinary native pañchâṅgs. By this system, as worked out according to our methods A and B, the English equivalents of all subsequent tithis will be found as often correct as if the first had been taken as a mean tithi;—probably more often.

101. The figures given in cols. 21 and 22, except in those cases where a minus sign is found prefixed (*e.g.*, Kali 4074 current), constitute a first approximation showing how much of chaitra śukla pratipadâ had expired on the occurrence of mean sunrise at Ujjain on the day given in cols. 19 and 20. Col. 21 gives the expired lunation-parts or tithi-index, and col. 22 shews the same period in tithi-parts, *i.e.*, decimals of a tithi. The meaning of both of these is explained above (*Arts. 80 and 81*). We differ from the ordinary pañchâṅgs in one respect, viz., that while they give the portion of the tithi which has to run after mean sunrise, we have given, as in some ways more convenient, the portion already elapsed at sunrise. Thus, the entry 286 in col. 21 means that 286 lunation-parts of Chaitra śukla 1st had expired at mean sunrise. The new moon therefore took place 286 lunation-parts before mean sunrise, and by Table X., col. 3, 286 lunation-parts are equal to (14 h. 10 m. + 6 h. 6 m. =) 20 h. 16 m. The new moon therefore took place 20 h. 16 m. before sunrise, or at 9.44 a.m. on the previous day by European reckoning. The ending-moment of Chaitra śukla pratipadâ can be calculated in the same way, remembering that there are 333 lunation-parts to a tithi.

We allude in the last paragraph to those entries in cols. 21 and 22 which stand with a minus sign prefixed. Their meaning is as follows:—Just as other tithis have sometimes to be expunged so it occasionally happens that Chaitra śukla 1st has to be expunged. In other words, the last tithi of Phâlguna, or the tithi called amâvâsyâ, is current at sunrise on one civil day and the 2nd tithi of Chaitra (Chaitra śukla dvitîyâ) at sunrise on the following civil day. In such a case the first of these is the civil day corresponding to Chaitra śukla 1st; and accordingly we give this civil day in cols. 19 and 20. But since the amâvâsyâ-tithi (the last tithi of Phâlguna) was actually current at sunrise on that civil day we give in cols. 21 and 22 the lunation-parts and tithi-parts of the amâvâsya-tithi which have to run after sunrise with a minus sign prefixed to them. Thus, "—12" in col. 21 means that the tithi-index at sunrise was 10,000—12 = or 9988, and that the amâvâsyâ-tithi (Phâlguna Kṛishṇa 15 or 30) *(Table VIII., col. 3)* will end 12 lunation-parts after sunrise, while the next tithi will end 333 lunation-parts after that.

102. (*a, b. c, cols. 23, 24, 25*). The moment of any new moon, or that moment in each lunation when the sun and moon are nearest together, in other words when the longitudes of the sun and moon are equal, cannot be ascertained without fixing the following three elements,—(*a*) The eastward distance of the moon from the sun in mean longitude, (*b*) the moon's mean anomaly (*Art. 15 and note*), which is here taken to be her distance from her perigee in mean longitude, (*c*) the sun's mean anomaly, or his distance from his perigee in mean longitude. And thus our "*a*", "*b*", "*c*", have the above meanings; "*a*" being expressed in 10,000ths of a circle reduced by 200.6 for purposes of convenience of use, all calculations being then additive, "*b*" and "*c*" being given in 1000ths of the circle. To take an example. At Ujjain mean sunrise on Chaitra śukla pratipadâ of the Kali year 3402 (Friday, 8th March, A.D. 300), the mean longitudes calculated direct from the *Sûrya-Siddhânta* were as follow: The sun, 349° 22′ 27″.92.

The sun's perigee, 257° 14′ 22″.86. The moon, 355° 55′ 35″.32. The moon's perigee, 33° 39′ 58″.03. The moon's distance from the sun therefore was (355° 55′ 35″.32—349° 22′ 27″.92 =) 6° 33′ 7″.4 = .0182 of the orbit of 360°. This (1.0182) reduced by 0 0200,6 comes to 0.99814; and consequently "*a*" for that moment is 9981·41. The moon's mean anomaly "*b*" was (355° 55′ 35″.32—33° 39′ 58″.03 =) 322° 15′ 37″.29 = 895·17. And the sun's mean anomaly "*c*" was (349° 22′ 27″.92—257° 14′ 22″.86 =) 92° 8′ 5″.06 = 255·93.[1] We therefore give $a = 9981$, $b = 895$, $c = 256$. The figures for any other year can if necessary be calculated from the following Table, which represents the motion. The increase in *a, b, c,* for the several lengths of the luni-solar year and for 1 day, is given under their respective heads; the figures in brackets in the first column representing the day of the week, and the first figures the number of days in the year.

Increase of a, b, c, in one year, and in one day.

Number of days in the year.	*a.*	*b. without bîja.*	*b. with bîja.*	*c.*
354(4)	9875.703337	847.2197487	847.220646	969.1758567
355(5)	214.335267	883.5113299	883.512230	971.9136416
383(5)	9696.029305	899.675604	899.676575	48.57161909
384(6)	34.661235	935.967185	935.968158	51.3094039
385(0)	373.293166	972.258766	972.259742	54.04789
1(1)	338.63193033	36.291581211	36.291583746	2.737784906

103. *Table II.*, Part i., of this table will speak for itself (*see also Art. 51 above*). In the second part is given, in the first five columns, the correspondence of a cycle of twelve lunar months of a number of different eras with the twelve lunar months of the Śaka year 1000,[2] which itself corresponds exactly with Kali 4179, Chaitrâdi Vikrama 1135, and Gupta 738. Cols. 8 to 13 give a similar concurrence of months of the solar year Śaka 1000. The concurrence of parts of solar months and of parts of the European months with the luni-solar months is given in cols. 6 and 7, and of the same parts with the solar months in cols. 14 and 15. Thus, the luni-solar amânta month Âshâḍha of the Chaitrâdi Saka year 1000 corresponds with amânta Âshâḍha of Kali 4179, of Chaitrâdi Vikrama 1135, and of the Gupta era 758; of the Âshâḍhâdi Vikrama year 1135, and of the Chedi or Kaḷachuri 828; of the Kârttikâdi Vikrama year 1134, and of the Nêvâr year 198. Parts of the solar months Mithuna and Karka, and parts of June and July of 1077 A.D. correspond with it; in some years parts of the other

[1] Calculating by Prof. Jacobi's Tables, *a, b, c,* are 9980, 896 and 255, each of which is wrong by 1.

The above figures were submitted by me to Dr. Downing of the Nautical Almanack office, with a request that he would test the results by scientific European methods. In reply he gave me the following quantities, for the sun from Leverrier's Tables, and and for the moon from Hansen's Tables (for the epoch A.D. 300, March 8th, 6 am., for the meridian of Ujjain). Mean long of sun 345° 51′ 47″·7, Do. of sun's perigee 253° 54′ 58″·5, Do. of moon 353° 0′ 36″·0, Do. of moon's perigee 36° 9′ 48″·4. He also verified the statement that the sunrise on the morning of March 8th was that immediately following new moon. The difference in result is partly caused by the fact that Leverrier's and Hansen's longitudes are tropical. and those of the *Sûrya-Siddhânta* sidereal. Comparing the two results we find a difference of 0° 35′ 40″·9 in "*a*", 5° 24′ 49″·69 in "*b*", 0° 11′ 15″·87 in "*c*". The closeness of the results obtained from the use of (1) purely Hindu (2) purely European methods is remarkable. Our Tables being for Indian documents and inscriptions we of course work by the former. [R. S.]

[4] This year Śaka 1000 is chosen for convenience of addition or substraction when calculating other years, and therefore we have not taken into account the fact that Ś 1000 was really an intercalary year, having both an Adhika Jyeshṭha and a Nija Jyeshṭha month. That peculiarity affects only that one year and not the concurrence of other months of previous or subsequent years in other eras.

two Christian months noted in col. 7 will correspond with it. In the year Śaka 1000, taken as a Meshâdi solar year, the month Siṁha corresponds with the Bengali Bhâdrapada and the Tamil Âvaṇi of the Meshâdi Kali 4179, and Meshâdi Vikrama 1135; with Âvaṇi of the Siṁhâdi Tinnevelly year 253; with Chingam of the South Malayâḷam Siṁhâdi Kollam âṇḍu 253, and of the North Malayâḷam Kanyâdi Kollam âṇḍu 252. Parts of the lunar months Śrâvaṇa and Bhâdrapada correspond with it, as well as parts of July and August of the European year 1077 A.D; in some years parts of August and September will correspond with it.

All the years in this Table are current years, and all the lunar months are amânta.

It will be noticed that the Tuḷu names of lunar months and the Tamil and Tinnevelly names of solar months are corruptions of the original Sanskrit names of lunar months; while the north and south Malayâḷam names of solar months are corruptions of the original Sanskṛit sign-names. Corruptions differing from these are likely to be found in use in many parts of India. In the Tamil Districts and the district of Tinnevelly the solar sign-names are also in use in some places.

104. *Table II.*, Part iii. This portion of the Table, when read with the notes printed below would seem to be simple and easy to be understood, but to make it still clearer we give the following rules:—

I. Rule for turning into a Chaitrâdi or Meshâdi year (for example, into a luni-solar Saka, or solar Śaka, year) a year of another era, whether earlier or later, which is non-Chaitrâdi or non-Meshâdi.

(*a*) *For an earlier era.* When the given date falls between the first moment of Chaitra or Mesha and the first moment of the month in which, as shewn by the heading, the year of the given earlier era begins, subtract from the given year the first, otherwise the second, of the double figures given under the heading of the earlier era along the line of the year 0 of the required Chaitrâdi or Meshâdi era (*e.g.*, the Śaka).

Examples. (1) To turn Vaiśâkha Śukla 1st of the Âshâḍhâdi Vikrama year 1837, or Srâvaṇa śukla 1st of the Kârttikâdi Vikrama year 1837 into corresponding Śaka reckoning. The year is (1837—134 =) 1703 Śaka. The day and month are the same in each case. (2) To turn Mâgha śukla 1st of the Kârttikâdi Vikrama samvat 1838 into the corresponding Śaka date. The year is (1838—135 =) 1703 Śaka. The day and month are the same. (3) Given 1st December, 1822 A.D. The year is (1822—77 =) 1745 Śaka current. (4) Given 2nd January, 1823 A.D. The year is (1823—78 =) 1745 Śaka current.

(*b*) *For a later era.* When the given day falls between the first moment of Chaitra or Mesha and the first moment of the month in which, as shewn by the heading, the later era begins, add to the number of the given year the figure in the Table under the heading of the required Chaitrâdi or Meshâdi era along the line of the year 0 1 of the given later era. In the reverse case add that number reduced by one.

Examples. (1) To turn the 1st day of Mithuna 1061 of the South Malayâḷam Kollam Âṇḍu into the corresponding Śaka date. The year is (1061 + 748 =) Śaka 1809 current. The day and month are the same. (2) To turn the 1st day of Makara 1062 of the South Malayâḷam Kollum Âṇḍu into the corresponding Śaka date. The year is (1062 + 747 =) 1809 Śaka current. The day and month are the same.

II. Rule for turning a Chaitrâdi or Meshâdi (*e.g.*, a Śaka) year into a non-Chaitrâdi or non-Meshâdi year of an earlier or later era.

(*a*) *For an earlier era.* When the given day falls between the first moment of Chaitra or Mesha and the first moment of the month in which, as shown by the heading, the year of the earlier era begins, add to the given Chaitrâdi or Meshâdi year the first, otherwise the second, of the double figures given under the heading of the earlier era along the line of the year 0 of the Chaitrâdi or Meshâdi era given.

Examples. (1) To turn Bhâdrapada kṛishṇa 30th of the Śaka year 1699 into the corresponding Kârttikâdi Vikrama year. The year is (1699 + 134 =) 1833 of the Kârttikâdi Vikrama era. The day and month are the same. (2) To turn the same Bhâdrapada kṛishṇa 30th, Śaka 1699, into the corresponding Âshâḍhâdi Vikrama year. The year is (1699 + 135 =) 1834 of the Âshâḍhâdi Vikrama era. The day and month are the same.

(*b*) *For a later era.* When the given day falls between the first moment of Chaitra or Mesha and the first moment of the month in which, as shown by the heading, the later era begins, subtract from the given year the number under the heading of the given Chaitrâdi or Meshâdi era along the line of the year 0/1 of the given later era; in the reverse case subtract that number reduced by one.

Examples. (1) To turn the 20th day of Siṁha Śaka 1727 current into the corresponding North Malayâḷam Kollam Âṇḍu date. The day and month are the same. The era is a Kanyâdi era, and therefore the required year is (1727—748 =) 979 of the required era. (2) To turn the 20th day of Siṁha Saka 1727 current into the corresponding South Malayâḷam (Tinnevelly) Kollam Âṇḍu date. The day and month are the same. The era is Siṁhâdi, and therefore the required year is (1727—747 =) 980 of the required era.

III. Rule for turning a year of one Chaitrâdi or Meshâdi era into one of another Chaitrâdi or Meshâdi era. This is obviously so simple that no explanations or examples are required.

IV. Rule for turning a year of a non-Chaitrâdi or non-Meshâdi era into one of another year equally non-Chaitrâdi or non-Meshâdi These are not required for our methods, but if any reader is curious he can easily do it for himself.

This Table must be used for all our three methods of conversion of dates.

105. *Table III.*—The numbers given in columns 3*a* and 10 are intended for use when calculation is made approximately by means of our method "*B*" (*Arts. 137, 138*).

It will be observed that the number of days in lunar months given in col. 3*a* is alternately 30 and 29; but such is not always the case in actual fact. In all the twelve months it occurs that the number of days is sometimes 29 and sometimes 30. Thus Bhâdrapada has by our Table 29 days, whereas it will be seen from the pañchâṅg extract printed in Art. 30 above that in A.D. 1894 (Śaka 1816 expired) it had 30 days.

The numbers given in col. 10 also are only approximate, as will be seen by comparing them with those given in cols. 6 to 9.

Thus all calculations made by use of cols. 3*a* and 10 will be sometimes wrong by a day. This is unavoidable, since the condition of things changes every year, so that no single Table can be positively accurate in this respect; but, other elements of the date being certain, calculations so made will *only* be wrong by one day, and if the week-day is given in the document or inscription concerned the date may be fixed with a fair pretence to accuracy. If entire accuracy is demanded, our method "C" must be followed. *(See Arts. 2 and 126.)*

The details in cols. 3, and 6 to 9, are exactly accurate to the unit of a pala, or 24 seconds. The figure in brackets, or week-day index (*w*), is the remainder after casting out sevens from the number of days; thus, casting out sevens from 30 the remainder is 2, and this is the (*w*) for 30. To guard against mistakes it may be mentioned that the figure "2" does not of course mean that the Mesha or Vṛishabha saṅkrânti always takes place on (2) Monday.

106. *Tables IV. and V.* These tables give the value of (*w*) (week-day) and (*a*) (*b*) and

(*c*) for any required number of civil days, hours, and minutes, according to the *Sûrya Siddhânta*. It will be seen that the figures given in these Tables are calculated by the value for one day given in Art. 102.

Table IV. is Prof. Jacobi's *Indian Antiquary* (Vol. XVII.) Table 7, slightly modified to suit our purposes; the days being run on instead of being divided into months, and the figures being given for the end of each period of 24 hours, instead of at its commencement. Table V. is Prof. Jacobi's Table 8.

107. *Tables VI. and VII.* These are Prof. Jacobi's Tables 9 and 10 re-arranged. It will be well that their meaning and use should be understood before the reader undertakes computations according to our method "C". It will be observed that the centre column of each column-triplet gives a figure constituting the equation for each figure of the argument from 0 to 1000, the centre figure corresponding to either of the figures to right or left. These last are given only in periods of 10 for convenience, an auxiliary Table being added to enable the proper equation to be determined for all arguments. Table VI. gives the lunar equation of the centre, Table VII. the solar equation of the centre. (*Art. 15 note 3 above*). The argument-figures are expressed in 1000ths of the circle, while the equation-figures are expressed in 10,000ths to correspond with the figures of our "*a*," to which they have to be added. Our (*b*) and (*c*) give the mean anomaly of the moon and sun for any moment, (*a*) being the mean longitudinal distance of the moon from the sun. To convert this last (*a*) into true longitudinal distance the equation of the centre for both moon and sun must be discovered and applied to (*a*) and these Tables give the requisite quantities. The case may perhaps be better understood if more simply explained. The moon and earth are constantly in motion in their orbits, and for calculation of a tithi we have to ascertain their relative positions with regard to the sun. Now supposing a railway train runs from one station to another twenty miles off in an hour. The average rate of running will be twenty miles an hour, but the actual speed will vary, being slower at starting and stopping than in the middle. Thus at the end of the first quarter of an hour it will not be quite five miles from the start, but some little distance short of this, say *m* yards. This distance is made up as full speed is acquired, and after three-quarters of an hour the train will be rather *more* than 15 miles from the start, since the speed will be slackened in approaching the station,—say *n* yards more than the 15 miles. These distances of *m* yards and *n* yards, the one in defect and the other in excess, correspond to the "Equation of the Centre" in planetary motion. The planetary motions are not uniform and a planet is thus sometimes behind, sometimes in front of, its mean or average place. To get the true longitude we must apply to the mean longitude the equation of the centre. And this last for both sun (or earth) and moon is what we give in these two Tables. All the requisite data for calculating the mean anomalies of the sun and moon, and the equations of the centre for each planet, are given in the Indian *Siddhântas* and *Karaṇas*, the details being obtained from actual observation; and since our Tables generally are worked according to the *Sûrya Siddhânta*, we have given in Tables VI. and VII. the equations of the centre by that authority.

Thus the Tables enable us to ascertain (*a*) the mean distance of moon from sun at any moment, (*b*) the correction for the moon's true (or apparent) place with reference to the earth, and (*c*) the correction for the earth's true (or apparent) place with reference to the sun; and with these corrections applied to the (*a*) we have the true (or apparent) distance of the moon from the sun, which marks the occurrence of the true (or apparent) tithi; and this result is our tithi-index, or (*t*). From this tithi-index (*t*) the tithi current at any given moment is found from Table VIII., and the time equivalent is found by Table X. Full explanation for actual work is given in Part IV. below (Arts. 139—160).

The method for calculating a nakshatra or yoga is explained in Art. 133.

108. Since the planet's true motion is sometimes greater and sometimes less than its mean motion it follows that the two equations of the centre found from (*b*) and (*c*) by our Tables VI. and VII. have sometimes to be added to and sometimes subtracted from the mean longitudinal distance (*a*), if it is required to find the true (or apparent) longitudinal distance (*t*). But to simplify calculation it is advisable to eliminate this inconvenient element, and to prepare the Tables so that the sum to be worked may always be one of addition. Now it is clear that this can be done by increasing every figure of each equation by its largest amount, and decreasing the figure (*a*) by the sum of the largest amount of both, and this is what has been done in the Tables. According to the *Sûrya Siddhânta* the greatest possible lunar equation of the centre is $5^{\circ}\ 2'\ 47''.17$ (=.0140,2 in our tithi-index computation), and the greatest possible solar equation of the centre is $2^{\circ}\ 10'\ 32''.35$ (=.0060,4). But the solar equation of the centre, or the equation for the earth, must be introduced into the figure representing the distance of the moon from the sun *with reversed sign*, because a positive correction to the earth's longitude implies a negative correction to the distance of moon from sun. This will be clear from a diagram.

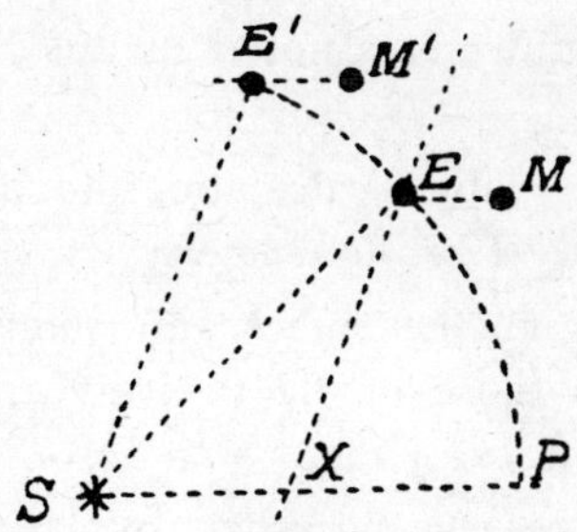

Let S be the sun, M the moon, E the earth, P the direction of perigee. Then the angle SEM represents the distance of moon from sun. But if we add a positive correction to (*i.e.*, increase) the earth's longitude PSE and make it PSE' (greater than PSE by ESE') we thereby *decrease* the angle SEM to SE'M', and we decrease it by exactly the same amount, since the angle SEM = $\angle$ SE'M' + $\angle$ ESE', as may be seen if we draw the line EX parallel to E'S; for the angle SEX = $\angle$ ESE' by Euclid.

Every figure of each equation is thus increased in our Tables VI. and VII. by its greatest value, *i.e.*, that of the moon by 140,2 and that of the sun by 60,4, and every figure of (*a*) is decreased by the sum of both, or (140,2 + 60,4 =) 200,6. [1]

In conclusion, Table VI. yields the lunar equation of the centre calculated by the *Sûrya Siddhânta*, turned into 10,000ths of a circle, and increased by 140.2; and Table VII. yields the solar equation of the centre calculated by the *Sûrya Siddhânta*, with sign reversed, converted into 10,000ths of a circle, and increased by 60.4. [2] This explains why for argument 0 the equation given is lunar 140 and solar 60. If there were no such alteration made the lunar equation for Arg. 0 would be ± 0, for Arg. 250 (or 90°) + 140, for Arg. 500 (180°) ± 0, and for Arg. 750 (or 270°) —140, and so on.

109. The lunar and solar equations of the centre for every degree of anomaly are given

[1] Prof. Jacobi gives this as 200.5, but after most careful calculation I find it to be 200.6. [S. B. D.]

[2] Prof. Jacobi has not explained these Tables.

in the *Makaranda,* and from these the figures given by us for every $\frac{1}{100}$th of a circle, or 10 units of the argument of the Tables, are easily deduced.

110. The use of the auxiliary Table is fully explained on the Table itself.

111. *Table VIII.* This is designed for use with our method *C,* the rules for which are given in Arts. 139—160. As regards the tithi-index, see Art. 80. The period of a nakshatra or yoga is the 27th part of a circle, that is 13° 20′ or $\frac{10000}{27} = 370\frac{10}{27}$. Thus, the index for the ending point of the first nakshatra or yoga is 370 and so on.[1] Tables VIII.A. and VIII.B. speak for themselves. They have been inserted for convenience of reference.

112. *Table IX.* is used in both methods *B* and *C.* See the rules for work.

113. *Table X.* (*See the rules for work by method C.*) The mean values in solar time of the several elements noted herein, as calculated by the *Sûrya-Siddhânta,* are as follow:—

A tithi	= 1417.46822	minutes.
A lunation	= 42524.046642	do.
A sidereal month	= 39343.21	do.
A yoga-chakra	= 36605.116	do.

From these values the time-equivalents noted in this Table[2] have been calculated. (*See also note to Art. 82.*)

114. *Table XI.* This Table enables calculations to be made for observations at different places in India. (*See Art. 36, and the rules for working by our method C.*)

115. *Table XII.* We here give the names and numbers of the samvatsaras, or years of the sixty-year cycle of Jupiter, with those of the twelve-year cycle corresponding thereto. (*See the description of these cycles given above, Arts. 53 to 63.*)

116. *Table XIII.* This Table was furnished by Dr. Burgess and is designed to enable the week-day corresponding to any European date to be ascertained. It explains itself. Results of calculations made by all our methods may be tested and verified by the use of this Table.

117. *Tables XIV. and XV.* are for use by our method *A* (*see the rules*), and were invented and prepared by Mr. T. Lakshmiah Naidu of Madras.

Table XVI. is explained in Part V.

PART IV.

USE OF THE TABLES.

118. The Tables now published may be used for several purposes, of which some are enumerated below.

(1) For finding the year and month of the Christian or any Indian era corresponding to a given year and month in any of the eras under consideration.

[1] This Table contains Prof. Jacobi's Table 11 (*Ind. Ant., XVII., p.* 147) and his Table 17, p. 181, in a modified form [S. B. D.]

[2] The Table contains Prof. Jacobi's Table 11 (*Ind. Ant., XVII., p.* 172), as well as his Table 17 Part II. (*id. p.* 181) modified and enlarged. I have also added the equivalents for tithi parts, and an explanation. [S. B. D.]

(2) For finding the samvatsara of the sixty-year cycle of Jupiter, whether in the southern (luni-solar) or northern (mean-sign) scheme. and of the twelve-year cycle of Jupiter, corresponding to the beginning of a solar (Meshâdi) year. or for any day of such a year.

(3) For finding the added or suppressed months, if any, in any year.

But the chief and most important use of them are;

(4) The conversion of any Indian date—luni-solar (tithi) or solar—into the corresponding date A.D. and vice versâ, from A.D. 300 to 1900, and finding the week-day of any such date;

(5) Finding the karaṇa. nakshatra. and yoga for any moment of any Indian or European date, and thereby verifying any given Indian date;

(6) Turning a Hindu solar date into a luni-solar date, and vice versâ.

(7) Conversion of a Muhammadan Hijra date into the corresponding date A.D., and vice versâ. This is fully explained in Part V. below.

119. (1) *For the first purpose* Table I., cols. 1 to 5, or Table II., must be used, with the explanation given in Part III. above. For eras not noted in these two Tables see the description of them given in Art. 71. In the case of obscure eras whose exact nature is not yet well known, the results will only be approximate.

(N.B.—It will be observed that in Table II., Part ii., portions of two solar months or of four [1] Christian months are made to correspond to a lunar month and vice versâ, and therefore that if this Table *only* be used the results may not be exact).

The following note, though not yielding very accurate results, will be found useful for finding the corresponding parts of lunar and solar months. The tithi corresponding to the Mesha-saṅkrânti can be approximately [2] found by comparing its English date (Table I., col. 13) with that of the luni-solar Chaitra śukla 1st (Table I., col. 19); generally the saṅkrântis from Vṛishabha to Tulâ fall in successive lunar months, either one or two tithis later than the given one. Tulâ falls about 10 tithis later in the month than Mesha; and the saṅkrântis from Vṛischika to Mîna generally fall on the same tithi as that of Tulâ. Thus, if the Mesha saṅkrânti falls on śukla pañchamî (5th) the Vṛishabha saṅkrânti will fall on śukla shasṭhî (6th) or saptamî (7th), the Mithuna saṅkrânti on śukla ashṭamî (8th) or navamî (9th), and so on.

120. (2) *For the samvatsara* of the southern sixty-year cycle see col. 6 of Table I., or calculate it by the rule given in Art. 62. For that of the sixty-year cycle of Jupiter of the mean sign system, according to *Sûrya Siddhânta* calculations, current at the beginning of the solar year, *i.e.*, at the true (or apparent) Mesha saṅkrânti, see col. 7 of Table I.; and for that current on any day in the year according to either the *Sûrya* or *Ârya Siddhântas*, use the rules in Art. 59. To find the samvatsara of the twelve-year cycle of the mean-sign system corresponding to that of the Jupiter sixty-year cycle see Table XII.

121. (2) *To find the added or suppressed month* according to the *Sûrya Siddhânta* by the true (apparent) system see col. 8 of Table I. throughout; and for an added month of the mean system according to either the Original or Present *Sûrya Siddhântas*, or by the *Ârya Siddhânta*, see col. 8*a* of Table I. for any year from A. D. 300 to 1100.

122. (4) *For conversion of an Indian date into a date A. D. and vice versâ, and to find the week day of any given date*, we give below three methods, with rules and examples for work.

123. The first method A (Arts. 135, 136), the invention of Mr. T. Lakshmiah Naidu of

1 Of course only two in a single case, but four during the entire period of 1600 years covered by our Tables.

2 The exact tithi can be calculated by Arts. 149 and 151.

Madras, is a method for obtaining approximate results without any calculation by the careful use of mere eye-tables, viz., Tables XIV. and XV. These, with the proper use of Table I., are alone necessary. But it must never be forgotten that this result may differ by one, or at the utmost two, days from the true one, and that it is not safe to trust to them unless the era and bases of calculation of the given date are clearly known. (*See Art. 126 below.*)

124. By our second method B (Arts. 137, 138), which follows the system established by Mr. W. S. Kṛishṇasvâmi Naidu of Madras, author of "*South Indian Chronological Tables*" (Madras 1889), and which is intended to enable an approximation to be made by a very simple calculation, a generally accurate correspondence of dates can be obtained by the use of Tables I., III., and IX. The calculation is so easy that it can be done in the head after a little practice. It is liable to precisely the same inaccuracies as method A, neither more nor less.

125. Tables II. and III. will also be sometimes required for both these methods.

126. The result obtained by either of these methods will thus be correct to within one or two days, and as often as not will be found to be quite correct; but there must always be an element of uncertainty connected with their use. If, however, the era and original bases of calculation of the given date are certainly known, the result arrived at from the use of these eye-Tables may be corrected by the week-day if that has been stated; since the day of the month and year will not be wrong by more than a day, or two at the most, and the day of the week will determine the corresponding civil day. Suppose, for instance, that the given Hindu date is Wednesday, Vaiśâkha śukla 5th, and it is found by method A or method B that the corresponding day according to European reckoning fell on a Thursday, it may be assumed, presuming that all other calculations for the year and month have been correctly made, that the civil date A.D. corresponding to the Wednesday is the real equivalentof Vaiśâkha śukla 5th. But these rough methods should never be trusted to in important cases. For a specimen of a date where the bases of calculation are not known see example xxv., Art. 160 below.

127. When Tables XIV. and XV. are once understood (and they are perfectly simple) it will probably be found advisable to use method A in preference to method B.

128. As already stated, our method "C" enables the conversion of dates to be made with precise accuracy; the exact moments of the beginning and ending of every tithi can be ascertained; and the corresponding date is obtained, simultaneously with the week-day, in the required reckoning.

129. The week-day for any European date can be found independently by Table XIII., which was supplied by Dr. Burgess.

131[1] (5) *To find the karaṇa, nakshatra, or yoga current on any Indian or European date; and to verify any Indian date.*

Method C includes calculations for the karaṇa, nakshatra and yoga current at any given moment of any given day, as well as the instants of their beginnings and endings; but for this purpose, if the given date is other than a tithi or a European date, it must be first turned into one or the other according to our rules *(Art. 139 to 152.)*

132. It is impossible, of course, to verify any tithi or solar date unless the week-day, nakshatra, karaṇa, or yoga, or more than one of these, is also given; but when this requirement is satisfied our method C will afford proof as to the correctness of the date. To verify a solar date it must first be turned into a tithi or European date. *(Art. 134 or 149.)*

133. For an explanation of the method of calculating tithis and half-tithis (karaṇas) see Art. 107 above. Our method of calculation for nakshatras and yogas requires a little

[1] Art. 130 has been omitted.

more explanation. The moon's nakshatra (Arts. 8, 38) is found from her apparent longitude. By our method C we shew how to find t (= the difference of the apparent longitudes of sun and moon), and equation[1] c (= the solar equation of the centre) for any given moment. To obtain (t) the sun's apparent longitude is subtracted from that of the moon, so that if we add the sun's apparent longitude to (t) we shall have the moon's apparent longitude. Our (c) (Table I., last column) is the sun's mean anomaly, being the mean sun's distance from his perigee. If we add the longitude of the sun's perigee to (c), we have the sun's mean longitude, and if we apply to this the solar equation of the centre (+ or —) we have the sun's apparent longitude.[2] According to the *Sûrya-Siddhânta* the sun's perigee has only a very slight motion, amounting to 3′ 5″.8 in 1600 years. Its longitude for A.D. 1100, the middle of the period covered by our Tables, was 257° 15′ 55″.7 or .7146,3 of a circle, and therefore this may be taken as a constant for all the years covered by our Tables.

Now, true or apparent sun = mean sun + equation of centre. But we have not tabulated in Table VII., col. 2, the exact equation of the centre; we have tabulated a quantity (say x) the value of which is expressed thus;—

x = 60,4—equation of centre (*see Art. 108*).

So that equation of centre = 60,4—x.

Hence, apparent sun = mean sun + 60,4—x.

But mean sun = c + perigee, (which is 7146,3 in tithi-indices.)

= c + 7146,3.

Hence apparent sun (which we call s) = c + 7146,3 + 60,4—x.

= c + 7206,7—x; or, say, = c + 7207—x

where x is, as stated, the quantity tabulated in col. 2, Table VII.

(c) is expressed in 1000ths, while 7207 and the solar equation in Table VII. are given in 10000ths of the circle, and therefore we must multiply (c) by 10. $t + s$ = apparent moon = n (the index of a nakshatra.) This explains the rule given below for work *(Art. 156)*.

For a yoga, the addition of the apparent longitude of the sun (s) and moon (n) is required. $s + n = y$ (the index of a yoga.) And so the rule in Art. 159.

134. (6) *To turn a solar date into its corresponding luni-solar date and vice versâ.*

First turn the given date into its European equivalent by either of our three methods and then turn it into the required one. The problem can be worked direct by anyone who has thoroughly grasped the principle of these methods.

Method A.

APPROXIMATE COMPUTATION OF DATES BY USE OF THE EYE-TABLE.

This is the method invented by Mr. T. Lakshmiah Naidu, nephew of the late W. S. Kṛishṇasvâmi Naidu of Madras, author of "South Indian Chronological Tables."

Results found by this method *may* be inaccurate by as much as two days, but not more. If the era and bases of calculation of the given Hindu date are clearly known, and if the given date mentions a week-day, the day found by the Tables may be altered to suit it. Thus, if the Table yield result Jan. 10th, Thursday, but the inscription mentions the week-day as "Tuesday", then Tuesday, January 8th, may be assumed to be the correct date A.D. corresponding to the given Hindu date, if the principle on which the Hindu date was fixed is known. If not, this method must not be trusted to.

135. (A.) *Conversion of a Hindu solar date into the corresponding date A. D.* Work by the following rules, always bearing in mind that when using the Kaliyuga or Śaka year Hindus

[1] Equation c is the equation in Table VII.

[2] Reference to the diagram in Art. 108 will make all this plain, if PSE be taken as the sun's mean anomaly, and ESE′ the equation of the centre, PSE′ + longitude of the sun's perigee being the sun's true or apparent longitude.

usually give the number of the expired year, and not that astronomically current, (*e.g.*, Kaliyuga 4904 means in full phrase "after 4904 years of the Kaliyuga had elapsed")—but when using the name of the cyclic year they give that of the one then current. All the years given in Table I. are current years. The Table to work by is Table XIV.

Rule I. From Table I., cols. 1 to 7, and Table II., as the case may be, find the year (current) and its initial date, and week-day (cols. 13, 14, Table I.). But if the given Hindu date belongs to any of the months printed in italics at the head of Table XIV., take the next following initial date and week day in cols. 13, 14 of Table I. The months printed in the heading in capitals are the initial months of the years according to the different reckonings.

Rule II. For either of the modes of reckoning given at the left of the head-columns of months, find the given month, and under it the given date.

Rule III. From the given date so found, run the eye to the left and find the week-day in the same line under the week-day number found by Rule I. This is the required week-day.

Rule IV. Note number in brackets in the same line on extreme left.

Rule V. In the columns to left of the *body* of the Table choose that headed by the bracket-number so found, and run the eye down till the initial date found by Rule I. is obtained.

Rule VI. From the month and date in the upper columns (found by Rule II.) run the eye down to the point of junction (vertical and horizontal lines) of this with the initial date found by Rule V. This is the required date A. D.

Rule VII. If the date A. D. falls on or after 1st January in columns to the right, it belongs to the next following year. If such next following year is a leap-year (marked by an asterisk in Table I.) and the date falls after February 28th in the above columns, reduce the date by one day.

N.B.—The dates A.D. obtained from this Table for solar years are Old Style dates up to 8th April, 1753, inclusive.

EXAMPLE. Find date A.D. corresponding to 20th Paṅguni of the Tamil year Rudhirodgâri, Kali 4904 expired.

By Rule I. Kali 4905 current, 2 (Monday), 11th April, 1803.
" " II. Tamil Panguni 20.
" " III. (under "2") Friday.
" " IV. Bracket-number (5).
" " V. [Under (5)]. Run down to April 11th.
" " VI. (Point of junctions) March 31st.
" " VII. March 30th. (1804 is a leap year.)

Answer.—Friday, March 30th, 1804 N.S. (See example 11, p. 74.)

(B.) *Conversion of a date A.D. into the corresponding Hindu solar date.* (See Rule V., method B. Art. 137, p. 70.) Use Table XIV.

Rule I. From Tables I., cols. 1 to 7 and 13, 14, and Table II., as the case may be, find the Hindu year, and its initial date and week-day, opposite the given year A.D. If the given date falls before such initial date, take the next previous Hindu year and its initial date and week-day A.D.

Rule II. From the columns to the left of the *body* of Table XIV. find that initial date found by Rule I. which is in a line, when carrying the eye horizontally to the right, with the given A.D. date, and note point of junction.

Rule III. Note the bracket-figure at head of the column on left so selected.

Rule IV. From the point of junction (Rule II.) run the eye vertically up to the Hindu date-columns above, and select that date which is in the same horizontal line as the bracket-figure on the extreme left corresponding with that found by Rule III. This is the required date.

Rule V. If the given date falls in the columns to the right after the 28th February in a leap-year (marked with an asterisk in Table I.), add 1 to the resulting date.

Rule VI. From the date found by Rule IV. or V., as the case may be, carry the eye horizontally to the week-day columns at the top on the left, and select the day which lies under the week-day number found from Table I. (Rule I.). This is the required week-day.

Rule VII. If the Hindu date arrived at falls under any of the months printed in italics in the Hindu month-columns at head of Table, the required year is the one next previous to that given in Table I. (Rule I.).

EXAMPLE. Find the Tamil solar date corresponding to March 30th, 1804 (N.S.).

(By Rule I.) Rudhirodgâri, Kali 4905 current. 2 (Monday) April 11th. (March 30th precedes April 11th.)

(By Rules II., III.) The point of junction of March 30th (body of Table), and April 11th, (columns on left) is under "(4)." Other entries of April 11th do not correspond with any entry of March 30).

(By Rule IV.) The date at the junction of the vertical column containing this "March 30th" with "(4)" horizontal is 19th Paṅguni.

(By Rule V.) (1804 is a leap-year) 20th Paṅguni.

(By Rule VI.) Under "2" (Rule I.), Friday.

Answer.—Friday, 20th Paṅguni, of Rudhirodgâri, Kali 4905 current. (See example 15, p. 76.

136. (A.) *Conversion of a Hindu luni-solar date into the corresponding date A.D.* Work by the following rules, using Tables XV.A., and XV.B.

Rule I. From Table I. find the current year and its initial day and week-day in A.D. reckoning, remembering that if the given Hindu date falls in one of the months printed in italics at the head of Table XV. the calculation must be made for the next following A.D. year. (The months printed in capitals are the initial months of the years according to the different reckonings enumerated in the column to the left.)

Rule II. (*a.*) Find the given month, and under it the given date, in the columns at the head of Table XV., in the same line with the appropriate mode of reckoning given in the column to the left. The dates printed in black type are kṛishṇa, or dark fortnight, dates.

(*b*) In intercalary years (cols. 8 to 12, 8*a* to 12*a* of Table I.), if the given month is itself an adhika mâsa (intercalary month), read it, for purpose of this Table, as if it were not so; but if the given month is styled *nija*, or if it falls after a repeated month, but before an expunged one (if any), work in this Table for the month next following the given one, as if that and not the given month had been given. If the given month is preceded by both an intercalated and a suppressed month, work as if the year were an ordinary one.

Rule III. From the date found by Rule II. carry the eye to the left, and find the week-day in the same horizontal line, but directly under the initial week-day found by Rule I.

Rule IV. Note the number in brackets on the extreme left opposite the week-day last found.

Rule V. In the columns to the left of the body of the Table choose that headed by the bracket-number so found, and run the eye down till the initial date found by Rule I. is obtained.

Rule VI. From the Hindu date found by Rule II. run the eye down to the point of junction, (vertical and horizontal lines) of this date with the date found by Rule V. The result is the required date A.D.

Rule VII (*a.*) If the date A.D. falls on or after January 1st in the columns to the right, it belongs to the next following year A.D.

(*b.*) If it is after February 28th in a leap-year (marked by an asterisk in col. 5, Table I.) reduce the date by one day, except in a leap-year in which the initial date (found in Table I.) itself falls after February 28th.

(*c.*) The dates obtained up to April 3rd, A.D. 1753, are Old Style dates.

EXAMPLE. To find the date A. D. corresponding to amânta Kârttika kṛishṇa 2nd of Kali 4923 expired, Śaka 1744 expired, Kârttikâdi Vikrama 1878 expired, Chaitrâdi Vikrama 1879 expired (1880 current), "Vijaya" in the Bṛihaspati cycle, "Chitrabhânu" in the luni-solar 60-year cycle.

(By Rule I.) (Kali 4924 current), 1 Sunday, March 24th, 1822.

(By Rule II.) (Kârttika, the 8th month, falls after the repeated month, 7 Âśvina, and before the suppressed month, 10 Pausha), Mârgaśîrsha kṛishṇa 2nd.

(By Rule III.) (Under "1"), 1 Sunday.

(By Rule IV.) Bracket-number (1).

(By Rule V.) Under (1) run down to March 24th (Rule I.)

(By Rule VI.) (Point of junction) December 1st.

Answer.—Sunday, December 1st, 1822.

(B.) *Conversion of a date A. D. into the corresponding luni-solar Hindu date.* (See Rule V. method B, p. 67 below). Use Tables XV.A., XV.B.

Rule I. From Table I. find the Hindu year, and its initial date and week-day, using also Table II., Parts ii., iii. If the given date falls before such initial date take the next previous Hindu year, and its initial date and week-day.

Rule II. In the columns to the left of the body of Table XV. note the initial date found by Rule I., which is in the same horizontal line with the given date in the body of the Table.

Rule III. Carrying the eye upwards, note the bracket-figure at the head of the initial date-column so noted.

Rule IV. From the given date found in the body of the Table (Rule II.) run the eye upwards to the Hindu date-columns above, and select the date which is in the same horizontal line as the bracket-figure in the extreme left found by Rule III. This is the required Hindu date.

Rule V. Note in Table I. if the year is an intercalary one (cols. 8 to 12, and 8*a* to 12*a*). If it is so, note if the Hindu month found by Rule IV. (*a*) precedes the first intercalary month, (*b*) follows one intercalated and one suppressed month, (*c*) follows an intercalated, but precedes a suppressed month, (*d*) follows two intercalated months and one suppressed month. In cases (*a*) and (*b*) work as though the year were a common year, *i.e.*, make no alteration in the date found by Rule IV. In cases (*c*) and (*d*) if the found month immediately follows the intercalated month, the name of the required Hindu month is to be the name of the intercalated month with the prefix "nija," and not the name of the month actually found; and if the found month does not immediately follow the intercalated month, then the required Hindu month is the month immediately preceding the found month. If the found month is itself intercalary, it retains its name, but with the prefix "adhika." If the found month is itself suppressed, the required month is the month immediately preceding the found month.

Rule VI. If the given date A.D. falls after February 29th in the columns to the right, in a leap-year (marked with an asterisk in Table I.), add 1 to the resulting Hindu date.

Rule VII. From the date found by Rule IV. carry the eye horizontally to the week-day columns on the left, and select the day which lies under the initial week-day number found by Rule I. This is the required week-day.

Rule VIII. If the Hindu date arrived at falls under any of the months printed in italics in the Hindu month-columns at head of the table, the required year is the one next previous to that given by Table I. (Rule I. above.)

EXAMPLE. Find the Telugu luni-solar date corresponding to Sunday, December 1st, 1822.

(By Rule I.) A.D. 1822—23, Sunday, March 24th, Kali 4923 expired, Śaka 1744 expired, Chitrabhânu samvatsara in the luni-solar 60-year or southern cycle reckoning, Vijaya in the northern cycle.

(By Rules II., III.) (Bracket-figure) 1.

(By Rule IV.) Mârgaśirsha kṛishṇa 2nd.

(By Rule V*c*.) (Âśvina being intercalated and Pausha suppressed in that year), Kârttika kṛishṇa 2nd.

(By Rule VI.) The year was not a leap-year.

(By Rule VII.) Sunday.

(By Rule VIII.) Does not apply.

Answer.—Sunday, Kârttika kṛishṇa 2nd, Kali 4923 expired, Śaka 1744 expired. (This can be applied to all Chaitrâdi years.) (See example 12 below, p. 75.)

Method B.

APPROXIMATE COMPUTATION OF DATES BY A SIMPLE PROCESS.

This is the system introduced by Mr. W. S. Kṛishṇasvâmi Naidu of Madras into his "South-Indian Chronological Tables"

137. (A.) *Conversion of Hindu dates into dates A.D.* (See Art. 135 above, para. 1.)

Rule I. Given a Hindu year, month and date. Convert it if necessary by cols. 1 to 5 of Table I., and by Table II., into a Chaitrâdi Kali or Śaka year, and the month into an amânta month. (See Art. 104.) Write down in a horizontal line (*d*) the date-indicator given in brackets in col. 13 or 19 of Table I., following the names of the initial civil day and month of the year in question as so converted, and (*w*) the week-day number (col. 14 or 20) corresponding to the initial date A.D. given in cols. 13 or 19. To both (*d*) and (*w*) add, from Table III., the collective duration of days from the beginning of the year as given in cols. 3*a* or 10 as the case may be, up to the end of the month preceding the given month, and also add the number of given Hindu days in the given month minus 1. If the given date is luni-solar and belongs to the kṛishṇa paksha, add 15 to the collective duration and proceed as before.

Rule II. From the sum of the first addition find in Table IX. (top and side columns) the required English date, remembering that when this is over 365 in a common year or 366 in a leap-year the date A.D. falls in the ensuing A.D. year.

Rule III. From the sum of the second addition cut out sevens. The remainder shews the required day of the week.

Rule IV. If the Hindu date is in a luni-solar year where, according to cols. 8 to 12, there was an added (*adhika*) or suppressed (*kshaya*) month, and falls after such month, the addition or suppression or both must be allowed for in calculating the collective duration of days; *i.e.*, add 30 days for an added month, and deduct 30 for a suppressed month.

Rule V. The results are Old Style dates up to, and New Style dates from, 1752 A.D. The New style in England was introduced with effect from after 2nd September, 1752. Since the initial dates of 1752, 1753 only are given, remember to apply the correction (+ 11 days) to any date between 2nd September, 1752, and 9th April, 1753, in calculating by the Hindu solar year, or between 2nd September, 1752, and 4th April, 1753, in calculating by the Hindu luni-solar year, so as to bring out the result in New Style dates A.D. The day of the week requires no alteration.

Rule VI. If the date A.D. found as above falls after February 29th in a leap-year, it must be reduced by one day.

(a) Luni-Solar Dates.

EXAMPLE 1. Required the A.D. equivalent of (luni-solar) Vaiśâkha śukla shashṭhî (6th), year Śârvari, Śaka 1702 expired, (1703 current).

The A.D. year is 1780 (a leap-year). The initial date *(d)* = 5th April (96), and (*w*) = 4 Wednesday, (Table I., cols. 5, 19, 20).

	d.		*w.*
State this accordingly	96		4
Collective duration (Table III., col. 3*a*)	30		30
Given date (6)—1	5		5
	131		
	1	(Rule VI.)	
	130		39÷7 = Rem. 4

The result gives 130 (Table IX.) = May 10th, and 4 = Wednesday. The required date is therefore Wednesday, May 10th, A.D. 1780.

EXAMPLE 2. Required the A.D. equivalent of (luni-solar) Kârttika śukla pañchamî (5th) Śaka 1698 expired (1699 current).

The A.D. year is 1776, and the initial date is (*d*) = 20th March (80), (*w*) = Wednesday (4). This is a leap-year, and the Table shews us that the month (6) Bhâdrapada was intercalated. So there is both an adhika Bhâdrapada and a nija Bhâdrapada in this year, which compels us to treat the given month Kârttika as if it were the succeeding month Mârgaśîrsha in order to get at the proper figure for the collective duration.

	d.	*w.*
The given figures are . . .	80	4
Collective duration (Table III.) for Mârgaśîrsha	236	236
Given date (5)—1	4	4
	320	
	—1 (Rule VI.)	
	319	244 ÷ 7 = Rem. 6.

319 = (Table IX.) November 15th. 6 = Friday

Answer.—Friday, November 15th, A.D. 1776.

EXAMPLE 3. Required the A.D. equivalent of Kârttika kṛishṇa pañchamî (5th) of the same luni-solar year.

	d.	*w.*
As before	80	4
Collective duration (Table III., col. 3a.)	236	236
Given date (5 + 15)—1	19	19
	335	
	—1 (Rule VI.)	
	334	259 ÷ 7, Rem. 0.

334 = (Table IX.) November 30th. 0 = Saturday.

Answer.—Saturday, November 30th, A.D. 1776.

EXAMPLE 4. Required the A.D. equivalent of Mâgha kṛishṇa pâdyami (1st) of K.Y. 4923 expired (4924 current). This corresponds (Table I., col. 5) to A.D. 1822, the Chitrabhânu samvatsara, and col. 8 shews us that the month Âśvina was intercalated *(adhika)*, and the month Pausha suppressed *(kshaya)*. We have therefore to add 30 days for the adhika month and subtract 30 days for the kshaya month, since Mâgha comes after Pausha. Hence the relative place of the month Mâgha remains unaltered,

Table I. gives 24th March (83), (1) Sunday, as the initial day.

	d.	*w.*
Initial date	83	1
Collective duration (Table III., col. 3a) .	295	295
Given date (1 + 15)—1	15 (Rule I.)	15
	393	311 ÷ 7, Rem. 3.

3 = Tuesday. 393 = January 28th of the following A.D. year (Table IX.).

Answer.—Tuesday, January 28th, A.D. 1823.

This is correct by the Tables, but as there happened to be an expunged tithi in Mâgha śukla, the first fortnight of Mâgha, the result is wrong by one day. The corresponding day was really Monday, January 27th, and to this we should have been guided if the given date had included the mention of Monday as the week-day. That is, we should have fixed Monday, January 27th, as the required day A.D. because our result gave Tuesday, January 28th, and we knew that the date given fell on a Monday,

EXAMPLE 5. Required the A.D. equivalent of Pausha śukla trayodaśî (13th) K.Y. 4853 expired, Aṅgiras samvatsara in luni-solar or southern reckoning. This is K. Y. 4854 current.

The year (Table I., col. 5) is A.D. 1752, a leap-year. The initial date (cols. 19, 20) is 5th March (65), (5) Thursday. The month Âshâḍha was intercalated. Therefore the given month (Pausha) must be treated, for collective duration, as if it were the succeeding month Mâgha.

	d.	*w.*
Initial date	65	5
Collective duration (Table III., col. 3a)	295	295
Given date (13)—1	12	12
	372	
	—1 (Rule VI)	
	371	312 ÷ 7, Rem. 4.

We must add eleven days to the amount 371 to make it a New Style date, because it falls after September 2nd, 1752, and before 4th April, 1753, (after which all dates will be in New Style by the Tables). 371 + 11 = 382 = January 17th (Table IX.). 4 = Wednesday.

Answer.—Wednesday, January 17th, A.D. 1753.

EXAMPLE 6. Required the A.D. equivalent of Vikrama samvatsara 1879 Âshâḍha kṛishṇa dvitîyâ (2nd). If this is a southern Vikrama year, as used in Gujarât, Western India, and countries south of the Narmadâ, the year is Kârttikâdi and amânta, *i.e.*, the sequence of fortnights makes the month begin with śukla 1st. The first process is to convert the date by Table II., Part iii., col. 3, Table II., Part ii., and Table I., into a Chaitrâdi year and month. Thus—Âshâḍha is the ninth month of the year and corresponds to Âshâḍha of the following Chaitrâdi Kali year, so that the given month Âshâḍha of Vikrama 1879 corresponds to Âshâḍha of Kali 4924. Work as before, using Table I. for Kali 4924. Initial date, 24th March (83), (1) Sunday.

	d.	*w.*
Initial date	83	1
Collective duration (Table III., col. 3*a*)	89	89
Given date (2 + 15)—1	16	16
	188	106 ÷ 7 Rem. 1

188 (Table IX.) = July 7th. 1 = Sunday.

Answer.—Sunday, July 7th, A.D. 1822.[1]

If the year given be a northern Vikrama year, as used in Mâlwa, Benares, Ujjain, and countries north of the Narmadâ, the Vikrama year is Chaitrâdi and corresponds to the Kali 4923, except that, being pûrṇimânta, the sequence of fortnights differs (see Table II., Part i.). In such a case Âshâḍha kṛishṇa of the Vikrama year corresponds to Jyeshṭha kṛishṇa in amânta months, and we must work for Kali 4923 Jyeshṭha kṛishṇa 2nd. By Table I. the initial date is April 3rd (93), (3) Tuesday. The A.D. year is 1821—22.

1 This is actually wrong by one day, owing to the approximate collective duration of days (Table III., 3*a*) being taken as 89. It might equally well be taken as 88. If it is desired to convert tithis into days (p. 75, note 2) a 64th part should be subtracted. The collective duration of the last day of Jyeshtha in tithis is 90. 90 ÷ 64 = 1.40. 90 — 1.40 = 88.60. If taken as 88 the answer would be Saturday, July 6th, which is actually correct. This serves to shew how errors may arise in days when calculation is only made approximately.

	d.	*w.*
	93	3
Collective duration (Table III., col. 3*a*)	59	59
Given date (2 + 15)—1	16	16
	168	78÷7, Rem. 1.

168 = June 17th. 1 = Sunday.

Answer.—Sunday, June 17th, A.D. 1821.

(*b*) *Solar Dates.*

EXAMPLE 7. Required the date A.D. corresponding to the Tamil (solar) 18th Puraṭṭâśi of Rudhirodgârin = K.Y. 4904 expired, or 4905 current.

Table I., cols. 13 and 14, give (*d*) = April 11th (101), (*w*) = (2) Monday, and the year A.D. 1803.

	d.	*w.*
Initial date	101	2
Collective duration (Table III., col. 10)	156	156
Given date (18)—1	17	17
	274	175÷7, Rem. 0.

274 (Table IX.) gives October 1st. 0 = Saturday.

Answer.—Saturday, October 1st, A.D. 1803.

EXAMPLE 8. Required the equivalent A.D. of the Tinnevelly Âṇḍu 1024, 20th Âvaṇi.

The reckoning is the same as the Tamil as regards months, but the year begins with Âvaṇi. Âṇḍu 1024 = K.Y. 4950. It is a solar year beginning (see Table I.) 11th April (102), (3) Tuesday, A.D. 1848 (a leap-year).

	d.	*w.*
Initial date	102	3
Tables II., Part ii., cols. 10 & 7, and III., col. 10.	125	125
Given date (20)—1	19	19
	246	
	—1 (Rule VI.)	
	245	147 ÷ 7, Rem. 0.

0 = Saturday; 245 = (Table IX.) September 2nd.

Answer.—Saturday, September 2nd, A.D. 1848.

EXAMPLE 9. Required the equivalent date A.D. of the South Malayâḷam Âṇḍu 1024, 20th Chiṅgam. The corresponding Tamil month and date (Table II., Part ii., cols. 9 and 11) is 20th Âvaṇi K.Y. 4950, and the answer is the same as in the last example.

EXAMPLE 10. Required the equivalent date A.D. of the North Malayâḷam (Kollam) Âṇḍu 1023, 20th Chiṅgam. This (Chiṅgam) is the 12th month of the Kollam Âṇḍu year which begins with Kanni. It corresponds with the Tamil 20th Âvaṇi K.Y. 4950 (Table II., Part ii., cols. 9, 12, and Table II., Part iii.), and the answer is similar to that in the two previous examples.

[The difference in the years will of course be noted. The same Tamil date corresponds to South Malayâḷam Âṇḍu 1024, 20th Chiṅgam, and to the same day of the month in the North Malayâḷam (Kollam) Âṇḍu 1023, the reason being that in the former reckoning the year begins with Chiṅgam, and in the latter with Kanni.]

EXAMPLE 11. Required the A.D. equivalent of the Tamil date, 20th Paṅguni of Rudhirodgârin, K.Y. 4905 current (or 4904 expired.)

Table I. gives (*d*) 11th April (101), 1803 A. D. as the initial date of the solar year, and its week-day (*w*) is (2) Monday.

	d.	*w.*
Initial date	101	2
Collective duration (Table III., col. 10)	335	335
Given date, (20)—1	19	19
	455	
	—1 (Rule VI.)	
	454	356 ÷ 7, Rem. 6.

6 = Friday; 454 (Table IX.) = March 30th in the following A.D. year, 1804.

Answer.—Friday, March 30th, 1804. (See example 1, above.)

138. (B.) *Conversion of dates A.D. into Hindu dates.* (See Art. 135 above, par. 1.)

Rule I. Given a year, month, and date A.D. Write down in a horizontal line (*d*) the date-indicator of the initial date [in brackets (Table I., cols. 13 or 19, as the case may be)] of the corresponding Hindu year required, and (*w*) the week-day number of that initial date (col. 14 or 20), remembering that, if the given date A.D. is earlier than such initial date, the (*d*) and (*w*) of the previous Hindu year must be taken. Subtract the date-indicator from the date number of the given A.D. date in Table IX., remembering that, if the previous Hindu year has been taken down, the number to be taken from Table IX. is that on the right-hand side of the Table and not that on the left. From the result subtract (Table III., col. 3*a* or 10) the collective-duration-figure which is nearest to, but lower than, that amount, and add 1 to the total so obtained; and to the (*w*) add the figure resulting from the second process under (*d*), and divide by 7. The result gives the required week-day. The resulting (*d*) gives the day of the Hindu month following that whose collective duration was subtracted.

Rule II. Observe (Table I., cols. 8 or 8a) if there has been an addition or suppression of a month prior to the month found by Rule I. and proceed accordingly.

An easy rule for dealing with the added and suppressed month is the following. When the intercalated month (Table I., col. 8 or 8a) precedes the month immediately preceding the one found, such immediately preceding month is the required month; when the intercalated month immediately precedes the one found, such immediately preceding month with the prefix "nija," natural, is the required month; when the intercalated month is the same as that found, such month with the prefix "adhika" is the required month. When a suppressed month precedes the month found, the required month is the same as that found, because there is never a suppression of a month without the intercalation of a previous month, which nullifies the suppression so far as regards the collective duration of preceding days. But if the given month falls after two intercalations and one suppression, act as above for one intercalation only.

Rule III. See Art. 137 (A) Rule V. (p. 70), but subtract the eleven days instead of adding.

Rule IV. If the given A.D. date falls in a leap-year after 29th February, or if its date-number (right-hand side of Table IX.) is more than 365, and the year next preceding it was a leap-year, add 1 to the date-number of the given European date found by Table IX., before subtracting the figure of the date-indicator

Rule V. Where the required date is a Hindu luni-solar date the second total, if less than 15, indicates a śukla date. If more than 15, deduct 15, and the remainder will be a kṛishṇa date. Kṛishṇa 15 is generally termed kṛishṇa 30; and often śukla 15 is called "pûrṇimâ" (full-moon day), and kṛishṇa 15 (or "30") is called amâvâsyâ (new-moon day).

(*a*) *Luni-Solar Dates.*

EXAMPLE 12. Required the Telugu or Tuḷu equivalent of December 1st, 1822. The luni-solar year began 24th March (83) on (1) Sunday (Table I., cols. 19 and 20.)

	d.	*w.*
(*d*) and (*w*) of initial date (Table I.)	83	1
(Table IX.) 1st December (335)	(335— 83 =)252	252
(Table III.) Collective duration to end of Kârttika	—236	
Add 1 to remainder	16 + 1 = 17	253 ÷ 7, Rem. 1.

17 indicates a kṛishṇa date. Deduct 15. Remainder 2. The right-hand remainder shews (1) Sunday.

The result so far is Sunday Mârgaśîrsha kṛishṇa 2nd. But see Table I., col. 8. Previous to this month Âśvina was intercalated. (The suppression of Pausha need not be considered because that month comes after Mârgaśîrsha.) Therefore the required month is not Mârgaśîrsha, but Kârttika; and the answer is Sunday Kârttika kṛishṇa 2nd (Telugu), or Jarde (Tuḷu), of the year Chitrabhânu, K.Y. 4923 expired, Śaka 1744 expired. (See the example on p. 69.)

(Note.) As in example 6 above, this date is actually wrong by one day, because it happened that in Kârttika śukla there was a tithi, the 12th, suppressed, and consequently the real day corresponding to the civil day was Sunday Kârttika kṛishṇa 3rd. These differences cannot possibly be avoided in methods A and B, nor by any method unless the duration of every tithi of every year be separately calculated. (See example xvii., p. 92.)

EXAMPLE 13. Required the Chaitrâdi Northern Vikrama date corresponding to April 9th 1822. By Table I. A.D. 1822—23 = Chaitrâdi Vikrama 1880 current. The reckoning is luni-solar. Initial day (*d*) March 24th (83), (*w*) 1 Sunday

	d.	*w.*
From Table I.	83	1
(Table IX.) April 9th (99)	99—83 = 16	16
Add	1	
	17	
For śukla dates	—15	
	2	17 ÷ 7, Rem. 3.

This is Tuesday, amanta Chaitra kṛishṇa 2nd.[1] But it should be converted into Vaiśâkha kṛishṇa 2nd, because of the custom of beginning the month with the full-moon (Table II., Part i.).

[1] The actual date was Tuesday, amânta Chaitra kṛishṇa 3rd, the difference being caused by a tithi having been expunged in the śukla fortnight of the same month *(see note to examples 6 and 12 above)*.

Since the Chaitrâdi Vikrama year begins with Chaitra, the required Vikrama year is 1880 current, 1879 expired. But if the required date were in the Southern reckoning, the year would be 1878 expired, since 1879 in that reckoning does not begin till Kârttika.

(*b*) *Solar Dates.*

EXAMPLE 14. 1. Required the Tamil equivalent of May 30th, 1803 A.D.

Table I. gives the initial date April 11th (101), and week-day number 2 Monday.

	d.	*w.*
From Table I.	101	2
(Table IX.) May 30th (150) . . . . 150—101 =	49	49
(Table III.) Collective duration to end of Śittirai (Mesha) .	—31	
	18	
Add 1	+ 1	
	19	51 ÷ 7, Rem. 2.

The day is the 19th; the month is Vaiyâśi, the month following Śittirai; the week-day is (2) Monday.

Answer.—Monday, 19th Vaiyâśi of the year Rudhirodgârin, K.Y. 4904 expired, Śaka 1725 expired.

EXAMPLE 15. Required the Tamil equivalent of March 30th, 1804. The given date precedes the initial date in 1804 A.D. (Table I., col. 13) April 10th, so the preceding Hindu year must be taken. Its initial day is 11th April (101), and the initial week-day is (2) Monday. 1804 was a leap-year.

	d.	*w.*
From Table I.	101	2
(Table IX.) (March 30th) 454 + 1 for leap-year, 455—101 =	354	354
(Table III., col. 10) Collective duration to end of Mâśi = Kumbha (Table II., Part ii.)	—335	
	19	
Add 1	+ 1	
	20	356 ÷ 7, Rem. 6.

Answer.—Friday 20th Paṅguṇi of the year Rudhirodgârin K.Y. 4904 expired, Śaka 1725 expired. (See the example on p. 67.)

EXAMPLE 16. Required the North Malayaḷam Âṇḍu equivalent of September 2nd, 1848. Work as by the Chaitrâdi year. The year is solar. 1848 is a leap-year.

	d.	*w.*
From Table I.	102	3
(Table IX.) September 2nd (245) + 1 for leap year . . . . 246 — 102 =	144	144
Coll. duration to end of Karka	—125	
	19	
Add 1	+ 1	
	20	147 ÷ 7, Rem. 0

Answer.—Saturday 20th Chiṅgam. This is the 12th month of the North Malayâḷam Âṇḍu which begins with Kanni. The year therefore is 1023.

If the date required had been in South Malayâḷam reckoning, the date would be the same, 20th Chiṅgam, but as the South Malayâlis begin the year with Chiṅgam as the first month, the required South Malayâḷam year would be Âṇḍu 1024.

Method C.

EXACT CALCULATION OF DATES.

(A.) *Conversion of Hindu luni-solar dates into dates A.D.*

139. *To calculate the week-day, the equivalent date A.D., and the moment of beginning or ending of a tithi.* Given a Hindu year, month, and tithi.—Turn the given year into a Chaitrâdi Kali, Śaka, or Vikrama year, and the given month into an amânta month (if they are not already so) and find the corresponding year A.D., by the aid of columns 1 to 5 [1] of Table I., and Table II., Parts i., ii., iii. Referring to Table I., carry the eye along the line of the Chaitrâdi year so found, and write down [2] in a horizontal line the following five quantities corresponding to the day of commencement (Chaitra śukla pratipadâ) of that Chaitrâdi-year, viz., (*d*) the date-indicator given in brackets after the day and month A.D. (Table I., col. 19), (*w*) the week-day number (col. 20), and (*a*), (*b*), (*c*) (cols. 23, 24, 25). Find the number of tithis which have intervened between the initial day of the year (Chaitra śukla pratipadâ), and the given tithi, by adding together the number of tithis (collective duration) up to the end of the month previous to the given one (col. 3, Table III.), and the number of elapsed tithis of the given month (that is the serial number of the given tithi reduced by one), taking into account the extra 15 days of the śukla paksha if the tithi belongs to the kṛishṇa paksha, and also the intervening intercalary month,[3] if any, given in col. 8 (or 8*a*) of Table I. This would give the result in tithis. But days, not tithis, are required. To reduce the tithis to days, reduce the sum of the tithis by its 60th part,[4] taking fractions larger than a half as one, and neglecting half or less. The result is the (*d*), the approximate number of days which have intervened since the initial day of the Hindu year. Write this number under head (*d*), and write under their respective heads, the (*w*), (*a*), (*b*), (*c*) for that number of days from Table IV. Add together the two lines of five quantities, but in the case of (*w*) divide the result by 7 and write only the remainder, in the case of (*a*) write only the remainder under 10000, and in the case of (*b*) and (*c*) only the remainder under 1000.[5] Find separately the equations to arguments (*b*) and (*c*) in Tables VI. and VII. respectively, and add them to the total under (*a*). The sum (*t*) is the tithi-index, which, by cols. 2 and 3 of Table VIII., will indicate the tithi current at mean sunrise on the week-day found under (*w*). If the number of the tithi so indicated is not the same as that of the given one, but is greater or less by one (or by two in rare cases), subtract one (or two) from, or add

[1] The initial days in cols 13 and 19, Table I., belong to the first of the double years A.D. given in col. 5.

[2] It will be well for a beginner to take an example at once, and work it out according to the rule. After a little practice the calculations can be made rapidly.

[3] When the intercalary month is Chaitra, count that also. See Art. 99 above.

[4] This number is taken for easy calculation. Properly speaking, to convert tithis into days the 64th part should be subtracted. The difference does not introduce any material error.

[5] Generally with regard to (*w*), (*a*), (*b*), (*c*) in working addition sums, take only the remainder respectively over 7, 10000, 1000 and 1000; and in subtracting, if the sum to be subtracted be greater, add respectively 7, 10000, 1000 and 1000 to the figure above.

one (or two) to, both (*d*) and (*w*);[1] subtract from, or add to, the (*a*) (*b*) (*c*) already found, their value for one (or two) days (Table IV.); add to (*a*) the equations for (*b*) and (*c*) (Tables VI. and VII.) and the sum (*t*) will then indicate the tithi. If this is the same as given (if not, proceed again as before till it corresponds), the (*w*) is its week-day, and the date shewn in the top line and side columns of Table IX. corresponding with the ascertained (*d*) is its equivalent date A.D. The year A.D. is found on the line of the given Chaitrâdi year in col. 5, Table I. Double figures are given in that column; if (*d*) is not greater than 365 in a common year, or 366 in a leap-year, the first, otherwise the second, of the double figures shows the proper A.D. year.

140. For all practical purposes and for some ordinary religious purposes a tithi is connected with that week-day at whose sunrise it is current. For some religious purposes, however, and sometimes even for practical purposes also, a tithi which is current at any particular moment of a week-day is connected with that week-day. (*See Art. 31 above.*)

141. In the case of an expunged tithi, the day on which it begins and ends is its week-day and equivalent. In the case of a repeated tithi, both the civil days at whose sunrise it is current,[2] are its week-days and equivalents.

142. *A clue for finding when a tithi is probably repeated or expunged.* When the tithi-index corresponding to a sunrise is greater or less, within 40, than the ending index of a tithi, and when the equation for (*b*) (Table VI.) is decreasing, a repetition of the same or another tithi takes place shortly after or before that sunrise; and when the equation for (*b*) is increasing an expunction of a tithi (different from the one in question) takes place shortly before or after it.

143. The identification of the date A.D. with the week-day arrived at by the above method, may be verified by Table XIII. The verification, however, is not in itself proof of the correctness of our results.

144. *To find the moment of the ending of a tithi.* Find the difference between the (*t*) on the given day at sunrise and the (*t*) of the tithi-index which shews the ending point of that tithi (Table VIII.). With this difference as argument find the corresponding time either in ghaṭikâs and palas, or hours and minutes, according to choice, from Table X. The given tithi ends after the given sunrise by the interval of time so found. But this interval is not always absolutely accurate. (*See Art. 82*). If accuracy is desired add the (*a*) (*b*) (*c*) for this interval of time (Table V.) to the (*a*) (*b*) (*c*) already obtained for sunrise. Add as before to (*a*) the equations of (*b*) and (*c*) from Tables VI. and VII., and find the difference between the (*t*) thus arrived at and the (*t*) of the ending point of the tithi (Table VIII.). The time corresponding to that difference, found from Table X., will show the ending of the tithi before or after the first found time. If still greater accuracy is desired, proceed until (*t*) amounts exactly to the (*t*) of the ending point (Table VIII.) For ordinary purposes, however, the first found time, or at least that arrived at after one more process, is sufficiently accurate.

145. The moment of the beginning of a tithi is the same as the moment of ending of the tithi next preceding it; and this can be found either by calculating backwards from the (*t*) of the same tithi, or independently from the (*t*) of the preceding tithi.

146. The moment of beginning or ending of tithis thus found is in mean time, and is applicable to all places on the meridian of Ujjain, which is the same as that of Laṅkâ. If the

1 Thus far the process will give the correct result if there be no probability by the rule given below of the expunction (*kshaya*) or repetition (*vṛiddhi*) of a tithi shortly preceding or following; and the (*d*) and (*w*) arrived at at this stage will indicate by use of Table IX. the A.D. equivalent, and the week-day of the given tithi.

2 For the definitions of expunged and repeated tithis see Art. 32 above.

exact mean time for other places is required, apply the correction given in Table XI., according to the rule given under that Table. If after this correction the ending time of a tithi is found to fall on the previous or following day the (*d*) and (*w*) should be altered accordingly.

Mean time is used throughout the parts of the Tables used for these rules, and it may sometimes differ from the true, used, at least in theory, in Hindu pañchâṅgs or almanacks.

The ending time of a tithi arrived at by these Tables may also somewhat differ from the ending time as arrived at from authorities other than the *Sûrya Siddhânta* which is used by us. The results, however, arrived at by the present Tables, may be safely relied on for all ordinary purposes.[1]

147. *N.B. i.* Up to 1100 A.D. both mean and true intercalary months are given in Table I. (*see Art.* 47 *above*). When it is not certain whether the given year is an expired or current year, whether it is a Chaitrâdi year or one of another kind, whether the given month is amânta or pûrṇimânta, and whether the intercalary month, if any, was taken true or mean, the only course is to try all possible years and months.

N.B. ii. The results are all Old Style dates up to, and New Style dates from, 1753 A.D The New Style was introduced with effect from after 2nd September, 1752. Since only the initial dates of 1752 and 1753 are given, remember to apply the correction (+ 11 days) to any date between 2nd September, 1752, and 9th April, 1753, in calculating by the Hindu solar year, and between 2nd September, 1752, and 4th April, 1753, in calculating by the Hindu luni-solar year, so as to bring out the result in New Style dates A.D. The day of the week requires no alteration.

N.B. iii. If the date A.D. found above falls after February 28th in a leap-year, it must be reduced by 1.

N.B. iv. The Hindus generally use expired (*gata*) years, while *current* years are given throughout the Tables. For example, for Śaka year 1702 "expired" 1703 current is given.

148. EXAMPLE I. Required the week-day and the A.D. year, month, and day corresponding to Jyeshṭha śukla pañchamî (5th), year Śârvari, Śaka year 1702 expired (1703 current), and the ending and beginning time of that tithi.

The given year is Chaitrâdi (see N.B. ii., Table II., Part iii.). It does not matter whether the month is amânta or pûrṇimânta, because the fortnight belongs to Jyeshṭha by both systems (see Table II., Part i.). Looking to Table I. along the given current Śaka year 1703, we find that its initial day falls in A.D. 1780 (see note 1 to Art. 139), a leap-year, on the 5th April, Wednesday; and that *d* (col. 19). *w* (col. 20), *a* (col. 23), *b* (col. 24) and *c* (col. 25) are 96, 4, 1, 657 and 267 respectively. We write them in a horizontal line (see the working of the example below). From Table I., col. 8, we find that there is no added month in the year. The number therefore of tithis between Chaitra ś. 1 and Jyeshṭha ś. 5 was 64, viz., 60 up to the end of Vaiśâkha (see Table III., col. 3), the month preceding the given one, and 4 in Jyeshṭha. The sixtieth part of 64 (neglecting the fraction $\frac{4}{60}$ because it is not more than half) is 1. Reduce 64 by one and we have 63 as the approximate number of days between Chaitra ś. 1 and Jyeshṭha ś. 5. We write this number under (*d*). Turning to Table IV. with the argument 63 we find under (*w*) (*a*) (*b*) (*c*) the numbers 0, 1334, 286, 172, respectively, and we write them under their respective heads, and add together the two quantities under each head. With the argument (*b*) (943) we turn to Table VI. for the equation. We do not find exactly the number 943 given, but we have 940 and 950 and must see the difference between the corresponding equation-figures and fix the appropriate figure for 943. The auxiliary table given will fix this, but in practice it can be easily calculated in the head. (The

[1] See Arts. 36 and 37 in which all the points noted in this article are fully treated of.

full numbers are not given so as to avoid cumbrousness in the tables.) Thus the equation for (*b*) (943) is found to be 90, and from Table VII. the equation for (*c*) is found to be 38. Adding 90 and 38 to (*a*) (1335) we get 1463, which is the required tithi-index (*t*). Turning with this to Table VIII., col. 3, we find by col. 2 that the tithi current was śukla 5, *i.e.*, the given date. Then (*w*) 4, Wednesday, was its week-day; and the tithi was current at mean sunrise on the meridian of Ujjain on that week-day. Turning with (*d*) 159 to Table IX., we find that the equivalent date A.D. was 8th June; but as this was after 28th February in a leap-year, we fix 7th June, A.D. 1780, (see N.B. iii., Art. 147) as the equivalent of the given tithi. As (*t*) is not within 40 of 1667, the (*t*) of the 5th tithi (Table VIII.), there is no probability of an expunction or repetition shortly preceding or following (Art. 142). The answer therefore is Wednesday, June 7th, A.D. 1780.

To find the ending time of the tithi. (*t*) at sunrise is 1463; and Table VIII., col. 3, shews that the tithi will end when (*t*) amounts to 1667. (1667—1463 =) 204 = (Table X.) 14 hours, 27 minutes, and this process shews us that the tithi will end 14 hours, 27 minutes, after sunrise on Wednesday, June 7th. This time is, however, approximate. To find the time more accurately we add the increase in (*a*) (*b*) (*c*) for 14 h. 27 m. (Table V.) to the already calculated (*a*) (*b*) (*c*) at sunrise; and adding to (*a*) as before the equations of (*b*) and (*c*) (Tables VI. and VII.) we find that the resulting (*t*) amounts to 1686. 1686—1667 = 19 = 1 hour and 21 minutes (Table X.). But this is a period beyond the end of the tithi, and the amount must be deducted from the 14 h. 27 m. first found to get the true end. The true end then is 13 h. 6 m. after sunrise on June 7th. This time is accurate for ordinary purposes, but for still further accuracy we proceed again as before. We may either add the increase in (*a*) (*b*) (*c*) for 13 h. 6 m. to the value of (*a*) (*b*) (*c*) at sunrise, or subtract the increase of (*a*) (*b*) (*c*) for 1 h. 21 m. from their value at 14 h. 27 m. By either process we obtain (*t*) = 1665. Proceed again. 1667—1665 = 2 = (Table X.) 9 minutes after 13 h. 6 m. or 13 h. 15 m. Work through again for 13 h. 15 m. and we obtain (*t*) = 1668. Proceed again. 1668—1667 = 1 = (Table X.) 4 minutes before 13 h. 15 m. or 13 h. 11 m. Work for 13 h. 11 m., and we at last have 1667, the known ending point. It is thus proved that 13 h. 11 m. after sunrise is the absolutely accurate mean ending time of the tithi in question by the *Sûrya-Siddhânta.*

To find the beginning time of the given tithi. We may find this independently by calculating as before the (*t*) at sunrise for the preceding tithi, (in this case śukla 4th) and thence finding its ending time. But in the example given we calculate it from the (*t*) of the given tithi. The tithi begins when (*t*) amounts to 1333 (Table VIII.). or (1463—1333) 130 before sunrise on June 7th. 130 is (Table X.) 9 h. 13 m. Proceed as before, but deduct the (*a*) (*b*) (*c*) instead of adding, and (see working below) we eventually find that (*t*) amounts exactly to 1333 and therefore the tithi begins at 8 h. 26 m. before sunrise on June 7th, that is 15 h. 34 m. after sunrise on Tuesday the 6th. The beginning and ending times are by Ujjain or Laṅkâ mean time. If we want the time, for instance, for Benares the difference in longitude in time, 29 minutes, should be added to the above result (See Table XI.). This, however, does not affect the day.

It is often very necessary to know the moments of beginning and ending of a tithi. Thus our result brings out Wednesday, June 7th, but since the 5th tithi began 15 h. 34 m. after sunrise on Tuesday, *i.e.*, about 9 h. 34 m. p.m., it might well happen that an inscription might record a ceremony that took place at 10 p.m., and therefore fix the day as Tuesday the 5th tithi, which, unless the facts were known, would appear incorrect.

From Table XII. we find that 7th June, A.D. 1780, was a Wednesday, and this helps to fix that day as current.

We now give the working of EXAMPLE I.

WORKING OF EXAMPLE I.

	d.	w.	a.	b.	c.
(*a*) *The day corresponding to Jyeshṭha śukla 5th.*					
Śaka 1703 current, Chaitra śukla 1st, (Table I., cols. 19, 20, 23, 24, 25)	96	4	1	657	267
Approximate number of days from Chaitra śukla 1st to Jyeshṭha śuk. 5th, (64 tithis reduced by a 60th part, neglecting fractions, = 63) with its (*w*) (*a*) (*b*) (*c*) (Table IV.)	63	0	1334	286	172
	159	4	1335	943	439
Equation for (*b*) (943) (Table VI.)			90		
Do. (*c*) (439) (Table VII.)			38		
			1463 = *t*.		

(*t*) gives śukla 5th (Table VIII., cols. 2, 3) (the same as the given tithi).
(*d*)—1, (*N. B. iii.*, Art. 147), or the number of days elapsed from January 1st, = ... 158

158 = June 7th (Table IX.). A.D. 1780 is the corresponding year, and 4 (*w*) Wednesday is the week-day of the given tithi.

Answer.—Wednesday, June 7th, 1780 A.D.

(*b*) *The ending of the tithi Jyeshṭha śuk.* 5. (Table VIII.) 1667—1463 = 204 = (14 h. 10 m. + 0 h. 17 m.) = 14 h. 27 m. (Table X.). Therefore the tithi ends at 14 h. 27 m. after mean sunrise on Wednesday. For more accurate time we proceed as follows:

	a.	b.	c.
At sunrise on Wednesday (*see above*)	1335	943	439
For 14 hours (Table V.)	198	21	2
For 27 minutes, (Do.)	6	1	0
	1539	965	441
Equation for (*b*) (965) (Table VI.)	109		
Do. (*c*) (441) (Do. VII.)	38		
	1686 = *t*.		

1686—1667 (Table VIII.) = 19 = 1 h. 21 m.; and 1 h. 21 m. deducted from 14 h. 27 m. gives 13 h. 6 m. after sunrise on Wednesday as the moment when the tithi ended. This is sufficient for all practical purposes. For absolute accuracy we proceed again.

	a.	b.	c.
For sunrise (*as before*)	1335	943	439
For 13 hours (Table V.)	183	20	1
For 6 minutes (Do.)	1	0	0
	1519	963	440
Equation for (*b*) (963) (Table VI.)	108		
Do. (*c*) (440) (Do. VII.)	38		
	1665 = *t*.		

1667—1665 = 2 = 9 m. after 13 h. 6 m. = 13 h. 15 h.

	a.	b.	c.
Again for sunrise (*as before*)	1335	943	439
For 13 hours (Table V.)	183	20	1
For 15 minutes (Do.)	4	0	0
	1522	963	440
Equation for (*b*) (963)	108		
Do. (*c*) (440)	38		
	1668 = *t*.		

1668—1667 = 1 = 4 m. before 13 h. 15 m. = 13 h. 11 m.

	a.	b.	c.
Again for sunrise (*as before*)	1335	943	439
For 13 hours (Table V.)	183	20	1
For 11 minutes (Do.)	3	0	0
	1521	963	440
Equation for (*b*) (963)	108		
Do. (*c*) (440)	38		
Actual end of the tithi	1667 = *t*.		

Thus 13 h. 11 m. after sunrise is the absolutely accurate ending time of the tithi.

(*c*) *The beginning of the tithi, Jyeshṭha śuk. 5.* Now for the beginning. 1463 (the original *t.* as found)—1333 (beginning of the tithi, (Table VIII.) = 130 = (Table X.) (7 h. 5 m. + 2 h. 8 m.) = 9 h. 13 m.; and we have this as the point of time before sunrise on Wednesday when the tithi begins.

	a.	b.	c.	a.	b.	c.
For sunrise (*as before*)				1335	943	439
For 9 h. (Table V.)	127	14	1			
For 13 m. (Do.)	3	0	0			
Deduct	130	14	1	130	14	1
				1205	929	438
Equation for *b*. (929)				79		
Do. *c*. (438)				37		
				1321 = *t*.		

(The beginning of the tithi) 1333—1321 = 12 = Table X.) 51 m. after the above time (9 h 13 m.), and this gives 8 h. 22 m. before sunrise. We proceed again.

	a.	b.	c.
For 9 h. 13 m. before sunrise (*found above*)	1205	929	438
Plus for 51 minutes (Table V.)	12	1	0
	1217	930	438
Equation for *b*. (930)	80		
Do. *c*. (438)	37		
	1334 = *t*.		

1334—1333 = 1 = 4 m. before the above time (viz., 8 h. 22 m.) *i.e.*, 8 h. 26 m. before sunrise. Proceed again.

	a.	*b.*	*c.*
For 8 h. 22 m. before sunrise (*found above*)	1217	930	438
Deduct for 4 m. (Table V.)	1	0	0
	1216	930	438
Equation for *b*. (930)	80		
Do. *c*. (438)	37		
	1333 = *t*.		

The result is precisely the same as the beginning point of the tithi (Table VIII.), and we know that the tithi actually began 8 hours 26 minutes before sunrise on Wednesday, or at 15 h. 34 m. after sunrise on Tuesday, 6th June.

EXAMPLE II. Required the week-day and equivalent A.D. of Jyeshṭha śuk. dasamî (10th) of the southern Vikrama year 1836 expired, 1837 current. The given year is *not* Chaitrâdi. Referring to Table II., Parts ii., and iii., we find, by comparing the non-Chaitrâdi Vikrama year with the Śaka, that the corresponding Śaka year is 1703 current, that is the same as in the first example. We know that the months are amânta.

	d.	*w.*	*a.*	*b.*	*c.*
State the figures for the initial day (Table I., cols. 19, 20, 23, 24, 25)	96	4	1	657	267
The number of intervened tithis down to end of Vaiśâkha, 60, (Table III.) + the number of the given date minus 1, is 69; reduced by a 60th part = 68, and by Table IV. we have	68	5	3027	468	186
	164	2	3028	125	453
Equation for (*b*) 125 (Table VI.)			239		
Do. (*c*) 453 (Table VII.)			42		
			3309 = *t*.		

(*d*) (164)—1 (*N. B. iii.*, Art. 147) = 163.

The result, 3309, fixes the day as śukla 10th (Table VIII., cols. 2, 3), the same as given.

Answer.—(By Table IX.) 163 = June 12th, 2 = Monday. The year is A.D. 1780 (Table II., Part ii.). The tithi will end at (3333—3309 = 24, or by Table X.) 1 h. 42 m. after sunrise, since 3309 represents the state of that tithi at sunrise, and it then had 24 lunation-parts to run. Note that this (*t*) (3309) is less by 24 than 3333, the ending point of the 10th tithi; that 24 is less than 40; and that the equation for (*b*) is increasing. This shows that an expunction of a tithi will shortly occur (*Art. 142.*)

EXAMPLE III. Required the week-day and equivalent A.D. of Jyeshṭha śukla ekâdaśî (11th) of the same Śaka year as in example 2, *i.e.*, Ś. 1703 current.

	d.	w.	a.	b.	c.
See (Table I.) example 2	96	4	1	657	267
Intervened days (to end of Vaiśâkha 59, + 11 given days—1) = 69.					
By Table IV.	69	6	3366	504	189
	165	3	3367	161	456
Equation for (*b*) (161) (Table VI.)			258		
Do. (*c*) (456) (Table VII.)			43		
			3668 = *t*.		

This figure (*t* = 3668) by Table VIII., cols. 2, 3, indicates śukla 12th.

d—1 (*N.B. iii.*, Art. 147) = 164 and Table IX. gives this as June 13th. The (*w*) is 3 = Tuesday. The year (Table II. Part iii.) is 1780 A.D.

The figure of (*t*), 3668, shows that the 12th tithi and not the required tithi (11th) was current at sunrise on Tuesday; but we found in example 2 that the 10th tithi was current at sunrise on Monday, June 12th, and we therefore learn that the 11th tithi was expunged. It commenced 1 h. 42 min. after sunrise on Monday and ended 4 minutes before sunrise on Tuesday, 13th June.[1] The corresponding day answering to śukla 10th is therefore Monday, June 12th, and that answering to śukla 12 is Tuesday the 13th June.

EXAMPLE IV. Required the week-day and equivalent A.D. of the pûrṇimânta Âshâḍha kṛishṇa dvitîyâ (2) of the Northern Vikrama year 1837 expired, 1838 current. The northern Vikrama is a Chaitrâdi year, and so the year is the same as in the previous example, viz., A.D. 1780–1 (Table II., Part iii.). The corresponding amânta month is Jyeshṭha (Table II., Part i.). Work therefore for Jyeshṭha kṛishṇa 2nd in A.D. 1780–1 (Table I.).

	d.	w.	a.	b.	c.
See example 1 (Table I.)	96	4	1	657	267
60 (coll. dur. to end Vaiś.) + 15 (for kṛishṇa fortnight) + 1 (given date minus 1) = 76 tithis = 75 days (as before); Table IV. gives .	75	5	5397	722	205
	171	2	5398	379	472
Equation for (*b*) (379)			237		
Do. (*c*) (472)			50		
			5685 = *t*.		

(*d*)—1 (*N.B. iii.*, Art. 147) = 170 = (Table IX.) 19th June. (2) = Monday. The year is 1780 A.D.

So far we have Monday, 19th June, A.D. 1780. But the figure 5685 for (*t*) shows that kṛi. 3rd and not the 2nd was current at sunrise on Monday the 19th June. It commenced (5685—5667 = 18 =) 1 h. 17 m. before sunrise on Monday. (*t*) being greater, but within 40, than the ending point of kṛi. 2nd, and the equation for (*b*) decreasing, it appears that a repetition of a tithi will shortly follow (but not precede). And thus we know that Sunday the 18th June is the equivalent of kṛi. 2nd.

EXAMPLE V. Required the week-day and equivalent A.D. of the amânta Jyeshṭha kṛi. 3rd of the Śaka year 1703 current, the same as in the last 4 examples.

[1] This is shewn by (*t*) = 3668 at sunrise, the end being indicated by 3667. Difference 1 lunation-unit, or 4 minutes.

	d.	w.	a.	b.	c.
(See example 1)	96	4	1	657	267
60 (coll. dur. to end Vaiś.) + 15 + 2 = 77 tithis = 76 days. (Table IV.)	76	6	5736	758	208
	172	3	5737	415	475
Equation for (*b*) (415)			211		
Do. (*c*) (475)			51		
			5999		

This indicates kṛishṇa 3rd, the same tithi as given. (*d*)—1 = 171 = 20th June, 1780 A.D.

From these last two examples we learn that kṛishṇa 3rd stands at sunrise on Tuesday 20th as well as Monday 19th. It is therefore a repeated or *vṛiddhi* tithi, and both days 19th and 20th correspond to it. It ends on Tuesday (6000—5999 = 1 =) 4 minutes after sunrise.

EXAMPLE VI. Required the week-day and A.D. equivalent of Kârttika śukla 5th of the Northern Vikrama year 1833 expired (1834 current). (See example 2, page 70.)

The given year is Chaitrâdi. It matters not whether the month is amânta or pûrṇimânta because the given tithi is in the śukla fortnight. The initial day of the given year falls on (Table I., col. 19) 20th March (80), (col. 20) 4 Wednesday; and looking in Table I. along the line of the given year, we find in col. 8 that the month Bhâdrapada was intercalated or added *(adhika)* in it. So the number of months which intervened between the beginning of the year and the given tithi was 8, one more than in ordinary year.

	d.	w.	a.	b.	c.
(Table I., cols. 19, 20, 23, 24, 25)	80	4	9841	54	223
(Coll. dur.) 240 + 4 = 244 = 240 days (Table IV.,)	240	2	1272	710	657
	320	6	1113	764	880
Equation for (*b*) (764)			0		
Do. (*c*) (880)			102		
			1215 = *t*.		

This indicates, not kṛi. 5 as given, but kṛi. 4 (Table VIII.)

Adding 1 to (*d*) and (*w*) (see Rule above, Art. 139) 321 0

a—1 (*N.B. iii.*, Art. 147) 320 = (Table IX.) Nov. 16th, A.D. 1776. 0 = Saturday.

(*t*) being not within 40 of the ending point of the tithi there is no probability of a repetition or expunction shortly preceding or following, and therefore Saturday the 16th November, 1776 A.D., is the equivalent of the given tithi.

EXAMPLE VII. Required the week-day and A.D. equivalent of amânta Mâgha kṛishṇa 1st of Kali 4923 expired, 4924 current. (See example 4, page 71.)

The given year is Chaitrâdi. Looking in Table I. along the line of the given year, we see that its initial day falls on 24th March (83), 1822 A.D., 1 Sunday, and that (col. 8) the month (7) Âśvina was intercalated and (10) Pausha expunged. So that, in counting, the number of intervened months is the same, viz., 10, as in an ordinary year, Mâgha coming after Pausha.

	d.	*w.*	*a.*	*b.*	*c.*
(Table I., cols. 19, 20, 23, 24, 23)	83	1	212	899	229
(Coll. dur.) 300 + 15 (śukla paksha) + (1—1=) 0 = 315 tithis = 310 days. By (Table IV.)	310	2	4976	250	849
	393	3	5188	149	78
Equation for (*b*) (149) (Table VI.)			252		
Do. (*c*) (78) (Table VII.)			32		
			5472 = *t*.		

The figure 5472 indicates (Table VIII.) kṛi. 2nd, *i.e.*, not the same as given (1st), but the tithi following. We therefore subtract 1 from (*d*) and (*w*) (Art. 139) making them 392 and 2.

Since (*t*) is not within 40 of the ending point of the tithi, there is no probability of a *kshaya* or *vṛiddhi* shortly following or preceding. (*w*) 2 = Monday. 392 = (Table IX.) 27th January. And therefore 27th January, A.D. 1823, Monday, is the equivalent of the given tithi.

EXAMPLE VIII. Required the week-day and the A.D. equivalent of śukla 13th of the Tuḷu month Puntelu, Kali year 4853 expired, 4854 current, "Aṅgiras samvatsara" in the luni-solar or southern 60-year cycle. (See example 5, page 72.)

The initial day (Table I.) is Old Style 5th March (65), A.D. 1752, a leap-year, (5) Thursday; and Âshâḍha was intercalated. The Tuḷu month Puntelu corresponds to the Sanskṛit Pausha (Table II., Part ii.), ordinarily the 10th, but now the 11th, month on account of the intercalated Âshâḍha.

	d.	*w.*	*a.*	*b.*	*c.*
(Table I., cols. 19, 20, 23, 24, 25)	65	5	39	777	213
(Coll. dur.) 300 + 12 (given tithi minus 1) = 312 tithis = 307 days (Table IV.)	307	6	3960	142	840
	372	4	3999	919	53
Equation for (*b*) (919)			71		
Do. (*c*) (53)			40		
			4110 = *t*.		

The result, 4110, indicates śukla 13th, *i.e.*, the same tithi as that given.
(*d*)—1 (*N.B. iii., Art. 147*) = 371 = (by Table IX.) January 6th, A.D. 1753.

We must add 11 days to this to make it a New Style date, because it falls after September 2nd, 1752, and before 4th April, 1753, the week-day remaining unaltered (*see N.B. ii., Art. 147*), and 17th January, 1753 A.D., is therefore the equivalent of the given date.

(B.) *Conversion of Hindu solar dates into dates A.D.*

149. *To calculate the week-day and the equivalent date A.D.* Turn the given year into a Meshâdi Kali, Śaka, or Vikrama year, and the name of the given month into a sign-name, if they are not already given as such, and find the corresponding year A.D. by the aid of columns 1 to 5, Table I., and Table II., Parts ii., and iii. Looking in Table I. along the line of the Meshâdi year so obtained, write down in a horizontal line the following three quantities corresponding to the

commencement of that (Meshâdi) year, viz., (*d*) the date-indicator given in brackets after the day and month A.D. in col. 13, (*w*) the week-day number (*col. 14*), and the time—either in ghaṭikâs and palas, or in hours and minutes as desired—of the Mesha saṅkrânti according to the *Ârya-Siddhânta* (cols. 15, or 17). For a Bengali date falling between A.D. 1100 and 1900, take the time by the *Sûrya-Siddhânta* from cols. 15*a* or 17*a*. When the result is wanted for a place not on the meridian of Ujjain, apply to the Mesha saṅkrânti time the correction given in Table XI. Under these items write from Table III., cols. 6, 7, 8, or 9 as the case may be, the collective duration of time from the beginning of the year up to the end of the month preceding the given one—days under (*d*), week-day under (*w*), and hours and minutes or ghaṭikâs and palas under *h. m.*, or *gh. p* respectively. Add together the three quantities. If the sum of hours exceeds 24, or if the sum of ghaṭikâs exceeds 60, write down the remainder only, and add one each to (*w*) and (*d*). If the sum of (*w*) exceeds 7, cast out sevens from it. The result is the time of the astronomical beginning of the current (given) month. Determine its civil beginning by the rules given in Art. 28 above.

When the month begins civilly on the same day as, on the day following, or on the third day after, the saṅkrânti day, subtract 1 from, or add 0, or 1, to both (*d*) and (*w*), and then to each of them add the number of the given day, casting out sevens from it in the case of (*w*). (*w*) is then the required week-day, and (*d*) will show, by Table IX., the A.D. equivalent of the given day.

N.B. i. When it is not certain whether the given year is Meshâdi or of another kind, or what rule for the civil beginning of the month applies, all possible ways must be tried.

N.B. ii. See *N.B. ii., iii., iv.*, Art. 147, under the rules for the conversion of luni-solar dates.

EXAMPLE IX. Required the week-day and the date A.D. corresponding to (Tamil) 18th Puraṭṭâśi of Rudhirodgârin, Kali year 4904 expired, (4905 current). (See example 7, p. 73.)

The given year, taken as a solar year, is Meshâdi. The month Puraṭṭâdi, or Puraṭṭâśi, corresponds to Kanyâ (Table II., Part ii.), and the year is a Tamil (Southern) one, to which the *Ârya Siddhânta* is applicable (*see Art. 21*). Looking in Table I. along the line of the given year, we find that it commenced on 11th April (col. 13), A.D. 1803, and we write as follows:—

	d.	*w.*	*h.*	*m.*
(Table I., cols. 13, 14, 17)	101	2	10	7
(Table III., col. 7) collective duration up to the end of Siṁha	156	2	10	28
	257	4	20	35
This shows that the Kanyâ saṅkrânti took place on a (4) Wednesday, at 20 h. 35 m. after sunrise, or 2.35 a.m. on the European Thursday. (Always remember that the Hindu week-day begins at sunrise.) The month Kanyâ, therefore, begins civilly on Thursday.[1] (*Rule 2(a), Art. 28.*) We add, therefore 0 to (*d*) and (*w*)	0	0		
Add 18, the serial number of the given day, to (*d*) and, casting out sevens from the same figure, 18, add 4 to (*w*)	18	4		
	275	1		

Then (*w*) = 1, *i.e.*, Sunday, and 275 = (Table IX.) 2nd October.

Answer.—Sunday, 2nd October, 1803 A.D.

EXAMPLE X. Required the week-day and A.D. date corresponding to the 20th day of the Bengali (solar) month Phâlguna of Śaka 1776 expired, 1777 current, at Calcutta.

[1] It would have so begun if the saṅkrânti occurred at 7 p.m. on the Wednesday, or at any time after sunset (6 p.m.)

The year is Meshâdi and from Bengal, to which the *Sûrya Siddhânta* applies (*see Art. 21*). The Bengâli month Phâlguna corresponds to Kumbha (Table II., Part ii.). The year commenced on 11th April, 1854, A.D. (Table I.).

	d.	w.	h.	m.
(Table I., cols. 13, 14, 17*a*)	101	3	17	13
Difference of longitude for Calcutta (Table XI.)				+50
Collective duration up to the end of Makara (Table III., col. 9.)	305	4	2	2
	406	0	20	5

This result represents the moment of the astronomical beginning of Kumbha, which is after midnight on Saturday, for 20 h. 5 m. after sunrise is 2.5 a.m. on the European Sunday morning. The month, therefore, begins civilly on Monday (Art. 28, *Rule 1 above*).

	d.	w.
Add, therefore, 1 to (*d*) and (*w*)	1	1
Add 20 (given day) to (*d*), and, casting out sevens from 20, add 6 to (*w*)	20	6
0 = Saturday, 427 = 3rd March (Table IX.) . . .	427	0

Answer.—Saturday, 3rd March, A.D. 1855.

EXAMPLE XI. Required the week-day and A.D. date corresponding to the Tinnevelly Âṇḍu 1024, 20th day of Âvaṇi. (See example 8, p. 73.)

The year is South Indian. It is not Meshâdi, but Siṁhâdi. Its corresponding Śaka year is 1771 current; and the sign-name of the month corresponding to Âvaṇi is Siṁha (Table I., and Table II., Parts ii., and iii.) The Śaka year 1771 commenced on 11th April (102), A.D. 1848 (a leap-year), on (3) Tuesday. Work by the *Ârya-Siddhânta (Art. 21)*.

	d.	w.	h.	m.
(Table I., cols. 13, 14, 17)	102	3	1	30
Collective duration up to the end of Karka	125	6	9	38
	227	2	11	8

	d.	w.
The month begins civilly on the same day by one of the South Indian systems (Art. 28, Rule 2, *a*); therefore subtract 1 from both (*d*) and (*w*).	1	1
	226	1
Add 20, the serial number of the given day, to (*d*) and (less sevens) to (*w*)	20	6
	246	0
Deduct 1 for 29th February (*N.B. ii.*, Art. 149 and *N.B. iii.*, Art. 147)	1	
	245	

0 = Saturday. 245 = (Table IX.) Sept. 2nd.

Answer.—Saturday, September 2nd, 1848 A.D.

EXAMPLE XII. Required the week-day and A.D. date corresponding to the South Malayâḷam Âṇḍu 1024, 19th Chiṅgam. (The calculations in Example xi. shew that the South-Malayâḷam month Chiṅgam began civilly one day later (Art. 28, Rule *2b*). Therefore the Tamil 20th Âvaṇi was the 19th South-Malayâḷam.)

Referring to Table II., Part ii., we see that the date is the same as in the last example.

EXAMPLE XIII. Required the week-day and A.D. date corresponding to the North Malayâḷam Âṇḍu 1023, 20th Chiṅgam.

Referring to Table II., Part ii., we see that the date is the same as in the last two examples.

(C.) *Conversion into dates A.D. of tithis which are coupled with solar months.*

150. Many inscriptions have been discovered containing dates, in expressing which a tithi has been coupled, not with a lunar, but with a solar month. We therefore find it necessary to give rules for the conversion of such dates.

Parts of two lunar months corresponding to each solar month are noted in Table II., Part ii., col. 14. Determine by Art. 119, or in doubtful cases by direct calculation made under Arts. 149 and 151, to which of these two months the given tithi of the given fortnight belongs, and then proceed according to the rules given in Art. 139.

It sometimes happens that the same solar month contains the given tithi of both the lunar months noted in Table II., Part ii., col. 14, one occurring at the beginning of it and the other at the end. Thus, suppose that in a certain year the solar month Mesha commenced on the luni-solar tithi Chaitra śukla ashṭami (8th) and ended on Vaiśâkha śukla daśamî (10th). In this case the tithi śukla navamî (9th) of both the lunar months Chaitra and Vaiśâkha fell in the same solar month Mesha. In such a case the exact corresponding lunar month cannot be determined unless the vâra (week-day), nakshatra, or yoga is given, as well as the tithi. If it is given, examine the date for both months, and after ascertaining when the given details agree with the given tithi, determine the date accordingly.

EXAMPLE XIV. Required the A.D. year, month, and day corresponding to a date given as follows;—"Śaka 1187, on the day of the nakshatra Rohiṇî, which fell on Saturday the thirteenth tithi of the second fortnight in the month of Mithuna."[1]

It is not stated whether the Śaka year is expired or current. We will therefore try it first as expired. The current year therefore is 1188. Turning to Table I. we find that its initial day, Chaitra śukla 1st, falls on 20th March (79), Friday (6), A.D. 1265. From Table II., Part ii., col. 14, we find that parts of the lunar months Jyeshṭha and Âshâḍha correspond to the solar month Mithuna. The Mesha saṅkrânti in that year falls on (Table I., col. 13) 25th March, Wednesday, that is on or about Chaitra śukla shashṭhî (6th), and therefore the Mithuna saṅkrânti falls on (about) Jyeshṭha śukla daśamî (10th) and the Karka saṅkrânti on (about) Âshâḍha śukla dvâdaśî (12th) (*see Art. 119*). Thus we see that the thirteenth tithi of the second fortnight falling in the solar month of Mithuna of the given date must belong to amânta Jyêshṭha.

[1] This date is from an actual inscription in Southern India. (See *Ind. Ant., XXII., p.* 219)

	d.	w.	a.	b.	c.
S. 1188, Chaitra ś. 1st (Table I., cols. 19, 20, 23, 24, 25) . . .	79	6	287	879	265
Approximate number of days from Ch. ś. 1st to Jyesh. kṛi. 13th (87 tithis reduced by 60th part = 86) with its (w) (a) (b) (c) (Table IV.)	86	2	9122	121	235
	165	1	9409	0	500
Equation for (b) (0) (Table VI.)			140		
Do. (c) (500) Table VII.)			60		
			9609 = t.		

The resulting number 9609 fixes the tithi as kṛishṇa 14th (Table VIII., cols. 2, 3), *i.e.*, the tithi immediately following the given tithi. There is no probability of a *kshaya* or *vṛiddhi* shortly before or after this (*Art 142*). Deduct, therefore, 1 from (*d*) and (*w*) 1 1

164 0

164 = (Table IX.) 13th June; 0 = Saturday.
Answer.—13th June, 1265 A.D., Saturday, (as required).[1]

(D.) *Conversion of dates A.D.*[2] *into Hindu luni-solar dates.*

151. Given a year, month, and date A.D., write down in a horizontal line (*w*) the week-day number, and (*a*), (*b*), (*c*) (Table I., cols. 20, 23, 24, 25) of the initial day (Chaitra ś. 1) of the Hindu Chaitrâdi (Śaka) year corresponding to the given year; remembering that if the given date A.D. is earlier than such initial day, the (*w*) (*a*) (*b*) (*c*) of the previous Hindu year[3] must be taken. Subtract the date-indicator of the initial date (in brackets, Table I., col. 19) from the date number of the given date (Table IX.), remembering that, if the initial day of the previous Hindu year has been taken, the number to be taken from Table IX. is that on the right-hand side, and not that on the left (*see also N.B. ii. below*). The remainder is the number of days which have intervened between the beginning of the Hindu year and the required date. Write down, under their respective heads, the (*w*) (*a*) (*b*) (*c*) of the number of intervening days from Table IV., and add them together as before (*see rules for conversion of luni-solar dates into dates A.D.*). Add to (*a*) the equation for (*b*) and (*c*) (Tables VI., VII.) and the sum (*t*) will indicate the tithi (Table VIII.) at sunrise of the given day; (*w*) is its week-day. To the number of intervening days add its sixtieth[4] part. See the number of tithis next lower than this total[5] (Table III., col. 3) and the lunar month along the same line (col. 2). Then this month is the month preceding the required month, and the following month is the required month.

When there is an added month in the year, as shown along the line in col. 8 or 8*a* of Table I., if it comes prior to the resulting month, the month next preceding the resulting month

[1] It is found by actual calculation under Art. 156 that the given nakshatra falls on the same date, and therefore we know that the above result is correct.

[2] This problem is easier than its converse, the number of intervening days here being certain.

[3] If the Rule I(*a*) in Art. 104 (Table II., Part iii.) be applied, this latter part of the rule necessarily follows.

[4] A 59th part, or more properly 63rd, should be added, but by adding a 60th, which is more convenient, there will be no difference in the ultimate result. Neglect the fraction half or less, and take more than half as equivalent to one.

[5] This total is the approximate number of tithis which have intervened. When it is the same as, or very near to, the number of tithis forming the collective duration up to the end of a month (as given in col. 3, Table III.), there will be some doubt about the required month; but this difficulty will be easily solved by comparing together the resulting tithi and the number of tithis which have intervened.

is the required month; if the added month is the same as the resulting month, the date belongs to that added month itself; and if the resulting month comes earlier than the added month, the result is not affected.

When there is a suppressed month in the year, if it is the same as, or prior to, the resulting month, the month next following the resulting month is the required month. If it is subsequent to the resulting month the result is not affected. If the resulting month falls after both an added and suppressed month the result is unaffected.

From the date in a Chaitrâdi year thus found, any other Hindu year corresponding to it can be found, if required, by reference to Table II., Parts ii., and iii.

The tithi thus found is the tithi corresponding to the given date A.D.; but sometimes a tithi which is current at any moment of an A.D. date may be said to be its corresponding tithi.

N.B. i. See *N.B. ii.*, Art. 147; but for "+ 11" read "—11".

N.B. ii. If the given A.D. date falls in a leap-year after 29th February, or if its date-number is more than 365 (taken from the right-hand side of Table IX.) and the year next preceding it was a leap-year, add 1 to the date-number before subtracting the date-indicator from it.

EXAMPLE XV. Required the tithi and month in the Śaka year corresponding to 7th June, 1780 A.D.

The Śaka year corresponding to the given date is 1703 current. Its initial day falls on (4) Wednesday, 5th April, the date-indicator being 96.

		w.	*a.*	*b.*	*c.*
(Table I., cols. 20, 23, 24, 25)		4	1	657	267
7th June = ...	158 (Table IX.)				
Add	+ 1 for leap-year (*N.B. ii.*)				
	159				
Deduct	96 the (*d*) of the initial date (Table I., col. 19).				
Days that have intervened 63. By Table IV. 63 = ...		0	1334	286	172
		4	1335	943	439
Equation for (*b*) (943) (Table VI.)			90		
Do. (*c*) (439) (Table VII.)			38		
		4	1463 = *t*.		

Śukla 5th (Table VIII.) is the required tithi, and (4) Wednesday is the week-day. Now $63 + \frac{63}{60} = 64\frac{3}{60}$. The next lowest number in col. 3, Table III., is 60, which shows Vaiśâkha to be the preceding month. Jyeshṭha is therefore the required month.

Answer.—Śaka 1703 current, Jyeshṭha śukla 5th, Wednesday.

If the exact beginning or ending time of the tithi is required, proceed as in example 1 above (*Art. 148.*)

We have seen in example 1 above (*Art. 148*) that this Jyeshṭha 5th ended, and śukla 6th commenced, at 13 h. 11 m. after sunrise on the given date; and after that hour śukla 6th corresponded with the given date. Śukla 6th therefore may be sometimes said to correspond to the given date as well as śukla 5th.

EXAMPLE XVI.—Required the tithi and month in the southern Vikrama year corresponding to 12th September, 1776 A.D.

The Śaka year corresponding to the given date is 1699 current. Its initial date falls on 20th March (80), 4 Wednesday, A.D. 1776. Bhâdrapada was intercalated in that year.

		w.	*a.*	*b.*	*c.*
(Table I., cols. 20, 23, 24, 25)		4	9841	54	223
12 September = ...	255 (Table IX.)				
Add	1 for leap-year (*N.B. ii.*)				
	256				
Deduct	80 the (*d*) of the initial day.				
Days that have intervened	176 = (Table IV.)	1	9599	387	482
		5	9440	441	705
Equation for (*b*) (441) (Table VI.)			191		
Do. (*c*) (705) (Table VII.)			118		
		5	9749 = *t*.		

This indicates (Table VIII.) kṛishṇa 30th (amâvâsyâ, or new moon day), Thursday.

The intervening tithis are $176 + \frac{176}{60} = 179$. The number next below this in col. 3, Table III., is 150, and shows that Śrâvaṇa preceded the required month. But Bhâdrapada was intercalated this year and it immediately followed Śrâvaṇa. Therefore the resulting tithi belongs to the intercalated or adhika Bhâdrapada.

Answer.—Adhika Bhâdrapada kṛi: 30th of Śaka 1699 current, that is adhika Bhâdrapada kṛi. 30th of the Southern Vikrama Kârttikâdi year 1833 current, 1832 expired. (Table II., Part ii.).

EXAMPLE XVII. Required the Telugu and Tuḷu equivalents of December 1st, 1822 A.D.

The corresponding Telugu or Tuḷu Chaitrâdi Śaka year is 1745 current. Âśvina was intercalary and Pausha was expunged (col. 8, Table I.). Its initial date falls on 24 March (83), A.D. 1822, (1) Sunday.

		w.	*a.*	*b.*	*c.*
Table I., cols. 20, 23, 24, 25)		1	212	899	229
1st December = ...	335 (Table IX.)				
Deduct	83 (The *d.* of the initial day)				
Days that have intervened	252 = (Table IV.)	0	5335	145	690
		1	5547	44	919
Equation for (*b*) (44) (Table IV.)			180		
Do. (*c*) (919) (Do. VII.)			90		
The results give us kṛishṇa 3, Sunday (1), (Table VIII.) . .		1	5817 = *t*.		

$252 + \frac{252}{60} = 256$. The number next below 256 in col. 3, Table III., is 240, and shews that Kârttika preceded the required month, and the required month would therefore be Mârgaśîrsha. But Âśvina, which is prior to Mârgasîrsha, was intercalated. Kârttika therefore is the required month. Pausha was expunged, but being later than Kârttika the result is not affected.

Answer.—Sunday, Kârttika (Telugu), or Jârde (Tuḷu) (Table II., Part ii.), kṛ. 3rd of the year Chitrabhânu, Śaka 1745 (1744 expired), Kali year 4923 expired.

Example xviii. Required the tithi and pûrṇimânta month in the Śaka year corresponding to 18th January, 1541 A.D.

The given date is prior to Chaitra śukla 1 in the given year. We take therefore the initial day in the previous year, A.D. 1540, which falls on Tuesday the 9th March (69). The corresponding Śaka year is 1463 current.

		w.	*a.*	*b.*	*c.*
(Table I., cols. 20, 23, 24, 25)		3	108	756	229
18th January = . .	383 (Table IX.)				
Add for leap-year . .	1 (*N.B. ii.*, latter part.)				
	384				
Deduct	69 (The *d.* of the initial day.)				
No. of intervening days. .	315 = (by Table IV.)	0	6669	432	862
		3	6777	188	91
Equation for (*b*) (188) (Table VI.)			269		
Do. (*c*) (91) (Do. VII.)			28		
		3	7074 = *t.*		

The result gives us kṛishṇa 7th, Tuesday (3) (Table VIII.).

$315 + \frac{315}{60} = 320$ tithis. The next lower number to 320 in col. 3, Table III., is 300, which shews Pausha as preceding the required month, and the required month would therefore be Mâgha. Âsvina, however, which is prior to Mâgha, was intercalary in this year; Pausha, therefore, would be the required month; but it was expunged; Mâgha, therefore, becomes again the required month. Adhika Âśvina and kshaya Pausha being both prior to Mâgha, they do not affect the result. By Table II. amânta Mâgha kṛishṇa is pûrṇimânta Phâlguna kṛishṇa. Therefore pûrṇimânta Phâlguna kṛishṇa 7th, Tuesday, Śaka 1463 current, is the required date.

(E.) *Conversion of A.D. dates into Hindu solar dates.*

152. Given a year, month, and date A.D., write down from Table I. in a horizontal line the (*d*) (*w*) and (*h*) (*m*) (the time) of the Mesha saṅkrânti, by the *Ârya* or *Sûrya-Siddhânta* [1] as the case may require, of the Hindu Meshâdi year, remembering that if the given day A.D. is earlier than the Mesha saṅkranti day in that year the previous [2] Hindu year must be taken. Subtract the date-indicator of the Mesha saṅkrânti day from the date-number of the given date (Table IX.), remembering that if the Mesha saṅkrânti time of the previous Hindu year is taken the number to be taken from Table IX. is that on the right-hand side, and not that on the left (*see also Art. 151, N.B. ii.*); the remainder is the number of days which intervened between the Mesha saṅkrânti and the given day. Find from Table III., cols. 6, 7, 8 or 9, as the case may be, the number next below that number of intervening days. Write its three quantities (*d*), (*w*), and the time of the saṅkrânti (*h. m.*), under their respective heads, and add together the three quantities separately (*See Art. 149*

[1] See Art. 21, and notes 1 and 2, and Arts. 93 and 96.

[2] See note 4, p. 90.

above). The sum is the time of the astronomical beginning of the required month, and the month next following that given in col. 5, on the line of the next lowest number, is the month required.

Ascertain the day of the civil beginning of the current required month by the rules in Art. 28. When it falls on the same day as the saṅkrânti day, or the following, or the third day, respectively, subtract 1 from, or add 0 or 1 to, both (*d*) and (*w*). Subtract (*d*) from the date-number of the given date. The remainder is the required Hindu day. Add that remainder, casting out sevens from it, to (*w*). The sum is the week-day required.

From the Meshâdi year and the sign-name of the month thus found, any other corresponding Hindu year can be found by reference to Table III., Parts ii., and iii.

Observe the cautions contained in *N.B. i.* and *ii.* to Art. 151.

EXAMPLE XIX. Required the Tamil, Tinnevelly, and South and North Malayâḷam equivalents of 30th May, 1803 A.D. (See example 14, p. 76.)

The corresponding Meshâdi Śaka year current is 1726. Its Mesha saṅkrânti falls on April 11th (101), 2 Monday. The *Ârya Siddhânta* applies. (*See Art. 21.*)

	d.	*w.*	*h.*	*m.*
(Table I., cols. 13 14, 17)	101	2	10	7
May 30th = . 150 (Table IX.)				
Deduct . . . 101, the (*d*) of the initial day.				
Intervening days 49				
The number next below 49, (Table III., col. 7), for the end of Mesha and beginning of Vṛishabha, is 30, and we have	30	2	22	12
[Total of hours = 32. 1 day of 24 hours carried over to (*d*) and (*w*).]				
Astronomical beginning of Vṛishabha	132	5	8	19
By all South Indian reckonings, except that in the South Malayâḷam country, the month begins civilly on the same day as the saṅkrânti. Subtract, therefore, 1 from (*d*) and (*w*)	1	1		
	131	4		
Subtract 131 (*d*) from the number of the given date . . .	150			
Remainder, 19, is the required date in the month of Vṛishabha.	19			
Add 19, casting out sevens, to (*w*)		5		
Required week-day		2		

Answer.—Monday, 19th day of the month Vṛishabha, Tamil Vaigâśi, of Śaka 1726 current (1725 expired); Kali 4904 expired (Table I., or Table II., Part iii.); Tinnevelly Âṇḍu 978, Vaigâśi 19th; North Malayâḷam Âṇḍu 978, Eḍavam 19th.

The Vṛishabha saṅkrânti took place 8 h. 19 m. after sunrise, viz., not within the first $\frac{3}{5}$ths of the day. Therefore by the South Malayâḷam system the month Vṛishabha began civilly, not on (5) Thursday, but on the following day (6) Friday. Therefore we have to add or subtract nothing from 132 and 5. Subtracting 132 from 150, the remainder, 18th, is the required day. Adding (18 ÷ 7) to 5 (*w*) we get (2) Monday as the required week-day. Therefore Monday 18th of Eḍavam, Kollam Âṇḍu 978, is the required South Malayâḷam equivalent.

EXAMPLE XX. Required the week-day and Bengali date at Calcutta corresponding to March 3rd, 1855 A.D. The *Sûrya-Siddhânta* is the authority in Bengal. The given day is earlier than the Mesha saṅkrânti in the year given. We must take therefore as our starting-point the Mesha saṅkrânti of the previous year, which falls on 11th April (101), Tuesday, (3) Śaka 1777 current, A.D. 1854.

		d.	*w.*	*h.*	*m.*
(Table I., cols. 13, 14, 17a)		101	3	17	13
Difference of longitude for Calcutta (Table XI.)					+ 50
March 3rd, 1855 = . .	427 (Table IX.)				
Deduct (*d*) of the initial day	101				
Intervening days . . .	326				
The number next below 326 (Table III. col. 9), for the end of Makara and beginning of Kumbha is		305	4	2	2
The astronomical beginning of Kumbha, after midnight on Saturday =		406	0	20	5
The civil beginning falls on the third day, Monday (Art. 28). We add therefore 1 to (*d*) and (*w*)		1	1		
The last civil day of Makara = ...		407	1		
Subtract (*d*) 407 from the date number of 3rd March . . .		427			
Remainder 20, and the required date is 20th Kumbha. . .		20			
Add 20 to (*w*) casting out sevens			6		
The required week-day is Saturday			0		

The Bengali month corresponding to Kumbha is Phâlguna (Table II., Part ii.).

Answer.—The 20th day of Phâlguna, Saturday, Śaka, 1776 expired. (See example x above.)

EXAMPLE XXI. Required the South Indian solar dates equivalent to 2nd September, 1848 A.D.

The corresponding Meshâdi Śaka year (current) is 1771. It commenced on 11th April (102), Tuesday (3).

		d.	*w.*	*h.*	*m.*
(Table I., cols. 13, 14, 17)		102	3	1	30
2nd September = ...	245 (Table IX.)				
Add 1 for leap-year . . .	1 (*N.B. ii*, Art. 151.)				
Date-number of the given day	246				
Deduct (*d*) of the initial day .	102				
Intervening days	144				
The number next below 144, (col. 7, Table III.), for the end of Karka and beginning of Siṁha is 125, and we write		125	6	9	38
The astronomical beginning of Siṁha is		227	2	11	8

This is the civil beginning by one of the Southern systems.

	d.	w.	h.	m.
(Brought over)	277	2	11	8
Subtract 1 from (*d*) and (*w*)	1	1		
Last civil day of Karka = ...	226	1		
Subtract 226 from the date number 246 (Table IX.) of the given day	246			
Required date in the month Siṁha	20			
Add this to (*w*) casting out sevens		6		
The required week-day is Saturday		0		

The equivalents are therefore:—(see Table II., Part ii.)

Saturday	19th	Chiṅgam,	South Malayâḷam Âṇḍu	1024	(See example XII., p. 89.)
Do.	20th	Do.	North Do.	1023	
Do.	20th	Avaṇi	Tinnevelly Âṇḍu	1024	
Do.	20th	Do.	Tamil Śaka year	1771	(current).

(F.) *Determination of Karaṇas.*

153. We now proceed to give rules for finding the karaṇas on a given day,—the exact moments of their beginning and ending, and the karaṇa current at sunrise on any given day, or at any moment of any given day.

The karaṇas[1] of a given tithi may be found by the following rule. Multiply the number of expired tithis by two. Divide this by 7; and the remainder is the karaṇa for the current half of the tithi. *Example.*—Find the karaṇa for the second half of kṛishṇa 8th. The number of expired tithis from the beginning of the month is $(15 + 7\frac{1}{2} =)$ $22\frac{1}{2}$. $22\frac{1}{2} \times 2 = 45$. Casting out sevens the 3rd, or Kaulava, is the required karaṇa.

154. To find the exact moments on which the karaṇas corresponding to a given tithi begin and end. Find the duration of the tithi from its beginning and ending moments, as calculated by the method given in Arts. 139, 144, and 145 above. The first half of the tithi is the period of duration of its first karaṇa, and the second half that of the second.

EXAMPLE XXII. Find the karaṇas, and the periods of their duration, current on Jyeshṭha śukla pañchamî (5th) of the Śaka year 1702 expired (1703 current). From Table VIII., cols. 4 and 5 we observe that (1) Bava is the first, and (2) Bâlava is the second, karaṇa corresponding to the 5th tithi. In the first example above (*Art. 148*) we have found that the tithi commenced on Tuesday, 6th June, A.D. 1780. at 15 h. 34 m. after mean sunrise, and that it ended on Wednesday, 7th June, at 13 h. 11 m. after mean sunrise. It lasted therefore for 21 h. 37 m. (8 h. 26 m. on Tuesday and 13 h. 11 m. on Wednesday). Half of this duration is 10 h. 48 m. The Bava karaṇa lasted therefore from 15 h. 34 m. after mean sunrise on Tuesday, June 6th, to 2 h. 22 m. after mean sunrise on Wednesday, June 7th, and the Bâlava karaṇa lasted thence to the end of the tithi.

155. The karaṇa at sunrise or at any other time can of course easily be found by the above method. It can also be calculated independently by finding the (*t*) for the time given. Its beginning or ending time also can be found, with its index, by the same method as is used for that of a tithi. The index of a karaṇa can be easily found from that of a tithi by finding the middle point of the latter. For example, the index of the middle point of śukla 14th

[1] For the definition of karaṇas, and other information regarding them, see Arts. 10 and 40.

is 4500, or 4333 + half the difference between 4333 and 4667 (*Table VIII.*), and therefore the indices for the beginning and ending of the 5th karaṇa on śukla 14th are 4333 and 4500, and of the 6th karaṇa on the same tithi 4500 and 4667.

EXAMPLE XXII(*a*). Find the karaṇa at sunrise on Wednesday the 7th June, A.D. 1780, Jyeshṭha śukla 5th, Śaka 1702 expired (1703 current).

In examples i. and xv. above we have found (*t*) at the given sunrise to be 1463. Turning with this to Table VIII. we see that the karaṇa was the 1st or 2nd. The index of the first is 1333 to 1500, and therefore the first karaṇa, Bava, was current at the given sunrise.

(G) *Determination of Nakshatras.*

156. *To find the nakshatra at sunrise, or at any other moment, of an Indian or European date.* If the given date be other than a tithi or a European date, turn it into one or other of these. Find the (*a*) (*b*) (*c*) and (*t*) for the given moment by the method given in Arts. 139, 148 or 151, *(Examples i. or xv.)* above. Multiply (*c*) by ten; add 7207 to the product, and from this sum subtract the equation for (*c*) (Table VII.). Call the remainder (*s*). Add (*s*) to (*t*). Call the result (*n*). Taken as an index, (*n*) shows, by Table VIII., col. 6, 7, 8, the nakshatra current at the given moment as calculated by the ordinary system.

157. If the nakshatra according to the Garga or Brahma Siddhânta system is required, use cols. 9 or 10 respectively of Table VIII.

158. The beginning or ending time of the nakshatra can be calculated in the same manner as that of a tithi. Since (*c*) is expressed in 1000ths, and 10000ths of it are neglected, the time will not be absolutely correct.

EXAMPLE XXIII. Find the nakshatra current at sunrise on Wednesday, Jyeshṭha śukla 5th, Śaka 1702 expired, (7th June, 1780 A.D.)

	t.	*c.*		*Equation for c.* (Table VII.)
As calculated in Example i. or xv. above	1463	439		38
Multiply (*c*) by 10		439 × 10 =	4390	
Add			7207	
			1597	
Subtract equation for (*c*)			38	
Add (*s*) to (*t*)	1559		1559 = (*s*)	
	3022 = (*n*)			

This result (*n*) gives Aśleshâ (Table VIII., cols. 6, 7, 8) as the required current nakshatra

The (*n*) so found 3022—2963 (index to beginning point of Aśleshâ) = 59. Therefore Aśleshâ begins 3 h. 52 m. (Table X., col. 4) before sunrise on the Wednesday.

3333 (end of Aśleshâ)—3022(*n*) = 311, and therefore Aśleshâ ends (19 h. 40 m. + 43 m. =) 20 h. 23 m. after sunrise on the Wednesday.

For greater accuracy we may proceed as in Example 1 (*Art. 148.*)

(H.) *Determination of Yogas.*

159. *The next problem is to find the yoga* at sunrise or at any other moment of an Indian or European date. If the given date is other than a tithi or a European date, turn it

into one or the other of these. Find (*a*) (*b*) (*c*) (*t*) (*s*) and (*n*) for the given moment as above (*Art. 156*). Add (*s*) to (*n*). Call the sum (*y*). This, as index, shews by Table VIII., cols. 11, 12, 13, the yoga current at the given moment.

EXAMPLE XXIV. Find the yoga at sunrise on Jyeshṭha śukla 5th, Saka 1702 expired, 7th June, 1780 A.D.

As calculated in example xviii. (*s*) = 1559 (*n*) = 3022
Add (*n*) to (*s*) . . . . (*n*) = 3022

Required yoga (*y*) = . . . 4581 = (13) Vyâghâta (Table VIII.).

We find the beginning point of Vyâghâta from this.

The (*y*) so found 4581—4444 (beginning point of Vyâghâta) = 137 = (6 h. 6 m. + 2 h. 15 m. =) 8 h. 21 m. before sunrise on Wednesday (Table X., col. 5).

The end of Vyâghâta is found thus:

(End of Vyâghâta) 4815—4581 (*y*) = 234 = (12 h. 12 m. + 2 h. 4 m. =) 14 h. 16 m. after sunrise on Wednesday.

(I.) *Verification of Indian dates.*

160. (*See Art. 132.*) The following is an example of the facility afforded by the Tables in this volume for verifying Indian dates.

EXAMPLE XXV. Suppose an inscription to contain the following record of its date,—"Śaka 666, Kârttika kṛishṇa amâvâsyâ (30), Sunday, nakshatra Hasta." The problem is to verify this date and find its equivalent A.D. There is nothing here to shew whether the given year is current or expired, whether the given month is amânta or pûrṇimânta, and whether, if the year be the current one, the intercalary month in it was taken as true or mean.[1]

First let us suppose that the year is an expired one (667 current) and the month amânta. There was no intercalary month in that year. The given month would therefore be the eighth, and the number of intervening months from the beginning of the year is 7.

	d.	*w.*	*a.*	*b.*	*c.*
Śaka 667 current. (Table I., cols. 19, 20, 23, 24, 25)	80	6	324	773	278
210 (7 months) + 15 (śukla) + 14 (kṛ. amâvâsyâ is 15, and 1 must be substracted by rule) = 239 tithis = 235 days	235	4	9578	529	643
	315	3	9902	302	921
Equation for (*b*) (302) (Table VI.)			271		
Do. (*c*) (921) (Do. VII.)			90		
		3	263 = *t*.		

This gives us Tuesday, śukla 1st (Table VIII.). Index, $t = 263$, proves that 263 parts of the tithi had expired at sunrise on Tuesday, and thence we learn that this śukla 1st commenced on Monday, and that the preceding tithi kṛi. 30 would possibly commence on Sunday. If so, can we connect the tithi kṛi. 30 with the Sunday? Let us see.

[1] This will illustrate the danger of trusting to Tables XIV. and XV. in important cases.

	d.	*w.*	*a.*	*b.*	*c.*
Already obtained	315	3	9902	302	921
Subtract value for two days (Table IV.)	2	2	677	73	5
	313	1	9225	229	916
Equation for (*b*) (229) (Table VI.)			279		
Do. (*c*) (916) (Do. VII.)			91		
		1	9595 = *t*.		

This index gives us kṛishṇa 14th (Table VIII.) as current at sunrise on Sunday (1). The tithi ended and kṛi. 30 commenced (9667—9595 = 72 =) 5 h. 6 m. after sunrise on Sunday. This kṛi. 30 therefore can be connected with a Sunday, and if the nakshatra comes right—Hasta—then this would be the given date. We calculate the nakshatra at sunrise on Sunday.

	t.	*c.*
As calculated above	9595	916
(*c*) multiplied by 10		916 × 10 = 9160
Add constant		7207
		6367
Subtract the equation for (*c*) (Table VII.)		91
Add (*s*) to (*t*)	6276	6276 = (*s*)
	5871 = (*n*)	

This index (*n*) gives nakshatra No. 16 Visâkhâ (Table VIII., col. 6, 7, 8). Therefore No. 13 Hasta had already passed, and this proves that the date obtained above is incorrect.

Now if Kârttika in the given record be pûrṇimânta, the amânta month corresponding (Table II., Part i) would be Âśvina, the 7th month, and it is possible that Âśvina kṛi. 30, falling back as it does 29 or 30 days from the date calculated, might fall on a Sunday. Let us see if it did so.

	d.	*w.*	*a.*	*b.*	*c.*
Chaitra śukla 1, Śaka 667 current (*as above*)	80	6	324	773	278
180 (6 expired months) + 15 (śukla) + 14 (*see above*) = 209 tithis = 206 days	206	3	9758	476	564
	286	2	82	249	842
Equation for (*b*) (249) (Table VI.)			280		
Do. (*c*) (842) (Do. VII.)			111		
		2	473 = (*t*)		

The result gives us Monday, śukla 2nd. [1]

[1] Note that this approximate calculation, which is the same as that by method B, comes out actually wrong by two days.

	d.	w.	a.	b.	c.
State the figures for this	286	2	82	249	842
Subtract value for two days (Table IV.)	2	2	677	73	5
	284	0	9405	176	837
Equation for (*b*) (176) (Table VI.)			265		
Do. (*c*) (842) (Do. VII.)			112		
		0	9782		

This gives Saturday kṛishṇa (30), amâvâsyâ, *i.e.*, that tithi had (10,000 − 9782) 218 parts to run at sunrise on Saturday. Therefore it ended on Saturday, and cannot be connected with a Sunday. Here again we have not the correct date.

Now let us suppose that the given year 666 is a *current* amânta year. Then the given month, Kârttika, is amânta, and the intercalary month was Bhâdrapada. The given month would be the 9th.

	d.	w.	a.	b.	c.
Chaitra śukla 1st, Śaka 666 current (Table I.)	61	0	289	837	227
240 (for 8 months) + 15 (śukla) + 14 (*as above*) = 269 tithies = 265 days (Table IV.)	265	6	9737	617	726
	326	6	26	454	953
Equation for (*b*) (454) (Table VI.)			180		
Do (*c*) (953) (Do. VII.)			78		
		6	284 = (*t*)		

This gives us Friday, śukla 1st. The preceding day is kṛishṇa amâvâsyâ, and this therefore ends on Thursday and can in no way be connected with a Sunday. This date is therefore again wrong. The amâvâsyâ of the previous month (29 days back) would end on a Wednesday or perhaps Tuesday, so that cannot help us. If we go back yet a month more, it is possible that the kṛishṇa amâvâsyâ might fall on a Sunday. That month could only be called Kârttika if it were treated according to the pûrṇimânta system and if there were no intercalary month. The given month would then be the 7th in the year. We test this as usual.

	d.	w.	a.	b.	c.
Chaitra śukla 1st, Saka 666 current	61	0	289	837	227
180 (6 expired months) + 15 śukla + 14 (*as before*) = 209 tithis = 206 days (Table IV.)	206	3	9758	476	564
	267	3	47	313	791
Equation for (*b*) (313) (Table VI.)			269		
Do. (*c*) (791) (Do. VII.)			119		
		3	435 = *t*.		

This gives Tuesday,[1] śukla 2nd, two tithis in advance of the required one.

1 In this case the result by the approximate method A or B will be wrong by two days.

We may either subtract the value of (*w*) (*a*) (*b*) (*c*) for two days from their value as already obtained, or may add the value for (206—2 =) 204 days to the value at the beginning of the year. We try the latter.

	d.	*w.*	*a.*	*b.*	*c.*
Chaitra śukla 1st, Śaka 666 current (Table I.)	61	0	289	837	227
204 days (Table IV.)	204	1	9081	403	559
	265	1	9370	240	786
Equation for (*b*) (240) (Table VI.)			280		
Do. (*c*) (786) (Do. VII.)			119		
		1	9769 = *t*.		

This gives us kṛishṇa amâvâsyâ, (1) Sunday, as required.

(*d*) = 265 = (Table IX.) 22nd September, 743 A.D. (Table I.). From Table XIII. we see that the week-day is right. If the nakshatra Hasta comes right, then this is the given date. We calculate it according to rule.

	t.	*c.*
As already obtained	9769	786
(*c*) multiplied by 10		7860
Add constant		7207
		5067
Subtract the equation for (*c*) (786) (Table VII.)		119
Add (*s*) to (*t*)	4948	4948 = (*s*)
	4717 = (*n*)	

This result gives No. 13 Hasta (Table VIII.) as required.

This therefore is the given date. Its equivalent A.D. is 22nd September, 743 A.D. The data were imaginary. If they had been taken from an actual record they would have proved that mean and not true intercalary months were in use in A.D. 743, because we have found that there was no intercalary month prior to the given month Kârttika. The mean intercalary month in that year (Table I.) was the 9th month, Mârgaśirsha, and of course Kârttika was unaffected by it.

160(*A*). See page of Addenda and Errata.

PART V.

THE MUHAMMADAN CALENDAR.

161. The Muhammadan era of the *Hijra*, or "flight," dates from the flight of Muhammad (Anglicé Mahomet) which took place, according to the Hissabi or astronomical reckoning, on the evening of July 15th, A.D. 622. But in the *Helali*, or chronological reckoning, Friday, July 16th, is made the initial date. The era was introduced by the Khalif Umar.

162. The year is purely lunar, and the month begins with the first heliacal rising of the moon after the new moon. The year is one of 354 days, and of 355 in intercalary years. The months have alternately 30 and 29 days each (*but see below*), with an extra day added to the last month eleven times in a cycle of thirty years. These are usually taken as the 2nd, 5th, 7th, 10th, 13th, 15th, 18th, 21st, 24th, 26th, and 29th in the cycle, but Jervis gives the 8th, 16th, 19th, and 27th as intercalary instead of the 7th, 15th, 18th and 26th, though he mentions the usual list. Ulug Beg mentions the 16th as a leap-year. It may be taken as certain that the practice varies in different countries, and sometimes even at different periods in the same country.

30 years are equal to $(354 \times 30 + 11 =)$ 10,631 days and the mean length of the year is $354\frac{11}{30}$ days.[1]

Since each Hijra year begins 10 or 11 civil days earlier than the last, in the course of 33 years the beginning of the Muhammadan year runs through the whole course of the seasons.

163. Table XVI. gives a complete list of the initial dates of the Muhammadan Hijra years from A.D. 300 to A.D. 1900. The asterisk in col. 1 shews the leap-years, when the year consists of 355 days, an extra day being added to the last month Zî'l-ḥijjat. The numbers in brackets following the date in col. 3 refer to Table IX. (*see above, Art. 95*), and are for purposes of calculation as shewn below.

Muhammadan Months.

		Days.	Collective duration.			Days.	Collective duration.
1	2	3	4	1	2	3	4
1	Muḥarram	30	30	7	Rajab	30	207
2	Śafar	29	59	8	Sha'bân	29	236
3	Rabî-ul awwal	30	89	9	Ramazân	30	266
4	Rabî-ul âkhir, or Rabi-uś śânî.	29	118	10	Shawwâl	29	295
5	Jumâda'l awwal	30	148	11	Zî-l-ka'da	30	325
6	Jumâda'l âkhir, or Jumâda-ś śânî	29	177	12	Zî-l-ḥijja	29	354
					In leap-years . . .	30	355

164. Since the Muhammadan year invariably begins with the heliacal rising of the moon, or her first observed appearance on the western horizon shortly after the sunset following the new-moon (the amâvâsyâ day of the Hindu luni-solar calendar), it follows that this rising is due about the end of the first tithi (śukla pratipadâ) of every lunar month, and that she is actually seen on the evening of the civil day corresponding to the 1st or 2nd tithi of the śukla (bright) fortnight. As, however, the Muhammadan day—contrary to Hindu practice, which counts the day from sunrise to sunrise—consists of the period from sunset to sunset, the first date of a Muhammadan month is always entered in Hindu almanacks as corresponding with the next following Hindu civil day. For instance, if the heliacal rising of the moon takes place shortly after sunset on a Saturday, the 1st day of the Muhammadan month is, in Hindu pañchâṅgs, coupled with the

[1] A year of the Hijra = 0.970223 of a Gregorian year, and a Gregorian year = 1.03069 years of the Hijra. Thus 32 Gregorian years are about equal to 33 years of the Hijra, or more nearly 163 Gregorian years are within less than a day of 168 Hijra years.

Sunday which begins at the next sunrise. But the Muhammadan day and the first day of the Muhammadan month begin with the Saturday sunset. (*See Art. 30, and the pañchâṅg extract attached.*)

165. It will be well to note that where the first tithi of a month ends not less than 5 ghaṭikâs, about two hours, before sunset, the heliacal rising of the moon will most probably take place on the same evening; but where the first tithi ends 5 ghaṭikâs or more after sunset the heliacal rising will probably not take place till the following evening. When the first tithi ends within these two periods, *i.e.*, 5 ghaṭikâs before or after sunset, the day of the heliacal rising can only be ascertained by elaborate calculations. In the pañchâṅg extract appended to Art. 30 it is noted that the heliacal rising of the moon takes place on the day corresponding to September 1st.

166. It must also be specially noted that variation of latitude and longitude sometimes causes a difference in the number of days in a month; for since the beginning of the Muhammadan month depends on the heliacal rising of the moon, the month may begin a day earlier at one place than at another, and therefore the following month may contain in one case a day more than in the other. Hence it is not right to lay down a law for all places in the world where Muhammadan reckoning is used, asserting that invariably months have alternately 29 and 30 days. The month Śafar, for instance, is said to have 29 days, but in the pañchâṅg extract given above (*Art. 30*) it has 30 days. No universal rule can be made, therefore, and each case can only be a matter of calculation.[1] The rule may be accepted as fairly accurate.

167. The days of the week are named as in the following Table.

Days of the Week.

	Hindustâni.	*Persian.*	*Arabic.*	*Hindî.*
1. Sun.	Itwâr.	Yak-shamba.	Yaumu'l-aḥad.	Rabî-bâr.
2. Mon.	Somwâr, or Pîr.	Do-shamba.	„ -iśnain.	Som-bâr.
3. Tues.	Mangal.	Sih-shamba.	„ -śalâsa'.	Mangal-bâr.
4. Wed.	Budh.	Chahâr-shamba.	„ -arbâ'.	Budh-bâr.
5. Thurs.	Jum'a-rât.	Panj-shamba.	„ -khamîs.	Brihaspati-bâr.
6. Fri.	Jum'a.	Âdîna.	„ -Jum'ah.	Śukra-bâr.
7. Sat.	Sanîchar.	Shamba, or Hafta.	Yaumu's-sab't.	Sanî-bâr.

Old and New style.

168. The New Style was introduced into all the Roman Catholic countries in Europe from October 5th, 1582 A.D., the year 1600 remaining a leap-year, while it was ordained that 1700, 1800, and 1900 should be common and not leap-years. This was not introduced into England till September 3rd, A.D. 1752. In the Table of Muhammadan initial dates we have given the comparative dates according to English computation, and if it is desired to assimilate the date to that of any Catholic country, 10 days must be added to the initial dates given by us from Hijra 991 to Hijra 1111 inclusive, and 11 days from H. 1112 to 1165 inclusive. Thus, for Catholic countries H. 1002 must be taken as beginning on September 27th, A.D. 1593.

[1] So far as I know no European chronologist of the present century has noticed this point. Tables could be constructed for the heliacal rising of the moon in every month of every year, but it would be too great a work for the present publication. [S. B. D.]

The Catholic dates will be found in Professor R. Wüstenfeld's "*Vergleichungs-Tabellen der Muhammadanischen und Christlichen Zeitrechnung*" (*Leipzic 1854*).

To convert a date A.H. into a date A.D.

169. Rule 1. Given a Muhammadan year, month, and date. Take down (*w*) the week-day number of the initial day of the given year from Table XVI., col. 2, and (*d*) the date-indicator in brackets given in col. 3 of the same Table (*Art. 163 and 95 above.*) Add to each the collective duration up to the end of the month preceding the one given, as also the moment of the given date minus 1 (*Table in Art. 163 above*). Of the two totals the first gives the day of the week by casting out sevens, and the second gives the day of the month with reference to Table IX.

Rule 2. Where the day indicated by the second total falls on or after February 29th in an English leap-year, reduce the total by one day.

Rule 3. For Old and New Style between Hijra 991 and 1165 see the preceding article.

EXAMPLE 1. Required the English equivalent of 20th Muharram, A.H. 1260.
A.H. 1260 begins (Table XVI.) January 22nd, 1844.

	(*w*) *Col. 2*	(*d*) *Col. 3*
	2	22
Given date minus 1 =	19	19
	21	41 = (Table IX.) Feb. 10th.
Cast out sevens =	21	
	0 = Saturday.	

Answer.—Saturday, February 10th, A.D. 1844.

EXAMPLE 2. Required the English equivalent of 9th Rajab, A.H. 1311.
A.H. 1311 begins July 15th, 1893.

	w.	*d.*
	0	196
9th Rajab = (177 + 8) =	185	185
	7 | 185	381 = Jan. 16th, 1894.
	(26) 3 = Tuesday.	

Answer.—Tuesday, January 16th, A.D. 1894.

This last example has been designedly introduced to prove the point we have insisted on viz., that care must be exercised in dealing with Muhammadan dates. According to Traill's *Indian Diary, Comparative Table of Dates*, giving the correspondence of English, Bengali, N.W. Fasali, "Samvat", Muhammadan, and Burmese dates, Rajab 1st corresponded with January 9th, and therefore Rajab 9th was Wednesday, January 17th, but Letts and Whitaker give Rajab 1st as corresponding with January 8th, and therefore Rajab 9th = Tuesday, January 16th, as by our Tables.

To convert a date A.D. into a date A.H.

170. Rule 1. Take down (*w*) the week-day number of the initial day of the corresponding Muhammadan year, or the year previous if the given date falls before its initial date, from Table XVI., col. 2, and (*d*) the corresponding date-indicator in brackets as given in col. 3. Subtract (*d*) from the collective duration up to the given A.D. date, as given in Table IX., Parts i. or ii. as the case may be. Add the remainder to (*w*). From the same remainder subtract the collective duration given in the Table in Art. 163 above which is next lowest, and add 1. Of these two totals (*w*) gives, by casting out sevens, the day of the week, and (*d*) the date of the Muhammadan month following that whose collective duration was taken.

Rule 2. When the given English date is in a leap-year, and falls on or after February 29th, or when its date-number is more than 365 (taken from the right-hand side of Table IX.), and the year preceding it was a leap-year, add 1 to the collective duration given in Table IX.

Rule 3. For Old and New Style see above, Art. 167.

EXAMPLE. Required the Muhammadan equivalent of January 16th, 894 A.D.

Since by Table XVI. we see that A.H. 1312 began July 5th, 1894 A.D., it is clear that we must take the figures of the previous year. This gives us the following:

(*w*)		(*d*)
0		196
	Jan. 16th (Table IX.) =	381
		− 196
185	. . . .	185
7 | 185		
(26) 3 = Tuesday.	Coll. dur. (Art. 163) −	177
		8
		+ 1
		9

Answer.—Tuesday, Rajab 9th, A.H. 1311.

Perpetual Muhammadan Calendar.

By the kindness of Dr. J. Burgess we are able to publish the following perpetual Muhammadan Calendar, which is very simple and may be found of use. Where the week-day is known this Calendar gives a choice of four or five days in the month. But where it is not known it must be found, and in that case our own process will be the simpler, besides fixing the day exactly instead of merely giving a choice of several days.

PERPETUAL MUHAMMADAN CALENDAR.

For odd years.							Years A.H.						
							0	30	60	90	120	150	180
							210	240	270	300	330	360	390
							420	450	480	510	540	570	600
							630	660	690	720	750	780	810
							840	870	900	930	960	990	1020
							1050	1080	1110	1140	1170	1200	1230
							1260	1290	1320	1350	1380	1410	1440
							Dominical Letters.						
0	5*	8	13*		21*	29*	G	B	D	F	A	C	E
1		9		17		25	C	E	G	B	D	F	A
2*		10*		18*		26*	F	A	C	E	G	B	D
3		11	16*	19	24*	27	A	C	E	G	B	D	F
4		12		20		28	D	F	A	C	E	G	B
	6		14		22		B	D	F	A	C	E	G
	7*		15		23		E	G	B	D	F	A	C

Month							
1 Muharram . . . . 10 Shawwâl	A	G	F	E	D	C	B
2 Śafar . . . . 7 Rajab	C	B	A	G	F	E	D
3 Rabî'l-âwwal . . . . . . 12 Zî'l-ḥijjat	D	C	B	A	G	F	E
4 Rabî'l-âkhir . . . . . . 9 Ramaḍan	F	E	D	C	B	A	G
5 Jamâda-l-âwwal	G	F	E	D	C	B	A
6 Jamâda-l-âkhir . . . . . 11 Zî'l-ka'dat	B	A	G	F	E	D	C
8 Shaʻbân	E	D	C	B	A	G	F

1	8	15	22	29	Sun.	Mon.	Tues.	Wed.	Thur.	Fri.	Sat.
2	9	16	23	30	Mon.	Tues.	Wed.	Thur.	Fri.	Sat.	Sun.
3	10	17	24		Tues.	Wed.	Thur.	Fri.	Sat.	Sun.	Mon.
4	11	18	25		Wed.	Thur.	Fri.	Sat.	Sun.	Mon.	Tues.
5	12	19	26		Thur.	Fri.	Sat.	Sun.	Mon.	Tues.	Wed.
6	13	20	27		Fri.	Sat.	Sun.	Mon.	Tues.	Wed.	Thur.
7	14	21	28		Sat.	Sun	Mon.	Tues.	Wed.	Thur.	Fri.

From the Hijra date subtract the next greatest at the head of the first Table, and in that column find the Dominical letter corresponding to the remainder. In the second Table, with the Dominical letter opposite the given month, run down to the week-days, and on the left will be found the dates and vice versa.

EXAMPLE. For Ramaḍan, A.H. 1310. The nearest year above is 1290, difference 20; in the same column with 1290, and in line with 20, is F. In line with Ramaḍan and the column F we find Sunday 1st, 8th, 15th, 22nd, 29th, etc.

* In the 11 years marked with an asterisk the month Zî'l-ka'dat has 30 days; in all others 29. Thus A.H. 1306 (1290 + 16) had 355 days, the 30th of Zî'l-ka'dat being Sunday.

TABLES.

TABLE I.

Lunation-parts = 10,000*ths of a circle. A tithi* = $^1/_{30}$*th of the moon's synodic revolution.*

I. CONCURRENT YEAR.								II. ADDED LUNAR MONTHS.				
						Samvatsara.		True.				
Kali.	Śaka.	Chaitrâdi. Vikrama.	Meshâdi (Solar) year in Bengal.	Kollam.	A. D.	(Southern.)	Bṛihaspati cycle (Northern) current at Mesha saṅkrânti.	Name of month.	Time of the preceding saṅkrânti expressed in		Time of the succeeding saṅkrânti expressed in	
									Lunation parts. (*t.*)	Tithis.	Lunation parts. (*t.*)	Tithis.
1	2	3	3a	4	5	6	7	8	9	10	11	12
3402	223	358	—	—	*300- 1	....	47 Pramâdin..........	....	......	....	......	......
3403	224	359	—	—	301- 2	....	48 Ânanda............	7 Âśvina	9950	29.850	287	0.861
3404	225	360	—	—	302- 3	....	49 Râkshasa..........	....	......	....	......	......
3405	226	361	—	—	303- 4	....	50 Anala.............	....	......	....	......	......
3406	227	362	—	—	*304- 5	....	51 Piṅgala...........	5 Śrâvaṇa.....	9585	28.755	248	0.744
3407	228	363	—	—	305- 6	....	52 Kâlayukta.........	....	......	....	......	......
3408	229	364	—	—	306- 7	....	53 Siddhârthin.......	....	......	....	......	......
3409	230	365	—	—	307- 8	....	54 Raudra............	3 Jyeshṭha....	9442	28.326	152	0.456
3410	231	366	—	—	*308- 9	....	55 Durmati...........	....	......	....	......	......
3411	232	367	—	—	309-10	....	56 Dundubhi..........	....	......	....	......	......
3412	233	368	—	—	310-11	....	57 Rudhirodgârin.....	2 Vaiśâkha....	9781	29.343	321	0.963
3413	234	369	—	—	311-12	....	58 Raktâksha 1)......	....	......	....	......	......
3414	235	370	—	—	*312-13	....	60 Kshaya............	6 Bhâdrapada..	9767	29.301	374	1.122
3415	236	371	—	—	313-14	....	1 Prabhava...........	....	......	....	......	......
3416	237	372	—	—	314-15	....	2 Vibhava............	....	......	....	......	......
3417	238	373	—	—	315-16	....	3 Sukla..............	4 Âshâḍha....	9648	28.944	306	0.918
3418	239	374	—	—	*316-17	....	4 Pramoda............	....	......	....	......	......
3419	240	375	—	—	317-18	....	5 Prajâpati,.........	....	......	....	......	......
3420	241	376	—	—	318-19	....	6 Aṅgiras............	3 Jyeshṭha....	9861	29.583	648	1.944
3421	242	377	—	—	319-20	....	7 Śrîmukha...........	....	......	....	......	......
3422	243	378	—	—	*320-21	....	8 Bhâva..............	7 Âśvina	9919	29.757	312	0.936
3423	244	379	—	—	321-22	....	9 Yuvan..............	....	......	....	......	......
3424	245	380	—	—	322-23	....	10 Dhâtṛi............	....	......	....	......	......
3425	246	381	—	—	323-24	....	11 Îśvara............	5 Śrâvaṇa.....	9770	29.310	349	1.047
3426	247	382	—	—	*324-25	....	12 Bahudhânya........	....	......	....	......	......
3427	248	383	—	—	325-26	....	13 Pramâthin.........	....	......	....	......	......
3428	249	384	—	—	326-27	....	14 Vikrama...........	3 Jyeshṭha....	9409	28.227	186	0.558
3429	250	385	—	—	327-28	....	15 Vṛisha............	....	......	....	......	......
3430	251	386	—	—	*328-29	....	16 Chitrabhânu.......	....	......	....	......	......
3431	252	387	—	—	329-30	....	17 Subhânu...........	2 Vaiśâkha....	9897	29.691	348	1.044
3432	253	388	—	—	330-31	....	18 Târaṇa............	....	......	....	......	......
3433	254	389	—	—	331-32	....	19 Pârthiva..........	6 Bhâdrapada..	9835	29.505	360	1.080
3434	255	390	—	—	*332-33	....	20 Vyaya.............	....	......	....	......	......

1) Krodhana, No. 59, was suppressed.

TABLE I.

(Col. 23) a = Distance of moon from sun. (Col. 24) b = moon's mean anomaly. (Col. 25) c = sun's mean anomaly.

II. ADDED LUNAR MONTHS *(continued.)*					III. COMMENCEMENT OF THE													
Mean.					Solar year.						Luni-Solar year. (Civil day of Chaitra Śukla 1st.)							
	Time of the preceding saṅkrânti expressed in		Time of the succeeding saṅkrânti expressed in			(Time of the Mesha saṅkrânti.)							At Sunrise on meridian of Ujjain.					
							By the Ârya Siddhânta.						Moon's Age.					
Name of month.	Lunation parts. (*t.*)	Tithis.	Lunation parts. (*t.*)	Tithis.	Day and Month A. D.	Week day.	Gh.	Pa.	H.	M.	Day and Month A. D.	Week day.	Lunat. parts elapsed. (*t.*)	Tithis elapsed.	*a*	*b.*	*c.*	Kali.
8a	9a	10a	11a	12a	13	14	15		17		19	20	21	22	23	24	25	1
....	...	...	...	...	16 Mar. (76)	0 Sat.	37	30	15	0	8 Mar. (68)	6 Fri.	34	.102	9981	895	256	3402
10 Pausha.....	9980	29.940	287	0.862	16 Mar. (75)	1 Sun.	53	1	21	12	26 Feb. (57)	4 Wed.	199	.597	196	779	228	3403
....	...	...	...	...	17 Mar. (76)	3 Tues.	8	32	3	25	17 Mar. (76)	3 Tues.	235	.705	230	715	279	3404
....	...	...	...	...	17 Mar. (76)	4 Wed.	24	4	9	37	6 Mar. (65)	0 Sat.	192	.576	106	562	248	3405
6 Bhâdrapada..	9815	29.446	123	0.368	16 Mar. (76)	5 Thur.	39	35	15	50	23 Feb. (54)	4 Wed.	199	.597	9982	409	218	3406
....	...	...	...	...	16 Mar. (75)	6 Fri.	55	6	22	2	13 Mar. (72)	3 Tues.	272	.816	16	345	269	3407
....	...	...	...	...	17 Mar. (76)	1 Sun.	10	37	4	15	2 Mar. (61)	0 Sat.	163	.489	9892	192	238	3408
3 Jyeshṭha....	9958	29.874	265	0.796	17 Mar. (76)	2 Mon.	26	9	10	27	20 Feb. (51)	5 Thur.	314	.942	107	76	210	3409
....	...	...	...	...	16 Mar. (76)	3 Tues.	41	40	16	40	10 Mar. (70)	4 Wed.	292	.876	141	12	261	3410
11 Mâgha.....	9793	29.380	101	0.302	16 Mar. (75)	4 Wed.	57	11	22	52	27 Feb. (58)	1 Sun.	49	.147	17	859	230	3411
....	...	...	...	...	17 Mar. (76)	6 Fri.	12	42	5	5	17 Feb. (48)	6 Fri.	234	.702	231	743	202	3412
....	...	...	...	...	17 Mar. (76)	0 Sat.	28	14	11	17	8 Mar. (67)	5 Thur.	280	.840	266	678	254	3413
8 Kârttika....	9936	29.809	244	0.731	16 Mar. (76)	1 Sun.	43	45	17	30	25 Feb. (56)	2 Mon.	260	.780	142	526	223	3414
....	...	...	...	...	16 Mar. (75)	2 Mon.	59	16	23	42	14 Mar. (73)	0 Sat.	42	.126	9838	425	271	3415
....	...	...	...	...	17 Mar. (76)	4 Wed.	14	47	5	55	4 Mar. (63)	5 Thur.	322	.966	52	309	243	3416
4 Âshâḍha....	9772	29.315	79	0.237	17 Mar. (76)	5 Thur.	30	19	12	7	21 Feb. (52)	2 Mon.	186	.558	9928	156	213	3417
....	...	...	...	...	16 Mar. (76)	6 Fri.	45	50	18	20	11 Mar. (71)	1 Sun.	179	.537	9962	92	264	3418
....	...	...	...	...	17 Mar. (76)	1 Sun.	1	21	0	32	1 Mar. (60)	6 Fri.	296	.888	177	976	236	3419
1 Chaitra.....	9914	29.743	222	0.665	17 Mar. (76)	2 Mon.	16	52	6	45	18 Feb. (49)	3 Tues.	69	.207	52	823	205	3420
....	...	...	...	...	17 Mar. (76)	3 Tues.	32	24	12	57	9 Mar. (68)	2 Mon.	87	.261	87	759	256	3421
9 Mârgaśîrsha.	9750	29.249	57	0.171	16 Mar. (76)	4 Wed.	47	55	19	10	26 Feb. (57)	6 Fri.	17	.051	9963	606	225	3422
....	...	...	...	...	17 Mar. (76)	6 Fri.	3	26	1	22	16 Mar. (75)	5 Thur.	101	.303	9997	542	277	3423
....	...	...	...	...	17 Mar. (76)	0 Sat.	18	57	7	35	5 Mar. (64)	2 Mon.	104	.312	9873	389	246	3424
6 Bhâdrapada..	9893	29.678	200	0.600	17 Mar. (76)	1 Sun.	34	29	13	47	22 Feb. (53)	6 Fri.	31	.093	9749	236	215	3425
....	...	...	...	...	16 Mar. (76)	2 Mon.	50	0	20	0	12 Mar. (72)	5 Thur.	47	.141	9783	172	266	3426
....	...	...	...	...	17 Mar. (76)	4 Wed.	5	31	2	12	2 Mar. (61)	3 Tues.	187	.561	9998	56	238	3427
2 Vaiśâkha....	9728	29.184	35	0.106	17 Mar. (76)	5 Thur.	21	2	8	25	20 Feb. (51)	1 Sun.	302	.906	212	939	210	3428
....	...	...	...	...	17 Mar. (76)	6 Fri.	36	34	14	37	11 Mar. (70)	0 Sat.	288	.864	247	875	261	3429
11 Mâgha......	9871	29.612	178	0.534	16 Mar. (76)	0 Sat.	52	5	20	50	28 Feb. (59)	4 Wed.	124	.372	122	723	231	3430
....	...	...	...	...	17 Mar. (76)	2 Mon.	7	36	3	2	16 Feb. (47)	1 Sun.	81	.243	9998	570	200	3431
....	...	...	...	...	17 Mar. (76)	3 Tues.	23	7	9	15	7 Mar. (66)	0 Sat.	268	.804	33	506	251	3432
7 Aśvina......	9706	29.118	13	0.040	17 Mar. (76)	4 Wed.	38	39	15	27	24 Feb. (55)	4 Wed.	161	.483	9908	353	220	3433
....	...	...	...	...	16 Mar. (76)	5 Thur.	54	10	21	40	14 Mar. (74)	3 Tues.	219	.657	9943	289	272	3434

TABLE I.

Lunation-parts = 10,000ths of a circle. A tithi = 1/30th of the moon's synodic revolution.

I. CONCURRENT YEAR.								II. ADDED LUNAR MONTHS.				
						Samvatsara.		True.				
Kali.	Śaka.	Chaitrâdi. Vikrama.	Meshâdi (Solar) year in Bengal.	Kollam.	A. D.	(Southern.)	Bṛihaspati cycle (Northern) current at Mesha saṅkrânti.	Name of month.	Time of the preceding saṅkrânti expressed in: Lunation parts. (*t.*)	Tithis.	Time of the succeeding saṅkrânti expressed in: Lunation parts. (*t.*)	Tithis.
1	2	3	3a	4	5	6	7	8	9	10	11	12
3435	256	391	—	—	333-34	21 Sarvajit						
3436	257	392	—	—	334-35	22 Sarvadhârin		4 Âshâḍha	9718	29.154	474	1.422
3437	258	393	—	—	335-36	23 Virodhin						
3438	259	394	—	—	*336-37	24 Vikṛita						
3439	260	395	—	—	337-38	25 Khara		3 Jyeshṭha	9861	29.583	607	1.821
3440	261	396	—	—	338-39	26 Nandana						
3441	262	397	—	—	339-40	27 Vijaya		7 Âśvina	9888	29.664	275	0.825
3442	263	398	—	—	*340-41	28 Jaya						
3443	264	399	—	—	341-42	29 Manmatha						
3444	265	400	—	—	342-43	30 Durmukha		5 Śrâvaṇa	9957	29.871	532	1.596
3445	266	401	—	—	343-44	31 Hemalamba						
3446	267	402	—	—	*344-45	32 Vilamba						
3447	268	403	—	—	345-46	33 Vikârin		3 Jyeshṭha	9384	28.152	152	0.456
3448	269	404	—	—	346-47	34 Śârvari						
3449	270	405	—	—	347-48	35 Plava						
3450	271	406	—	—	*348-49	36 Śubhakṛit		1 Chaitra	9890	29.670	86	0.258
3451	272	407	—	—	349-50	37 Śobhana						
3452	273	408	—	—	350-51	38 Krodhin		6 Bhâdrapada	9998	29.994	438	1.314
3453	274	409	—	—	351-52	39 Viśvâvasu						
3454	275	410	—	—	*352-53	40 Parâbhava						
3455	276	411	—	—	353-54	41 Plavaṅga		4 Âshâḍha	9701	29.103	550	1.650
3456	277	412	—	—	354-55	42 Kîlaka						
3457	278	413	—	—	355-56	43 Saumya						
3458	279	414	—	—	*356-57	44 Sâdhâraṇa		3 Jyeshṭha	9956	29.868	603	1.809
3459	280	415	—	—	357-58	45 Virodhakṛit						
3460	281	416	—	—	358-59	46 Paridhâvin		7 Âśvina	9933	29.799	256	0.768
3461	282	417	—	—	359-60	47 Pramâdin						
3462	283	418	—	—	*360-61	48 Ânanda						
3463	284	419	—	—	361-62	49 Râkshasa		4 Ashâḍha	9245	27.735	67	0.201
3464	285	420	—	—	362-63	50 Anala						
3465	286	421	—	—	363-64	51 Piṅgala						
3466	287	422	—	—	*364-65	52 Kâlayukta		3 Jyeshṭha	9443	28.329	192	0.576
3467	288	423	—	—	365-66	53 Siddhârthin						

TABLE I.

(*Col.* 23) *a* = *Distance of moon from sun.* (*Col.* 24) *b* = *moon's mean anomaly.* (*Col.* 25) *c* = *sun's mean anomaly.*

II. ADDED LUNAR MONTHS (*continued.*)					III. COMMENCEMENT OF THE														
Mean.					Solar year.						Luni-Solar year. (Civil day of Chaitra Śukla 1st.)								
Name of month.	Time of the preceding saṅkrânti expressed in: Lunation parts. (*t.*)	Tithis.	Time of the succeeding saṅkrânti expressed in: Lunation parts. (*t.*)	Tithis.	Day and Month A. D.	(Time of the Mesha saṅkrânti.) Week day.	By the Ârya Siddhânta. Gh.	Pa	H.	M.	Day and Month A. D.	Week day.	At Sunrise on meridian of Ujjain. Moon's Age. Lunat. parts elapsed. (*t.*)	Tithis elapsed.	*a.*	*b.*	*c.*	Kali.	
8a	9a	10a	11a	12a	13	14	15		17		19	20	21	22	23	24	25	1	
....	....	....	....	....	17 Mar. (76)	0 Sat.	9	41	3	52	4 Mar. (63)	1 Sun.	321	.963	157	172	244	3435	
4 Âshâḍha....	9849	29.547	156	0.469	17 Mar. (76)	1 Sun.	25	12	10	5	21 Feb. (52)	5 Thur.	192	.579	33	20	213	3436	
....	....	....	....	....	17 Mar. (76)	2 Mon.	40	44	16	17	12 Mar. (71)	4 Wed.	170	.510	68	956	264	3437	
....	....	....	....	....	16 Mar. (76)	3 Tues.	56	15	22	30	1 Mar. (61)	2 Mon.	303	.909	282	839	236	3438	
1 Chaitra.....	9992	29.975	299	0.897	17 Mar. (76)	5 Thur.	11	46	4	42	18 Feb. (49)	6 Fri.	172	.516	158	686	205	3439	
....	....	....	....	....	17 Mar. (76)	6 Fri.	27	17	10	55	9 Mar. (68)	5 Thur.	235	.705	192	622	256	3440	
9 Mârgaśîrsha.	9827	29.481	134	0.403	17 Mar. (76)	0 Sat.	42	49	17	7	26 Feb. (57)	2 Mon.	236	.708	68	469	225	3441	
....	....	....	....	....	16 Mar. (76)	1 Sun.	58	20	23	20	16 Mar. (76)	1 Sun.	322	.966	103	406	277	3442	
....	....	....	....	....	17 Mar. (76)	3 Tues.	13	51	5	32	5 Mar. (64)	5 Thur.	259	.777	9979	253	246	3443	
6 Bhâdrapada..	9970	29.909	277	0.832	17 Mar. (76)	4 Wed.	29	22	11	45	22 Feb. (53)	2 Mon.	79	.237	9854	100	215	3444	
....	....	....	....	....	17 Mar. (76)	5 Thur.	44	54	17	57	13 Mar. (72)	1 Sun.	60	.180	9889	36	266	3445	
....	....	....	....	....	17 Mar. (77)	0 Sat.	0	25	0	10	2 Mar. (62)	6 Fri.	175	.525	103	920	239	3446	
2 Vaiśâkha....	9805	29.416	113	0.338	17 Mar. (76)	1 Sun.	15	56	6	22	20 Feb. (51)	4 Wed.	328	.984	318	803	210	3447	
....	....	....	....	....	17 Mar. (76)	2 Mon.	31	27	12	35	10 Mar. (69)	2 Mon.	20	.060	14	703	259	3448	
11 Mâgha......	9948	29.844	255	0.766	17 Mar. (76)	3 Tues.	46	59	18	47	28 Feb. (59)	0 Sat.	296	.888	228	586	231	3449	
....	....	....	....	....	17 Mar. (77)	5 Thur.	2	30	1	0	17 Feb. (48)	4 Wed.	304	.912	104	433	200	3450	
....	....	....	....	....	17 Mar. (76)	6 Fri.	18	1	7	12	6 Mar. (65)	2 Mon.	62	.186	9800	333	249	3451	
7 Âśvina......	9783	29.350	91	0.272	17 Mar. (76)	0 Sat.	33	32	13	25	24 Feb. (55)	0 Sat.	292	.876	14	217	221	3452	
....	....	....	....	....	17 Mar. (76)	1 Sun.	49	4	19	37	15 Mar. (74)	6 Fri.	303	.909	49	152	272	3453	
....	....	....	....	....	17 Mar. (77)	3 Tues.	4	35	1	50	3 Mar. (63)	3 Tues.	64	.192	9924	1000	241	3454	
4 Âshâḍha....	9926	29.778	234	0.701	17 Mar. (76)	4 Wed.	20	6	8	2	21 Feb. (52)	1 Sun.	187	.561	139	883	213	3455	
....	....	....	....	....	17 Mar. (76)	5 Thur.	35	37	14	15	12 Mar. (71)	0 Sat.	186	.558	173	819	264	3456	
12 Phâlguna....	9762	29.285	69	0.207	17 Mar. (76)	6 Fri.	51	9	20	27	1 Mar. (60)	4 Wed.	68	.204	49	666	234	3457	
....	....	....	....	....	17 Mar. (77)	1 Sun.	6	40	2	40	18 Feb. (49)	1 Sun.	55	.165	9925	514	202	3458	
....	....	....	....	....	17 Mar. (76)	2 Mon.	22	11	8	52	8 Mar. (67)	0 Sat.	144	.432	9960	450	254	3459	
9 Mârgaśîrsha.	9904	29.713	212	0.635	17 Mar. (76)	3 Tues.	37	42	15	5	25 Feb. (56)	4 Wed.	110	.330	9835	297	223	3460	
....	....	....	....	....	17 Mar. (76)	4 Wed.	53	14	21	17	16 Mar. (75)	3 Tues.	148	.444	9870	233	274	3461	
....	....	....	....	....	17 Mar. (77)	6 Fri.	8	45	3	30	5 Mar. (65)	1 Sun.	318	.954	83	116	246	3462	
5 Śrâvaṇa.....	9740	29.219	47	0.141	17 Mar. (76)	0 Sat.	24	16	9	42	22 Feb. (53)	5 Thur.	70	.210	9960	963	215	3463	
....	....	....	....	....	17 Mar. (76)	1 Sun.	39	47	15	55	13 Mar. (72)	4 Wed.	52	.156	9994	900	267	3464	
....	....	....	....	....	17 Mar. (76)	2 Mon.	55	19	22	7	3 Mar. (62)	2 Mon.	212	.636	209	783	239	3465	
2 Vaiśâkha....	9882	29.647	190	0.570	17 Mar. (77)	4 Wed.	10	50	4	20	20 Feb. (51)	6 Fri.	124	.372	84	630	208	3466	
....	....	....	....	....	17 Mar. (76)	5 Thur.	26	21	10	32	10 Mar. (69)	5 Thur.	202	.606	119	566	259	3467	

TABLE I.

Lunation-parts = 10,000ths of a circle. A tithi = 1/30th of the moon's synodic revolution.

I CONCURRENT YEAR.								II. ADDED LUNAR MONTHS.				
						Samvatsara.		True.				
Kali.	Śaka.	Chaitrâdi. Vikrama.	Meshâdi (Solar) year in Bengal.	Kollam.	A. D.	(Southern.)	Bṛihaspati cycle (Northern) current at Mesha saṅkrânti.	Name of month.	Time of the preceding saṅkrânti expressed in Lunation parts. (*l.*)	Time of the preceding saṅkrânti expressed in Tithis.	Time of the succeeding saṅkrânti expressed in Lunation parts. (*l.*)	Time of the succeeding saṅkrânti expressed in Tithis.
1	2	3	3a	4	5	6	7	8	9	10	11	12
3468	289	424	—	—	366-67	54 Raudra		12 Phâlguna	9914	29.742	16	0.048
3469	290	425	—	—	367-68	55 Durmati						
3470	291	426	—	—	*368-69	56 Dundubhi						
3471	292	427	—	—	369-70	57 Rudhirodgârin		5 Śrâvaṇa	9574	28.722	196	0.588
3472	293	428	—	—	370-71	58 Raktâksha						
3473	294	429	—	—	371-72	59 Krodhana						
3474	295	430	—	—	*372-73	60 Kshaya		4 Ashâḍha	9658	28.974	531	1.593
3475	296	431	—	—	373-74	1 Prabhava						
3476	297	432	—	—	374-75	2 Vibhava						
3477	298	433	—	—	375-76	3 Śukla		2 Vaiśâkha	9747	29.241	136	0.408
3478	299	434	—	—	*376-77	4 Pramoda						
3479	300	435	—	—	377-78	5 Prajâpati		6 Bhâdrapada	9663	28.989	77	0.231
3480	301	436	—	—	378-79	6 Aṅgiras						
3481	302	437	—	—	379-80	7 Śrîmukha						
3482	303	438	—	—	*380-81	8 Bhâva		4 Âshâḍha	9202	27.606	140	0.420
3483	304	439	—	—	381-82	9 Yuvan						
3484	305	440	—	—	382-83	10 Dhâtri						
3485	306	441	—	—	383-84	11 Îśvara		3 Jyeshṭha	9602	28.806	186	0.558
3486	307	442	—	—	*384-85	12 Bahudhânya						
3487	308	443	—	—	385-86	13 Pramâthin		12 Phâlguna	9895	29.685	41	0.123
3488	309	444	—	—	386-87	14 Vikrama						
3489	310	445	—	—	387-88	15 Vṛisha						
3490	311	446	—	—	*388-89	16 Chitrabhânu		5 Śravâṇa	9613	28.839	336	1.008
3491	312	447	—	—	389-90	17 Subhânu						
3492	313	448	—	—	390-91	18 Târaṇa						
3493	314	449	—	—	391-92	19 Pârthiva		4 Âshâḍha	9687	29.061	491	1.473
3494	315	450	—	—	*392-93	20 Vyaya						
3495	316	451	—	—	393-94	21 Sarvajit						
3496	317	452	—	—	394-95	22 Sarvadhârin		2 Vaiśâkha	9875	29.625	323	0.969
3497	318	453	—	—	395-96	23 Virodhin						
3498	319	454	—	—	*396-97	24 Vikṛita		6 Bhâdrapada	9831	29.493	270	0.810
3499	320	455	—	—	397-98	25 Khara [1]						
3500	321	456	—	—	398-99	27 Vijaya						

[1] Nandana, No. 26, was suppressed.

TABLE I.

(*Col.* 23) *a* = *Distance of moon from sun.* (*Col.* 24) *b* = *moon's mean anomaly.* (*Col.* 25) *c* = *sun's mean anomaly.*

II. ADDED LUNAR MONTHS (*continued.*)					III. COMMENCEMENT OF THE													
Mean.					Solar year.					Luni-Solar year. (Civil day of Chaitra Śukla 1st.)								
	Time of the preceding saṅkrânti expressed in		Time of the succeeding saṅkrânti expressed in			(Time of the Mesha saṅkrânti.)						At Sunrise on meridian of Ujjain.						
							By the Ârya Siddhânta.					Moon's Age.						
Name of month.	Lunation parts. (*t.*)	Tithis.	Lunation parts. (*t.*)	Tithis.	Day and Month A. D.	Week day.	Gh.	Pa.	H.	M.	Day and Month A. D.	Week day.	Lunat. parts elapsed. (*t.*)	Tithis elapsed.	*a.*	*b.*	*c.*	Kali.
8a	**9a**	**10a**	**11a**	**12a**	**13**	**14**	**15**		**17**		**19**	**20**	**21**	**22**	**23**	**24**	**25**	**1**
10 Pausha	9718	29.154	25	0.076	17 Mar. (76)	6 Fri.	41	52	16	45	27 Feb. (58)	2 Mon.	207	.621	9995	414	228	3468
...					17 Mar. (76)	0 Sat.	57	24	22	57	18 Mar. (77)	1 Sun.	284	.852	30	349	279	3469
...					17 Mar. (77)	2 Mon.	12	55	5	10	6 Mar. (66)	5 Thur.	177	.531	9905	197	249	3470
7 Aśvina	9861	29.582	168	0.504	17 Mar. (76)	3 Tues.	28	26	11	22	24 Feb. (55)	3 Tues.	329	.987	120	80	221	3471
...					17 Mar. (76)	4 Wed.	43	57	17	35	15 Mar. (74)	2 Mon.	308	.924	154	16	272	3472
...					17 Mar. (76)	5 Thur.	59	29	23	47	4 Mar. (63)	6 Fri.	64	.192	30	863	241	3473
3 Jyeshṭha	9696	29.088	3	0.010	17 Mar. (77)	0 Sat.	15	0	6	0	22 Feb. (53)	4 Wed.	246	.738	244	747	213	3474
...					17 Mar. (76)	1 Sun.	30	31	12	12	12 Mar. (71)	3 Tues.	291	.873	279	683	265	3475
12 Phâlguna	9839	29.517	146	0.439	17 Mar. (76)	2 Mon.	46	2	18	25	1 Mar. (60)	0 Sat.	269	.807	155	530	234	3476
...					18 Mar. (77)	4 Wed.	1	34	0	37	18 Feb. (49)	4 Wed.	271	.813	30	377	203	3477
...					17 Mar. (77)	5 Thur.	17	5	6	50	7 Mar. (67)	2 Mon.	3	.009	9726	277	252	3478
9 Mârgaśîrsha	9982	29.945	289	0.867	17 Mar. (76)	6 Fri.	32	36	13	2	25 Feb. (56)	0 Sat.	200	.600	9941	160	223	3479
...					17 Mar. (76)	0 Sat.	48	7	19	15	16 Mar. (75)	6 Fri.	197	.591	9975	97	275	3480
...					18 Mar. (77)	2 Mon.	3	39	1	27	6 Mar. (65)	4 Wed.	312	.936	190	980	246	3481
5 Śrâvaṇa	9817	29.451	124	0.373	17 Mar. (77)	3 Tues.	19	10	7	40	23 Feb. (54)	1 Sun.	82	.246	65	827	216	3482
...					17 Mar. (76)	4 Wed.	34	41	13	52	13 Mar. (72)	0 Sat.	100	.300	100	763	267	3483
...					17 Mar. (76)	5 Thur.	50	12	20	5	2 Mar. (61)	4 Wed.	26	.078	9976	610	236	3484
2 Vaiśâkha	9960	29.879	267	0.801	18 Mar. (77)	0 Sat.	5	44	2	17	19 Feb. (50)	1 Sun.	32	.096	9851	457	205	3485
...					17 Mar. (77)	1 Sun.	21	15	8	30	9 Mar. (69)	0 Sat.	113	.339	9886	394	257	3486
10 Pausha	9795	29.386	103	0.308	17 Mar. (79)	2 Mon.	36	46	14	42	26 Feb. (57)	4 Wed.	42	.126	9762	241	226	3487
...					17 Mar. (76)	3 Tues.	52	17	20	55	17 Mar. (76)	3 Tues.	63	.189	9796	177	277	3488
...					18 Mar. (77)	5 Thur.	7	49	3	7	7 Mar. (66)	1 Sun.	203	.609	11	60	249	3489
7 Aśvina	9938	29.814	245	0.736	17 Mar. (77)	6 Fri.	23	20	9	20	25 Feb. (56)	6 Fri.	317	.951	225	944	221	3490
...					17 Mar. (76)	0 Sat.	38	51	15	32	15 Mar. (74)	5 Thur.	304	.912	260	880	272	3491
...					17 Mar. (76)	1 Sun.	54	22	21	45	4 Mar. (63)	2 Mon.	138	.414	136	727	242	3492
3 Jyeshṭha	9773	29.320	81	0.242	18 Mar. (77)	3 Tues.	9	54	3	57	21 Feb. (52)	6 Fri.	90	.270	11	574	211	3493
...					17 Mar. (77)	4 Wed.	25	25	10	10	11 Mar. (71)	5 Thur.	177	.531	46	510	262	3494
12 Phâlguna	9916	29.748	223	0.670	17 Mar. (76)	5 Thur.	40	56	16	22	28 Feb. (59)	2 Mon.	172	.516	9922	357	231	3495
...					17 Mar. (76)	6 Fri.	56	27	22	35	17 Feb. (48)	6 Fri.	74	.222	9797	205	200	3496
...					18 Mar. (77)	1 Sun.	11	59	4	47	8 Mar. (67)	5 Thur.	80	.240	9832	140	252	3497
8 Kârttika	9752	29.255	59	0.177	17 Mar. (77)	2 Mon.	27	30	11	0	26 Feb. (57)	3 Tues.	208	.624	46	24	223	3498
...					17 Mar. (76)	3 Tues.	43	1	17	12	16 Mar. (75)	2 Mon.	187	.561	81	960	275	3499
...					17 Mar. (76)	4 Wed.	58	32	23	25	6 Mar. (65)	0 Sat.	319	.957	295	844	247	3500

TABLE I.

Lunation-parts = 10,000*ths of a circle. A tithi* = $^{1}/_{30}$*th of the moon's synodic revolution.*

I. CONCURRENT YEAR.								II. ADDED LUNAR MONTHS.				
						Samvatsara.		True.				
									Time of the preceding saṅkrânti expressed in		Time of the succeeding saṅkrânti expressed in	
Kali.	Śaka.	Chaitrâdi. Vikrama.	Meshâdi (Solar) year in Bengal.	Kollam.	A. D.	(Southern.)	Bṛihaspati cycle (Northern) current at Mesha saṅkrânti.	Name of month.	Lunation parts. (*t.*)	Tithis.	Lunation parts. (*t.*)	Tithis.
1	2	3	3a	4	5	6	7	8	9	10	11	12
3501	322	457	—	—	399-400	.... 28 Jaya		4 Âshâḍha	9199	27.597	34	0.102
3502	323	458	—	—	*400-401	.... 29 Manmatha		....	......	....	......	......
3503	324	459	—	—	401- 2	.... 30 Durmukha		....	......	....	......	......
3504	325	460	—	—	402- 3	.... 31 Hemalamba.........		3 Jyeshṭha	9777	29.331	343	1.029
3505	326	461	—	—	403- 4	.... 32 Vilamba		....	......	....	......	......
			—	—				8 Kârttika ...	9957	29.871	20	0.060
3506	327	462	—	—	*404- 5	.... 33 Vikârin...........		9 *Mârgaś.*(*Ksh.*)	20	0.060	9968	29.904
								12 Phâlguna....	9859	29.577	2	0.006
3507	328	463	—	—	405- 6	.... 34 Śârvari		....	......	....	......	......
3508	329	464			406- 7	.... 35 Plava..............		....	......	....	......	......
3509	330	465	—	—	407- 8	.... 36 Śubhakṛit..........		5 Śrâvaṇa.....	9586	28.758	374	1.122
3510	331	466	—	—	*408- 9	.... 37 Śobhana...........		....	......	....	......	......
3511	332	467	—	—	409- 10	.... 38 Krodhin		....	......	....	......	......
3512	333	468	—	—	410- 11	.... 39 Viśvâvasu..........		4 Âshâḍha	9813	29.439	515	1.545
3513	334	469	—	—	411- 12	.... 40 Parâbhava		....	......	....	......	......
3514	335	470	—	—	*412- 13	.... 41 Plavaṅga		....	......	....	......	......
3515	336	471	—	—	413- 14	.... 42 Kîlaka.............		2 Vaiśâkha....	9908	29.724	445	1.335
3516	337	472	—	—	414- 15	.... 43 Saumya............		....	......	....	......	......
3517	338	473	—	—	415- 16	.... 44 Sádhâraṇa..........		6 Bhâdrapada..	9911	29.733	434	1.302
3518	339	474	—	—	*416- 17	.... 45 Virodhakṛit.........		....	......	....	......	......
3519	340	475	—	—	417- 18	.... 46 Paridhâvin		....	......	....	......	......
3520	341	476	—	—	418- 19	.... 47 Pramâdin..........		4 Âshâḍha	9294	27.882	30	0.090
3521	342	477	—	—	419- 20	.... 48 Ânanda............		....	......	....	......	......
3522	343	478	—	—	*420- 21	.... 49 Râkshasa...........		....	......	....	......	......
3528	344	479	—	—	421- 22	.... 50 Anala		3 Jyeshṭha....	9949	29.847	542	1.626
3524	345	480	—	—	422- 23	.... 51 Piṅgala............		....	......	....	......	......
			—	—				7 Âśvina......	9920	29.760	154	0.462
3525	346	481	—	—	423- 24	.... 52 Kâlayukta..........		10 *Pausha* (*Ksh.*)	93	0.279	9955	29.865
3526	347	482			*424- 25	.... 53 Siddhârthin		1 Chaitra.....	9985	29.955	324	0.972
			—	—								
3527	348	483			425- 26	.... 54 Raudra		....	......	....	......	......
3528	349	484	—	—	426- 27	.... 55 Durmati............		5 Śrâvaṇa.....	9554	28.662	349	1.047
3529	350	485	—	—	427- 28	.... 56 Dundubhi...........		....	......	....	......	......
3530	351	486	—	—	*428- 29	.... 57 Rudhirodgârin		....	......	....	......	......

TABLE I.

(*Col.* 23) *a* = *Distance of moon from sun.* (*Col.* 24) *b* = *moon's mean anomaly.* (*Col.* 25) *c* = *sun's mean anomaly.*

II. ADDED LUNAR MONTHS (*continued.*)					III. COMMENCEMENT OF THE													
Mean.					Solar year.						Luni-Solar year. (Civil day of Chaitra Śukla 1st.)							
Name of month.	Time of the preceding saṅkrânti expressed in		Time of the succeeding saṅkrânti expressed in		Day and Month A. D.	(Time of the Mesha saṅkrânti.)					Day and Month A. D.	Week day.	At Sunrise on meridian of Ujjain.					Kali.
	Lunation parts. (*t.*)	Tithis.	Lunation parts. (*t.*)	Tithis.		Week day.	By the Ârya Siddhânta.						Moon's Age.		*a.*	*b.*	*c.*	
							Gh.	Pa.	H.	M.			Lunat. parts elapsed. (*t.*)	Tithis elapsed.				
8a	9a	10a	11a	12a	13	14	15	15	17	17	19	20	21	22	23	24	25	1
5 Śrâvaṇa.....	9894	29.683	202	0.605	18 Mar. (77)	6 Fri.	14	4	5	37	23 Feb. (54)	4 Wed.	182	.546	171	691	216	3501
....	....	....	....	......	17 Mar. (77)	0 Sat.	29	35	11	50	13 Mar. (73)	3 Tues.	246	.738	206	627	267	3502
....	....	....	....	......	17 Mar. (76)	1 Sun.	45	6	18	2	2 Mar. (61)	0 Sat.	246	.738	82	474	236	3503
1 Chaitra.....	9730	29.189	37	0.111	18 Mar. (77)	3 Tues.	0	37	0	15	19 Feb. (50)	4 Wed.	226	.678	9957	321	206	3504
....	....	....	....	......	18 Mar. (77)	4 Wed.	16	9	6	27	10 Mar. (69)	3 Tues.	272	.816	9992	257	257	3505
}10 Pausha....	9872	29.617	180	0.539	17 Mar. (77)	5 Thur.	31	40	12	40	27 Feb. (58)	0 Sat.	94	.282	9868	104	226	3506
....	....	....	....	......	17 Mar. (76)	6 Fri.	47	11	18	52	17 Mar. (76)	6 Fri.	78	.234	9902	40	277	3507
....	....	....	....	......	18 Mar. (77)	1 Sun.	2	42	1	5	7 Mar. (66)	4 Wed.	192	.576	117	924	249	3508
6 Bhâdrapada..	9708	29.124	15	0.046	18 Mar. (77)	2 Mon.	18	14	7	17	24 Feb. (55)	1 Sun.	⊙ −6	−.018	9992	771	219	3509
....	....	....	....	......	17 Mar. (77)	3 Tues.	33	45	13	30	14 Mar. (74)	0 Sat.	32	.096	27	707	270	3510
....	....	....	....	......	17 Mar. (76)	4 Wed.	49	16	19	42	4 Mar. (63)	5 Thur.	306	.918	241	590	242	3511
3 Jyeshṭha....	9851	29.552	158	0.474	18 Mar. (77)	6 Fri.	4	47	1	55	21 Feb. (52)	2 Mon.	313	.939	117	438	211	3512
....	....	....	....	......	18 Mar. (77)	0 Sat.	20	19	8	7	11 Mar. (70)	0 Sat.	73	.219	9813	337	260	3513
12 Phâlguna....	9993	29.980	301	0.902	17 Mar. (77)	1 Sun.	35	50	14	20	29 Feb. (60)	5 Thur.	304	.912	27	221	231	3514
....	....	....	....	......	17 Mar. (76)	2 Mon.	51	21	20	32	17 Feb. (48)	2 Mon.	104	.312	9903	68	201	3515
....	....	....	....	......	18 Mar. (77)	4 Wed.	6	52	2	45	8 Mar. (67)	1 Sun.	82	.246	9938	4	252	3516
8 Kârttika.....	9829	29.486	136	0.408	18 Mar. (77)	5 Thur.	22	14	8	57	26 Feb. (57)	6 Fri.	201	.606	152	887	224	3517
....	....	....	....	......	17 Mar. (77)	6 Fri.	37	55	15	10	16 Mar. (76)	5 Thur.	202	.606	187	824	275	3518
....	....	....	....	......	17 Mar. (76)	0 Sat.	53	26	21	22	5 Mar. (64)	2 Mon.	80	.240	63	671	244	3519
5 Śrâvaṇa.....	9972	29.915	279	0.837	18 Mar. (77)	2 Mon.	8	57	3	35	22 Feb. (53)	6 Fri.	64	.192	9938	518	213	3520
....	....	....	....	......	18 Mar. (77)	3 Tues.	24	29	9	47	13 Mar. (72)	5 Thur.	153	.459	9973	454	265	3521
....	....	....	....	......	17 Mar. (77)	4 Wed.	40	0	16	0	1 Mar. (61)	2 Mon.	122	.366	9849	301	234	3522
1 Chaitra.....	9807	29.421	114	0.343	17 Mar. (76)	5 Thur.	55	31	22	12	18 Feb. (49)	6 Fri.	⊙−21	−.063	9724	148	203	3523
....	....	....	....	......	18 Mar. (77)	0 Sat.	11	2	4	25	9 Mar. (68)	5 Thur.	⊙−30	−.090	9759	84	255	3524
}10 Pausha....	9950	29.849	257	0.771	18 Mar. (77)	1 Sun.	26	34	10	37	27 Feb. (58)	3 Tues.	85	.255	9973	968	226	3525
....	....	....	....	......	17 Mar. (77)	2 Mon.	42	5	16	50	17 Feb. (48)	1 Sun.	219	.657	188	851	198	3526
....	....	....	....	......	17 Mar. (76)	3 Tues.	57	36	23	2	7 Mar. (66)	0 Sat.	226	.678	222	787	250	3527
6 Bhâdrapada..	9785	29.355	93	0.278	18 Mar. (77)	5 Thur.	13	7	5	15	24 Feb. (55)	4 Wed.	134	.402	98	635	219	3528
....	....	....	....	......	18 Mar. (77)	6 Fri.	28	39	11	27	15 Mar (74)	3 Tues.	213	.639	133	570	270	3529
....	....	....	....	......	17 Mar. (77)	0 Sat.	44	10	17	40	3 Mar. (63)	0 Sat.	217	.651	8	418	239	3530

⊙ See Text. Art. 101 above, para. 2.

TABLE I.

Lunation-parts = 10,000ths of a circle. A tithi = 1/30th of the moon's synodic revolution.

I. CONCURRENT YEAR.								II. ADDED LUNAR MONTHS.				
						Samvatsara.		True.				
Kali.	Śaka.	Chaitrâdi. Vikrama.	Meshâdi (Solar) year in Bengal.	Kollam.	A. D.	(Southern.)	Bṛihaspati cycle (Northern) current at Mesha saṅkrânti.	Name of month.	Time of the preceding saṅkrânti expressed in Lunation parts. (t.)	Tithis.	Time of the succeeding saṅkrânti expressed in Lunation parts. (t.)	Tithis.
1	2	3	3a	4	5	6	7	8	9	10	11	12
3531	352	487	—	—	429-30	58 Raktâksha		3 Jyeshṭha	9440	28.320	8	0.024
3532	353	488	—	—	430-31	59 Krodhana						
3533	354	489	—	—	431-32	60 Kshaya						
3534	355	490	—	—	*432-33	1 Prabhava		2 Vaiśâkha	9870	29.610	462	1.386
3535	356	491	—	—	433-34	2 Vibhava						
3536	357	492	—	—	434-35	3 Śukla		6 Bhâdrapada	9895	29.685	502	1.506
3537	358	493	—	—	435-36	4 Pramoda						
3538	359	494	—	—	*436-37	5 Prajâpati						
3539	360	495	—	—	437-38	6 Aṅgiras		4 Ashâḍha	9475	28.425	118	0.354
3540	361	496	—	—	438-39	7 Śrîmukha						
3541	362	497	—	—	439-40	8 Bhâva						
3542	363	498	—	—	*440-41	9 Yuvan		3 Jyeshṭha	9998	29.994	689	2.067
3543	364	499	—	—	441-42	10 Dhâtṛi						
3544	365	500	—	—	442-43	11 Îśvara		6 Bhâdrapada	9440	28.320	22	0.066
3545	366	501	—	—	443-44	12 Bahudhânya						
3546	367	502	—	—	*444-45	13 Pramâthin						
3547	368	503	—	—	445-46	14 Vikrama		5 Śrâvaṇa	9608	28.824	319	0.957
3548	369	504	—	—	446-47	15 Vṛisha						
3549	370	505	—	—	447-48	16 Chitrabhânu						
3550	371	506	—	—	*448-49	17 Subhânu		3 Jyeshṭha	9524	28.572	182	0.546
3551	372	507	—	—	449-50	18 Târaṇa						
3552	373	508	—	—	450-51	19 Pârthiva						
3553	374	509	—	—	451-52	20 Vyaya		2 Vaiśâkha	9847	29.541	423	1.269
3554	375	510	—	—	*452-53	21 Sarvajit						
3555	376	511	—	—	453-54	22 Sarvadhârin		6 Bhâdrapada	9858	29.574	485	1.455
3556	377	512	—	—	454-55	23 Virodhin						
3557	378	513	—	—	455-56	24 Vikṛita						
3558	379	514	—	—	*456-57	25 Khara		4 Âshâḍha	9663	28.989	291	0.873
3559	380	515	—	—	457-58	26 Nandana						
3560	381	516	—	—	458-59	27 Vijaya						
3561	382	517	—	—	459-60	28 Jaya		3 Jyeshṭha	9670	29.010	674	2.022
3562	383	518	—	—	*460-61	29 Manmatha						
3563	384	519	—	—	461-62	30 Durmukha		6 Bhâdrapada	9398	28.194	28	0.084

TABLE I.

(*Col.* 23) *a* = *Distance of moon from sun.* (*Col.* 24) *b* = *moon's mean anomaly.* (*Col.* 25) *c* = *sun's mean anomaly.*

II. ADDED LUNAR MONTHS (*continued.*)					III. COMMENCEMENT OF THE													
Mean.					Solar year.						Luni-Solar year. (Civil day of Chaitra Śukla 1st.)							
	Time of the preceding saṅkrânti expressed in		Time of the succeeding saṅkrânti expressed in			(Time of the Mesha saṅkrânti.)							At Sunrise on meridian of Ujjain.					
							By the Arya Siddhânta.						Moon's Age.					
Name of month.	Lunation parts. (*t.*)	Tithis.	Lunation parts. (*t.*)	Tithis.	Day and Month A. D.	Week day.	Gh.	Pa.	H.	M.	Day and Month A. D.	Week day.	Lunat. parts elapsed. (*t.*)	Tithis elapsed.	*a.*	*b.*	*c.*	Kali.
8a	9a	10a	11a	12a	13	14	15		17		19	20	21	22	23	24	25	1
3 Jyeshṭha....	9928	29.784	235	0.706	17 Mar. (76)	1 Sun.	59	41	23	52	20 Feb. (51)	4 Wed.	166	.498	9884	265	208	3531
....	....	....	....	......	18 Mar. (77)	3 Tues.	15	12	6	5	11 Mar. (70)	3 Tues.	192	.576	9919	201	260	3532
11 Mâgha......	9763	29.290	71	0.212	18 Mar. (77)	4 Wed.	30	44	12	17	28 Feb. (59)	0 Sat.	⊙−24	−.072	9794	48	229	3533
....	....	....	....	......	17 Mar. (77)	5 Thur.	46	15	18	30	18 Feb. (49)	5 Thur.	93	.279	8	932	201	3534
....	....	....	....	......	18 Mar. (77)	0 Sat.	1	46	0	42	8 Mar. (67)	4 Wed.	79	.237	43	868	252	3535
8 Kârttika....	9906	29.718	213	0.640	18 Mar. (77)	1 Sun.	17	17	6	55	26 Feb. (57)	2 Mon.	258	.774	257	751	224	3536
....	....	....	....	......	18 Mar. (77)	2 Mon.	32	49	13	7	17 Mar. (76)	1 Sun.	304	.912	292	687	275	3537
....	....	....	....	......	17 Mar. (77)	3 Tues.	48	20	19	20	5 Mar. (65)	5 Thur	278	.834	168	534	245	3538
4 Âshâḍha....	9741	29.224	49	0.147	18 Mar. (77)	5 Thur.	3	51	1	32	22 Feb. (53)	2 Mon.	281	.843	44	381	214	3539
....	....	....	....	......	18 Mar. (77)	6 Fri.	19	22	7	45	12 Mar. (71)	0 Sat.	17	.051	9740	281	262	3540
....	....	....	....	......	18 Mar. (77)	0 Sat.	34	54	13	57	2 Mar. (61)	5 Thur.	214	.642	9954	165	234	3541
1 Chaitra.....	9884	29.653	192	0.575	17 Mar. (77)	1 Sun.	50	25	20	10	19 Feb. (50)	2 Mon.	⊙−16	−.048	9830	12	203	3542
....	....	....	....	......	18 Mar. (77)	3 Tues.	5	56	2	22	10 Mar. (69)	2 Mon.	329	987	203	984	257	3543
9 Margaśîrsha..	9720	29.159	27	0.081	18 Mar. (77)	4 Wed.	21	27	8	35	27 Feb. (58)	6 Fri.	97	.291	79	832	227	3544
....	....	....	....	......	18 Mar. (77)	5 Thur.	36	59	14	47	18 Mar. (77)	5 Thur.	115	.345	113	767	278	3545
....	....	....	....	......	17 Mar. (77)	6 Fri.	52	30	21	0	6 Mar. (66)	2 Mon.	36	.108	9989	615	247	3546
6 Bhâdrapada..	9862	29.587	170	0.509	18 Mar. (77)	1 Sun.	8	1	3	12	23 Feb. (54)	6 Fri.	39	.117	9865	462	216	3547
....	....	....	....	......	18 Mar. (77)	2 Mon.	23	32	9	25	14 Mar (73)	5 Thur.	124	.372	9900	398	268	3548
....	....	....	....	......	18 Mar. (77)	3 Tues.	39	4	15	37	3 Mar. (62)	2 Mon.	55	.165	9775	245	237	3549
2 Vaiśâkha....	9698	29.093	5	0.016	17 Mar. (77)	4 Wed.	54	35	21	50	21 Feb. (52)	0 Sat.	232	.696	9989	129	209	3550
....	....	....	....	......	18 Mar. (77)	6 Fri.	10	6	4	2	11 Mar. (70)	6 Fri.	219	.657	24	64	260	3551
11 Mâgha......	9841	29.522	148	0.444	18 Mar. (77)	0 Sat.	25	37	10	15	1 Mar. (60)	4 Wed.	332	.996	238	948	232	3552
....	....	....	....	......	18 Mar. (77)	1 Sun.	41	9	16	27	18 Feb. (49)	1 Sun.	122	.366	114	795	201	3553
....	....	....	....	......	17 Mar. (77)	2 Mon.	56	40	22	40	8 Mar. (68)	0 Sat.	150	.450	149	731	252	3554
8 Kârttika....	9983	29.950	291	0.872	18 Mar. (77)	4 Wed.	12	11	4	52	25 Feb. (56)	4 Wed.	99	.297	24	578	221	3555
....	....	....	....	......	18 Mar. (77)	5 Thur.	27	42	11	5	16 Mar. (75)	3 Tues.	186	.558	59	515	274	3556
....	....	....	....	......	18 Mar. (77)	6 Fri.	43	14	17	17	5 Mar. (64)	0 Sat.	182	.546	9935	361	242	3557
4 Âshâḍha....	9819	29.456	126	0.378	17 Mar. (77)	0 Sat.	58	45	23	30	22 Feb. (53)	4 Wed.	89	.267	9811	209	211	3558
....	....	....	....	......	18 Mar. (77)	2 Mon.	14	16	5	42	12 Mar. (71)	3 Tues.	96	.288	9845	145	262	3559
....	....	....	....	......	18 Mar. (77)	3 Tues.	29	47	11	55	2 Mar. (61)	1 Sun.	224	.672	60	28	234	3560
1 Chaitra.....	9962	29.885	269	0.807	18 Mar. (77)	4 Wed.	45	19	18	7	19 Feb. (50)	5 Thur.	⊙−21	−.063	9935	875	204	3561
....	....	....	....	......	18 Mar. (78)	6 Fri.	0	50	0	20	9 Mar. (69)	4 Wed.	⊙−19	−.057	9970	812	255	3562
9 Mârgaśîrsha..	9797	29.391	104	0.313	18 Mar. (77)	0 Sat.	16	21	6	32	27 Feb. (58)	2 Mon.	194	.582	185	695	227	3563

⊙ See Text. Art. 101 above, para. 2.

TABLE I.

Lunation-parts = 10,000*ths of a circle. A tithi* = $^1/_{30}$*th of the moon's synodic revolution.*

I. CONCURRENT YEAR.								II. ADDED LUNAR MONTHS.				
						Samvatsara.		True.				
Kali.	Śaka.	Chaitrâdi. Vikrama.	Meshâdi (Solar) year in Bengal.	Kollam.	A. D.	(Southern.)	Bṛihaspati cycle (Northern) current at Mesha saṅkrânti.	Name of month.	Time of the preceding saṅkrânti expressed in Lunation parts. (t.)	Time of the preceding saṅkrânti expressed in Tithis.	Time of the succeeding saṅkrânti expressed in Lunation parts. (t.)	Time of the succeeding saṅkrânti expressed in Tithis.
1	2	3	3a	4	5	6	7	8	9	10	11	12
3564	385	520	—	—	462-63	31 Hemalamba						
3565	386	521	—	—	463-64	32 Vilamba						
3566	387	522	—	—	*464-65	33 Vikârin		5 Śrâvaṇa	9758	29.274	371	1.113
3567	388	523	—	—	465-66	34 Śârvari						
3568	389	524	—	—	466-67	35 Plava						
3569	390	525	—	—	467-68	36 Śubhakṛit		3 Jyeshṭha	9518	28.554	268	0.804
3570	391	526	—	—	*468-69	37 Śobhana						
3571	392	527	—	—	469-70	38 Krodhin						
3572	393	528	—	—	470-71	39 Viśvâvasu		2 Vaiśâkha	9914	29.742	409	1.227
3573	394	529	—	—	471-72	40 Parâbhava						
3574	395	530	—	—	*472-73	41 Plavaṅga		6 Bhâdrapada	9876	29.628	443	1.329
3575	396	531	—	—	473-74	42 Kîlaka						
3576	397	532	—	—	474-75	43 Saumya						
3577	398	533	—	—	475-76	44 Sâdhâraṇa		4 Âshâḍha	9783	29.349	482	1.446
3578	399	534	—	—	*476-77	45 Virodhakṛit						
3579	400	535	—	—	477-78	46 Paridhâvin						
3580	401	536	—	—	478-79	47 Pramâdin		3 Jyeshṭha	9937	29.811	712	2.136
3581	402	537	—	—	479-80	48 Ananda						
3882	403	538	—	—	*480-81	49 Râkshasa		7 Âśvina	9984	29.952	385	1.155
3583	404	539	—	—	481-82	50 Anala						
3584	405	540	—	—	482-83	51 Piṅgala [1])						
3585	406	541	—	—	483-84	53 Siddhârthin		5 Śrâvaṇa	9953	29.859	521	1.563
3586	407	542	—	—	*484-85	54 Raudra						
3587	408	543	—	—	485-86	55 Durmati						
3588	409	544	—	—	486-87	56 Dundubhi		3 Jyeshṭha	9476	28.428	261	0.783
3589	410	545	—	—	487-88	57 Rudhirodgârin						
3590	411	546	—	—	*488-89	58 Raktâksha		8 Kârttika 10 *Pausha* (*Ksh.*)	9928 64	29.784 0.192	86 9950	0.258 29.850
3591	412	547	—	—	489-90	59 Krodhana		1 Chaitra	9887	29.661	73	0.219
3592	413	548	—	—	490-91	60 Kshaya						
3893	414	549	—	—	491-92	1 Prabhava		6 Bhâdrapada	9993	29.979	472	1.416
3594	415	550	—	—	*492-93	2 Vibhava						
3595	416	551	—	—	493-94	3 Śukla						

1) Kâlayukta, No. 52, was suppressed.

TABLE I.

(Col. 23) a = Distance of moon from sun. (Col. 24) b = moon's mean anomaly. (Col. 25) c = sun's mean anomaly.

II. ADDED LUNAR MONTHS (continued.)					III. COMMENCEMENT OF THE													
Mean.					Solar year.						Luni-Solar year. (Civil day of Chaitra Śukla 1st.)							Kali.
Name of month.	Time of the preceding saṅkrânti expressed in		Time of the succeeding saṅkrânti expressed in		Day and Month A. D.	(Time of the Mesha saṅkrânti.)					Day and Month A. D.	Week day.	At Sunrise on meridian of Ujjain.					
						Week day.	By the Ârya Siddhânta.						Moon's Age.		a.	b.	c.	
	Lunation parts. (*l.*)	Tithis.	Lunation parts. (*l.*)	Tithis.			Gh.	Pa.	H.	M.			Lunat. parts elapsed. (*l.*)	Tithis elapsed.				
8a	9a	10a	11a	12a	13	14	15		17		19	20	21	22	23	24	25	1
....	...	......	...	......	18 Mar. (77)	1 Sun.	31	52	12	45	18 Mar. (77)	1 Sun.	257	.771	219	631	278	3564
....	...	......	...	......	18 Mar. (77)	2 Mon.	47	24	18	57	7 Mar. (66)	5 Thur.	255	.765	95	478	247	3565
6 Bhâdrapada..	9940	29.819	247	0.741	18 Mar. (78)	4 Wed.	2	55	1	10	24 Feb. (55)	2 Mon.	235	.705	9970	326	216	3566
....	...	......	...	......	18 Mar. (77)	5 Thur.	18	26	7	22	14 Mar. (73)	1 Sun.	285	.855	5	261	268	3567
....	...	......	...	......	18 Mar. (77)	6 Fri.	33	57	13	35	3 Mar. (62)	5 Thur.	110	.330	9881	109	237	3568
2 Vaiśâkha....	9775	29.325	82	0.247	18 Mar. (77)	0 Sat.	49	29	19	47	21 Feb. (52)	3 Tues.	230	.690	95	992	209	3569
....	...	......	...	......	18 Mar. (78)	2 Mon.	5	0	2	0	11 Mar. (71)	2 Mon.	208	.624	130	928	260	3570
11 Mâgha......	9918	29.754	225	0.676	18 Mar. (77)	3 Tues.	20	31	8	12	28 Feb. (59)	6 Fri.	7	.021	5	775	229	3571
....	...	......	...	......	18 Mar. (77)	4 Wed.	36	2	14	25	18 Feb. (49)	4 Wed.	246	.738	220	659	201	3572
....	...	......	...	......	18 Mar. (77)	5 Thur.	51	34	20	37	8 Mar. (67)	2 Mon.	6	.018	9916	558	250	3573
7 Âśvina......	9753	29.260	61	0.182	18 Mar. (78)	0 Sat.	7	5	2	50	26 Feb. (57)	0 Sat.	321	.963	130	442	222	3574
....	...	......	...	......	18 Mar. (77)	1 Sun.	22	36	9	2	15 Mar. (74)	5 Thur.	83	.249	9826	342	270	3575
....	...	......	...	......	18 Mar. (77)	2 Mon.	38	7	15	15	5 Mar. (64)	3 Tues.	319	.957	41	225	242	3576
4 Ashâḍha....	9896	29.688	203	0.610	18 Mar. (77)	3 Tues.	53	39	21	27	22 Feb. (53)	0 Sat.	120	.360	9916	72	211	3577
....	...	......	...	......	18 Mar. (78)	5 Thur.	9	10	3	40	12 Mar. (72)	6 Fri.	99	.297	9951	9	263	3578
12 Phâlguna....	9731	29.194	39	0.116	18 Mar. (77)	6 Fri.	24	41	9	52	2 Mar. (61)	4 Wed.	216	.648	165	892	235	3579
....	...	......	...	......	18 Mar. (77)	0 Sat.	40	12	16	5	19 Feb. (50)	1 Sun.	44	.132	41	739	204	3580
....	...	......	...	......	18 Mar. (77)	1 Sun.	55	44	22	17	10 Mar. (69)	0 Sat.	91	273	76	675	255	3581
9 Mârgaśîrsha.	9874	29.623	182	0.545	18 Mar. (78)	3 Tues.	11	15	4	30	27 Feb. (58)	4 Wed.	71	.213	9951	522	224	3582
....	...	......	...	......	18 Mar. (77)	4 Wed.	26	46	10	42	17 Mar. (76)	3 Tues.	164	.492	9986	458	276	3583
....	...	......	...	......	18 Mar. (77)	5 Thur.	42	17	16	55	6 Mar. (65)	0 Sat.	132	.396	9861	306	245	3584
5 Śrâvaṇa.....	9710	29.129	17	0.051	18 Mar. (77)	6 Fri.	57	49	23	7	23 Feb. (54)	4 Wed.	⊙ −7	−.021	9737	153	214	3585
....	...	......	...	......	18 Mar. (78)	1 Sun.	13	20	5	20	13 Mar. (73)	3 Tues.	⊙ −14	−.042	9772	89	265	3586
....	...	......	...	......	18 Mar. (77)	2 Mon.	28	51	11	32	3 Mar. (62)	1 Sun.	102	.306	9986	972	237	3587
2 Vaiśâkha....	9853	29.557	160	0.479	18 Mar. (77)	3 Tues.	44	22	17	45	21 Feb. (52)	6 Fri.	233	.699	201	856	209	3588
....	...	......	...	......	18 Mar. (77)	4 Wed.	59	54	23	57	12 Mar. (71)	5 Thur.	239	.717	235	792	260	3589
} 11 Mâgha.....	9995	29.985	303	0.908	18 Mar. (78)	6 Fri.	15	25	6	10	29 Feb. (60)	2 Mon.	144	.432	111	639	230	3590
....	...	......	...	......	18 Mar. (77)	0 Sat.	30	56	12	22	17 Feb. (48)	6 Fri.	143	.429	9987	486	199	3591
....	...	......	...	......	18 Mar. (77)	1 Sun.	46	27	18	35	8 Mar. (67)	5 Thur.	227	.681	21	422	250	3592
7 Aśvina......	9831	29.492	138	0.414	19 Mar. (78)	3 Tues.	1	59	0	47	25 Feb. (56)	2 Mon.	177	.531	9897	269	219	3593
....	...	......	...	......	18 Mar. (78)	4 Wed.	17	30	7	0	15 Mar. (75)	1 Sun.	207	.621	9932	205	271	3594
....	...	......	...	......	18 Mar. (77)	5 Thur.	33	1	13	12	4 Mar. (63)	5 Thur.	⊙ −7	−.021	9807	52	240	3595

⊙ See Text. Art. 101 above, para. 2.

TABLE I.

Lunation-parts = 10,000*ths of a circle. A tithi* = 1/30*th of the moon's synodic revolution.*

I. CONCURRENT YEAR.								II. ADDED LUNAR MONTHS.				
						Samvatsara.		True.				
Kali.	Śaka.	Chaitrâdi. Vikrama.	Meshâdi (Solar) year in Bengal.	Kollam.	A. D.	(Southern.)	Bṛihaspati cycle (Northern) current at Mesha saṅkrânti.	Name of month.	Time of the preceding saṅkrânti expressed in: Lunation parts. (*t.*)	Time of the preceding saṅkrânti expressed in: Tithis.	Time of the succeeding saṅkrânti expressed in: Lunation parts. (*t.*)	Time of the succeeding saṅkrânti expressed in: Tithis.
1	2	3	3a	4	5	6	7	8	9	10	11	12
3596	417	552	—	—	494- 95	......	4 Pramoda...........	4 Âshâḍha....	9803	29.409	610	1.830
3597	418	553	—	—	495- 96	......	5 Prajâpati	....	......	......	......	......
3598	419	554	—	—	*496- 97	......	6 Aṅgiras..........	....	......	......	......	......
3599	420	555	—	—	497- 98	......	7 Srîmukha..........	3 Jyeshṭha....	9982	29.946	681	2.043
3600	421	556	—	—	498- 99	......	8 Bhâva...........	....	......	......	......	......
3601	422	557	—	—	499-500	......	9 Yuvan............	7 Âśvina.....	9988	29.964	348	1.044
3602	423	558	—	—	*500- 1	......	10 Dhâtṛi	....	......	......	......	......
3603	424	559	—	—	501- 2	......	11 Îśvara............	....	......	......	......	......
3604	425	560	—	—	502- 3	......	12 Bahudhânya..	4 Âshâḍha....	9336	28.008	109	0.327
3605	426	561	—	—	503- 4	......	13 Pramâthin.........	....	......	......	......	......
3606	427	562	—	—	*504- 5	......	14 Vikrama..........	....	......	......	......	......
3607	428	563	—	—	505- 6	......	15 Vṛisha............	3 Jyeshṭha....	9487	28.461	219	0.657
3608	429	564	—	—	506- 7	......	16 Chitrabhânu........	....	......	......	......	......
3609	430	565	—	—	507- 8	......	17 Subhânu...........	12 Phâlguna....	9983	29.949	52	0.156
3610	431	566	—	—	*508- 9	......	18 Târaṇa...........	....	......	......	......	......
3611	432	567	—	—	509- 10	......	19 Pârthiva..........	....	......	......	......	......
3612	433	568	—	—	510- 11	......	20 Vyaya............	5 Śrâvaṇa.....	9597	28.791	184	0.552
3613	434	569	—	—	511- 12	......	21 Sarvajit	....	......	......	......	......
3614	435	570	—	—	*512- 13	......	22 Sarvadhârin	....	......	......	......	......
3615	436	571	—	—	513- 14	......	23 Virodhin	4 Âshâḍha....	9764	29.292	635	1.905
3616	437	572	—	—	514- 15	......	24 Vikṛita...........	....	......	......	......	......
3617	438	573	—	—	515- 16	......	25 Khara............	....	......	......	......	......
3618	439	574	—	—	*516- 17	......	26 Nandana...........	2 Vaiśâkha....	9737	29.211	122	0.366
3619	440	575	—	—	517- 18	......	27 Vijaya............	....	......	......	......	......
3620	441	576	—	—	518- 19	......	28 Jaya...............	6 Bhâdrapada..	9648	28.944	78	0.234
3621	442	577	—	—	519- 20	......	29 Manmatha.........	....	......	......	......	......
3622	443	578	—	—	*520- 21	......	30 Durmukha.........	....	......	......	......	......
3623	444	579	—	—	521- 22	......	31 Hemalamba.........	4 Ashâḍha....	9310	27.930	167	0.501
3624	445	580	—	—	522- 23	......	32 Vilamba..........	....	......	......	......	......
3625	446	581	—	—	523- 24	......	33 Vikârin...........	....	......	......	......	......
3626	447	582	—	—	*524- 25	......	34 Śârvari............	3 Jyeshṭha....	9598	28.794	229	0.687
3627	448	583	—	—	525- 26	......	35 Plava.............	....	......	......	......	......

TABLE I.

(*Col.* 23) *a* = *Distance of moon from sun.* (*Col.* 24) *b* = *moon's mean anomaly.* (*Col.* 25) *c* = *sun's mean anomaly.*

II. ADDED LUNAR MONTHS (*continued.*)					III. COMMENCEMENT OF THE													
Mean.					Solar year.						Luni-Solar year. (Civil day of Chaitra Śukla 1st.)							Kali.
Name of month.	Time of the preceding saṅkrânti expressed in: Lunation parts. (*t.*)	Tithis.	Time of the succeeding saṅkrânti expressed in: Lunation parts. (*t.*)	Tithis.	Day and Month A. D.	(Time of the Mesha saṅkrânti.) Week day.	By the Ârya Siddhânta. Gh.	Pa.	H.	M.	Day and Month A. D.	Week day.	At Sunrise on meridian of Ujjain. Moon's Age. Lunat. parts elapsed. (*t.*)	Tithis elapsed.	*a.*	*b.*	*c.*	
8a	9a	10a	11a	12a	13	14	15		17		19	20	21	22	23	24	25	1
4 Âshâḍha....	9973	29.920	281	0.842	18 Mar. (77)	6 Fri.	48	32	19	25	22 Feb. (53)	3 Tues.	109	.327	22	936	212	3596
....	...	......	...	......	19 Mar. (78)	1 Sun.	4	4	1	37	13 Mar. (72)	2 Mon.	96	.288	57	872	263	3597
12 Phâlguna....	9809	29.426	116	0.348	18 Mar. (78)	2 Mon.	19	35	7	50	2 Mar. (62)	0 Sat.	271	.813	271	756	235	3598
....	...	......	...	......	18 Mar. (77)	3 Tues.	35	6	14	2	19 Feb. (50)	4 Wed.	206	.618	147	603	204	3599
....	...	......	...	......	18 Mar. (77)	4 Wed.	50	37	20	15	10 Mar. (69)	3 Tues.	287	.861	181	539	255	3600
9 Mârgaśirsha..	9951	29.854	259	0.777	19 Mar. (78)	6 Fri.	6	9	2	27	27 Feb. (58)	0 Sat.	289	.867	57	386	225	3601
....	...	......	...	......	18 Mar. (78)	0 Sat.	21	40	8	40	16 Mar. (76)	5 Thur.	29	.087	9753	286	273	3602
....	...	......	...	......	18 Mar. (77)	1 Sun.	37	11	14	52	6 Mar. (65)	3 Tues.	229	.687	9967	169	245	3603
5 Śrâvaṇa.....	9787	29.361	94	0.283	18 Mar. (77)	2 Mon.	52	42	21	5	23 Feb. (54)	0 Sat.	⊙ −1	−.003	9843	16	214	3604
....	...	......	...	......	19 Mar. (78)	4 Wed.	8	14	3	17	14 Mar. (73)	6 Fri.	⊙ −24	−.072	9878	952	265	3605
....	...	......	...	......	18 Mar. (78)	5 Thur.	23	45	9	30	3 Mar. (63)	4 Wed.	112	.336	92	836	237	3606
2 Vaiśâkha....	9930	29.789	237	0.711	18 Mar. (77)	6 Fri.	39	16	15	42	21 Feb. (52)	2 Mon.	311	.933	306	719	209	3607
....	...	......	...	......	18 Mar. (77)	0 Sat.	54	47	21	55	11 Mar. (70)	0 Sat.	47	.141	2	619	258	3608
10 Pausha......	9765	29.295	72	0.217	19 Mar. (78)	2 Mon.	10	19	4	7	28 Feb. (59)	4 Wed.	48	.144	9878	466	227	3609
....	...	......	...	......	18 Mar. (78)	3 Tues	25	50	10	20	18 Mar. (78)	3 Tues.	135	.405	9912	402	278	3610
....	...	......	...	......	18 Mar. (77)	4 Wed.	41	21	16	32	7 Mar. (66)	0 Sat.	68	.204	9788	249	248	3611
7 Âśvina......	9908	29.724	215	0.646	18 Mar. (77)	5 Thur.	56	52	22	45	25 Feb. (56)	5 Thur	248	.744	3	133	219	3612
....	...	......	...	......	19 Mar. (78)	0 Sat.	12	24	4	57	16 Mar. (75)	4 Wed.	236	.708	37	69	271	3613
....	...	......	...	......	18 Mar. (78)	1 Sun.	27	55	11	10	4 Mar. (64)	1 Sun.	⊙ −18	−.054	9913	916	240	3614
3 Jyeshtha....	9743	29.230	51	0.152	18 Mar. (77)	2 Mon.	43	26	17	22	22 Feb. (53)	6 Fri.	137	.411	128	799	212	3615
....	...	......	...	......	18 Mar. (77)	3 Tues.	58	57	23	35	13 Mar. (72)	5 Thur.	162	.486	162	736	263	3616
12 Phâlguna....	9886	29.658	193	0.580	19 Mar. (78)	5 Thur.	14	29	5	47	2 Mar. (61)	2 Mon.	108	.324	38	583	232	3617
....	...	......	...	......	18 Mar. (78)	6 Fri.	30	0	12	0	19 Feb. (50)	6 Fri.	116	.348	9913	430	201	3618
....	...	......	...	......	18 Mar. (77)	0 Sat.	45	31	18	12	9 Mar. (68)	5 Thur.	192	.576	9948	366	253	3619
8 Kârttika....	9721	29.164	29	0.086	19 Mar. (78)	2 Mon.	1	2	0	25	26 Feb. (57)	2 Mon.	101	.303	9824	213	222	3620
....	...	......	...	......	19 Mar. (78)	3 Tues.	16	34	6	37	17 Mar. (76)	1 Sun.	110	.330	9858	149	273	3621
....	...	......	...	......	18 Mar. (78)	4 Wed.	32	5	12	50	6 Mar. (66)	6 Fri.	242	.726	73	33	245	3622
5 Śrâvaṇa.....	9864	29.593	172	0.515	18 Mar. (77)	5 Thur.	47	36	19	2	23 Feb. (54)	3 Tues.	⊙ −5	−.015	9949	880	214	3623
....	...	......	...	......	19 Mar. (78)	0 Sat.	3	7	1	15	14 Mar. (73)	2 Mon.	⊙ −5	−.015	9983	816	266	3624
....	...	......	...	......	19 Mar. (78)	1 Sun.	18	39	7	27	4 Mar. (63)	0 Sat.	204	.612	197	699	238	3625
1 Chaitra.....	9700	29.099	7	0.021	18 Mar. (78)	2 Mon.	34	10	13	40	21 Feb. (52)	4 Wed.	174	.522	73	547	207	3626
....	...	......	...	......	18 Mar. (77)	3 Tues.	49	41	19	52	11 Mar. (70)	3 Tues.	264	.792	108	482	258	3627

⊙ See Text, Art. 101, para. 2.

TABLE I.

Lunation-parts = 10,000*ths of a circle. A tithi* = ¹/₃₀*th of the moon's synodic revolution.*

I. CONCURRENT YEAR.								II. ADDED LUNAR MONTHS.				
						Samvatsara.		True.				
Kali.	Śaka.	Chaitrâdi. Vikrama.	Meshâdi (Solar) year in Bengal.	Kollam.	A. D.	(Southern.)	Bṛihaspati cycle (Northern) current at Mesha saṅkrânti.	Name of month.	Time of the preceding saṅkrânti expressed in Lunation parts. (*t.*)	Tithis.	Time of the succeeding saṅkrânti expressed in Lunation parts. (*t.*)	Tithis.
1	2	3	3a	4	5	6	7	8	9	10	11	12
3628	449	584	—	—	526-27	...... 36 Śubhakṛit		8 Kârttika.... 10 *Pausha* (*Ksh.*) 12 Phâlguna....	9878 15 9998	29.634 0.045 29.994	28 9998 126	0.084 29.994 0.378
3629	450	585	—	—	527-28	...... 37 Śobhana...........		....	......	....	....	......
3630	451	586	—	—	*528-29	...... 38 Krodhin		....	......	....	....	......
3631	452	587	—	—	529-30	...... 39 Viśvâvasu...........		5 Śrâvaṇa.....	9691	29.073	364	1.092
3632	453	588	—	—	530-31	...... 40 Parâbhava..........		....	......	....	....	......
3633	454	589	—	—	531-32	...... 41 Plavaṅga...........		....	......	....	....	......
3634	455	590	—	—	*532-33	...... 42 Kîlaka.............		4 Âshâḍha	9747	29.241	596	1.788
3635	456	591	—	—	533-34	...... 43 Saumya............		....	......	....	....	......
3636	457	592	—	—	534-35	...... 44 Sâdhâraṇa..........		....	......	....	....	......
3637	458	593	—	—	535-36	...... 45 Virodhakṛit		2 Vaiśâkha....	9909	29.727	320	0.960
3638	459	594	—	—	*536-37	...... 46 Paridhâvin..........		....	......	....	....	......
3639	460	595	—	—	537-38	...... 47 Pramâdin...........		6 Bhâdrapada..	9844	29.532	260	0.780
3640	461	596	—	—	538-39	...... 48 Ânanda............		....	......	....	....	......
3641	462	597	—	—	539-40	...... 49 Râkshasa		....	......	....	....	......
3642	463	598	—	—	*540-41	...... 50 Anala		4 Âshâḍha	9277	27.831	146	0.438
3643	464	599	—	—	541-42	...... 51 Piṅgala............		....	......	....	....	......
3644	465	600	—	—	542-43	...... 52 Kâlayukta..........		....	......	....	....	......
3645	466	601	—	—	543-44	...... 53 Siddhârthin		3 Jyeshṭha	9784	29.352	340	1.020
3646	467	602	—	—	*544-45	...... 54 Raudra............		....	......	....	....	......
3647	468	603	—	—	545-46	...... 55 Durmati...........		8 Kârttika.... 10 *Pausha* (*Ksh.*) 12 Phâlguna....	9965 30 9958	29.895 0.090 29.874	55 9961 110	0.165 29.883 0.330
3648	469	604	—	—	546-47	...... 56 Dundubhi...........		....	......	....	....	......
3649	470	605	—	—	547-48	...... 57 Rudhirodgârin		....	......	....	....	......
3650	471	606	—	—	*548-49	...... 58 Raktâksha...........		5 Śrâvaṇa.....	9690	29.070	457	1.371
3651	472	607	—	—	549-50	...... 59 Krodhana		....	......	....	....	......
3652	473	608	—	—	550-51	...... 60 Kshaya		....	......	....	....	......
3653	474	609	—	—	551-52	...... 1 Prabhava...........		4 Âshâḍha	9824	29.472	577	1.731
3654	475	610	—	—	*552-53	...... 2 Vibhava............		....	......	....	....	......
3655	476	611	—	—	553-54	...... 3 Śukla..............		....	......	....	....	......
3656	477	612	—	—	554-55	...... 4 Pramoda............		2 Vaiśâkha....	9990	29.970	482	1.446

TABLE I.

(*Col.* 23) *a* = *Distance of moon from sun.* (*Col.* 24) *b* = *moon's mean anomaly.* (*Col.* 25) *c* = *sun's mean anomaly.*

II ADDED LUNAR MONTHS (*continued.*)					III. COMMENCEMENT OF THE											
Mean.					Solar year.				Luni-Solar year. (Civil day of Chaitra Śukla 1st.)							Kali.
Name of month.	Time of the preceding saṅkrânti expressed in		Time of the succeeding saṅkrânti expressed in		Day and Month A. D.	(Time of the Mesha saṅkrânti.)			Day and Month A. D.	Week day.	At Sunrise on meridian of Ujjain.					
	Lunation parts. (*t.*)	Tithis.	Lunation parts. (*t.*)	Tithis.		Week day.	By the Ârya Siddhânta. Gh. Pa.	H. M.			Moon's Age. Lunat. parts elapsed. (*t.*)	Tithis elapsed.	*a.*	*b.*	*c.*	
8a	9a	10a	11a	12a	13	14	15	17	19	20	21	22	23	24	25	1
10 Pausha....	9842	29.527	150	0.449	19 Mar. (78)	5 Thur.	5 12	2 5	28 Feb. (59)	0 Sat.	247	.741	9984	330	227	3628
....	....	....	....	......	19 Mar. (78)	6 Fri.	20 44	8 17	19 Mar. (78)	6 Fri.	298	.894	18	266	278	3629
....	....	....	....	......	18 Mar. (78)	0 Sat.	36 15	14 30	7 Mar. (67)	3 Tues.	126	.378	9894	113	248	3630
7 Âśvina......	9985	29.955	292	0.877	18 Mar. (77)	1 Sun.	51 46	20 42	25 Feb. (56)	1 Sun.	245	.735	108	996	220	3631
....	....	....	....	......	19 Mar. (78)	3 Tues.	7 17	2 55	16 Mar. (75)	0 Sat.	225	675	143	932	271	3632
....	....	....	....	......	19 Mar. (78)	4 Wed.	22 49	9 7	5 Mar. (64)	4 Wed.	22	.066	19	780	240	3633
3 Jyeshṭha....	9821	29.462	128	0.384	18 Mar. (78)	5 Thur.	38 20	15 20	23 Feb. (54)	2 Mon.	256	.768	233	663	212	3634
....	....	....	....	......	18 Mar. (77)	6 Fri.	53 51	21 32	12 Mar. (71)	0 Sat.	15	.045	9929	563	261	3635
12 Phâlguna....	9963	29.890	271	0.812	19 Mar. (78)	1 Sun.	9 22	3 45	2 Mar. (61)	5 Thur.	330	.990	143	446	232	3636
....	....	....	....	......	19 Mar. (78)	2 Mon.	24 54	9 57	19 Feb. (50)	2 Mon.	297	.891	19	293	202	3637
....	....	....	....	......	18 Mar. (78)	3 Tues.	40 25	16 10	9 Mar. (69)	1 Sun.	333	.999	54	230	253	3638
8 Kârttika....	9799	29.396	106	0.318	18 Mar. (77)	4 Wed.	55 56	22 22	26 Feb. (57)	5 Thur.	136	.408	9930	77	222	3639
....	....	....	....	......	19 Mar. (78)	6 Fri.	11 27	4 35	17 Mar. (76)	4 Wed.	116	.348	9964	13	273	3640
....	....	....	....	......	19 Mar. (78)	0 Sat.	26 59	10 47	7 Mar. (66)	2 Mon.	232	.696	178	896	245	3641
5 Śrâvaṇa.....	9941	29.824	249	0.746	18 Mar. (78)	1 Sun.	42 30	17 0	24 Feb. (55)	6 Fri.	56	.168	54	743	215	3642
....	....	....	....	......	18 Mar. (77)	2 Mon.	58 1	23 12	14 Mar. (73)	5 Thur.	102	.306	89	679	266	3643
....	....	....	....	......	19 Mar. (78)	4 Wed.	13 32	5 25	3 Mar. (62)	2 Mon.	81	.243	9965	527	235	3644
1 Chaitra.....	9777	29.331	84	0.253	19 Mar. (78)	5 Thur.	29 4	11 37	20 Feb. (51)	6 Fri.	83	.249	9840	374	204	3645
....	....	....	....	......	18 Mar. (78)	6 Fri.	44 35	17 50	10 Mar. (70)	5 Thur.	145	.435	9875	310	256	3646
10 Pausha....	9920	29.759	227	0.681	19 Mar. (78)	1 Sun.	0 6	0 2	27 Feb. (58)	2 Mon.	8	.024	9751	157	225	3647
....	....	....	....	......	19 Mar. (78)	2 Mon.	15 37	6 15	18 Mar. (77)	1 Sun.	3	.009	9785	93	276	3648
....	....	....	....	......	19 Mar. (78)	3 Tues.	31 9	12 27	8 Mar. (67)	6 Fri.	119	.357	0	976	248	3649
6 Bhâdrapada..	9755	29.265	62	0.187	18 Mar. (78)	4 Wed.	46 40	18 40	26 Feb. (57)	4 Wed.	247	.741	214	860	220	3650
....	....	....	....	......	19 Mar. (78)	6 Fri.	2 11	0 52	16 Mar. (75)	3 Tues.	255	.765	249	796	271	3651
....	....	....	....	......	19 Mar. (78)	0 Sat.	17 42	7 5	5 Mar. (64)	0 Sat.	155	.465	124	643	240	3652
3 Jyeshṭha....	9898	29.693	205	0.615	19 Mar. (78)	1 Sun.	33 14	13 17	22 Feb. (53)	4 Wed.	151	.453	0	490	209	3653
....	....	....	....	......	18 Mar. (78)	2 Mon.	48 45	19 30	12 Mar. (72)	3 Tues.	237	.711	35	426	261	3654
11 Mâgha......	9733	29.200	41	0.122	19 Mar. (78)	4 Wed.	4 16	1 42	1 Mar. (60)	0 Sat.	188	.564	9910	274	230	3655
....	....	....	....	......	19 Mar. (78)	5 Thur.	19 47	7 55	18 Feb. (49)	4 Wed.	26	.078	9786	121	199	3656

TABLE I.

Lunation-parts = 10,000*ths of a circle. A tithi* = 1/30*th of the moon's synodic revolution.*

I. CONCURRENT YEAR.								II. ADDED LUNAR MONTHS.				
						Samvatsara.		True.				
									Time of the preceding saṅkrânti expressed in		Time of the succeeding saṅkrânti expressed in	
Kali.	Śaka.	Chaitrâdi. Vikrama.	Meshâdi (Solar) year in Bengal.	Kollam.	A. D.	(Southern.)	Bṛihaspati cycle (Northern) current at Mesha saṅkrânti.	Name of month.	Lunation parts. (*t.*)	Tithis.	Lunation parts. (*t.*)	Tithis.
1	2	3	3a	4	5	6	7	8	9	10	11	12
3657	478	613	—	—	555-56	5 Prajâpati						
3658	479	614	—	—	*556-57	6 Aṅgiras		6 Bhâdrapada	9970	29.910	448	1.344
3659	480	615	—	—	557-58	7 Śrîmukha						
3660	481	616	—	—	558-59	8 Bhâva						
3661	482	617	—	—	559-60	9 Yuvan		4 Âshâḍha	9320	27.960	108	0.324
3662	483	618	—	—	*560-61	10 Dhâtṛi						
3663	484	619	—	—	561-62	11 Îśvara						
3664	485	620	—	—	562-63	12 Bahudhânya		3 Jyeshṭha	9967	29.901	527	1.581
3665	486	621	—	—	563-64	13 Pramâthin						
3666	487	622	—	—	*564-65	14 Vikrama		7 Aśvina	9921	29.763	140	0.420
								10 *Pausha* (*Ksh.*)	104	0.312	9989	29.967
								12 Phâlguna	9948	29.844	70	0.210
3667	488	623	—	—	565-66	15 Vṛisha						
3668	489	624	—	—	566-67	16 Chitrabhânu						
3669	490	625	—	—	567-68	17 Subhânu [1])		5 Śrâvaṇa	9648	28.944	455	1.365
3670	491	626	—	—	*568-69	19 Pârthiva						
3671	492	627	—	—	569-70	20 Vyaya						
3672	493	628	—	—	570-71	21 Sarvajit		4 Âshâḍha	9993	29.979	648	1.944
3673	494	629	—	—	571-72	22 Sarvadhârin						
3674	495	630	—	—	*572-73	23 Virodhin						
3675	496	631	—	—	573-74	24 Vikṛita		2 Vaiśâkha	9980	29.940	551	1.653
3676	497	632	—	—	574-75	25 Khara						
3677	498	633	—	—	575-76	26 Nandana		6 Bhâdrapada	9997	29.991	567	1.701
3678	499	634	—	—	*576-77	27 Vijaya						
3679	500	635	—	—	577-78	28 Jaya						
3680	501	636	—	—	578-79	29 Manmatha		4 Ashâḍha	9462	28.386	144	0.432
3681	502	637	—	—	579-80	30 Durmukha						
3682	503	638	—	—	*580-81	31 Hemalamba						
3683	504	639	—	—	581-82	32 Vilamba		2 Vaiśâkha	9522	28.566	71	0.213
3684	505	640	—	—	582-83	33 Vikârin						
3685	506	641	—	—	583-84	34 Śârvari		6 Bhâdrapada	9530	28.590	71	0.213
3686	507	642	—	—	*584-85	35 Plava						
3687	508	643	—	—	585-86	36 Śubhakṛit						

1) Târaṇa, No. 18, was suppressed.

TABLE I.

(*Col.* 23) *a* = *Distance of moon from sun.* (*Col.* 24) *b* = *moon's mean anomaly.* (*Col.* 25) *c* = *sun's mean anomaly.*

II. ADDED LUNAR MONTHS *(continued.)*					III. COMMENCEMENT OF THE														
Mean.					Solar year.						Luni-Solar year. (Civil day of Chaitra Śukla 1st.)								
Name of month.	Time of the preceding saṅkrânti expressed in		Time of the succeeding saṅkrânti expressed in		Day and Month A. D.	(Time of the Mesha saṅkrânti.)					Day and Month A. D.	Week day.	At Sunrise on meridian of Ujjain.						Kali.
	Lunation parts. (*t.*)	Tithis.	Lunation parts. (*t.*)	Tithis.		Week day.	By the Ârya Siddhânta.						Moon's Age.						
							Gh.	Pa	H.	M.			Lunat. parts elapsed. (*t.*)	Tithis elapsed.	*a.*	*b.*	*c.*		
8a	**9a**	**10a**	**11a**	**12a**	**13**	**14**	**15**		**17**		**19**	**20**	**21**	**22**	**23**	**24**	**25**		**1**
...	...	...	...	...	19 Mar. (78)	6 Fri.	35	19	14	7	9 Mar. (68)	3 Tues.	11	.033	9821	57	250		3657
8 Kârttika	9876	29.628	183	0.550	18 Mar. (78)	0 Sat.	50	50	20	20	27 Feb. (58)	1 Sun.	124	.372	35	940	222		3658
...	...	...	...	...	19 Mar. (78)	2 Mon.	6	21	2	32	17 Mar. (76)	0 Sat.	112	.336	70	876	274		3659
...	...	...	...	...	19 Mar. (78)	3 Tues.	21	52	8	45	7 Mar. (66)	5 Thur.	284	.852	284	760	246		3660
4 Âshâḍha	9711	29.134	19	0.056	19 Mar. (78)	4 Wed.	37	24	14	57	24 Feb. (55)	2 Mon.	214	.642	160	607	215		3661
...	...	...	...	...	18 Mar. (78)	5 Thur.	52	55	21	10	14 Mar. (74)	1 Sun.	296	.888	194	543	266		3662
...	...	...	...	...	19 Mar. (78)	0 Sat.	8	26	3	22	3 Mar. (62)	5 Thur.	300	.900	70	390	235		3663
1 Chaitra	9854	29.562	161	0.484	19 Mar. (78)	1 Sun.	23	57	9	35	20 Feb. (51)	2 Mon.	229	.687	9946	237	205		3664
...	...	...	...	...	19 Mar. (78)	2 Mon.	39	29	15	47	11 Mar. (70)	1 Sun.	245	.735	9981	173	256		3665
}10 Pausha	9997	29.991	304	0.913	18 Mar. (78)	3 Tues.	55	0	22	0	28 Feb. (59)	5 Thur.	16	.048	9856	21	225		3666
...	...	...	...	...	19 Mar. (78)	5 Thur.	10	31	4	12	18 Mar. (77)	4 Wed.	⊙ −6	−.018	9891	957	276		3667
...	...	...	...	...	19 Mar. (78)	6 Fri.	26	2	10	25	8 Mar. (67)	2 Mon.	127	.381	105	840	248		3668
6 Bhâdrapada	9832	29.497	140	0.419	19 Mar. (78)	0 Sat.	41	34	16	37	26 Feb. (57)	0 Sat.	322	.966	319	723	220		3669
...	...	...	...	...	18 Mar. (78)	1 Sun.	57	5	22	50	15 Mar. (75)	5 Thur.	58	.174	16	623	269		3670
...	...	...	...	...	19 Mar. (78)	3 Tues.	12	36	5	2	4 Mar. (63)	2 Mon.	57	.171	9891	470	238		3671
3 Jyeshtha	9975	29.925	282	0.847	19 Mar. (78)	4 Wed.	28	7	11	15	21 Feb. (52)	6 Fri.	37	.111	9767	318	207		3672
...	...	...	...	...	19 Mar. (78)	5 Thur.	43	39	17	27	12 Mar. (71)	5 Thur.	82	.246	9802	254	258		3673
11 Mâgha	9810	29.431	118	0.354	18 Mar. (78)	6 Fri.	59	10	23	40	1 Mar. (61)	3 Tues.	262	.786	16	137	230		3674
...	...	...	...	...	19 Mar. (78)	1 Sun.	14	41	5	52	18 Feb. (49)	0 Sat.	21	.063	9892	984	199		3675
...	...	...	...	...	19 Mar. (78)	2 Mon.	30	12	12	5	9 Mar. (68)	6 Fri.	⊙ −2	−.006	9926	920	251		3676
8 Kârttika	9953	29.860	261	0.782	19 Mar. (78)	3 Tues.	45	44	18	17	27 Feb. (58)	4 Wed.	150	.450	141	804	223		3677
...	...	...	...	...	19 Mar. (79)	5 Thur.	1	15	0	30	17 Mar. (77)	3 Tues.	175	.525	175	740	274		3678
...	...	...	...	...	19 Mar. (78)	6 Fri.	16	46	6	42	6 Mar. (65)	0 Sat.	118	.354	51	587	243		3679
4 Ashâḍha	9789	29.366	96	0.288	19 Mar. (78)	0 Sat.	32	17	12	55	23 Feb. (54)	4 Wed.	126	.378	9927	434	212		3680
...	...	...	...	...	19 Mar. (78)	1 Sun.	47	49	19	7	14 Mar. (73)	3 Tues.	203	.609	9961	370	264		3681
...	...	...	...	...	19 Mar. (79)	3 Tues.	3	20	1	20	2 Mar. (62)	0 Sat.	114	.342	9837	218	233		3682
1 Chaitra	9931	29.794	239	0.716	19 Mar. (78)	4 Wed.	18	51	7	32	20 Feb. (51)	5 Thur.	278	.834	51	101	205		3683
...	...	...	...	...	19 Mar. (78)	5 Thur.	34	22	13	45	11 Mar. (70)	4 Wed.	258	.774	86	37	256		3684
9 Mârgaśirsha	9767	29.300	74	0.223	19 Mar. (78)	6 Fri.	49	54	19	57	28 Feb. (59)	1 Sun.	9	.027	9962	884	225		3685
...	...	...	...	...	19 Mar. (79)	1 Sun.	5	25	2	10	18 Mar. (78)	0 Sat.	10	.030	9996	820	277		3686
...	...	...	...	...	19 Mar. (78)	2 Mon.	20	56	8	22	8 Mar. (67)	5 Thur.	217	.651	211	704	248		3687

⊙ See Text. Art. 101 above, para. 2.

TABLE I.

Lunation-parts = 10,000*ths of a circle. A tithi* = $^{1}/_{30}$*th of the moon's synodic revolution.*

I. CONCURRENT YEAR.								II. ADDED LUNAR MONTHS.				
						Samvatsara.		True.				
Kali.	Śaka.	Chaitrâdi. Vikrama.	Meshâdi (Solar) year in Bengal.	Kollam.	A. D.	(Southern.)	Bṛihaspati cycle (Northern) current at Mesha saṅkrânti.	Name of month.	Time of the preceding saṅkrânti expressed in: Lunation parts. (*t.*)	Tithis.	Time of the succeeding saṅkrânti expressed in: Lunation parts. (*t.*)	Tithis.
1	2	3	3a	4	5	6	7	8	9	10	11	12
3688	509	644	—	—	586- 87	...... 37 Śobhana............		5 Śrâvaṇa.....	9654	28.962	416	1.248
3689	510	645	—	—	587- 88	...... 38 Krodhin............		....	......	......	......	......
3690	511	646	—	—	*588- 89	...... 39 Viśvâvasu..........		....	......	......	......	......
3691	512	647	—	—	589- 90	...... 40 Parâbhava..........		3 Jyeshṭha....	9581	28.743	189	0.567
3692	513	648	—	—	590- 91	...... 41 Plavaṅga...........		....	......	......	......	......
3693	514	649	—	—	591- 92	...... 42 Kîlaka.............		....	......	......	......	......
3694	515	650	—	—	*592- 93	...... 43 Saumya.............		2 Vaiśâkha....	9938	29.814	527	1.581
3695	516	651	—	—	593- 94	...... 44 Sâdhâraṇa..........		....	......	......	......	......
3696	517	652	1	—	594- 95	...... 45 Virodhakṛit........		6 Bhâdrapada..	9960	29.880	584	1.752
3697	518	653	2	—	595- 96	...... 46 Paridhâvin.........		....	......	......	......	......
3698	519	654	3	—	*596- 97	...... 47 Pramâdin...........		....	......	......	......	......
3699	520	655	4	—	597- 98	...... 48 Ananda.............		4 Âshâḍha....	9679	29.037	281	0.843
3700	521	656	5	—	598- 99	...... 49 Râkshasa...........		....	......	......	......	......
3701	522	657	6	—	599-600	...... 50 Anala..............		....	......	......	......	......
3702	523	658	7	—	*600- 1	...... 51 Piṅgala............		2 Vaiśâkha....	9482	28.446	76	0.228
3703	524	659	8	—	601- 2	...... 52 Kâlayukta..........		....	......	......	......	......
3704	525	660	9	—	602- 3	...... 53 Siddhârthin........		6 Bhâdrapada..	9506	28.518	119	0.357
3705	526	661	10	—	603- 4	...... 54 Raudra.............		....	......	......	......	......
3706	527	662	11	—	*604- 5	...... 55 Durmati............		....	......	......	......	......
3707	528	663	12	—	605- 6	...... 56 Dundubhi...........		5 Śrâvaṇa.....	9759	29.277	418	1.254
3708	529	664	13	—	606- 7	...... 57 Rudhirodgârin......		....	......	......	......	......
3709	530	665	14	—	607- 8	...... 58 Raktâksha..........		....	......	......	......	......
3710	531	666	15	—	*608- 9	...... 59 Krodhana...........		3 Jyeshṭha....	9613	28.839	323	0.969
3711	532	667	16	—	609- 10	...... 60 Kshaya.............		....	......	......	......	......
3712	533	668	17	—	610- 11	...... 1 Prabhava...........		8 Kârttika.... 9 *Mârgaś.*(*Ksh.*)	9960 30	29.880 0.090	30 9937	0.090 29.811
3713	534	669	18	—	611- 12	...... 2 Vibhava............		2 Vaiśâkha....	9954	29.862	492	1.476
3714	535	670	19	—	*612- 13	...... 3 Śukla..............		....	......	......	......	......
3715	536	671	20	—	613- 14	...... 4 Pramoda............		6 Bhâdrapada..	9940	29.820	545	1.635
3716	537	672	21	—	614- 15	...... 5 Prajâpati..........		....	......	......	......	......
3717	538	673	22	—	615- 16	...... 6 Aṅgiras............		....	......	......	......	......
3718	539	674	23	—	*616- 17	...... 7 Śrîmukha...........		4 Âshâḍha....	9819	29.457	476	1.428
3719	540	675	24	—	617- 18	...... 8 Bhâva..............		....	......	......	......	......

TABLE I.

(*Col.* 23) *a* = *Distance of moon from sun.* (*Col.* 24) *b* = *moon's mean anomaly.* (*Col.* 25) *c* = *sun's mean anomaly.*

II. ADDED LUNAR MONTHS (*continued.*)					III. COMMENCEMENT OF THE													
Mean.					Solar year						Luni-Solar year. (Civil day of Chaitra Śukla 1st.)							
Name of month.	Time of the preceding saṅkrânti expressed in: Lunation parts. (*t.*)	Time of the preceding saṅkrânti expressed in: Tithis.	Time of the succeeding saṅkrânti expressed in: Lunation parts. (*t.*)	Time of the succeeding saṅkrânti expressed in: Tithis.	Day and Month A. D.	(Time of the Mesha saṅkrânti.) Week day.	By the Ârya Siddhânta. Gh.	Pa	H.	M.	Day and Month A. D.	Week day.	At Sunrise on meridian of Ujjain. Moon's Age. Lunat. parts elapsed. (*t.*)	Tithis elapsed.	*a.*	*b.*	*c.*	Kali.
8a	9a	10a	11a	12a	13	14	15		17		19	20	21	22	23	24	25	1
6 Bhâdrapada..	9910	29.729	217	0.651	19 Mar. (78)	3 Tues.	36	27	14	35	25 Feb. (56)	2 Mon.	183	.549	87	551	218	3688
....	....	....	....	....	19 Mar. (78)	4 Wed.	51	59	20	47	16 Mar. (75)	1 Sun.	273	.819	121	487	269	3689
....	....	....	....	....	19 Mar. (79)	6 Fri.	7	30	3	0	4 Mar. (64)	5 Thur.	258	.774	9997	334	238	3690
2 Vaiśâkha....	9745	29.235	52	0.157	19 Mar. (78)	0 Sat.	23	1	9	12	21 Feb. (52)	2 Mon.	141	.423	9872	181	207	3691
....	....	....	....	....	19 Mar. (78)	1 Sun.	38	32	15	25	12 Mar. (71)	1 Sun.	141	.423	9907	117	259	3692
11 Mâgha.....	9888	29.663	195	0.585	19 Mar. (78)	2 Mon.	54	4	21	37	2 Mar. (61)	6 Fri.	262	.786	122	1	230	3693
....	....	....	....	....	19 Mar. (79)	4 Wed.	9	35	3	50	19 Feb. (50)	3 Tues.	26	.078	9997	848	200	3694
....	....	....	....	....	19 Mar. (78)	5 Thur.	25	6	10	2	9 Mar. (68)	2 Mon.	35	.105	32	784	251	3695
7 Âśvina......	9723	29.170	31	0.092	19 Mar. (78)	6 Fri.	40	37	16	15	27 Feb. (58)	0 Sat.	265	.795	246	668	223	3696
....	....	....	....	....	19 Mar. (78)	0 Sat.	56	9	22	27	17 Mar. (76)	5 Thur.	24	.072	9942	567	271	3697
....	....	....	....	....	19 Mar. (79)	2 Mon.	11	40	4	40	5 Mar. (65)	2 Mon.	29	.087	9817	414	241	3698
4 Âshâḍha....	9866	29.598	173	0.520	19 Mar. (78)	3 Tues.	27	11	10	52	23 Feb. (54)	0 Sat.	308	.924	32	298	212	3699
....	....	....	....	....	19 Mar. (78)	4 Wed.	42	42	17	5	13 Mar. (72)	5 Thur.	⊙ −0	−.000	9728	198	261	3700
12 Phâlguna....	9701	29.104	9	0.026	19 Mar. (78)	5 Thur.	58	14	23	17	3 Mar. (62)	3 Tues.	152	.456	9943	81	233	3701
....	....	....	....	....	19 Mar. (79)	0 Sat.	13	45	5	30	21 Feb. (52)	1 Sun.	270	.810	157	965	205	3702
....	....	....	....	....	19 Mar. (78)	1 Sun.	29	16	11	42	11 Mar. (70)	0 Sat.	249	.747	192	900	256	3703
9 Mârgaśîrsha.	9844	29.532	151	0.454	19 Mar. (78)	2 Mon.	44	47	17	55	28 Feb. (59)	4 Wed.	67	.201	67	748	225	3704
....	....	....	....	....	20 Mar. (79)	4 Wed.	0	19	0	7	19 Mar. (78)	3 Tues.	115	.345	102	684	277	3705
....	....	....	....	....	19 Mar. (79)	5 Thur.	15	50	6	20	7 Mar. (67)	0 Sat.	91	.273	9978	531	246	3706
6 Bhâdrapada..	9987	29.961	294	0.883	19 Mar. (78)	6 Fri.	31	21	12	32	24 Feb. (55)	4 Wed.	92	.276	9854	378	215	3707
....	....	....	....	....	19 Mar. (78)	0 Sat.	46	52	18	45	15 Mar. (74)	3 Tues.	157	.471	9888	314	266	3708
....	....	....	....	....	20 Mar. (79)	2 Mon.	2	24	0	57	4 Mar. (63)	0 Sat.	22	.066	9764	161	236	3709
2 Vaiśâkha....	9822	29.467	130	0.389	19 Mar. (79)	3 Tues.	17	55	7	10	22 Feb. (53)	5 Thur.	160	.480	9978	45	208	3710
....	....	....	....	....	19 Mar. (78)	4 Wed.	33	26	13	22	12 Mar. (71)	4 Wed.	135	.405	13	981	259	3711
} 11 Mâgha.....	9965	29.895	272	0.817	19 Mar (78)	5 Thur.	48	57	19	35	2 Mar. (61)	2 Mon.	261	.783	227	864	231	3712
....	....	....	....	....	20 Mar. (79)	0 Sat.	4	29	1	47	19 Feb. (50)	6 Fri.	110	.330	103	711	200	3713
....	....	....	....	....	19 Mar. (79)	1 Sun.	20	0	8	0	9 Mar. (69)	5 Thur.	166	.498	138	648	251	3714
7 Âśvina......	9800	29.401	108	0.323	19 Mar. (78)	2 Mon.	35	31	14	12	26 Feb (57)	2 Mon.	159	.477	13	495	220	3715
....	....	....	....	....	19 Mar. (78)	3 Tues.	51	2	20	25	17 Mar. (76)	1 Sun.	247	.741	48	431	272	3716
....	....	....	....	....	20 Mar. (79)	5 Thur.	6	34	2	37	6 Mar. (65)	5 Thur.	201	.603	9924	278	241	3717
4 Âshâḍha....	9943	29.830	251	0.752	19 Mar. (79)	6 Fri.	22	5	8	50	23 Feb. (54)	2 Mon.	40	.120	9799	125	210	3718
....	....	....	....	....	19 Mar. (78)	0 Sat.	37	36	15	2	13 Mar. (72)	1 Sun.	28	.084	9834	61	261	3719

⊙ See Text. Art. 101 above, para 2.

TABLE I.

Lunation-parts = 10,000*ths of a circle. A tithi* = 1/30*th of the moon's synodic revolution.*

I. CONCURRENT YEAR.								II. ADDED LUNAR MONTHS.				
						Samvatsara.		True.				
Kali.	Śaka.	Chaitrâdi. Vikrama.	Meshâdi (Solar) year in Bengal.	Kollam.	A. D.	(Southern.)	Bṛihaspati cycle (Northern) current at Mesha saṅkrânti.	Name of month.	Time of the preceding saṅkrânti expressed in Lunation parts. (*l.*)	Time of the preceding saṅkrânti expressed in Tithis.	Time of the succeeding saṅkrânti expressed in Lunation parts. (*l.*)	Time of the succeeding saṅkrânti expressed in Tithis.
1	2	3	3a	4	5	6	7	8	9	10	11	12
3720	541	676	25	—	618-19	9 Yuvan						
3721	542	677	26	—	619-20	10 Dhâtṛi		2 Vaiśâkha	9469	28.407	35	0.105
3722	543	678	27	—	*620-21	11 Îśvara						
3723	544	679	28	—	621-22	12 Bahudhânya		6 Bhâdrapada	9467	28.401	92	0.276
3724	545	680	29	—	622-23	13 Pramâthin						
3725	546	681	30	—	623-24	14 Vikrama						
3726	547	682	31	—	*624-25	15 Vṛisha		5 Śrâvaṇa	9942	29.826	520	1.560
3727	548	683	32	—	625-26	16 Chitrabhânu						
3728	549	684	33	—	626-27	17 Subhânu						
3729	550	685	34	—	627-28	18 Târaṇa		3 Jyeshṭha	9580	28.740	358	1.074
3730	551	686	35	—	*628-29	19 Pârthiva						
3731	552	687	36	—	629-30	20 Vyaya		7 Âśvina 10 *Pausha* (*Ksh.*)	9640 101	28.920 0.303	19 9968	0.057 29.904
3732	553	688	37	—	630-31	21 Sarvajit		1 Chaitra	9870	29.610	70	0.210
3733	554	689	38	—	631-32	22 Sarvadhârin						
3734	555	690	39	—	*632-33	23 Virodhin		5 Srâvaṇa	9406	28.218	7	0.021
3735	556	691	40	—	633-34	24 Vikṛita						
3736	557	692	41	—	634-35	25 Khara						
3737	558	693	42	—	635-36	26 Nandana		4 Ashâḍha	9890	29.670	644	1.932
3738	559	694	43	—	*636-37	27 Vijaya						
3739	560	695	44	—	637-38	28 Jaya						
3740	561	696	45	—	638-39	29 Manmatha		2 Vaiśâkha	9551	28.653	31	0.093
3741	562	697	46	—	639-40	30 Durmukha						
3742	563	698	47	—	*640-41	31 Hemalamba		6 Bhâdrapada	9504	28.512	60	0.180
3743	564	699	48	—	641-42	32 Vilamba						
3744	565	700	49	—	642-43	33 Vikârin						
3745	566	701	50	—	643-44	34 Śârvari		4 Âshâḍha	9408	28.224	129	0.387
3746	567	702	51	—	*644-45	35 Plava						
3747	568	703	52	—	645-46	36 Śubhakṛit						
3748	569	704	53	—	646-47	37 Śobhana		3 Jyeshṭha	9555	28.665	323	0.969
3749	570	705	54	—	647-48	38 Krodhin						
3750	571	706	55	—	*648-49	39 Viśvâvasu		8 Kârttika	9994	29.982	171	0.518
3751	572	707	56	—	649-50	40 Parâbhava						

TABLE I.

(*Col.* 23) *a* = *Distance of moon from sun*. (*Col.* 24) *b* = *moon's mean anomaly*. (*Col.* 25) *c* = *sun's mean anomaly*.

II. ADDED LUNAR MONTHS (continued.)					III. COMMENCEMENT OF THE													
Mean.					Solar year.						Luni-Solar year. (Civil day of Chaitra Śukla 1st.)							
Name of month.	Time of the preceding saṅkrânti expressed in: Lunation parts. (*t.*)	Tithis.	Time of the succeeding saṅkrânti expressed in: Lunation parts. (*t.*)	Tithis.	Day and Month A. D.	(Time of the Mesha saṅkrânti.) Week day.	By the Ârya Siddhânta. Gh.	Pa.	H.	M.	Day and Month A. D.	Week day.	At Sunrise on meridian of Ujjain. Moon's Age. Lunat. parts elapsed. (*t.*)	Tithis elapsed.	*a.*	*b.*	*c.*	Kali.
8a	9a	10a	11a	12a	13	14	15		17		19	20	21	22	23	24	25	1
12 Phâlguna....	9779	29.336	86	0.258	19 Mar. (78)	1 Sun.	53	7	21	15	3 Mar. (62)	6 Fri.	140	.420	48	945	233	3720
....	....	....	....	....	20 Mar. (79)	3 Tues.	8	39	3	27	21 Feb. (52)	4 Wed.	281	.843	263	828	205	3721
....	....	....	....	....	19 Mar. (79)	4 Wed.	24	10	9	40	11 Mar. (71)	3 Tues.	297	.891	297	764	256	3722
9 Mârgaśîrsha .	9921	29.764	229	0 686	19 Mar. (78)	5 Thur.	39	41	15	52	28 Feb. (59)	0 Sat.	222	.666	173	611	226	3723
....	....	....	....	....	19 Mar. (78)	6 Fri.	55	12	22	5	19 Mar. (78)	6 Fri.	308	.624	208	547	277	3724
....	....	....	....	....	20 Mar. (79)	1 Sun.	10	44	4	17	8 Mar. (67)	3 Tues.	310	.930	83	394	246	3725
5 Srâvaṇa.....	9757	29.270	64	0.192	19 Mar. (79)	2 Mon.	26	15	10	30	25 Feb. (56)	0 Sat.	240	.720	9959	242	215	3726
....	....	....	....	....	19 Mar. (78)	3 Tues.	41	46	16	42	15 Mar. (74)	6 Fri.	260	.780	9994	178	267	3727
....	....	....	....	....	19 Mar. (78)	4 Wed.	57	17	22	55	4 Mar. (63)	3 Tues.	31	.093	9869	25	236	3728
2 Vaiśâkha....	9900	29.699	207	0.621	20 Mar. (79)	6 Fri.	12	49	5	7	22 Feb. (53)	1 Sun.	149	.447	84	908	208	3729
....	....	....	....	....	19 Mar. (79)	0 Sat.	28	20	11	20	12 Mar. (72)	0 Sat.	142	.426	118	844	259	3730
}10 Pausha....	9735	29.205	42	0.127	19 Mar. (78)	1 Sun.	43	51	17	32	1 Mar. (60)	4 Wed.	4	.012	9994	691	228	3731
....	....	....	....	....	19 Mar. (78)	2 Mon.	59	22	23	45	19 Feb. (50)	2 Mon.	287	.861	208	575	200	3732
....	....	....	....	....	20 Mar. (79)	4 Wed.	14	54	5	57	9 Mar. (68)	0 Sat.	66	.193	9904	475	249	3733
7 Aśvina......	9878	29.633	185	0.555	19 Mar. (79)	5 Thur.	30	25	12	10	26 Feb. (57)	4 Wed.	47	.141	9780	322	218	3734
....	....	....	....	....	19 Mar. (78)	6 Fri.	45	56	18	22	16 Mar. (75)	3 Tues.	95	.285	9815	258	269	3735
....	....	....	....	....	20 Mar. (79)	1 Sun.	1	27	0	35	6 Mar. (65)	1 Sun.	278	.834	29	142	241	3736
3 Jyeshṭha....	9713	29.139	20	0.061	20 Mar. (79)	2 Mon.	16	59	6	47	23 Feb. (54)	5 Thur.	37	.111	9905	989	210	3737
....	....	....	....	....	19 Mar. (79)	3 Tues.	32	30	13	0	13 Mar. (73)	4 Wed.	16	.048	9940	925	262	3738
12 Phâlguna..	9856	29.568	163	0.490	19 Mar. (78)	4 Wed.	48	1	19	12	3 Mar. (62)	2 Mon.	163	.489	154	808	234	3739
....	....	....	....	....	20 Mar. (79)	6 Fri.	3	32	1	.25	20 Feb. (51)	6 Fri.	57	.171	30	655	203	3740
....	....	....	....	....	20 Mar. (79)	0 Sat.	19	4	7	37	11 Mar. (70)	5 Thur.	128	.384	64	591	254	3741
9 Mârgaśîrsha .	9999	29.996	306	0.918	19 Mar. (79)	1 Sun.	34	35	13	50	28 Feb. (59)	2 Mon.	134	.402	9940	439	223	3742
....	....	....	....	....	19 Mar. (78)	2 Mon.	50	6	20	2	18 Mar. (77)	1 Sun.	215	.645	9975	374	274	3743
....	....	....	....	....	20 Mar. (79)	4 Wed.	5	37	2	15	7 Mar. (66)	5 Thur.	127	.381	9850	222	244	3744
5 Śrâvaṇa.....	9834	29.502	141	0.424	20 Mar. (79)	5 Thur.	21	9	8	27	25 Feb. (56)	3 Tues.	292	.876	65	105	216	3745
....	....	....	....	....	19 Mar. (79)	6 Fri.	36	40	14	40	15 Mar. (75)	2 Mon.	275	.825	99	41	267	3746
....	....	....	....	....	19 Mar. (78)	0 Sat.	52	11	20	52	4 Mar. (63)	6 Fri.	24	.072	9975	888	236	3747
2 Vaiśâkha....	9977	29.930	284	0.853	20 Mar. (79)	2 Mon.	7	42	3	5	22 Feb. (53)	4 Wed.	192	.576	189	772	208	3748
....	....	....	....	....	20 Mar. (79)	3 Tues.	23	14	9	17	13 Mar. (72)	3 Tues.	227	.681	224	708	259	3749
10 Pausha......	9812	29.437	120	0.359	19 Mar. (79)	4 Wed.	38	45	15	30	1 Mar. (61)	0 Sat.	192	.576	100	555	228	3750
....	....	....	....	....	19 Mar. (78)	5 Thur.	54	16	21	42	20 Mar. (79)	6 Fri.	285	.855	134	491	280	3751

TABLE I.

Lunation-parts = 10,000*ths of a circle. A tithi* = 1/30*th of the moon's synodic revolution.*

I. CONCURRENT YEAR.								II. ADDED LUNAR MONTHS.				
						Samvatsara.		True.				
Kali.	Śaka.	Chaitrâdi. Vikrama.	Meshâdi (Solar) year in Bengal.	Kollam.	A. D.	(Southern.)	Bṛihaspati cycle (Northern) current at Mesha saṅkrânti.	Name of month.	Time of the preceding saṅkrânti expressed in: Lunation parts. (*t.*)	Time of the preceding saṅkrânti expressed in: Tithis.	Time of the succeeding saṅkrânti expressed in: Lunation parts. (*t.*)	Time of the succeeding saṅkrânti expressed in: Tithis.
1	2	3	3a	4	5	6	7	8	9	10	11	12
3752	573	708	57	—	650-51	.... 41 Plavanga...........		....	......	....	......	....
3753	574	709	58	—	651-52	.... 42 Kîlaka.............		5 Śrâvaṇa.....	9604	28.812	168	0.504
3754	575	710	59	—	*652-53	.... 43 Saumya............		....	......	....	......	....
3755	576	711	60	—	653-54	.... 44 Sâdhâraṇa[1])........		....	......	....	......	....
3756	577	712	61	—	654-55	.... 46 Paridhâvin........		4 Âshâḍha	9871	29.613	722	2.166
3757	578	713	62	—	655-56	.... 47 Pramâdin..........		....	......	....	......	....
3758	579	714	63	—	*656-57	.... 48 Ânauda............		....	......	....	......	....
3759	580	715	64	—	657-58	.... 49 Râkshasa		2 Vaiśâkha....	9725	29.175	127	0.381
3760	581	716	65	—	658-59	.... 50 Anala..............		....	......	....	......	....
3761	582	717	66	—	659-60	.... 51 Piṅgala............		6 Bhâdrapada..	9638	28.914	104	0.312
3762	583	718	67	—	*660-61	.... 52 Kâlayukta..........		....	......	....	......	....
3763	584	719	68	—	661-62	.... 53 Siddhârthin........		....	......	....	......	....
3764	585	720	69	—	662-63	.... 54 Raudra............		4 Ashâḍha	9415	28.245	238	0.714
3765	586	721	70	—	663-64	.... 55 Durmati...........		....	......	....	......	....
3766	587	722	71	—	*664-65	.... 56 Dundubhi..........		....	......	....	......	....
3767	588	723	72	—	665-66	.... 57 Rudhirodgârin.......		3 Jyeshṭha....	9615	28.845	290	0.870
3768	589	724	73	—	666-67	.... 58 Raktâksha..........		....	......	....	......	....
3769	590	725	74	—	667-68	.... 59 Krodhana..........		8 Kârttika	9959	29.877	132	0.396
3770	591	726	75	—	*668-69	.... 60 Kshaya............		....	......	....	......	....
3771	592	727	76	—	669-70	.... 1 Prabhava...........		....	......	....	......	....
3772	593	728	77	—	670-71	.... 2 Vibhava............		5 Śrâvaṇa.....	9746	29.238	365	1.095
3773	594	729	78	—	671-72	.... 3 Śukla..............		....	......	....	......	....
3774	595	730	79	—	*672-73	.... 4 Pramoda............		....	......	....	......	....
3775	596	731	80	—	673-74	.... 5 Prajâpati..........		4 Âshâḍha	9833	29.499	706	2.118
3776	597	732	81	—	674-75	.... 6 Aṅgiras............		....	......	....	......	....
3777	598	733	82	—	675-76	.... 7 Śrîmukha...........		....	......	....	......	....
3778	599	734	83	—	*676-77	.... 8 Bhâva..............		2 Vaiśâkha....	9915	29.745	303	0.909
3779	600	735	84	—	677-78	.... 9 Yuvan..............		....	......	....	......	....
3780	601	736	85	—	678-79	.... 10 Dhâtṛi............		6 Bhâdrapada..	9831	29.493	246	0.738
3781	602	737	86	—	679-80	.... 11 Îśvara.............		....	......	....	......	....
3782	603	738	87	—	*680-81	.... 12 Bahudhânya.........		....	......	....	......	....
3783	604	739	88	—	681-82	.... 13 Pramâthin..........		4 Âshâḍha	9373	28.119	248	0.744
3784	605	740	89	—	682-83	.... 14 Vikrama............		....	......	....	......	....

1) Virodhakṛit, No. 45, was suppressed.

TABLE I.

(*Col.* 23) *a* = *Distance of moon from sun.* (*Col.* 24) *b* = *moon's mean anomaly.* (*Col.* 25) *c* = *sun's mean anomaly.*

II. ADDED LUNAR MONTHS (*continued.*)					III. COMMENCEMENT OF THE													
Mean.					Solar year.						Luni-Solar year. (Civil day of Chaitra Śukla 1st.)							
Name of month.	Time of the preceding saṅkrânti expressed in: Lunation parts. (*t.*)	Time of the preceding saṅkrânti expressed in: Tithis.	Time of the succeeding saṅkrânti expressed in: Lunation parts. (*t.*)	Time of the succeeding saṅkrânti expressed in: Tithis.	Day and Month A. D.	(Time of the Mesha saṅkrânti.) Week day.	By the Ârya Siddhânta. Gh.	Pa.	H.	M.	Day and Month A. D.	Week day.	At Sunrise on meridian of Ujjain. Moon's Age. Lunat. parts elapsed. (*t.*)	Tithis elapsed.	*a.*	*b.*	*c.*	Kali.
8a	9a	10a	11a	12a	13	14	15		17		19	20	21	22	23	24	25	1
....	....	....	....	......	20 Mar. (79)	0 Sat.	9	47	3	55	9 Mar. (68)	3 Tues.	267	.801	10	338	249	3752
7 Aśvina	9955	29.865	262	0.787	20 Mar. (79)	1 Sun.	25	19	10	7	26 Feb. (57)	0 Sat.	155	.465	9886	186	218	3753
....	....	....	....	......	19 Mar. (79)	2 Mon.	40	50	16	20	16 Mar. (76)	6 Fri.	157	.471	9920	122	269	3754
....	....	....	....	......	19 Mar. (78)	3 Tues.	56	21	22	32	6 Mar. (65)	4 Wed.	279	.837	135	5	241	3755
3 Jyeshṭha	9790	29.371	98	0.293	20 Mar. (79)	5 Thur.	11	52	4	45	23 Feb. (54)	1 Sun.	40	.120	10	852	211	3756
....	....	....	....	......	20 Mar. (79)	6 Fri.	27	24	10	57	14 Mar. (73)	0 Sat.	49	.147	45	788	262	3757
12 Phâlguna....	9933	29.800	241	0.722	19 Mar. (79)	0 Sat.	42	55	17	10	3 Mar. (63)	5 Thur.	275	.825	259	672	234	3758
....	....	....	....	......	19 Mar. (78)	1 Sun.	58	26	23	22	20 Feb. (51)	2 Mon.	261	.783	135	519	203	3759
....	....	....	....	......	20 Mar. (79)	3 Tues.	13	57	5	35	10 Mar. (69)	0 Sat.	40	.120	9831	419	252	3760
8 Kârttika	9769	29.306	76	0.228	20 Mar. (79)	4 Wed.	29	29	11	47	28 Feb. (59)	5 Thur.	319	.957	46	302	223	3761
....	....	....	....	......	19 Mar. (79)	5 Thur.	45	0	18	0	17 Mar. (77)	3 Tues.	16	.048	9742	202	272	3762
....	....	....	....	......	20 Mar (79)	0 Sat.	0	31	0	12	7 Mar. (66)	1 Sun.	167	.501	9956	85	244	3763
5 Śrâvaṇa.....	9911	29.734	219	0.656	20 Mar. (79)	1 Sun.	16	2	6	25	25 Feb. (56)	6 Fri.	284	.852	170	969	216	3764
....	....	....	....	......	20 Mar. (79)	2 Mon.	31	34	12	37	16 Mar. (75)	5 Thur.	266	.798	205	905	267	3765
....	....	....	....	......	19 Mar. (79)	3 Tues.	47	5	18	50	4 Mar. (64)	2 Mon.	81	.243	81	752	236	3766
1 Chaitra.....	9747	29.240	54	0.162	20 Mar. (79)	5 Thur.	2	36	1	2	21 Feb. (52)	6 Fri.	16	.048	9956	599	205	3767
....	....	....	....	......	20 Mar. (79)	6 Fri.	18	7	7	15	12 Mar. (71)	5 Thur.	101	.303	9991	535	257	3768
10 Pausha......	9890	29.669	197	0.591	20 Mar. (79)	0 Sat.	33	39	13	27	1 Mar. (60)	2 Mon.	102	.306	9867	382	226	3769
....	....	....	....	......	19 Mar. (79)	1 Sun.	49	10	19	40	19 Mar. (79)	1 Sun.	170	.510	9901	318	277	3770
....	....	....	....	......	20 Mar. (79)	3 Tues.	4	41	1	52	8 Mar. (67)	5 Thur.	38	.114	9777	166	246	3771
6 Bhâdrapada..	9725	29.175	32	0.097	20 Mar. (79)	4 Wed.	20	12	8	5	26 Feb. (57)	3 Tues.	175	.525	9991	49	218	3772
....	....	....	....	......	20 Mar. (79)	5 Thur.	35	44	14	17	17 Mar. (76)	2 Mon.	152	.456	26	985	270	3773
....	....	....	....	......	19 Mar. (79)	6 Fri.	51	15	20	30	6 Mar. (66)	0 Sat.	277	.831	240	869	242	3774
3 Jyeshṭha	9868	29.603	175	0.525	20 Mar. (79)	1 Sun.	6	46	2	42	23 Feb. (54)	4 Wed.	121	.363	116	716	211	3775
....	....	....	....	......	20 Mar. (79)	2 Mon.	22	17	8	55	14 Mar. (73)	3 Tues.	177	.531	151	652	262	3776
11 Mâgha......	9703	29.109	10	0.031	20 Mar. (79)	3 Tues.	37	49	15	7	3 Mar. (62)	0 Sat.	168	.504	27	499	231	3777
....	....	....	....	......	19 Mar. (79)	4 Wed.	53	20	21	20	20 Feb. (51)	4 Wed.	160	.480	9902	346	200	3778
....	....	....	....	......	20 Mar. (79)	6 Fri.	8	51	3	32	10 Mar. (69)	3 Tues.	214	.642	9937	282	252	3779
8 Kârttika	9846	29.538	153	0.460	20 Mar. (79)	0 Sat.	24	22	9	45	27 Feb. (58)	0 Sat.	56	.168	9813	130	221	3780
....	....	....	....	......	20 Mar. (79)	1 Sun.	39	54	15	57	18 Mar. (77)	6 Fri.	43	.129	9847	65	272	3781
....	....	....	....	......	19 Mar. (79)	2 Mon.	55	25	22	10	7 Mar. (67)	4 Wed.	157	.471	62	949	244	3782
5 Śrâvaṇa.....	9989	29.966	296	0.888	20 Mar. (79)	4 Wed.	10	56	4	22	25 Feb. (56)	2 Mon.	295	.885	276	832	216	3783
....	....	....	....	......	20 Mar. (79)	5 Thur.	26	27	10	35	16 Mar. (75)	1 Sun.	311	.933	310	769	267	3784

TABLE I.

Lunation-parts = 10,000*ths of a circle. A tithi* = $^1/_{30}$*th of the moon's synodic revolution.*

I. CONCURRENT YEAR.								II. ADDED LUNAR MONTHS.				
						Samvatsara.		True.				
Kali.	Śaka.	Chaitrâdi. Vikrama.	Meshâdi (Solar) year in Bengal.	Kollam.	A. D.	(Southern.)	Bṛihaspati cycle (Northern) current at Mesha saṅkrânti.	Name of month.	Time of the preceding saṅkrânti expressed in: Lunation parts. (*t.*)	Time of the preceding saṅkrânti expressed in: Tithis.	Time of the succeeding saṅkrânti expressed in: Lunation parts. (*t.*)	Time of the succeeding saṅkrânti expressed in: Tithis.
1	2	3	3a	4	5	6	7	8	9	10	11	12
3785	606	741	90	—	683- 84	.... 15 Vṛisha.............		....	......	....	......	....
3786	607	742	91	—	*684- 85	.... 16 Chitrabhânu.........		3 Jyeshṭha....	9770	29.310	358	1.074
3787	608	743	92	—	685- 86	.... 17 Subhânu...........		....	......	....	......	....
3788	609	744	93	—	686- 87	.... 18 Târaṇa.............		8 Kârttika....	9994	29.982	116	0.348
3789	610	745	94	—	687- 88	.... 19 Pârthiva...........		....	......	....	......	....
3790	611	746	95	—	*688- 89	.... 20 Vyaya..............		....	......	....	......	....
3791	612	747	96	—	689- 90	.... 21 Sarvajit............		5 Śrâvaṇa	9787	29.361	510	1.530
3792	613	748	97	—	690- 91	.... 22 Sarvadhârin.........		....	......	....	......	....
3793	614	749	98	—	691- 92	.... 23 Virodhin............		....	......	....	......	....
3794	615	750	99	—	*692- 93	.... 24 Vikṛita.............		4 Âshâḍha....	9859	29.577	666	1.998
3795	616	751	100	—	693- 94	.... 25 Khara..............		....	......	....	......	....
3796	617	752	101	—	694- 95	.... 26 Nandana............		....	......	....	......	....
3797	618	753	102	—	695- 96	.... 27 Vijaya.............		1 Chaitra.....	9748	29.244	48	0.144
3798	619	754	103	—	*696- 97	.... 28 Jaya...............		....	......	....	......	....
3799	620	755	104	—	697- 98	.... 29 Manmatha...........		5 Śrâvaṇa.....	9316	27.948	3	0.009
3800	621	756	105	—	698- 99	.... 30 Durmukha...........		....	......	....	......	....
3801	622	757	106	—	699-700	.... 31 Hemalamba..........		....	......	....	......	....
3802	623	758	107	—	*700- 1	.... 32 Vilamba............		4 Âshâḍha....	9372	28.116	209	0.627
3803	624	759	108	—	701- 2	.... 33 Vikârin............		....	......	....	......	....
3804	625	760	109	—	702- 3	.... 34 Śârvari............		....	......	....	......	....
3805	626	761	110	—	703- 4	.... 35 Plava..............		3 Jyeshṭha....	9969	29.907	515	1.545
3806	627	762	111	—	*704- 5	.... 36 Śubhakṛit..........		....	......	....	......	....
3807	628	763	112	—	705- 6	.... 37 Śobhana............		7 Aśvina......	9901	29.703	131	0.393
3808	629	764	113	—	706- 7	.... 38 Krodhin............		....	......	....	......	....
3809	630	765	114	—	707- 8	.... 39 Viśvâvasu..........		....	......	....	......	....
3810	631	766	115	—	*708- 9	.... 40 Parâbhava..........		5 Srâvaṇa.....	9755	29.265	554	1.662
3811	632	767	116	—	709- 10	.... 41 Plavaṅga...........		....	......	....	......	....
3812	633	768	117	—	710- 11	.... 42 Kîlaka.............		....	......	....	......	....
3813	634	769	118	—	711- 12	.... 43 Saumya.............		4 Âshâḍha....	9987	29.961	685	2.055
3814	635	770	119	—	*712- 13	.... 44 Sâdhâraṇa..........		....	......	....	......	....
3815	636	771	120	—	713- 14	.... 45 Virodhakṛit........		....	......	....	......	....
3816	637	772	121	—	714- 15	.... 46 Paridhâvin.........		1 Chaitra.....	9723	29.169	80	0.240
3817	638	773	122	—	715- 16	.... 47 Pramâdin...........		....	......	....	......	....

TABLE I.

(*Col.* 23) *a* = *Distance of moon from sun.* (*Col.* 24) *b* = *moon's mean anomaly.* (*Col.* 25) *c* = *sun's mean anomaly.*

II. ADDED LUNAR MONTHS (*continued.*)					III. COMMENCEMENT OF THE													
Mean.					Solar year.						Luni-Solar year. (Civil day of Chaitra Śukla 1st.)							
Name of month.	Time of the preceding saṅkrânti expressed in		Time of the succeeding saṅkrânti expressed in		Day and Month A. D.	(Time of the Mesha saṅkrânti.)					Day and Month A. D.	Week day.	At Sunrise on meridian of Ujjain.					Kali.
						Week day.	By the Ârya Siddhânta.						Moon's Age.					
	Lunation parts. (*l.*)	Tithis.	Lunation parts. (*t.*)	Tithis.			Gh.	Pa	H.	M.			Lunat. parts elapsed. (*t.*)	Tithis elapsed.	*a.*	*b.*	*c.*	
8a	9a	10a	11a	12a	13	14	15		17		19	20	21	22	23	24	25	1
......	...	......	...	......	20 Mar. (79)	6 Fri	41	59	16	47	5 Mar. (64)	5 Thur	233	.699	186	616	236	3785
1 Chaitra.....	9824	29.472	131	0.394	19 Mar. (79)	0 Sat.	57	30	23	0	22 Feb. (53)	2 Mon.	236	.708	62	463	206	3786
......	...	......	...	......	20 Mar. (79)	2 Mon.	13	1	5	12	12 Mar. (71)	1 Sun.	321	.963	97	399	257	3787
10 Pausha......	9967	29.900	274	0.823	20 Mar. (79)	3 Tues.	28	32	11	25	1 Mar. (60)	5 Thur.	252	.756	9972	246	226	3788
......	...	......	...	......	20 Mar. (79)	4 Wed.	44	4	17	37	20 Mar. (79)	4 Wed.	276	.828	7	182	277	3789
......	...	......	...	......	19 Mar. (79)	5 Thur.	59	35	23	50	8 Mar. (68)	1 Sun.	48	.144	9883	29	247	3790
6 Bhâdrapada..	9802	29.407	110	0.329	20 Mar. (79)	0 Sat.	15	6	6	2	26 Feb. (57)	6 Fri.	165	.495	97	913	219	3791
......	...	......	...	......	20 Mar. (79)	1 Sun.	30	37	12	15	17 Mar. (76)	5 Thur.	158	.474	132	849	270	3792
......	...	......	...	......	20 Mar. (79)	2 Mon.	46	9	18	27	6 Mar. (65)	2 Mon.	15	.045	7	696	239	3793
3 Jyeshṭha....	9945	29.835	252	0.757	20 Mar. (80)	4 Wed.	1	40	0	40	24 Feb. (55)	0 Sat.	296	.888	222	580	211	3794
......	...	......	...	......	20 Mar. (79)	5 Thur.	17	11	6	52	13 Mar. (72)	5 Thur.	77	.231	9918	479	259	3795
11 Mâgha......	9780	29.341	88	0.263	20 Mar. (79)	6 Fri.	32	42	13	5	2 Mar. (61)	2 Mon.	57	.171	9793	326	229	3796
......	...	......	...	......	20 Mar. (79)	0 Sat.	48	14	19	17	20 Feb. (51)	0 Sat.	287	.861	8	210	201	3797
......	...	......	...	......	20 Mar (80)	2 Mon.	3	45	1	30	10 Mar. (70)	6 Fri.	293	.879	42	146	252	3798
8 Kârttika....	9923	29.769	231	0.691	20 Mar. (79)	3 Tues.	19	16	7	42	27 Feb. (58)	3 Tues.	53	.159	9918	993	221	3799
......	...	......	...	......	20 Mar. (79)	4 Wed.	34	47	13	55	18 Mar. (77)	2 Mon.	32	.096	9953	929	272	3800
......	...	......	...	......	20 Mar. (79)	5 Thur.	50	19	20	7	8 Mar. (67)	0 Sat.	178	.534	167	812	244	3801
4 Âshâḍha....	9759	29.276	66	0.198	20 Mar. (80)	0 Sat.	5	50	2	20	25 Feb. (56)	4 Wed.	67	.201	43	660	213	3802
......	...	......	...	......	20 Mar. (79)	1 Sun.	21	21	8	32	15 Mar. (74)	3 Tues.	139	.417	78	596	265	3803
......	...	......	...	......	20 Mar. (79)	2 Mon.	36	52	14	45	4 Mar. (63)	0 Sat.	141	.423	9953	443	234	3804
1 Chaitra.....	9901	29.704	209	0.626	20 Mar. (79)	3 Tues.	52	24	20	57	21 Feb. (52)	4 Wed.	108	.324	9829	290	203	3805
......	...	......	...	......	20 Mar. (80)	5 Thur.	7	55	3	10	11 Mar. (71)	3 Tues.	142	.426	9864	226	254	3806
9 Mârgaśîrsha.	9737	29.210	44	0.132	20 Mar. (79)	6 Fri	23	26	9	22	1 Mar. (60)	1 Sun.	308	.924	78	110	226	3807
......	...	......	...	......	20 Mar. (79)	0 Sat.	38	57	15	35	20 Mar. (79)	0 Sat.	294	.882	113	46	278	3808
......	...	......	...	......	20 Mar. (79)	1 Sun.	54	29	21	47	9 Mar. (68)	4 Wed.	40	.120	9988	893	247	3809
6 Bhâdrapada..	9879	29.638	187	0.561	20 Mar. (80)	3 Tues.	10	0	4	0	27 Feb. (58)	2 Mon.	206	.618	203	776	219	3810
......	...	......	...	......	20 Mar. (79)	4 Wed.	25	31	10	12	17 Mar. (76)	1 Sun.	241	.723	237	712	270	3811
......	...	......	...	......	20 Mar. (79)	5 Thur.	41	2	16	25	6 Mar. (65)	5 Thur.	201	.603	113	560	239	3812
2 Vaiśâkha....	9715	29.145	22	0.067	20 Mar. (79)	6 Fri.	56	34	22	37	23 Feb. (54)	2 Mon.	209	.627	9989	407	208	3813
......	...	......	...	......	20 Mar. (80)	1 Sun.	12	5	4	50	13 Mar. (73)	1 Sun.	280	.840	23	343	260	3814
11 Mâgha......	9858	29.573	165	0.495	20 Mar (79)	2 Mon.	27	36	11	2	2 Mar. (61)	5 Thur.	169	.507	9899	190	229	3815
......	...	......	...	......	20 Mar. (79)	3 Tues.	43	7	17	15	20 Feb. (51)	3 Tues.	318	.954	113	73	201	3816
......	...	......	...	......	20 Mar. (79)	4 Wed.	58	39	23	27	11 Mar. (70)	2 Mon.	296	.888	148	9	252	3817

TABLE I.

Lunation-parts = 10,000*ths of a circle. A tithi* = 1/30*th of the moon's synodic revolution.*

I. CONCURRENT YEAR.								II. ADDED LUNAR MONTHS.				
						Samvatsara.		True.				
Kali.	Śaka.	Chaitrâdi. Vikrama.	Meshâdi (Solar) year in Bengal.	Kollam.	A. D.	(Southern.)	Bṛihaspati cycle (Northern) current at Mesha saṅkrânti.	Name of month.	Time of the preceding saṅkrânti expressed in Lunation parts. (*t.*)	Time of the preceding saṅkrânti expressed in Tithis.	Time of the succeeding saṅkrânti expressed in Lunation parts. (*t.*)	Time of the succeeding saṅkrânti expressed in Tithis.
1	2	3	3a	4	5	6	7	8	9	10	11	12
3818	639	774	123	—	*716-17	....	48 Ananda	5 Śrâvaṇa	9301	27.903	83	0.249
3819	640	775	124	—	717-18	....	49 Râkshasa					
3820	641	776	125	—	718-19	....	50 Anala					
3821	642	777	126	—	719-20	....	51 Piṅgala	4 Âshâḍha	9466	28.398	201	0.603
3822	643	778	127	—	*720-21	....	52 Kâlayukta					
3823	644	779	128	—	721-22	....	53 Siddhârtin					
3824	645	780	129	—	722-23	....	54 Raudra	2 Vaiśâkha	9611	28.833	118	0.354
3825	646	781	130	—	723-24	....	55 Durmati					
3826	647	782	131	—	*724-25	....	56 Dundubhi	6 Bhâdrapada	9600	28.800	90	0.270
3827	648	783	132	—	725-26	....	57 Rudhirodgârin					
3828	649	784	133	—	726-27	....	58 Raktâksha					
3829	650	785	134	—	727-28	....	59 Krodhana	5 Śrâvaṇa	9728	29.184	522	1.566
3830	651	786	135	—	*728-29	....	60 Kshaya					
3831	652	787	136	—	729-30	....	1 Prabhava					
3832	653	788	137	—	730-31	....	2 Vibhava	3 Jyeshṭha	9610	28.830	178	0.534
3833	654	789	138	—	731-32	....	3 Śukla					
3834	655	790	139	—	*732-33	....	4 Pramoda					
3835	656	791	140	—	733-34	....	5 Prajâpati	1 Chaitra	9690	29.070	44	0.132
3836	657	792	141	—	734-35	....	6 Aṅgiras					
3837	658	793	142	—	735-36	....	7 Śrîmukha	5 Śrâvaṇa	9261	27.783	68	0.204
3838	659	794	143	—	*736-37	....	8 Bhâva					
3839	660	795	144	—	737-38	....	9 Yuvan					
3840	661	796	145	—	738-39	....	10 Dhâtṛi [1]	4 Âshâḍha	9643	28.929	288	0.864
3841	662	797	146	—	739-40	....	12 Bahudhânya					
3842	663	798	147	—	*740-41	....	13 Pramâthin					
3843	664	799	148	—	741-42	....	14 Vikrama	2 Vaiśâkha	9590	28.770	172	0.516
3844	665	800	149	—	742-43	....	15 Vṛisha					
3845	666	801	150	—	743-44	....	16 Chitrabhânu	6 Bhâdrapada	9612	28.836	194	0.582
3846	667	802	151	—	*744-45	....	17 Subhânu					
3847	668	803	152	—	745-46	....	18 Târaṇa					
3848	669	804	153	—	746-47	....	19 Pârthiva	5 Śrâvaṇa	9780	29.340	492	1.476
3849	670	805	154	—	747-48	....	20 Vyaya					
3850	671	806	155	—	*748-49	....	21 Sarvajit					

[1] Îśvara, No. 11, was suppressed.

TABLE I.

(*Col.* 23) *a* = *Distance of moon from sun.* (*Col.* 24) *b* = *moon's mean anomaly.* (*Col.* 25) *c* = *sun's mean anomaly.*

II. ADDED LUNAR MONTHS (*continued.*)					III. COMMENCEMENT OF THE										
Mean.					Solar year.				Luni-Solar year. (Civil day of Chaitra Śukla 1st.)						Kali.
Name of month.	Time of the preceding saṅkrânti expressed in		Time of the succeeding saṅkrânti expressed in		Day and Month A. D.	(Time of the Mesha saṅkrânti.)			Day and Month A. D.	Week day.	At Sunrise on meridian of Ujjain.				
						Week day.	By the Ârya Siddhânta.				Moon's Age.				
	Lunation parts. (*t.*)	Tithis.	Lunation parts. (*t.*)	Tithis.			Gh. Pa	H. M.			Lunat. parts elapsed. (*t.*)	Tithis elapsed	*a.*	*b.*	*c.*	
8a	9a	10a	11a	12a	13	14	15	17	19	20	21	22	23	24	25	1
7 Âśvina......	9693	29.079	0	0.001	20 Mar. (80)	6 Fri.	14 10	5 40	28 Feb. (59)	6 Fri.	55	.165	24	857	221	3818
....	....	......	....	......	20 Mar. (79)	0 Sat.	29 41	11 52	18 Mar. (77)	5 Thur.	63	.189	58	792	273	3819
....	....	......	....	......	20 Mar. (79)	1 Sun.	45 12	18 5	8 Mar. (67)	3 Tues.	287	.861	273	676	245	3820
4 Âshâḍha....	9836	29.507	143	0.430	21 Mar (80)	3 Tues.	0 44	0 17	25 Feb. (56)	0 Sat.	269	.807	148	523	214	3821
....	....	......	....	......	20 Mar. (80)	4 Wed.	16 15	6 30	14 Mar. (74)	5 Thur.	51	.153	9845	423	262	3822
....	....	......	....	......	20 Mar (79)	5 Thur.	31 46	12 42	4 Mar. (63)	3 Tues.	330	.990	59	306	234	3823
1 Chaitra.....	9979	29.936	286	0.858	20 Mar. (79)	6 Fri.	47 17	18 55	21 Feb. (52)	0 Sat.	193	.579	9935	154	203	3824
....	....	......	....	......	21 Mar. (80)	1 Sun.	2 49	1 7	12 Mar. (71)	6 Fri.	184	.552	9969	90	255	3825
9 Mârgaśîrsha.	9814	29.442	121	0.364	20 Mar. (80)	2 Mon.	18 20	7 20	1 Mar. (61)	4 Wed.	300	.900	184	973	227	3826
....	....	......	....	......	20 Mar. (79)	3 Tues.	33 51	13 32	20 Mar. (79)	3 Tues.	283	.849	218	909	278	3827
....	....	......	....	......	20 Mar. (79)	4 Wed.	49 22	19 45	9 Mar. (68)	0 Sat.	94	.282	94	756	247	3828
6 Bhâdrapada..	9957	29.870	264	0.792	21 Mar. (80)	6 Fri.	4 54	1 57	26 Feb. (57)	4 Wed.	26	.078	9970	603	216	3829
....	....	......	....	......	20 Mar. (80)	0 Sat.	20 25	8 10	16 Mar. (76)	3 Tues.	109	.327	4	540	267	3830
....	....	......	....	......	20 Mar. (79)	1 Sun.	35 56	14 22	5 Mar. (64)	0 Sat.	112	.336	9880	387	237	3831
2 Vaiśâkha....	9792	29.376	100	0.299	20 Mar. (79)	2 Mon.	51 27	20 35	22 Feb. (53)	4 Wed.	37	.111	9756	234	206	3832
....	....	......	....	......	21 Mar. (80)	4 Wed.	6 59	2 47	13 Mar. (72)	3 Tues.	53	.159	9790	170	257	3833
11 Mâgha......	9935	29.805	242	0.727	20 Mar. (80)	5 Thur.	22 30	9 0	2 Mar. (62)	1 Sun.	192	.576	5	54	229	3834
....	....	......	....	......	20 Mar. (79)	6 Fri.	38 1	15 12	20 Feb. (51)	6 Fri.	308	.924	219	937	201	3835
....	....	......	....	......	20 Mar. (79)	0 Sat.	53 32	21 25	11 Mar. (70)	5 Thur.	294	.882	254	873	252	3836
7 Âśvina......	9770	29.311	78	0.233	21 Mar. (80)	2 Mon.	9 4	3 37	28 Feb. (59)	2 Mon.	133	.399	129	720	222	3837
....	....	......	....	......	20 Mar. (80)	3 Tues.	24 35	9 50	18 Mar. (78)	1 Sun.	188	.564	164	656	273	3838
....	....	......	....	......	20 Mar. (79)	4 Wed.	40 6	16 2	7 Mar. (66)	5 Thur.	177	.531	40	503	242	3839
4 Âshâḍha....	9913	29.739	220	0.661	20 Mar. (79)	5 Thur.	55 37	22 15	24 Feb. (55)	2 Mon.	170	.510	9915	351	211	3840
....	....	......	....	......	21 Mar. (80)	0 Sat.	11 9	4 27	15 Mar. (74)	1 Sun.	226	.678	9950	286	262	3841
12 Phâlguna...	9749	29.246	56	C.168	20 Mar. (80)	1 Sun.	26 40	10 40	3 Mar. (63)	5 Thur.	70	.210	9826	134	232	3842
....	....	......	....	......	20 Mar. (79)	2 Mon.	42 11	16 52	21 Feb. (52)	3 Tues.	198	.594	40	17	204	3843
....	....	......	....	......	20 Mar. (79)	3 Tues.	57 42	23 5	12 Mar. (71)	2 Mon.	174	.522	75	953	255	3844
9 Mârgaśîrsha.	9891	29.674	199	0.596	21 Mar. (80)	5 Thur.	13 14	5 17	2 Mar. (61)	0 Sat.	309	.927	289	837	227	3845
....	....	......	....	......	20 Mar. (80)	6 Fri.	28 45	11 30	20 Mar. (80)	6 Fri.	327	.981	324	773	278	3846
....	....	......	....	......	20 Mar. (79)	0 Sat	44 16	17 42	9 Mar. (68)	3 Tues.	244	.732	200	620	247	3847
5 Śrâvaṇa.....	9727	29.180	34	0.102	20 Mar. (79)	1 Sun.	59 47	23 55	26 Feb. (57)	0 Sat.	245	.735	75	467	216	3848
....	....	......	....	......	21 Mar. (80)	3 Tues.	15 19	6 7	17 Mar. (76)	6 Fri.	331	.993	110	403	268	3849
....	....	......	....	......	20 Mar. (80)	4 Wed.	30 50	12 20	5 Mar. (65)	3 Tues.	265	.795	9985	250	237	3850

TABLE I.

Lunation-parts = 10,000*ths of a circle. A tithi* = 1/30*th of the moon's synodic revolution.*

I. CONCURRENT YEAR.								II. ADDED LUNAR MONTHS.				
						Samvatsara.		True.				
Kali.	Śaka.	Chaitrâdi. Vikrama.	Meshâdi (Solar) year in Bengal.	Kollam.	A. D.	(Southern.)	Bṛihaspati cycle (Northern) current at Mesha saṅkrânti.	Name of month.	Time of the preceding saṅkrânti expressed in: Lunation parts. (*t*.)	Time of the preceding saṅkrânti expressed in: Tithis.	Time of the succeeding saṅkrânti expressed in: Lunation parts. (*t*.)	Time of the succeeding saṅkrânti expressed in: Tithis.
1	2	3	3a	4	5	6	7	8	9	10	11	12
3851	672	807	156	—	749-50	.... 22 Sarvadhârin		3 Jyeshṭha....	9697	29.091	353	1.059
3852	673	808	157	—	750-51	.... 23 Virodhin						
3853	674	809	158	—	751-52	.... 24 Vikṛita						
3854	675	810	159	—	*752-53	.... 25 Khara		1 Chaitra.....	9723	29.169	22	0.066
3855	676	811	160	—	753-54	.... 26 Nandana						
3856	677	812	161	—	754-55	.... 27 Vijaya		5 Śrâvaṇa.....	9283	27.849.	29	0.087
3857	678	813	162	—	755-56	.... 28 Jaya						
3858	679	814	163	—	*756-57	.... 29 Manmatha						
3859	680	815	164	—	757-58	.... 30 Durmukha		4 Âshâḍha	9835	29.505	463	1.389
3860	681	816	165	—	758-59	.... 31 Hemalamba						
3861	682	817	166	—	759-60	.... 32 Vilamba						
3862	683	818	167	—	*760-61	.... 33 Vikârin		2 Vaiśâkha....	9554	28.662	142	0.426
3863	684	819	168	—	761-62	.... 34 Śârvari						
3864	685	820	169	—	762-63	.... 35 Plava		6 Bhâdrapada..	9570	28.710	199	0.597
3865	686	821	170	—	763-64	.... 36 Śubhakṛit						
3866	687	822	171	—	*764-65	.... 37 Śobhana						
3867	688	823	172	—	765-66	.... 38 Krodhin		5 Śrâvaṇa.....	9929	29.787	543	1.629
3868	689	824	173	—	766-67	.... 39 Visvâvasu						
3869	690	825	174	—	767-68	.... 40 Parâbhava						
3870	691	826	175	—	*768-69	.... 41 Plavaṅga		3 Jyeshṭha	9691	29.073	440	1.320
3871	692	827	176	—	769-70	.... 42 Kîlaka						
3872	693	828	177	—	770-71	.... 43 Saumya		{ 7 Âśvina...... 10 *Pausha* (*Ksh.*)	9740 115	29.220 0.345	88 9964	0.264 29.892 }
3873	694	829	178	—	771-72	.... 44 Sâdhâraṇa		1 Chaitra.....	9860	29.580	86	0.258
3874	695	830	179	—	*772-73	.... 45 Virodhakṛit						
3875	696	831	180	—	773-74	.... 46 Paridhâvin		5 Śrâvaṇa.....	9404	28.212	48	0.144
3876	697	832	181	—	774-75	.... 47 Pramâdhin						
3877	698	833	182	—	775-76	.... 48 Ânanda						
3878	699	834	183	—	*776-77	.... 49 Râkshasa		4 Âshâḍha	9955	29.865	655	1.965
3879	700	835	184	—	777-78	.... 50 Anala						
3880	701	836	185	—	778-79	.... 51 Piṅgala						
3881	702	837	186	—	779-80	.... 52 Kâlayukta		2 Vaiśâkha....	9584	28.752	111	0.333
3882	703	838	187	—	*780-81	.... 53 Siddhârthin						

TABLE I.

(*Col.* 23) *a* = *Distance of moon from sun.* (*Col.* 24) *b* = *moon's mean anomaly.* (*Col.* 25) *c* = *sun's mean anomaly.*

II. ADDED LUNAR MONTHS (*continued.*)					III. COMMENCEMENT OF THE													
Mean.					Solar year.						Luni-Solar year. (Civil day of Chaitra Śukla 1st.)							
	Time of the preceding saṅkrânti expressed in		Time of the succeeding saṅkrânti expressed in			(Time of the Mesha saṅkrânti.)							At Sunrise on meridian of Ujjain.					
							By the Ârya Siddhânta.						Moon's Age.					
Name of month.	Lunation parts. (*l.*)	Tithis.	Lunation parts. (*l.*)	Tithis.	Day and Month A. D.	Week day.	Gh.	Pa.	H.	M.	Day and Month A. D.	Week day.	Lunat. parts elapsed. (*l.*)	Tithis elapsed.	*a.*	*b.*	*c.*	Kali.
8a	**9a**	**10a**	**11a**	**12a**	**13**	**14**	**15**		**17**		**19**	**20**	**21**	**22**	**23**	**24**	**25**	**1**
2 Vaiśâkha....	9869	29.608	177	0.530	20 Mar. (79)	5 Thur.	46	21	18	32	22 Feb. (53)	0 Sat.	84	.252	9861	97	206	3851
....	....	....	....	....	21 Mar. (80)	0 Sat.	1	52	0	45	13 Mar. (72)	6 Fri.	66	.198	9896	34	257	3852
10 Pausha	9705	29.115	12	0.037	21 Mar. (80)	1 Sun.	17	24	6	57	3 Mar. (62)	4 Wed.	181	.543	111	917	229	3853
....	....	....	....	....	20 Mar. (80)	2 Mon	32	55	13	10	20 Feb. (51)	1 Sun.	⊙−11	−.033	9986	764	198	3854
....	....	....	....	....	20 Mar. (79)	3 Tues.	48	26	19	22	10 Mar. (69)	0 Sat.	28	.084	21	700	250	3855
7 Âśvina......	9848	29.543	155	0.465	21 Mar. (80)	5 Thur.	3	57	1	35	28 Feb. (59)	5 Thur.	305	.915	235	584	222	3856
....	....	....	....	....	21 Mar. (80)	6 Fri.	19	29	7	47	18 Mar. (77)	3 Tues.	86	.258	9931	483	270	3857
....	....	....	....	....	20 Mar. (80)	0 Sat.	35	0	14	0	6 Mar. (66)	0 Sat.	70	.210	9807	331	239	3858
4 Ashâḍha	9990	29.971	298	0.893	20 Mar. (79)	1 Sun.	50	31	20	12	24 Feb. (55)	5 Thur.	299	.897	21	214	211	3859
....	....	....	....	....	21 Mar. (80)	3 Tues.	6	2	2	25	15 Mar. (74)	4 Wed.	309	.927	56	150	263	3860
12 Phâlguna....	9826	29.477	133	0.399	21 Mar. (80)	4 Wed.	21	34	8	37	4 Mar. (63)	1 Sun.	68	.204	9931	997	232	3861
....	....	....	....	....	20 Mar. (80)	5 Thur.	37	5	14	50	22 Feb. (53)	6 Fri.	194	.582	146	881	204	3862
....	....	....	....	....	20 Mar. (79)	6 Fri.	52	36	21	2	12 Mar. (71)	5 Thur.	192	.576	180	817	255	3863
9 Mârgaśirsha .	9969	29.906	276	0.828	21 Mar. (80)	1 Sun.	8	7	3	15	1 Mar. (60)	2 Mon.	77	.231	56	664	224	3864
....	....	....	....	....	21 Mar. (80)	2 Mon.	23	39	9	27	20 Mar. (79)	1 Sun.	148	.444	91	600	276	3865
....	....	....	....	....	20 Mar. (80)	3 Tues.	39	10	15	40	8 Mar. (68)	5 Thur.	152	.456	9966	447	245	3866
5 Śrâvaṇa.....	9804	29.412	111	0.334	20 Mar. (79)	4 Wed.	54	41	21	52	25 Feb. (56)	2 Mon.	119	.357	9842	294	214	3867
....	....	....	....	....	21 Mar. (80)	6 Fri.	10	12	4	5	16 Mar. (75)	1 Sun.	156	.468	9877	231	265	3868
....	....	....	....	....	21 Mar. (80)	0 Sat.	25	44	10	17	6 Mar. (65)	6 Fri.	323	.969	91	114	237	3869
2 Vaiśâkha....	9947	29.840	254	0.762	20 Mar. (80)	1 Sun.	41	15	16	30	23 Feb. (54)	3 Tues.	75	.225	9967	961	206	3870
....	....	....	....	....	20 Mar. (79)	2 Mon.	56	46	22	42	13 Mar. (72)	2 Mon.	56	.168	1	897	258	3871
}10 Pausha	9782	29.346	89	0.268	21 Mar. (80)	4 Wed.	12	17	4	55	3 Mar. (62)	0 Sat.	219	.657	216	781	230	3872
....	....	....	....	....	21 Mar. (80)	5 Thur.	27	49	11	7	20 Feb. (51)	4 Wed.	134	.402	92	628	199	3873
....	....	....	....	....	20 Mar. (80)	6 Fri.	43	20	17	20	10 Mar. (70)	3 Tues.	211	.633	126	564	250	3874
7 Âśvina......	9925	29.775	232	0.697	20 Mar. (79)	0 Sat.	58	51	23	32	27 Feb. (58)	0 Sat.	217	.651	2	411	219	3875
....	....	....	....	....	21 Mar. (80)	2 Mon.	14	22	5	45	18 Mar. (77)	6 Fri.	292	.876	37	347	271	3876
....	....	....	....	....	21 Mar. (80)	3 Tues.	29	54	11	57	7 Mar. (66)	3 Tues.	183	.549	9912	194	240	3877
3 Jyeshṭha	9760	29.281	68	0.203	20 Mar. (80)	4 Wed.	45	25	18	10	24 Feb. (55)	0 Sat.	⊙−34	−.102	9788	41	209	3878
....	....	....	....	....	21 Mar. (80)	6 Fri.	0	56	0	22	15 Mar. (74)	0 Sat.	313	.939	161	14	263	3879
12 Phâlguna....	9903	29.709	210	0.631	21 Mar. (80)	0 Sat.	16	27	6	35	4 Mar. (63)	4 Wed.	70	.210	37	861	232	3880
....	....	....	....	....	21 Mar. (80)	1 Sun.	31	59	12	47	22 Feb. (53)	2 Mon.	254	.762	251	744	204	3881
....	....	....	....	....	20 Mar. (80)	2 Mon.	47	30	19	0	12 Mar. (72)	1 Sun.	299	.897	286	680	255	3882

⊙ See Text. Art. 101 above, para. 2.

TABLE I.

Lunation-parts = 10,000ths of a circle. A tithi = 1/30th of the moon's synodic revolution.

I. CONCURRENT YEAR.								II. ADDED LUNAR MONTHS.				
						Samvatsara.		True.				
Kali.	Śaka.	Chaitrâdi. Vikrama.	Meshâdi (Solar) year in Bengal.	Kollam.	A. D.	(Southern.)	Bṛihaspati cycle (Northern) current at Mesha saṅkrânti.	Name of month.	Time of the preceding saṅkrânti expressed in		Time of the succeeding saṅkrânti expressed in	
									Lunation parts. (*l.*)	Tithis.	Lunation parts. (*l.*)	Tithis.
1	2	3	3a	4	5	6	7	8	9	10	11	12
3883	704	839	188	—	781- 82	54 Raudra		6 Bhâdrapada	9563	28.689	158	0.474
3884	705	840	189	—	782- 83	55 Durmati						
3885	706	841	190	—	783- 84	56 Dundubhi						
3886	707	842	191	—	*784- 85	57 Rudhirodgârin		4 Âshâḍha	9457	28.371	127	0.381
3887	708	843	192	—	785- 86	58 Raktâksha						
3888	709	844	193	—	786- 87	59 Krodhana						
3889	710	845	194	—	787- 88	60 Kshaya		3 Jyeshṭha	9647	28.941	434	1.302
3890	711	846	195	—	*788- 89	1 Prabhava						
3891	712	847	196	—	789- 90	2 Vibhava		7 Âśvina	9703	29.109	98	0.294
3892	713	848	197	—	790- 91	3 Śukla						
3893	714	849	198	—	791- 92	4 Pramoda						
3894	715	850	199	—	*792- 93	5 Prajâpati		5 Śrâvaṇa	9591	28.773	165	0.495
3895	716	851	200	—	793- 94	6 Aṅgiras						
3896	717	852	201	—	794- 95	7 Śrîmukha						
3897	718	853	202	—	795- 96	8 Bhâva		4 Âshâḍha	9976	29.928	792	2.376
3898	719	854	203	—	*796- 97	9 Yuvan						
3899	720	855	204	—	797- 98	10 Dhâtṛi						
3900	721	856	205	—	798- 99	11 Îśvara		2 Vaiśâkha	9715	29.145	152	0.456
3901	722	857	206	—	799-800	12 Bahudhânya						
3902	723	858	207	--	*800- 1	13 Pramâthin		6 Bhâdrapada	9648	28.944	155	0.465
3903	724	859	208	--	801- 2	14 Vikrama						
3904	725	860	209	—	802- 3	15 Vṛisha						
3905	726	861	210	—	803- 4	16 Chitrabhânu		4 Âshâḍha	9510	28.530	282	0.846
3906	727	862	211	—	*804- 5	17 Subhânu						
3907	728	863	212	—	805- 6	18 Târaṇa						
3908	729	864	213	—	806- 7	19 Pârthiva		3 Jyeshṭha	9660	28.980	392	1.176
3909	730	865	214	—	807- 8	20 Vyaya						
3910	731	866	215	—	*808- 9	21 Sarvajit		7 Âśvina	9680	29.040	58	0.174
3911	732	867	216	—	809- 10	22 Sarvadhârin						
3912	733	868	217	—	810- 11	23 Virodhin						
3913	734	869	218	—	811- 12	24 Vikṛita		5 Śrâvaṇa	9772	29.316	355	1.065
3914	735	870	219	—	*812- 13	25 Khara						
3915	736	871	220	—	813- 14	26 Nandana						

TABLE I.

(*Col.* 23) *a* = *Distance of moon from sun.* (*Col.* 24) *b* = *moon's mean anomaly.* (*Col.* 25) *c* = *sun's mean anomaly.*

II. ADDED LUNAR MONTHS (*continued.*)					III. COMMENCEMENT OF THE													
Mean.					Solar year.						Luni-Solar year. (Civil day of Chaitra Śukla 1st.)							
Name of month.	Time of the preceding saṅkrânti expressed in		Time of the succeeding saṅkrânti expressed in		Day and Month A. D.	(Time of the Mesha saṅkrânti.)					Day and Month A. D.	Week day.	At Sunrise on meridian of Ujjain.					Kali.
						Week day.	By the Ârya Siddhânta.						Moon's Age.					
	Lunation parts. (*t.*)	Tithis.	Lunation parts. (*t.*)	Tithis.			Gh.	Pa.	H.	M.			Lunat. parts elapsed. (*t.*)	Tithis elapsed.	*a.*	*b.*	*c.*	
8a	**9a**	**10a**	**11a**	**12a**	**13**	**14**	**15**		**17**		**19**	**20**	**21**	**22**	**23**	**24**	**25**	**1**
8 Kârttika....	9738	29.215	46	0.137	21 Mar. (80)	4 Wed.	3	1	1	12	1 Mar. (60)	5 Thur.	278	.834	162	528	225	3883
....	...	......	...	......	21 Mar. (80)	5 Thur.	18	32	7	25	19 Mar. (78)	3 Tues.	60	.180	9858	427	273	3884
....	...	......	...	......	21 Mar. (80)	6 Fri.	34	4	13	37	8 Mar. (67)	0 Sat.	11	.033	9733	274	242	3885
5 Śrâvaṇa.....	9881	29.644	189	0.566	20 Mar. (80)	0 Sat.	49	35	19	50	26 Feb. (57)	5 Thur.	207	.621	9948	158	214	3886
....	...	......	...	......	21 Mar. (80)	2 Mon.	5	6	2	2	16 Mar. (75)	4 Wed.	200	.600	9982	94	266	3887
....	...	......	...	......	21 Mar. (80)	3 Tues.	20	37	8	15	6 Mar. (65)	2 Mon.	317	.951	197	978	237	3888
1 Chaitra.....	9717	29.150	24	0.072	21 Mar. (80)	4 Wed.	36	9	14	27	23 Feb. (54)	6 Fri.	89	.267	72	825	207	3889
....	...	......	...	......	20 Mar. (80)	5 Thur.	51	40	20	40	13 Mar. (73)	5 Thur.	107	.321	107	761	258	3890
10 Pausha.....	9859	29.578	167	0.500	21 Mar. (80)	0 Sat.	7	11	2	52	2 Mar. (61)	2 Mon.	35	.105	9983	608	227	3891
....	...	......	...	......	21 Mar. (80)	1 Sun.	22	42	9	5	21 Mar. (80)	1 Sun.	119	.357	17	544	278	3892
....	...	......	...	......	21 Mar. (80)	2 Mon.	38	14	15	17	10 Mar. (69)	5 Thur.	122	.366	9893	391	247	3893
6 Bhâdrapada..	9695	29.084	2	0.007	20 Mar. (80)	3 Tues.	53	45	21	30	27 Feb. (58)	2 Mon.	50	.150	9769	238	217	3894
....	...	......	...	......	21 Mar. (80)	5 Thur.	9	16	3	42	17 Mar. (76)	1 Sun.	68	.204	9804	174	268	3895
....	...	......	...	......	21 Mar. (80)	6 Fri.	24	47	9	55	7 Mar. (66)	6 Fri.	208	.624	18	58	240	3896
3 Jyeshṭha. ..	9838	29.513	145	0.435	21 Mar. (80)	0 Sat.	40	19	16	7	25 Feb. (56)	4 Wed.	323	.969	232	941	212	3897
....	...	......	...	......	20 Mar. (80)	1 Sun.	55	50	22	20	15 Mar. (75)	3 Tues.	309	.927	267	877	263	3898
12 Phâlguna....	9980	29.941	288	0.863	21 Mar. (80)	3 Tues.	11	21	4	32	4 Mar. (63)	0 Sat.	145	.435	143	724	232	3899
....	...	......	...	......	21 Mar. (80)	4 Wed.	26	52	10	45	21 Feb. (52)	4 Wed.	99	.297	18	572	202	3900
....	...	......	...	......	21 Mar. (80)	5 Thur.	42	24	16	57	12 Mar. (71)	3 Tues.	186	.558	53	508	253	3901
8 Kârttika....	9816	29.447	123	0.369	20 Mar. (80)	6 Fri.	57	55	23	10	29 Feb. (60)	0 Sat.	181	.543	9929	355	222	3902
....	...	......	...	......	21 Mar. (80)	1 Sun.	13	26	5	22	19 Mar. (78)	6 Fri.	239	.717	9963	291	273	3903
....	...	......	...	......	21 Mar. (80)	2 Mon.	28	57	11	35	8 Mar. (67)	3 Tues.	88	.264	9839	138	243	3904
5 Śrâvaṇa.....	9959	29.876	266	0.798	21 Mar. (80)	3 Tues.	44	29	17	47	26 Feb. (57)	1 Sun.	214	.642	53	21	214	3905
....	...	......	...	......	21 Mar. (81)	5 Thur.	0	0	0	0	16 Mar. (76)	0 Sat.	191	.573	88	958	266	3906
....	...	......	...	......	21 Mar. (80)	6 Fri.	15	31	6	12	6 Mar. (65)	5 Thur.	324	.972	302	841	238	3907
1 Chaitra.....	9794	29.382	101	0.304	21 Mar. (80)	0 Sat.	31	2	12	25	23 Feb. (54)	2 Mon.	191	.573	178	688	207	3908
....	...	......	...	......	21 Mar. (80)	1 Sun.	46	34	18	37	14 Mar. (73)	1 Sun.	255	.765	213	624	258	3909
10 Pausha......	9937	29.810	244	0.732	21 Mar. (81)	3 Tues.	2	5	0	50	2 Mar. (62)	5 Thur.	252	.756	88	472	227	3910
....	...	......	...	......	21 Mar. (80)	4 Wed.	17	36	7	2	20 Mar. (79)	3 Tues.	26	.078	9784	371	276	3911
....	...	......	...	......	21 Mar (80)	5 Thur.	33	7	13	15	10 Mar. (69)	1 Sun.	279	.837	9999	255	248	3912
6 Bhâdrapada..	9772	29.316	79	0 238	21 Mar. (80)	6 Fri.	48	39	19	27	27 Feb. (58)	5 Thur.	100	.300	9875	102	217	3913
....	...	......	...	......	21 Mar. (81)	1 Sun.	4	10	1	40	17 Mar. (77)	4 Wed.	82	.246	9909	38	268	3914
....	...	......	...	......	21 Mar. (80)	2 Mon.	19	41	7	52	7 Mar (66)	2 Mon.	197	.591	124	921	240	3915

TABLE I.

Lunation-parts = 10,000*ths of a circle. A tithi* = $^1/_{30}$*th of the moon's synodic revolution.*

I. CONCURRENT YEAR.								II. ADDED LUNAR MONTHS.				
						Samvatsara.		True.				
Kali.	Śaka.	Chaitrâdi. Vikrama.	Meshâdi (Solar) year in Bengal.	Kollam.	A. D.	(Southern.)	Bṛihaspati cycle (Northern) current at Mesha saṅkrânti.	Name of month.	Time of the preceding saṅkrânti expressed in Lunation parts. (*l.*)	Time of the preceding saṅkrânti expressed in Tithis.	Time of the succeeding saṅkrânti expressed in Lunation parts. (*l.*)	Time of the succeeding saṅkrânti expressed in Tithis.
1	2	3	3a	4	5	6	7	8	9	10	11	12
3916	737	872	221	—	814-15	27 Vijaya		4 Âshâḍha	9935	29.805	807	2.421
3917	738	873	222	—	815-16	28 Jaya						
3918	739	874	223	—	*816-17	29 Manmatha						
3919	740	875	224	—	817-18	30 Durmukha		2 Vaiśâkha	9910	29.730	296	0.888
3920	741	876	225	—	818-19	31 Hemalamba						
3921	742	877	226	—	819-20	32 Vilamba		6 Bhâdrapada	9821	29.463	251	0.753
3922	743	878	227	—	*820-21	33 Vikârin						
3923	744	879	228	—	821-22	34 Śârvarin						
3924	745	880	229	—	822-23	35 Plava		4 Âshâḍha	9482	28.446	340	1.020
3925	746	881	230	—	823-24	36 Śubhakṛit 1)						
3926	747	882	231	—	*824-25	38 Krodhin						
3927	748	883	232	0- 1	825-26	39 Viśvâvasu		3 Jyeshṭha	9773	29.319	403	1.209
3928	749	884	233	1- 2	826-27	40 Parâbhavu						
3929	750	885	234	2- 3	827-28	41 Plavaṅga		7 Âśvina	9740	29.220	51	0.153
3930	751	886	235	3- 4	*828-29	42 Kîlaka						
3931	752	887	236	4- 5	829-30	43 Saumya						
3932	753	888	237	5- 6	830-31	44 Sâdhâraṇa		5 Śrâvaṇa	9865	29.595	533	1.599
3933	754	889	238	6- 7	831-32	45 Virodhakṛit						
3934	755	890	239	7- 8	*832-33	46 Paridhâvin						
3935	756	891	240	8- 9	833-34	47 Pramâdin		4 Âshâḍha	9920	29.760	770	2.310
3936	757	892	241	9-10	834-35	48 Ânanda						
3937	758	893	242	10-11	835-36	49 Râkshasa						
3938	759	894	243	11-12	*836-37	50 Anala		1 Chaitra	9817	29.451	81	0.243
3939	760	895	244	12-13	837-38	51 Piṅgala						
3940	761	896	245	13-14	838-39	52 Kâlayukta		5 Śrâvaṇa	9377	28.131	13	0.039
3941	762	897	246	14-15	839-40	53 Siddhârthin						
3942	763	898	247	15-16	*840-41	54 Raudra						
3943	764	899	248	16-17	841-42	55 Durmati		4 Âshâḍha	9449	28.347	316	0.948
3944	765	900	249	17-18	842-43	56 Dundubhi						
3945	766	901	250	18-19	843-44	57 Rudhirodgârin						
3946	767	902	251	19-20	*844-45	58 Raktâksha		3 Jyeshṭha	9956	29.868	513	1.539
3947	768	903	252	20-21	845-46	59 Krodhana						

1) Śobhana, No. 37, was suppressed.

TABLE I.

(*Col.* 23) *a* = *Distance of moon from sun.* (*Col.* 24) *b* = *moon's mean anomaly.* (*Col.* 25) *c* = *sun's mean anomaly.*

II. ADDED LUNAR MONTHS (*continued.*)					III. COMMENCEMENT OF THE													
Mean.					Solar year.						Luni-Solar year. (Civil day of Chaitra Śukla 1st.)							
	Time of the preceding saṅkrânti expressed in		Time of the succeeding saṅkrânti expressed in			(Time of the Mesha saṅkrânti.)							At Sunrise on meridian of Ujjain.					
							By the Ârya Siddhânta.						Moon's Age.					
Name of month.	Lunation parts. (*t.*)	Tithis.	Lunation parts. (*t.*)	Tithis.	Day and Month A. D.	Week day.	Gh.	Pa.	H.	M.	Day and Month A. D.	Week day.	Lunat. parts elapsed. (*t.*)	Tithis elapsed.	*a*	*b.*	*c.*	Kali.
8a	9a	10a	11a	12a	13	14	15		17		19	20	21	22	23	24	25	1
3 Jyeshtha....	9915	29.745	222	0.667	21 Mar. (80)	3 Tues.	35	12	14	5	24 Feb. (55)	6 Fri.	2	.006	9999	769	210	3916
....	...	....	...	....	21 Mar. (80)	4 Wed.	50	44	20	17	15 Mar. (74)	5 Thur.	40	.120	34	704	261	3917
11 Mâgha......	9750	29.251	58	0.173	21 Mar. (81)	6 Fri.	6	15	2	30	3 Mar. (63)	2 Mon.	3	.009	9909	552	230	3918
....	...	....	...	....	21 Mar. (80)	0 Sat.	21	46	8	42	21 Feb. (52)	0 Sat.	323	.969	124	435	202	3919
....	...	....	...	....	21 Mar. (80)	1 Sun.	37	17	14	55	11 Mar. (70)	5 Thur.	81	.243	9820	335	250	3920
8 Kârttika....	9893	29.679	200	0.601	21 Mar. (80)	2 Mon.	52	49	21	7	1 Mar. (60)	3 Tues.	312	.936	34	218	222	3921
....	...	....	...	....	21 Mar. (81)	4 Wed.	8	20	3	20	19 Mar. (79)	2 Mon.	324	.972	69	154	274	3922
....	...	....	...	....	21 Mar. (80)	5 Thur.	23	51	9	32	8 Mar. (67)	6 Fri.	87	.261	9945	2	243	3923
4 Âshâḍha....	9728	29.185	36	0.107	21 Mar. (80)	6 Fri.	39	22	15	45	26 Feb. (57)	4 Wed.	208	.624	159	885	215	3924
....	...	....	...	....	21 Mar. (80)	0 Sat.	54	54	21	57	17 Mar. (76)	3 Tues.	206	.618	194	821	266	3925
....	...	....	...	....	21 Mar. (81)	2 Mon.	10	25	4	10	5 Mar. (65)	0 Sat.	87	.261	69	668	235	3926
1 Chaitra.....	9871	29.614	179	0.536	21 Mar. (80)	3 Tues.	25	56	10	22	22 Feb. (53)	4 Wed.	76	.228	9945	515	204	3927
....	...	....	...	....	21 Mar. (80)	4 Wed.	41	27	16	35	13 Mar. (72)	3 Tues.	162	.486	9980	452	256	3928
9 Mârgaśîrsha .	9707	29.120	14	0.042	21 Mar. (80)	5 Thur.	56	59	22	47	2 Mar. (61)	0 Sat.	131	.393	9855	299	225	3929
....	...	....	...	....	21 Mar. (81)	0 Sat.	12	30	5	0	20 Mar. (80)	6 Fri.	171	.513	9890	235	276	3930
....	...	....	...	....	21 Mar. (80)	1 Sun.	28	1	11	12	9 Mar. (68)	3 Tues.	⊙−25	−.075	9766	82	245	3931
6 Bhâdrapada..	9849	29.548	157	0.470	21 Mar. (80)	2 Mon.	43	32	17	25	27 Feb. (58)	1 Sun.	91	.273	9980	965	217	3932
....	...	....	...	....	21 Mar. (80)	3 Tues.	59	4	23	37	18 Mar. (77)	0 Sat.	73	.219	15	901	269	3933
....	...	....	...	....	21 Mar. (81)	5 Thur.	14	35	5	50	7 Mar. (67)	5 Thur.	232	.696	229	785	240	3934
3 Jyeshtha....	9992	29.976	299	0.898	21 Mar. (80)	6 Fri.	30	6	12	2	24 Feb. (55)	2 Mon.	144	.432	105	632	210	3935
....	...	....	...	....	21 Mar. (80)	0 Sat.	45	37	18	15	15 Mar. (74)	1 Sun.	221	.663	139	568	261	3936
11 Mâgha......	9828	29.483	135	0.405	22 Mar. (81)	2 Mon.	1	9	0	27	4 Mar. (63)	5 Thur.	226	.678	15	415	230	3937
....	...	....	...	....	21 Mar. (81)	3 Tues.	16	40	6	40	21 Feb. (52)	2 Mon.	174	.522	9891	263	199	3938
....	...	....	...	....	21 Mar. (80)	4 Wed.	32	11	12	52	11 Mar. (70)	1 Sun.	199	.597	9926	198	251	3939
8 Kârttika....	9970	29.911	278	0.833	21 Mar. (80)	5 Thur.	47	42	19	5	28 Feb. (59)	5 Thur.	⊙−17	−.051	9801	46	220	3940
....	...	....	...	....	22 Mar. (81)	0 Sat.	3	14	1	17	20 Mar. (79)	5 Thur.	330	.990	174	18	274	3941
....	...	....	...	....	21 Mar. (81)	1 Sun.	18	45	7	30	8 Mar. (68)	2 Mon.	86	.268	50	865	243	3942
4 Âshâḍha....	9806	29.417	113	0.339	21 Mar. (80)	2 Mon.	34	16	13	42	26 Feb. (57)	0 Sat.	267	.801	265	749	215	3943
....	...	....	...	....	21 Mar. (80)	3 Tues.	49	47	19	55	17 Mar. (76)	6 Fri.	311	.933	299	685	266	3944
....	...	....	...	....	22 Mar. (81)	5 Thur.	5	19	2	7	6 Mar. (65)	3 Tues.	286	.858	175	532	235	3945
1 Chaitra.....	9948	29.845	256	0.767	21 Mar. (81)	6 Fri.	20	50	8	20	23 Feb. (54)	0 Sat.	289	.867	51	379	205	3946
....	...	....	...	....	21 Mar. (80)	0 Sat.	36	21	14	32	12 Mar. (71)	5 Thur.	24	.072	9747	279	253	3947

⊙ See Text. Art. 101 above, para. 2.

TABLE I.

Lunation-parts = 10,000ths of a circle. A tithi = 1/30th of the moon's synodic revolution.

I. CONCURRENT YEAR.								II. ADDED LUNAR MONTHS.				
						Samvatsara.		True.				
Kali.	Śaka.	Chaitrâdi. Vikrama.	Meshâdi (Solar) year in Bengal.	Kollam.	A. D.	(Southern.)	Bṛihaspati cycle (Northern) current at Mesha saṅkrânti.	Name of month.	Time of the preceding saṅkrânti expressed in Lunation parts. (*l.*)	Time of the preceding saṅkrânti expressed in Tithis.	Time of the succeeding saṅkrânti expressed in Lunation parts. (*l.*)	Time of the succeeding saṅkrânti expressed in Tithis.
1	2	3	3a	4	5	6	7	8	9	10	11	12
3948	769	904	253	21-22	846-47	.... 60 Kshaya............		7 Âśvina......	9894	29.682	136	0.408
3949	770	905	254	22-23	847-48	.... 1 Prabhava..........		......	......	......	......	......
3950	771	906	255	23-24	*848-49	.... 2 Vibhava..........		......	......	......	......	......
3951	772	907	256	24-25	849-50	.... 3 Śukla.............		5 Śrâvaṇa.....	9862	29.586	630	1.890
3952	773	908	257	25-26	850-51	.... 4 Pramoda..........		......	......	......	......	......
3953	774	909	258	26-27	851-52	.... 5 Prajâpati.........		......	......	......	......	......
3954	775	910	259	27-28	*852-53	.... 6 Aṅgiras............		4 Âshâḍha....	9996	29.988	750	2.250
3955	776	911	260	28-29	853-54	.... 7 Śrîmukha..........		......	......	......	......	......
3956	777	912	261	29-30	854-55	.... 8 Bhâva.............		......	......	......	......	......
3957	778	913	262	30-31	855-56	.... 9 Yuvan.............		1 Chaitra.....	9827	29.481	162	0.486
3958	779	914	263	31-32	*856-57	.... 10 Dhâtṛi...........		......	......	......	......	......
3959	780	915	264	32-33	857-58	.... 11 Îśvara...........		5 Śrâvaṇa....	9406	28.218	142	0.426
3960	781	916	265	33-34	858-59	.... 12 Bahudhânya........		......	......	......	......	......
3961	782	917	266	34-35	859-60	.... 13 Pramâthin.........		......	......	......	......	......
3962	783	918	267	35-36	*860-61	.... 14 Vikrama...........		4 Âshâḍha....	9491	28.473	281	0.843
3963	784	919	268	36-37	861-62	.... 15 Vṛisha............		......	......	......	......	......
3964	785	920	269	37-38	862-63	.... 16 Chitrabhânu........		......	......	......	......	......
3965	786	921	270	38-39	863-64	.... 17 Subhânu...........		2 Vaiśâkha....	9679	29.037	140	0.420
3966	787	922	271	39-40	*864-65	.... 18 Târaṇa...........		......	......	......	......	......
3967	788	923	272	40-41	865-66	.... 19 Pârthiva...........		6 Bhâdrapada..	9642	28.926	92	0.276
3968	789	924	273	41-42	866-67	.... 20 Vyaya.............		......	......	......	......	......
3969	790	925	274	42-43	867-68	.... 21 Sarvajit...........		......	......	......	......	......
3970	791	926	275	43-44	*868-69	.... 22 Sarvadhârin.........		5 Śrâvaṇa.....	9821	29.463	630	1.890
3971	792	927	276	44-45	869-70	.... 23 Virodhin..........		......	......	......	......	......
3972	793	928	277	45-46	870-71	.... 24 Vikṛita...........		......	......	......	......	......
3973	794	929	278	46-47	871-72	.... 25 Khara............		3 Jyeshṭha....	9616	28.848	163	0.489
3974	795	930	279	47-48	*872-73	.... 26 Nandana..........		......	......	......	......	......
3975	796	931	280	48-49	873-74	.... 27 Vijaya...........		......	......	......	......	......
3976	797	932	281	49-50	874-75	.... 28 Jaya..............		1 Chaitra.....	9786	29.358	151	0.453
3977	798	933	282	50-51	875-76	.... 29 Manmatha.........		......	......	......	......	......
3978	799	934	283	51-52	*876-77	.... 30 Durmukha..........		5 Śrâvaṇa.....	9365	28.095	170	0.510
3979	800	935	284	52-53	877-78	.... 31 Hemalamba........		......	......	......	......	......

TABLE I.

(*Col.* 23) *a* = *Distance of moon from sun.* (*Col.* 24) *b* = *moon's mean anomaly.* (*Col.* 25) *c* = *sun's mean anomaly.*

II. ADDED LUNAR MONTHS (*continued.*)					III. COMMENCEMENT OF THE													
	Mean.				Solar year.						Luni-Solar year. (Civil day of Chaitra Śukla 1st.)							
Name of month.	Time of the preceding saṅkrânti expressed in		Time of the succeeding saṅkrânti expressed in		Day and Month A. D.	(Time of the Mesha saṅkrânti.)					Day and Month A. D.	Week day.	At Sunrise on meridian of Ujjain.					Kali.
						Week day.	By the Ârya Siddhânta.						Moon's Age.					
	Lunation parts. (*t.*)	Tithis.	Lunation parts. (*t.*)	Tithis.			Gh.	Pa.	H.	M.			Lunat. parts elapsed. (*t.*)	Tithis elapsed.	*a*	*b.*	*c.*	
8a	9a	10a	11a	12a	13	14	15		17		19	20	21	22	23	24	25	1
9 Mârgaśîrsha..	9784	29.352	91	0.274	21 Mar. (80)	1 Sun.	51	52	20	45	2 Mar. (61)	3 Tues.	220	.660	9961	162	225	3948
....	....	....	....	....	22 Mar. (81)	3 Tues.	7	24	2	57	21 Mar. (80)	2 Mon.	218	.654	9996	98	276	3949
....	....	....	....	....	21 Mar. (81)	4 Wed.	22	55	9	10	9 Mar. (69)	6 Fri.	⊙−36	−.108	9871	946	246	3950
6 Bhâdrapada..	9927	29.780	234	0.702	21 Mar. (80)	5 Thur.	38	26	15	22	27 Feb. (58)	4 Wed.	104	.312	86	829	217	3951
....	....	....	....	....	21 Mar. (80)	6 Fri.	53	57	21	35	18 Mar. (77)	3 Tues.	120	.360	120	765	269	3952
....	....	....	....	....	22 Mar. (81)	1 Sun.	9	29	3	47	7 Mar. (66)	0 Sat.	45	.135	9996	612	238	3953
2 Vaiśâkha....	9762	29.286	69	0.208	21 Mar. (81)	2 Mon.	25	0	10	0	24 Feb. (55)	4 Wed.	49	.147	9872	459	207	3954
....	....	....	....	....	21 Mar. (80)	3 Tues.	40	31	16	12	14 Mar. (73)	3 Tues.	135	.405	9906	395	258	3955
11 Mâgha......	9905	29.714	212	0.637	21 Mar. (80)	4 Wed.	56	2	22	25	3 Mar. (62)	0 Sat.	63	.189	9783	243	228	3956
....	....	....	....	....	22 Mar. (81)	6 Fri.	11	34	4	37	21 Feb. (52)	5 Thur.	239	.717	9996	126	200	3957
....	....	....	....	....	21 Mar. (81)	0 Sat.	27	5	10	50	11 Mar. (71)	4 Wed.	225	.675	31	62	251	3958
7 Âśvina......	9740	29.221	48	0.143	21 Mar. (80)	1 Sun.	42	36	17	2	28 Feb. (59)	1 Sun.	⊙−27	−.081	9907	909	220	3959
....	....	....	....	....	21 Mar. (80)	2 Mon.	58	7	23	15	20 Mar. (79)	1 Sun.	325	.975	280	882	274	3960
....	....	....	....	....	22 Mar. (81)	4 Wed.	13	39	5	27	9 Mar. (68)	5 Thur.	157	.471	156	729	243	3961
4 Âshâḍha	9883	29.649	190	0.571	21 Mar. (81)	5 Thur.	29	10	11	40	26 Feb. (57)	2 Mon.	108	.324	31	576	212	3962
....	....	....	....	....	21 Mar. (80)	6 Fri.	44	41	17	52	16 Mar. (75)	1 Sun	196	.588	66	512	264	3963
12 Phâlguna....	9718	29.155	26	0.077	22 Mar. (81)	1 Sun.	0	12	0	5	5 Mar. (64)	5 Thur.	191	.573	9942	359	233	3964
....	....	....	....	....	22 Mar. (81)	2 Mon.	15	44	6	17	22 Feb. (53)	2 Mon.	96	.288	9818	206	202	3965
....	....	....	....	....	21 Mar. (81)	3 Tues.	31	15	12	30	12 Mar. (72)	1 Sun.	101	.303	9852	142	253	3966
9 Mârgaśîrsha .	9861	29.583	169	0.506	21 Mar. (80)	4 Wed.	46	46	18	42	2 Mar. (61)	6 Fri.	229	.687	67	26	225	3967
....	....	....	....	....	22 Mar. (81)	6 Fri.	2	17	0	55	21 Mar. (80)	5 Thur.	209	.627	101	962	277	3968
....	....	....	....	....	22 Mar. (81)	0 Sat.	17	49	7	7	10 Mar. (69)	2 Mon.	⊙−13	−.039	9977	809	246	3969
5 Śrâvaṇa.....	9697	29.090	4	0.012	21 Mar. (81)	1 Sun.	33	20	13	20	28 Feb. (59)	0 Sat.	202	.606	191	693	218	3970
....	....	....	....	....	21 Mar. (80)	2 Mon.	48	51	19	32	18 Mar. (77)	6 Fri.	266	.798	226	628	269	3971
....	....	....	....	....	22 Mar. (81)	4 Wed.	4	22	1	45	7 Mar. (66)	3 Tues.	263	.789	102	476	238	3972
2 Vaiśâkha....	9839	29.518	147	0.440	22 Mar. (81)	5 Thur	19	54	7	57	24 Feb (55)	0 Sat.	245	.735	9977	323	207	3973
....	....	....	....	....	21 Mar. (81)	6 Fri.	35	25	14	10	14 Mar. (74)	6 Fri.	292	.876	12	259	259	3974
11 Mâgha......	9982	29.946	289	0.868	21 Mar. (80)	0 Sat.	50	56	20	22	3 Mar. (62)	3 Tues.	116	.348	9888	106	228	3975
....	....	....	....	....	22 Mar. (81)	2 Mon.	6	27	2	35	21 Feb. (52)	1 Sun.	236	.708	102	990	200	3976
....	....	....	....	....	22 Mar. (81)	3 Tues.	21	59	8	47	12 Mar. (71)	0 Sat.	213	.639	137	926	251	3977
7 Âśvina......	9818	29.453	125	0.375	21 Mar. (81)	4 Wed.	37	30	15	0	29 Feb. (60)	4 Wed.	15	.045	12	773	220	3978
....	....	....	....	....	21 Mar. (80)	5 Thur.	53	1	21	12	19 Mar. (78)	3 Tues.	53	.159	47	709	272	3979

⊙ See Text. Art. 101 above, para. 2.

TABLE I.

Lunation-parts = 10,000*ths of a circle.* *A tithi* = 1/30*th of the moon's synodic revolution.*

I. CONCURRENT YEAR.								II. ADDED LUNAR MONTHS.				
						Samvatsara.		True.				
Kali.	Śaka.	Chaitrâdi. Vikrama.	Meshâdi (Solar) year in Bengal.	Kollam.	A. D.	(Southern.)	Bṛihaspati cycle (Northern) current at Mesha saṅkrânti.	Name of month.	Time of the preceding saṅkrânti expressed in: Lunation parts. (*l.*)	Time of the preceding saṅkrânti expressed in: Tithis.	Time of the succeeding saṅkrânti expressed in: Lunation parts. (*l.*)	Time of the succeeding saṅkrânti expressed in: Tithis.
1	2	3	3a	4	5	6	7	8	9	10	11	12
3980	801	936	285	53-54	878- 79	32 Vilamba						
3981	802	937	286	54-55	879- 80	33 Vikârin		4 Âshâḍha	9633	28.899	316	0.948
3982	803	938	287	55-56	*880- 81	34 Śârvari						
3983	804	939	288	56-57	881- 82	35 Plava						
3984	805	940	289	57-58	882- 83	36 Śubhakṛit		2 Vaiśâkha	9694	29.082	241	0.723
3985	806	941	290	58-59	883- 84	37 Śobhana						
3986	807	942	291	59-60	*884- 85	38 Krodhin		6 Bhâdrapada	9702	29.106	243	0.729
3987	808	943	292	60-61	885- 86	39 Viśvâvasu						
3988	809	944	293	61-62	886- 87	40 Parâbhava						
3989	810	945	294	62-63	887- 88	41 Plavaṅga		5 Śrâvaṇa	9825	29.475	588	1.764
3990	811	946	295	63-64	*888- 89	42 Kîlaka						
3991	812	947	296	64-65	889- 90	43 Saumya						
3992	813	948	297	65-66	890- 91	44 Sâdhâraṇa		3 Jyeshṭha	9753	29.259	359	1.077
3993	814	949	298	66-67	891- 92	45 Virodhakṛit						
3994	815	950	299	67-68	*892- 93	46 Paridhâvin		{ 8 Kârttika 9 *Mârgaś.(Ksh.)*	9974 8	29.922 0.024	8 9912	0 024 } 29.736 }
3995	816	951	300	68-69	893- 94	47 Pramâdin		1 Chaitra	9780	29.340	111	0.333
3996	817	952	301	69-70	894- 95	48 Ânanda						
3997	818	953	302	70-71	895- 96	49 Râkshasa		5 Srâvaṇa	9347	28.041	132	0.396
3998	819	954	303	71-72	*896- 97	50 Anala						
3999	820	955	304	72-73	897- 98	51 Piṅgala						
4000	821	956	305	73-74	898- 99	52 Kâlayukta		4 Âshâḍha	9829	29.487	452	1.356
4001	822	957	306	74-75	899-900	53 Siddhârthin						
4002	823	958	307	75-76	*900- 1	54 Raudra						
4003	824	959	308	76-77	901- 2	55 Durmati		2 Vaiśâkha	9654	28.962	250	0.750
4004	825	960	309	77-78	902- 3	56 Dundubhi						
4005	826	961	310	78-79	903- 4	57 Rudhirodgârin		6 Bhâdrapada	9671	29.013	292	0.876
4006	827	962	311	79-80	*904- 5	58 Raktâksha						
4007	828	963	312	80-81	905- 6	59 Krodhana						
4008	829	964	313	81-82	906- 7	60 Kshaya		5 Śrâvaṇa	9930	29.790	591	1.773
4009	830	965	314	82-83	907- 8	1 Prabhava						
4010	831	966	315	83-84	*908- 9	2 Vibhava [1]						

[1] Śukla, No. 3, was suppressed in the north, but by southern reckoning there has been no suppression since this date.

TABLE I.

(*Col.* 23) *a* = *Distance of moon from sun.* (*Col.* 24) *b* = *moon's mean anomaly.* (*Col.* 25) *c* = *sun's mean anomaly.*

II. ADDED LUNAR MONTHS (continued.)					III. COMMENCEMENT OF THE														
Mean.					Solar year.						Luni-Solar year. (Civil day of Chaitra Śukla 1st.)								
Name of month.	Time of the preceding saṅkrânti expressed in		Time of the succeeding saṅkrânti expressed in		Day and Month A. D.	(Time of the Mesha saṅkrânti.)					Day and Month A. D.	Week day.	At Sunrise on meridian of Ujjain.						Kali.
	Lunation parts. (*t.*)	Tithis.	Lunation parts. (*t.*)	Tithis.		Week day.	By the Ârya Siddhânta.						Moon's Age.						
							Gh.	Pa.	H.	M.			Lunat. parts elapsed. (*t.*)	Tithis elapsed.	*a.*	*b.*	*c.*		
8a	9a	10a	11a	12a	13	14	15		17		19	20	21	22	23	24	25		1
....	....	....	....	....	22 Mar. (81)	0 Sat.	8	32	3	25	8 Mar. (67)	0 Sat.	14	.042	9923	556	241		3980
4 Âshâḍha....	9960	29.881	268	0.803	22 Mar. (81)	1 Sun.	24	4	9	37	26 Feb. (57)	5 Thur.	332	.996	137	439	212		3981
....	....	....	....	....	21 Mar. (81)	2 Mon.	39	35	15	50	15 Mar. (75)	3 Tues.	91	.273	9833	339	261		3982
12 Phâlguna....	9796	29.387	103	0.309	21 Mar. (80)	3 Tues.	55	6	22	2	5 Mar. (64)	1 Sun.	325	.975	47	223	233		3983
....	....	....	....	....	22 Mar. (81)	5 Thur.	10	37	4	15	22 Feb. (53)	5 Thur.	126	.378	9923	70	202		3984
....	....	....	....	....	22 Mar. (81)	6 Fri.	26	9	10	27	13 Mar. (72)	4 Wed.	103	.309	9958	6	254		3985
9 Mârgaśîrsha..	9938	29.815	246	0.737	21 Mar. (81)	0 Sat.	41	40	16	40	2 Mar. (62)	2 Mon.	223	.669	172	890	226		3986
....	....	....	....	....	21 Mar. (80)	1 Sun.	57	11	22	52	21 Mar. (80)	1 Sun.	224	.672	207	825	277		3987
....	....	....	....	....	22 Mar. (81)	3 Tues.	12	42	5	5	10 Mar. (69)	5 Thur.	99	.297	83	673	246		3988
5 Srâvaṇa.....	9774	29.322	81	0.244	22 Mar. (81)	4 Wed.	28	14	11	17	27 Feb. (58)	2 Mon.	82	.246	9958	520	215		3989
....	....	....	....	....	21 Mar. (81)	5 Thur.	43	45	17	30	17 Mar. (77)	1 Sun.	172	.516	9993	456	266		3990
....	....	....	....	....	21 Mar. (80)	6 Fri.	59	16	23	42	6 Mar. (65)	5 Thur.	141	.423	9869	303	236		3991
2 Vaiśâkha....	9917	29.750	224	0.672	22 Mar. (81)	1 Sun.	14	47	5	55	23 Feb. (54)	2 Mon.	⊙ −0	−.000	9744	150	205		3992
....	....	....	....	....	22 Mar. (81)	2 Mon.	30	19	12	7	14 Mar. (73)	1 Sun.	⊙ −8	−.024	9779	86	256		3993
}10 Pausha.....	9752	29.256	59	0.178	21 Mar. (81)	3 Tues.	45	50	18	20	3 Mar. (63)	6 Fri.	7	.021	9993	970	228		3994
....	....	....	....	....	22 Mar. (81)	5 Thur.	1	21	0	32	21 Feb. (52)	4 Wed.	239	.717	208	853	200		3995
....	....	....	....	....	22 Mar. (81)	6 Fri.	16	52	6	45	12 Mar. (71)	3 Tues.	246	.738	242	789	251		3996
7 Âśvina......	9895	29.684	202	0.606	22 Mar. (81)	0 Sat.	32	24	12	57	1 Mar. (60)	0 Sat.	153	.459	118	636	220		3997
....	....	....	....	....	21 Mar. (81)	1 Sun.	47	55	19	10	19 Mar. (79)	6 Fri.	230	.690	153	572	272		3998
....	....	....	....	....	22 Mar. (81)	3 Tues.	3	26	1	22	8 Mar. (67)	3 Tues.	238	.714	28	420	241		3999
3 Jyeshṭha....	9730	29.191	38	0.113	22 Mar. (81)	4 Wed.	18	57	7	35	25 Feb. (56)	0 Sat.	285	.855	9904	267	210		4000
....	....	....	....	....	22 Mar. (81)	5 Thur.	34	29	13	47	16 Mar. (75)	6 Fri.	213	.639	9939	203	261		4001
12 Phâlguna....	9873	29.619	180	0.541	21 Mar. (81)	6 Fri.	50	0	20	0	4 Mar. (64)	3 Tues.	⊙ −1	−.003	9814	50	231		4002
....	....	....	....	....	22 Mar. (81)	1 Sun.	5	31	2	12	22 Feb. (53)	1 Sun.	114	.342	29	933	202		4003
....	....	....	....	....	22 Mar. (81)	2 Mon.	21	2	8	25	13 Mar. (72)	0 Sat.	101	.303	63	870	254		4004
8 Kârttika.....	9708	29.125	16	0.047	22 Mar. (81)	3 Tues.	36	34	14	37	3 Mar. (62)	5 Thur.	278	.834	278	753	226		4005
....	....	....	....	....	21 Mar. (81)	4 Wed.	52	5	20	50	21 Mar. (81)	4 Wed.	324	.972	312	689	277		4006
....	....	....	....	....	22 Mar. (81)	6 Fri.	7	36	3	2	10 Mar. (69)	1 Sun.	298	.894	188	536	246		4007
5 Śrâvaṇa.....	9851	29.553	158	0.475	22 Mar. (81)	0 Sat.	23	7	9	15	27 Feb. (58)	5 Thur.	299	.897	64	383	215		4008
....	....	....	....	....	22 Mar. (81)	1 Sun.	38	39	15	27	17 Mar. (76)	3 Tues.	36	.108	9760	283	264		4009
....	....	....	....	....	21 Mar. (81)	2 Mon.	54	10	21	40	6 Mar (66)	1 Sun.	235	.705	9974	167	236		4010

⊙ See Text. Art. 101 above, para. 2.

TABLE I.

Lunation-parts = 10,000*ths of a circle. A tithi* = $^1/_{30}$*th of the moon's synodic revolution.*

I. CONCURRENT YEAR.								II. ADDED LUNAR MONTHS.				
						Samvatsara.		True.				
Kali.	Śaka.	Chaitrâdi. Vikrama.	Meshâdi (Solar) year in Bengal.	Kollam.	A. D.	Luni-Solar cycle. (Southern.)	Bṛihaspati cycle (Northern) current at Mesha saṅkrânti.	Name of month.	Time of the preceding saṅkrânti expressed in Lunation parts. (*t*.)	Time of the preceding saṅkrânti expressed in Tithis.	Time of the succeeding saṅkrânti expressed in Lunation parts. (*t*.)	Time of the succeeding saṅkrânti expressed in Tithis.
1	2	3	3a	4	5	6	7	8	9	10	11	12
4011	832	967	316	84- 85	909-10	3 Śukla	4 Pramoda [1]	3 Jyeshṭha	9788	29.364	496	1.488
4012	833	968	317	85- 86	910-11	4 Pramoda	5 Prajâpati					
4013	834	969	318	86- 87	911-12	5 Prajâpati	6 Aṅgiras	7 Âśvina 10 *Pausha* (*Ksh.*)	9818 108	29.454 0.324	131 9947	0.393 29.841
4014	835	970	319	87- 88	*912-13	6 Aṅgiras	7 Śrîmukha	1 Chaitra	9865	29.595	125	0.375
4015	836	971	320	88- 89	913-14	7 Śrîmukha	8 Bhâva					
4016	837	972	321	89- 90	914-15	8 Bhâva	9 Yuvan	5 Śrâvaṇa	9416	28.248	112	0.336
4017	838	973	322	90- 91	915-16	9 Yuvan	10 Dhâtṛi					
4018	839	974	323	91- 92	*916-17	10 Dhâtṛi	11 Îśvara					
4019	840	975	324	92- 93	917-18	11 Îśvara	12 Bahudhânya	4 Âshâḍha	9967	29.901	646	1.938
4020	841	976	325	93- 94	918-19	12 Bahudhânya	13 Pramâthin					
4021	842	977	326	94- 95	919-20	13 Pramâthin	14 Vikrama					
4022	843	978	327	95- 96	*920-21	14 Vikrama	15 Vṛisha	2 Vaiśâkha	9642	28.926	206	0.618
4023	844	979	328	96- 97	921-22	15 Vṛisha	16 Chitrabhânu					
4024	845	980	329	97- 98	922-23	16 Chitrabhânu	17 Subhânu	6 Bhâdrapada	9643	28.929	266	0.798
4025	846	981	330	98- 99	923-24	17 Subhânu	18 Târaṇa					
4026	847	982	331	99-100	*924-25	18 Târaṇa	19 Pârthiva					
4027	848	983	332	100- 1	925-26	19 Pârthiva	20 Vyaya	4 Âshâḍha	9480	28.440	113	0.339
4028	849	984	333	101- 2	926-27	20 Vyaya	21 Sarvajit					
4029	850	985	334	102- 3	927-28	21 Sarvajit	22 Sarvadhârin					
4030	851	986	335	103- 4	*928-29	22 Sarvadhâri	23 Virodhin	3 Jyeshṭha	9753	29.259	530	1.590
4031	852	987	336	104- 5	929-30	23 Virodhin	24 Vikṛita					
4032	853	988	337	105- 6	930-31	24 Vikṛita	25 Khara	7 Âśvina	9813	29.439	192	0.576
4033	854	989	338	106- 7	931-32	25 Khara	26 Nandana					
4034	855	990	339	107- 8	*932-33	26 Nandana	27 Vijaya					
4035	856	991	340	108- 9	933-34	27 Vijaya	28 Jaya	5 Śrâvaṇa	9579	28.737	180	0.540
4036	857	992	341	109- 10	934-35	28 Jaya	29 Manmatha					
4037	858	993	342	110- 11	935-36	29 Manmatha	30 Durmukha					
4038	859	994	343	111- 12	*936-37	30 Durmukha	31 Hemalamba	3 Jyeshṭha	9302	27.906	37	0.111
4039	860	995	344	112- 13	937-38	31 Hemalamba	32 Vilamba					
4040	861	996	345	113- 14	938-39	32 Vilamba	33 Vikârin					
4041	862	997	346	114- 15	939-40	33 Vikârin	34 Śârvari	2 Vaiśâkha	9724	29.172	204	0.612
4042	863	998	347	115- 16	*940-41	34 Śârvari	35 Plava					

[1] See note 1, last page.

TABLE I.

(*Col.* 23) *a* = *Distance of moon from sun.* (*Col.* 24) *b* = *moon's mean anomaly.* (*Col.* 25) *c* = *sun's mean anomaly.*

II. ADDED LUNAR MONTHS (*continued.*)					III. COMMENCEMENT OF THE													
Mean.					Solar year.						Luni-Solar year. (Civil day of Chaitra Śukla 1st.)							
Name of month.	Time of the preceding saṅkrânti expressed in		Time of the succeeding saṅkrânti expressed in		Day and Month A. D.	(Time of the Mesha saṅkrânti.)					Day and Month A. D.	Week day.	At Sunrise on meridian of Ujjain.					Kali.
						Week day.	By the Ârya Siddhânta.						Moon's Age.					
	Lunation parts. (*t.*)	Tithis.	Lunation parts. (*t.*)	Tithis.			Gh.	Pa.	H.	M.			Lunat. parts elapsed. (*t.*)	Tithis elapsed.	*a.*	*b.*	*c.*	
8a	**9a**	**10a**	**11a**	**12a**	**13**	**14**	**15**		**17**		**19**	**20**	**21**	**22**	**23**	**24**	**25**	**1**
2 Vaiśâkha....	9994	29.982	301	0.904	22 Mar. (81)	4 Wed.	9	41	3	52	23 Feb. (54)	5 Thur.	4	.012	9850	14	205	4011
....	....	......	....	......	22 Mar. (81)	5 Thur.	25	12	10	5	14 Mar. (73)	4 Wed.	⊙−19	−.057	9885	950	256	4012
}10 Pausha....	9829	29.488	137	0.410	22 Mar. (81)	6 Fri.	40	44	16	17	4 Mar. (63)	2 Mon.	117	.351	99	833	228	4013
....	....	......	....	......	21 Mar. (81)	0 Sat.	56	15	22	30	22 Feb. (53)	0 Sat.	319	.957	313	717	200	4014
....	....	......	....	......	22 Mar. (81)	2 Mon.	11	46	4	42	11 Mar. (70)	5 Thur.	56	.168	9	616	249	4015
7 Âśvina......	9972	29.916	279	0.838	22 Mar. (81)	3 Tues.	27	17	10	55	28 Feb. (59)	2 Mon.	57	.171	9885	464	218	4016
....	....	......	....	......	22 Mar. (81)	4 Wed.	42	49	17	7	19 Mar. (78)	1 Sun.	144	.432	9920	400	269	4017
....	....	......	....	......	21 Mar. (81)	5 Thur.	58	20	23	20	7 Mar. (67)	5 Thur.	75	.225	9795	247	238	4018
3 Jyeshṭha....	9807	29.422	115	0.344	22 Mar. (81)	0 Sat.	13	51	5	32	25 Feb. (56)	3 Tues.	254	.762	10	130	210	4019
....	....	......	....	......	22 Mar. (81)	1 Sun.	29	22	11	45	16 Mar. (75)	2 Mon.	242	.726	44	66	262	4020
12 Phâlguna....	9950	29.851	258	0.773	22 Mar. (81)	2 Mon.	44	54	17	57	5 Mar. (64)	6 Fri.	⊙−13	−.039	9920	914	231	4021
....	....	......	....	......	22 Mar. (82)	4 Wed.	0	25	0	10	23 Feb. (54)	4 Wed.	143	.429	134	797	203	4022
....	....	......	....	......	22 Mar. (81)	5 Thur.	15	56	6	22	13 Mar. (72)	3 Tues.	171	.513	169	733	254	4023
8 Kârttika....	9786	29.357	93	0.279	22 Mar. (81)	6 Fri.	31	27	12	35	2 Mar. (61)	0 Sat.	118	.354	45	580	223	4024
....	....	......	....	......	22 Mar. (81)	0 Sat.	46	59	18	47	21 Mar. (80)	6 Fri.	205	.615	79	516	275	4025
....	....	......	....	......	22 Mar. (82)	2 Mon.	2	30	1	0	9 Mar. (69)	3 Tues.	201	.603	9955	364	244	4026
5 Śrâvaṇa....	9928	20.785	236	0.707	22 Mar. (81)	3 Tues.	18	1	7	12	26 Feb. (57)	0 Sat.	109	327	9831	211	213	4027
....	....	......	....	......	22 Mar. (81)	4 Wed.	33	32	13	25	17 Mar. (76)	6 Fri.	116	.348	9865	147	264	4028
....	....	......	....	......	22 Mar. (81)	5 Thur.	49	4	19	37	7 Mar. (66)	4 Wed.	246	.738	80	30	236	4029
1 Chaitra....	9764	29.291	71	0.213	22 Mar. (82)	0 Sat.	4	35	1	50	24 Feb. (55)	1 Sun.	⊙ −0	−.000	9955	877	205	4030
....	....	......	....	......	22 Mar. (81)	1 Sun.	20	6	8	2	14 Mar. (73)	0 Sat.	2	.006	9990	813	257	4031
10 Pausha......	9907	29.720	214	0.642	22 Mar. (81)	2 Mon.	35	37	14	15	4 Mar. (63)	5 Thur.	212	.636	204	697	228	4032
....	....	......	....	......	22 Mar. (81)	3 Tues.	51	9	20	27	23 Mar. (82)	4 Wed.	276	.828	239	633	280	4033
....	....	......	....	......	22 Mar. (82)	5 Thur.	6	40	2	40	11 Mar. (71)	1 Sun.	272	.816	115	480	249	4034
6 Bhâdrapada..	9742	29.226	49	0.148	22 Mar. (81)	6 Fri.	22	11	8	52	28 Feb. (59)	5 Thur.	256	.768	9991	327	218	4035
....	....	......	....	......	22 Mar. (81)	0 Sat.	37	42	15	5	19 Mar. (78)	4 Wed.	305	.915	25	263	269	4036
....	....	......	....	......	22 Mar. (81)	1 Sun.	53	14	21	17	8 Mar. (67)	1 Sun.	131	.393	9901	110	239	4037
3 Jyeshṭha....	9885	29.654	192	0.576	22 Mar. (82)	3 Tues.	8	45	3	30	26 Feb. (57)	6 Fri.	252	.756	115	994	211	4038
....	....	......	....	......	22 Mar. (81)	4 Wed.	24	16	9	42	16 Mar. (75)	5 Thur.	231	.693	150	930	262	4039
11 Mâgha......	9720	29.160	28	0.083	22 Mar. (81)	5 Thur.	39	47	15	55	5 Mar. (64)	2 Mon.	28	.084	26	777	231	4040
....	....	......	....	......	22 Mar. (81)	6 Fri.	55	19	22	7	23 Feb. (54)	0 Sat.	264	.792	240	661	203	4041
....	....	......	....	......	22 Mar. (82)	1 Sun.	10	50	4	20	12 Mar. (72)	5 Thur.	23	.069	9936	560	252	4042

⊙ See Text. Art. 101 above, para. 2.

TABLE I.

Lunation-parts = 10,000*ths of a circle. A tithi* = 1/30*th of the moon's synodic revolution.*

I. CONCURRENT YEAR.								II. ADDED LUNAR MONTHS.				
						Samvatsara.		True.				
Kali.	Śaka.	Chaitrâdi. Vikrama.	Meshâdi (Solar) year in Bengal.	Kollam.	A. D.	Luni-Solar cycle. (Southern.)	Bṛihaspati cycle (Northern) current at Mesha saṅkrânti.	Name of month.	Time of the preceding saṅkrânti expressed in: Lunation parts. (*l.*)	Tithis.	Time of the succeeding saṅkrânti expressed in: Lunation parts. (*l.*)	Tithis.
1	2	3	3a	4	5	6	7	8	9	10	11	12
4043	864	999	348	116-17	941-42	35 Plava	36 Śubhakṛit	6 Bhâdrapada	9677	29.031	233	0.699
4044	865	1000	349	117-18	942-43	36 Śubhakṛit	37 Śobhana					
4045	866	1001	350	118-19	943-44	37 Śobhana	38 Krodhin					
4046	867	1002	351	119-20	*944-45	38 Krodhin	39 Viśvâvasu	4 Âshâḍha	9581	28.743	298	0.894
4047	868	1003	352	120-21	945-46	39 Viśvâvasu	40 Parâbhava					
4048	869	1004	353	121-22	946-47	40 Parâbhava	41 Plavaṅga					
4049	870	1005	354	122-23	947-48	41 Plavaṅga	42 Kîlaka	3 Jyeshṭha	9727	29.181	495	1.485
4050	871	1006	355	123-24	*948-49	42 Kîlaka	43 Saumya					
4051	872	1007	356	124-25	949-50	43 Saumya	44 Sâdhâraṇa	7 Âśvina	9768	29.304	167	0.501
4052	873	1008	357	125-26	950-51	44 Sâdhâraṇa	45 Virodhakṛit					
4053	874	1009	358	126-27	951-52	45 Virodhakṛit	46 Paridhâvin					
4054	875	1010	359	127-28	*952-53	46 Paridhâvi	47 Pramâdin	5 Srâvaṇa	9773	29.319	340	1.020
4055	876	1011	360	128-29	953-54	47 Pramâdin	48 Ânanda					
4056	877	1012	361	129-30	954-55	48 Ânanda	49 Râkshasa					
4057	878	1013	362	130-31	955-56	49 Râkshasa	50 Anala	3 Jyeshṭha	9260	27.780	42	0.126
4058	879	1014	363	131-32	*956-57	50 Anala	51 Piṅgala					
4059	880	1015	364	132-33	957-58	51 Piṅgala	52 Kâlayukta					
4060	881	1016	365	133-34	958-59	52 Kâlayukta	53 Siddhârthin	2 Vaiśâkha	9894	29.682	298	0.894
4061	882	1017	366	134-35	959-60	53 Siddhârthin	54 Raudra					
4062	883	1018	367	135-36	*960-61	54 Raudra	55 Durmati	6 Bhâdrapada	9809	29.427	274	0.822
4063	884	1019	368	136-37	961-62	55 Durmati	56 Dundubhi					
4064	885	1020	369	137-38	962-63	56 Dundubhi	57 Rudhirodgârin					
4065	886	1021	370	138-39	963-64	57 Rudhirodgârin	58 Raktâksha	4 Âshâḍha	9588	28.764	411	1.233
4066	887	1022	371	139-40	*964-65	58 Raktâksha	59 Krodhana					
4067	888	1023	372	140-41	965-66	59 Krodhana	60 Kshaya					
4068	889	1024	373	141-42	966-67	60 Kshaya	1 Prabhava	3 Jyeshṭha	9786	29.358	472	1.416
4069	890	1025	374	142-43	967-68	1 Prabhava	2 Vibhava					
4070	891	1026	375	143-44	*968-69	2 Vibhava	3 Śukla	7 Âśvina	9783	29.349	131	0.393
4071	892	1027	376	144-45	969-70	3 Śukla	4 Pramoda					
4072	893	1028	377	145-46	970-71	4 Pramoda	5 Prajâpati					
4073	894	1029	378	146-47	971-72	5 Prajâpati	6 Aṅgiras	5 Śrâvaṇa	9916	29.748	537	1.611
4074	895	1030	379	147-48	*972-73	6 Aṅgiras	7 Śrîmukha					
4075	896	1031	380	148-49	973-74	7 Śrîmukha	8 Bhâva					

TABLE I.

(*Col.* 23) *a* = *Distance of moon from sun.* (*Col.* 24) *b* = *moon's mean anomaly.* (*Col.* 25) *c* = *sun's mean anomaly.*

II. ADDED LUNAR MONTHS (*continued.*)					III. COMMENCEMENT OF THE													
Mean.					Solar year.						Luni-Solar year. (Civil day of Chaitra Śukla 1st.)							Kali.
Name of month.	Time of the preceding saṅkrânti expressed in		Time of the succeeding saṅkrânti expressed in		Day and Month A. D.	(Time of the Mesha saṅkrânti.)					Day and Month A. D.	Week day.	At Sunrise on meridian of Ujjain.					
	Lunation parts. (*l.*)	Tithis.	Lunation parts. (*l.*)	Tithis.		Week day.	By the Ârya Siddhânta.						Moon's Age.		*a.*	*b.*	*c.*	
							Gh.	Pa	H.	M.			Lunat. parts elapsed. (*l.*)	Tithis elapsed.				
8a	9a	10a	11a	12a	13	14	15		17		19	20	21	22	23	24	25	1
8 Kârttika....	9863	29.589	170	0.511	22 Mar. (81)	2 Mon.	26	21	10	32	1 Mar. (60)	2 Mon.	30	.090	9812	408	223	4043
....	....	....	....	....	22 Mar. (81)	3 Tues.	41	52	16	45	20 Mar. (79)	1 Sun.	104	.312	9846	344	272	4044
....	....	....	....	....	22 Mar. (81)	4 Wed.	57	24	22	57	9 Mar. (68)	5 Thur.	⊙ −8	−.024	9722	191	241	4045
4 Âshâḍha....	9698	29.095	6	0.017	22 Mar (82)	6 Fri.	12	55	5	10	27 Feb. (58)	3 Tues.	142	.426	9936	74	213	4046
....	....	....	....	....	22 Mar. (81)	0 Sat.	28	26	11	22	17 Mar. (76)	2 Mon.	120	.360	9971	10	264	4047
....	....	....	....	....	22 Mar. (81)	1 Sun.	43	57	17	35	7 Mar. (66)	0 Sat.	238	.714	185	894	236	4048
1 Chaitra.....	9841	29.523	148	0.445	22 Mar. (81)	2 Mon.	59	29	23	47	24 Feb. (55)	4 Wed.	63	.189	61	741	206	4049
....	....	....	....	....	22 Mar. (82)	4 Wed.	15	0	6	0	14 Mar. (74)	3 Tues.	110	.330	96	677	257	4050
10 Pausha.....	9984	29.952	291	0.874	22 Mar. (81)	5 Thur.	30	31	12	12	3 Mar (62)	0 Sat.	90	.270	9971	524	226	4051
....	....	....	....	....	22 Mar. (81)	6 Fri.	46	2	18	25	22 Mar. (81)	6 Fri.	182	.546	6	460	277	4052
....	....	....	....	....	23 Mar. (82)	1 Sun.	1	34	0	37	11 Mar. (70)	3 Tues.	153	.459	9882	307	247	4053
6 Bhâdrapada..	9819	29.458	127	0.380	22 Mar. (82)	2 Mon.	17	5	6	50	28 Feb. (59)	0 Sat.	14	.042	9758	155	216	4054
....	....	....	....	....	22 Mar. (81)	3 Tues.	32	36	13	2	18 Mar. (77)	6 Fri.	7	.021	9792	91	267	4055
....	....	....	....	....	22 Mar. (81)	4 Wed.	48	7	19	15	8 Mar. (67)	4 Wed.	125	.375	7	974	239	4056
3 Jyeshṭha....	9962	29.886	269	0.808	23 Mar. (82)	6 Fri.	3	39	1	27	26 Feb. (57)	2 Mon.	254	.762	221	858	211	4057
....	....	....	....	....	22 Mar. (82)	0 Sat.	19	10	7	40	16 Mar. (76)	1 Sun.	260	.780	255	794	262	4058
11 Mâgha......	9797	29.392	105	0.314	22 Mar. (81)	1 Sun.	34	41	13	52	5 Mar. (64)	5 Thur.	163	.489	131	641	231	4059
....	....	....	....	....	22 Mar. (81)	2 Mon.	50	12	20	5	22 Feb. (53)	2 Mon.	161	.483	7	488	200	4060
....	....	....	....	....	23 Mar. (82)	4 Wed.	5	44	2	17	13 Mar. (72)	1 Sun.	247	.741	42	424	252	4061
8 Kârttika....	9940	29.821	248	0.743	22 Mar. (82)	5 Thur.	21	15	8	30	1 Mar. (61)	5 Thur.	197	.591	9917	271	221	4062
....	....	....	....	....	22 Mar. (81)	6 Fri.	36	46	14	42	20 Mar. (79)	4 Wed.	227	.681	9932	207	272	4063
....	....	....	....	....	22 Mar. (81)	0 Sat.	52	17	20	55	9 Mar. (68)	1 Sun.	16	.048	9828	54	242	4064
4 Âshâḍha....	9776	29.327	83	0.249	23 Mar. (82)	2 Mon.	7	49	3	7	27 Feb. (58)	6 Fri.	130	.390	42	938	213	4065
....	....	....	....	....	22 Mar. (82)	3 Tues.	23	20	9	20	17 Mar. (77)	5 Thur.	117	.351	77	874	265	4066
....	....	....	....	....	22 Mar. (81)	4 Wed.	38	51	15	32	7 Mar. (66)	3 Tues.	291	.873	291	757	237	4067
1 Chaitra.....	9918	29.755	226	0.677	22 Mar. (81)	5 Thur.	54	22	21	45	24 Feb. (55)	0 Sat.	223	.669	167	605	206	4068
....	....	....	....	....	23 Mar. (82)	0 Sat.	9	54	3	57	15 Mar. (74)	6 Fri.	305	.915	201	541	257	4069
9 Mârgaśîrsha.	9754	29.261	61	0.183	22 Mar. (82)	1 Sun.	25	25	10	10	3 Mar. (63)	3 Tues.	308	.924	77	388	226	4070
....	....	....	....	....	22 Mar. (81)	2 Mon.	40	56	16	22	21 Mar. (80)	1 Sun.	49	.147	9773	287	275	4071
....	....	....	....	....	22 Mar. (81)	3 Tues.	56	27	22	35	11 Mar. (70)	6 Fri.	250	.750	9987	171	247	4072
6 Bhâdrapada..	9897	29.690	204	0.612	23 Mar. (82)	5 Thur.	11	59	4	47	28 Feb. (59)	3 Tues.	20	.060	9863	18	216	4073
....	....	....	....	....	22 Mar. (82)	6 Fri.	27	30	11	0	18 Mar. (78)	2 Mon.	⊙ −2	−.006	9898	954	267	4074
....	....	....	....	....	22 Mar. (81)	0 Sat.	43	1	17	12	8 Mar. (67)	0 Sat.	133	.399	112	838	239	4075

⊙ See Text. Art. 101 above, para. 2.

TABLE I.

Lunation-parts = 10,000*ths of a circle. A tithi* = $^1/_{30}$*th of the moon's synodic revolution.*

I. CONCURRENT YEAR.								II. ADDED LUNAR MONTHS.				
						Samvatsara.		True.				
Kali.	Śaka.	Chaitrâdi. Vikrama.	Meshâdi (Solar) year in Bengal.	Kollam.	A. D.	Luni-Solar cycle. (Southern.)	Bṛihaspati cycle (Northern) current at Mesha saṅkrânti.	Name of month.	Time of the preceding saṅkrânti expressed in Lunation parts. (*l.*)	Time of the preceding saṅkrânti expressed in Tithis.	Time of the succeeding saṅkrânti expressed in Lunation parts. (*l.*)	Time of the succeeding saṅkrânti expressed in Tithis.
1	2	3	3a	4	5	6	7	8	9	10	11	12
4076	897	1032	381	149-50	974- 75	8 Bhâva	9 Yuvan	3 Jyeshṭha	9287	27.861	5	0.015
4077	898	1033	382	150-51	975- 76	9 Yuvan	10 Dhâtṛi					
4078	899	1034	383	151-52	*976- 77	10 Dhâtṛi	11 Îśvara					
4079	900	1035	384	152-53	977- 78	11 Îśvara	12 Bahudhânya	1 Chaitra	9862	29.586	91	0.273
4080	901	1036	385	153-54	978- 79	12 Bahudhânya	13 Pramâthin					
4081	902	1037	386	154-55	979- 80	13 Pramâthin	14 Vikrama	5 Śrâvaṇa	9411	28.233	4	0.012
4082	903	1038	387	155-56	*980- 81	14 Vikrama	15 Vṛisha					
4083	904	1039	388	156-57	981- 82	15 Vṛisha	16 Chitrabhânu					
4084	905	1040	389	157-58	982- 83	16 Chitrabhânu	17 Subhânu	4 Âshâḍha	9545	28.635	421	1.263
4085	906	1041	390	158-59	983- 84	17 Subhânu	18 Târaṇa					
4086	907	1042	391	159-60	*984- 85	18 Târaṇa	19 Pârthiva					
4087	908	1043	392	160-61	985- 86	19 Pârthiva	20 Vyaya	3 Jyeshṭha	9944	29.832	529	1.587
4088	909	1044	393	161-62	986- 87	20 Vyaya	21 Sarvajit					
4089	910	1045	394	162-63	987- 88	21 Sarvajit	22 Sarvadhârin	7 Âśvina	9892	29.676	165	0.495
4090	911	1046	395	163-64	*988- 89	22 Sarvadhârin	23 Virodhin					
4091	912	1047	396	164-65	989- 90	23 Virodhin	24 Vikṛita					
4092	913	1048	397	165-66	990- 91	24 Vikṛita	25 Khara	5 Śrâvaṇa	9960	29.880	679	2.037
4093	914	1049	398	166-67	991- 92	25 Khara	26 Nandana					
4094	915	1050	399	167-68	*992- 93	26 Nandana	27 Vijaya					
4095	916	1051	400	168-69	993- 94	27 Vijaya	28 Jaya	3 Jyeshṭha	9414	28.242	30	0.090
4096	917	1052	401	169-70	994- 95	28 Jaya	29 Manmatha [1]					
4097	918	1053	402	170-71	995- 96	29 Manmatha	31 Hemalamba					
4098	919	1054	403	171-72	*996- 97	30 Durmukha	32 Vilamba	1 Chaitra	9918	29.754	219	0.657
4099	920	1055	404	172-73	997- 98	31 Hemalamba	33 Vikârin					
4100	921	1056	405	173-74	998- 99	32 Vilamba	34 Śârvari	5 Śrâvaṇa	9488	28.464	172	0.516
4101	922	1057	406	174-75	999-1000	33 Vikârin	35 Plava					
4102	923	1058	407	175-76	*1000- 1	34 Śârvari	36 Śubhakṛit					
4103	924	1059	408	176-77	1001- 2	35 Plava	37 Śobhana	4 Âshâḍha	9545	28.635	379	1.137
4104	925	1060	409	177-78	1002- 3	36 Śubhakṛit	38 Krodhin					
4105	926	1061	410	178-79	1003- 4	37 Śobhana	39 Viśvâvasu					
4106	927	1062	411	179-80	*1004- 5	38 Krodhin	40 Parâbhava	2 Vaiśâkha	9717	29.151	139	0.417
4107	928	1063	412	180-81	1005- 6	39 Viśvâvasu	41 Plavaṅga					

[1] Durmukha, No. 30, was suppressed in the north.

TABLE I.

(*Col.* 23) *a* = *Distance of moon from sun.* (*Col.* 24) *b* = *moon's mean anomaly.* (*Col.* 25) *c* = *sun's mean anomaly.*

II. ADDED LUNAR MONTHS (*continued.*)					III. COMMENCEMENT OF THE													
Mean.					Solar year.						Luni-Solar year. (Civil day of Chaitra Śukla 1st.)							
Name of month.	Time of the preceding saṅkrânti expressed in: Lunation parts. (*t.*)	Tithis.	Time of the succeeding saṅkrânti expressed in: Lunation parts. (*t.*)	Tithis.	Day and Month A. D.	(Time of the Mesha saṅkrânti.) Week day.	By the Ârya Siddhânta. Gh.	Pa	H.	M.	Day and Month A. D.	Week day.	At Sunrise on meridian of Ujjain. Moon's Age. Lunat. parts elapsed. (*t.*)	Tithis elapsed.	*a.*	*b.*	*c.*	Kali.
8a	9a	10a	11a	12a	13	14	15		17		19	20	21	22	23	24	25	1
2 Vaiśâkha....	9732	29.196	39	0.118	22 Mar. (81)	1 Sun.	58	32	23	25	25 Feb. (56)	4 Wed.	2	.006	9988	685	208	4076
....	....	....	....	....	23 Mar. (82)	3 Tues.	14	4	5	37	16 Mar. (75)	3 Tues.	65	.195	22	621	260	4077
11 Mâgha......	9875	29.624	182	0.546	22 Mar. (82)	4 Wed.	29	35	11	50	4 Mar. (64)	0 Sat.	66	.198	9898	468	229	4078
....	....	....	....	....	22 Mar. (81)	5 Thur.	45	6	18	2	21 Feb. (52)	4 Wed.	46	.138	9774	315	198	4079
....	....	....	....	....	23 Mar. (82)	0 Sat.	0	37	0	15	12 Mar. (71)	3 Tues.	88	.264	9808	251	249	4080
7 Âśvina......	9710	29.130	17	0.052	23 Mar. (82)	1 Sun	16	9	6	27	2 Mar. (61)	1 Sun.	269	.807	23	135	221	4081
....	....	....	....	....	22 Mar. (82)	2 Mon.	31	40	12	40	20 Mar. (80)	0 Sat.	258	.774	57	71	273	4082
....	....	....	....	....	22 Mar. (81)	3 Tues.	47	11	18	52	9 Mar. (68)	4 Wed.	4	.016	9933	918	242	4083
4 Âshâḍha	9853	29.559	160	0.481	23 Mar. (82)	5 Thur.	2	42	1	5	27 Feb. (58)	2 Mon.	157	.471	148	801	214	4084
....	....	....	....	....	23 Mar. (82)	6 Fri.	18	14	7	17	18 Mar. (77)	1 Sun.	182	.546	182	737	265	4085
....	....	....	....	....	22 Mar. (82)	0 Sat.	33	45	13	30	6 Mar. (66)	5 Thur.	127	.381	58	585	234	4086
1 Chaitra.....	9996	29.987	303	0.909	22 Mar. (81)	1 Sun.	49	16	19	42	23 Feb. (54)	2 Mon.	136	.408	9934	432	203	4087
....	....	....	....	....	23 Mar. (82)	3 Tues.	4	47	1	55	14 Mar. (73)	1 Sun.	211	633	9968	368	255	4088
9 Mârgaśîrsha .	9831	29.493	138	0.415	23 Mar. (82)	4 Wed.	20	19	8	7	4 Mar. (63)	6 Fri.	277	.831	183	251	226	4089
....	....	....	....	....	22 Mar. (82)	5 Thur.	35	50	14	20	21 Mar. (81)	4 Wed.	132	.396	9879	151	275	4090
....	....	....	....	....	22 Mar. (81)	6 Fri.	51	21	20	32	11 Mar. (70)	2 Mon.	263	.789	93	34	247	4091
6 Bhâdrapada ..	9974	29.921	281	0.844	23 Mar. (82)	1 Sun.	6	52	2	45	28 Feb. (59)	6 Fri.	15	.045	9969	882	216	4092
....	....	....	....	....	23 Mar. (82)	2 Mon.	22	24	8	57	19 Mar. (78)	5 Thur.	16	.048	3	818	267	4093
....	....	....	....	....	22 Mar. (82)	3 Tues.	37	55	15	10	8 Mar. (68)	3 Tues.	224	.672	218	701	239	4094
2 Vaiśâkha....	9809	29.428	117	0.350	22 Mar. (81)	4 Wed.	53	26	21	22	25 Feb. (56)	0 Sat.	193	.579	93	548	209	4095
....	....	....	....	....	23 Mar. (82)	6 Fri.	8	57	3	35	16 Mar. (75)	6 Fri.	282	.846	128	484	260	4096
11 Mâgha......	9952	29.856	259	0.778	23 Mar. (82)	0 Sat.	24	29	9	47	5 Mar. (64)	3 Tues.	268	.804	4	332	229	4097
....	....	....	....	....	22 Mar. (82)	1 Sun.	40	0	16	0	22 Feb. (53)	0 Sat.	149	.447	9879	179	198	4098
....	....	....	....	....	22 Mar. (81)	2 Mon.	55	31	22	12	12 Mar. (71)	6 Fri.	147	.441	9914	115	250	4099
7 Âśvina......	9787	29.362	95	0.284	23 Mar. (82)	4 Wed.	11	2	4	25	2 Mar. (61)	4 Wed.	267	.801	128	998	221	4100
....	....	....	....	....	23 Mar. (82)	5 Thur.	26	34	10	37	21 Mar. (80)	3 Tues.	246	.738	163	934	273	4101
....	....	....	....	....	22 Mar. (82)	6 Fri.	42	5	16	50	9 Mar. (69)	0 Sat.	42	.126	39	782	242	4102
4 Âshâḍha	9930	29.790	238	0.713	22 Mar. (81)	0 Sat.	57	36	23	2	27 Feb. (58)	5 Thur.	275	.825	253	665	214	4103
....	....	....	....	....	23 Mar. (82)	2 Mon.	13	7	5	15	17 Mar. (76)	3 Tues.	33	.099	9949	565	262	4104
12 Phâlguna....	9766	29.297	73	0.219	23 Mar. (82)	3 Tues.	28	39	11	27	6 Mar. (65)	0 Sat.	39	.117	9825	412	231	4105
....	....	....	....	....	22 Mar. (82)	4 Wed.	44	10	17	40	24 Feb. (55)	5 Thur.	316	.948	39	295	203	4106
....	....	....	....	....	22 Mar. (81)	5 Thur.	59	41	23	52	13 Mar. (72)	3 Tues.	6	.018	9735	195	252	4107

TABLE I.

Lunation-parts = 10,000ths of a circle. A tithi = 1/30th of the moon's synodic revolution.

I. CONCURRENT YEAR.								II. ADDED LUNAR MONTHS.				
						Samvatsara.		True.				
Kali.	Śaka.	Chaitrâdi. Vikrama.	Meshâdi (Solar) year in Bengal.	Kollam.	A. D.	Luni-Solar cycle. (Southern.)	Bṛihaspati cycle (Northern) current at Mesha saṅkrânti.	Name of month.	Time of the preceding saṅkrânti expressed in: Lunation parts. (*t.*)	Tithis.	Time of the succeeding saṅkrânti expressed in: Lunation parts. (*t.*)	Tithis.
1	2	3	3a	4	5	6	7	8	9	10	11	12
4108	929	1064	413	181- 82	1006- 7	40 Parâbhava	42 Kîlaka	6 Bhâdrapada	9657	28.971	80	0.240
4109	930	1065	414	182- 83	1007- 8	41 Plavaṅga	43 Saumya					
4110	931	1066	415	183- 84	*1008- 9	42 Kîlaka	44 Sâdhâraṇa					
4111	932	1067	416	184- 85	1009-10	43 Saumya	45 Virodhakṛit	5 Śrâvaṇa	9924	29.772	725	2.175
4112	933	1068	417	185- 86	1010-11	44 Sâdhâraṇa	46 Paridhâvin					
4113	934	1069	418	186- 87	1011-12	45 Virodhakṛit	47 Pramâdin					
4114	935	1070	419	187- 88	*1012-13	46 Paridhâvin	48 Ânanda	3 Jyeshṭha	9606	28.818	155	0.465
4115	936	1071	420	188- 89	1013-14	47 Pramâdin	49 Râkshasa					
4116	937	1072	421	189- 90	1014-15	48 Ananda	50 Anala					
4117	938	1073	422	190- 91	1015-16	49 Râkshasa	51 Piṅgala	1 Chaitra	9896	29.688	251	0.753
4118	939	1074	423	191- 92	*1016-17	50 Anala	52 Kâlayukta					
4119	940	1075	424	192- 93	1017-18	51 Piṅgala	53 Siddhârthin	5 Śrâvaṇa	9474	28.422	253	0.759
4120	941	1076	425	193- 94	1018-19	52 Kâlayukta	54 Raudra					
4121	942	1077	426	194- 95	1019-20	53 Siddhârthin	55 Durmati					
4122	943	1078	427	195- 96	*1020-21	54 Raudra	56 Dundubhi	4 Âshâḍha	9635	28.905	373	1.119
4123	944	1079	428	196- 97	1021-22	55 Durmati	57 Rudhirodgârin					
4124	945	1080	429	197- 98	1022-23	56 Dundubhi	58 Raktâksha					
4125	946	1081	430	198- 99	1023-24	57 Rudhirodgârin	59 Krodhana	2 Vaiśâkha	9783	29.349	288	0.864
4126	947	1082	431	199-200	*1024-25	58 Raktâksha	60 Kshaya					
4127	948	1083	432	200- 1	1025-26	59 Krodhana	1 Prabhava	6 Bhâdrapada	9770	29.310	263	0.789
4128	949	1084	433	201- 2	1026-27	60 Kshaya	2 Vibhava					
4129	950	1085	434	202- 3	1027-28	1 Prabhava	3 Sukla					
4130	951	1086	435	203- 4	*1028-29	2 Vibhava	4 Pramoda	5 Śrâvaṇa	9898	29.694	693	2.079
4131	952	1087	436	204- 5	1029-30	3 Śukla	5 Prajâpati					
4132	953	1088	437	205- 6	1030-31	4 Pramoda	6 Aṅgiras					
4133	954	1089	438	206- 7	1031-32	5 Prajâpati	7 Śrîmukha	3 Jyeshṭha	9781	29.343	347	1.041
4134	955	1090	439	207- 8	*1032-33	6 Aṅgiras	8 Bhâva					
4135	956	1091	440	208- 9	1033-34	7 Śrîmukha	9 Yuvan					
4136	957	1092	441	209- 10	1034-35	8 Bhâva	10 Dhâtṛi	1 Chaitra	9859	29.577	215	0.645
4137	958	1093	442	210- 11	1035-36	9 Yuvan	11 Îśvara					
4138	959	1094	443	211- 12	*1036-37	10 Dhâtṛi	12 Bahudhânya	5 Śrâvaṇa	9438	28.314	241	0.723
4139	960	1095	444	212- 13	1037-38	11 Îśvara	13 Pramâthin					

TABLE I.

(*Col.* 23) *a* = *Distance of moon from sun.* (*Col.* 24) *b* = *moon's mean anomaly.* (*Col.* 25) *c* = *sun's mean anomaly.*

II. ADDED LUNAR MONTHS (*continued.*)					III. COMMENCEMENT OF THE													
Mean.					Solar year.						Luni-Solar year. (Civil day of Chaitra Śukla 1st.)							Kali.
Name of month.	Time of the preceding saṅkrânti expressed in: Lunation parts. (*t.*)	Time of the preceding saṅkrânti expressed in: Tithis.	Time of the succeeding saṅkrânti expressed in: Lunation parts. (*t.*)	Time of the succeeding saṅkrânti expressed in: Tithis.	Day and Month A. D.	(Time of the Mesha saṅkrânti.) Week day.	By the Ârya Siddhânta. Gh.	Pa.	H.	M.	Day and Month A. D.	Week day.	At Sunrise on meridian of Ujjain. Moon's Age. Lunat. parts elapsed. (*t.*)	Tithis elapsed.	*a.*	*b.*	*c.*	
8a	9a	10a	11a	12a	13	14	15		17		19	20	21	22	23	24	25	1
9 Mârgaśîrsha	9908	29.725	216	0.647	23 Mar. (82)	0 Sat.	15	12	6	5	3 Mar. (62)	1 Sun.	158	.474	9950	79	224	4108
...	...	...	...	...	23 Mar. (82)	1 Sun.	30	44	12	17	22 Mar. (81)	0 Sat.	137	.411	9984	14	275	4109
...	...	...	...	...	22 Mar. (82)	2 Mon.	46	15	18	30	11 Mar. (71)	5 Thur.	255	.765	199	898	247	4110
5 Śrâvaṇa	9744	29.231	51	0.153	23 Mar. (82)	4 Wed.	1	46	0	42	28 Feb. (59)	2 Mon.	75	.227	74	745	216	4111
...	...	...	...	...	23 Mar. (82)	5 Thur.	17	17	6	55	19 Mar. (78)	1 Sun.	122	.366	109	681	268	4112
...	...	...	...	...	23 Mar. (82)	6 Fri.	32	49	13	7	8 Mar. (67)	5 Thur.	101	.303	9985	528	237	4113
2 Vaiśâkha	9886	29.659	194	0.582	22 Mar. (82)	0 Sat.	48	20	19	20	25 Feb. (56)	2 Mon.	100	.300	9860	376	206	4114
...	...	...	...	...	23 Mar. (82)	2 Mon.	3	51	1	32	15 Mar. (74)	1 Sun.	165	.495	9895	312	257	4115
10 Pausha	9722	29.166	29	0.088	23 Mar. (82)	3 Tues.	19	22	7	45	4 Mar. (63)	5 Thur.	28	.084	9771	159	226	4116
...	...	...	...	...	23 Mar. (82)	4 Wed.	34	54	13	57	22 Feb. (53)	3 Tues.	165	.495	9985	42	198	4117
...	...	...	...	...	22 Mar. (82)	5 Thur.	50	25	20	10	12 Mar. (72)	2 Mon.	140	.420	20	978	250	4118
7 Âśvina	9865	29.594	172	0.516	23 Mar. (82)	0 Sat.	5	56	2	22	2 Mar. (61)	0 Sat.	268	.804	234	862	221	4119
...	...	...	...	...	23 Mar. (82)	1 Sun.	21	27	8	35	21 Mar. (80)	6 Fri.	275	.825	269	798	273	4120
...	...	...	...	...	23 Mar. (82)	2 Mon.	36	59	14	47	10 Mar. (69)	3 Tues.	174	.522	144	645	242	4121
3 Jyeshṭha	9700	29.100	7	0.022	22 Mar. (82)	3 Tues.	52	30	21	0	27 Feb. (58)	0 Sat.	168	.504	20	492	211	4122
...	...	...	...	...	23 Mar. (82)	5 Thur.	8	1	3	12	17 Mar. (76)	6 Fri.	257	.771	55	428	262	4123
12 Phâlguna	9843	29.529	150	0.451	23 Mar. (82)	6 Fri.	23	32	9	25	6 Mar. (65)	3 Tues.	208	.624	9930	276	232	4124
...	...	...	...	...	23 Mar. (82)	0 Sat.	39	4	15	37	23 Feb. (54)	0 Sat.	47	.141	9806	123	201	4125
...	...	...	...	...	22 Mar. (82)	1 Sun.	54	35	21	50	13 Mar. (73)	6 Fri.	32	.096	9841	59	252	4126
9 Mârgaśîrsha	9986	29.957	293	0.879	23 Mar. (82)	3 Tues.	10	6	4	2	3 Mar. (62)	4 Wed.	146	.438	55	942	224	4127
...	...	...	...	...	23 Mar. (82)	4 Wed.	25	37	10	15	22 Mar. (81)	3 Tues.	133	.399	90	878	275	4128
...	...	...	...	...	23 Mar. (82)	5 Thur	41	9	16	27	12 Mar. (71)	1 Sun.	304	.912	304	762	247	4129
5 Śrâvaṇa	9821	29.463	128	0.385	22 Mar. (82)	6 Fri.	56	40	22	40	29 Feb. (60)	5 Thur.	232	.696	180	609	217	4130
...	...	...	...	...	23 Mar. (82)	1 Sun.	12	11	4	52	19 Mar. (78)	4 Wed.	316	.948	215	545	268	4131
...	...	...	...	...	23 Mar. (82)	2 Mon.	27	42	11	5	8 Mar. (67)	1 Sun.	319	.957	90	392	237	4132
2 Vaiśâkha	9964	29.891	271	0.813	23 Mar. (82)	3 Tues.	43	14	17	17	25 Feb. (56)	5 Thur.	248	.744	9966	239	206	4133
...	...	...	...	...	22 Mar. (82)	4 Wed.	58	45	23	30	15 Mar. (75)	4 Wed.	266	.798	1	175	258	4134
10 Pausha	9799	29.398	107	0.320	23 Mar. (82)	6 Fri.	14	16	5	42	4 Mar. (63)	1 Sun.	36	.108	9876	22	227	4135
...	...	...	...	...	23 Mar. (82)	0 Sat.	29	47	11	55	22 Feb. (53)	6 Fri.	156	.468	91	906	199	4136
...	...	...	...	...	23 Mar. (82)	1 Sun.	45	19	18	7	13 Mar. (72)	5 Thur.	148	.444	125	842	250	4137
7 Âśvina	9942	29.826	249	0.748	23 Mar. (83)	3 Tues.	0	50	0	20	1 Mar. (61)	2 Mon.	12	.036	1	689	219	4138
...	...	...	...	...	23 Mar. (82)	4 Wed.	16	21	6	32	20 Mar. (79)	1 Sun.	77	.231	36	625	270	4139

TABLE I.

Lunation-parts = 10,000*ths of a circle. A tithi* = $^1/_{30}$*th of the moon's synodic revolution.*

I. CONCURRENT YEAR.								II. ADDED LUNAR MONTHS.				
						Samvatsara.		True.				
Kali.	Śaka.	Chaitrâdi. Vikrama.	Meshâdi (Solar) year in Bengal.	Kollam.	A. D.	Luni-Solar cycle, (Southern.)	Bṛihaspati cycle (Northern) current at Mesha saṅkrânti.	Name of month.	Time of the preceding saṅkrânti expressed in: Lunation parts. (*l.*)	Tithis.	Time of the succeeding saṅkrânti expressed in: Lunation parts. (*l.*)	Tithis.
1	2	3	3a	4	5	6	7	8	9	10	11	12
4140	961	1096	445	213- 14	1038-39	12 Bahudhânya..	14 Vikrama.....	....	......	......	......	......
4141	962	1097	446	214- 15	1039-40	13 Pramâthin...	15 Vṛisha......	4 Âshâḍha....	9811	29.433	606	1.818
4142	963	1098	447	215- 16	*1040-41	14 Vikrama.....	16 Chitrabhânu..	....	......	......	......	......
4143	964	1099	448	216- 17	1041-42	15 Vṛisha.......	17 Subhânu.....	....	......	......	......	......
4144	965	1100	449	217- 18	1042-43	16 Chitrabhânu..	18 Târaṇa......	2 Vaiśâkha....	9763	29.289	343	1.029
4145	966	1101	450	218- 19	1043-44	17 Subhânu.....	19 Pârthiva.....	....	......	......	......	......
4146	967	1102	451	219- 20	*1044-45	18 Târaṇa.......	20 Vyaya.......	6 Bhâdrapada..	9785	29.355	465	1.395
4147	968	1103	452	220- 21	1045-46	19 Pârthiva.....	21 Sarvajit......	....	......	......	......	......
4148	969	1104	453	221- 22	1046-47	20 Vyaya.......	22 Sarvadhârin...	....	......	......	......	......
4149	970	1105	454	222- 23	1047-48	21 Sarvajit......	23 Virodhin,....	5 Śrâvaṇa.....	9288	27.864	666	1.998
4150	971	1106	455	223- 24	*1048-49	22 Sarvadhârin..	24 Vikṛita......	....	......	......	......	......
4151	972	1107	456	224- 25	1049-50	23 Virodhin.....	25 Khara.......	....	......	......	......	......
4152	973	1108	457	225- 26	1050-51	24 Vikṛita......	26 Nandana.....	3 Jyeshṭha....	9867	29.601	522	1.566
4153	974	1109	458	226- 27	1051-52	25 Khara.......	27 Vijaya.......	....	......	......	......	......
4154	975	1110	459	227- 28	*1052-53	26 Nandana.....	28 Jaya........	7 Âśvina...... 10 *Pausha* (*Ksh.*)	9874 93	29.622 0.279	147 9938	0.441 29.814
4155	976	1111	460	228- 29	1053-54	27 Vijaya.......	29 Manmatha....	1 Chaitra.....	9896	29.688	193	0.579
4156	977	1112	461	229- 30	1054-55	28 Jaya........	30 Durmukha...	....	......	......	......	......
4157	978	1113	462	230- 31	1055-56	29 Manmatha....	31 Hemalamba...	5 Śrâvaṇa.....	9452	28.356	200	0.600
4158	979	1114	463	231- 32	*1056-57	30 Durmukha...	32 Vilamba.....	....	......	......	......	......
4159	980	1115	464	232- 33	1057-58	31 Hemalamba...	33 Vikârin.....	....	......	......	......	......
4160	981	1116	465	233- 34	1058-59	32 Vilamba......	34 Śârvari......	3 Jyeshṭha....	9382	28.146	5	0.015
4161	982	1117	466	234- 35	1059-60	33 Vikârin......	35 Plava.......	....	......	......	......	......
4162	983	1118	467	235- 36	*1060-61	34 Śârvari......	36 Śubhakṛit....	....	......	......	......	......
4163	984	1119	468	236- 37	1061-62	35 Plava........	37 Śobhana......	2 Vaiśâkha....	9726	29.178	316	0.948
4164	985	1120	469	237- 38	1062-63	36 Śubhakṛit....	38 Krodhin......	....	......	......	......	......
4165	986	1121	470	238- 39	1063-64	37 Śobhana......	39 Viśvâvasu....	6 Bhâdrapada..	9743	29.229	370	1.110
4166	987	1122	471	239- 40	*1064-65	38 Krodhin.....	40 Parâbhava....	....	......	......	......	......
4167	988	1123	472	240- 41	1065-66	39 Viśvâvasu....	41 Plavaṅga.....	....	......	......	......	......
4168	989	1124	473	241- 42	1066-67	40 Parâbhava....	42 Kîlaka......	4 Âshâḍha....	9475	28.425	97	0.291
4169	990	1125	474	242- 43	1067-68	41 Plavaṅga.....	43 Saumya......	....	......	......	......	......
4170	991	1126	475	243- 44	*1068-69	42 Kîlaka......	44 Sâdhâraṇa....	....	......	......	......	......

TABLE I.

(*Col.* 23) *a* = *Distance of moon from sun.* (*Col.* 24) *b* = *moon's mean anomaly.* (*Col.* 25) *c* = *sun's mean anomaly.*

II. ADDED LUNAR MONTHS (*continued.*)					III. COMMENCEMENT OF THE													
Mean.					Solar year.						Luni-Solar year. (Civil day of Chaitra Śukla 1st.)							Kali.
Name of month.	Time of the preceding saṅkrânti expressed in		Time of the succeeding saṅkrânti expressed in		Day and Month A. D.	(Time of the Mesha saṅkrânti.)					Day and Month A. D.	Week day.	At Sunrise on meridian of Ujjain.					
						Week day.	By the Ârya Siddhânta.						Moon's Age.					
	Lunation parts. (*t.*)	Tithis.	Lunation parts. (*t.*)	Tithis.			Gh.	Pa.	H.	M.			Lunat. parts elapsed. (*t.*)	Tithis elapsed.	*a*	*b.*	*c.*	
8a	**9a**	**10a**	**11a**	**12a**	**13**	**14**	**15**		**17**		**19**	**20**	**21**	**22**	**23**	**24**	**25**	**1**
....	....	....	....	......	23 Mar. (82)	5 Thur.	31	52	12	45	9 Mar. (68)	5 Thur.	74	.222	9911	474	240	4140
3 Jyeshṭha....	9777	29.332	85	0.254	23 Mar. (82)	6 Fri.	47	24	18	57	26 Feb. (57)	2 Mon.	56	.168	9787	320	209	4141
....	....	....	....	......	23 Mar. (83)	1 Sun.	2	55	1	10	16 Mar. (76)	1 Sun.	102	.306	9822	256	260	4142
12 Phâlguna...	9920	29.760	227	0.682	23 Mar. (82)	2 Mon.	18	26	7	22	6 Mar. (65)	6 Fri.	283	.849	36	139	232	4143
....	....	....	....	......	23 Mar. (82)	3 Tues.	33	57	13	35	23 Feb. (54)	3 Tues.	42	.126	9912	986	201	4144
....	....	....	....	......	23 Mar. (82)	4 Wed.	49	29	19	47	14 Mar. (73)	2 Mon.	20	.060	9946	922	252	4145
8 Kârttika....	9756	29.267	63	0.189	23 Mar. (83)	6 Fri.	5	0	2	0	3 Mar. (63)	0 Sat.	171	.513	161	806	224	4146
....	....	....	....	......	23 Mar. (82)	0 Sat.	20	31	8	12	22 Mar. (81)	6 Fri.	195	.585	195	742	276	4147
....	....	....	....	......	23 Mar. (82)	1 Sun.	36	2	14	25	11 Mar. (70)	3 Tues.	137	.411	71	589	245	4148
5 Srâvaṇa....	9898	29.695	206	0.617	23 Mar. (82)	2 Mon.	51	34	20	37	28 Feb. (59)	0 Sat.	144	.432	9947	436	214	4149
....	....	....	....	......	23 Mar. (83)	4 Wed.	7	5	2	50	18 Mar. (78)	6 Fri.	222	.666	9981	372	265	4150
....	....	....	....	......	23 Mar. (82)	5 Thur.	22	36	9	2	7 Mar. (66)	3 Tues.	134	.402	9857	219	235	4151
1 Chaitra.....	9734	29.201	41	0.123	23 Mar. (82)	6 Fri.	38	7	15	15	25 Feb. (56)	1 Sun.	298	.894	71	103	206	4152
....	....	....	....	......	23 Mar. (82)	0 Sat.	53	39	21	27	16 Mar. (75)	0 Sat.	280	.540	106	39	258	4153
}10 Pausha.....	9876	29.629	184	0.551	23 Mar. (83)	2 Mon.	9	10	3	40	4 Mar. (64)	4 Wed.	30	.090	9982	886	227	4154
....	....	....	....	......	23 Mar. (82)	3 Tues.	24	41	9	52	22 Feb. (53)	2 Mon.	200	.600	196	769	199	4155
....	....	....	....	......	23 Mar. (82)	4 Wed.	40	12	16	5	13 Mar. (72)	1 Sun.	236	.708	231	705	250	4156
6 Bhâdrapada..	9712	29.136	19	0.058	23 Mar. (82)	5 Thur.	55	44	22	17	2 Mar. (61)	5 Thur.	202	.606	107	553	219	4157
....	....	....	....	......	23 Mar. (83)	0 Sat.	11	15	4	30	20 Mar. (80)	4 Wed.	291	.873	141	489	271	4158
....	....	....	....	......	23 Mar. (82)	1 Sun.	26	46	10	42	9 Mar. (68)	1 Sun.	277	.831	17	336	240	4159
3 Jyeshṭha....	9855	29.564	162	0.486	23 Mar. (82)	2 Mon.	42	17	16	55	26 Feb. (57)	5 Thur.	162	.486	9892	183	209	4160
....	....	....	....	......	23 Mar. (82)	3 Tues.	57	49	23	7	17 Mar. (76)	4 Wed.	162	.486	9927	119	260	4161
12 Phâlguna....	9997	29.992	305	0.914	23 Mar. (83)	5 Thur.	13	20	5	20	6 Mar. (66)	2 Mon.	285	.855	142	3	232	4162
....	....	....	....	......	23 Mar. (82)	6 Fri.	28	51	11	32	23 Feb. (54)	6 Fri.	47	.141	17	850	201	4163
....	....	....	....	......	23 Mar. (82)	0 Sat.	44	22	17	45	14 Mar. (73)	5 Thur.	56	.168	52	786	253	4164
8 Kârttika....	9833	29.498	140	0.420	23 Mar. (82)	1 Sun.	59	54	23	57	4 Mar. (63)	3 Tues.	285	.855	266	669	225	4165
....	....	....	....	......	23 Mar. (83)	3 Tues.	15	25	6	10	21 Mar. (81)	1 Sun.	43	.129	9962	569	273	4166
....	....	....	....	......	23 Mar. (82)	4 Wed.	30	56	12	22	10 Mar. (69)	5 Thur.	49	.147	9838	416	242	4167
5 Śrâvaṇa.....	9976	29.927	283	0.849	23 Mar. (82)	5 Thur.	46	27	18	35	28 Feb. (59)	3 Tues.	327	.981	52	300	214	4168
....	....	....	....	......	24 Mar. (83)	0 Sat.	1	59	0	47	18 Mar. (77)	1 Sun.	21	.063	9748	199	263	4169
....	....	....	....	......	23 Mar. (83)	1 Sun.	17	30	7	0	7 Mar. (67)	6 Fri.	173	.519	9963	83	235	4170

TABLE I.

Lunation-parts = 10,000ths of a circle. A tithi = 1/30th of the moon's synodic revolution.

I. CONCURRENT YEAR.								II. ADDED LUNAR MONTHS.				
						Samvatsara.		True.				
Kali.	Śaka.	Chaitrâdi. Vikrama.	Meshâdi (Solar) year in Bengal.	Kollam.	A. D.	Luni-Solar cycle. (Southern.)	Bṛihaspati cycle (Northern) current at Mesha saṅkrânti.	Name of month.	Time of the preceding saṅkrânti expressed in		Time of the succeeding saṅkrânti expressed in	
									Lunation parts. (*l*.)	Tithis.	Lunation parts. (*l*.)	Tithis.
1	2	3	3a	4	5	6	7	8	9	10	11	12
4171	992	1127	476	244-45	1069- 70	43 Saumya......	45 Virodhakṛit...	3 Jyeshṭha....	9864	29.592	612	1.836
4172	993	1128	477	245-46	1070- 71	44 Sâdhâraṇa ...	46 Paridhâvin...	....	......	....	......	......
4173	994	1129	478	246-47	1071- 72	45 Virodhakṛit...	47 Pramâdin....	7 Âśvina......	9901	29.703	258	0.774
4174	995	1130	479	247-48	*1072- 73	46 Paridhâvin...	48 Ânanda......	....	......	....	......	......
4175	996	1131	480	248-49	1073- 74	47 Pramâdin....	49 Râkshasa.....	....	......	....	......	......
4176	997	1132	481	249-50	1074- 75	48 Ânanda......	50 Anala	5 Śrâvaṇa.....	9571	28.713	217	0.651
4177	998	1133	482	250-51	1075- 76	49 Râkshasa.....	51 Piṅgala......	....	......	....	......	......
4178	999	1134	483	251-52	*1076- 77	50 Anala........	52 Kâlayukta....	....	......	....	......	......
4179	1000	1135	484	252-53	1077- 78	51 Piṅgala......	53 Siddhârthin ..	3 Jyeshṭha....	9404	28.212	125	0.375
4180	1001	1136	485	253-54	1078- 79	52 Kâlayukta....	54 Raudra	....	......	....	......	......
4181	1002	1137	486	254-55	1079- 80	53 Siddhârthin ..	55 Durmati [1])....	....	......	....	......	......
4182	1003	1138	487	255-56	*1080- 81	54 Raudra	57 Rudhirodgârin	2 Vaiśâkha....	9756	29.268	281	0.843
4183	1004	1139	488	256-57	1081- 82	55 Durmati.....	58 Raktâksha....	....	......	....	......	......
4184	1005	1140	489	257-58	1082- 83	56 Dundubhi....	59 Krodhana	6 Bhâdrapada..	9733	29.199	329	0.987
4185	1006	1141	490	258-59	1083- 84	57 Rudhirodgârin	60 Kshaya......	....	......	....	......	......
4186	1007	1142	491	259-60	*1084- 85	58 Raktâksha....	1 Prabhava.....	....	......	....	......	......
4187	1008	1143	492	260-61	1085- 86	59 Krodhana....	2 Vibhava......	4 Âshâḍha....	9629	28.887	282	0.846
4188	1009	1144	493	261-62	1086- 87	60 Kshaya......	3 Śukla........	....	......	....	......	......
4189	1010	1145	494	262-63	1087- 88	1 Prabhava.....	4 Pramoda......	....	......	....	......	......
4190	1011	1146	495	263-64	*1088- 89	2 Vibhava......	5 Prajâpati.....	3 Jyeshṭha....	9819	29.457	605	1.815
4191	1012	1147	496	264-65	1089- 90	3 Śukla........	6 Aṅgiras......	....	......	....	......	......
4192	1013	1148	497	265-66	1090- 91	4 Pramoda.....	7 Śrîmukha	7 Âśvina......	9875	29.625	271	0.813
4193	1014	1149	498	266-67	1091- 92	5 Prajâpati.....	8 Bhâva.......	....	......	....	......	......
4194	1015	1150	499	267-68	*1092- 93	6 Aṅgiras......	9 Yuvan.......	....	......	....	......	......
4195	1016	1151	500	268-69	1093- 94	7 Śrîmukha....	10 Dhâtṛi.......	5 Śrâvaṇa.....	9763	29.289	336	1.008
4196	1017	1152	501	269-70	1094- 95	8 Bhâva.......	11 Îśvara.......	....	......	....	......	......
4197	1018	1153	502	270-71	1095- 96	9 Yuvan.......	12 Bahudhânya...	....	......	....	......	......
4198	1019	1154	503	271-72	*1096- 97	10 Dhâtṛi.......	13 Pramâthin....	3 Jyeshṭha....	9363	28.089	147	0.441
4199	1020	1155	504	272-73	1097- 98	11 Îśvara.......	14 Vikrama	....	......	....	......	......
4200	1021	1156	505	273-74	1098- 99	12 Bahudhânya..	15 Vṛisha.......	....	......	....	......	......
4201	1022	1157	506	274-75	1099-100	13 Pramâthin....	16 Chitrabhânu..	2 Vaiśâkha....	9885	29.655	323	0.969
4202	1023	1158	507	275-76	*1100- 1	14 Vikrama.....	17 Subhânu.....	....	......	....	......	......

[1]) Dundubhi, No. 56, was suppressed in the north.

TABLE I.

(*Col.* 23) *a* = *Distance of moon from sun.* (*Col.* 24) *b* = *moon's mean anomaly.* (*Col.* 25) *c* = *sun's mean anomaly.*

II. ADDED LUNAR MONTHS (*continued.*)					III. COMMENCEMENT OF THE													
Mean.					Solar year.						Luni-Solar year. (Civil day of Chaitra Śukla 1st.)							Kali.
Name of month.	Time of the preceding saṅkrânti expressed in: Lunation parts. (*t.*)	Tithis.	Time of the succeeding saṅkrânti expressed in: Lunation parts. (*t.*)	Tithis.	Day and Month A. D.	(Time of the Mesha saṅkrânti.) Week day.	By the Ârya Siddhânta. Gh.	Pa.	H.	M.	Day and Month A. D.	Week day.	At Sunrise on meridian of Ujjain. Moon's Age. Lunat. parts elapsed. (*t.*)	Tithis elapsed.	*a*	*b.*	*c.*	
8a	9a	10a	11a	12a	13	14	15		17		19	20	21	22	23	24	25	1
1 Chaitra.....	9811	29.433	118	0.355	23 Mar. (82)	2 Mon.	33	1	13	12	25 Feb. (56)	4 Wed.	289	.867	177	966	207	4171
....	....	....	...	......	23 Mar. (82)	3 Tues.	48	32	19	25	16 Mar. (75)	3 Tues.	271	.813	212	902	258	4172
10 Pausha......	9954	29.861	261	0.783	24 Mar. (83)	5 Thur.	4	4	1	37	5 Mar. (64)	0 Sat.	87	.261	87	749	227	4173
....	....	....	...	......	23 Mar. (83)	6 Fri.	19	35	7	50	23 Mar. (83)	6 Fri.	134	.402	122	686	278	4174
....	....	....	...	......	23 Mar. (82)	0 Sat.	35	6	14	2	12 Mar. (71)	3 Tues.	110	.330	9998	533	248	4175
6 Bhâdrapada..	9789	29.367	97	0.290	23 Mar. (82)	1 Sun.	50	37	20	15	1 Mar. (60)	0 Sat.	111	.333	9874	380	217	4176
....	....	....	...	......	24 Mar. (83)	3 Tues.	6	9	2	27	20 Mar. (79)	6 Fri.	176	.528	9908	316	268	4177
....	....	....	...	......	23 Mar. (83)	4 Wed.	21	40	8	40	8 Mar. (68)	3 Tues.	44	.132	9784	165	237	4178
3 Jyeshtha....	9932	29.796	239	0.718	23 Mar. (82)	5 Thur.	37	11	14	52	26 Feb. (57)	1 Sun.	181	.543	9998	47	209	4179
....	....	....	...	......	23 Mar. (82)	6 Fri.	52	42	21	5	17 Mar. (76)	0 Sat.	158	.474	33	983	260	4180
11 Mâgha......	9767	29.302	75	0.224	24 Mar. (83)	1 Sun.	8	14	3	17	7 Mar. (66)	5 Thur.	283	.849	247	866	232	4181
....	....	....	...	......	23 Mar. (83)	2 Mon.	23	45	9	30	24 Feb. (55)	2 Mon.	130	.390	123	713	202	4182
....	....	....	...	......	23 Mar. (82)	3 Tues.	39	16	15	42	14 Mar. (73)	1 Sun.	186	.558	158	649	253	4183
8 Kârttika.....	9910	29.730	217	0.652	23 Mar. (82)	4 Wed.	54	47	21	55	3 Mar. (62)	5 Thur.	177	.531	33	497	222	4184
....	....	....	...	......	24 Mar. (83)	6 Fri.	10	19	4	7	22 Mar. (81)	4 Wed.	266	.798	68	432	273	4185
....	....	....	...	......	23 Mar. (83)	0 Sat.	25	50	10	20	10 Mar. (70)	1 Sun.	221	.663	9944	280	243	4186
4 Âshâḍha....	9745	29.236	53	0.159	23 Mar. (82)	1 Sun.	41	21	16	32	27 Feb. (58)	5 Thur.	61	.183	9819	127	212	4187
....	....	....	...	......	23 Mar. (82)	2 Mon.	56	52	22	45	18 Mar. (77)	4 Wed.	48	.144	9854	63	263	4188
....	....	....	...	......	24 Mar. (83)	4 Wed.	12	24	4	57	8 Mar. (67)	2 Mon.	161	.483	68	946	235	4189
1 Chaitra.....	9888	29.665	196	0.587	23 Mar. (83)	5 Thur.	27	55	11	10	26 Feb. (57)	0 Sat.	302	.906	283	830	207	4190
....	....	....	...	......	23 Mar. (82)	6 Fri.	43	26	17	22	16 Mar. (75)	6 Fri.	318	.954	317	766	258	4191
9 Mârgaśîrsha.	9724	29.171	31	0.093	23 Mar. (82)	0 Sat.	58	57	23	35	5 Mar. (64)	3 Tues.	241	.723	193	613	227	4192
....	....	....	...	......	24 Mar. (85)	2 Mon.	14	29	5	47	23 Mar. (82)	1 Sun.	18	.054	9889	513	276	4193
....	....	....	...	......	23 Mar. (83)	3 Tues.	30	0	12	0	12 Mar. (72)	6 Fri.	328	.984	103	396	248	4194
6 Bhâdrapada..	9866	29.599	174	0.521	23 Mar. (82)	4 Wed.	45	31	18	12	1 Mar. (60)	3 Tues.	260	.780	9979	243	217	4195
....	....	....	...	......	24 Mar. (83)	6 Fri.	1	2	0	25	20 Mar. (79)	2 Mon.	281	.843	14	180	268	4196
....	....	....	...	......	24 Mar. (83)	0 Sat.	16	34	6	37	9 Mar. (68)	6 Fri.	52	.156	9889	27	237	4197
2 Vaiśâkha....	9702	29.105	9	0.028	23 Mar. (83)	1 Sun.	32	5	12	50	27 Feb. (58)	4 Wed.	171	.513	104	910	209	4198
....	....	....	...	......	23 Mar. (82)	2 Mon.	47	36	19	2	17 Mar. (76)	3 Tues.	163	.489	138	846	261	4199
11 Mâgha......	9845	29.534	152	0.456	24 Mar. (83)	4 Wed.	3	7	1	15	6 Mar. (65)	0 Sat.	23	.069	14	693	230	4200
....	....	....	...	......	24 Mar. (83)	5 Thur	18	39	7	27	24 Feb. (55)	5 Thur.	306	.918	229	577	202	4201
....	....	....	...	......	23 Mar. (83)	6 Fri.	34	10	13	40	13 Mar. (73)	3 Tues.	85	.255	9925	477	250	4202

TABLE I.

Lunation-parts = 10,000*ths of a circle. A tithi* = 1/30*th of the moon's synodic revolution.*

I. CONCURRENT YEAR.								II. ADDED LUNAR MONTHS.				
						Samvatsara.		True.				
Kali.	Śaka.	Chaitrâdi. Vikrama.	Meshâdi (Solar) year in Bengal.	Kollam.	A. D.	Luni-Solar cycle. (Southern.)	Bṛihaspati cycle (Northern) current at Mesha saṅkrânti.	Name of month.	Time of the preceding saṅkrânti expressed in		Time of the succeeding saṅkrânti expressed in	
									Lunation parts. (*l.*)	Tithis.	Lunation parts. (*l.*)	Tithis.
1	2	3	3a	4	5	6	7	8	9	10	11	12
4203	1024	1159	508	276- 77	1101- 2	15 Vṛisha	18 Târaṇa	6 Bhâdrapada	9818	29.454	328	0.984
4204	1025	1160	509	277- 78	1102- 3	16 Chitrabhânu	19 Pârthiva					
4205	1026	1161	510	278- 79	1103- 4	17 Subhânu	20 Vyaya					
4206	1027	1162	511	279- 80	*1104- 5	18 Târaṇa	21 Sarvajit	4 Âshâḍha	9677	29.031	453	1.359
4207	1028	1163	512	280- 81	1105- 6	19 Pârthiva	22 Sarvadhârin					
4208	1029	1164	513	281- 82	1106- 7	20 Vyaya	23 Virodhin					
4209	1030	1165	514	282- 83	1107- 8	21 Sarvajit	24 Vikṛita	3 Jyeshṭha	9830	29.490	563	1.689
4210	1031	1166	515	283- 84	*1108- 9	22 Sarvadhârin	25 Khara					
4211	1032	1167	516	284- 85	1109-10	23 Virodhin	26 Nandana	7 Âśvina	9852	29.556	230	0.690
4212	1033	1168	517	285- 86	1110-11	24 Vikṛita	27 Vijaya					
4213	1034	1169	518	286- 87	1111-12	25 Khara	28 Jaya					
4214	1035	1170	519	287- 88	*1112-13	26 Nandana	29 Manmatha	5 Śrâvaṇa	9941	29.823	524	1.572
4215	1036	1171	520	288- 89	1113-14	27 Vijaya	30 Durmukha					
4216	1037	1172	521	289- 90	1114-15	28 Jaya	31 Hemalamba					
4217	1038	1173	522	290- 91	1115-16	29 Manmatha	32 Vilamba	3 Jyeshṭha	9349	28.047	107	0.321
4218	1039	1174	523	291- 92	*1116-17	30 Durmukha	33 Vikârin					
4219	1040	1175	524	292- 93	1117-18	31 Hemalamba	34 Śârvari					
4220	1041	1176	525	293- 94	1118-19	32 Vilamba	35 Plava	1 Chaitra	9876	29.628	78	0.234
4221	1042	1177	526	294- 95	1119-20	33 Vikârin	36 Śubhakṛit					
4222	1043	1178	527	295- 96	*1120-21	34 Śârvari	37 Śobhana	6 Bhâdrapada	9990	29.970	421	1.263
4223	1044	1179	528	296- 97	1121-22	35 Plava	38 Krodhin					
4224	1045	1180	529	297- 98	1122-23	36 Śubhakṛit	39 Viśvâvasu					
4225	1046	1181	530	298- 99	1123-24	37 Śobhana	40 Parâbhava	4 Âshâḍha	9655	28.965	512	1.536
4226	1047	1182	531	299-300	*1124-25	38 Krodhin	41 Plavaṅga					
4227	1048	1183	532	300- 1	1125-26	39 Viśvâvasu	42 Kîlaka					
4228	1049	1184	533	301- 2	1126-27	40 Parâbhava	43 Saumya	3 Jyeshṭha	9939	29.817	575	1.725
4229	1050	1185	534	302- 3	1127-28	41 Plavaṅga	44 Sâdhâraṇa					
4230	1051	1186	535	303- 4	*1128-29	42 Kîlaka	45 Virodhakṛit	7 Âśvina	9910	29.730	223	0.669
4231	1052	1187	536	304- 5	1129-30	43 Saumya	46 Paridhâvin					
4232	1053	1188	537	305- 6	1130-31	44 Sâdhâraṇa	47 Pramâdin					
4233	1054	1189	538	306- 7	1131-32	45 Virodhakṛit	48 Ânanda	4 Âshâḍha	9201	27.603	37	0.111
4234	1055	1190	539	307- 8	*1132-33	46 Paridhâvin	49 Râkshasa					
4235	1056	1191	540	308- 9	1133-34	47 Pramâdin	50 Anala					

TABLE I.

(*Col.* 23) a = *Distance of moon from sun.* (*Col.* 24) b = *moon's mean anomaly.* (*Col.* 25) c = *sun's mean anomaly.*

III. COMMENCEMENT OF THE																	
Solar year.										Luni-Solar year. (Civil day of Chaitra Śukla 1st.)							Kali.
Day and Month. A. D.	(Time of the Mesha saṅkrânti.)									Day and Month. A. D.	Week day.	At Sunrise on meridian of Ujjain.					
	Week day.	By the Ârya Siddhânta.				By the Sûrya Siddhânta.						Moon's Age.		a.	b.	c.	
		Gh.	Pa.	H.	M.	Gh.	Pa.	H.	M.			Lunat. parts elapsed. (t.)	Tithis elapsed.				
13	14	15		17		15a		17a		19	20	21	22	23	24	25	1
23 Mar. (82)..	0 Sat.....	49	41	19	52	52	27	20	59	2 Mar. (61)..	0 Sat.....	66	.198	9800	324	220	4203
24 Mar. (83)..	2 Mon....	5	12	2	5	7	58	3	11	21 Mar. (80)..	6 Fri,....	115	.345	9835	260	271	4204
24 Mar. (83)..	3 Tues....	20	44	8	17	23	30	9	24	11 Mar. (70)..	4 Wed....	298	.894	49	143	243	4205
23 Mar. (83)..	4 Wed....	36	15	14	30	39	1.	15	36	28 Feb. (59)..	1 Sun....	59	.177	9925	991	212	4206
23 Mar. (82)..	5 Thur...	51	46	20	42	54	33	21	49	18 Mar (77)..	0 Sat.....	38	.114	9960	927	263	4207
24 Mar. (83)..	0 Sat.....	7	17	2	55	10	4	4	2	8 Mar. (67)..	5 Thur...	184	.552	174	810	235	4208
24 Mar. (83)..	1 Sun....	22	49	9	7	25	36	10	14	25 Feb. (56)..	2 Mon....	77	.231	50	657	204	4209
23 Mar. (83)..	2 Mon....	38	20	15	20	41	7	16	27	15 Mar. (75)..	1 Sun....	146	.438	84	593	256	4210
23 Mar. (82)..	3 Tues....	53	51	21	32	56	39	22	39	4 Mar. (63)..	5 Thur...	152	.456	9960	440	225	4211
24 Mar. (83)..	5 Thur...	9	22	3	45	12	10	4	52	23 Mar. (82)..	4 Wed....	234	.702	9995	376	276	4212
24 Mar. (83)..	6 Fri.....	24	54	9	57	27	42	11	5	12 Mar. (71)..	1 Sun....	148	.444	9870	224	245	4213
23 Mar. (83)..	0 Sat.....	40	25	16	10	43	13	17	17	1 Mar. (61)..	6 Fri.....	314	.942	85	107	217	4214
23 Mar. (82)..	1 Sun....	55	56	22	22	58	45	23	30	20 Mar. (79)..	5 Thur...	297	.891	119	43	269	4215
24 Mar. (83)..	3 Tues....	11	27	4	35	14	16	5	43	9 Mar. (68)..	2 Mon....	45	.135	9995	890	238	4216
24 Mar. (83)..	4 Wed....	26	59	10	47	29	48	11	55	27 Feb. (58)..	0 Ṡat.....	214	.642	210	774	210	4217
23 Mar. (83)..	5 Thur...	42	30	17	0	45	19	18	8	17 Mar. (77)..	6 Fri.....	248	.744	244	710	261	4218
23 Mar. (82)..	6 Fri.....	58	1	23	12	†0	51	†0	20	6 Mar. (65)..	3 Tues....	210	.630	120	557	230	4219
24 Mar. (83)..	1 Sun....	13	32	5	25	16	22	6	33	23 Feb. (54)..	0 Sat.....	218	.654	9995	404	199	4220
24 Mar. (83)..	2 Mon....	29	4	11	37	31	54	12	46	14 Mar. (73)..	6 Fri,....	288	.864	30	340	251	4221
23 Mar. (83)..	3 Tues....	44	35	17	50	47	25	18	58	2 Mar. (62)..	3 Tues....	176	.528	9906	187	220	4222
24 Mar. (83)..	5 Thur...	0	6	0	2	2	57	1	11	21 Mar. (80)..	2 Mon....	179	.537	9941	123	271	4223
24 Mar. (83)..	6 Fri.....	15	37	6	15	18	29	7	23	11 Mar. (70)..	0 Sat.....	301	.903	155	7	243	4224
24 Mar. (83)..	0 Sat.....	31	9	12	27	34	0	13	36	28 Feb. (59)..	4 Wed....	62	.186	31	854	212	4225
23 Mar. (83)..	1 Sun....	46	40	18	40	49	32	19	49	18 Mar. (78)..	3 Tues....	69	.207	65	790	264	4226
24 Mar. (83)..	3 Tues....	2	11	0	52	5	3	2	1	8 Mar. (67)..	1 Sun....	296	.888	280	674	235	4227
24 Mar. (83)..	4 Wed....	17	42	7	5	20	35	8	14	25 Feb. (56)..	5 Thur...	279	.837	155	521	205	4228
24 Mar. (83)..	5 Thur...	33	14	13	17	36	6	14	26	15 Mar. (74)..	3 Tues....	59	.177	9851	420	253	4229
23 Mar. (83)..	6 Fri.....	48	45	19	30	51	38	20	39	3 Mar. (63)..	0 Sat.....	7	.021	9727	268	222	4230
24 Mar. (83)..	1 Sun....	4	16	1	42	7	9	2	52	22 Mar. (81)..	6 Fri.....	36	.108	9762	204	274	4231
24 Mar. (83)..	2 Mon ...	19	47	7	55	22	41	9	4	12 Mar. (71)..	4 Wed....	189	.567	9976	87	246	4232
24 Mar. (83)..	3 Tues....	35	19	14	7	38	12	15	17	2 Mar. (61)..	2 Mon....	306	.918	190	971	218	4233
23 Mar. (83)..	4 Wed ...	50	50	20	20	53	44	21	30	20 Mar. (80)..	1 Sun....	288	.864	225	907	269	4234
24 Mar. (83)..	6 Fri.....	6	21	2	32	9	15	3	42	9 Mar. (68)..	5 Thur...	101	.303	101	754	238	4235

† Wherever these marks occur the day of the month and week-day in cols 13, 14 should, for Sûrya Siddhânta calculations, be advanced by 1. Thus in A.D. 1117-18 the Mesha saṅkrânti date by the Sûrya Siddhânta is March 24th. (0) Saturday.

TABLE I.

Lunation-parts = 10,000*ths of a circle. A tithi* = $^1/_{30}$*th of the moon's synodic revolution.*

I. CONCURRENT YEAR.								II. ADDED LUNAR MONTHS.				
						Samvatsara.		True.				
Kali.	Śaka.	Chaitrâdi. Vikrama.	Meshâdi (Solar) year in Bengal.	Kollam.	A. D.	Luni-Solar cycle. (Southern.)	Bṛihaspati cycle (Northern) current at Mesha saṅkrânti.	Name of month.	Time of the preceding saṅkrânti expressed in: Lunation parts. (*t.*)	Time of the preceding saṅkrânti expressed in: Tithis.	Time of the succeeding saṅkrânti expressed in: Lunation parts. (*t.*)	Time of the succeeding saṅkrânti expressed in: Tithis.
1	2	3	3a	4	5	6	7	8	9	10	11	12
4236	1057	1192	541	309–10	1134–35	48 Ânanda	51 Piṅgala	3 Jyeshṭha	9422	28.266	92	0.276
4237	1058	1193	542	310–11	1135–36	49 Râkshasa	52 Kâlayukta					
4238	1059	1194	543	311–12	*1136–37	50 Anala	53 Siddhârthin					
4239	1060	1195	544	312–13	1137–38	51 Piṅgala	54 Raudra	1 Chaitra	9987	29.961	212	0.636
4240	1061	1196	545	313–14	1138–39	52 Kâlayukta	55 Durmati					
4241	1062	1197	546	314–15	1139–40	53 Siddhârthin	56 Dundubhi	5 Śrâvaṇa	9547	28.641	182	0.546
4242	1063	1198	547	315–16	*1140–41	54 Raudra	57 Rudhirodgârin					
4243	1064	1199	548	316–17	1141–42	55 Durmati	58 Raktâksha					
4244	1065	1200	549	317–18	1142–43	56 Dundubhi	59 Krodhana	4 Âshâḍha	9623	28.869	490	1.470
4245	1066	1201	550	318–19	1143–44	57 Rudhirodgârin	60 Kshaya					
4246	1067	1202	551	319–20	*1144–45	58 Raktâksha	1 Prabhava					
4247	1068	1203	552	320–21	1145–46	59 Krodhana	2 Vibhava	2 Vaiśâkha	9733	29.199	136	0.408
4248	1069	1204	553	321–22	1146–47	60 Kshaya	3 Śukla					
4249	1070	1205	554	322–23	1147–48	1 Prabhava	4 Pramoda	6 Bhâdrapada	9653	28.959	65	0.195
4250	1071	1206	555	323–24	*1148–49	2 Vibhava	5 Prajâpati					
4251	1072	1207	556	324–25	1149–50	3 Śukla	6 Aṅgiras					
4252	1073	1208	557	325–26	1150–51	4 Pramoda	7 Śrîmukha	4 Âshâḍha	9160	27.480	35	0.105
4253	1074	1209	558	326–27	1151–52	5 Prajâpati	8 Bhâva					
4254	1075	1210	559	327–28	*1152–53	6 Aṅgiras	9 Yuvan					
4255	1076	1211	560	328–29	1153–54	7 Śrîmukha	10 Dhâtṛi	3 Jyeshṭha	9591	28.773	169	0.507
4256	1077	1212	561	329–30	1154–55	8 Bhâva	11 Îśvara					
4257	1078	1213	562	330–31	1155–56	9 Yuvan	12 Bahudhânya	12 Phâlguna	9851	29.553	0	0.001
4258	1079	1214	563	331–32	*1156–57	10 Dhâtṛi	13 Pramâthin					
4259	1080	1215	564	332–33	1157–58	11 Îśvara	14 Vikrama					
4260	1081	1216	565	333–34	1158–59	12 Bahudhânya	15 Vṛisha	5 Śrâvaṇa	9578	28.734	314	0.942
4261	1082	1217	566	334–35	1159–60	13 Pramâthin	16 Chitrabhânu					
4262	1083	1218	567	335–36	*1160–61	14 Vikrama	17 Subhânu					
4263	1084	1219	568	336–37	1161–62	15 Vṛisha	18 Târaṇa	4 Âshâḍha	9664	28.992	455	1.365
4264	1085	1220	569	337–38	1162–63	16 Chitrabhânu	19 Pârthiva					
4265	1086	1221	570	338–39	1163–64	17 Subhânu	20 Vyaya					
4266	1087	1222	571	339–40	*1164–65	18 Târaṇa	21 Sarvajit [1])	2 Vaiśâkha	9849	29.547	310	0.930
4267	1088	1223	572	340–41	1165–66	19 Pârthiva	23 Virodhin					
4268	1089	1224	573	341–42	1166–67	20 Vyaya	24 Vikṛita	6 Bhâdrapada	9813	29.439	261	0.783

1) Sarvadhârin, No. 22, was suppressed in the north.

TABLE I.

(*Col.* 23) *a* = *Distance of moon from sun.* (*Col.* 24) *b* = *moon's mean anomaly.* (*Col.* 25) *c* = *sun's mean anomaly.*

III. COMMENCEMENT OF THE

Solar year.										Luni-Solar year. (Civil day of Chaitra Śukla 1st.)							Kali.
Day and Month. A. D.	(Time of the Mesha saṅkrânti.)									Day and Month. A. D.	Week day.	At Sunrise on meridian of Ujjain.					
	Week day.	By the Ârya Siddhânta.				By the Sûrya Siddhânta.						Moon's Age.					
		Gh.	Pa.	H.	M.	Gh.	Pa.	H.	M.			Lunat. parts elapsed. (*t.*)	Tithis elapsed.	*a.*	*b.*	*c.*	
13	14	15		17		15a		17a		19	20	21	22	23	24	25	1
24 Mar. (83)..	0 Sat....	21	52	8	45	24	47	9	55	26 Feb. (57)..	2 Mon....	34	.102	9976	601	207	4236
24 Mar. (83)..	1 Sun....	37	24	14	57	40	18	16	7	17 Mar. (76)..	1 Sun....	119	.357	11	537	258	4237
23 Mar. (83)..	2 Mon....	52	55	21	10	55	50	22	20	5 Mar. (65)..	5 Thur...	121	.363	9887	384	228	4238
24 Mar. (83)..	4 Wed....	8	26	3	22	11	21	4	33	22 Feb. (53)..	2 Mon....	45	.135	9763	232	197	4239
24 Mar. (83)..	5 Thur...	23	57	9	35	26	53	10	45	13 Mar. (72)..	1 Sun....	59	.177	9797	168	248	4240
24 Mar. (83)..	6 Fri.....	39	29	15	47	42	24	16	58	3 Mar. (62)..	6 Fri.....	198	.594	12	51	220	4241
23 Mar. (83)..	0 Sat.....	55	0	22	0	57	56	23	10	21 Mar. (81)..	5 Thur...	174	.522	46	987	271	4242
24 Mar. (83)..	2 Mon....	10	31	4	12	13	27	5	23	11 Mar. (70)..	3 Tues....	299	.897	261	870	243	4243
24 Mar. (83)..	3 Tues....	26	2	10	25	28	59	11	36	28 Feb. (59)..	0 Sat.....	141	.423	136	718	212	4244
24 Mar. (83)..	4 Wed....	41	34	16	37	44	31	17	48	19 Mar. (78)..	6 Fri.....	196	.589	171	654	264	4245
23 Mar. (83)..	5 Thur...	57	5	22	50	†0	2	†0	1	7 Mar. (67)..	3 Tues....	186	.558	47	501	233	4246
24 Mar. (83)..	0 Sat.....	12	36	5	2	15	34	6	13	24 Feb. (55)..	0 Sat.....	179	.537	9922	348	202	4247
24 Mar. (83)..	1 Sun....	28	7	11	15	31	5	12	26	15 Mar. (74)..	6 Fri.....	234	.702	9957	284	253	4248
24 Mar. (83)..	2 Mon....	43	39	17	27	46	37	18	39	4 Mar. (63)..	3 Tues....	77	.231	9833	131	223	4249
23 Mar. (83)..	3 Tues....	59	10	23	40	†2	8	†0	51	22 Mar. (82)..	2 Mon....	65	.195	9867	67	274	4250
24 Mar. (83)..	5 Thur...	14	41	5	52	17	40	7	4	12 Mar. (71)..	0 Sat.....	179	.537	82	951	246	4251
24 Mar. (83)..	6 Fri.....	30	12	12	5	33	11	13	16	2 Mar. (61)..	5 Thur...	316	.948	296	834	218	4252
24 Mar. (83)..	0 Sat.....	45	44	18	17	48	43	19	29	21 Mar. (80)..	4 Wed....	332	.996	331	770	269	4253
24 Mar. (84)..	2 Mon....	1	15	0	30	4	14	1	42	9 Mar. (69)..	1 Sun....	251	.753	206	618	238	4254
24 Mar. (83)..	3 Tues....	16	46	6	42	19	46	7	54	26 Feb. (57)..	5 Thur...	255	.765	82	465	207	4255
24 Mar. (83)..	4 Wed....	32	17	12	55	35	17	14	7	16 Mar. (75)..	3 Tues....	23	.069	9778	364	256	4256
24 Mar. (83)..	5 Thur...	47	49	19	7	50	49	20	20	6 Mar. (65)..	1 Sun....	272	.816	9992	248	228	4257
24 Mar. (84)..	0 Sat.....	3	20	1	20	6	20	2	32	24 Mar. (84)..	0 Sat.....	296	.888	27	184	279	4258
24 Mar. (83)..	1 Sun....	18	51	7	32	21	52	8	45	13 Mar. (72)..	4 Wed....	70	.210	9903	31	248	4259
24 Mar. (83)..	2 Mon....	34	22	13	45	37	23	14	57	3 Mar. (62)..	2 Mon....	186	.558	117	915	220	4260
24 Mar. (83)..	3 Tues....	49	54	19	57	52	55	21	10	22 Mar. (81)..	1 Sun....	179	.537	152	851	272	4261
24 Mar. (84)..	5 Thur...	5	25	2	10	8	26	3	23	10 Mar. (70)..	5 Thur...	36	.108	28	698	241	4262
24 Mar. (83)..	6 Fri.....	20	56	8	22	23	58	9	35	27 Feb. (58)..	2 Mon....	6	.018	9903	545	210	4263
24 Mar. (83)..	0 Sat.....	36	27	14	35	39	29	15	48	18 Mar. (77)..	1 Sun....	95	.285	9938	481	261	4264
24 Mar. (83)..	1 Sun....	51	59	20	47	55	1	22	0	7 Mar. (66)..	5 Thur...	78	.234	9814	328	230	4265
24 Mar. (84)..	3 Tues....	7	30	3	0	10	33	4	13	25 Feb. (56)..	3 Tues....	307	.921	28	212	202	4266
24 Mar. (83)..	4 Wed....	23	1	9	12	26	4	10	26	15 Mar. (74)..	2 Mon....	315	.945	63	148	254	4267
24 Mar. (83)..	5 Thur...	38	32	15	25	41	36	16	38	4 Mar. (63)..	6 Fri.....	74	.222	9938	995	223	4268

† See footnote p. liii above.

TABLE I.

Lunation-parts = 10,000ths of a circle. A tithi = 1/30th of the moon's synodic revolution.

I. CONCURRENT YEAR.								II. ADDED LUNAR MONTHS.				
						Samvatsara.		True.				
									Time of the preceding saṅkrânti expressed in		Time of the succeeding saṅkrânti expressed in	
Kali.	Śaka.	Chaitrâdi. Vikrama.	Meshâdi (Solar) year in Bengal.	Kollam.	A. D.	Luni-Solar cycle. (Southern.)	Bṛihaspati cycle (Northern) current at Mesha saṅkrânti.	Name of month.	Lunation parts. (t.)	Tithis.	Lunation parts. (t.)	Tithis.
1	2	3	3a	4	5	6	7	8	9	10	11	12
4269	1090	1225	574	342-43	1167-68	21 Sarvajit	25 Khara					
4270	1091	1226	575	343-44	*1168-69	22 Sarvadhârin	26 Nandana					
4271	1092	1227	576	344-45	1169-70	23 Virodhin	27 Vijaya	5 Śrâvaṇa	9993	29.979	803	2.409
4272	1093	1228	577	345-46	1170-71	24 Vikṛita	28 Jaya					
4273	1094	1229	578	346-47	1171-72	25 Khara	29 Manmatha					
4274	1095	1230	579	347-48	*1172-73	26 Nandana	30 Durmukha	3 Jyeshṭha	9787	29.361	334	1.002
4275	1096	1231	580	348-49	1173-74	27 Vijaya	31 Hemalamba					
4276	1097	1232	581	349-50	1174-75	28 Jaya	32 Vilamba					
4277	1098	1233	582	350-51	1175-76	29 Manmatha	33 Vikârin	1 Chaitra	9959	29.877	324	0.972
4278	1099	1234	583	351-52	*1176-77	30 Durmukha	34 Sârvari					
4279	1100	1235	584	352-53	1177-78	31 Hemalamba	35 Plava	5 Śrâvaṇa	9538	28.614	342	1.026
4280	1101	1236	585	353-54	1178-79	32 Vilamba	36 Śubhakṛit					
4281	1102	1237	586	354-55	1179-80	33 Vikârin	37 Śobhana					
4282	1103	1238	587	355-56	*1180-81	34 Sârvari	38 Krodhin	4 Âshâḍha	9802	29.406	487	1.461
4283	1104	1239	588	356-57	1181-82	35 Plava	39 Viśvâvasu					
4284	1105	1240	589	357-58	1182-83	36 Śubhakṛit	40 Parâbhava					
4285	1106	1241	590	358-59	1183-84	37 Śobhana	41 Plavaṅga	2 Vaiśâkha	9866	29.598	414	1.242
4286	1107	1242	591	359-60	*1184-85	38 Krodhin	42 Kîlaka					
4287	1108	1243	592	360-61	1185-86	39 Viśvâvasu	43 Saumya	6 Bhâdrapada	9875	29.625	414	1.242
4288	1109	1244	593	361-62	1186-87	40 Parâbhava	44 Sâdhâraṇa					
4289	1110	1245	594	362-63	1187-88	41 Plavaṅga	45 Virodhakṛit					
4290	1111	1246	595	363-64	*1188-89	42 Kîlaka	46 Paridhâvin	5 Śrâvaṇa	9997	29.991	760	2.280
4291	1112	1247	596	364-65	1189-90	43 Saumya	47 Pramâdin					
4292	1113	1248	597	365-66	1190-91	44 Sâdhâraṇa	48 Ânanda					
4293	1114	1249	598	366-67	1191-92	45 Virodhakṛit	49 Râkshasa	3 Jyeshṭha	9924	29.772	530	1.590
4294	1115	1250	599	367-68	*1192-93	46 Paridhâvin	50 Anala					
4295	1116	1251	600	368-69	1193-94	47 Pramâdin	51 Piṅgala	7 Âśvina 10 *Pausha (Ksh.)*	9906 82	29.718 0.246	145 9941	0.435 29.823
4296	1117	1252	601	369-70	1194-95	48 Ananda	52 Kâlayukta	1 Chaitra	9951	29.853	282	0.846
4297	1118	1253	602	370-71	1195-96	49 Râkshasa	53 Siddhârthin					
4298	1119	1254	603	371-72	*1196-97	50 Anala	54 Raudra	5 Śrâvaṇa	9518	28.554	314	0.942
4299	1120	1255	604	372-73	1197-98	51 Piṅgala	55 Durmati					
4300	1121	1256	605	373-74	1198-99	52 Kâlayukta	56 Dundubhi					

TABLE I.

(Col. 23) a = Distance of moon from sun. (Col. 24) b = moon's mean anomaly. (Col. 25) c = sun's mean anomaly.

III. COMMENCEMENT OF THE

Solar year.										Luni-Solar year. (Civil day of Chaitra Śukla 1st.)							
Day and Month. A. D.	(Time of the Mesha saṅkrânti.)									Day and Month. A. D.	Week day.	At Sunrise on meridian of Ujjain.					Kali.
	Week day.	By the Ârya Siddhânta.				By the Sûrya Siddhânta.						Moon's Age.					
		Gh.	Pa.	H.	M.	Gh.	Pa.	H.	M.			Lunat. parts elapsed. (t.)	Tithis elapsed.	a.	b.	c.	
13	14	15		17		15a		17a		19	20	21	22	23	24	25	1
24 Mar. (83)..	6 Fri.....	54	4	21	37	57	7	22	51	23 Mar. (82)..	5 Thur...	54	.162	9973	931	274	4269
24 Mar. (84)..	1 Sun....	9	35	3	50	12	39	5	3	12 Mar. (72)..	3 Tues....	198	.594	187	814	246	4270
24 Mar. (83)..	2 Mon....	25	6	10	2	28	10	11	16	1 Mar. (60)..	0 Sat.....	85	.255	63	662	215	4271
24 Mar. (83)..	3 Tues....	40	37	16	15	43	42	17	29	20 Mar. (79)..	6 Fri.....	157	.471	98	598	267	4272
24 Mar. (83) .	4 Wed....	56	9	22	27	59	13	23	41	9 Mar. (68)..	3 Tues....	161	.483	9973	445	236	4273
24 Mar. (84)..	6 Fri.....	11	40	4	40	14	45	5	54	26 Feb. (57)..	0 Sat.....	127	.381	9849	292	205	4274
24 Mar. (83)..	0 Sat.....	27	11	10	52	30	16	12	6	16 Mar. (75)..	6 Fri.....	163	.489	9884	228	256	4275
24 Mar. (83)..	1 Sun....	42	42	17	5	45	48	18	19	6 Mar. (65)..	4 Wed....	329	.987	98	112	228	4276
24 Mar. (83)..	2 Mon....	58	14	23	17	†1	19	†0	32	23 Feb. (54)..	1 Sun....	81	.243	9974	959	197	4277
24 Mar. (84)..	4 Wed....	13	45	5	30	16	51	6	44	13 Mar. (73)..	0 Sat.....	61	.183	8	895	249	4278
24 Mar. (83)..	5 Thur...	29	16	11	42	32	22	12	57	3 Mar. (62)..	5 Thur...	227	.681	223	778	221	4279
24 Mar. (83)..	6 Fri.....	44	47	17	55	47	54	19	10	22 Mar. (81)..	4 Wed....	261	.783	257	714	272	4280
25 Mar. (84)..	1 Sun....	0	19	0	7	3	25	1	22	11 Mar. (70)..	1 Sun....	220	.660	133	561	241	4281
24 Mar. (84)..	2 Mon....	15	50	6	20	18	57	7	35	28 Feb. (59)..	5 Thur...	227	.681	9	409	210	4282
24 Mar. (83)..	3 Tues....	31	21	12	32	34	28	13	47	18 Mar. (77)..	4 Wed....	299	.897	43	345	262	4283
24 Mar. (83)..	4 Wed....	46	52	18	45	50	0	2	0	7 Mar. (66)..	1 Sun....	190	.570	9919	192	231	4284
25 Mar. (84)..	6 Fri.....	2	24	0	57	5	31	2	13	24 Feb. (55)..	5 Thur...	⊙−28	−.084	9795	39	200	4285
24 Mar. (84)..	0 Sat.....	17	55	7	10	21	3	8	25	15 Mar. (75)..	5 Thur...	318	.954	168	11	254	4286
24 Mar. (83)..	1 Sun....	33	26	13	22	36	35	14	38	4 Mar. (63)..	2 Mon....	76	.228	44	858	223	4287
24 Mar. (83)..	2 Mon....	48	57	19	35	52	6	20	50	23 Mar. (82)..	1 Sun....	84	.252	79	795	274	4288
25 Mar. (84)..	4 Wed....	4	29	1	47	7	38	3	3	13 Mar. (72)..	6 Fri.....	307	.921	293	678	246	4289
24 Mar. (84)..	5 Thur...	20	0	8	0	23	9	9	16	1 Mar. (61)..	3 Tues....	289	.867	169	525	215	4290
24 Mar. (83)..	6 Fri.....	35	31	14	12	38	41	15	28	19 Mar. (78)..	1 Sun....	69	.207	9865	425	264	4291
24 Mar. (83)..	0 Sat.....	51	2	20	25	54	12	21	41	8 Mar. (67)..	5 Thur...	19	.057	9740	272	233	4292
25 Mar. (84)..	2 Mon....	6	34	2	37	9	44	3	53	26 Feb. (57)..	3 Tues....	213	.639	9955	156	205	4293
24 Mar. (84)..	3 Tues....	22	5	8	50	25	15	10	6	16 Mar. (76)..	2 Mon....	206	.618	9989	92	256	4294
24 Mar. (83)..	4 Wed....	37	36	15	2	40	47	16	19	6 Mar. (65)..	0 Sat.....	322	.966	204	975	228	4295
24 Mar. (83)..	5 Thur...	53	7	21	15	56	18	22	31	23 Feb. (54)..	4 Wed....	96	.288	79	822	198	4296
25 Mar. (84)..	0 Sat.....	8	39	3	27	11	50	4	44	14 Mar. (73)..	3 Tues....	114	.342	114	758	249	4297
24 Mar. (84)..	1 Sun....	24	10	9	40	27	21	10	57	2 Mar. (62)..	0 Sat.....	44	.132	9990	606	218	4298
24 Mar. (83)..	2 Mon....	39	41	15	52	42	53	17	9	21 Mar. (80)..	6 Fri.....	128	.384	24	541	269	4299
24 Mar. (83)..	3 Tues....	55	12	22	5	58	24	23	22	10 Mar. (69)..	3 Tues....	131	.393	9900	389	239	4300

† See footnote p. liii above. ⊙ See Text. Art. 101 above, para. 2.

TABLE I.

Lunation-parts = 10,000*ths of a circle. A tithi* = 1/30*th of the moon's synodic revolution.*

I. CONCURRENT YEAR.								II. ADDED LUNAR MONTHS.				
						Samvatsara.		True.				
Kali.	Śaka.	Chaitrâdi. Vikrama.	Meshâdi (Solar) year in Bengal.	Kollam.	A. D.	Luni-Solar cycle. (Southern.)	Bṛihaspati cycle (Northern) current at Mesha saṅkrânti.	Name of month.	Time of the preceding saṅkrânti expressed in: Lunation parts. (*l.*)	Time of the preceding saṅkrânti expressed in: Tithis.	Time of the succeeding saṅkrânti expressed in: Lunation parts. (*l.*)	Time of the succeeding saṅkrânti expressed in: Tithis.
1	2	3	3a	4	5	6	7	8	9	10	11	12
4301	1122	1257	606	374- 75	1199-200	53 Siddhârthin...	57 Rudhirodgârin	4 Âshâḍha....	9999	29.997	623	1.869
4302	1123	1258	607	375- 76	*1200- 1	54 Raudra......	58 Raktâksha....	......	......	......	......	......
4303	1124	1259	608	376- 77	1201- 2	55 Durmati.....	59 Krodhana....	......	......	......	......	......
4304	1125	1260	609	377- 78	1202- 3	56 Dundubhi....	60 Kshaya......	2 Vaiśâkha....	9826	29.478	422	1.266
4305	1126	1261	610	378- 79	1203- 4	57 Rudhirodgârin	1 Prabhava.....	......	......	......	......	......
4306	1127	1262	611	379- 80	*1204- 5	58 Raktâksha....	2 Vibhava......	6 Bhâdrapada..	9854	29.562	466	1.398
4307	1128	1263	612	380- 81	1205- 6	59 Krodhana....	3 Śukla........	......	......	......	......	......
4308	1129	1264	613	381- 82	1206- 7	60 Kshaya......	4 Pramoda.....	......	......	......	......	......
4309	1130	1265	614	382- 83	1207- 8	1 Prabhava.....	5 Prajâpati.....	4 Âshâḍha....	9462	28.386	100	0.300
4310	1131	1266	615	383- 84	*1208- 9	2 Vibhava......	6 Aṅgiras......	......	......	......	......	......
4311	1132	1267	616	384- 85	1209- 10	3 Śukla........	7 Śrîmukha....	......	......	......	......	......
4312	1133	1268	617	385- 86	1210- 11	4 Pramoda.....	8 Bhâva.......	3 Jyeshṭha....	9960	29.880	667	2.001
4313	1134	1269	618	386- 87	1211- 12	5 Prajâpati.....	9 Yuvan.......	......	......	......	......	......
4314	1135	1270	619	387- 88	*1212- 13	6 Aṅgiras......	10 Dhâtṛi.....	7 Âśvina......	9991	29.973	304	0.912
4315	1136	1271	620	388- 89	1213- 14	7 Śrîmukha....	11 Îśvara.......	......	......	......	......	......
4316	1137	1272	621	389- 90	1214- 15	8 Bhâva.......	12 Bahudhânya..	......	......	......	......	......
4317	1138	1273	622	390- 91	1215- 16	9 Yuvan.......	13 Pramâthin...	5 Śrâvaṇa.....	9588	28.764	284	0.852
4318	1139	1274	623	391- 92	*1216- 17	10 Dhâtṛi.......	14 Vikrama.....	......	......	......	......	......
4319	1140	1275	624	392- 93	1217- 18	11 Îśvara.......	15 Vṛisha.......	......	......	......	......	......
4320	1141	1276	625	393- 94	1218- 19	12 Bahudhânya..	16 Chitrabhânu..	3 Jyeshṭha....	9500	28.500	162	0.486
4321	1142	1277	626	394- 95	1219- 20	13 Pramâthin....	17 Subhânu.....	......	......	......	......	......
4322	1143	1278	627	395- 96	*1220- 21	14 Vikrama.....	18 Târaṇa.......	......	......	......	......	......
4323	1144	1279	628	396- 97	1221- 22	15 Vṛisha.......	19 Pârthiva.....	2 Vaiśâkha....	9816	29.448	380	1.140
4324	1145	1280	629	397- 98	1222- 23	16 Chitrabhânu..	20 Vyaya.......	......	......	......	......	......
4325	1146	1281	630	398- 99	1223- 24	17 Subhânu.....	21 Sarvajit......	6 Bhâdrapada..	9814	29.442	435	1.305
4326	1147	1282	631	399-400	*1224- 25	18 Târaṇa.......	22 Sarvadhârin..	......	......	......	......	......
4327	1148	1283	632	400- 1	1225- 26	19 Pârthiva.....	23 Virodhin.....	......	......	......	......	......
4328	1149	1284	633	401- 2	1226- 27	20 Vyaya.......	24 Vikṛita......	4 Âshâḍha....	9648	28.944	281	0.843
4329	1150	1285	634	402- 3	1227- 28	21 Sarvajit......	25 Khara.......	......	......	......	......	......
4330	1151	1286	635	403- 4	*1228- 29	22 Sarvadhârin..	26 Nandana.....	......	......	......	......	......
4331	1152	1287	636	404- 5	1229- 30	23 Virodhin.....	27 Vijaya.......	3 Jyeshṭha....	9925	29.775	705	2.115
4332	1153	1288	637	405- 6	1230- 31	24 Vikṛita......	28 Jaya........	......	......	......	......	......
4333	1154	1289	638	406- 7	1231- 32	25 Khara.......	29 Manmatha....	7 Aśvina......	9984	29.952	364	1.092

TABLE I.

(*Col.* 23) *a* = *Distance of moon from sun.* (*Col.* 24) *b* = *moon's mean anomaly.* (*Col.* 25) *c* = *sun's mean anomaly.*

III. COMMENCEMENT OF THE

Solar year. Day and Month A. D.	Solar year. (Time of the Mesha saṅkrânti.) Week day.	By the Ârya Siddhânta. Gh.	By the Ârya Siddhânta. Pa.	By the Ârya Siddhânta. H.	By the Ârya Siddhânta. M.	By the Sûrya Siddhânta. Gh.	By the Sûrya Siddhânta. Pa.	By the Sûrya Siddhânta. H.	By the Sûrya Siddhânta. M.
13	14	15		17		15a		17a	
25 Mar. (84)..	5 Thur...	10	44	4	17	13	56	5	34
24 Mar. (84)..	6 Fri....	26	15	10	30	29	27	11	47
24 Mar. (83)..	0 Sat....	41	46	16	42	44	59	18	0
24 Mar. (83)..	1 Sun....	57	17	22	55	†0	30	†0	12
25 Mar. (84)..	3 Tues....	12	49	5	7	16	2	6	25
24 Mar. (84)..	4 Wed....	28	20	11	20	31	33	12	37
24 Mar. (83)..	5 Thur...	43	51	17	32	47	5	18	50
24 Mar. (83)..	6 Fri	59	22	23	45	†2	36	†1	3
25 Mar. (84)..	1 Sun....	14	54	5	57	18	8	7	15
24 Mar. (84)..	2 Mon....	30	25	12	10	33	40	13	28
24 Mar. (83)..	3 Tues....	45	56	18	22	49	10	19	40
25 Mar. (84)..	5 Thur...	1	27	0	35	4	43	1	53
25 Mar. (84)..	6 Fri.....	16	59	6	47	20	14	8	6
24 Mar. (84)..	0 Sat.....	32	30	13	0	35	46	14	18
24 Mar. (83)..	1 Sun....	48	1	19	12	51	17	20	31
25 Mar. (84)..	3 Tues...	3	32	1	25	6	49	2	43
25 Mar. (84)..	4 Wed....	19	4	7	37	22	20	8	56
24 Mar. (84)..	5 Thur...	34	35	13	50	37	52	15	9
24 Mar. (83)..	6 Fri.....	50	6	20	2	53	23	21	21
25 Mar. (84)..	1 Sun....	5	37	2	15	8	55	3	34
25 Mar. (84)..	2 Mon....	21	9	8	27	24	26	9	46
24 Mar. (84)..	3 Tues....	36	40	14	40	39	58	15	59
24 Mar. (83)..	4 Wed....	52	11	20	52	55	29	22	12
25 Mar. (84)..	6 Fri.....	7	42	3	5	11	1	4	24
25 Mar. (84)..	0 Sat.....	23	14	9	17	26	32	10	37
24 Mar. (84) ..	1 Sun....	38	45	15	30	42	4	16	50
24 Mar. (83)..	2 Mon....	54	16	21	42	57	35	23	2
25 Mar. (84)..	4 Wed....	9	47	3	55	13	7	5	15
25 Mar. (84)..	5 Thur...	25	19	10	7	28	38	11	27
24 Mar. (84)..	6 Fri.....	40	50	16	20	44	10	17	40
24 Mar. (83)..	0 Sat.....	56	21	22	32	59	42	23	53
25 Mar. (84)..	2 Mon....	11	52	4	45	15	13	6	5
25 Mar. (84)..	3 Tues....	27	24	10	57	30	45	12	18

Luni-Solar year. (Civil day of Chaitra Śukla 1st.) Day and Month A. D.	Week day.	At Sunrise on meridian of Ujjain. Moon's Age. Lunat. parts elapsed. (*t*.)	Moon's Age. Tithis elapsed.	*a*.	*b*.	*c*.	Kali.
19	20	21	22	23	24	25	1
27 Feb. (58)..	0 Sat.....	58	.174	9776	236	208	4301
17 Mar. (77)..	6 Fri.....	74	222	9810	172	259	4302
7 Mar. (66)..	4 Wed....	213	.639	25	55	231	4303
25 Feb. (56)..	2 Mon....	329	.987	239	939	203	4304
16 Mar. (75)..	1 Sun....	315	.945	274	875	254	4305
4 Mar. (64)..	5 Thur...	153	.459	149	722	223	4306
23 Mar. (82)..	4 Wed....	205	.615	184	658	275	4307
12 Mar. (71)..	1 Sun....	196	.588	60	505	244	4308
1 Mar. (60)..	5 Thur...	189	.567	9935	352	213	4309
19 Mar. (79)..	4 Wed....	246	.738	9970	288	264	4310
8 Mar. (67)..	1 Sun....	92	276	9846	136	233	4311
26 Feb. (57)..	6 Fri.....	220	.660	60	19	205	4312
17 Mar. (76)..	5 Thur...	195	.585	95	955	257	4313
6 Mar. (66)..	3 Tues....	330	.990	309	839	228	4314
24 Mar. (83)..	1 Sun....	6	.018	5	738	277	4315
14 Mar. (73)..	6 Fri.....	263	.789	220	622	249	4316
3 Mar. (62)..	3 Tues....	260	.780	95	469	218	4317
20 Mar. (80)..	1 Sun....	34	.102	9791	369	267	4318
10 Mar. (69)..	6 Fri.....	286	.858	6	252	239	4319
27 Feb. (58)..	3 Tues....	106	.318	9881	99	208	4320
18 Mar. (77)..	2 Mon....	86	.258	9916	35	259	4321
7 Mar. (67)..	0 Sat.....	201	.603	130	919	231	4322
24 Feb. (55)..	4 Wed....	10	.030	6	766	200	4323
15 Mar: (74)..	3 Tues....	47	.141	41	702	252	4324
4 Mar. (63)..	0 Sat.....	14	.042	9916	549	221	4325
22 Mar. (82)..	6 Fri.....	104	.312	9951	485	272	4326
11 Mar. (70)..	3 Tues....	89	.267	9827	332	241	4327
1 Mar. (60)..	1 Sun....	320	.960	41	216	213	4328
20 Mar. (79)..	0 Sat.....	330	.990	76	152	264	4329
8 Mar. (68)..	4 Wed....	91	.273	9951	999	234	4330
26 Feb. (57)..	2 Mon....	214	.642	166	883	205	4331
17 Mar. (76)..	1 Sun....	213	.639	200	819	257	4332
6 Mar. (65)..	5 Thur...	95	.285	76	666	226	4333

† See footnote p. liii above.

TABLE I.

Lunation-parts = 10,000ths of a circle. A tithi = 1/30th of the moon's synodic revolution.

I. CONCURRENT YEAR.								II. ADDED LUNAR MONTHS.				
						Samvatsara.		True.				
Kali.	Śaka.	Chaitrâdi. Vikrama.	Meshâdi (Solar) year in Bengal.	Kollam.	A. D.	Luni-Solar cycle. (Southern.)	Bṛihaspati cycle (Northern) current at Mesha saṅkrânti.	Name of month.	Time of the preceding saṅkrânti expressed in: Lunation parts. (*t.*)	Time of the preceding saṅkrânti expressed in: Tithis.	Time of the succeeding saṅkrânti expressed in: Lunation parts. (*t.*)	Time of the succeeding saṅkrânti expressed in: Tithis.
1	2	3	3a	4	5	6	7	8	9	10	11	12
4334	1155	1290	639	407- 8	*1232-33	26 Nandana	30 Durmukha					
4335	1156	1291	640	408- 9	1233-34	27 Vijaya	31 Hemalamba					
4336	1157	1292	641	409-10	1234-35	28 Jaya	32 Vilamba	5 Śrâvaṇa	9746	29.238	349	1.047
4337	1158	1293	642	410-11	1235-36	29 Manmatha	33 Vikârin					
4338	1159	1294	643	411-12	*1236-37	30 Durmukha	34 Śârvari					
4339	1160	1295	644	412-13	1237-38	31 Hemalamba	35 Plava	3 Jyeshṭha	9473	28.419	237	0.711
4340	1161	1296	645	413-14	1238-39	32 Vilamba	36 Śubhakṛit					
4341	1162	1297	646	414-15	1239-40	33 Vikârin	37 Śobhana					
4342	1163	1298	647	415-16	*1240-41	34 Śârvari	38 Krodhin	2 Vaiśâkha	9892	29.676	377	1.131
4343	1164	1299	648	416-17	1241-42	35 Plava	39 Viśvâvasu					
4344	1165	1300	649	417-18	1242-43	36 Śubhakṛit	40 Parâbhava	6 Bhâdrapada	9848	29.544	406	1.218
4345	1166	1301	650	418-19	1243-44	37 Śobhana	41 Plavaṅga					
4346	1167	1302	651	419-20	*1244-45	38 Krodhin	42 Kîlaka					
4347	1168	1303	652	420-21	1245-46	39 Viśvâvasu	43 Saumya	4 Âshâḍha	9755	29.265	471	1.413
4348	1169	1304	653	421-22	1246-47	40 Parâbhava	44 Sâdhâraṇa					
4349	1170	1305	654	422-23	1247-48	41 Plavaṅga	45 Virodhakṛit					
4350	1171	1306	655	423-24	*1248-49	42 Kîlaka	46 Paridhâvin	3 Jyeshṭha	9900	29.700	670	2.010
4351	1172	1307	656	424-25	1249-50	43 Saumya	47 Pramâdin					
4352	1173	1308	657	425-26	1250-51	44 Sâdhâraṇa	48 Ananda [1]	7 Aśvina	9943	29.829	342	1.026
4353	1174	1309	658	426-27	1251-52	45 Virodhakṛit	50 Anala					
4354	1175	1310	659	427-28	*1252-53	46 Paridhâvin	51 Piṅgala					
4355	1176	1311	660	428-29	1253-54	47 Pramâdin	52 Kâlayukta	5 Śrâvaṇa	9945	29.835	510	1.530
4356	1177	1312	661	429-30	1254-55	48 Ânanda	53 Siddhârthin					
4357	1178	1313	662	430-31	1255-56	49 Râkshasa	54 Raudra					
4358	1179	1314	663	431-32	*1256-57	50 Anala	55 Durmati	3 Jyeshṭha	9434	28.302	218	0.654
4359	1180	1315	664	432-33	1257-58	51 Piṅgala	56 Dundubhi					
4360	1181	1316	665	433-34	1258-59	52 Kâlayukta	57 Rudhirodgâr.	{ 8 Kârttika 10 *Pausha (Ksh.)*	9886 35	29.658 0.105	51 9930	0.153 } 29.790 }
4361	1182	1317	666	434-35	1259-60	53 Siddhârthin	58 Raktâksha	1 Chaitra	9876	29.628	65	0.195
4362	1183	1318	667	435-36	*1260-61	54 Raudra	59 Krodhana					
4363	1184	1319	668	436-37	1261-62	55 Durmati	60 Kshaya	6 Bhâdrapada	9981	29.943	447	1.341
4364	1185	1320	669	437-38	1262-63	56 Dundubhi	1 Prabhava					
4365	1186	1321	670	438-39	1263-64	57 Rudhirodgârin	2 Vibhava					

1) Râkshasa, No. 49, was suppressed in the north.

TABLE I.

(Col. 23) a = Distance of moon from sun. (Col. 24) b = moon's mean anomaly. (Col. 25) c = sun's mean anomaly.

III. COMMENCEMENT OF THE																	
Solar year.										Luni-Solar year. (Civil day of Chaitra Śukla 1st.)							Kali.
Day and Month A. D.	(Time of the Mesha saṅkrânti.)									Day and Month A. D.	Week day.	At Sunrise on meridian of Ujjain.					
	Week day.	By the Ârya Siddhânta.				By the Sûrya Siddhânta.						Moon's Age.		*a.*	*b.*	*c.*	
		Gh.	Pa.	H.	M.	Gh.	Pa.	H.	M.			Lunat. parts elapsed. (*t.*)	Tithis elapsed.				
13	**14**	**15**		**17**		**15a**		**17a**		**19**	**20**	**21**	**22**	**23**	**24**	**25**	**1**
24 Mar. (84)..	4 Wed....	42	55	17	10	46	16	18	30	24 Mar. (84)..	4 Wed....	168	.504	111	602	277	4334
24 Mar. (83)..	5 Thur...	58	26	23	22	†1	48	†0	43	13 Mar. (72)..	1 Sun....	172	.516	9987	449	246	4335
25 Mar. (84)..	0 Sat.....	13	57	5	35	17	19	6	56	2 Mar. (61)..	5 Thur...	137	.411	9862	296	216	4336
25 Mar. (84)..	1 Sun....	29	29	11	47	32	51	13	8	21 Mar. (80)..	4 Wed....	176	.528	9897	232	267	4337
24 Mar. (84)..	2 Mon....	45	0	18	0	48	22	19	21	9 Mar. (69)..	1 Sun....	⊙−19	−.057	9773	80	236	4338
25 Mar. (84)..	4 Wed....	0	31	0	12	3	54	1	33	27 Feb. (58)..	6 Fri.....	97	.291	9987	963	208	4339
25 Mar. (84)..	5 Thur...	16	2	6	25	19	25	7	46	18 Mar. (77)..	5 Thur...	78	.234	22	899	259	4340
25 Mar. (84)..	6 Fri.....	31	34	12	37	34	57	13	59	8 Mar. (67)..	3 Tues....	239	.717	236	782	231	4341
24 Mar. (84)..	0 Sat.....	47	5	18	50	50	28	20	11	25 Feb. (56)..	0 Sat.....	153	.459	112	630	200	4342
25 Mar. (84)..	2 Mon....	2	36	1	2	6	0	2	24	15 Mar. (74)..	6 Fri.....	229	.687	146	566	252	4343
25 Mar. (84)..	3 Tues....	18	7	7	15	21	31	8	37	4 Mar. (63)..	3 Tues....	236	.708	22	413	221	4344
25 Mar. (84)..	4 Wed....	33	39	13	27	37	3	14	49	23 Mar. (82)..	2 Mon....	311	.933	57	349	272	4345
24 Mar. (84)..	5 Thur...	49	10	19	40	52	34	21	2	11 Mar. (71)..	6 Fri.....	204	.612	9932	196	241	4346
25 Mar. (84)..	0 Sat.....	4	41	1	52	8	6	3	14	28 Feb. (59)..	3 Tues....	⊙−12	−.036	9808	43	211	4347
25 Mar. (84)..	1 Sun....	20	12	8	5	23	37	9	27	19 Mar. (78)..	2 Mon....	⊙−36	−.108	9843	979	262	4348
25 Mar. (84)..	2 Mon....	35	44	14	17	39	9	15	40	9 Mar. (68)..	0 Sat.....	91	.273	57	863	234	4349
24 Mar. (84)..	3 Tues....	51	15	20	30	54	40	21	52	27 Feb. (58)..	5 Thur...	273	.819	271	746	206	4350
25 Mar. (84)..	5 Thur...	6	46	2	42	10	12	4	5	17 Mar. (76)..	4 Wed....	318	.954	306	682	257	4351
25 Mar. (84)..	6 Fri.....	22	17	8	55	25	44	10	17	6 Mar. (65)..	1 Sun....	296	.888	182	530	226	4352
25 Mar. (84)..	0 Sat.....	37	49	15	7	41	15	16	30	24 Mar. (83)..	6 Fri.....	79	.237	9878	429	275	4353
24 Mar. (84)..	1 Sun....	53	20	21	20	56	47	22	43	12 Mar. (72)..	3 Tues....	32	.096	9754	276	244	4354
25 Mar. (84)..	3 Tues....	8	51	3	32	12	18	4	55	2 Mar. (61)..	1 Sun....	227	.681	9968	160	216	4355
25 Mar. (84)..	4 Wed....	24	22	9	45	27	50	11	8	21 Mar. (80)..	0 Sat.....	233	.699	3	96	267	4356
25 Mar. (84)..	5 Thur...	39	54	15	57	43	21	17	20	10 Mar. (69)..	4 Wed....	⊙−32	−.096	9878	943	236	4357
24 Mar. (84)..	6 Fri.....	55	25	22	10	58	53	23	33	28 Feb. (59)..	2 Mon....	111	.333	93	827	208	4358
25 Mar. (84)..	1 Sun....	10	56	4	22	14	24	5	46	18 Mar. (77)..	1 Sun....	127	.381	127	763	260	4359
}25 Mar. (84)..	2 Mon....	26	27	10	35	29	56	11	58	7 Mar. (66)..	5 Thur...	53	.159	3	610	229	4360
25 Mar. (84)..	3 Tues....	41	59	16	47	45	27	18	11	24 Feb. (55)..	2 Mon....	50	.150	9879	457	198	4361
24 Mar. (84)..	4 Wed....	57	30	23	0	†0	59	†0	24	14 Mar. (74)..	1 Sun....	141	.423	9913	393	249	4362
25 Mar. (84)..	6 Fri.....	13	1	5	12	16	30	6	36	3 Mar. (62)..	5 Thur...	70	.210	9789	240	218	4363
25 Mar. (84)..	0 Sat.....	28	32	11	25	32	2	12	49	22 Mar. (81)..	4 Wed....	89	.267	9824	176	270	4364
25 Mar. (84)..	1 Sun....	44	4	17	37	47	33	19	1	12 Mar. (71)..	2 Mon....	230	.690	38	60	242	4365

† See footnote p. liii above. ⊙ See Text Art. 101, para. 2.

TABLE I.

Lunation-parts = 10,000ths of a circle. A tithi = 1/30th of the moon's synodic revolution.

I. CONCURRENT YEAR.								II. ADDED LUNAR MONTHS.				
						Samvatsara.		True.				
Kali.	Śaka.	Chaitrâdi. Vikrama.	Meshâdi (Solar) year in Bengal.	Kollam.	A. D.	Luni-Solar cycle. (Southern.)	Bṛihaspati cycle (Northern) current at Mesha saṅkrânti.	Name of month.	Time of the preceding saṅkrânti expressed in: Lunation parts. (t.)	Time of the preceding saṅkrânti expressed in: Tithis.	Time of the succeeding saṅkrânti expressed in: Lunation parts. (t.)	Time of the succeeding saṅkrânti expressed in: Tithis.
1	2	3	3a	4	5	6	7	8	9	10	11	12
4366	1187	1322	671	439-40	*1264-65	58 Raktâksha....	3 Śukla........	4 Ashâḍha	9759	29.277	582	1.746
4367	1188	1323	672	440-41	1265-66	59 Krodhana	4 Pramoda.....	....	.....	.....	.....	.....
4368	1189	1324	673	441-42	1266-67	60 Kshaya	5 Prajâpati.....	....	.....	.....	.....	.....
4369	1190	1325	674	442-43	1267-68	1 Prabhava.....	6 Aṅgiras	3 Jyeshṭha. ..	9958	29.874	643	1.929
4370	1191	1326	675	443-44	*1268-69	2 Vibhava......	7 Śrîmukha	....	.....	.....	.....	.....
4371	1192	1327	676	444-45	1269-70	3 Śukla........	8 Bhâva.......	7 Âśvina......	9954	29.862	306	0.918
4372	1193	1328	677	445-46	1270-71	4 Pramoda.....	9 Yuvan.......	....	.....	.....	.....	.....
4373	1194	1329	678	446-47	1271-72	5 Prajâpati.....	10 Dhâtṛi.......	....	.....	.....	.....	.....
4374	1195	1330	679	447-48	*1272-73	6 Aṅgiras......	11 Îśvara.......	4 Âshâḍha	9301	27.903	88	0.264
4375	1196	1331	680	448-49	1273-74	7 Śrîmukha	12 Bahudhânya..	....	.....	.....	.....	.....
4376	1197	1332	681	449-50	1274-75	8 Bhâva.......	13 Pramâthin....	....	.....	.....	.....	.....
4377	1198	1333	682	450-51	1275-76	9 Yuvan.......	14 Vikrama.....	3 Jyeshṭha....	9460	28.380	167	0.501
4378	1199	1334	683	451-52	*1276-77	10 Dhâtṛi.......	15 Vṛisha.......	....	.....	.....	.....	.....
4379	1200	1335	684	452-53	1277-78	11 Îśvara.......	16 Chitrabhânu.	8 Kârttika	9846	29.538	25	0.075
								10 *Pausha (Ksh.)*	45	0.135	9982	29.946
								12 Phâlguna....	9955	29.865	32	0.096
4380	1201	1336	685	453-54	1278-79	12 Bahudhânya..	17 Subhânu.....	....	.....	.....	.....	.....
4381	1202	1337	686	454-55	1279-80	13 Pramâthin....	18 Târaṇa.......	....	.....	.....	.....	.....
4382	1203	1338	687	455-56	*1280-81	14 Vikrama.....	19 Pârthiva.....	5 Śrâvaṇa.....	9580	28.740	174	0.522
4383	1204	1339	688	456-57	1281-82	15 Vṛisha... ...	20 Vyaya.......	....	.....	.....	.....	.....
4384	1205	1340	689	457-58	1282-83	16 Chitrabhânu..	21 Sarvajit......	....	.....	.....	.....	.....
4385	1206	1341	690	458-59	1283-84	17 Subhânu.....	22 Sarvadhârin ..	4 Âshâḍha	9721	29.163	595	1.785
4386	1207	1342	691	459-60	*1284-85	18 Târaṇa.......	23 Virodhin.....	....	.....	.....	.....	.....
4387	1208	1343	692	460-61	1285-86	19 Pârthiva.....	24 Vikṛita......	....	.....	.....	.....	.....
4388	1209	1344	693	461-62	1286-87	20 Vyaya.......	25 Khara.......	2 Vaiśâkha....	9730	29.190	113	0.339
4389	1210	1345	694	462-63	1287-88	21 Sarvajit......	26 Nandana.....	....	.....	.....	.....	.....
4390	1211	1346	695	463-64	*1288-89	22 Sarvadhârin ..	27 Vijaya.......	6 Bhâdrapada..	9640	28.920	63	0.189
4391	1212	1347	696	464-65	1289-90	23 Virodhin.....	28 Jaya.........	....	.....	.....	.....	.....
4392	1213	1348	697	465-66	1290-91	24 Vikṛita......	29 Manmatha....	....	.....	.....	.....	.....
4393	1214	1349	698	466-67	1291-92	25 Khara.......	30 Durmukha ...	4 Âshâḍha....	9266	27.798	133	0.399
4394	1215	1350	699	467-68	*1292-93	26 Nandana.....	31 Hemalamba..	....	.....	.....	.....	.....
4395	1216	1351	700	468-69	1293-94	27 Vijaya.......	32 Vilamba......	....	.....	.....	.....	.....
4396	1217	1352	701	469-70	1294-95	28 Jaya.........	33 Vikârin.....	3 Jyeshṭha....	9584	28.752	202	0.606

TABLE I.

(*Col.* 23) *a* = *Distance of moon from sun.* (*Col.* 24) *b* = *moon's mean anomaly.* (*Col.* 25) *c* = *sun's mean anomaly.*

III. COMMENCEMENT OF THE																	
Solar year.										Luni-Solar year. (Civil day of Chaitra Śukla 1st.)							Kali.
Day and Month A. D.	(Time of the Mesha saṅkrânti.)									Day and Month A. D.	Week day.	At Sunrise on meridian of Ujjain.					
	Week day.	By the Ârya Siddhânta.				By the Sûrya Siddhânta.						Moon's Age.		*a.*	*b.*	*c.*	
		Gh.	Pa.	H.	M.	Gh.	Pa.	H.	M.			Lunat. parts elapsed. (*t.*)	Tithis elapsed.				
13	**14**	**15**		**17**		**15a**		**17a**		**19**	**20**	**21**	**22**	**23**	**24**	**25**	**1**
24 Mar. (84)..	2 Mon....	59	35	23	50	†3	5	†1	14	29 Feb. (60)..	6 Fri.....	⊙–21	–.063	9914	907	211	4366
25 Mar. (84)..	4 Wed ...	15	6	6	2	18	36	7	27	20 Mar. (79)..	6 Fri.....	330	.990	287	879	265	4367
25 Mar. (84)..	5 Thur...	30	37	12	15	34	8	13	39	9 Mar. (68)..	3 Tues...	165	.495	163	726	234	4368
25 Mar. (84)..	6 Fri.....	46	9	18	27	49	39	19	52	26 Feb. (57)..	0 Sat.. ..	118	.354	38	574	203	4369
25 Mar. (85)..	1 Sun....	1	40	0	40	5	11	2	4	16 Mar. (76)..	6 Fri.....	204	.612	73	510	255	4370
25 Mar. (84)..	2 Mon....	17	11	6	52	20	42	8	17	5 Mar. (64)..	3 Tues....	200	.600	9949	357	224	4371
25 Mar. (84)..	3 Tues....	32	42	13	5	36	14	14	30	24 Mar. (83)..	2 Mon....	259	.777	9983	293	275	4372
25 Mar. (84)..	4 Wed....	48	14	19	17	51	46	20	42	13 Mar. (72)..	6 Fri.....	107	.321	9859	140	244	4373
25 Mar. (85)..	6 Fri.....	3	45	1	30	7	17	2	55	2 Mar. (62)..	4 Wed....	235	.705	73	23	216	4374
25 Mar. (84)..	0 Sat.....	19	16	7	42	22	49	9	7	21 Mar. (80)..	3 Tues....	212	.636	108	959	267	4375
25 Mar. (84)..	1 Sun.. .	34	47	13	55	38	20	15	20	10 Mar. (69)..	0 Sat.....	⊙ –7	–.021	9984	807	237	4376
25 Mar. (84)..	2 Mon....	50	19	20	7	53	52	21	33	28 Feb. (59)..	5 Thur...	210	.630	198	690	208	4377
25 Mar. (85)..	4 Wed....	5	50	2	20	9	23	3	45	18 Mar. (78)..	4 Wed....	273	.819	233	626	260	4378
}25 Mar. (84)..	5 Thur...	21	21	8	32	24	55	9	58	7 Mar. (66)..	1 Sun....	212	.636	109	473	229	4379
25 Mar. (84)..	6 Fri.....	36	52	14	45	40	26	16	10	25 Mar. (84)..	6 Fri.....	45	.135	9804	373	278	4380
25 Mar. (84)..	0 Sat.....	52	24	20	57	55	58	22	23	15 Mar. (74) .	4 Wed....	299	.897	19	257	249	4381
25 Mar. (85)..	2 Mon....	7	55	3	10	11	29	4	36	3 Mar. (63)..	1 Sun...	121	.363	9894	104	219	4382
25 Mar. (84)..	3 Tues....	23	26	9	22	27	1	10	48	22 Mar. (81)..	0 Sat.....	104	.312	9929	40	270	4383
25 Mar. (84)..	4 Wed....	38	57	15	35	42	32	17	1	12 Mar. (71)..	5 Thur...	217	.651	143	923	242	4384
25 Mar (84)..	5 Thur...	54	29	21	47	58	4	23	14	1 Mar. (60)..	2 Mon....	22	.066	19	770	211	4385
25 Mar. (85)..	0 Sat.....	10	0	4	0	13	35	5	26	19 Mar. (79)..	1 Sun....	59	.177	54	706	263	4386
25 Mar. (84)..	1 Sun....	25	31	10	12	29	7	11	39	8 Mar. (67)..	5 Thur...	22	.066	9930	554	232	4387
25 Mar. (84)..	2 Mon....	41	2	16	25	44	38	17	51	25 Feb. (56)..	2 Mon....	31	.093	9805	401	201	4388
25 Mar. (84)..	3 Tues....	56	34	22	37	†0	10	†0	4	16 Mar. (75)..	1 Sun....	100	.300	9840	337	252	4389
25 Mar. (85)..	5 Thur...	12	5	4	50	15	41	6	17	5 Mar. (65)..	6 Fri.....	332	.996	54	220	224	4390
25 Mar. (84)..	6 Fri.....	27	36	11	2	31	13	12	29	23 Mar. (82)..	4 Wed....	⊙–14	–.042	9750	120	273	4391
25 Mar. (84)..	0 Sat.....	43	7	17	15	46	44	18	42	13 Mar. (72)..	2 Mon....	109	.327	9965	4	244	4392
25 Mar. (84)..	1 Sun....	58	39	23	27	†2	16	†0	54	3 Mar. (62)..	0 Sat.....	228	.684	179	887	216	4393
25 Mar. (85)..	3 Tues....	14	10	5	40	17	48	7	7	21 Mar. (81)..	6 Fri.....	228	.684	214	823	268	4394
25 Mar. (84)..	4 Wed....	29	41	11	52	33	19	13	20	10 Mar. (69)..	3 Tues....	106	.318	89	670	237	4395
25 Mar. (84)..	5 Thur...	45	12	18	5	48	51	19	32	27 Feb. (58)..	0 Sat.....	91	.273	9965	517	206	4396

† See footnote p. liii above. ⊙ See Text. Art. 101, para. 2.

TABLE I.

Lunation-parts = 10,000*ths of a circle. A tithi* = $^{1}/_{30}$*th of the moon's synodic revolution.*

I. CONCURRENT YEAR.								II. ADDED LUNAR MONTHS.				
						Samvatsara.		True.				
Kali.	Śaka.	Chaitrâdi. Vikrama.	Meshâdi (Solar) year in Bengal.	Kollam.	A. D.	Luni-Solar cycle. (Southern.)	Bṛihaspati cycle (Northern) current at Mesha saṅkrânti.	Name of month.	Time of the preceding saṅkrânti expressed in: Lunation parts. (*t.*)	Tithis.	Time of the succeeding saṅkrânti expressed in: Lunation parts. (*t.*)	Tithis.
1	2	3	3a	4	5	6	7	8	9	10	11	12
4397	1218	1353	702	470-71	1295- 96	29 Manmatha....	34 Śârvari......	....	......	....	......	......
4398	1219	1354	703	471-72	*1296- 97	30 Durmukha....	35 Plava.......	9 Mârgaśîrsha . 10 *Pausha (Ksh.)* 12 Phâlguna...	9991 1 9964	29.973 0.003 29.892	1 9954 91	0.003 29.862 0.273
4399	1220	1355	704	472-73	1297- 98	31 Hemalamba...	36 Śubhakṛit....	....	......	....	......	......
4400	1221	1356	705	473-74	1298- 99	32 Vilamba......	37 Śobhanu.....	....	......	....	......	......
4401	1222	1357	706	474-75	1299-300	33 Vikârin......	38 Krodhin......	5 Śrâvaṇa.....	9661	28.983	344	1.032
4402	1223	1358	707	475-76	*1300- 1	34 Śârvari......	39 Viśvâvasu....	....	......	....	......	......
4403	1224	1359	708	476-77	1301- 2	35 Plava........	40 Parâbhava....	....	......	....	......	......
4404	1225	1360	709	477-78	1302- 3	36 Śubhakṛit....	41 Plavaṅga.....	4 Âshâḍha	9715	29.145	554	1.662
4405	1226	1361	710	478-79	1303- 4	37 Śobhana......	42 Kîlaka.......	....	......	....	......	......
4406	1227	1362	711	479-80	*1304- 5	38 Krodhin.....	43 Saumya......	....	......	....	......	......
4407	1228	1363	712	480-81	1305- 6	39 Viśvâvasu....	44 Sâdhâraṇa....	2 Vaiśâkha....	9889	29.667	310	0.930
4408	1229	1364	713	481-82	1306- 7	40 Parâbhava...	45 Virodhakṛit...	....	......	....	......	......
4409	1230	1365	714	482-83	1307- 8	41 Plavaṅga.....	46 Paridhâvin...	6 Bhâdrapada..	9827	29 481	250	0.750
4410	1231	1366	715	483-84	*1308- 9	42 Kîlaka.......	47 Pramâdin....	....	......	....	......	......
4411	1232	1367	716	484-85	1309- 10	43 Saumya......	48 Ânanda......	....	......	....	......	......
4412	1233	1368	717	485-86	1310- 11	44 Sâdhâraṇa ...	49 Râkshasa.....	4 Âshâḍha	9239	27.717	101	0.303
4413	1234	1369	718	486-87	1311- 12	45 Virodhakṛit..	50 Anala........	....	......	....	......	......
4414	1235	1370	719	487-88	*1312- 13	46 Paridhâvin...	51 Piṅgala......	....	......	....	......	......
4415	1236	1371	720	488-89	1313- 14	47 Pramâdin....	52 Kâlayukta....	3 Jyeshṭha....	9776	29.328	328	0.984
4416	1237	1372	721	489-90	1314- 15	48 Ânanda......	53 Siddhârthin...	....	......	....	......	......
4417	1238	1373	722	490-91	1315- 16	49 Râkshasa.....	54 Raudra.....	8 Kârttika.... 9 *Mârgaś.(Ksh.)* 12 Phâlguna....	9950 31 9917	29.850 0.093 29.751	31 9996 67	0.093 29.988 0.201
4418	1239	1374	723	491-92	*1316- 17	50 Anala......	55 Durmati.....	....	......	....	......	......
4419	1240	1375	724	492-93	1317- 18	51 Piṅgala......	56 Dundubhi....	....	......	....	......	......
4420	1241	1376	725	493-94	1318- 19	52 Kâlayukta....	57 Rudhirodgârin	5 Śrâvaṇa.....	9648	28.944	425	1.275
4421	1242	1377	726	494-95	1319- 20	53 Siddhârthin..	58 Raktâksha....	....	......	....	......	......
4422	1243	1378	727	495-96	*1320- 21	54 Raudra......	59 Krodhana....	....	......	....	......	......
4423	1244	1379	728	496-97	1321- 22	55 Durmati.....	60 Kshaya......	4 Âshâḍha	9800	29.400	547	1.641
4424	1245	1380	729	497-98	1322- 23	56 Dundubhi....	1 Prabhava.....	....	......	....	......	......
4425	1246	1381	730	498-99	1323- 24	57 Rudhirodgârin	2 Vibhava......	....	......	....	......	......

TABLE I.

(*Col.* 23) *a* = *Distance of moon from sun.* (*Col.* 24) *b* = *moon's mean anomaly.* (*Col.* 25) *c* = *sun's mean anomaly.*

III. COMMENCEMENT OF THE

Solar year.										Luni-Solar year. (Civil day of Chaitra Śukla 1st.)								
Day and Month A. D.	(Time of the Mesha saṅkrânti.)									Day and Month A. D.	Week day.	At Sunrise on meridian of Ujjain.						Kali.
	Week day.	By the Ârya Siddhânta.				By the Sûrya Siddhânta.						Moon's Age.						
		Gh.	Pa.	H.	M.	Gh.	Pa.	H.	M.			Lunat. parts elapsed. (*t*.)	Tithis elapsed.	*a*.	*b*.	*c*.		
13	14	15		17		15a		17a		19	20	21	22	23	24	25	1	
26 Mar. (85)..	0 Sat....	0	44	0	17	4	22	1	45	18 Mar. (77)..	6 Fri....	181	.543	0	453	257	4397	
25 Mar. (85)..	1 Sun....	16	15	6	30	19	54	7	57	6 Mar. (66)..	3 Tues....	148	.444	9875	301	226	4398	
25 Mar. (84)..	2 Mon....	31	46	12	42	35	25	14	10	25 Mar. (84)..	2 Mon....	191	.573	9910	237	278	4399	
25 Mar. (84)..	3 Tues....	47	17	18	55	50	57	20	23	14 Mar. (73)..	6 Fri....	⊙ −3	−.009	9786	84	247	4400	
26 Mar. (85)..	5 Thur...	2	49	1	7	6	28	2	35	4 Mar. (63)..	4 Wed....	112	.336	0	967	219	4401	
25 Mar. (85)..	6 Fri.....	18	20	7	20	22	0	8	48	22 Mar. (82)..	3 Tues....	95	.285	35	903	270	4402	
25 Mar. (84)..	0 Sat.....	33	51	13	32	37	31	15	0	12 Mar. (71)..	1 Sun....	253	.759	249	787	242	4403	
25 Mar. (84)..	1 Sun....	49	22	19	45	53	3	21	13	1 Mar. (60)..	5 Thur...	163	.489	125	634	211	4404	
26 Mar. (85)..	3 Tues....	4	54	1	57	8	34	3	26	20 Mar. (79)..	4 Wed....	239	.717	159	570	263	4405	
25 Mar. (85)..	4 Wed....	20	25	8	10	24	6	9	38	8 Mar. (68)..	1 Sun....	245	.735	35	417	232	4406	
25 Mar. (84)..	5 Thur...	35	56	14	22	39	37	15	51	25 Feb. (56)..	5 Thur. .	194	.582	9911	264	201	4407	
25 Mar. (84)..	6 Fri.....	51	27	20	35	55	9	22	4	16 Mar. (75)..	4 Wed.. .	219	.657	9946	200	252	4408	
26 Mar. (85)..	1 Sun....	6	59	2	47	10	40	4	16	5 Mar. (64)..	1 Sun....	4	.012	9821	48	221	4409	
25 Mar. (85)..	2 Mon....	22	30	9	0	26	12	10	29	23 Mar. (83)..	0 Sat....	⊙−18	−.054	9856	984	273	4410	
25 Mar. (84)..	3 Tues....	38	1	15	12	41	43	16	41	13 Mar. (72)..	5 Thur...	106	.318	70	867	245	4411	
25 Mar. (84)..	4 Wed....	53	32	21	25	57	15	22	54	3 Mar. (62)..	3 Tues....	286	.858	285	751	217	4412	
26 Mar. (85)..	6 Fri.....	9	4	3	37	12	46	5	7	21 Mar. (80)..	1 Sun.. .	8	.024	9981	650	265	4413	
25 Mar. (85)..	0 Sat.....	24	35	9	50	28	18	11	19	10 Mar. (70)..	6 Fri.....	305	.915	195	534	237	4414	
25 Mar. (84)..	1 Sun....	40	6	16	2	43	49	17	32	27 Feb. (58)..	3 Tues....	308	.924	71	381	206	4415	
25 Mar. (84)..	2 Mon....	55	37	22	15	59	21	23	44	17 Mar. (76)..	1 Sun....	42	.126	9767	281	255	4416	
26 Mar. (85)..	4 Wed....	11	9	4	27	14	53	5	57	7 Mar. (66)..	6 Fri.....	242	.726	9981	164	227	4417	
25 Mar. (85)..	5 Thur...	26	40	10	40	30	24	12	10	25 Mar. (85)..	5 Thur...	240	.720	16	100	278	4418	
25 Mar. (84)..	6 Fri.....	42	11	16	52	45	56	18	22	14 Mar. (73)..	2 Mon....	⊙−15	−.045	9891	947	247	4419	
25 Mar. (84)..	0 Sat.....	57	42	23	5	†1	27	†0	35	4 Mar. (63)..	0 Sat.....	124	.372	106	831	219	4420	
26 Mar. (85)..	2 Mon....	13	14	5	17	16	59	6	47	23 Mar. (82)..	6 Fri.....	141	.423	140	767	270	4421	
25 Mar. (85)..	3 Tues ...	28	45	11	30	32	30	13	0	11 Mar (71)..	3 Tues....	64	.192	16	614	240	4422	
25 Mar. (84)..	4 Wed....	44	16	17	42	48	2	19	13	28 Feb. (59)..	0 Sat.....	68	.204	9892	461	209	4423	
25 Mar. (84)..	5 Thur...	59	47	23	55	†3	33	†1	25	19 Mar. (78)..	6 Fri.....	151	.453	9926	397	260	4424	
26 Mar. (85)..	0 Sat.....	15	19	6	7	19	5	7	38	8 Mar. (67)..	3 Tues....	82	.246	9802	244	229	4425	

† See footnote p. liii above. ⊙ See Text. Art. 101, para. 2.

TABLE I.

Lunation-parts = 10,000ths of a circle. A tithi = 1/30th of the moon's synodic revolution.

I. CONCURRENT YEAR.								II. ADDED LUNAR MONTHS.				
						Samvatsara.		True.				
Kali.	Śaka.	Chaitrâdi. Vikrama.	Meshâdi (Solar) year in Bengal.	Kollam.	A. D.	Luni-Solar cycle. (Southern.)	Bṛihaspati cycle (Northern) current at Mesha saṅkrânti.	Name of month.	Time of the preceding saṅkrânti expressed in Lunation parts. (*t.*)	Time of the preceding saṅkrânti expressed in Tithis.	Time of the succeeding saṅkrânti expressed in Lunation parts. (*t.*)	Time of the succeeding saṅkrânti expressed in Tithis.
1	2	3	3a	4	5	6	7	8	9	10	11	12
4426	1247	1382	731	499-500	*1324-25	58 Raktâksha	3 Śukla	2 Vaiśâkha	9956	29.868	461	1.383
4427	1248	1383	732	500- 1	1325-26	59 Krodhana	4 Pramoda					
4428	1249	1384	733	501- 2	1326-27	60 Kshaya	5 Prajâpati	6 Bhâdrapada	9942	29.826	433	1.299
4429	1250	1385	734	502- 3	1327-28	1 Prabhava	6 Aṅgiras					
4430	1251	1386	735	503- 4	*1328-29	2 Vibhava	7 Śrîmukha					
4431	1252	1387	736	504- 5	1329-30	3 Śukla	8 Bhâva	4 Âshâḍha	9297	27.891	74	0.222
4432	1253	1388	737	505- 6	1330-31	4 Pramoda	9 Yuvan					
4433	1254	1389	738	506- 7	1331-32	5 Prajâpati	10 Dhâtṛi					
4434	1255	1390	739	507- 8	*1332-33	6 Aṅgiras	11 Îśvara	3 Jyeshṭha	9950	29.850	515	1.545
4435	1256	1391	740	508- 9	1333-34	7 Śrîmukha	12 Bahudhânya					
4436	1257	1392	741	509- 10	1334-35	8 Bhâva	13 Pramâthin	7 Âśvina 10 *Pausha* (*Ksh.*) 12 Phâlguna	9909 9 9915	29.727 0.027 29.745	130 9942 33	0.390 29.826 0.099
4437	1258	1393	742	510- 11	1335-36	9 Yuvan	14 Vikrama [1])					
4438	1259	1394	743	511- 12	*1336-37	10 Dhâtṛi	16 Chitrabhânu					
4439	1260	1395	744	512- 13	1337-38	11 Îśvara	17 Subhânu	5 Śrâvaṇa	9609	28.827	415	1.245
4440	1261	1396	745	513- 14	1338-39	12 Bahudhânya	18 Târaṇa					
4441	1262	1397	746	514- 15	1339-40	13 Pramâthin	19 Pârthiva					
4442	1263	1398	747	515- 16	*1340-41	14 Vikrama	20 Vyaya	4 Ashâḍha	9982	29.946	627	1.881
4443	1264	1399	748	516- 17	1341-42	15 Vṛisha	21 Sarvajit					
4444	1265	1400	749	517- 18	1342-43	16 Chitrabhânu	22 Sarvadhârin					
4445	1266	1401	750	518- 19	1343-44	17 Subhânu	23 Virodhin	2 Vaiśâkha	9934	29.802	514	1.542
4446	1267	1402	751	519- 20	*1344-45	18 Târaṇa	24 Vikṛita					
4447	1268	1403	752	520- 21	1345-46	19 Pârthiva	25 Khara	6 Bhâdrapada	9957	29.871	538	1.614
4448	1269	1404	753	521- 22	1346-47	20 Vyaya	26 Nandana					
4449	1270	1405	754	522- 23	1347-48	21 Sarvajit	27 Vijaya					
4450	1271	1406	755	523- 24	*1348-49	22 Sarvadhârin	28 Jaya	4 Âshâḍha	9448	28.344	121	0.363
4451	1272	1407	756	524- 25	1349-50	23 Virodhin	29 Manmatha					
4452	1273	1408	757	525- 26	1350-51	24 Vikṛita	30 Durmukha					
4453	1274	1409	758	526- 27	1351-52	25 Khara	31 Hemalamba	2 Vaiśâkha	9471	28.413	40	0.120
4454	1275	1410	759	527- 28	*1352-53	26 Nandana	32 Vilamba					
4455	1276	1411	760	528- 29	1353-54	27 Vijaya	33 Vikârin	6 Bhâdrapada	9495	28.485	47	0.141
4456	1277	1412	761	529- 30	1354-55	28 Jaya	34 Śârvari					

[1]) Vṛisha, No. 15, was suppressed in the north.

TABLE I.

(*Col.* 23) *a* = *Distance of moon from sun.* (*Col.* 24) *b* = *moon's mean anomaly.* (*Col.* 25) *c* = *sun's mean anomaly.*

III. COMMENCEMENT OF THE

Solar year. Day and Month A. D.	Solar year. (Time of the Mesha saṅkrânti.) Week day.	By the Ârya Siddhânta. Gh.	Pa.	H.	M.	By the Sûrya Siddhânta. Gh.	Pa.	H.	M.	Luni-Solar year. (Civil day of Chaitra Śukla 1st.) Day and Month A. D.	Week day.	At Sunrise on meridian of Ujjain. Moon's Age. Lunat. parts elapsed. (*t.*)	Tithis elapsed.	*a.*	*b.*	*c.*	Kali.
13	14	15		17		15a		17a		19	20	21	22	23	24	25	1
25 Mar. (85)..	1 Sun....	30	50	12	20	34	36	13	50	26 Feb. (57)..	1 Sun....	260	.780	16	128	201	4426
25 Mar. (84)..	2 Mon....	46	21	18	32	50	8	20	3	16 Mar. (75)..	0 Sat.....	246	.738	51	64	252	4427
26 Mar. (85)..	4 Wed....	1	52	0	45	5	39	2	16	5 Mar. (64)..	4 Wed....	⊙ −6	−.018	9927	911	222	4428
26 Mar. (85)..	5 Thur...	17	24	6	57	21	11	8	28	24 Mar. (83)..	3 Tues....	⊙−12	−.036	9962	847	273	4429
25 Mar. (85)..	6 Fri.....	32	55	13	10	36	42	14	41	13 Mar. (73)..	1 Sun....	177	.531	176	731	245	4430
25 Mar (84)..	0 Sat.....	48	26	19	22	52	14	20	54	2 Mar. (61)..	5 Thur...	128	.384	52	578	214	4431
26 Mar. (85)..	2 Mon....	3	57	1	35	7	45	3	6	21 Mar. (80)..	4 Wed....	213	.639	86	514	265	4432
26 Mar. (85)..	3 Tues....	19	29	7	47	23	17	9	19	10 Mar. (69)..	1 Sun....	209	.627	9962	361	235	4433
25 Mar. (85)..	4 Wed....	35	0	14	0	38	48	15	31	27 Feb. (58)..	5 Thur ..	116	.348	9838	208	204	4434
25 Mar. (84)..	5 Thur...	50	31	20	12	54	20	21	44	17 Mar. (76)..	4 Wed....	122	.366	9872	144	255	4435
} 26 Mar. (85)..	0 Sat.....	6	2	2	25	9	51	3	57	7 Mar. (66)..	2 Mon....	251	.753	87	28	227	4436
26 Mar. (85)..	1 Sun....	21	34	8	37	25	23	10	9	26 Mar. (85)..	1 Sun....	231	.693	121	964	278	4437
25 Mar. (85)..	2 Mon....	37	5	14	50	40	55	16	22	14 Mar. (74)..	5 Thur...	7	.021	9997	811	247	4438
25 Mar. (84)..	3 Tues....	52	36	21	2	56	26	22	34	4 Mar. (63) .	3 Tues....	221	.663	211	694	219	4439
26 Mar. (85)..	5 Thur...	8	7	3	15	11	58	4	47	23 Mar. (8?)..	2 Mon....	284	.852	246	630	271	4440
26 Mar. (85)..	6 Fri.....	23	39	9	27	27	29	11	0	12 Mar. (71)..	6 Fri.....	282	.846	122	478	240	4441
25 Mar. (85)..	0 Sat.....	39	10	15	40	43	1	17	12	29 Feb. (60)..	3 Tues....	264	.792	9997	325	209	4442
25 Mar. (84)..	1 Sun....	54	41	21	52	58	32	23	25	19 Mar. (78)..	2 Mon....	312	.936	32	261	260	4443
26 Mar. (85)..	3 Tues...	10	12	4	5	14	4	5	37	8 Mar. (67)..	6 Fri.....	137	.411	9908	109	230	4444
26 Mar. (85)..	4 Wed....	25	44	10	17	29	35	11	50	26 Feb. (57)..	4 Wed....	258	.774	122	992	201	4445
25 Mar. (85)..	5 Thur...	41	15	16	30	45	7	18	3	16 Mar. (76)..	3 Tues....	235	.705	157	928	253	4446
25 Mar. (84)..	6 Fri.....	56	46	22	42	†0	38	†0	15	5 Mar. (64)..	0 Sat.....	35	.105	32	775	222	4447
26 Mar. (85)..	1 Sun....	12	17	4	55	16	10	6	28	24 Mar. (83)..	6 Fri.....	71	.213	67	711	273	4448
26 Mar. (85)..	2 Mon....	27	49	11	7	31	41	12	41	13 Mar. (72)..	3 Tues....	33	.099	9943	558	242	4449
25 Mar. (85)..	3 Tues....	43	20	17	20	47	13	18	53	1 Mar. (61)..	0 Sat.....	39	.117	9818	405	212	4450
25 Mar. (84)..	4 Wed....	58	51	23	32	†2	44	†1	6	20 Mar. (79)..	6 Fri.....	111	.333	9853	341	263	4451
26 Mar. (85)..	6 Fri.....	14	22	5	45	18	16	7	18	9 Mar. (68)..	3 Tues....	⊙ −2	−.006	9729	188	232	4452
26 Mar. (85)..	0 Sat.....	29	54	11	57	33	47	13	31	27 Feb. (58) .	1 Sun....	148	.444	9943	72	204	4453
25 Mar. (85)..	1 Sun....	45	25	18	10	49	19	19	44	17 Mar. (77)..	0 Sat.....	125	.375	9978	8	255	4454
26 Mar. (85)..	3 Tues....	0	56	0	22	4	50	1	56	7 Mar. (66)..	5 Thur...	243	.729	192	891	227	4455
26 Mar. (85)..	4 Wed....	16	27	6	35	20	22	8	9	26 Mar. (85)..	4 Wed....	244	.732	227	827	279	4456

† See footnote p. liii above. ⊙ See Text. Art. 101 above, para. 2.

TABLE I.

Lunation-parts = 10,000*ths of a circle. A tithi* = $^1/_{30}$*th of the moon's synodic revolution.*

I. CONCURRENT YEAR.								II. ADDED LUNAR MONTHS.				
						Samvatsara.		True.				
Kali.	Śaka.	Chaitrâdi. Vikrama.	Meshâdi (Solar) year in Bengal.	Kollam.	A. D.	Luni-Solar cycle. (Southern.)	Bṛihaspati cycle (Northern) current at Mesha saṅkrânti.	Name of month.	Time of the preceding saṅkrânti expressed in: Lunation parts. (*l.*)	Time of the preceding saṅkrânti expressed in: Tithis.	Time of the succeeding saṅkrânti expressed in: Lunation parts. (*l.*)	Time of the succeeding saṅkrânti expressed in: Tithis.
1	2	3	3a	4	5	6	7	8	9	10	11	12
4457	1278	1413	762	530-31	1355-56	29 Manmatha	35 Plava					
4458	1279	1414	763	531-32	*1356-57	30 Durmukha	36 Śubhakṛit	5 Śrâvaṇa	9624	28.872	374	1.122
4459	1280	1415	764	532-33	1357-58	31 Hemalamba	37 Śobhana					
4460	1281	1416	765	533-34	1358-59	32 Vilamba	38 Krodhin					
4461	1282	1417	766	534-35	1359-60	33 Vikârin	39 Viśvâvasu	3 Jyeshṭha	9556	28.668	174	0.522
4462	1283	1418	767	535-36	*1360-61	34 Śârvari	40 Parâbhava					
4463	1284	1419	768	536-37	1361-62	35 Plava	41 Plavaṅga					
4464	1285	1420	769	537-38	1362-63	36 Śubhakṛit	42 Kîlaka	2 Vaiśâkha	9898	29.694	490	1.470
4465	1286	1421	770	538-39	1363-64	37 Śobhana	43 Saumya					
4466	1287	1422	771	539-40	*1364-65	38 Krodhin	44 Sâdhâraṇa	6 Bhâdrapada	9918	29.754	544	1.632
4467	1288	1423	772	540-41	1365-66	39 Viśvâvasu	45 Virodhakṛit					
4468	1289	1424	773	541-42	1366-67	40 Parâbhava	46 Paridhâvin					
4469	1290	1425	774	542-43	1367-68	41 Plavaṅga	47 Pramâdin	4 Âshâḍha	9647	28.941	268	0.804
4470	1291	1426	775	543-44	*1368-69	42 Kîlaka	48 Ânanda					
4471	1292	1427	776	544-45	1369-70	43 Saumya	49 Râkshasa					
4472	1293	1428	777	545-46	1370-71	44 Sâdhâraṇa	50 Anala	2 Vaiśâkha	9438	28.314	36	0.108
4473	1294	1429	778	546-47	1371-72	45 Virodhakṛit	51 Piṅgala					
4474	1295	1430	779	547-48	*1372-73	46 Paridhâvin	52 Kâlayukta	6 Bhâdrapada	9464	28.392	83	0.249
4475	1296	1431	780	548-49	1373-74	47 Pramâdin	53 Sidhârthin					
4476	1297	1432	781	549-50	1374-75	48 Ânanda	54 Raudra					
4477	1298	1433	782	550-51	1375-76	49 Râkshasa	55 Durmati	5 Śrâvaṇa	9743	29.229	389	1.167
4478	1299	1434	783	551-52	*1376-77	50 Anala	56 Dundubhi					
4479	1300	1435	784	552-53	1377-78	51 Piṅgala	57 Rudhirodgârin					
4480	1301	1436	785	553-54	1378-79	52 Kâlayukta	58 Raktâksha	3 Jyeshṭha	9577	28.731	296	0.888
4481	1302	1437	786	554-55	1379-80	53 Siddhârthin	58 Krodhana					
4482	1303	1438	787	555-56	*1380-81	54 Raudra	60 Kshaya	8 Kârttika 9 *Mârgaś.*(*Ksh*)	9937 15	29.811 0.045	15 9927	0.045 29.781
4483	1304	1439	788	556-57	1381-82	55 Durmati	1 Prabhava	2 Vaiśâkha	9927	29.781	455	1.365
4484	1305	1440	789	557-58	1382-83	56 Dundubhi	2 Vibhava					
4485	1306	1441	790	558-59	1383-84	57 Rudhirodgârin	3 Śukla	6 Bhâdrapada	9906	29.718	500	1.500
4486	1307	1442	791	559-60	*1384-85	58 Raktâksha	4 Pramoda					
4487	1308	1443	792	560-61	1385-86	59 Krodhana	5 Prajâpati					
4488	1309	1444	793	561-62	1386-87	60 Kshaya	6 Aṅgiras	4 Âshâḍha	9799	29.397	427	1.281

TABLE I.

(Col. 23) a = Distance of moon from sun. (Col. 24) b = moon's mean anomaly. (Col. 25) c = sun's mean anomaly.

III. COMMENCEMENT OF THE																	
Solar year.										Luni-Solar year. (Civil day of Chaitra Śukla 1st.)							Kali.
Day and Month A. D.	(Time of the Mesha saṅkrânti.)									Day and Month A. D.	Week day.	At Sunrise on meridian of Ujjain.					
	Week day.	By the Ârya Siddhânta.				By the Sûrya Siddhânta.						Moon's Age.		a.	b.	c.	
		Gh.	Pa.	H.	M.	Gh.	Pa.	H.	M.			Lunat. parts elapsed. (t.)	Tithis elapsed.				
13	14	15		17		15a		17a		19	20	21	22	23	24	25	1
26 Mar. (85)..	5 Thur...	31	59	12	47	35	53	14	21	15 Mar. (74)..	1 Sun....	118	.354	103	674	248	4457
25 Mar. (85)..	6 Fri.....	47	30	19	0	51	25	20	34	3 Mar. (63)..	5 Thur...	99	.297	9978	522	217	4458
26 Mar. (85)..	1 Sun....	3	1	1	12	6	57	2	47	22 Mar. (81)..	4 Wed....	180	.540	13	458	268	4459
26 Mar. (85)..	2 Mon....	18	32	7	25	22	28	8	59	11 Mar. (70)..	1 Sun ...	161	.483	9889	305	237	4460
26 Mar. (85)..	3 Tues....	34	4	13	37	38	0	15	12	28 Feb. (59)..	5 Thur...	20	.060	9764	152	207	4461
25 Mar. (85)..	4 Wed....	49	35	19	50	53	31	21	24	18 Mar. (78)..	4 Wed....	13	.039	9799	88	258	4462
26 Mar. (85)..	6 Fri.....	5	6	2	2	9	3	3	37	8 Mar. (67)..	2 Mon....	139	.417	13	972	230	4463
26 Mar. (85)..	0 Sat.....	20	37	8	15	24	34	9	50	26 Feb. (57)..	0 Sat.....	260	.780	228	855	202	4464
26 Mar. (85)..	1 Sun....	36	9	14	27	40	6	16	2	17 Mar. (76)..	6 Fri.....	266	.798	262	791	253	4465
25 Mar. (85)..	2 Mon....	51	40	20	40	55	37	22	15	5 Mar. (65)..	3 Tues....	173	.519	138	638	222	4466
26 Mar. (85)..	4 Wed....	7	11	2	52	11	9	4	27	24 Mar. (83)..	2 Mon....	250	.750	173	574	273	4467
26 Mar. (85)..	5 Thur...	22	42	9	5	26	40	10	40	13 Mar. (72)..	6 Fri.....	254	.762	48	422	243	4468
26 Mar. (85)..	6 Fri.....	38	14	15	17	42	12	16	53	2 Mar. (61)..	3 Tues....	205	.615	9924	269	212	4469
25 Mar. (85)..	0 Sat.....	53	45	21	30	57	43	23	5	20 Mar. (80)..	2 Mon....	233	.699	9959	205	263	4470
26 Mar. (85)..	2 Mon....	9	16	3	42	13	15	5	18	9 Mar. (68)..	6 Fri.....	21	.063	9835	52	232	4471
26 Mar. (85)..	3 Tues....	24	47	9	55	28	46	11	31	27 Feb. (58)..	4 Wed....	137	.411	49	936	204	4472
26 Mar. (85)..	4 Wed....	40	19	16	7	44	18	17	43	18 Mar. (77)..	3 Tues....	122	.366	83	871	256	4473
25 Mar. (85)..	5 Thur...	55	50	22	20	59	49	23	56	7 Mar. (67)..	1 Sun....	298	.894	298	755	227	4474
26 Mar. (85)..	0 Sat.....	11	21	4	32	15	21	6	8	25 Mar. (84)..	6 Fri.....	20	.060	9994	655	276	4475
26 Mar. (85)..	1 Sun....	26	52	10	45	30	52	12	21	15 Mar. (74)..	4 Wed....	315	.945	208	538	248	4476
26 Mar. (85)..	2 Mon....	42	24	16	57	46	24	18	34	4 Mar. (63)..	1 Sun....	318	.954	84	385	217	4477
25 Mar. (85)..	3 Tues ...	57	55	23	10	†1	55	†0	46	21 Mar. (81)..	6 Fri.....	57	.171	9780	285	266	4478
26 Mar. (85) .	5 Thur...	13	26	5	22	17	27	6	59	11 Mar. (70)..	4 Wed....	256	.768	9994	168	238	4479
26 Mar. (85)..	6 Fri.....	28	57	11	35	32	59	13	11	28 Feb. (59)..	1 Sun....	26	.078	9870	16	207	4480
26 Mar. (85)..	0 Sat.....	44	29	17	47	48	30	19	24	19 Mar. (78)..	0 Sat.....	3	.009	9905	952	258	4481
}26 Mar. (86)..	2 Mon....	0	0	0	0	4	2	1	37	8 Mar. (68)..	5 Thur...	138	.414	119	835	230	4482
26 Mar. (85)..	3 Tues....	15	31	6	12	19	33	7	49	25 Feb. (56)..	2 Mon....	10	.030	9995	682	199	4483
26 Mar. (85)..	4 Wed....	31	2	12	25	35	5	14	2	16 Mar. (75)..	1 Sun....	74	.222	29	618	250	4484
26 Mar. (85)..	5 Thur...	46	34	18	37	50	36	20	14	5 Mar. (64)..	5 Thur...	77	.231	9905	466	220	4485
26 Mar. (86)..	0 Sat.....	2	5	0	50	6	8	2	27	23 Mar. (83)..	4 Wed....	161	.483	9940	402	271	4486
26 Mar. (85)..	1 Sun....	17	36	7	2	21	39	8	40	12 Mar. (71)..	1 Sun....	95	.285	9815	249	240	4487
26 Mar. (85)..	2 Mon....	33	7	13	15	37	11	14	52	2 Mar. (61)..	6 Fri.....	275	.825	30	132	212	4488

† See footnote p. liii above.

TABLE I.

Lunation-parts = 10,000ths of a circle. A tithi = 1/30th of the moon's synodic revolution.

I. CONCURRENT YEAR.								II. ADDED LUNAR MONTHS.				
						Samvatsara.		True.				
Kali.	Śaka.	Chaitrâdi. Vikrama.	Meshâdi (Solar) year in Bengal.	Kollam.	A. D.	Luni-Solar cycle. (Southern.)	Bṛihaspati cycle (Northern) current at Mesha saṅkrânti.	Name of month.	Time of the preceding saṅkrânti expressed in: Lunation parts. (*l.*)	Tithis.	Time of the succeeding saṅkrânti expressed in: Lunation parts. (*l.*)	Tithis.
1	2	3	3a	4	5	6	7	8	9	10	11	12
4489	1310	1445	794	562-63	1387- 88	1 Prabhava	7 Śrîmukha	...	...	...	...	...
4490	1311	1446	795	563-64	*1388- 89	2 Vibhava	8 Bhâva	...	...	...	...	...
4491	1312	1447	796	564-65	1389- 90	3 Śukla	9 Yuvan	3 Jyeshṭha	9991	29.973	879	2.637
4492	1313	1448	797	565-66	1390- 91	4 Pramoda	10 Dhâtṛi	...	...	...	...	...
4493	1314	1449	798	566-67	1391- 92	5 Prajâpati	11 Îśvara	6 Bhâdrapada	9433	28.299	48	0.144
4494	1315	1450	799	567-68	*1392- 93	6 Aṅgiras	12 Bahudhânya	...	...	...	...	...
4495	1316	1451	800	568-69	1393- 94	7 Śrîmukha	13 Pramâthin	...	...	...	...	...
4496	1317	1452	801	569-70	1394- 95	8 Bhâva	14 Vikrama	5 Śrâvaṇa	9932	29.796	501	1.503
4497	1318	1453	802	570-71	1395- 96	9 Yuvan	15 Vṛisha	...	...	...	...	...
4498	1319	1454	803	571-72	*1396- 97	10 Dhâtṛi	16 Chitrabhânu	...	...	...	...	...
4499	1320	1455	804	572-73	1397- 98	11 Îśvara	17 Subhânu	3 Jyeshṭha	9538	28.614	327	0.981
4500	1321	1456	805	573-74	1398- 99	12 Bahudhânya	18 Târaṇa	...	...	...	...	...
4501	1322	1457	806	574-75	1399-400	13 Pramâthin	19 Pârthiva	8 Kârttika	9981	29.943	121	0.363
								10 *Pausha* (*Ksh.*)	80	0.240	9950	29.850
4502	1323	1458	807	575-76	*1400- 1	14 Vikrama	20 Vyaya	1 Chaitra	9862	29.586	56	0.168
4503	1324	1459	808	576-77	1401- 2	15 Vṛisha	21 Sarvajit	...	...	...	...	...
4504	1325	1460	809	577-78	1402- 3	16 Chitrabhânu	22 Sarvadhârin	6 Bhâdrapada	9989	29.967	499	1.497
4505	1326	1461	810	578-79	1403- 4	17 Subhânu	23 Virodhin	...	...	...	...	...
4506	1327	1462	811	579-80	*1404- 5	18 Târaṇa	24 Vikṛita	...	...	...	...	...
4507	1328	1463	812	580-81	1405- 6	19 Pârthiva	25 Khara	4 Âshâḍha	9855	29.565	625	1.875
4508	1329	1464	813	581-82	1406- 7	20 Vyaya	26 Nandana	...	...	...	...	...
4509	1330	1465	814	582-83	1407- 8	21 Sarvajit	27 Vijaya	...	...	...	...	...
4510	1331	1466	815	583-84	*1408- 9	22 Sarvadhârin	28 Jaya	2 Vaiśâkha	9535	28.605	1	0.003
4511	1332	1467	816	584-85	1409- 10	23 Virodhin	29 Manmatha	...	...	...	...	...
4512	1333	1468	817	585-86	1410- 11	24 Vikṛita	30 Durmukha	6 Bhâdrapada	9483	28.449	23	0.069
4513	1334	1469	818	586-87	1411- 12	25 Khara	31 Hemalamba	...	...	...	...	...
4514	1335	1470	819	587-88	*1412- 13	26 Nandana	32 Vilamba	...	...	...	...	...
4515	1336	1471	820	588-89	1413- 14	27 Vijaya	33 Vikârin	4 Âshâḍha	9380	28.140	112	0.336
4516	1337	1472	821	589-90	1414- 15	28 Jaya	34 Śârvari	...	...	...	...	...
4517	1338	1473	822	590-91	1415- 16	29 Manmatha	35 Plava	...	...	...	...	...
4518	1339	1474	823	591-92	*1416- 17	30 Durmukha	36 Śubhakṛit	3 Jyeshṭha	9536	28.608	282	0.846
4519	1340	1475	824	592-93	1417- 18	31 Hemalamba	37 Śobhana	...	...	...	...	...
4520	1341	1476	825	593-94	1418- 19	32 Vilamba	38 Krodhin	8 Kârttika	9951	29.853	130	0.390

TABLE I.

(*Col.* 23) *a* = *Distance of moon from sun.* (*Col.* 24) *b* = *moon's mean anomaly.* (*Col.* 25) *c* = *sun's mean anomaly.*

III. COMMENCEMENT OF THE																	
Solar year.										Luni-Solar year. (Civil day of Chaitra Śukla 1st.)							Kali.
Day and Month. A. D.	(Time of the Mesha saṅkrânti.)									Day and Month. A. D.	Week day.	At Sunrise on meridian of Ujjain.					
	Week day.	By the Ârya Siddhânta.				By the Sûrya Siddhânta.						Moon's Age.		a.	b.	c.	
		Gh.	Pa.	H.	M.	Gh.	Pa.	H.	M.			Lunat. parts elapsed. (*t*.)	Tithis elapsed.				
13	**14**	**15**		**17**		**15a**		**17a**		**19**	**20**	**21**	**22**	**23**	**24**	**25**	**1**
26 Mar. (85)..	3 Tues....	48	39	19	27	52	42	21	5	21 Mar. (80)..	5 Thur...	262	.786	64	68	263	4489
26 Mar. (86)..	5 Thur...	4	10	1	40	8	14	3	17	9 Mar. (69)..	2 Mon....	9	.027	9940	916	232	4490
26 Mar. (85)..	6 Fri.....	19	41	7	52	23	45	9	30	27 Feb. (58)..	0 Sat.....	164	.492	154	799	204	4491
26 Mar. (85)..	0 Sat.....	35	12	14	5	39	17	15	43	18 Mar. (77)..	6 Fri.....	190	.570	189	735	256	4492
26 Mar. (85)..	1 Sun....	50	44	20	17	54	48	21	55	7 Mar. (66)..	3 Tues....	136	.408	65	582	225	4493
26 Mar. (86)..	3 Tues....	6	15	2	30	10	20	4	8	25 Mar. (85)..	2 Mon....	224	.672	99	518	276	4494
26 Mar. (85)..	4 Wed....	21	46	8	42	25	51	10	21	14 Mar. (73)..	6 Fri.....	220	.660	9975	365	245	4495
26 Mar. (85)..	5 Thur...	37	17	14	55	41	23	16	33	3 Mar. (62)..	3 Tues....	129	.387	9851	213	215	4496
26 Mar. (85)..	6 Fri.....	52	49	21	7	56	54	22	46	22 Mar. (81)..	2 Mon....	138	.414	9886	149	266	4497
26 Mar. (86)..	1 Sun....	8	20	3	20	12	26	4	58	11 Mar. (71)..	0 Sat.....	268	.804	100	32	238	4498
26 Mar. (85)..	2 Mon....	23	51	9	32	27	57	11	11	28 Feb. (59)..	4 Wed....	21	.063	9976	879	207	4499
26 Mar. (85)..	3 Tues....	39	22	15	45	43	29	17	24	19 Mar. (78)..	3 Tues....	21	.063	10	815	258	4500
}26 Mar. (85)..	4 Wed....	54	54	21	57	59	1	23	36	9 Mar. (68)..	1 Sun....	231	.693	224	699	230	4501
26 Mar. (86)..	6 Fri.....	10	25	4	10	14	32	5	49	26 Feb. (57)..	5 Thur...	203	.609	100	546	199	4502
26 Mar. (85)..	0 Sat.....	25	56	10	22	30	4	12	1	16 Mar. (75)..	4 Wed....	291	.873	135	482	251	4503
26 Mar. (85)..	1 Sun....	41	27	16	35	45	35	18	14	5 Mar. (64)..	1 Sun....	275	.825	11	329	220	4504
26 Mar. (85)..	2 Mon....	56	59	22	47	†1	7	†0	27	24 Mar. (83)..	0 Sat.....	325	.973	45	265	271	4505
26 Mar. (86)..	4 Wed....	12	30	5	0	16	38	6	39	12 Mar. (72)..	4 Wed....	152	.456	9921	112	240	4506
26 Mar. (85)..	5 Thur...	28	1	11	12	32	10	12	52	2 Mar. (61)..	2 Mon....	273	.819	135	996	212	4507
26 Mar. (85)..	6 Fri.....	43	32	17	25	47	41	19	4	21 Mar. (80)..	1 Sun....	252	.756	170	932	264	4508
26 Mar. (85)..	0 Sat.....	59	4	23	37	†3	13	†1	17	10 Mar. (69)..	5 Thur...	49	.147	46	779	233	4509
26 Mar. (86)..	2 Mon....	14	35	5	50	18	44	7	30	28 Feb. (59)..	3 Tues....	285	.855	260	663	205	4510
26 Mar. (85)..	3 Tues....	30	6	12	2	34	16	13	42	17 Mar. (76)..	1 Sun....	42	.126	9956	562	253	4511
26 Mar. (85)..	4 Wed....	45	37	18	15	49	47	19	55	6 Mar. (65)..	5 Thur...	48	.144	9832	410	222	4512
27 Mar. (86)..	6 Fri.....	1	9	0	27	5	19	2	8	25 Mar. (84)..	4 Wed....	122	.366	9866	345	274	4513
26 Mar. (86)..	0 Sat.....	16	40	6	40	20	50	8	20	13 Mar. (73)..	1 Sun...	13	.039	9742	193	243	4514
26 Mar. (85)..	1 Sun....	32	11	12	52	36	22	14	33	3 Mar. (62)..	6 Fri.....	163	.489	9956	76	215	4515
26 Mar. (85)..	2 Mon....	47	42	19	5	51	53	20	45	22 Mar. (81)..	5 Thur...	142	.426	9991	12	266	4516
27 Mar. (86)..	4 Wed....	3	14	1	17	7	25	2	58	12 Mar. (71)..	3 Tues....	259	.777	205	896	238	4517
26 Mar. (86),..	5 Thur...	18	45	7	30	22	56	9	11	29 Feb. (60)..	0 Sat.....	83	.249	81	743	207	4518
26 Mar. (85)..	6 Fri....	34	16	13	42	38	28	15	23	19 Mar. (78)..	6 Fri.....	129	.387	116	679	259	4519
26 Mar. (85)..	0 Sat.....	49	47	19	55	53	59	21	36	8 Mar. (67)..	3 Tues....	109	.327	9992	526	228	4520

† See footnote p. liii above.

TABLE I.

Lunation-parts = 10,000ths of a circle. A tithi = 1/30th of the moon's synodic revolution.

I. CONCURRENT YEAR.								II. ADDED LUNAR MONTHS.				
						Samvatsara.		True.				
									Time of the preceding saṅkrânti expressed in		Time of the succeeding saṅkrânti expressed in	
Kali.	Śaka.	Chaitrâdi. Vikrama.	Meshâdi (Solar) year in Bengal.	Kollam.	A. D.	Luni-Solar cycle. (Southern.)	Bṛihaspati cycle (Northern) current at Mesha saṅkrânti.	Name of month.	Lunation parts. (*l.*)	Tithis.	Lunation parts. (*l.*)	Tithis.
1	2	3	3a	4	5	6	7	8	9	10	11	12
4521	1342	1477	826	594- 95	1419-20	33 Vikârin......	39 Viśvâvasu....	....	......	......	......	......
4522	1343	1478	827	595- 96	*1420-21	34 Sârvari......	40 Parâbhava [1]..	....	......	......	......	......
4523	1344	1479	828	596- 97	1421-22	35 Plava.......	42 Kîlaka.......	5 Śrâvaṇa.....	9592	28.776	162	0.486
4524	1345	1480	829	597- 98	1422-23	36 Śubhakṛit....	43 Saumya......	....	......	......	......	......
4525	1346	1481	830	598- 99	1423-24	37 Śobhana......	44 Sâdhâraṇa....	....	......	......	......	......
4526	1347	1482	831	599-600	*1424-25	38 Krodhin.....	45 Virodhakṛit...	4 Âshâḍha....	9829	29.487	686	2.058
4527	1348	1483	832	600- 1	1425-26	39 Viśvâvasu....	46 Paridhâvin...	....	......	......	......	......
4528	1349	1484	833	601- 2	1426-27	40 Parâbhava....	47 Pramâdin....	....	......	......	......	......
4529	1350	1485	834	602- 3	1427-28	41 Plavaṅga.....	48 Ânanda......	2 Vaiśâkha....	9715	29.145	111	0.333
4530	1351	1486	835	603- 4	*1428-29	42 Kîlaka.......	49 Râkshasa.....	....	......	......	......	......
4531	1352	1487	836	604- 5	1429-30	43 Saumya......	50 Anala.......	6 Bhâdrapada..	9629	28.887	81	0.243
4532	1353	1488	837	605- 6	1430-31	44 Sâdhâraṇa....	51 Piṅgala......	....	......	......	......	......
4533	1354	1489	838	606- 7	1431-32	45 Virodhakṛit...	52 Kâlayukta....	....	......	......	......	......
4534	1355	1490	839	607- 8	*1432-33	46 Paridhâvin...	53 Siddhârthin...	4 Âshâḍha....	9374	28.122	173	0.519
4535	1356	1491	840	608- 9	1433-34	47 Pramâdin....	54 Raudra......	....	......	......	......	......
4536	1357	1492	841	609- 10	1434-35	48 Ânanda......	55 Durmati.....	....	......	......	......	......
4537	1358	1493	842	610- 11	1435-36	49 Râkshasa.....	56 Dundubhi....	3 Jyeshṭha....	9596	28.788	264	0.792
4538	1359	1494	843	611- 12	*1436-37	50 Anala.......	57 Rudhirodgârin	....	......	......	......	......
4539	1360	1495	844	612- 13	1437-38	51 Piṅgala......	58 Raktâksha....	8 Kârttika....	9922	29.766	90	0.270
4540	1361	1496	845	613- 14	1438-39	52 Kâlayukta....	59 Krodhana....	....	......	......	......	......
4541	1362	1497	846	614- 15	1439-40	53 Siddhârthin..	60 Kshaya......	....	......	......	......	......
4542	1363	1498	847	615- 16	*1440-41	54 Raudra......	1 Prabhava.....	5 Śrâvaṇa.....	9721	29.163	355	1.065
4543	1364	1499	848	616- 17	1441-42	55 Durmati.....	2 Vibhava......	....	......	......	......	......
4544	1365	1500	849	617- 18	1442-43	56 Dundubhi....	3 Śukla........	....	......	......	......	......
4545	1366	1501	850	618- 19	1443-44	57 Rudhirodgârin	4 Pramoda.....	4 Âshâḍha....	9795	29.385	664	1.992
4546	1367	1502	851	619- 20	*1444-45	58 Raktâksha....	5 Prajâpati....	....	......	......	......	......
4547	1368	1503	852	620- 21	1445-46	59 Krodhana....	6 Aṅgiras......	....	......	......	......	......
4548	1369	1504	853	621- 22	1446-47	60 Kshaya......	7 Śrîmukha....	2 Vaiśâkha....	9904	29.712	297	0.891
4549	1370	1505	854	622- 23	1447-48	1 Prabhava.....	8 Bhâva.......	....	......	......	......	......
4550	1371	1506	855	623- 24	*1448-49	2 Vibhava......	9 Yuvan.......	6 Bhâdrapada..	9825	29.475	236	0.708
4551	1372	1507	856	624- 25	1449-50	3 Śukla........	10 Dhâtṛi......	....	......	......	......	......
4552	1373	1508	857	625- 26	1450-51	4 Pramoda.....	11 Îśvara......	....	......	......	......	......
4553	1374	1509	858	626- 27	1451-52	5 Prajâpati....	12 Bahudhânya..	4 Âshâḍha....	9332	27.996	209	0.627

[1] Plavaṅga No. 41 was suppressed in the North.

TABLE I.

(*Col.* 23) *a* = *Distance of moon from sun.* (*Col.* 24) *b* = *moon's mean anomaly.* (*Col.* 25) *c* = *sun's mean anomaly.*

III. COMMENCEMENT OF THE																	
Solar year.										Luni-Solar year. (Civil day of Chaitra Śukla 1st.)							Kali.
Day and Month. A. D.	(Time of the Mesha saṅkrânti.) Week day.	By the Ârya Siddhânta. Gh.	Pa.	H.	M.	By the Sûrya Siddhânta. Gh.	Pa.	H.	M.	Day and Month. A. D.	Week day.	At Sunrise on meridian of Ujjain. Moon's Age. Lunat. parts elapsed. (*t.*)	Tithis elapsed.	*a.*	*b.*	*c.*	
13	14	15		17		15a		17a		19	20	21	22	23	24	25	1
27 Mar. (86)..	2 Mon....	5	19	2	7	9	31	3	48	27 Mar. (86)..	2 Mon....	200	.600	26	462	279	4521
26 Mar. (86)..	3 Tues....	20	50	8	20	25	2	10	1	15 Mar. (75)..	6 Fri.....	172	.516	9902	309	248	4522
26 Mar. (85)..	4 Wed....	36	21	14	32	40	34	16	14	4 Mar. (63)..	3 Tues....	35	.105	9778	156	217	4523
26 Mar. (85)..	5 Thur...	51	52	20	45	56	6	22	26	23 Mar. (82)..	2 Mon....	29	.087	9812	92	269	4524
27 Mar. (86)..	0 Sat....	7	24	2	57	11	37	4	39	13 Mar. (72)..	0 Sat.....	146	.438	27	976	241	4525
26 Mar. (86)..	1 Sun....	22	55	9	10	27	9	10	51	2 Mar. (62)..	5 Thur...	275	.825	241	860	213	4526
26 Mar. (85)..	2 Mon....	38	26	15	22	42	40	17	4	21 Mar. (80)..	4 Wed....	282	.846	276	795	264	4527
26 Mar. (85)..	3 Tues....	53	57	21	35	58	12	23	17	10 Mar. (69)..	1 Sun.....	182	.546	151	643	233	4528
27 Mar. (86)..	5 Thur...	9	29	3	47	13	43	5	29	27 Feb. (58)..	5 Thur...	179	.537	27	490	202	4529
26 Mar. (86)..	6 Fri.....	25	0	10	0	29	15	11	42	17 Mar. (77)..	4 Wed....	265	.795	62	426	253	4530
26 Mar. (85)..	0 Sat.....	40	31	16	12	44	46	17	54	6 Mar. (65)..	1 Sun.....	216	.648	9937	273	223	4531
26 Mar. (85)..	1 Sun....	56	2	22	25	†0	18	†0	7	25 Mar. (84)..	0 Sat.....	248	.744	9972	209	274	4532
27 Mar. (86)..	3 Tues....	11	34	4	37	15	49	6	20	14 Mar. (73)..	4 Wed....	37	.111	9848	56	243	4533
26 Mar. (86)..	4 Wed....	27	5	10	50	31	21	12	32	3 Mar. (63)..	2 Mon....	151	.453	62	940	215	4534
26 Mar. (85)..	5 Thur...	42	36	17	2	46	52	18	45	22 Mar. (81)..	1 Sun.....	139	.417	97	876	266	4535
26 Mar. (85)..	6 Fri.....	58	7	23	15	†2	24	†0	57	12 Mar. (71)..	6 Fri.....	311	.933	311	759	238	4536
27 Mar. (86)..	1 Sun....	13	39	5	27	17	55	7	10	1 Mar. (60)..	3 Tues....	242	.726	187	606	207	4537
26 Mar. (86)..	2 Mon....	29	10	11	40	33	27	13	23	19 Mar. (79)..	2 Mon....	324	972	221	542	259	4538
26 Mar. (85)..	3 Tues....	44	41	17	52	48	58	19	35	8 Mar. (67).	6 Fri.....	327	.981	97	390	228	4539
27 Mar. (86)..	5 Thur...	0	12	0	5	4	30	1	48	26 Mar. (85)..	4 Wed....	70	.210	9793	289	276	4540
27 Mar. (86)..	6 Fri.....	15	44	6	17	20	1	8	1	16 Mar. (75)..	2 Mon....	272	.816	8	173	248	4541
26 Mar. (86)..	0 Sat.....	31	15	12	30	35	33	14	13	4 Mar. (64)..	6 Fri.....	42	.126	9883	20	218	4542
26 Mar. (85)..	1 Sun....	46	46	18	42	51	4	20	26	23 Mar. (82)..	5 Thur...	19	.057	9918	956	269	4543
27 Mar. (86)..	3 Tues....	2	17	0	55	6	36	2	38	13 Mar. (72)..	3 Tues....	154	.462	132	840	241	4544
27 Mar. (86)..	4 Wed....	17	49	7	7	22	8	8	51	2 Mar. (61)..	0 Sat.....	21	.063	8	687	210	4545
26 Mar. (86)..	5 Thur...	33	20	13	20	37	39	15	4	20 Mar. (80)..	6 Fri.....	85	.255	43	623	261	4546
26 Mar. (85)..	6 Fri.....	48	51	19	32	53	11	21	16	9 Mar. (68)..	3 Tues....	84	.252	9918	470	230	4547
27 Mar. (86)..	1 Sun....	4	22	1	45	8	42	3	29	26 Feb. (57)..	0 Sat.....	65	.195	9794	317	200	4548
27 Mar. (86)..	2 Mon....	19	54	7	57	24	14	9	41	17 Mar. (76)..	6 Fri.....	109	.327	9829	253	251	4549
26 Mar. (86)..	3 Tues....	35	25	14	10	39	45	15	54	6 Mar. (66)..	4 Wed....	290	.870	43	137	223	4550
26 Mar. (85)..	4 Wed....	50	56	20	22	55	17	22	7	25 Mar. (84)..	3 Tues....	280	.840	78	73	274	4551
27 Mar. (86)..	6 Fri.....	6	27	2	35	10	48	4	19	14 Mar. (73)..	0 Sat.....	25	.075	9953	920	243	4552
27 Mar. (86)..	0 Sat.....	21	59	8	47	26	20	10	32	4 Mar. (63)..	5 Thur...	177	.531	168	803	215	4553

† See footnote p. liii above.

TABLE I.

Lunation-parts = 10,000*ths of a circle. A tithi* = $^1/_{30}$*th of the moon's synodic revolution.*

I. CONCURRENT YEAR.								II. ADDED LUNAR MONTHS.				
						Samvatsara.		True.				
Kali.	Śaka.	Chaitrâdi. Vikrama.	Meshâdi (Solar) year in Bengal.	Kollam.	A. D.	Luni-Solar cycle. (Southern.)	Bṛihaspati cycle (Northern) current at Mesha saṅkrânti.	Name of month.	Time of the preceding saṅkrânti expressed in: Lunation parts. (*t.*)	Time of the preceding saṅkrânti expressed in: Tithis.	Time of the succeeding saṅkrânti expressed in: Lunation parts. (*t.*)	Time of the succeeding saṅkrânti expressed in: Tithis.
1	2	3	3a	4	5	6	7	8	9	10	11	12
4554	1375	1510	859	627–28	*1452–53	6 Aṅgiras	13 Pramâthin					
4555	1376	1511	860	628–29	1453–54	7 Śrîmukha	14 Vikrama					
4556	1377	1512	861	629–30	1454–55	8 Bhâva	15 Vṛisha	3 Jyeshṭha	9764	29.292	338	1.014
4557	1378	1513	862	630–31	1455–56	9 Yuvan	16 Chitrabhânu					
4558	1379	1514	863	631–32	*1456–57	10 Dhâtṛi	17 Subhânu	8 Kârttika	9971	29.913	84	0.252
4559	1380	1515	864	632–33	1457–58	11 Îśvara	18 Târaṇa					
4560	1381	1516	865	633–34	1458–59	12 Bahudhânya	19 Pârthiva					
4561	1382	1517	866	634–35	1459–60	13 Pramâthin	20 Vyaya	5 Śrâvaṇa	9750	29.250	485	1.455
4562	1383	1518	867	635–36	*1460–61	14 Vikrama	21 Sarvajit					
4563	1384	1519	868	636–37	1461–62	15 Vṛisha	22 Sarvadhârin					
4564	1385	1520	869	637–38	1462–63	16 Chitrabhânu	23 Virodhin	4 Âshâḍha	9836	29.508	626	1.878
4565	1386	1521	870	638–39	1463–64	17 Subhânu	24 Vikṛita					
4566	1387	1522	871	639–40	*1464–65	18 Târaṇa	25 Khara					
4567	1388	1523	872	640–41	1465–66	19 Pârthiva	26 Nandana	1 Chaitra	9712	29.136	21	0.063
4568	1389	1524	873	641–42	1466–67	20 Vyaya	27 Vijaya					
4569	1390	1525	874	642–43	1467–68	21 Sarvajit	28 Jaya	6 Bhâdrapada	9983	29.949	433	1.299
4570	1391	1526	875	643–44	*1468–69	22 Sarvadhârin	29 Manmatha					
4571	1392	1527	876	644–45	1469–70	23 Virodhin	30 Durmukha					
4572	1393	1528	877	645–46	1470–71	24 Vikṛita	31 Hemalamba	4 Âshâḍha	9342	28.026	164	0.492
4573	1394	1529	878	646–47	1471–72	25 Khara	32 Vilamba					
4574	1395	1530	879	647–48	*1472–73	26 Nandana	33 Vikârin					
4575	1396	1531	880	648–49	1473–74	27 Vijaya	34 Śârvari	3 Jyeshṭha	9959	29.877	507	1.521
4576	1397	1532	881	649–50	1474–75	28 Jaya	35 Plava					
4577	1398	1533	882	650–51	1475–76	29 Manmatha	36 Subhakṛit	7 Âśvina 11 *Mâgha* (*Ksh.*) 12 Phâlguna	9902 16 9990	29.706 0.048 29.970	121 9990 131	0.363 29.970 0.393
4578	1399	1534	883	651–52	*1476–77	30 Durmukha	37 Śobhana					
4579	1400	1535	884	652–53	1477–78	31 Hemalamba	38 Krodhin					
4580	1401	1536	885	653–54	1478–79	32 Vilamba	39 Viśvâvasu	5 Śravaṇa	9712	29.136	516	1.548
4581	1402	1537	886	654–55	1479–80	33 Vikârin	40 Parâbhava					
4582	1403	1538	887	655–56	*1480–81	34 Śârvari	41 Plavaṅga					
4583	1404	1539	888	656–57	1481–82	35 Plava	42 Kîlaka	4 Âshâḍha	9974	29.922	661	1.983
4584	1405	1540	889	657–58	1482–83	36 Śubhakṛit	43 Saumya					

TABLE I.

(*Col.* 23) *a* = *Distance of moon from sun.* (*Col.* 24) *b* = *moon's mean anomaly.* (*Col.* 25) *c* = *sun's mean anomaly.*

III. COMMENCEMENT OF THE																	
Solar year.										Luni-Solar year. (Civil day of Chaitra Śukla 1st.)							Kali.
Day and Month A. D.	(Time of the Mesha saṅkrânti.)									Day and Month A. D.	Week day.	At Sunrise on meridian of Ujjain.					
	Week day.	By the Ârya Siddhânta.				By the Sûrya Siddhânta.						Moon's Age.					
		Gh.	Pa.	H.	M.	Gh.	Pa.	H.	M.			Lunat. parts elapsed. (*t.*)	Tithis elapsed.	*a.*	*b.*	*c.*	
13	14	15		17		15a		17a		19	20	21	22	23	24	25	1
26 Mar. (86)..	1 Sun....	37	30	15	0	41	51	16	44	22 Mar. (82)..	4 Wed....	202	.606	202	739	267	4554
26 Mar. (85)..	2 Mon....	53	1	21	12	57	23	22	57	11 Mar. (70)..	1 Sun....	146	.438	78	586	236	4555
27 Mar. (86)..	4 Wed....	8	32	3	25	12	54	5	10	28 Feb. (59)..	5 Thur...	154	.462	9954	434	205	4556
27 Mar. (86)..	5 Thur...	24	4	9	37	28	26	11	22	19 Mar. (78)..	4 Wed....	230	.690	9988	370	256	4557
26 Mar. (86)..	6 Fri.....	39	35	15	50	43	57	17	35	7 Mar. (67)..	1 Sun....	142	.426	9864	217	225	4558
26 Mar. (85)..	0 Sat.....	55	6	22	2	59	29	23	48	26 Mar. (85)..	0 Sat.....	155	.465	9899	153	277	4559
27 Mar. (86)..	2 Mon....	10	37	4	15	15	0	6	0	16 Mar. (75)..	5 Thur...	284	.852	113	36	249	4560
27 Mar. (86)..	3 Tues....	26	9	10	27	30	32	12	13	5 Mar. (64)..	2 Mon....	36	.108	9989	884	218	4561
26 Mar. (86)..	4 Wed....	41	40	16	40	46	3	18	25	23 Mar. (83)..	1 Sun....	36	.108	23	820	269	4562
26 Mar. (85)..	5 Thur...	57	11	22	52	†1	35	†0	38	13 Mar. (72)..	6 Fri.....	244	.732	238	703	241	4563
27 Mar. (86)..	0 Sat.....	12	42	5	5	17	6	6	51	2 Mar. (61)..	3 Tues....	212	.636	114	550	210	4564
27 Mar. (86)..	1 Sun....	28	14	11	17	32	38	13	3	21 Mar. (80)..	2 Mon....	301	.903	148	486	262	4565
26 Mar. (86)..	2 Mon....	43	45	17	30	48	10	19	16	9 Mar. (69)..	6 Fri.....	285	.855	24	334	231	4566
26 Mar. (85)..	3 Tues....	59	16	23	42	†3	41	†1	28	26 Feb. (57)..	3 Tues....	170	.510	9900	181	200	4567
27 Mar. (86)..	5 Thur...	14	47	5	55	19	13	7	41	17 Mar. (76)..	2 Mon....	168	.504	9934	117	251	4568
27 Mar. (86)..	6 Fri.....	30	19	12	7	34	44	13	54	7 Mar. (66)..	0 Sat.....	290	.870	149	0	223	4569
26 Mar. (86)..	0 Sat.....	45	50	18	20	50	16	20	6	25 Mar. (85)..	6 Fri.....	268	.804	183	936	274	4570
27 Mar. (86)..	2 Mon....	1	21	0	32	5	47	2	19	14 Mar. (73)..	3 Tues ...	62	.186	59	783	244	4571
27 Mar. (86)..	3 Tues....	16	52	6	45	21	19	8	31	4 Mar. (63)..	1 Sun....	293	.879	273	667	216	4572
27 Mar. (86)..	4 Wed....	32	24	12	57	36	50	14	44	22 Mar. (81)..	6 Fri.....	51	.153	9969	567	264	4573
26 Mar. (86)..	5 Thur...	47	55	19	10	52	22	20	57	10 Mar. (70).	3 Tues....	57	.171	9845	414	233	4574
27 Mar. (86)..	0 Sat.....	3	26	1	22	7	53	3	9	27 Feb. (58)..	0 Sat.....	4	.012	9721	261	203	4575
27 Mar. (86)..	1 Sun....	18	57	7	35	23	25	9	22	18 Mar. (77)..	6 Fri.....	27	.081	9755	197	254	4576
}27 Mar. (86)..	2 Mon....	34	29	13	47	38	56	15	35	8 Mar. (67) .	4 Wed....	178	.534	9970	80	226	4577
26 Mar. (86)..	3 Tues....	50	0	20	0	54	28	21	47	26 Mar. (86)..	3 Tues....	160	.480	4	17	277	4578
27 Mar. (86)..	5 Thur...	5	31	2	12	9	59	4	0	16 Mar. (75)..	1 Sun....	276	.828	219	900	249	4579
27 Mar. (86)..	6 Fri.....	21	2	8	25	25	31	10	12	5 Mar. (64)..	5 Thur...	95	.285	94	747	218	4580
27 Mar. (86)..	0 Sat.....	36	34	14	37	41	2	16	25	24 Mar. (83)..	4 Wed....	141	.423	129	683	269	4581
26 Mar. (86)..	1 Sun....	52	5	20	50	56	34	22	38	12 Mar. (72)..	1 Sun....	118	.354	5	531	239	4582
27 Mar. (86)..	3 Tues....	7	36	3	2	12	5	4	50	1 Mar. (60)..	5 Thur...	119	.357	9880	378	208	4583
27 Mar. (86)..	4 Wed....	23	7	9	15	27	37	11	3	20 Mar. (79)..	4 Wed....	184	.552	9915	314	259	4584

† See footnote p. liii above.

TABLE I.

Lunation-parts = 10,000*ths of a circle.* *A tithi* = $^1/_{30}$*th of the moon's synodic revolution.*

I. CONCURRENT YEAR.								II. ADDED LUNAR MONTHS.				
						Samvatsara.		True.				
Kali.	Śaka.	Chaitrâdi. Vikrama.	Meshâdi (Solar) year in Bengal.	Kollam.	A. D.	Luni-Solar cycle. (Southern.)	Bṛihaspati cycle (Northern) current at Mesha saṅkrânti.	Name of month.	Time of the preceding saṅkrânti expressed in		Time of the succeeding saṅkrânti expressed in	
									Lunation parts. (*t.*)	Tithis.	Lunation parts. (*t.*)	Tithis.
1	2	3	3a	4	5	6	7	8	9	10	11	12
4585	1406	1541	890	658-59	1483- 84	37 Śobhana	44 Sâdhâraṇa	...	...	...	...	...
4586	1407	1542	891	659-60	*1484- 85	38 Krodhin	45 Virodhakṛit	1 Chaitra	9679	29.037	41	0.123
4587	1408	1543	892	660-61	1485- 86	39 Viśvâvasu	46 Paridhâvin	...	...	...	...	...
4588	1409	1544	893	661-62	1486- 87	40 Parâbhava	47 Pramâdin	5 Śrâvaṇa	9259	27.777	48	0.144
4589	1410	1545	894	662-63	1487- 88	41 Plavaṅga	48 Ânanda	...	...	...	...	...
4590	1411	1546	895	663-64	*1488- 89	42 Kîlaka	49 Râkshasa	...	...	...	...	...
4591	1412	1547	896	664-65	1489- 90	43 Saumya,	50 Anala	4 Âshâḍha	9451	28.353	170	0.510
4592	1413	1548	897	665-66	1490- 91	44 Sâdhâraṇa	51 Piṅgala	...	...	...	...	...
4593	1414	1549	898	666-67	1491- 92	45 Virodhakṛit	52 Kâlayukta	...	...	...	...	...
4594	1415	1550	899	667-68	*1492- 93	46 Paridhâvin	53 Siddhârthin	2 Vaiśâkha	9575	28.725	94	0.282
4595	1416	1551	900	668-69	1493- 94	47 Pramâdin	54 Raudra	...	...	...	...	...
4596	1417	1552	901	669-70	1494- 95	48 Ânanda	55 Durmati	6 Bhâdrapada	9569	28.707	75	0.225
4597	1418	1553	902	670-71	1495- 96	49 Râkshasa	56 Dundubhi	...	...	...	...	...
4598	1419	1554	903	671-72	*1496- 97	50 Anala	57 Rudhirodgârin	...	...	...	...	...
4599	1420	1555	904	672-73	1497- 98	51 Piṅgala	58 Raktâksha	5 Śrâvaṇa	9689	29.067	478	1.434
4600	1421	1556	905	673-74	1498- 99	52 Kâlayukta	59 Krodhana	...	...	...	...	...
4601	1422	1557	906	674-75	1499-500	53 Siddhârthin	60 Kshaya	...	...	...	...	...
4602	1423	1558	907	675-76	*1500- 1	54 Randra	1 Prabhava	3 Jyeshṭha	9590	28.770	167	0.501
4603	1424	1559	908	676-77	1501- 2	55 Durmati	2 Vikhava	...	...	...	...	...
4604	1425	1560	909	677-78	1502- 3	56 Dundubhi	3 Śukla	...	...	...	...	...
4605	1426	1561	910	678-79	1503- 4	57 Rudhirodgârin	4 Pramoda	1 Chaitra	9653	28.959	4	0.012
4606	1427	1562	911	679-80	*1504- 5	58 Raktâksha	5 Prajâpati	...	...	...	...	...
4607	1428	1563	912	680-81	1505- 6	59 Krodhana	6 Aṅgiras	5 Śrâvaṇa	9225	27.675	28	0.084
4608	1429	1564	913	681-82	1506- 7	60 Kshaya	7 Śrîmukha	...	...	...	...	...
4609	1430	1565	914	682-83	1507- 8	1 Prabhava	8 Bhâva	...	...	...	...	...
4610	1431	1566	915	683-84	*1508- 9	2 Vibhava	9 Yuvan	4 Âshâḍha	9630	28.890	269	0.807
4611	1432	1567	916	684-85	1509- 10	3 Śukla	10 Dhâtṛi	...	...	...	...	...
4612	1433	1568	917	685-86	1510- 11	4 Pramoda	11 Îśvara	...	...	...	...	...
4613	1434	1569	918	686-87	1511- 12	5 Prajâpati	12 Bahudhânya	2 Vaiśâkha	9551	28.653	137	0.411
4614	1435	1570	919	687-88	*1512- 13	6 Aṅgiras	13 Pramâthin	...	...	...	...	...
4615	1436	1571	920	688-89	1513- 14	7 Śrîmukha	14 Vikrama	6 Bhâdrapada	9574	28.722	145	0.435
4616	1437	1572	921	689-90	1514- 15	8 Bhâva	15 Vṛisha [1])	...	...	...	...	...
4617	1438	1573	922	690-91	1515- 16	9 Yuvan	17 Subhânu	...	...	...	...	...

[1]) Chitrabhânu, No. 16, was suppressed in the north.

TABLE I.

(*Col.* 23) *a* = *Distance of moon from sun.* (*Col.* 24) *b* = *moon's mean anomaly.* (*Col.* 25) *c* = *sun's mean anomaly.*

III. COMMENCEMENT OF THE

Solar year.										Luni-Solar year. (Civil day of Chaitra Śukla 1st.)							Kali.
Day and Month A. D.	(Time of the Mesha saṅkrânti.)									Day and Month A. D.	Week day.	At Sunrise on meridian of Ujjain.					
	Week day.	By the Ârya Siddhânta.				By the Sûrya Siddhânta.						Moon's Age.					
		Gh.	Pa.	H.	M.	Gh.	Pa.	H.	M.			Lunat. parts elapsed. (*t*.)	Tithis elapsed.	*a*.	*b*.	*c*.	
13	14	15		17		15a		17a		19	20	21	22	23	24	25	1
27 Mar. (86)..	5 Thur...	38	39	15	27	43	8	17	15	9 Mar. (68)..	1 Sun....	49	.147	9791	161	228	4585
26 Mar. (86)..	6 Fri.....	54	10	21	40	58	40	23	28	27 Feb. (58)..	6 Fri.....	187	.561	5	44	200	4586
27 Mar. (86)..	1 Sun....	9	41	3	52	14	12	5	41	17 Mar. (76)..	5 Thur...	162	.486	40	980	251	4587
27 Mar. (86)..	2 Mon....	25	12	10	5	29	43	11	53	7 Mar. (66)..	3 Tues....	289	.867	254	864	223	4588
27 Mar. (86)..	3 Tues....	40	44	16	17	45	15	18	6	26 Mar. (85)..	2 Mon....	296	.888	289	800	275	4589
26 Mar. (86)..	4 Wed....	56	15	22	30	†0	46	†0	18	14 Mar. (74)..	6 Fri.....	194	.582	165	647	244	4590
27 Mar. (86)..	6 Fri.....	11	46	4	42	16	18	6	31	3 Mar. (62)..	3 Tues....	187	.561	40	494	212	4591
27 Mar. (86)..	0 Sat.....	27	17	10	55	31	49	12	44	22 Mar. (81)..	2 Mon....	275	.825	75	430	264	4592
27 Mar. (86)..	1 Sun....	42	49	17	7	47	21	18	56	11 Mar. (70)..	6 Fri.....	229	.687	9951	277	234	4593
26 Mar. (86)..	2 Mon....	58	20	23	20	†2	52	†1	9	28 Feb. (59)..	3 Tues....	68	.204	9826	125	203	4594
27 Mar. (86)..	4 Wed....	13	51	5	32	18	24	7	21	18 Mar. (77)..	2 Mon....	54	.162	9861	61	254	4595
27 Mar. (86)..	5 Thur...	29	22	11	45	33	55	13	34	8 Mar. (67)..	0 Sat.....	166	.498	75	944	226	4596
27 Mar. (86)..	6 Fri.....	44	54	17	57	49	27	19	47	27 Mar. (86)..	6 Fri.....	155	.465	110	880	277	4597
27 Mar. (86)..	1 Sun....	0	25	0	10	4	58	1	59	16 Mar. (76)..	4 Wed....	324	.972	324	764	249	4598
27 Mar. (86)..	2 Mon....	15	56	6	22	20	30	8	12	5 Mar. (64)..	1 Sun....	250	.750	200	611	218	4599
27 Mar. (86)..	3 Tues....	31	27	12	35	36	1	14	25	23 Mar. (82)..	6 Fri.....	26	.078	9896	511	267	4600
27 Mar. (86)..	4 Wed....	46	59	18	47	51	33	20	37	12 Mar. (71)..	3 Tues....	21	.063	9772	358	236	4601
27 Mar. (87)..	6 Fri.....	2	30	1	0	7	4	2	50	1 Mar. (61)..	1 Sun....	268	.804	9986	241	208	4602
27 Mar. (86)..	0 Sat.....	18	1	7	12	22	36	9	2	20 Mar. (79)..	0 Sat.....	288	.864	21	181	259	4603
27 Mar. (86)..	1 Sun....	33	32	13	25	38	7	15	15	9 Mar. (68)..	4 Wed....	61	.183	9896	29	228	4604
27 Mar. (86)..	2 Mon....	49	4	19	37	53	39	21	28	27 Feb. (58)..	2 Mon....	180	.540	111	912	200	4605
27 Mar. (87)..	4 Wed....	4	35	1	50	9	10	3	40	17 Mar. (77)..	1 Sun....	171	.513	145	848	252	4606
27 Mar. (86)..	5 Thur...	20	6	8	2	24	42	9	53	6 Mar. (65)..	5 Thur...	31	.093	21	695	221	4607
27 Mar. (86)..	6 Fri.....	35	37	14	15	40	13	16	5	25 Mar. (84)..	4 Wed....	93	.279	56	631	272	4608
27 Mar. (86)..	0 Sat.....	51	9	20	27	55	45	22	18	14 Mar. (73)..	1 Sun....	90	270	9931	479	241	4609
27 Mar. (87)..	2 Mon....	6	40	2	40	11	17	4	31	2 Mar. (62)..	5 Thur...	74	.222	9807	326	210	4610
27 Mar. (86)..	3 Tues....	22	11	8	52	26	48	10	43	21 Mar. (80)..	4 Wed....	122	.366	9842	262	262	4611
27 Mar. (86)..	4 Wed....	37	42	15	5	42	20	16	56	11 Mar. (70)..	2 Mon....	307	.921	56	145	234	4612
27 Mar. (86)..	5 Thur...	53	14	21	17	57	51	23	8	28 Feb. (59)..	6 Fri.....	68	.204	9932	992	203	4613
27 Mar. (87)..	0 Sat.....	8	45	3	30	13	23	5	21	18 Mar. (78)..	5 Thur...	45	.135	9967	928	254	4614
27 Mar. (86)..	1 Sun....	24	16	9	42	28	54	11	34	8 Mar. (67)..	3 Tues....	192	.576	181	812	226	4615
27 Mar. (86)..	2 Mon....	39	47	15	55	44	26	17	46	27 Mar. (86)..	2 Mon. ..	217	.651	216	748	277	4616
27 Mar. (86)..	3 Tues....	55	19	22	7	59	57	23	59	16 Mar. (75)..	6 Fri.....	152	.456	91	595	247	4617

† See footnote p. liii above.

TABLE I.

Lunation-parts = 10,000*ths of a circle. A tithi* = 1/30*th of the moon's synodic revolution.*

I. CONCURRENT YEAR.								II. ADDED LUNAR MONTHS.				
						Samvatsara.		True.				
									Time of the preceding saṅkrânti expressed in		Time of the succeeding saṅkrânti expressed in	
Kali.	Saka.	Chaitrâdi. Vikrama.	Meshâdi (Solar) year in Bengal.	Kollam.	A. D.	Luni-Solar cycle. (Southern.)	Bṛihaspati cycle (Northern) current at Mesha saṅkrânti.	Name of month.	Lunation parts. (*t*.)	Tithis.	Lunation parts. (*t*.)	Tithis.
1	2	3	3a	4	5	6	7	8	9	10	11	12
4618	1439	1574	923	691- 92	*1516-17	10 Dhâtṛi	18 Târaṇa	5 Śrâvaṇa	9756	29.268	458	1.374
4619	1440	1575	924	692- 93	1517-18	11 Îśvara	19 Pârthiva					
4620	1441	1576	925	693- 94	1518-19	12 Bahudhânya	20 Vyaya					
4621	1442	1577	926	694- 95	1519-20	13 Pramâthin	21 Sarvajit	3 Jyeshṭha	9665	28.995	334	1.002
4622	1443	1578	927	695- 96	*1520-21	14 Vikrama	22 Sarvadhârin					
4623	1444	1579	928	696- 97	1521-22	15 Vṛisha	23 Virodhin	8 Kârttika	9961	29.883	12	0.036
								9 *Mârgaś.*(*Ksh.*)	12	0.036	9911	29.733
4624	1445	1580	929	697- 98	1522-23	16 Chitrabhânu	24 Vikṛita	2 Vaiśâkha	9989	29.967	558	1.674
4625	1446	1581	930	698- 99	1523-24	17 Subhânu	25 Khara					
4626	1447	1582	931	699-700	*1524-25	18 Târaṇa	26 Nandana	6 Bhâdrapada	9992	29.976	616	1.848
4627	1448	1583	932	700- 1	1525-26	19 Pârthiva	27 Vijaya					
4628	1449	1584	933	701- 2	1526-27	20 Vyaya	28 Jaya					
4629	1450	1585	934	702- 3	1527-28	21 Sarvajit	29 Manmatha	4 Âshâḍha	9818	29.454	450	1.350
4630	1451	1586	935	703- 4	*1528-29	22 Sarvadhârin	30 Durmukha					
4631	1452	1587	936	704- 5	1529-30	23 Virodhin	31 Hemalamba					
4632	1453	1588	937	705- 6	1530-31	24 Vikṛita	32 Vilamba	2 Vaiśâkha	9517	28.551	103	0.309
4633	1454	1589	938	706- 7	1531-32	25 Khara	33 Vikârin					
4634	1455	1590	939	707- 8	*1532-33	26 Nandana	34 Śârvari	6 Bhâdrapada	9532	28.596	249	0.747
4635	1456	1591	940	708- 9	1533-34	27 Vijaya	35 Plava					
4636	1457	1592	941	709- 10	1534-35	28 Jaya	36 Śubhakṛit					
4637	1458	1593	942	710- 11	1535-36	29 Manmatha	37 Śobhana	5 Śrâvaṇa	9916	29.748	519	1.557
4638	1459	1594	943	711- 12	*1536-37	30 Durmukha	38 Krodhin					
4639	1460	1595	944	712- 13	1537-38	31 Hemalamba	39 Viśvâvasu					
4640	1461	1596	945	713- 14	1538-39	32 Vilamba	40 Parâbhava	3 Jyeshṭha	9649	28.947	408	1.224
4641	1462	1597	946	714- 15	1539-40	33 Vikârin	41 Plavaṅga					
4642	1463	1598	947	715- 16	*1540-41	34 Śârvari	42 Kîlaka	7 Âśvina	9704	29.112	60	0.180
								10 *Pausha*(*Ksh.*)	96	0.288	9948	29.844
4643	1464	1599	948	716- 17	1541-42	35 Plava	43 Saumya	1 Chaitra	9847	29.541	65	0.195
4644	1465	1600	949	717- 18	1542-43	36 Śubhakṛit	44 Sâdhâraṇa					
4645	1466	1601	950	718- 19	1543-44	37 Śobhana	45 Virodhakṛit	5 Śrâvaṇa	9348	28.044	18	0.054
4646	1467	1602	951	719- 20	*1544-45	38 Krodhin	46 Paridhâvin					
4647	1468	1603	952	720- 21	1545-46	39 Visvâvasu	47 Pramâdin					
4648	1469	1604	953	721- 22	1546-47	40 Parâbhava	48 Ânanda	4 Âshâḍha	9927	29.781	637	1.911

TABLE I.

(*Col.* 23) *a* = *Distance of moon from sun.* (*Col.* 24) *b* = *moon's mean anomaly.* (*Col.* 25) *c* = *sun's mean anomaly.*

III. COMMENCEMENT OF THE

Solar year.										Luni-Solar year. (Civil day of Chaitra Śukla 1st.)							Kali.
Day and Month A. D.	(Time of the Mesha saṅkrânti.)									Day and Month A. D.	Week day.	At Sunrise on meridian of Ujjain.					
	Week day.	By the Ârya Siddhânta.				By the Sûrya Siddhânta.						Moon's Age.					
		Gh.	Pa.	H.	M.	Gh.	Pa.	H.	M.			Lunat. parts elapsed. (*t.*)	Tithis elapsed.	*a.*	*b.*	*c.*	
13	**14**	**15**		**17**		**15a**		**17a**		**19**	**20**	**21**	**22**	**23**	**24**	**25**	**1**
27 Mar. (87)..	5 Thur...	10	50	4	20	15	29	6	11	4 Mar. (64)..	3 Tues....	158	.474	9967	442	216	4618
27 Mar. (86)..	6 Fri.....	26	21	10	32	31	0	12	24	23 Mar. (82)..	2 Mon....	239	.717	2	378	267	4619
27 Mar. (86)..	0 Sat.....	41	52	16	45	46	32	18	37	12 Mar. (71)..	6 Fri.....	155	.465	9877	226	236	4620
27 Mar. (86)..	1 Sun....	57	24	22	57	†2	3	†0	49	2 Mar. (61)..	4 Wed....	323	.969	92	109	208	4621
27 Mar. (87)..	3 Tues....	12	55	5	10	17	35	7	2	20 Mar. (80)..	3 Tues....	306	.918	126	45	259	4622
}27 Mar. (86)..	4 Wed....	28	26	11	22	33	6	13	15	9 Mar. (68)..	0 Sat.....	53	.159	2	892	229	4623
27 Mar. (86)..	5 Thur...	43	57	17	35	48	38	19	27	27 Feb. (58)..	5 Thur...	221	.663	216	776	201	4624
27 Mar. (86)..	6 Fri.....	59	29	23	47	†4	9	†1	40	18 Mar. (77)..	4 Wed....	255	.765	251	712	252	4625
27 Mar. (87)..	1 Sun....	15	0	6	0	19	41	7	52	6 Mar. (66)..	1 Sun....	217	.651	127	559	221	4626
27 Mar. (86)..	2 Mon....	30	31	12	12	35	12	14	5	25 Mar. (84)..	0 Sat.....	306	.918	161	495	272	4627
27 Mar. (86)..	3 Tues....	46	2	18	25	50	44	20	18	14 Mar. (73)..	4 Wed....	294	.882	37	342	241	4628
28 Mar. (87)..	5 Thur...	1	34	0	37	6	15	2	30	3 Mar. (62)..	1 Sun....	185	.555	9913	189	211	4629
27 Mar (87)..	6 Fri.....	17	5	6	50	21	47	8	43	21 Mar. (81)..	0 Sat.....	187	.561	9947	125	262	4630
27 Mar. (86)..	0 Sat.....	32	36	13	2	37	19	14	55	11 Mar. (70)..	5 Thur...	310	.930	162	9	234	4631
27 Mar. (86)..	1 Sun....	48	7	19	15	52	50	21	8	28 Feb. (59)..	2 Mon....	70	.210	37	856	203	4632
28 Mar. (87)..	3 Tues....	3	39	1	27	8	22	3	21	19 Mar. (78)..	1 Sun....	77	.231	72	792	254	4633
27 Mar. (87)..	4 Wed....	19	10	7	40	23	53	9	33	8 Mar. (68)..	6 Fri.....	301	.903	286	675	226	4634
27 Mar. (86)..	5 Thur...	34	41	13	52	39	25	15	46	26 Mar. (85)..	4 Wed....	58	.174	9982	575	275	4635
27 Mar. (86)..	6 Fri.....	50	12	20	5	54	56	21	58	15 Mar. (74)..	1 Sun....	64	.192	9858	422	244	4636
28 Mar. (87)..	1 Sun....	5	44	2	17	10	28	4	11	4 Mar. (63)..	5 Thur...	15	.045	9734	270	213	4637
27 Mar. (87)..	2 Mon....	21	15	8	30	25	59	10	24	22 Mar. (82)..	4 Wed....	44	.132	9769	206	265	4638
27 Mar. (86)..	3 Tues....	36	46	14	42	41	31	16	36	12 Mar. (71)..	2 Mon....	197	.591	9983	89	236	4639
27 Mar. (86)..	4 Wed....	52	17	20	55	57	2	22	49	2 Mar. (61)..	0 Sat.....	315	.945	197	973	208	4640
28 Mar. (87)..	6 Fri.....	7	49	3	7	12	34	5	2	21 Mar. (80)..	6 Fri.....	296	.888	232	909	260	4641
}27 Mar. (87)..	0 Sat.....	23	20	9	20	28	5	11	14	9 Mar. (69)..	3 Tues....	108	.324	108	756	229	4642
27 Mar. (86)..	1 Sun....	38	51	15	32	43	37	17	27	26 Feb. (57)..	0 Sat.....	41	.123	9983	603	198	4643
27 Mar. (86)..	2 Mon....	54	22	21	45	59	8	23	39	17 Mar. (76)..	6 Fri.....	124	.372	18	539	249	4644
28 Mar. (87)..	4 Wed....	9	54	3	57	14	40	5	52	6 Mar. (65)..	3 Tues....	127	.381	9894	386	218	4645
27 Mar. (87)..	5 Thur...	25	25	10	10	30	11	12	5	24 Mar. (84)..	2 Mon....	194	.582	9928	322	270	4646
27 Mar. (86)..	6 Fri	40	56	16	22	45	43	18	17	13 Mar. (72)..	6 Fri.....	67	.201	9804	169	239	4647
27 Mar. (86)..	0 Sat.....	56	27	22	35	†1	14	0	30	3 Mar. (62)..	4 Wed....	206	.618	18	53	211	4648

† See footnote p. liii above.

TABLE I.

Lunation-parts = 10,000*ths of a circle. A tithi* = 1/30*th of the moon's synodic revolution.*

I. CONCURRENT YEAR.								II. ADDED LUNAR MONTHS.				
						Samvatsara.		True.				
Kali.	Śaka.	Chaitrâdi. Vikrama.	Meshâdi (Solar) year in Bengal.	Kollam.	A. D.	Luni-Solar cycle. (Southern.)	Bṛihaspati cycle (Northern) current at Mesha saṅkrânti.	Name of month.	Time of the preceding saṅkrânti expressed in		Time of the succeeding saṅkrânti expressed in	
									Lunation parts. (*t*.)	Tithis.	Lunation parts. (*t*.)	Tithis.
1	2	3	3a	4	5	6	7	8	9	10	11	12
4649	1470	1605	954	722-23	1547-48	41 Plavaṅga	49 Râkshasa					
4650	1471	1606	955	723-24	*1548-49	42 Kîlaka	50 Anala					
4651	1472	1607	956	724-25	1549-50	43 Saumya	51 Piṅgala	2 Vaiśâkha	9559	28.677	75	0.225
4552	1473	1608	957	725-26	1550-51	44 Sâdhâraṇa	52 Kâlayukta					
4653	1474	1609	958	726-27	1551-52	45 Virodhakṛit	53 Siddhârthin	6 Bhâdrapada	9533	28.599	121	0.363
4654	1475	1610	959	727-28	*1552-53	46 Paridhâvin	54 Raudra					
4655	1476	1611	960	728-29	1553-54	47 Pramâdin	55 Durmati					
4656	1477	1612	961	729-30	1554-55	48 Ânanda	56 Dundubhi	4 Âshâḍha	9435	28.305	115	0.345
4657	1478	1613	962	730-31	1555-56	49 Râkshasa	57 Rudhirodgârin					
4658	1479	1614	963	731-32	*1556-57	50 Anala	58 Raktâksha					
4659	1480	1615	964	732-33	1557-58	51 Piṅgala	59 Krodhana	3 Jyeshṭha	9611	28.833	394	1.182
4660	1481	1616	965	733-34	1558-59	52 Kâlayukta	60 Kshaya					
4661	1482	1617	966	734-35	1559-60	53 Siddhârthin	1 Prabhava	7 Âśvina	9864	29.592	63	0.189
4662	1483	1618	967	735-36	*1560-61	54 Raudra	2 Vibhava					
4663	1484	1619	968	736-37	1561-62	55 Durmati	3 Śukla					
4664	1485	1620	969	737-38	1562-63	56 Dundubhi	4 Pramoda	5 Śrâvaṇa	9580	28.740	147	0.441
4665	1486	1621	970	738-39	1563-64	57 Rudhirodgârin	5 Prajâpati					
4666	1487	1622	971	739-40	*1564-65	58 Raktâksha	6 Aṅgiras					
4667	1488	1623	972	740-41	1565-66	59 Krodhana	7 Śrîmukha	4 Âshâḍha	9938	29.814	753	2.259
4668	1489	1624	973	741-42	1566-67	60 Kshaya	8 Bhâva					
4669	1490	1625	974	742-43	1567-68	1 Prabhava	9 Yuvan					
4670	1491	1626	975	743-44	*1568-69	2 Vibhava	10 Dhâtṛi	2 Vaiśâkha	9671	29.013	129	0.387
4671	1492	1627	976	744-45	1569-70	3 Śukla	11 Îśvara					
4672	1493	1628	977	745-46	1570-71	4 Pramoda	12 Bahudhânya	6 Bhâdrapada	9628	28.884	126	0.378
4673	1494	1629	978	746-47	1571-72	5 Prajâpati	13 Pramâthin					
4674	1495	1630	979	747-48	*1572-73	6 Aṅgiras	14 Vikrama					
4675	1496	1631	980	748-49	1573-74	7 Śrîmukha	15 Vṛisha	4 Âshâḍha	9477	28.431	258	0.774
4676	1497	1632	981	749-50	1574-75	8 Bhâva	16 Chitrabhânu					
4677	1498	1633	982	750-51	1575-76	9 Yuvan	17 Subhânu					
4678	1499	1634	983	751-52	*1576-77	10 Dhâtṛi	18 Târaṇa	3 Jyeshṭha	9631	28.893	352	1.056
4679	1500	1635	984	752-53	1577-78	11 Îśvara	19 Pârthiva					
4680	1501	1636	985	753-54	1578-79	12 Bahudhânya	20 Vyaya	7 Âśvina	9645	28.935	19	0.057
4681	1502	1637	986	754-55	1579-80	13 Pramâthin	21 Sarvajit					

TABLE I.

(*Col.* 23) a = *Distance of moon from sun.* (*Col.* 24) b = *moon's mean anomaly.* (*Col.* 25) c = *sun's mean anomaly.*

III. COMMENCEMENT OF THE																	
Solar year.										Luni-Solar year. (Civil day of Chaitra Śukla 1st.)							Kali.
Day and Month A. D.	(Time of the Mesha saṅkrânti.)									Day and Month A. D.	Week day.	At Sunrise on meridian of Ujjain.					
	Week day.	By the Ârya Siddhânta.				By the Sûrya Siddhânta.						Moon's Age.		*a.*	*b.*	*c.*	
		Gh.	Pa.	H.	M.	Gh.	Pa.	H.	M.			Lunat. parts elapsed. (*t.*)	Tithis elapsed.				
13	14	15		17		15a		17a		19	20	21	22	23	24	25	1
28 Mar. (87)..	2 Mon....	11	59	4	47	16	46	6	42	22 Mar. (81)..	3 Tues....	183	.549	53	989	262	4649
27 Mar. (87)..	3 Tues....	27	30	11	0	32	17	12	55	11 Mar. (71)..	1 Sun....	306	.918	267	872	234	4650
27 Mar. (86)..	4 Wed....	43	1	17	12	47	49	19	8	28 Feb. (59)..	5 Thur...	149	.447	143	720	203	4651
27 Mar. (86)..	5 Thur...	58	32	23	25	†3	21	†1	20	19 Mar. (78)..	4 Wed....	202	.606	178	656	255	4652
28 Mar. (87)..	0 Sat.....	14	4	5	37	18	52	7	33	8 Mar. (67)..	1 Sun....	191	.573	53	503	224	4653
27 Mar. (87)..	1 Sun....	29	35	11	50	34	24	13	45	26 Mar. (86)..	0 Sat.....	281	.843	88	439	275	4654
27 Mar. (86)..	2 Mon....	45	6	18	2	49	55	19	58	15 Mar. (74)..	4 Wed....	240	.720	9964	286	244	4655
28 Mar. (87)..	4 Wed....	0	37	0	15	5	27	2	11	4 Mar. (63)..	1 Sun....	86	.258	9840	133	214	4656
28 Mar. (87)..	5 Thur...	16	9	6	27	20	58	8	23	23 Mar. (82)..	0 Sat.....	73	.219	9874	69	265	4657
27 Mar. (87)..	6 Fri.....	31	40	12	40	36	30	14	36	12 Mar. (72)..	5 Thur...	188	.564	89	953	237	4658
27 Mar. (86)..	0 Sat.....	47	11	18	52	52	1	20	48	2 Mar. (61)..	3 Tues....	325	.975	303	836	209	4659
28 Mar. (87)..	2 Mon....	2	42	1	5	7	33	3	1	20 Mar. (79)..	1 Sun....	⊙ −1	−.003	9999	736	257	4660
28 Mar. (87)..	3 Tues....	18	14	7	17	23	4	9	14	10 Mar. (69)..	6 Fri.....	258	.774	213	619	229	4661
27 Mar. (87)..	4 Wed....	33	45	13	30	38	36	15	26	27 Mar. (87)..	4 Wed....	33	.099	9909	519	278	4662
27 Mar. (86)..	5 Thur...	49	16	19	42	54	7	21	39	16 Mar. (75)..	1 Sun....	29	.087	9785	366	247	4663
28 Mar. (87)..	0 Sat.....	4	47	1	55	9	39	3	52	6 Mar. (65)..	6 Fri.....	280	.840	9999	250	219	4664
28 Mar. (87)..	1 Sun....	20	19	8	7	25	10	10	4	25 Mar. (84)..	5 Thur...	303	.909	34	186	270	4665
27 Mar. (87)..	2 Mon....	35	50	14	20	40	42	16	17	13 Mar (73)..	2 Mon....	79	.237	9910	33	239	4666
27 Mar. (86)..	3 Tues....	51	21	20	32	56	13	22	29	3 Mar. (62)..	0 Sat.....	196	.588	124	917	211	4667
28 Mar. (87)..	5 Thur...	6	52	2	45	11	45	4	42	22 Mar. (81)..	6 Fri.....	287	.861	159	852	262	4668
28 Mar. (87)..	6 Fri.....	22	24	8	57	27	16	10	55	11 Mar. (70)..	3 Tues....	41	.123	34	700	232	4669
27 Mar. (87)..	0 Sat.....	37	55	15	10	42	48	17	7	28 Feb. (59)..	0 Sat.....	12	.036	9910	547	201	4670
27 Mar. (86)..	1 Sun....	53	26	21	22	58	19	23	20	18 Mar. (77)..	6 Fri.....	101	.303	9945	483	252	4671
28 Mar. (87)..	3 Tues....	8	57	3	35	13	51	5	32	7 Mar. (66)..	3 Tues....	84	.252	9820	330	221	4672
28 Mar. (87)..	4 Wed....	24	29	9	47	29	23	11	45	26 Mar. (85)..	2 Mon....	134	.402	9855	266	273	4673
27 Mar. (87)..	5 Thur...	40	0	16	0	44	54	17	58	15 Mar. (75)..	0 Sat.....	322	.966	69	150	245	4674
27 Mar. (86)..	6 Fri.....	55	31	22	12	†0	26	†0	10	4 Mar. (63)..	4 Wed....	84	.252	9945	997	214	4675
28 Mar. (87)..	1 Sun....	11	2	4	25	15	57	6	23	23 Mar. (82)..	3 Tues....	62	.186	9980	933	265	4676
28 Mar. (87)..	2 Mon....	26	34	10	37	31	29	12	35	13 Mar. (72)..	1 Sun....	206	.618	194	816	237	4677
27 Mar. (87)..	3 Tues....	42	5	16	50	47	0	18	48	1 Mar. (61)..	5 Thur...	92	.276	70	664	206	4678
27 Mar. (86)..	4 Wed....	57	36	23	2	†2	32	†1	1	20 Mar. (79)..	4 Wed....	162	.486	105	600	257	4679
28 Mar. (87)..	6 Fri.....	13	7	5	15	18	3	7	13	9 Mar. (68)..	1 Sun....	166	.498	9980	447	227	4680
28 Mar. (87).	0 Sat.....	28	39	11	27	33	35	13	26	28 Mar. (87)..	0 Sat.....	250	.750	15	383	278	4681

† See footnote p. liii above. ⊙ See Text. Art. 101 above, para. 2.

TABLE I.

Lunation-parts = 10,000*ths of a circle. A tithi* = 1/30*th of the moon's synodic revolution.*

I. CONCURRENT YEAR.								II. ADDED LUNAR MONTHS.				
						Samvatsara.		True.				
Kali.	Śaka.	Chaitrâdi. Vikrama.	Meshâdi (Solar) year in Bengal.	Kollam.	A. D.	Luni-Solar cycle. (Southern.)	Bṛihaspati cycle (Northern) current at Mesha saṅkrânti.	Name of month.	Time of the preceding saṅkrânti expressed in: Lunation parts. (*l.*)	Time of the preceding saṅkrânti expressed in: Tithis.	Time of the succeeding saṅkrânti expressed in: Lunation parts. (*l.*)	Time of the succeeding saṅkrânti expressed in: Tithis.
1	2	3	3a	4	5	6	7	8	9	10	11	12
4682	1503	1638	987	755-56	*1580- 81	14 Vikrama.....	22 Sarvadhârin...	......	......	......	......	......
4683	1504	1639	988	756-57	1581- 82	15 Vṛisha.......	23 Virodhin.....	5 Śrâvaṇa.....	9752	29.256	347	1.041
4684	1505	1640	989	757-58	1582- 83	16 Chitrabhânu..	24 Vikṛita.....	......	......	......	......	......
4685	1506	1641	990	758-59	1583- 84	17 Subhânu.....	25 Khara.....	......	......	......	......	......
4686	1507	1642	991	759-60	*1584- 85	18 Târaṇa......	26 Nandana.....	4 Âshâḍha....	9894	29.682	772	2.316
4687	1508	1643	992	760-61	1585- 86	19 Parthiva.....	27 Vijaya.....	......	......	......	......	......
4688	1509	1644	993	761-62	1586- 87	20 Vyaya......	28 Jaya.....	......	......	......	......	......
4689	1510	1645	994	762-63	1587- 88	21 Sarvajit.....	29 Manmatha....	2 Vaiśâkha....	9894	29.682	280	0.840
4690	1511	1646	995	763-64	*1588- 89	22 Sarvadhârin..	30 Durmukha....	......	......	......	......	......
4691	1512	1647	996	764-65	1589- 90	23 Virodhin.....	31 Hemalamba...	6 Bhâdrapada..	9806	29.418	233	0.699
4692	1513	1648	997	765-66	1590- 91	24 Vikṛita......	32 Vilamba.....	......	......	......	......	......
4693	1514	1649	998	766-67	1591- 92	25 Khara.......	33 Vikârin.....	......	......	......	......	......
4694	1515	1650	999	767-68	*1592- 93	26 Nandana.....	34 Śârvari......	4 Âshaḍha....	9443	28.329	307	0.921
4695	1516	1651	1000	768-69	1593- 94	27 Vijaya.......	35 Plava.....	......	......	......	......	......
4696	1517	1652	1001	769-70	1594- 95	28 Jaya.........	36 Śubhakṛit....	......	......	......	......	......
4697	1518	1653	1002	770-71	1595- 96	29 Manmatha....	37 Śobhana......	3 Jyeshṭha....	9753	29.259	375	1.125
4698	1519	1654	1003	771-72	*1596- 97	30 Durmukha...	38 Krodhin.....	......	......	......	......	......
4699	1520	1655	1004	772-73	1597- 98	31 Hemalamba...	39 Viśvâvasu....	7 Âśvina......	9728	29.184	21	0.063
4700	1521	1656	1005	773-74	1598- 99	32 Vilamba.....	40 Parâbhava....	......	......	......	......	......
4701	1522	1657	1006	774-75	1599-600	33 Vikârin......	41 Plavaṅga....	......	......	......	......	......
4702	1523	1658	1007	775-76	*1600- 1	34 Śârvari......	42 Kîlaka [1])....	5 Śrâvaṇa.....	9934	29.802	515	1.545
4703	1524	1659	1008	776-77	1601- 2	35 Plava........	44 Sâdhâraṇa....	......	......	......	......	......
4704	1525	1660	1009	777-78	1602- 3	36 Śubhakṛit....	45 Virodhakṛit...	......	......	......	......	......
4705	1526	1661	1010	778-79	1603- 4	37 Sobhana......	46 Paridhâvin...	4 Âshâḍha....	9907	29.721	731	2.193
4706	1527	1662	1011	779-80	*1604- 5	38 Krodhin.....	47 Pramâdin....	......	......	......	......	......
4707	1528	1663	1012	780-81	1605- 6	39 Viśvâvasu....	48 Ânanda.....	......	......	......	......	......
4708	1529	1664	1013	781-82	1606- 7	40 Parâbhava....	49 Râkshasa.....	1 Chaitra.....	9789	29.367	60	0.180
4709	1530	1665	1014	782-83	1607- 8	41 Plavaṅga.....	50 Anala.....	......	......	......	......	......
4710	1531	1666	1015	783-84	*1608- 9	42 Kîlaka.......	51 Piṅgala......	6 Bhâdrapada..	9997	29.991	415	1.245
4711	1532	1667	1016	784-85	1609- 10	43 Saumya......	52 Kâlayukta....	......	......	......	......	......
4712	1533	1668	1017	785-86	1610- 11	44 Sâdhâraṇa....	53 Siddhârthin...	......	......	......	......	......
4713	1534	1669	1018	786-87	1611- 12	45 Virodhakṛit...	54 Raudra......	4 Âshâḍha....	9417	28.251	287	0.861
4714	1535	1670	1019	787-88	*1612- 13	46 Paridhâvin...	55 Durmati.....	......	......	......	......	......

[1]) Saumya, No. 43, was suppressed in the north.

TABLE I.

(*Col.* 23) *a* = *Distance of moon from sun.* (*Col.* 24) *b* = *moon's mean anomaly.* (*Col.* 25) *c* = *sun's mean anomaly.*

III. COMMENCEMENT OF THE																	
Solar year.										Luni-Solar year. (Civil day of Chaitra Śukla 1st.)							Kali.
Day and Month A. D.	(Time of the Mesha saṅkrânti.) Week day.	By the Ârya Siddhânta.				By the Sûrya Siddhânta.				Day and Month A. D.	Week day.	At Sunrise on meridian of Ujjain. Moon's Age. Lunat. parts elapsed. (*t.*)	Tithis elapsed.	*a.*	*b.*	*c.*	
		Gh.	Pa.	H.	M.	Gh.	Pa.	H.	M.								
13	14	15		17		15a		17a		19	20	21	22	23	24	25	1
27 Mar. (87)..	1 Sun....	44	10	17	40	49	6	19	38	16 Mar. (76)..	4 Wed....	169	.507	9890	230	247	4682
27 Mar. (86)..	2 Mon....	59	41	23	52	†4	38	†1	51	5 Mar. (64)..	1 Sun....	⊙−27	−.081	9766	77	216	4683
28 Mar. (87)..	4 Wed....	15	12	6	5	20	9	8	4	25 Mar. (84)..	1 Sun....	322	.966	139	49	270	4684
28 Mar. (87)..	5 Thur...	30	44	12	17	35	41	14	16	14 Mar. (73)..	5 Thur...	70	.210	15	897	239	4685
27 Mar. (87)..	6 Fri.....	46	15	18	30	51	12	20	29	3 Mar. (63)..	3 Tues....	235	.705	230	780	211	4686
28 Mar. (87)..	1 Sun....	1	46	0	42	6	44	2	42	22 Mar. (81)..	2 Mon....	267	.801	264	716	263	4687
28 Mar. (87)..	2 Mon....	17	17	6	55	22	15	8	54	11 Mar. (70)..	6 Fri.....	226	.678	140	563	232	4688
28 Mar. (87)..	3 Tues....	32	49	13	7	37	47	15	7	28 Feb. (59)..	3 Tues....	233	.699	16	411	201	4689
27 Mar. (87)..	4 Wed....	48	20	19	20	53	18	21	19	18 Mar. (78)..	2 Mon....	305	.915	50	347	252	4690
28 Mar. (87)..	6 Fri.....	3	51	1	32	8	50	3	32	7 Mar. (66)..	6 Fri.....	198	.594	9926	194	222	4691
28 Mar. (87)..	0 Sat.....	19	22	7	45	24	21	9	45	26 Mar. (85)..	5 Thur...	203	.609	9961	130	273	4692
28 Mar. (87)..	1 Sun....	34	54	13	57	39	53	15	57	16 Mar. (75)..	3 Tues....	327	.981	175	13	245	4693
27 Mar. (87)..	2 Mon....	50	25	20	10	55	25	22	10	4 Mar. (64)..	0 Sat.....	85	.255	51	860	214	4694
28 Mar. (87)..	4 Wed....	5	56	2	22	10	56	4	22	23 Mar. (82)..	6 Fri.....	91	.273	85	796	265	4695
28 Mar. (87)..	5 Thur...	21	27	8	35	26	28	10	35	13 Mar. (72)..	4 Wed....	313	.939	300	680	237	4696
28 Mar. (87)..	6 Fri.....	36	59	14	47	41	59	16	48	2 Mar. (61)..	1 Sun....	293	.879	175	527	206	4697
27 Mar. (87)..	0 Sat.....	52	30	21	0	57	31	23	0	19 Mar. (79)..	6 Fri.....	73	.219	9871	427	255	4698
28 Mar. (87)..	2 Mon....	8	1	3	12	13	2	5	13	8 Mar. (67)..	3 Tues....	26	.078	9747	274	224	4699
28 Mar. (87)..	3 Tues....	23	32	9	25	28	34	11	25	27 Mar. (86)..	2 Mon....	59	.177	9782	210	275	4700
28 Mar. (87)..	4 Wed....	39	4	15	37	44	5	17	38	17 Mar. (76)..	0 Sat.....	214	.642	9996	94	247	4701
27 Mar. (87)..	5 Thur...	54	35	21	50	59	37	23	51	6 Mar. (66)..	5 Thur...	331	.993	210	977	219	4702
28 Mar. (87)..	0 Sat.....	10	6	4	2	15	8	6	3	25 Mar. (84)..	4 Wed....	312	.936	245	913	271	4703
28 Mar. (87)..	1 Sun....	25	37	10	15	30	40	12	16	14 Mar. (73)..	1 Sun....	121	.363	121	760	240	4704
28 Mar. (87)..	2 Mon....	41	9	16	27	46	11	18	29	3 Mar. (62)..	5 Thur...	51	.153	9997	607	209	4705
27 Mar. (87)..	3 Tues....	56	40	22	40	†1	43	†0	41	21 Mar. (81)..	4 Wed....	133	.399	31	543	260	4706
28 Mar. (87)..	5 Thur...	12	11	4	52	17	14	6	54	10 Mar. (69)..	1 Sun....	136	.408	9907	391	229	4707
28 Mar. (87)..	6 Fri.....	27	42	11	5	32	46	13	6	27 Feb. (58)..	5 Thur...	66	.198	9783	238	199	4708
28 Mar. (87)..	0 Sat.....	43	14	17	17	48	17	19	19	18 Mar. (77)..	4 Wed....	82	.246	9817	174	250	4709
27 Mar. (87)..	1 Sun....	58	45	23	30	†3	49	†1	32	7 Mar. (67)..	2 Mon....	223	.669	32	57	222	4710
28 Mar. (87)..	3 Tues....	14	16	5	42	19	20	7	44	26 Mar. (85)..	1 Sun....	200	.600	66	993	273	4711
28 Mar. (87)..	4 Wed....	29	47	11	55	34	52	13	57	16 Mar. (75)..	6 Fri.....	323	.969	281	877	245	4712
28 Mar. (87)..	5 Thur...	45	19	18	7	50	23	20	9	5 Mar. (64)..	3 Tues....	160	.480	156	724	214	4713
28 Mar. (87)..	0 Sat.....	0	50	0	20	5	55	2	22	23 Mar. (88)..	2 Mon....	213	.639	191	660	265	4714

† See footnote p. liii above. ⊙ See Text. Art. 101 above, para. 2.

TABLE I.

Lunation-parts = 10,000*ths of a circle. A tithi* = 1/30*th of the moon's synodic revolution.*

I. CONCURRENT YEAR.								II. ADDED LUNAR MONTHS.				
						Samvatsara.		True.				
Kali.	Śaka.	Chaitrâdi. Vikrama.	Meshâdi (Solar) year in Bengal.	Kollam.	A. D.	Luni-Solar cycle. (Southern.)	Bṛihaspati cycle (Northern) current at Mesha saṅkrânti.	Name of month.	Time of the preceding saṅkrânti expressed in		Time of the succeeding saṅkrânti expressed in	
									Lunation parts. (*t.*)	Tithis.	Lunation parts. (*t.*)	Tithis.
1	2	3	3a	4	5	6	7	8	9	10	11	12
4715	1536	1671	1020	788- 89	1613-14	47 Pramâdin....	56 Dundubhi....	....	.....	......	.....	......
4716	1537	1672	1021	789- 90	1614-15	48 Ânanda......	57 Rudhirodgârin	3 Jyeshṭha....	9943	29.829	495	1.485
4717	1538	1673	1022	790- 91	1615-16	49 Râkshasa.....	58 Raktâksha....	....	.....	......	.....	......
4718	1539	1674	1023	791- 92	*1616-17	50 Anala.......	59 Krodhana....	7 Âśvina......	9880	29.640	119	0.357
4719	1540	1675	1024	792- 93	1617-18	51 Piṅgala......	60 Kshaya......	....	.....	......	.....	......
4720	1541	1676	1025	793- 94	1618-19	52 Kâlayukta....	1 Prabhava.....	....	.....	......	.....	......
4721	1542	1677	1026	794- 95	1619-20	53 Siddhârthin..	2 Vibhava......	5 Śrâvaṇa.....	9825	29.475	600	1.800
4722	1543	1678	1027	795- 96	*1620-21	54 Raudra......	3 Śukla........	....	.....	......	.....	......
4723	1544	1679	1028	796- 97	1621-22	55 Durmati.....	4 Pramoda.....	....	.....	......	.....	......
4724	1545	1680	1029	797- 98	1622-23	56 Dundubhi....	5 Prajâpati.....	4 Âshâḍha....	9967	29.901	720	2.160
4725	1546	1681	1030	798- 99	1623-24	57 Rudhirodgârin	6 Âṅgiras......	....	.....	......	.....	......
4726	1547	1682	1031	799-800	*1624-25	58 Raktâksha....	7 Śrîmukha....	....	.....	......	.....	......
4727	1548	1683	1032	800- 1	1625-26	59 Krodhana....	8 Bhâva.......	1 Chaitra.....	9791	29.373	132	0.396
4728	1549	1684	1033	801- 2	1626-27	60 Kshaya......	9 Yuvan.......	....	.....	......	.....	......
4729	1550	1685	1034	802- 3	1627-28	1 Prabhava.....	10 Dhâtṛi.......	5 Śrâvaṇa.....	9368	28.104	116	0.348
4730	1551	1686	1035	803- 4	*1628-29	2 Vibhava......	11 Îśvara.......	....	.....	......	.....	......
4731	1552	1687	1036	804- 5	1629-30	3 Śukla........	12 Bahudhânya..	....	.....	......	.....	......
4732	1553	1688	1037	805- 6	1630-31	4 Pramoda.....	13 Pramâthin...	4 Âshâḍha....	9469	28.407	249	0.747
4733	1554	1689	1038	806- 7	1631-32	5 Prajâpati.....	14 Vikrama.....	....	.....	......	.....	......
4734	1555	1690	1039	807- 8	*1632-33	6 Âṅgiras......	15 Vṛisha......	....	.....	......	.....	......
4735	1556	1691	1040	808- 9	1633-34	7 Śrîmukha....	16 Chitrabhânu..	2 Vaiśâkha....	9651	28.953	123	0.369
4736	1557	1692	1041	809- 10	1634-35	8 Bhâva.......	17 Subhanu.....	....	.....	......	.....	......
4737	1558	1693	1042	810- 11	1635-36	9 Yuvan.......	18 Târaṇa.......	6 Bhâdrapada..	9620	28.860	77	0.231
4738	1559	1694	1043	811- 12	*1636-37	10 Dhâtṛi.......	19 Pârthiva.....	....	.....	......	.....	......
4739	1560	1695	1044	812- 13	1637-38	11 Îśvara.......	20 Vyaya.......	....	.....	......	.....	......
4740	1561	1696	1045	813- 14	1638-39	12 Bahudhânya..	21 Sarvajit......	5 Śrâvaṇa.....	9805	29.415	593	1.779
4741	1562	1697	1046	814- 15	1639-40	13 Pramâthin....	22 Sarvadhârin..	....	.....	......	.....	......
4742	1563	1698	1047	815- 16	*1640-41	14 Vikrama.....	23 Virodhin.....	....	.....	......	.....	......
4743	1564	1699	1048	816- 17	1641-42	15 Vṛisha.......	24 Vikṛita......	3 Jyeshṭha....	9602	28.806	152	0.456
4744	1565	1700	1049	817- 18	1642-43	16 Chitrabhânu..	25 Khara.......	....	.....	......	.....	......
4745	1566	1701	1050	818- 19	1643-44	17 Subhânu.....	26 Nandana.....	....	.....	......	.....	......
4746	1567	1702	1051	819- 20	*1644-45	18 Târaṇa.......	27 Vijaya.......	1 Chaitra.....	9749	29.247	114	0.342
4747	1568	1703	1052	820- 21	1645-46	19 Pârthiva....	28 Jaya........	....	.....	......	.....	......

TABLE I.

(*Col.* 23) *a* = *Distance of moon from sun.* (*Col.* 24) *b* = *moon's mean anomaly.* (*Col.* 25) *c* = *sun's mean anomaly.*

III. COMMENCEMENT OF THE																	
Solar year.										Luni-Solar year. (Civil day of Chaitra Śukla 1st.)							Kali.
Day and Month A. D.	(Time of the Mesha saṅkrânti.)									Day and Month A. D.	Week day.	At Sunrise on meridian of Ujjain.					
	Week day.	By the Ârya Siddhânta.				By the Sûrya Siddhânta.						Moon's Age.					
		Gh.	Pa.	H.	M.	Gh.	Pa.	H.	M.			Lunat. parts elapsed. (*t.*)	Tithis elapsed.	*a.*	*b.*	*c.*	
13	14	15		17		15a		17a		19	20	21	22	23	24	25	1
28 Mar. (87)..	1 Sun....	16	21	6	32	21	26	8	35	12 Mar. (71)..	6 Fri.....	201	.603	67	507	235	4715
28 Mar. (87)..	2 Mon....	31	52	12	45	36	58	14	47	1 Mar. (60)..	3 Tues....	196	.588	9942	354	204	4716
28 Mar. (87)..	3 Tues....	47	24	18	57	52	30	21	0	20 Mar. (79)..	2 Mon....	253	.759	9977	290	255	4717
28 Mar. (88)..	5 Thur...	2	55	1	10	8	1	3	12	8 Mar. (68)..	6 Fri.....	101	.303	9853	138	224	4718
28 Mar. (87)..	6 Fri.....	18	26	7	22	23	33	9	25	27 Mar. (86)..	5 Thur...	92	.276	9888	74	276	4719
28 Mar. (87)..	0 Sat.....	33	57	13	35	39	4	15	38	17 Mar. (76)..	3 Tues....	204	.612	102	957	248	4720
28 Mar. (87)..	1 Sun....	49	29	19	47	54	36	21	50	6 Mar. (65)..	0 Sat.....	⊙−14	−.042	9977	804	217	4721
28 Mar. (88)..	3 Tues....	5	0	2	0	10	7	4	3	24 Mar. (84)..	6 Fri.....	12	.036	12	740	268	4722
28 Mar. (87)..	4 Wed....	20	31	8	12	25	39	10	15	14 Mar. (73)..	4 Wed....	268	.804	226	624	240	4723
28 Mar. (87)..	5 Thur...	36	2	14	25	41	10	16	28	3 Mar. (62)..	1 Sun....	269	.807	102	471	209	4724
28 Mar. (87)..	6 Fri.....	51	34	20	37	56	42	22	41	21 Mar. (80)..	6 Fri.....	39	.117	9798	371	258	4725
28 Mar. (88)..	1 Sun....	7	5	2	50	12	13	4	53	10 Mar. (70)..	4 Wed....	292	.876	12	254	230	4726
28 Mar. (87)..	2 Mon....	22	36	9	2	27	45	11	6	27 Feb. (58)..	1 Sun....	115	.345	9888	101	199	4727
28 Mar. (87)..	3 Tues....	38	7	15	15	43	16	17	19	18 Mar. (77)..	0 Sat.....	95	.285	9923	37	250	4728
28 Mar. (87)..	4 Wed....	53	39	21	27	58	48	23	31	8 Mar. (67)..	5 Thur...	211	.633	137	921	222	4729
28 Mar. (88)..	6 Fri.....	9	10	3	40	14	19	5	44	26 Mar. (86)..	4 Wed....	203	.609	172	857	273	4730
28 Mar. (87)..	0 Sat.....	24	41	9	52	29	51	11	56	15 Mar. (74)..	1 Sun....	54	.162	48	704	242	4731
28 Mar. (87)..	1 Sun....	40	12	16	5	45	22	18	9	5 Mar. (64)..	6 Fri.....	330	.990	262	588	214	4732
28 Mar. (87)..	2 Mon....	55	44	22	17	†0	54	†0	22	23 Mar. (82)..	4 Wed....	110	.330	9958	487	263	4733
28 Mar. (88)..	4 Wed....	11	15	4	30	16	25	6	34	11 Mar. (71)..	1 Sun....	94	.282	9834	335	232	4734
28 Mar. (87)..	5 Thur...	26	46	10	42	31	57	12	47	1 Mar. (60)..	6 Fri.....	328	.984	48	218	204	4735
28 Mar. (87)..	6 Fri.....	42	17	16	55	47	28	18	59	19 Mar. (78)..	4 Wed....	⊙−11	−.033	9744	118	253	4736
28 Mar. (87)..	0 Sat.....	57	49	23	7	†3	0	†1	12	9 Mar. (68)..	2 Mon....	100	.300	9958	1	225	4737
28 Mar. (88)..	2 Mon....	13	20	5	20	18	32	7	25	27 Mar. (87)..	1 Sun....	80	.240	9993	937	276	4738
28 Mar. (87)..	3 Tues....	28	51	11	32	34	3	13	37	17 Mar. (76)..	6 Fri.....	220	.660	207	821	248	4739
28 Mar. (87)..	4 Wed....	44	22	17	45	49	35	19	50	6 Mar. (65)..	3 Tues....	102	.306	83	668	217	4740
28 Mar. (87)..	5 Thur...	59	54	23	57	†5	6	†2	2	25 Mar. (84)..	2 Mon....	172	.516	118	604	268	4741
28 Mar. (88)..	0 Sat.....	15	25	6	10	20	38	8	15	13 Mar. (73)..	6 Fri.....	176	.528	9993	451	237	4742
28 Mar. (87)..	1 Sun....	30	56	12	22	36	9	14	28	2 Mar. (61)..	3 Tues....	145	.435	9869	298	207	4743
28 Mar. (87)..	2 Mon....	46	27	18	35	51	41	20	40	21 Mar. (80)..	2 Mon....	183	.549	9904	234	258	4744
29 Mar. (88)..	4 Wed....	1	59	0	47	7	12	2	53	10 Mar. (69)..	6 Fri.....	⊙−12	−.036	9779	82	227	4745
28 Mar. (88)..	5 Thur...	17	30	7	0	22	44	9	5	28 Feb. (59)..	4 Wed....	107	.321	9994	965	199	4746
28 Mar. (87)..	6 Fri.....	33	1	13	12	38	15	15	18	18 Mar. (77)..	3 Tues....	86	.258	28	901	250	4747

† See footnote p. liii above. ⊙ See Text. Art. 101 above, para. 2.

TABLE I.

Lunation-parts = 10,000*ths of a circle. A tithi* = $^1/_{30}$*th of the moon's synodic revolution.*

I. CONCURRENT YEAR.								II. ADDED LUNAR MONTHS.				
						Samvatsara.		True.				
Kali.	Śaka.	Chaitrâdi. Vikrama.	Meshâdi (Solar) year in Bengal.	Kollam.	A. D.	Luni-Solar cycle. (Southern.)	Bṛihaspati cycle (Northern) current at Mesha saṅkrânti.	Name of month.	Time of the preceding saṅkrânti expressed in Lunation parts. (t.)	Time of the preceding saṅkrânti expressed in Tithis.	Time of the succeeding saṅkrânti expressed in Lunation parts. (t.)	Time of the succeeding saṅkrânti expressed in Tithis.
1	2	3	3a	4	5	6	7	8	9	10	11	12
4748	1569	1704	1053	821-22	1646-47	20 Vyaya	29 Manmatha	5 Śrâvaṇa	9328	27.984	133	0.399
4749	1570	1705	1054	822-23	1647-48	21 Sarvajit	30 Durmukha					
4750	1571	1706	1055	823-24	*1648-49	22 Sarvadhârin	31 Hemalamba					
4751	1572	1707	1056	824-25	1649-50	23 Virodhin	32 Vilamba	4 Âshâḍha	9618	28.854	294	0.882
4752	1573	1708	1057	825-26	1650-51	24 Vikṛita	33 Vikârin					
4753	1574	1709	1058	826-27	1651-52	25 Khara	34 Śârvari					
4754	1575	1710	1059	827-28	*1652-53	26 Nandana	35 Plava	2 Vaiśâkha	9658	28.974	216	0.648
4755	1576	1711	1060	828-29	1653-54	27 Vijaya	36 Śubhakṛit					
4756	1577	1712	1061	829-30	1654-55	28 Jaya	37 Śobhana	6 Bhâdrapada	9670	29.010	219	0.657
4757	1578	1713	1062	830-31	1655-56	29 Manmatha	38 Krodhin					
4758	1579	1714	1063	831-32	*1656-57	30 Durmukha	39 Viśvâvasu					
4759	1580	1715	1064	832-33	1657-58	31 Hemalamba	40 Parâbhava	5 Śrâvaṇa	9800	29.400	552	1.656
4760	1581	1716	1065	833-34	1658-59	32 Vilamba	41 Plavaṅga					
4761	1582	1717	1066	834-35	1659-60	33 Vikârin	42 Kîlaka					
4762	1583	1718	1067	835-36	*1660-61	34 Śârvari	43 Saumya	3 Jyeshṭha	9727	29.181	343	1.029
4763	1584	1719	1068	836-37	1661-62	35 Plava	44 Sâdhâraṇa					
4764	1585	1720	1069	837-38	1662-63	36 Śubhakṛit	45 Virodhakṛit					
4765	1586	1721	1070	838-39	1663-64	37 Śobhana	46 Paridhâvin	1 Chaitra	9749	29.247	72	0.216
4766	1587	1722	1071	839-40	*1664-65	38 Krodhin	47 Pramâdin					
4767	1588	1723	1072	840-41	1665-66	39 Viśvâvasu	48 Ânanda	5 Śrâvaṇa	9319	27.957	94	0.282
4768	1589	1724	1073	841-42	1666-67	40 Parâbhava	49 Râkshasa					
4769	1590	1725	1074	842-43	1667-68	41 Plavaṅga	50 Anala					
4770	1591	1726	1075	843-44	*1668-69	42 Kîlaka	51 Piṅgala	4 Âshâḍha	9814	29.442	438	1.314
4771	1592	1727	1076	844-45	1669-70	43 Saumya	52 Kâlayukta					
4772	1593	1728	1077	845-46	1670-71	44 Sâdhâraṇa	53 Siddhârthin					
4773	1594	1729	1078	846-47	1671-72	45 Virodhakṛit	54 Raudra	2 Vaiśâkha	9616	28.848	212	0.636
4774	1595	1730	1079	847-48	*1672-73	46 Paridhâvin	55 Durmati					
4775	1596	1731	1080	848-49	1673-74	47 Pramâdin	56 Dundubhi	6 Bhâdrapada	9641	28.923	262	0.786
4776	1597	1732	1081	849-50	1674-75	48 Ânanda	57 Rudhirodgârin					
4777	1598	1733	1082	850-51	1675-76	49 Râkshasa	58 Raktâksha					
4778	1599	1734	1083	851-52	*1676-77	50 Anala,	59 Krodhana	5 Śrâvaṇa	9913	29.739	563	1.689
4779	1600	1735	1084	852-53	1677-78	51 Piṅgala	60 Kshaya					
4780	1601	1736	1085	853-54	1678-79	52 Kâlayukta	1 Prabhava					

TABLE I.

(*Col.* 23) *a* = *Distance of moon from sun.* (*Col.* 24) *b* = *moon's mean anomaly.* (*Col.* 25) *c* = *sun's mean anomaly.*

III. COMMENCEMENT OF THE

Solar year.									Luni-Solar year. (Civil day of Chaitra Śukla 1st.)						Kali.
Day and Month. A. D.	(Time of the Mesha saṅkrânti.) Week day.	By the Ârya Siddhânta.				By the Sûrya Siddhânta.			Day and Month. A. D.	Week day.	At Sunrise on meridian of Ujjain. Moon's Age. Lunat. parts elapsed. (*t.*)	Tithis elapsed.	*a.*	*b.*	*c.*	
		Gh.	Pa.	H.	M.	Gh.	Pa.	H.	M.							
13	14	15		17		15a		17a		19	20	21	22	23	24	25	1
28 Mar. (87)..	0 Sat.....	48	32	19	25	53	47	21	31	8 Mar. (67)..	1 Sun....	247	.741	243	784	222	4748
29 Mar. (88)..	2 Mon....	4	4	1	37	9	18	3	43	27 Mar. (86)..	0 Sat.....	280	.840	277	721	273	4749
28 Mar. (88)..	3 Tues....	19	35	7	50	24	50	9	56	15 Mar. (75)..	4 Wed....	235	.705	153	568	243	4750
28 Mar. (87)..	4 Wed....	35	6	14	2	40	21	16	9	4 Mar. (63)..	1 Sun ...	242	.726	29	415	212	4751
28 Mar. (87)..	5 Thur...	50	37	20	15	55	53	22	21	23 Mar. (82)..	0 Sat.....	315	.945	63	351	263	4752
29 Mar. (88)..	0 Sat.....	6	9	2	27	11	24	4	34	12 Mar. (71)..	4 Wed....	211	.633	9939	198	232	4753
28 Mar. (88)..	1 Sun....	21	40	8	40	26	56	10	46	29 Feb. (60)..	1 Sun....	⊙ −2	−.006	9815	45	202	4754
28 Mar. (87)..	2 Mon....	37	11	14	52	42	27	16	59	19 Mar. (78)..	0 Sat.....	⊙−27	−.081	9850	981	253	4755
28 Mar. (87)..	3 Tues....	52	42	21	5	57	59	23	12	9 Mar. (68)..	5 Thur...	100	.300	64	865	225	4756
29 Mar. (88)..	5 Thur...	8	14	3	17	13	30	5	24	28 Mar. (87)..	4 Wed....	107	.321	99	801	276	4757
28 Mar. (88)..	6 Fri.....	23	45	9	30	29	2	11	37	16 Mar. (76)..	1 Sun....	2	.006	9974	648	245	4758
28 Mar. (87)..	0 Sat.....	39	16	15	42	44	34	17	49	6 Mar. (65)..	6 Fri.....	302	.906	189	532	217	4759
28 Mar. (87)..	1 Sun....	54	47	21	55	†0	5	†0	2	24 Mar. (83)..	4 Wed....	84	.252	9885	431	266	4760
29 Mar. (88)..	3 Tues....	10	19	4	7	15	37	6	15	13 Mar. (72)..	1 Sun....	37	.112	9760	278	235	4761
28 Mar. (88)..	4 Wed....	25	50	10	20	31	8	12	27	2 Mar. (62)..	6 Fri.....	236	.708	9975	162	207	4762
28 Mar. (87)..	5 Thur...	41	21	16	32	46	40	18	40	21 Mar. (80)..	5 Thur...	230	.690	9	98	258	4763
28 Mar. (87)..	6 Fri.....	56	52	22	45	†2	11	†0	52	10 Mar. (69)..	2 Mon..	⊙−23	−.069	9885	945	227	4764
29 Mar. (88)..	1 Sat.....	12	24	4	57	17	43	7	5	28 Feb. (59)..	0 Sat.....	119	.357	99	829	199	4765
28 Mar. (88)..	2 Mon....	27	55	11	10	33	14	13	18	18 Mar. (78)..	6 Fri.....	134	.402	134	765	251	4766
28 Mar. (87)..	3 Tues....	43	26	17	22	48	46	19	30	7 Mar. (66)..	3 Tues....	60	.180	10	612	220	4767
28 Mar. (87)..	4 Wed....	58	57	23	35	†4	17	†1	43	26 Mar. (85)..	2 Mon....	142	.426	44	548	271	4768
29 Mar. (88)..	6 Fri.....	14	29	5	47	19	49	7	56	15 Mar. (74)..	6 Fri.....	147	.441	9920	395	240	4769
28 Mar. (88)..	0 Sat.....	30	0	12	0	35	20	14	8	3 Mar. (63)..	3 Tues....	78	.234	9796	242	209	4770
28 Mar. (87)..	1 Sun....	45	31	18	12	50	52	20	21	22 Mar. (81)..	2 Mon....	97	.293	9831	178	261	4771
29 Mar. (88)..	3 Tues....	1	2	0	25	6	23	2	33	12 Mar. (71)..	0 Sat.....	238	.714	44	62	233	4772
29 Mar. (88)..	4 Wed....	16	34	6	37	21	55	8	46	1 Mar. (60)..	4 Wed....	⊙−12	−.036	9921	909	202	4773
28 Mar. (88)..	5 Thur...	32	5	12	50	37	26	14	59	19 Mar. (80)..	3 Tues....	⊙−20	−.060	9955	845	253	4774
28 Mar. (87)..	6 Fri.....	47	36	19	2	52	58	21	11	9 Mar. (68)..	1 Sun....	172	.516	170	728	225	4775
29 Mar. (88)..	1 Sun....	3	7	1	15	8	29	3	24	28 Mar. (87)..	0 Sat.....	225	.675	204	664	276	4776
29 Mar. (88)..	2 Mon....	18	39	7	27	24	1	9	36	17 Mar. (76)..	4 Wed....	209	.627	80	512	245	4777
28 Mar. (88)..	3 Tues....	34	10	13	40	39	32	15	49	5 Mar. (65)..	1 Sun....	205	.615	9956	359	215	4778
28 Mar. (87)..	4 Wed....	49	41	19	52	55	4	22	2	24 Mar. (83)..	0 Sat.....	265	.795	9990	295	266	4779
29 Mar. (88)..	6 Fri.....	5	12	2	5	10	36	4	14	13 Mar. (72)..	4 Wed....	115	.345	9866	142	235	4780

† See footnote p. liii above. ⊙ See Text. Art. 101 above, para. 2.

TABLE I.

Lunation-parts = 10,000*ths of a circle. A tithi* = 1/30*th of the moon's synodic revolution.*

I. CONCURRENT YEAR.								II. ADDED LUNAR MONTHS.				
						Samvatsara.		True.				
Kali.	Śaka.	Chaitrâdi. Vikrama.	Meshâdi (Solar) year in Bengal.	Kollam.	A. D.	Luni-Solar cycle. (Southern.)	Bṛihaspati cycle (Northern) current at Mesha saṅkrânti.	Name of month.	Time of the preceding saṅkrânti expressed in: Lunation parts. (*t.*)	Tithis.	Time of the succeeding saṅkrânti expressed in: Lunation parts. (*t.*)	Tithis.
1	2	3	3a	4	5	6	7	8	9	10	11	12
4781	1602	1737	1086	854–55	1679– 80	53 Siddhârthin...	2 Vibhava......	3 Jyeshṭha....	9755	29.265	470	1.410
4782	1603	1738	1087	855–56	*1680– 81	54 Raudra......	3 Śukla....	....	....	....	....	....
4783	1604	1739	1088	856–57	1681– 82	55 Durmati.....	4 Pramoda....	7 Âśvina...... 10 *Pausha* (*Ksk.*)	9788 94	29.364 0.282	110 9936	0.330 29.808
4784	1605	1740	1089	857–58	1682– 83	56 Dundubhi....	5 Prajâpati.....	1 Chaitra.....	9920	29.760	99	0.297
4785	1606	1741	1090	858–59	1683– 84	57 Rudhirodgârin	6 Aṅgiras......	....	....	....	....	....
4786	1607	1742	1091	859–60	*1684– 85	58 Raktâksha....	7 Śrîmukha	5 Srâvaṇa.....	9394	28.182	82	0.246
4787	1608	1743	1092	860–61	1685– 86	59 Krodhana....	8 Bhâva [1])	....	....	....	....	....
4788	1609	1744	1093	861–62	1686– 87	60 Kshaya......	10 Dhâtṛi.......	....	....	....	....	....
4789	1610	1745	1094	862–63	1687– 88	1 Prabhava.....	11 Îśvara.......	4 Ashâḍha....	9971	29.913	634	1.902
4790	1611	1746	1095	863–64	*1688– 89	2 Vibhava......	12 Bahudhânya..	....	....	....	....	....
4791	1612	1747	1096	864–65	1689– 90	3 Śukla........	13 Pramâthin....	....	....	....	....	....
4792	1613	1748	1097	865–66	1690– 91	4 Pramoda.....	14 Vikrama.....	2 Vaiśâkha....	9613	28.839	169	0.507
4793	1614	1749	1098	866–67	1691– 92	5 Prajâpati.....	15 Vṛisha.......	....	....	....	....	....
4794	1615	1750	1099	867–68	*1692– 93	6 Aṅgiras......	16 Chitrabhânu..	6 Bhâdrapada..	9609	28.827	216	0.648
4795	1616	1751	1100	868–69	1693– 94	7 Śrîmukha....	17 Subhânu.....	....	....	....	....	....
4796	1617	1752	1101	869–70	1694– 95	8 Bhâva.......	18 Târaṇa......	....	....	....	....	....
4797	1618	1753	1102	870–71	1695– 96	9 Yuvan.......	19 Pârthiva.....	4 Âshâḍha....	9459	28.377	99	0.297
4798	1619	1754	1103	871–72	*1696– 97	10 Dhâtṛi.......	20 Vyaya.......	....	....	....	....	....
4799	1620	1755	1104	872–73	1697– 98	11 Îśvara.......	21 Sarvajit......	....	....	....	....	....
4800	1621	1756	1105	873–74	1698– 99	12 Bahudhânya..	22 Sarvadhârin...	3 Jyeshṭha....	9714	29.142	511	1.533
4801	1622	1757	1106	874–75	1699–700	13 Pramâthin ..	23 Virodhin.....	....	....	....	....	....
4802	1623	1758	1107	875–76	*1700– 1	14 Vikrama.....	24 Vikṛita......	7 Âśvina......	9772	29.316	147	0.441
4803	1624	1759	1108	876–77	1701– 2	15 Vṛisha.......	25 Khara.......	....	....	....	....	....
4804	1625	1760	1109	877–78	1702– 3	16 Chitrabhânu..	26 Nandana.....	....	....	....	....	....
4805	1626	1761	1110	878–79	1703– 4	17 Subhânu.....	27 Vijaya.......	5 Śrâvaṇa.....	9574	28.722	168	0.504
4806	1627	1762	1111	879–80	*1704– 5	18 Târaṇa......	28 Jaya........	....	....	....	....	....
4807	1628	1763	1112	880–81	1705– 6	19 Pârthiva.....	29 Manmatha....	....	....	....	....	....
4808	1629	1764	1113	881–82	1706– 7	20 Vyaya.......	30 Durmukha....	3 Jyeshṭha....	9270	27.810	30	0.090
4809	1630	1765	1114	882–83	1707– 8	21 Sarvajit......	31 Hemalamba..	....	....	....	....	....
4810	1631	1766	1115	883–84	*1708– 9	22 Sarvadhârin..	32 Vilamba......	....	....	....	....	....
4811	1632	1767	1116	884–85	1709– 10	23 Virodhin.....	33 Vikârin......	2 Vaiśâkha....	9706	29.118	187	0.561

[1]) Yuvan, No. 9, was suppressed in the north.

TABLE I.

(*Col.* 23) *a* = *Distance of moon from sun.* (*Col.* 24) *b* = *moon's mean anomaly.* (*Col.* 25) *c* = *sun's mean anomaly.*

III. COMMENCEMENT OF THE

Solar year.										Luni-Solar year. (Civil day of Chaitra Śukla 1st.)							
Day and Month. A. D.	(Time of the Mesha saṅkrânti.)									Day and Month. A. D.	Week day.	At Sunrise on meridian of Ujjain.					Kali.
	Week day.	By the Ârya Siddhânta.				By the Sûrya Siddhânta.						Moon's Age.		a.	b.	c.	
		Gh.	Pa.	H.	M.	Gh.	Pa.	H.	M.			Lunat. parts elapsed. (t.)	Tithis elapsed.				
13	14	15		17		15a		17a		19	20	21	22	23	24	25	1
29 Mar. (88)..	0 Sat.....	20	44	8	17	26	7	10	27	3 Mar. (62)..	2 Mon....	245	.735	80	26	207	4781
28 Mar. (88)..	1 Sun....	36	15	14	30	41	39	16	39	21 Mar. (81)..	1 Sun....	222	.666	115	962	258	4782
}28 Mar. (87)..	2 Mon....	51	46	20	42	57	10	22	52	10 Mar. (69)..	5 Thur...	1	.003	9991	809	228	4783
29 Mar. (88)..	4 Wed....	7	17	2	55	12	42	5	5	28 Feb. (59)..	3 Tues....	217	.651	205	694	199	4784
29 Mar. (88)..	5 Thur...	22	49	9	7	28	13	11	17	19 Mar. (78)..	2 Mon....	279	.837	240	628	251	4785
28 Mar. (88)..	6 Fri.....	38	20	15	20	43	45	17	30	7 Mar. (67)..	6 Fri.....	278	.834	115	475	220	4786
28 Mar. (87)..	0 Sat.....	53	51	21	32	59	16	23	42	25 Mar. (84)..	4 Wed....	50	.150	9811	375	269	4787
29 Mar. (88)..	2 Mon....	9	22	3	45	14	48	5	55	15 Mar. (74)..	2 Mon....	306	.918	26	259	240	4788
29 Mar. (88)..	3 Tues....	24	54	9	57	30	19	12	8	4 Mar. (63)..	6 Fri.....	130	.390	9901	106	210	4789
28 Mar. (88)..	4 Wed....	40	25	16	10	45	51	18	20	22 Mar. (82)..	5 Thur...	113	.339	9936	42	261	4790
28 Mar. (87)..	5 Thur...	55	56	22	22	†1	22	†0	33	12 Mar. (71)..	3 Tues....	226	.678	150	925	233	4791
29 Mar. (88)..	0 Sat.....	11	27	4	35	16	54	6	46	1 Mar. (60)..	0 Sat.....	31	.093	26	773	202	4792
29 Mar. (88)..	1 Sun....	26	59	10	47	32	25	12	58	20 Mar. (79)..	6 Fri.....	66	.198	61	708	253	4793
28 Mar. (88)..	2 Mon....	42	30	17	0	47	57	19	11	8 Mar. (68)..	3 Tues....	28	.084	9936	556	222	4794
28 Mar. (87)..	3 Tues....	58	1	23	12	†3	28	†1	23	27 Mar. (86)..	2 Mon....	118	.354	9971	492	274	4795
29 Mar. (88)..	5 Thur...	13	32	5	25	19	0	7	36	16 Mar. (75)..	6 Fri.....	105	.315	9847	339	243	4796
29 Mar. (88)..	6 Fri.....	29	4	11	37	34	31	13	49	5 Mar. (64)..	3 Tues....	⊙ −6	−.018	9723	186	212	4797
28 Mar. (88)..	0 Sat.....	44	35	17	50	50	3	20	1	23 Mar. (83)..	2 Mon....	⊙ −6	−.018	9757	122	263	4798
29 Mar. (88)..	2 Mon....	0	6	0	2	5	34	2	14	13 Mar. (72)..	0 Sat.....	117	.351	9972	6	235	4799
29 Mar. (88)..	3 Tues....	15	37	6	15	21	6	8	26	3 Mar. (62)..	5 Thur...	237	.711	186	889	207	4800
29 Mar. (88)..	4 Wed....	31	9	12	27	36	38	14	39	22 Mar. (81)..	4 Wed....	236	.708	221	825	259	4801
28 Mar. (88)..	5 Thur...	46	40	18	40	52	9	20	52	10 Mar. (70)..	1 Sun....	112	.336	96	672	228	4802
29 Mar. (88)..	0 Sat.....	2	11	0	52	7	41	3	4	29 Mar. (88)..	0 Sat.....	183	.549	131	608	279	4803
29 Mar. (88)..	1 Sun....	17	42	7	5	23	12	9	17	18 Mar. (77)..	4 Wed....	186	.558	7	455	248	4804
29 Mar. (88)..	2 Mon....	33	14	13	17	38	44	15	29	7 Mar. (66)..	1 Sun....	155	.465	9882	303	217	4805
28 Mar. (88)..	3 Tues....	48	45	19	30	54	15	21	42	25 Mar. (85)..	0 Sat.....	197	.591	9917	239	269	4806
29 Mar. (88)..	5 Thur...	4	16	1	42	9	47	3	55	14 Mar. (78)..	4 Wed. ..	5	.015	9793	86	238	4807
29 Mar. (88)..	6 Fri.....	19	47	7	55	25	18	10	7	4 Mar. (63)..	2 Mon....	122	.366	7	969	210	4808
29 Mar. (88)..	0 Sat.....	35	19	14	7	40	50	16	20	23 Mar. (82)..	1 Sun....	103	.309	42	905	261	4809
28 Mar. (88)..	1 Sun....	50	50	20	20	56	21	22	32	12 Mar. (72)..	6 Fri.....	260	.780	256	789	233	4810
29 Mar. (88)..	3 Tues....	6	21	2	32	11	53	4	45	1 Mar. (60)..	3 Tues....	169	.507	132	636	202	4811

† See footnote p. liii above. ⊙ See Text. Art. 101 above, para. 2.

TABLE I.

Lunation-parts = 10,000*ths of a circle. A tithi* = $^1/_{30}$*th of the moon's synodic revolution.*

I. CONCURRENT YEAR.								II. ADDED LUNAR MONTHS.				
						Samvatsara.		True.				
Kali.	Śaka.	Chaitrâdi. Vikrama.	Meshâdi (Solar) year in Bengal.	Kollam.	A. D.	Luni-Solar cycle. (Southern.)	Bṛihaspati cycle (Northern) current at Mesha saṅkrânti.	Name of month.	Time of the preceding saṅkrânti expressed in: Lunation parts. (t.)	Tithis.	Time of the succeeding saṅkrânti expressed in: Lunation parts. (t.)	Tithis.
1	2	3	3a	4	5	6	7	8	9	10	11	12
4812	1633	1768	1117	885- 86	1710-11	24 Vikṛita	34 Śârvari	......	......	......	......	......
4813	1634	1769	1118	886- 87	1711-12	25 Khara	35 Plava	6 Bhâdrapada	9654	28.962	200	0.600
4814	1635	1770	1119	887- 88	*1712-13	26 Nandana	36 Śubhakṛit	......	......	......	......	......
4815	1636	1771	1120	888- 89	1713-14	27 Vijaya	37 Śobhana	......	......	......	......	......
4816	1637	1772	1121	889- 90	1714-15	28 Jaya	38 Krodhin	4 Âshâḍha	9900	29.700	283	0.849
4817	1638	1773	1122	890- 91	1715-16	29 Manmatha	39 Viśvâvasu	......	......	......	......	......
4818	1639	1774	1123	891- 92	*1716-17	30 Durmukha	40 Parâbhava	......	......	......	......	......
4819	1640	1775	1124	892- 93	1717-18	31 Hemalamba	41 Plavaṅga	3 Jyeshṭha	9695	29.085	457	1.371
4820	1641	1776	1125	893- 94	1718-19	32 Vilamba	42 Kîlaka	......	......	......	......	......
4821	1642	1777	1126	894- 95	1719-20	33 Vikârin	43 Saumya	7 Âśvina	9733	29.199	128	0.384
4822	1643	1778	1127	895- 96	*1720-21	34 Śârvari	44 Sâdhâraṇa	......	......	......	......	......
4823	1644	1779	1128	896- 97	1721-22	35 Plava	45 Virodhakṛit	......	......	......	......	......
4824	1645	1780	1129	897- 98	1722-23	36 Śubhakṛit	46 Paridhâvin	5 Śrâvaṇa	9759	29.277	328	0.984
4825	1646	1781	1130	898- 99	1723-24	37 Śobhana	47 Pramâdin	......	......	......	......	......
4826	1647	1782	1131	899-900	*1724-25	38 Krodhin	48 Ânanda	......	......	......	......	......
4827	1648	1783	1132	900- 1	1725-26	39 Viśvâvasu	49 Râkshasa	3 Jyeshṭha	'9224	27.672	4	0.012
4828	1649	1784	1133	901- 2	1726-27	40 Parâbhava	50 Anala	......	......	......	......	......
4829	1650	1785	1134	902- 3	1727-28	41 Plavaṅga	51 Piṅgala	......	......	......	......	......
4830	1651	1786	1135	903- 4	*1728-29	42 Kîlaka	52 Kâlayukta	2 Vaiśâkha	9881	29.643	280	0.840
4831	1652	1787	1136	904- 5	1729-30	43 Saumya	53 Siddhârthin	......	......	......	......	......
4832	1653	1788	1137	905- 6	1730-31	44 Sâdhâraṇa	54 Raudra	6 Bhâdrapada	9796	29.388	252	0.756
4833	1654	1789	1138	906- 7	1731-32	45 Virodhakṛit	55 Durmati	......	......	......	......	......
4834	1655	1790	1139	907- 8	*1732-33	46 Paridhâvin	56 Dundubhi	......	......	......	......	......
4835	1656	1791	1140	908- 9	1733-34	47 Pramâdin	57 Rudhirodgârin	4 Ashâḍha	9552	28.656	381	1.143
4836	1657	1792	1141	909- 10	1734-35	48 Ananda	58 Raktâksha	......	......	......	......	......
4837	1658	1793	1142	910- 11	1735-36	49 Râkshasa	59 Krodhana	......	......	......	......	......
4838	1659	1794	1143	911- 12	*1736-37	50 Anala	60 Kshaya	3 Jyeshṭha	9763	29.289	458	1.374
4839	1660	1795	1144	912- 13	1737-38	51 Piṅgala	1 Prabhava	......	......	......	......	......
4840	1661	1796	1145	913- 14	1738-39	52 Kâlayukta	2 Vibhava	7 Âśvina	9754	29.262	96	0.288
4841	1662	1797	1146	914- 15	1739-40	53 Siddhârthin	3 Śukla	......	......	......	......	......
4842	1663	1798	1147	915- 16	*1740-41	54 Raudra	4 Pramoda	......	......	......	......	......
4843	1664	1799	1148	916- 17	1741-42	55 Durmati	5 Prajâpati	5 Śrâvaṇa	9892	29.676	523	1.569

TABLE I.

(*Col.* 23) *a* = *Distance of moon from sun.* (*Col.* 24) *b* = *moon's mean anomaly.* (*Col.* 25) *c* = *sun's mean anomaly.*

III. COMMENCEMENT OF THE

Solar year.										Luni-Solar year. (Civil day of Chaitra Śukla 1st.)							Kali.
Day and Month A. D.	(Time of the Mesha saṅkrânti.)									Day and Month A. D.	Week day.	At Sunrise on meridian of Ujjain.					
	Week day.	By the Ârya Siddhânta.				By the Sûrya Siddhânta.						Moon's Age.					
		Gh.	Pa.	H.	M.	Gh.	Pa.	H.	M.			Lunat. parts elapsed. (t.)	Tithis elapsed.	a.	b.	c.	
13	14	15		17		15a		17a		19	20	21	22	23	24	25	1
29 Mar. (88)..	4 Wed....	21	52	18	45	27	24	10	58	20 Mar. (79)..	2 Mon....	244	.732	166	572	254	4812
29 Mar. (88)..	5 Thur...	37	24	14	57	42	56	17	10	9 Mar. (68)..	6 Fri.....	252	.756	42	419	223	4813
28 Mar. (88)..	6 Fri.....	52	55	21	10	58	27	23	23	27 Mar. (87)..	5 Thur...	327	.981	77	355	274	4814
29 Mar. (88)..	1 Sun....	8	26	3	22	13	59	5	36	16 Mar. (75)..	2 Mon....	226	.678	9952	203	243	4815
29 Mar. (88)..	2 Mon....	23	57	9	35	29	30	11	48	5 Mar. (64)..	6 Fri.....	14	.042	9828	50	212	4816
29 Mar. (88)..	3 Tues....	39	29	15	47	45	2	18	1	24 Mar. (83)..	5 Thur...	⊙−10	−.030	9863	986	264	4817
28 Mar. (88)..	4 Wed....	55	0	22	0	†0	33	†0	13	13 Mar. (73)..	3 Tues....	114	.342	77	869	236	4818
29 Mar. (88)..	6 Fri.....	10	31	4	12	16	5	6	26	3 Mar. (62)..	1 Sun....	294	.882	292	753	207	4819
29 Mar. (88)..	0 Sat.....	26	2	10	25	31	36	12	38	21 Mar. (80)..	6 Fri.....	13	.039	9987	652	256	4820
29 Mar. (88)..	1 Sun....	41	34	16	37	47	8	18	51	11 Mar. (70)..	4 Wed....	311	.933	202	536	228	4821
28 Mar. (88)..	2 Mon....	57	5	22	50	†2	39	†1	4	28 Mar. (88)..	2 Mon....	94	.282	9898	436	276	4822
29 Mar. (88)..	4 Wed....	12	36	5	2	18	11	7	16	17 Mar. (76)..	6 Fri.....	51	.153	9774	283	246	4823
29 Mar. (88)..	5 Thur..	28	7	11	15	33	43	13	29	7 Mar. (66)..	4 Wed....	250	.750	9988	166	218	4824
29 Mar. (88)..	6 Fri.....	43	39	17	27	49	14	19	42	26 Mar. (85)..	3 Tues....	247	.741	23	102	269	4825
28 Mar. (88)..	0 Sat.....	59	10	23	40	†4	46	†1	54	14 Mar. (74)..	0 Sat.....	⊙ −7	−.021	9898	949	238	4826
29 Mar. (88)..	2 Mon....	14	41	5	52	20	17	8	7	4 Mar. (63)..	5 Thur...	133	.399	113	833	210	4827
29 Mar. (88)..	3 Tues....	30	12	12	5	35	49	14	19	23 Mar. (82)..	4 Wed....	148	.444	147	769	261	4828
29 Mar. (88)..	4 Wed....	45	44	18	17	51	20	20	32	12 Mar. (71)..	1 Sun....	69	.207	23	616	230	4829
29 Mar. (89)..	6 Fri.....	1	15	0	30	6	52	2	45	29 Feb. (60)..	5 Thur...	74	.222	9899	463	200	4830
29 Mar. (88)..	0 Sat.....	16	46	6	42	22	23	8	57	19 Mar. (78)..	4 Wed....	158	.474	9933	399	251	4831
29 Mar. (88)..	1 Sun....	32	17	12	55	37	55	15	10	8 Mar. (67)..	1 Sun....	90	.270	9809	247	220	4832
29 Mar. (88)..	2 Mon....	47	49	19	7	53	26	21	22	27 Mar. (86)..	0 Sat.....	112	.336	9844	183	272	4833
29 Mar. (89)..	4 Wed....	3	20	1	20	8	58	3	35	16 Mar. (76)..	5 Thur...	255	.765	58	66	243	4834
29 Mar. (88)..	5 Thur...	18	51	7	32	24	29	9	48	5 Mar. (64)..	2 Mon....	3	.009	9934	913	213	4835
29 Mar. (88)..	6 Fri.....	34	22	13	45	40	1	16	0	24 Mar. (83)..	1 Sun....	⊙ −5	−.015	9968	849	264	4836
29 Mar. (88)..	0 Sat....	49	54	19	57	55	32	22	13	14 Mar. (73)..	6 Fri.....	184	.552	183	733	236	4837
29 Mar. (89)..	2 Mon....	5	25	2	10	11	4	4	26	2 Mar. (62)..	3 Tues....	134	.402	59	580	205	4838
29 Mar. (88)..	3 Tues....	20	56	8	22	26	35	10	38	21 Mar. (80)..	2 Mon....	219	.657	93	516	256	4839
29 Mar. (88)..	4 Wed....	36	27	14	35	42	7	16	51	10 Mar. (69)..	6 Fri.....	215	.645	9969	363	225	4840
29 Mar. (88)..	5 Thur...	51	59	20	47	57	38	23	3	29 Mar. (88)..	5 Thur...	277	.831	3	299	277	4841
29 Mar. (89)..	0 Sat	7	30	3	0	13	10	5	16	17 Mar. (77)..	2 Mon....	130	.390	9879	146	246	4842
29 Mar. (88)..	1 Sun....	23	1	9	12	28	41	11	28	7 Mar. (66)..	0 Sat.....	260	.780	93	30	218	4843

† See footnote p. liii above. ⊙ See Text. Art. 101 above, para. 2.

TABLE I.

Lunation-parts = 10,000ths of a circle. A tithi = 1/30th of the moon's synodic revolution.

I. CONCURRENT YEAR.								II. ADDED LUNAR MONTHS.				
						Samvatsara.		True.				
Kali.	Śaka.	Chaitrâdi. Vikrama.	Meshâdi (Solar) year in Bengal.	Kollam.	A. D.	Luni-Solar cycle. (Southern.)	Bṛihaspati cycle (Northern) current at Mesha saṅkrânti.	Name of month.	Time of the preceding saṅkrânti expressed in: Lunation parts. (*l.*)	Time of the preceding saṅkrânti expressed in: Tithis.	Time of the succeeding saṅkrânti expressed in: Lunation parts. (*l.*)	Time of the succeeding saṅkrânti expressed in: Tithis.
1	2	3	3a	4	5	6	7	8	9	10	11	12
4844	1665	1800	1149	917–18	1742–43	56 Dundubhi	6 Aṅgiras					
4845	1666	1801	1150	918–19	1743–44	57 Rudhirodgârin	7 Śrîmukha					
4846	1667	1802	1151	919–20	*1744–45	58 Raktâksha	8 Bhâva	4 Âshâdha	9969	29.907	839	2.517
4847	1668	1803	1152	920–21	1745–46	59 Krodhana	9 Yuvan					
4848	1669	1804	1153	921–22	1746–47	60 Kshaya	10 Dhâtṛi					
4849	1670	1805	1154	922–23	1747–48	1 Prabhava	11 Îśvara	1 Chaitra	9837	29.511	73	0.219
4850	1671	1806	1155	923–24	*1748–49	2 Vibhava	12 Bahudhânya					
4851	1672	1807	1156	924–25	1749–50	3 Śukla	13 Pramâthin	6 Bhâdrapada	9993	29.979	404	1.212
4852	1673	1808	1157	925–26	1750–51	4 Pramoda	14 Vikrama					
4853	1674	1809	1158	926–27	1751–52	5 Prajâpati	15 Vṛisha					
4854	1675	1810	1159	927–28	*1752–53	6 Aṅgiras	16 Chitrabhânu	4 Âshâḍha	9509	28.527	385	1.155
4855	1676	1811	1160	928–29	1753–54	7 Śrîmukha	17 Subhânu					
4856	1677	1812	1161	929–30	1754–55	8 Bhâva	18 Târaṇa					
4857	1678	1813	1162	930–31	1755–56	9 Yuvan	19 Pârthiva	3 Jyeshṭha	9930	29.790	509	1.527
4858	1679	1814	1163	931–32	*1756–57	10 Dhâtṛi	20 Vyaya					
4859	1680	1815	1164	932–33	1757–58	11 Îśvara	21 Sarvajit	7 Âśvina	9878	29.634	143	0.429
4860	1681	1816	1165	933–34	1758–59	12 Bahudhânya	22 Sarvadhârin					
4861	1682	1817	1166	934–35	1759–60	13 Pramâthin	23 Virodhin					
4862	1683	1818	1167	935–36	*1760–61	14 Vikrama	24 Vikṛita	5 Śrâvaṇa	9924	29.772	657	1.971
4863	1684	1819	1168	936–37	1761–62	15 Vṛisha	25 Khara					
4864	1685	1820	1169	937–38	1762–63	16 Chitrabhânu	26 Nandana					
4865	1686	1821	1170	938–39	1763–64	17 Subhânu	27 Vijaya	3 Jyeshṭha	9398	28.194	5	0.015
4866	1687	1822	1171	939–40	*1764–65	18 Târaṇa	28 Jaya					
4867	1688	1823	1172	940–41	1765–66	19 Pârthiva	29 Manmatha					
4868	1689	1824	1173	941–42	1766–67	20 Vyaya	30 Durmukha	1 Chaitra	9880	29.640	194	0.582
4869	1690	1825	1174	942–43	1767–68	21 Sarvajit	31 Hemalamba					
4870	1691	1826	1175	943–44	*1768–69	22 Sarvadhârin	32 Vilamba	5 Śrâvana	9435	28.305	158	0.474
4871	1692	1827	1176	944–45	1769–70	23 Virodhin	33 Vikârin					
4872	1693	1828	1177	945–46	1770–71	24 Vikṛita	34 Śârvarin					
4873	1694	1829	1178	946–47	1771–72	25 Khara	35 Plava [1]	4 Âshâḍha	9779	29.337	342	1.026
4874	1695	1830	1179	947–48	*1772–73	26 Nandana	37 Śobhana					
4875	1696	1831	1180	948–49	1773–74	27 Vijaya	38 Krodhin					

[1] Śubhakṛit, No. 36, was suppressed in the north.

TABLE I.

(*Col.* 23) *a* = *Distance of moon from sun.* (*Col.* 24) *b* = *moon's mean anomaly.* (*Col.* 25) *c* = *sun's mean anomaly.*

III. COMMENCEMENT OF THE																	
Solar year.										Luni-Solar year. (Civil day of Chaitra Śukla 1st.)							
Day and Month A. D.	(Time of the Mesha saṅkrânti.) Week day.	By the Ârya Siddhânta.				By the Sûrya Siddhânta.				Day and Month A. D.	Week day.	At Sunrise on meridian of Ujjain. Moon's Age. Lunat. parts elapsed. (*t.*)	Tithis elapsed.	*a.*	*b.*	*c.*	Kali.
		Gh.	Pa.	H.	M.	Gh.	Pa.	H.	M.								
13	**14**	**15**		**17**		**15a**		**17a**		**19**	**20**	**21**	**22**	**23**	**24**	**25**	**1**
29 Mar. (88)..	2 Mon....	38	32	15	25	44	13	17	41	26 Mar. (85)..	6 Fri.....	238	.714	128	966	269	4844
29 Mar. (88)..	3 Tues....	54	4	21	37	59	45	23	54	15 Mar. (74)..	3 Tues....	15	.045	4	813	238	4845
29 Mar. (89)..	5 Thur...	9	35	3	50	15	16	6	6	4 Mar. (64)..	1 Sun....	228	.684	218	697	210	4846
29 Mar. (88)..	6 Fri.....	25	6	10	2	30	48	12	19	23 Mar. (82)..	0 Sat.....	290	.870	254	633	262	4847
29 Mar. (88)..	0 Sat.....	40	37	16	15	46	19	18	32	12 Mar. (71)..	4 Wed....	287	.861	129	480	231	4848
29 Mar. (88)..	1 Sun....	56	9	22	27	†1	51	†0	44	1 Mar. (60)..	1 Sun....	271	.813	4	327	200	4849
29 Mar. (89)..	3 Tues....	11	40	4	40	17	22	6	57	19 Mar. (79)..	0 Sat.....	319	.957	39	263	251	4850
29 Mar. (88)..	4 Wed....	27	11	10	52	32	54	13	9	8 Mar. (67)..	4 Wed....	146	.439	9915	110	220	4851
29 Mar. (88)..	5 Thur...	42	42	17	5	48	25	19	22	27 Mar. (86)..	3 Tues....	129	.387	9949	46	272	4852
29 Mar. (88)..	6 Fri.....	58	14	23	17	†3	57	†1	35	17 Mar. (76)..	1 Sun....	244	.732	164	930	244	4853
29 Mar. (89)..	1 Sun....	13	45	5	30	19	28	7	47	5 Mar. (65)..	5 Thur...	43	.129	39	777	213	4854
9 April (99) ×	2 Mon....	29	16	11	42	35	0	14	0	4 April (94) ×	4 Wed....	78	.234	74	713	264	4855
9 April (99)..	3 Tues....	44	47	17	55	50	31	20	13	24 Mar. (83)..	1 Sun....	38	.114	9950	560	233	4856
10 April (100).	5 Thur...	0	19	0	7	6	3	2	25	13 Mar. (72)..	5 Thur...	45	.135	9825	407	202	4857
9 April (100).	6 Fri.....	15	50	6	20	21	34	8	38	31 Mar. (91)..	4 Wed....	117	.351	9860	343	254	4858
9 April (99)..	0 Sat.....	31	21	12	32	37	6	14	50	20 Mar. (79)..	1 Sun....	7	.021	9736	190	223	4859
9 April (99)..	1 Sun....	46	52	18	45	52	37	21	3	8 April (98)..	0 Sat.....	10	.030	9770	126	274	4860
10 April (100).	3 Tues....	2	24	0	57	8	9	3	16	29 Mar. (88)..	5 Thur...	134	.402	9985	10	246	4861
9 April (100).	4 Wed....	17	55	7	10	23	40	9	28	18 Mar. (78)..	3 Tues....	252	.756	199	893	218	4862
9 April (99)..	5 Thur...	33	26	13	22	39	12	15	41	6 April (96)..	2 Mon....	251	.753	234	829	269	4863
9 April (99)..	6 Fri.....	48	57	19	35	54	43	21	53	26 Mar. (85)..	6 Fri.....	123	.369	109	677	239	4864
10 April (100).	1 Sun....	4	29	1	47	10	15	4	6	15 Mar. (74)..	3 Tues....	6	.018	9985	524	208	4865
9 April (100).	2 Mon....	20	0	8	0	25	47	10	19	2 April (93) .	2 Mon....	195	.585	20	460	259	4866
9 April (99)..	3 Tues....	35	31	14	12	41	18	16	31	22 Mar. (81)..	6 Fri.....	167	.501	9896	307	228	4867
9 April (99)..	4 Wed....	51	2	20	25	56	50	22	43	11 Mar. (70)..	3 Tues....	29	.087	9771	154	197	4868
10 April (100).	6 Fri.....	6	34	2	37	12	21	4	56	30 Mar. (89)..	2 Mon....	21	.063	9806	90	249	4869
9 April (100).	0 Sat.....	22	5	8	50	27	53	11	9	19 Mar. (79)..	0 Sat.....	138	.414	20	974	221	4870
9 April (99)..	1 Sun....	37	36	15	2	43	24	17	22	7 April (97)..	6 Fri.....	120	.360	55	910	272	4871
9 April (99)..	2 Mon....	53	7	21	15	58	56	23	34	28 Mar. (87)..	4 Wed....	274	.822	269	793	244	4872
10 April (100).	4 Wed....	8	39	3	27	14	27	5	47	17 Mar. (76)..	1 Sun....	179	.537	145	640	213	4873
9 April (100).	5 Thur...	24	10	9	40	29	59	11	59	4 April (95)..	0 Sat.....	255	.765	180	576	264	4874
9 April (99)..	6 Fri.....	39	41	15	52	45	30	18	12	24 Mar. (83)..	4 Wed....	260	.780	55	424	233	4875

† See footnote p. liii above. × From here (inclusive) forward the dates are New Style.

TABLE I.

Lunation-parts = 10,000*ths of a circle. A tithi* = $^1/_{30}$*th of the moon's synodic revolution.*

I. CONCURRENT YEAR.								II. ADDED LUNAR MONTHS.				
						Samvatsara.		True.				
Kali.	Śaka.	Chaitrâdi. Vikrama.	Meshâdi (Solar) year in Bengal.	Kollam.	A. D.	Luni-Solar cycle. (Southern.)	Bṛihaspati cycle (Northern) current at Mesha saṅkrânti.	Name of month.	Time of the preceding saṅkrânti expressed in: Lunation parts. (*t.*)	Tithis.	Time of the succeeding saṅkrânti expressed in: Lunation parts. (*t.*)	Tithis.
1	2	3	3a	4	5	6	7	8	9	10	11	12
4876	1697	1832	1181	949-50	1774- 75	28 Jaya	39 Viśvâvasu	2 Vaiśâkha	9696	29.088	124	0.372
4877	1698	1833	1182	950-51	1775- 76	29 Manmatha	40 Parâbhava					
4878	1699	1834	1183	951-52	*1776- 77	30 Durmukha	41 Plavaṅga	6 Bhâdrapada	9612	28.836	67	0.201
4879	1700	1835	1184	952-53	1777- 78	31 Hemalamba	42 Kîlaka					
4880	1701	1836	1185	953-54	1778- 79	32 Vilamba	43 Saumya					
4881	1702	1837	1186	954-55	1779- 80	33 Vikârin	44 Sâdhâraṇa	5 Śrâvaṇa	9972	29.916	690	2.070
4882	1703	1838	1187	955-56	*1780- 81	34 Śârvari	45 Virodhakṛit					
4883	1704	1839	1188	956-57	1781- 82	35 Plava	46 Paridhâvin					
4884	1705	1840	1189	957-58	1782- 83	36 Śubhakṛit	47 Pramâdin	3 Jyeshṭha	9593	28.779	142	0.426
4885	1706	1841	1190	958-59	1783- 84	37 Śobhana	48 Ânanda					
4886	1707	1842	1191	959-60	*1784- 85	38 Krodhin	49 Râkshasa					
4887	1708	1843	1192	960-61	1785- 86	39 Viśvâvasu	50 Anala	1 Chaitra	9855	29.565	217	0.651
4888	1709	1844	1193	961-62	1786- 87	40 Parâbhava	51 Piṅgala					
4889	1710	1845	1194	962-63	1787- 88	41 Plavaṅga	52 Kâlayukta	5 Śrâvaṇa	9433	28.299	221	0.663
4890	1711	1846	1195	963-64	*1788- 89	42 Kîlaka	53 Siddhârthin					
4891	1712	1847	1196	964-65	1789- 90	43 Saumya	54 Raudra					
4892	1713	1848	1197	965-66	1790- 91	44 Sâdhâraṇa	55 Durmati	4 Âshâḍha	9650	28.950	344	1.032
4893	1714	1849	1198	966-67	1791- 92	45 Virodhakṛit	56 Dundubhi					
4894	1715	1850	1199	967-68	*1792- 93	46 Paridhâvin	57 Rudhirodgârin					
4895	1716	1851	1200	968-69	1793- 94	47 Pramâdin	58 Raktâksha	2 Vaiśâkha	9751	29.253	268	0.804
4896	1717	1852	1201	969-70	1794- 95	48 Ananda	59 Krodhana					
4897	1718	1853	1202	970-71	1795- 96	49 Râkshasa	60 Kshaya	6 Bhâdrapada	9743	29.229	244	0.732
4898	1719	1854	1203	971-72	*1796- 97	50 Anala	1 Prabhava					
4899	1720	1855	1204	972-73	1797- 98	51 Piṅgala	2 Vibhava					
4900	1721	1856	1205	973-74	1798- 99	52 Kâlayukta	3 Śukla	5 Śrâvaṇa	9866	29.598	654	1.962
4901	1722	1857	1206	974-75	1799-800	53 Siddhârthin	4 Pramoda					
4902	1723	1858	1207	975-76	1800§- 1	54 Raudra	5 Prajâpati					
4903	1724	1859	1208	976-77	1801- 2	55 Durmati	6 Aṅgiras	3 Jyeshṭha	9760	29.280	233	0.699
4904	1725	1860	1209	977-78	1802- 3	56 Dundubhi	7 Śrîmukha					
4905	1726	1861	1210	978-79	1803- 4	57 Rudhirodgârin	8 Bhâva					
4906	1727	1862	1211	979-80	*1804- 5	58 Raktâksha	9 Yuvan	1 Chaitra	9228	27.684	178	0.534
4907	1728	1863	1212	980-81	1805- 6	59 Krodhana	10 Dhâtṛi					

§ The year 1800 was not a leap-year.

TABLE I.

(*Col.* 23) *a* = *Distance of moon from sun.* (*Col.* 24) *b* = *moon's mean anomaly.* (*Col.* 25) *c* = *sun's mean anomaly.*

III. COMMENCEMENT OF THE																	
Solar year.										Luni-Solar year. (Civil day of Chaitra Śukla 1st.)							
Day and Month A. D.	(Time of the Mesha saṅkrânti.)									Day and Month A. D.	Week day.	At Sunrise on meridian of Ujjain.					Kali.
	Week day.	By the Ârya Siddhânta.				By the Sûrya Siddhânta.						Moon's Age.		*a.*	*b.*	*c.*	
		Gh.	Pa.	H.	M.	Gh.	Pa.	H.	M.			Lunat. parts elapsed. (*t.*)	Tithis elapsed.				
13	**14**	**15**		**17**		**15a**		**17a**		**19**	**20**	**21**	**22**	**23**	**24**	**25**	**1**
9 April (99)..	0 Sat.....	55	12	22	5	†1	2	†0	25	13 Mar. (72)..	1 Sun.....	213	.639	9931	271	203	4876
10 April (100).	2 Mon....	10	44	4	17	16	33	6	37	1 April (91)..	0 Sat.....	241	.723	9966	207	254	4877
9 April (100).	3 Tues....	26	15	10	30	32	5	12	50	20 Mar. (80)..	4 Wed....	29	.087	9841	54	223	4878
9 April (99)..	4 Wed....	41	46	16	42	47	36	19	3	8 April (98)..	3 Tues...	8	.024	9876	990	275	4879
9 April (99)..	5 Thur...	57	17	22	55	†3	8	†1	15	29 Mar. (88)..	1 Sun.....	130	.390	90	874	246	4880
10 April (100).	0 Sat.....	12	49	5	7	18	39	7	28	19 Mar. (78)..	6 Fri.....	306	.918	305	757	218	4881
9 April (100).	1 Sun....	28	20	11	20	34	11	13	40	5 April (96)..	4 Wed....	24	.072	1	657	267	4882
9 April (99)..	2 Mon....	43	51	17	32	49	42	19	53	25 Mar. (84)..	1 Sun.....	12	.036	9876	504	236	4883
9 April (99)..	3 Tues....	59	22	23	45	†5	14	†2	6	14 Mar. (73)..	5 Thur...	8	.024	9752	351	205	4884
10 April (100).	5 Thur...	14	54	5	57	20	45	8	18	2 April (92)..	4 Wed....	63	.189	9787	287	256	4885
9 April (100).	6 Fri.....	30	25	12	10	36	17	14	31	22 Mar. (82)..	2 Mon....	264	.792	1	171	228	4886
9 April (99)..	0 Sat.....	45	56	18	22	51	49	20	43	11 Mar. (70)..	6 Fri.....	36	.108	9877	18	198	4887
10 April (100).	2 Mon....	1	27	0	35	7	20	2	56	30 Mar. (89)..	5 Thur...	11	.033	9911	954	249	4888
10 April (100).	3 Tues....	16	59	6	47	22	52	9	9	20 Mar. (79)..	3 Tues....	148	.444	126	837	221	4889
9 April (100).	4 Wed....	32	30	13	0	38	23	15	21	7 April (98)..	2 Mon....	163	.489	161	773	272	4890
9 April (99)..	5 Thur...	48	1	19	12	53	55	21	34	27 Mar. (86)..	6 Fri.....	79	.237	36	621	241	4891
10 April (100).	0 Sat.....	3	32	1	25	9	26	3	46	16 Mar. (75)..	3 Tues....	82	.246	9912	468	211	4892
10 April (100).	1 Sun....	19	4	7	37	24	58	9	59	4 April (94)..	2 Mon....	167	.501	9947	404	262	4893
9 April (100).	2 Mon....	34	35	13	50	40	29	16	12	23 Mar. (83)..	6 Fri.....	102	.306	9822	251	231	4894
9 April (99)..	3 Tues....	50	6	20	2	56	1	22	24	13 Mar. (72)..	4 Wed....	284	.852	37	134	203	4895
10 April (100).	5 Thur...	5	37	2	15	11	32	4	37	1 April (91)..	3 Tues....	271	.813	71	70	254	4896
10 April (100).	6 Fri....	21	9	8	27	27	4	10	49	21 Mar. (80)..	0 Sat.....	19	.057	9947	918	223	4897
9 April (100).	0 Sat.....	36	40	14	40	42	35	17	2	8 April (99)..	6 Fri.....	12	.036	9982	854	275	4898
9 April (99)..	1 Sun....	52	11	20	52	58	7	23	15	29 Mar. (88)..	4 Wed....	196	.588	196	737	247	4899
10 April (100).	3 Tues....	7	42	3	5	13	38	5	27	18 Mar. (77)..	1 Sun....	142	.426	72	584	216	4900
10 April (100).	4 Wed....	23	14	9	17	29	10	11	40	6 April (96)..	0 Sat.....	228	.684	106	520	267	4901
10 April (100).	5 Thur...	38	45	15	30	44	41	17	53	26 Mar. (85)..	4 Wed....	225	.675	9982	368	236	4902
10 April (100).	6 Fri.....	54	16	21	42	†0	13	†0	5	15 Mar. (74)..	1 Sun....	137	.411	9858	215	205	4903
11 April (101).	1 Sun....	9	47	3	55	15	44	6	18	3 April (93)..	0 Sat.....	146	.438	9892	151	257	4904
11 April (101).	2 Mon....	25	19	10	7	31	16	12	30	24 Mar. (83)..	5 Thur...	277	.831	107	34	229	4905
10 April (101).	3 Tues....	40	50	16	20	46	47	18	43	12 Mar. (72)..	2 Mon....	30	.090	9982	882	198	4906
10 April (100).	4 Wed....	56	21	22	32	†2	19	†0	55	31 Mar. (90)..	1 Sun....	29	.087	17	817	249	4907

† See footnote p. liii above.

TABLE I.

Lunation-parts = 10,000*ths of a circle. A tithi* = $^1/_{30}$*th of the moon's synodic revolution.*

I. CONCURRENT YEAR.								II. ADDED LUNAR MONTHS.				
						Samvatsara.		True.				
Kali.	Śaka.	Chaitrâdi. Vikrama.	Meshâdi (Solar) year in Bengal.	Kollam.	A. D.	Luni-Solar cycle. (Southern.)	Bṛihaspati cycle (Northern) current at Mesha saṅkrânti.	Name of month.	Time of the preceding saṅkrânti expressed in: Lunation parts. (*t.*)	Time of the preceding saṅkrânti expressed in: Tithis.	Time of the succeeding saṅkrânti expressed in: Lunation parts. (*t.*)	Time of the succeeding saṅkrânti expressed in: Tithis.
1	2	3	3a	4	5	6	7	8	9	10	11	12
4908	1729	1864	1213	981- 82	1806- 7	60 Kshaya......	11 Îśvara.......	5 Śrâvaṇa.....	9398	28.194	205	0 615
4909	1730	1865	1214	982- 83	1807- 8	1 Prabhava.....	12 Bahudhânya..	....	....	....	......	......
4910	1731	1866	1215	983- 84	*1808- 9	2 Vibhava......	13 Pramâthin....	....	....	....	......	......
4911	1732	1867	1216	984- 85	1809-10	3 Śukla.........	14 Vikrama.....	4 Âshâḍha....	9799	29.397	438	1.314
4912	1733	1868	1217	985- 86	1810-11	4 Pramoda.....	15 Vṛisha.......	....	....	....	......	......
4913	1734	1869	1218	986- 87	1811-12	5 Prajâpati.....	16 Chitrabhânu..	....	....	....	......	......
4914	1735	1870	1219	987- 88	*1812-13	6 Aṅgiras......	17 Subhânu.....	2 Vaiśâkha....	9726	29.178	308	0.924
4915	1736	1871	1220	988- 89	1813-14	7 Śrîmukha....	18 Târaṇa.......	....	....	....	......	......
4916	1737	1872	1221	989- 90	1814-15	8 Bhâva.......	19 Pârthiva.....	6 Bhâdrapada..	9748	29.244	336	1.008
4917	1738	1873	1222	990- 91	1815-16	9 Yuvan.......	20 Vyaya.......	....	....	....	......	......
4918	1739	1874	1223	991- 92	*1816-17	10 Dhâtṛi.......	21 Sarvajit......	....	....	....	......	......
4919	1740	1875	1224	992- 93	1817-18	11 Îśvara.......	22 Sarvadhârin..	5 Śrâvaṇa.....	9926	29.778	731	2.193
4920	1741	1876	1225	993- 94	1818-19	12 Bahudhânya..	23 Virodhin.....	....	....	....	......	......
4921	1742	1877	1226	994- 95	1819-20	13 Pramâthin...	24 Vikṛita......	....	....	....	......	......
4922	1743	1878	1227	995- 96	*1820-21	14 Vikrama.....	25 Khara.......	3 Jyeshṭha....	9838	29.514	501	1.503
4923	1744	1879	1228	996- 97	1821-22	15 Vṛisha.......	26 Nandana.....	....	....	....	......	......
4924	1745	1880	1229	997- 98	1822-23	16 Chitrabhânu..	27 Vijaya......	7 Âśvina...... 10 *Pausha* (*Ksh.*)	9848 74	29.544 0.222	127 9918	0.381 29.754
4925	1746	1881	1230	998- 99	1823-24	17 Subhânu.....	28 Jaya.........	1 Chaitra.....	9870	29 610	161	0.483
4826	1747	1882	1231	999-1000	*1824-25	18 Târaṇa......	29 Manmatha....	....	....	....	......	......
4927	1748	1883	1232	1000- 1	1825-26	19 Pârthiva.....	30 Durmukha....	5 Śrâvaṇa.....	9427	28.281	166	0.498
4928	1749	1884	1233	1001- 2	1826-27	20 Vyaya.......	31 Hemalamba..	....	....	....	......	......
4929	1750	1885	1234	1002- 3	1827-28	21 Sarvajit......	32 Vilamba.....	....	....	....	......	......
4930	1751	1886	1235	1003- 4	*1828-29	22 Sarvadhârin..	33 Vikârin......	4 Âshâḍha....	9984	29.952	615	1.845
4931	1752	1887	1236	1004- 5	1829-30	23 Virodhin.....	34 Śârvari......	....	....	....	......	......
4932	1753	1888	1237	1005- 6	1830-31	24 Vikṛita......	35 Plava.......	....	....	....	......	......
4933	1754	1889	1238	1006- 7	1831-32	25 Khara.......	36 Śubhakṛit....	2 Vaiśâkha....	9653	28.959	277	0.831
4934	1755	1890	1239	1007- 8	*1832-33	26 Nandana.....	37 Śobhana.....	....	....	....	......	......
4935	1756	1891	1240	1008- 9	1833-34	27 Vijaya.......	38 Krodhin.....	6 Bhâdrapada..	9707	29.121	335	1.005
4936	1757	1892	1241	1009- 10	1834-35	28 Jaya.........	39 Viśvâvasu....	....	....	....	......	......
4937	1758	1893	1242	1010- 11	1835-36	29 Manmatha....	40 Parâbhava....	....	....	....	......	......
4938	1759	1894	1243	1011- 12	*1836-37	30 Durmukha...	41 Plavaṅga.....	4 Âshâḍha....	9460	28.380	251	0.753

TABLE I.

(*Col.* 23) *a* = *Distance of moon from sun.* (*Col.* 24) *b* = *moon's mean anomaly.* (*Col.* 25) *c* = *sun's mean anomaly.*

III. COMMENCEMENT OF THE																	
Solar year.										Luni-Solar year. (Civil day of Chaitra Śukla 1st.)							Kali.
Day and Month A. D.	(Time of the Mesha saṅkrânti.) Week day.	By the Ârya Siddhânta.				By the Sûrya Siddhânta.				Day and Month A. D.	Week day.	At Sunrise on meridian of Ujjain. Moon's Age. Lunat. parts elapsed. (*t.*)	Tithis elapsed.	*a.*	*b.*	*c.*	
		Gh.	Pa.	H.	M.	Gh.	Pa.	H.	M.								
13	**14**	**15**		**17**		**15a**		**17a**		**19**	**20**	**21**	**22**	**23**	**24**	**25**	**1**
11 April (101).	6 Fri.....	11	52	4	45	17	50	7	8	21 Mar. (80)..	6 Fri.....	239	.717	231	701	221	4908
11 April (101).	0 Sat.....	27	24	10	57	33	22	13	21	9 April (99)..	5 Thur...	300	.900	266	637	272	4909
10 April (101).	1 Sun....	42	55	17	10	48	54	19	33	28 Mar. (88)..	2 Mon....	296	.888	142	484	242	4910
10 April (101).	2 Mon....	58	26	23	22	†4	25	†1	46	17 Mar. (76)..	6 Fri.....	281	.843	17	332	211	4911
11 April (101).	4 Wed....	13	57	5	35	19	57	7	59	5 April (95)..	5 Thur...	331	.993	52	267	262	4912
11 April (101).	5 Thur...	29	29	11	47	35	28	14	11	25 Mar. (84)..	2 Mon....	161	.483	9928	115	231	4913
10 April (101).	6 Fri.....	45	0	18	0	51	0	20	24	14 Mar. (74)..	0 Sat.....	283	.849	142	998	203	4914
11 April (101).	1 Sun....	0	31	0	12	6	31	2	36	2 April (92)..	6 Fri.....	260	.780	177	934	254	4915
11 April (101).	2 Mon....	16	2	6	25	22	3	8	49	22 Mar. (81)..	3 Tues....	57	.171	53	781	224	4916
11 April (101).	3 Tues....	31	34	12	37	37	34	15	2	10 April (100).	2 Mon....	91	.273	87	717	275	4917
10 April (101).	4 Wed....	47	5	18	50	53	6	21	14	29 Mar. (89)..	6 Fri.....	48	.144	9963	564	244	4918
11 April (101).	6 Fri.....	2	36	1	2	8	37	3	27	18 Mar. (77)..	3 Tues....	55	.165	9839	412	213	4919
11 April (101).	0 Sat.....	18	7	7	15	24	9	9	40	6 April (96)..	2 Mon....	127	.381	9873	348	265	4920
11 April (101).	1 Sun....	33	39	13	27	39	40	15	52	26 Mar. (85)..	6 Fri.....	21	.063	9749	195	234	4921
10 April (101).	2 Mon....	49	10	19	40	55	12	22	5	15 Mar. (75)..	4 Wed....	171	.513	9963	78	206	4922
11 April (101).	4 Wed....	4	41	1	52	10	43	4	17	3 April (93)..	3 Tues....	151	.453	9998	14	257	4923
11 April (101).	5 Thur...	20	12	8	5	26	15	10	30	24 Mar. (83)..	1 Sun....	268	.804	212	899	229	4924
11 April (101).	6 Fri.....	35	44	14	17	41	46	16	42	13 Mar. (72)..	5 Thur...	91	.273	88	746	197	4925
10 April (101).	0 Sat.....	51	15	20	30	57	18	22	55	31 Mar. (91)..	4 Wed....	135	.405	123	682	248	4926
11 April (101).	2 Mon....	6	46	2	42	12	49	5	8	20 Mar. (79)..	1 Sun....	114	.342	9998	529	218	4927
11 April (101).	3 Tues....	22	17	8	55	28	21	11	20	8 April (98)..	0 Sat.....	203	.609	33	465	269	4928
11 April (101).	4 Wed....	37	49	15	7	43	52	17	33	28 Mar. (87)..	4 Wed....	178	.534	9909	312	238	4929
10 April (101).	5 Thur...	53	20	21	20	59	24	23	46	16 Mar. (76)..	1 Sun....	44	.132	9784	160	207	4930
11 April (101).	0 Sat.....	8	51	3	32	14	56	5	58	4 April (94)..	0 Sat.....	39	.117	9819	96	259	4931
11 April (101).	1 Sun....	24	22	9	45	30	27	12	11	25 Mar. (84)..	5 Thur...	154	.462	33	979	230	4932
11 April (101).	2 Mon....	39	54	15	57	45	59	18	23	15 Mar. (74)..	3 Tues....	284	.852	248	863	202	4933
10 April (101).	3 Tues....	55	25	22	10	†1	30	†0	36	2 April (93)..	2 Mon....	289	.867	282	799	254	4934
11 April (101).	5 Thur...	10	56	4	22	17	2	6	49	22 Mar. (81)..	6 Fri.....	188	.564	158	646	223	4935
11 April (101).	6 Fri.....	26	27	10	35	32	33	13	1	10 April (100).	5 Thur...	264	.792	193	582	274	4936
11 April (101).	0 Sat.....	41	59	16	47	48	5	19	14	30 Mar. (89)..	2 Mon....	270	.810	69	429	243	4937
10 April (101).	1 Sun....	57	30	23	0	†3	36	†1	26	18 Mar. (78)..	6 Fri.....	225	.675	9945	276	213	4938

† See footnote p. liii above.

TABLE I.

Lunation-parts = 10,000ths of a circle. A tithi = 1/30th of the moon's synodic revolution.

I. CONCURRENT YEAR.								II. ADDED LUNAR MONTHS.				
						Samvatsara.		True.				
Kali.	Śaka.	Chaitrâdi. Vikrama.	Meshâdi (Solar) year in Bengal.	Kollam.	A. D.	Luni-Solar cycle. (Southern.)	Bṛihaspati cycle (Northern) current at Mesha saṅkrânti.	Name of month.	Time of the preceding saṅkrânti expressed in		Time of the succeeding saṅkrânti expressed in	
									Lunation parts. (*t.*)	Tithis.	Lunation parts. (*t.*)	Tithis.
1	2	3	3a	4	5	6	7	8	9	10	11	12
4939	1760	1895	1244	1012–13	1837–38	31 Hemalamba	42 Kîlaka	...	...	...	...	...
4940	1761	1896	1245	1013–14	1838–39	32 Vilamba	43 Saumya	...	...	...	...	...
4941	1762	1897	1246	1014–15	1839–40	33 Vikârin	44 Sâdhâraṇa	3 Jyeshṭha	9826	29.478	581	1.743
4942	1763	1898	1247	1015–16	*1840–41	34 Śârvari	45 Virodhakṛit	...	...	...	...	...
4943	1764	1899	1248	1016–17	1841–42	35 Plava	46 Paridhâvin	7 Âśvina	9876	29.628	232	0.696
4944	1765	1900	1249	1017–18	1842–43	36 Śubhakṛit	47 Pramâdin	...	...	...	...	...
4945	1766	1901	1250	1018–19	1843–44	37 Śobhana	48 Ânanda	...	...	...	...	...
4946	1767	1902	1251	1019–20	*1844–45	38 Krodhin	49 Râkshasa	5 Śrâvaṇa	9554	28.662	155	0.465
4947	1768	1903	1252	1020–21	1845–46	39 Viśvâvasu	50 Anala	...	...	...	...	...
4948	1769	1904	1253	1021–22	1846–47	40 Parâbhava	51 Piṅgala	...	...	...	...	...
4949	1770	1905	1254	1022–23	1847–48	41 Plavaṅga	52 Kâlayukta	3 Jyeshṭha	9368	28.104	98	0.294
4950	1771	1906	1255	1023–24	*1848–49	42 Kîlaka	53 Siddhârthin	...	...	...	...	...
4951	1772	1907	1256	1024–25	1849–50	43 Saumya	54 Raudra	...	...	...	...	...
4952	1773	1908	1257	1025–26	1850–51	44 Sâdhâraṇa	55 Durmati	2 Vaiśâkha	9729	29.187	248	0.744
4953	1774	1909	1258	1026–27	1851–52	45 Virodhakṛit	56 Dundubhi	...	...	...	...	...
4954	1775	1910	1259	1027–28	*1852–53	46 Paridhâvin	57 Rudhirodgârin	6 Bhâdrapada	9713	29.139	293	0.879
4955	1776	1911	1260	1028–29	1853–54	47 Pramâdin	58 Raktâksha	...	...	...	...	...
4956	1777	1912	1261	1029–30	1854–55	48 Ânanda	59 Krodhana	...	...	...	...	...
4957	1778	1913	1262	1030–31	1855–56	49 Râkshasa	60 Kshaya	4 Âshâḍha	9612	28.836	277	0.831
4958	1779	1914	1263	1031–32	*1856–57	50 Anala	1 Prabhava [1]	...	...	...	...	...
4959	1780	1915	1264	1032–33	1857–58	51 Piṅgala	3 Śukla	...	...	...	...	...
4960	1781	1916	1265	1033–34	1858–59	52 Kâlayukta	4 Pramoda	3 Jyeshṭha	9783	29.349	568	1.704
4961	1782	1917	1266	1034–35	1859–60	53 Siddhârthin	5 Prajâpati	...	...	...	...	...
4962	1783	1918	1267	1035–36	*1860–61	54 Raudra	6 Aṅgiras	7 Âśvina	9845	29.535	242	0.726
4963	1784	1919	1268	1036–37	1861–62	55 Durmati	7 Śrîmukha	...	...	...	...	...
4964	1785	1920	1269	1037–38	1862–63	56 Dundubhi	8 Bhâva	...	...	...	...	...
4965	1786	1921	1270	1038–39	1863–64	57 Rudhirodgârin	9 Yuvan	5 Śrâvaṇa	9744	29.232	316	0.948
4966	1787	1922	1271	1039–40	*1864–65	58 Raktâksha	10 Dhâtṛi	...	...	...	...	...
4967	1788	1923	1272	1040–41	1865–66	59 Krodhana	11 Îśvara	...	...	...	...	...
4968	1789	1924	1273	1041–42	1866–67	60 Kshaya	12 Bahudhânya	3 Jyeshṭha	9326	27.978	111	0.333
4969	1790	1925	1274	1042–43	1867–68	1 Prabhava	13 Pramâthin	...	...	...	...	...
4970	1791	1926	1275	1043–44	*1868–69	2 Vibhava	14 Vikrama	...	...	...	...	...

1) Vibhava, No. 2, was suppressed in the north.

TABLE I.

(*Col.* 23) a = *Distance of moon from sun.* (*Col.* 24) b = *moon's mean anomaly.* (*Col.* 25) c = *sun's mean anomaly.*

III. COMMENCEMENT OF THE

Solar year.										Luni-Solar year. (Civil day of Chaitra Śukla 1st.)							Kali.
Day and Month A. D.	(Time of the Mesha saṅkrânti.)									Day and Month A. D.	Week day.	At Sunrise on meridian of Ujjain.					
	Week day.	By the Ârya Siddhânta.				By the Sûrya Siddhânta.						Moon's Age.					
		Gh.	Pa.	H.	M.	Gh.	Pa.	H.	M.			Lunat. parts elapsed. (*t.*)	Tithis elapsed.	*a.*	*b.*	*c.*	
13	14	15		17		15a		17a		19	20	21	22	23	24	25	1
11 April (101)	3 Tues....	13	1	5	12	19	8	7	39	6 April (96)..	5 Thur...	255	.765	9979	212	264	4939
11 April (101).	4 Wed....	28	32	11	25	34	39	13	52	26 Mar. (85)..	2 Mon....	46	.138	9855	59	233	4940
11 April (101).	5 Thur...	44	4	17	37	50	11	20	4	16 Mar. (75)..	0 Sat.....	161	.483	69	942	205	4941
10 April (101).	6 Fri.....	59	35	23	50	†5	42	†2	17	3 April (94)..	6 Fri.....	147	.441	104	878	256	4942
11 April (101).	1 Sun....	15	6	6	2	21	14	8	29	24 Mar. (83)..	4 Wed....	318	.954	318	761	228	4943
11 April (101).	2 Mon....	30	37	12	15	36	45	14	42	11 April (101).	2 Mon....	36	.108	14	661	277	4944
11 April (101).	3 Tues....	46	9	18	27	52	17	20	55	31 Mar. (90)..	6 Fri.....	23	.069	9890	508	246	4945
11 April (102).	5 Thur...	1	40	0	40	7	48	3	7	19 Mar. (79)..	3 Tues....	16	.048	9765	356	215	4946
11 April (101).	6 Fri.....	17	11	6	52	23	20	9	20	7 April (97)..	2 Mon....	75	.225	9800	292	266	4947
11 April (101).	0 Sat.....	32	42	13	5	38	51	15	33	28 Mar. (87)..	0 Sat.....	279	.837	14	175	238	4948
11 April (101).	1 Sun....	48	14	19	17	54	23	21	45	17 Mar. (76)..	4 Wed....	52	.156	9890	22	208	4949
11 April (102).	3 Tues....	3	45	1	30	9	54	3	58	4 April (95)..	3 Tues....	28	.084	9925	958	259	4950
11 April (101).	4 Wed....	19	16	7	42	25	26	10	10	25 Mar. (84)..	1 Sun....	162	.486	139	842	231	4951
11 April (101).	5 Thur...	34	47	13	55	40	58	16	23	14 Mar. (73)..	5 Thur...	28	.084	15	689	200	4952
11 April (101).	6 Fri.....	50	19	20	7	56	29	22	36	2 April (92)..	4 Wed....	90	.270	49	625	251	4953
11 April (102).	1 Sun....	5	50	2	20	12	1	4	48	21 Mar. (81)..	1 Sun....	90	.270	9925	472	220	4954
11 April (101).	2 Mon....	21	21	8	32	27	32	11	1	9 April (99)..	0 Sat.....	177	.531	9960	408	272	4955
11 April (101).	3 Tues....	36	52	14	45	43	4	17	13	29 Mar. (88)..	4 Wed....	115	.345	9835	255	241	4956
11 April (101).	4 Wed....	52	24	20	57	58	35	23	26	19 Mar. (78)..	2 Mon....	299	.897	50	139	213	4957
11 April (102).	6 Fri.....	7	55	3	10	14	7	5	39	6 April (97)..	1 Sun....	288	.864	84	75	264	4958
11 April (101).	0 Sat.....	23	26	9	22	29	38	11	51	26 Mar. (85)..	5 Thur...	34	.102	9960	922	233	4959
11 April (101).	1 Sun....	38	57	15	35	45	10	18	4	16 Mar. (75)..	3 Tues....	186	.558	175	806	205	4960
11 April (101).	2 Mon....	54	29	21	47	†0	41	†0	16	4 April (94)..	2 Mon....	209	.627	209	741	257	4961
11 April (102).	4 Wed....	10	0	4	0	16	13	6	29	23 Mar. (83)..	6 Fri.....	151	.453	85	589	226	4962
11 April (101).	5 Thur...	25	31	10	12	31	44	12	42	11 April (101).	5 Thur...	239	.717	120	525	277	4963
11 April (101).	6 Fri.....	41	2	16	25	47	16	18	54	31 Mar. (90)..	2 Mon....	236	.708	9995	372	246	4964
11 April (101).	0 Sat.....	56	34	22	37	†2	47	†1	7	20 Mar. (79)..	6 Fri.....	149	.447	9871	219	215	4965
11 April (102).	2 Mon....	12	5	4	50	18	19	7	20	7 April (98)..	5 Thur...	161	.483	9906	155	267	4966
11 April (101).	3 Tues....	27	36	11	2	33	50	13	32	28 Mar. (87)..	3 Tues....	294	.882	120	89	239	4967
11 April (101).	4 Wed....	43	7	17	15	49	22	19	45	17 Mar. (76)..	0 Sat.....	46	.138	9996	886	208	4968
11 April (101).	5 Thur...	58	39	23	27	†4	53	†1	57	5 April (95)..	6 Fri.....	44	.132	30	822	259	4969
11 April (102).	0 Sat.....	14	10	5	40	20	25	8	10	25 Mar. (85)..	4 Wed....	250	.750	245	705	231	4970

† See footnote p. liii above.

TABLE I.

Lunation-parts = 10,000*ths of a circle. A tithi* = 1/30*th of the moon's synodic revolution.*

I. CONCURRENT YEAR.								II. ADDED LUNAR MONTHS.				
						Samvatsara.		True.				
Kali.	Śaka.	Chaitrâdi. Vikrama.	Meshâdi (Solar) year in Bengal.	Kollam.	A. D.	Luni-Solar cycle. (Southern.)	Bṛihaspati cycle (Northern) current at Mesha saṅkrânti.	Name of month.	Time of the preceding saṅkrânti expressed in: Lunation parts. (*t.*)	Time of the preceding saṅkrânti expressed in: Tithis.	Time of the succeeding saṅkrânti expressed in: Lunation parts. (*t.*)	Time of the succeeding saṅkrânti expressed in: Tithis.
1	2	3	3a	4	5	6	7	8	9	10	11	12
4971	1792	1927	1276	1044–45	1869– 70	3 Śukla	15 Vṛisha	2 Vaiśâkha	9869	29.607	299	0.897
4972	1793	1928	1277	1045–46	1870– 71	4 Pramoda	16 Chitrabhânu					
4973	1794	1929	1278	1046–47	1871– 72	5 Prajâpati	17 Subhânu	6 Bhâdrapada	9796	29.388	297	0.891
4974	1795	1930	1279	1047–48	*1872– 73	6 Aṅgiras	18 Târana					
4975	1796	1931	1280	1048–49	1873– 74	7 Śrîmukha	19 Pârthiva					
4976	1797	1932	1281	1049–50	1874– 75	8 Bhâva	20 Vyaya	4 Âshâḍha	9648	28.944	429	1.287
4977	1798	1933	1282	1050–51	1875– 76	9 Yuvan	21 Sarvajit					
4978	1799	1934	1283	1051–52	*1876– 77	10 Dhâtṛi	22 Sarvadhârin					
4979	1800	1935	1284	1052–53	1877– 78	11 Îśvara	23 Virodhin	3 Jyeshṭha	9802	29.406	527	1.581
4980	1801	1936	1285	1053–54	1878– 79	12 Bahudhânya	24 Vikṛita					
4981	1802	1937	1286	1054–55	1879– 80	13 Pramâthin	25 Khara	7 Âśvina	9818	29.454	194	0.582
4982	1803	1938	1287	1055–56	*1880– 81	14 Vikrama	26 Nandana					
4983	1804	1939	1288	1056–57	1881– 82	15 Vṛisha	27 Vijaya					
4984	1805	1940	1289	1057–58	1882– 83	16 Chitrabhânu	28 Jaya	5 Śrâvaṇa	9921	29.763	510	1.530
4985	1806	1941	1290	1058–59	1883– 84	17 Subhânu	29 Manmatha					
4986	1807	1942	1291	1059–60	*1884– 85	18 Târaṇa	30 Durmukha					
4987	1808	1943	1292	1060–61	1885– 86	19 Pârthiva	31 Hemalamba	3 Jyeshṭha	9328	27.984	70	0.210
4988	1809	1944	1293	1061–62	1886– 87	20 Vyaya	32 Vilamba					
4989	1810	1945	1294	1062–63	1887– 88	21 Sarvajit	33 Vikârin					
4990	1811	1946	1295	1063–64	*1888– 89	22 Sarvadhârin	34 Śârvari	1 Chaitra	9857	29.571	62	0.186
4991	1812	1947	1296	1064–65	1889– 90	23 Virodhin	35 Plava					
4992	1813	1948	1297	1065–66	1890– 91	24 Vikṛita	36 Śubhakrit	6 Bhâdrapada	9973	29.919	402	1.206
4993	1814	1949	1298	1066–67	1891– 92	25 Khara	37 Śobhana					
4994	1815	1950	1299	1067–68	*1892– 93	26 Nandana	38 Krodhin					
4995	1816	1951	1300	1068–69	1893– 94	27 Vijaya	39 Viśvâvasu	4 Âshâḍha	9616	28.848	479	1.437
4996	1817	1952	1301	1069–70	1894– 95	28 Jaya	40 Parâbhava					
4997	1818	1953	1302	1070–71	1895– 96	29 Manmatha	41 Plavaṅga					
4998	1819	1954	1303	1071–72	*1896– 97	30 Durmukha	42 Kîlaka	3 Jyeshṭha	9921	29.763	544	1.632
4999	1820	1955	1304	1072–73	1897– 98	31 Hemalamba	43 Saumya					
5000	1821	1956	1305	1073–74	1898– 99	32 Vilamba	44 Sâdhâraṇa	7 Âśvina	9888	29.664	189	0.567
5001	1822	1957	1306	1074–75	1899–900	33 Vikârin	45 Virodhakrit					
5002	1823	1958	1307	1075–76	1900§– 1	34 Śârvari	46 Paridhâvin					

§ The year 1900 A. D. will not be a leap-year.

TABLE I.

(*Col.* 23) *a* = *Distance of moon from sun.* (*Col.* 24) *b* = *moon's mean anomaly.* (*Col.* 25) *c* = *sun's mean anomaly.*

III. COMMENCEMENT OF THE																	
Solar year.										Luni-Solar year. (Civil day of Chaitra Śukla 1st.)							Kali.
Day and Month A. D.	(Time of the Mesha saṅkrânti.)									Day and Month A. D.	Week day.	At Sunrise on meridian of Ujjain.					
	Week day.	By the Ârya Siddhânta.				By the Sûrya Siddhânta.						Moon's Age.					
		Gh.	Pa.	H.	M.	Gh.	Pa.	H.	M.			Lunat. parts elapsed. (*t.*)	Tithis elapsed.	*a.*	*b.*	*c.*	
13	14	15		17		15a		17a		19	20	21	22	23	24	25	1
11 April (101).	1 Sun....	29	41	11	52	35	56	14	23	14 Mar. (73)..	1 Sun....	217	.651	120	553	200	4971
11 April (101).	2 Mon....	45	12	18	5	51	28	20	35	2 April (92)..	0 Sat.....	306	.918	155	488	251	4972
12 April (102).	4 Wed....	0	44	0	17	7	0	2	48	22 Mar. (81)..	4 Wed....	292	.876	31	336	221	4973
11 April (102).	5 Thur...	16	15	6	30	22	31	9	0	8 April (99)..	2 Mon....	7	.021	9727	235	269	4974
11 April (101).	6 Fri.....	31	46	12	42	38	3	15	13	29 Mar. (88)..	0 Sat.....	176	.528	9941	119	241	4975
11 April (101).	0 Sat.....	47	17	18	55	53	34	21	26	19 Mar. (78)..	5 Thur...	299	.897	155	2	213	4976
12 April (102).	2 Mon....	2	49	1	7	9	6	3	38	7 April (97)..	4 Wed....	276	.828	190	938	264	4977
11 April (102).	3 Tues....	18	20	7	20	24	37	9	51	26 Mar. (86)..	1 Sun....	70	.210	66	786	233	4978
11 April (101).	4 Wed....	33	51	13	32	40	9	16	3	16 Mar. (75)..	6 Fri.....	300	.900	280	669	205	4979
11 April (101).	5 Thur...	49	22	19	45	55	40	22	16	3 April (93)..	4 Wed....	57	.171	9976	569	254	4980
12 April (102).	0 Sat.....	4	54	1	57	11	12	4	29	23 Mar. (82)..	1 Sun....	63	.189	9852	416	223	4981
11 April (102).	1 Sun....	20	25	8	10	26	43	10	41	10 April (101).	0 Sat.....	139	.417	9887	352	274	4982
11 April (101).	2 Mon....	35	56	14	22	42	15	16	54	30 Mar. (89)..	4 Wed....	35	.105	9762	199	244	4983
11 April (101).	3 Tues....	51	27	20	35	57	46	23	7	20 Mar. (79)..	2 Mon...	188	.564	9977	83	215	4984
12 April (102).	5 Thur...	6	59	2	47	13	18	5	19	8 April (98)..	1 Sun....	168	.504	11	19	267	4985
11 April (102).	6 Fri.....	22	30	9	0	28	49	11	32	28 Mar. (88)..	6 Fri.....	285	.855	226	902	239	4986
11 April (101).	0 Sat.....	38	1	15	12	44	21	17	44	17 Mar. (76)..	3 Tues....	103	.309	101	749	208	4987
11 April (101).	1 Sun....	53	32	21	25	59	52	23	57	5 April (95)..	2 Mon....	147	.441	136	685	259	4988
12 April (102).	3 Tues....	9	4	3	37	15	24	6	9	25 Mar. (84)..	6 Fri.....	123	.369	12	533	229	4989
11 April (102).	4 Wed....	24	35	9	50	30	55	12	22	13 Mar. (73)..	3 Tues....	126	.378	9887	380	199	4990
11 April (101).	5 Thur...	40	6	16	2	46	27	18	35	1 April (91)..	2 Mon....	190	.570	9922	816	250	4991
11 April (101).	6 Fri.....	55	37	22	15	†1	58	†0	47	21 Mar. (80)..	6 Fri.....	49	.147	9798	163	219	4992
12 April (102).	1 Sun....	11	9	4	27	17	30	7	0	9 April (99)..	5 Thur...	54	.162	9832	99	270	4993
11 April (102).	2 Mon....	26	40	10	40	33	2	13	13	29 Mar. (89)..	3 Tues....	171	.513	47	982	242	4994
11 April (101).	3 Tues....	42	11	16	52	48	33	19	25	19 Mar. (78)..	1 Sun....	299	.897	261	866	214	4995
11 April (101).	4 Wed....	57	42	23	5	†4	5	†1	38	7 April (97)..	0 Sat.....	304	.912	296	802	265	4996
12 April (102).	6 Fri.....	13	14	5	17	19	36	7	50	27 Mar. (86)..	4 Wed....	198	.594	171	649	235	4997
11 April (102).	0 Sat.....	28	45	11	30	35	8	14	3	15 Mar. (75)..	1 Sun....	194	.582	47	496	204	4998
11 April (101).	1 Sun....	44	16	17	42	50	39	20	16	3 April (93)..	0 Sat.....	280	.840	82	432	255	4999
11 April (101).	2 Mon....	59	47	23	55	†6	11	†2	28	23 Mar. (82)..	4 Wed....	235	.705	9957	280	224	5000
12 April (102).	4 Wed....	15	19	6	7	21	42	8	41	11 April (101).	3 Tues....	270	.810	9992	216	276	5001
12 April (102).	5 Thur...	30	50	12	20	37	14	14	53	31 Mar. (90)..	0 Sat.....	62	.186	9868	63	245	5002

† See footnote p. liii above.

TABLE II. PART I.

CORRESPONDENCE OF AMANTA AND PÛRNIMANTA MONTHS

(*See Art.* 51.)

Amânta months.	Fortnights.	Pûrṇimânta months.
1	2	3
		Chaitra.
1 Chaitra........	Śukla...........	
	Kṛishṇa..........	Vaiśâkha.
2 Vaiśâkha.......	Śukla...........	
	Kṛishṇa..........	Jyeshṭha.
3 Jyeshṭha.......	Śukla...........	
	Kṛishṇa..........	Âshâḍha.
4 Âshâḍha........	Śukla...........	
	Kṛishṇa..........	Śrâvaṇa.
5 Śrâvaṇa........	Śukla...........	
	Kṛishṇa..........	Bhâdrapada
6 Bhâdrapada.....	Śukla...........	
	Kṛishṇa..........	Âśvina.
7 Âśvina.........	Śukla...........	
	Kṛishṇa..........	Kârttika.
8 Kârttika.......	Śukla...........	
	Kṛishṇa..........	Mârgaśîrsha.
9 Mârgaśîrsha....	Śukla...........	
	Kṛishṇa..........	Pausha.
10 Pausha........	Śukla...........	
	Kṛishṇa..........	Mâgha.
11 Mâgha.........	Śukla...........	
	Kṛishṇa..........	Phâlguna.
12 Phâlguna......	Śukla...........	
	Kṛishṇa..........	Chaitra.

Śukla = Śuddha and other synonyms.
Kṛishṇa = Bahula, Vadya, and other synonyms.

TABLE II. PART II.

CORRESPONDENCE OF MONTHS IN DIFFERENT ERAS.

(See Art. 103 *of the Text.)*

	LUNI-SOLAR YEAR.					Other months corresponding to Lunar months.	
	Chaitrâdi.		Âshâḍhâdi.	Âśvinâdi.	Kârttikâdi.		
	Sanskṛit names of months.	Tuḷu names.	Sanskṛit names of months.			Solar months.	Months A. D.
	1	2	3	4	5	6	7
	Kali 4179. Vikrama 1135.	Śaka 1000. Gupta 758.	Vikrama Samvat 1134.	Chedi (Kalachuri) 829.	Vikrama 1134. Nevâr 198.		A. D. 1077.
1	Chaitra.	Paggu.	Chaitra.	Chaitra.	Chaitra.	Mîna, Mesha.	Feb., March, April, May.
2	Vaiśâkha.	Beśâ.	Vaiśâkha.	Vaiśâkha.	Vaiśâkha.	Mesha, Vṛishabha.	March, April, May, June.
3	Jyeshṭha.	Kârtelu.	Jyeshṭha.	Jyeshṭha.	Jyeshṭha.	Vṛishabha, Mithuna.	April, May, June, July.
			1135.				
4	Âshâḍha.	Âṭi.	Âshâḍha.	Âshâḍha.	Âshâḍha.	Mithuna, Karka.	May, June, July, Aug.
5	Śrâvaṇa.	Sôṇa.	Śrâvaṇa.	Śrâvaṇa.	Śrâvaṇa.	Karka, Siṁha.	June, July, Aug., Sept.
6	Bhâdrapada.	Nirṇâla.	Bhâdrapada.	Bhâdrapada.	Bhâdrapada.	Siṁha, Kanyâ.	July, Aug., Sept., Oct.
				830.			
7	Âśvina.	Bontelu.	Âśvina.	Âśvina.	Âśvina.	Kanyâ, Tulâ.	Aug., Sept., Oct., Nov.
					1135; 199.		
8	Kârttika.	Jârde.	Kârttika.	Kârttika.	Kârttika.	Tulâ, Vṛiśchika	Sept., Oct., Nov., Dec.
							1078.
9	Mârgaśîrsha.	Perârde.	Mârgaśîrsha.	Mârgaśîrsha.	Mârgaśîrsha.	Vṛiśchika, Dhanus.	Oct., Nov., Dec., Jan.
10	Pausha.	Pûntelu.	Pausha.	Pausha.	Pausha.	Dhanus, Makara.	Nov., Dec., Jan., Feb.
11	Mâgha.	Mâyi.	Mâgha.	Mâgha.	Mâgha.	Makara, Kumbha.	Dec., Jan., Feb., March.
12	Phâlguna.	Suggi.	Phâlguna.	Phâlguna.	Phâlguna.	Kumbha, Mîna.	Jan., Feb., March, April.

N.B. i. All the years are current, and the lunar-months are amânta.

N.B. ii. *Chaitrâdi* = "beginning with Chaitra"; *Meshâdi* = "beginning with Mesha" and so on.

TABLE II. PART II. (CONTINUED.)

CORRESPONDENCE OF MONTHS IN DIFFERENT ERAS.

(See Art. 103 *of the Text.)*

	SOLAR YEAR.							Other months corresponding to Solar months.	
	Meshâdi.			Siṁhâdi.		Kanyâdi.			
	Sign names.	Bengali names.	Tamil names.	Tinnevelly names.	South Malayâḷam names.	North Malayâḷam names.	Orissa names.	Lunar months.	Months A. D.
	8	9	10	11	12	13		14	15
	Kali 4179. Śaka 1000.	Vikrama 1135. Bengali San 484.		Tinnevelly 252.	Kollam 252.	Kollam 252.	Vilâyatî 484.		A. D. 1077.
1	Mesha.	Vaiśâkha (Baisâk).	Chittirai (Śittirai).	Chittirai (Śittirai).	Mêḍam.	Mêḍam.	Baisâk.	Chait., Vaiś.	Mar., Apr., May.
2	Vṛishabha	Jyeshṭha (Joisṭho).	Vaigâśi, Vaiyâśi.	Vaigâśi (Vaiyâśi).	Eḍavam.	Eḍavam.	Joisṭho.	Vaiś., Jyesh.	Apr., May, June.
3	Mithuna.	Âshâḍha (Assar).	Âni.	Âni.	Midunam.	Midunam.	Assar.	Jyesh., Âshâ.	May, June, July.
4	Karka.	Śrâvaṇa (Shrâban).	Âḍi.	Âḍi.	Karkaḍakam	Karkadakam.	Sawun.	Âshâ., Śrâv.	June, July, Aug.
				253.	253.				
5	Siṁha.	Bhâdrapada (Bhâdro).	Âvaṇi.	Âvaṇi.	Chiṅgam.	Chiṅgam.	Bhâdro.	Śrâv., Bhâd.	July, Aug., Sept.
						253.	485.		
6	Kanyâ.	Âśvina (Âssin).	Puraṭṭâdi —(Puraṭṭâśi).	Puraṭṭâdi —(Puraṭṭâśi).	Kanni.	Kanni.	Âssin.	Bhâd., Âśv.	Aug., Sept., Oct.
7	Tulâ.	Kârttika (Kârttik).	Aippaśi (Arppiśi, —Appiśi).	Aippaśi (Arppiśi, —Appiśi).	Tuḷâm.	Tuḷâm.	Kârttik.	Âśv., Kârtt.	Sept.. Oct., Nov.
8	Vṛiśchika.	Mârgaśîrsha (Âghrân).	Kârttigai.	Kârttigai.	Vṛiśchikam.	Vṛiśchikam.	Âghrân.	Kârt., Mârg.	Oct., Nov., Dec.
									1078.
9	Dhanus.	Pausha (Paus).	Mârgaḷi.	Mârgaḷi.	Dhanu.	Dhanu.	Paus.	Mârg., Paus.	Nov., Dec., Jan.
10	Makara.	Mâgha.	Tai.	Tai.	Makaram.	Makaram.	Mâgha.	Paus., Mâgh.	Dec., Jan., Feb.
11	Kumbha.	Phâlguna (Falgûn).	Mâśi.	Mâśi.	Kumbham.	Kumbham.	Falgûn.	Mâgh., Phâl.	Jan., Feb., Mar.
12	Mîna.	Chaitra (Choitro).	Paṅguni.	Paṅguni.	Mînam.	Mînam.	Choitro.	Phâl., Chait.	Feb., Mar., Apr.

TABLE II. PART III.

CORRESPONDENCE OF YEARS OF DIFFERENT ERAS.

N.B. i. The month in which the year of a non-Chaitrâdi or non-Meshâdi era begins is given in brackets in the heading. An era which has no month printed under it in the heading is Chaitrâdi or Meshâdi.

N.B. ii. To turn a year of one era into that of another, use the year 0 under one and the corresponding year on the same horizontal line under the other. For instance, to turn a Saka year into a Vikrama year and vice versâ, Saka 0 = Chaitrâdi Vikrama 135 = Âshâḍhâdi or Kârttikâdi Vikrama 134–5. A. D. 0 = either kind of Vikrama 57–8; and so on. (See also Art. 104 of the text.)

Kali.																					
0	Saptarshi.																				
26	0	Vikrama.																			
3044	3018	0	Vikrama (Âshâḍha, Kârttika).																		
3044–5	3018–9	0–1	0	A. D. (January).																	
3101–2	3075–6	57–8	57–8	0	Saka.																
3179	3153	135	134–5	77–8	0	Chedi (Âśvina).															
3349–50	3323–4	305–6	305–6 304–5	247–8	170–1	0	Valabhi (Kârttika).														
3420–1	3394–5	376–7	376–7 376	318–9	241–2	71–2	0	Gupta.													
3421	3395	377	376–7	319–20	242	71–2	0–1	0	Fasali of South (June, July).												
3692–3	3666–7	648–9	648–9 647–8	590–1	513–4	342–3	271–2	271–2	0	Fasali of North (Âśvina) Vilâyati (Kanyâ) Amli (Bhâdrapada).											
3694–5	3668–9	650–1	650–1 649–50	592–3	515–6	344–5	273–4	273–4	2–3	0	Bengali.										
3695	3669	651	650–1	593–4	516	345–6	274–5	274	2–3	0–1	0	Sûr-San (June).									
3701–2	3675–6	657–8	656–7	599–600	522–3	351–2	280–1	280–1	8–9	6–7	6–7	0	Harsha.								
3708	3682	664	663–4	606–7	529	358–9	287–8	287	15–6	13–4	13	6–7	0	Mâgî.							
3740	3714	696	695–6	638–9	561	390–1	319–20	319	47–8	45–6	45	38–9	32	0	Kollam (Simha, Kanyâ).						
3926–7	3900–1	882–3	882–3 881–2	824–5	747–8	576–7	505–6	505–6	234–5	231–2 232	231–2	225–6	218–9	186–7	0	Nevâr (Kârttika).					
3980–1	3954–5	936–7	935–6 936	878–9	801–2	631–2	560	559–60	288–9	286–7	285–6	279–80	272–3	240–1	54–5	0	Châlukya (initial month doubtful).				
4177–8	4151–2	1133–4	1133–4	1075–6	998–9	828–9	757–8	756–7	485–6	483–4	482–3	476–7	469–70	437–8	251–2	197–8	0	Simha (Âshaḍha).			
4215–6	4189–90	1171–2	1171 1170–1	1113–4	1036–7	865–6	794–5	794–5	522–3 523–4	520–1	520–1	514–5 513–4	507–8	475–6	288–9	234–5	37–8	0	Lakshmana Sena (Kârttika).		
4220–1	4194–5	1176–7	1176–7 1176	1118–9	1041–2	871–2	800	799–800	528–9	526–7	525–6	519–20	512–3	480–1	294–5	240	42–3	5–6	0	Ilâhi.	
4656–7	4630–1	1612–3	1612–3	1555–6	1477–8	1307–8	1236–7	1235–6	964–5	962–3	961–2	955–6	948–9	916–7	730–1	676–7	479–80	441–2	436–7	0	Râjaśaka (Jyeshṭha).
4775–6	4749–50	1731–2	1730–1	1673–4	1596–7	1425–6	1354–5	1354–5	1082–3	1081–2	1080–1	1073–4	1067–8	1035–6	848–9	794–5	597–8	559–60	554–5	118–9	0

TABLE III.

COLLECTIVE DURATION OF MONTHS.

Part I.				Part II.																	
Luni-Solar year (Chaitrâdi).				Solar year (Meshâdi).																	
Serial number.	Name of Month.	Collective duration from the beginning of the year to the end of each month.		Serial number.	Name of Month.	Sankrânti at end of month in col. 5.	Collective duration (in days) from the beginning of the year to the end of the month in col. 5, or to the sankrânti in col. 5 a.														
							Exact.														Approximate.
							By the *Ârya Siddhânta.*						By the *Sûrya Siddhânta.*								
		Exactly in tithis.	Approximately in solar-days.				Hindu reckoning.			European reckoning.			Hindu reckoning.			European reckoning.					
							D.	GH.	P.	D.	H.	M.	D.	GH.	P.	D.	H.	M.			
1	**2**	**3**	**3a**	**4**	**5**	**5a**	**6**			**7**			**8**			**9**					**10**
1	Chaitra....	30	30	1	Mesha.....	Vṛishabha..	30(2)*	55	30	30(2)	22	12	30(2)	56	7	30(2)	22	27			31
2	Vaiśâkha...	60	59	2	Vṛishabha..	Mithuna...	62(6)	19	34	62(6)	7	49	62(6)	21	20	62(6)	8	32			62
3	Jyeshṭha...	90	89	3	Mithuna...	Karka.....	93(2)	56	0	93(2)	22	24	94(3)	0	1	94(3)	0	0			94
4	Âshâḍha...	120	118	4	Karka.....	Siṁha.....	125(6)	24	4	125(6)	9	38	125(6)	28	32	125(6)	11	25			125
5	Śrâvaṇa....	150	148	5	Siṁha.....	Kanyâ.....	156(2)	26	9	156(2)	10	28	156(2)	29	39	156(2)	11	52			156
6	Bhâdrapada.	180	177	6	Kanyâ	Tulâ......	186(4)	53	33	186(4)	21	25	186(4)	56	8	186(4)	22	27			187
7	Âśvina.....	210	207	7	Tulâ......	Vṛiśchika...	216(6)	47	45	216(6)	19	6	216(6)	49	44	216(6)	19	54			217
8	Kârttika....	240	236	8	Vṛiśchika..	Dhanus....	246(1)	18	16	246(1)	7	18	246(1)	19	9	246(1)	7	40			246
9	Mârgaśîrsha	270	266	9	Dhanus ...	Makara....	275(2)	39	18	275(2)	15	43	275(2)	38	13	275(2)	15	17			276
10	Pausha	300	295	10	Makara ...	Kumbha...	305(4)	6	42	305(4)	2	41	305(4)	5	6	305(4)	2	2			305
11	Mâgha.....	330	325	11	Kumbha...	Mîna......	334(5)	55	12	334(5)	22	5	334(5)	54	19	334(5)	21	44			335
12	Phâlguna... In intercalary years.	360 390	354 384	12	Mîna	Mesha (of the following year)†.	365(1)	15	31	365(1)	6	12	365(1)	15	32	365(1)	6	13			365

* The figures in brackets in columns 6, 7, 8, 9 give the (*w*) or weekday index.

† The moment of the Mesha sankrânti coincides with the exact beginning of the solar year.

TABLE IV.

(*W*) (*A*) (*B*) (*C*) FOR EVERY DAY IN THE YEAR.

(*Prof. Jacobi's Table 7 in Ind. Ant., Vol. XVII., modified and corrected*).

No. of days.	(*w.*)	(*a.*)	(*b.*)	(*c.*)	No. of days.	(*w.*)	(*a.*)	(*b.*)	(*c.*)	No. of days.	(*w.*)	(*a.*)	(*b.*)	(*c.*)
1	1	339	36	3	43	1	4561	561	118	85	1	8784	85	233
2	2	677	73	5	44	2	4900	597	120	86	2	9122	121	235
3	3	1016	109	8	45	3	5238	633	123	87	3	9461	157	238
4	4	1355	145	11	46	4	5577	669	126	88	4	9800	194	241
5	5	1693	181	14	47	5	5916	706	129	89	5	138	230	244
6	6	2032	218	16	48	6	6254	742	131	90	6	477	266	246
7	0	2370	254	19	49	0	6593	778	134	91	0	816	303	249
8	1	2709	290	22	50	1	6932	815	137	92	1	1154	339	252
9	2	3048	327	25	51	2	7270	851	140	93	2	1493	375	255
10	3	3386	363	27	52	3	7609	887	142	94	3	1831	411	257
11	4	3725	399	30	53	4	7947	923	145	95	4	2170	448	260
12	5	4064	435	33	54	5	8286	960	148	96	5	2509	484	263
13	6	4402	472	36	55	6	8625	996	151	97	6	2847	520	266
14	0	4741	508	38	56	0	8963	32	153	98	0	3186	557	268
15	1	5079	544	41	57	1	9302	69	156	99	1	3525	593	271
16	2	5418	581	44	58	2	9641	105	159	100	2	3863	629	274
17	3	5757	617	47	59	3	9979	141	162	101	3	4202	665	277
18	4	6095	653	49	60	4	318	177	164	102	4	4540	702	279
19	5	6434	690	52	61	5	657	214	167	103	5	4879	738	282
20	6	6773	726	55	62	6	995	250	170	104	6	5218	774	285
21	0	7111	762	57	63	0	1334	286	172	105	0	5556	811	287
22	1	7450	798	60	64	1	1672	323	175	106	1	5895	847	290
23	2	7789	835	63	65	2	2011	359	178	107	2	6234	883	293
24	3	8127	871	66	66	3	2350	395	181	108	3	6572	919	296
25	4	8466	907	68	67	4	2688	432	183	109	4	6911	956	298
26	5	8804	944	71	68	5	3027	468	186	110	5	7250	992	301
27	6	9143	980	74	69	6	3366	504	189	111	6	7588	28	304
28	0	9482	16	77	70	0	3704	540	192	112	0	7927	65	307
29	1	9820	52	79	71	1	4043	577	194	113	1	8265	101	309
30	2	159	89	82	72	2	4381	613	197	114	2	8604	137	312
31	3	498	125	85	73	3	4720	649	200	115	3	8943	174	315
32	4	836	161	88	74	4	5059	686	203	116	4	9281	210	318
33	5	1175	198	90	75	5	5397	722	205	117	5	9620	246	320
34	6	1513	234	93	76	6	5736	758	208	118	6	9959	282	323
35	0	1852	270	96	77	0	6075	794	211	119	0	297	319	326
36	1	2191	306	99	78	1	6413	831	214	120	1	636	355	329
37	2	2529	343	101	79	2	6752	867	216	121	2	974	391	331
38	3	2868	379	104	80	3	7091	903	219	122	3	1313	428	334
39	4	3207	415	107	81	4	7429	940	222	123	4	1652	464	337
40	5	3545	452	110	82	5	7768	976	224	124	5	1990	500	339
41	6	3884	488	112	83	6	8106	12	227	125	6	2329	536	342
42	0	4223	524	115	84	0	8445	48	230	126	0	2668	573	345

TABLE IV. (CONTINUED).

No. of days.	(w.)	(a.)	(b.)	(c.)	No. of days.	(w.)	(a.)	(b.)	(c.)	No. of days.	(w.)	(a.)	(b.)	(c.)
127	1	3006	609	348	171	3	7906	206	468	215	5	2806	803	589
128	2	3345	645	350	172	4	8245	242	471	216	6	3144	839	591
129	3	3684	682	353	173	5	8583	278	474	217	0	3483	875	594
130	4	4022	718	356	174	6	8922	315	476	218	1	3822	912	597
131	5	4361	754	359	175	0	9261	351	479	219	2	4160	948	600
132	6	4699	790	361	176	1	9599	387	482	220	3	4499	984	602
133	0	5038	827	364	177	2	9938	424	485	221	4	4838	20	605
134	1	5377	863	367	178	3	276	460	487	222	5	5176	57	608
135	2	5715	899	370	179	4	615	496	490	223	6	5515	93	611
136	3	6054	936	372	180	5	954	532	493	224	0	5854	129	613
137	4	6393	972	375	181	6	1292	569	496	225	1	6192	166	616
138	5	6731	8	378	182	0	1631	605	498	226	2	6531	202	619
139	6	7070	45	381	183	1	1970	641	501	227	3	6869	238	621
140	0	7408	81	383	184	2	2308	678	504	228	4	7208	274	624
141	1	7747	117	386	185	3	2647	714	506	229	5	7547	311	627
142	2	8086	153	389	186	4	2986	750	509	230	6	7885	347	630
143	3	8424	190	392	187	5	3324	787	512	231	0	8224	383	632
144	4	8763	226	394	188	6	3663	823	515	232	1	8563	420	635
145	5	9102	262	397	189	0	4001	859	517	233	2	8901	456	638
146	6	9440	299	400	190	1	4340	895	520	234	3	9240	492	641
147	0	9779	335	402	191	2	4679	932	523	235	4	9579	529	643
148	1	118	371	405	192	3	5017	968	526	236	5	9917	565	646
149	2	456	407	408	193	4	5356	4	528	237	6	256	601	649
150	3	795	444	411	194	5	5695	41	531	238	0	594	637	652
151	4	1133	480	413	195	6	6033	77	534	239	1	933	674	654
152	5	1472	516	416	196	0	6372	113	537	240	2	1272	710	657
153	6	1811	553	419	197	1	6710	149	539	241	3	1610	746	660
154	0	2149	589	422	198	2	7049	186	542	242	4	1949	783	663
155	1	2488	625	424	199	3	7388	222	545	243	5	2288	819	665
156	2	2827	661	427	200	4	7726	258	548	244	6	2626	855	668
157	3	3165	698	430	201	5	8065	295	550	245	0	2965	891	671
158	4	3504	734	433	202	6	8404	331	553	246	1	3303	928	673
159	5	3842	770	435	203	0	8742	367	556	247	2	3642	964	676
160	6	4181	807	438	204	1	9081	403	559	248	3	3981	0	679
161	0	4520	843	441	205	2	9420	440	561	249	4	4319	37	682
162	1	4858	879	444	206	3	9758	476	564	250	5	4658	73	684
163	2	5197	916	446	207	4	97	512	567	251	6	4997	109	687
164	3	5536	952	449	208	5	435	549	569	252	0	5335	145	690
165	4	5874	988	452	209	6	774	585	572	253	1	5674	182	693
166	5	6213	24	454	210	0	1113	621	575	254	2	6013	218	695
167	6	6552	61	457	211	1	1451	658	578	255	3	6351	254	698
168	0	6890	97	460	212	2	1790	694	580	256	4	6690	291	701
169	1	7229	133	463	213	3	2129	730	583	257	5	7028	327	704
170	2	7567	170	465	214	4	2467	766	586	258	6	7367	363	706

TABLE IV. (CONTINUED.)

No. of days.	(w.)	(a.)	(b.)	(c.)
259	0	7706	400	709
260	1	8044	436	712
261	2	8383	472	715
262	3	8722	508	717
263	4	9060	545	720
264	5	9399	581	723
265	6	9737	617	726
266	0	76	654	728
267	1	415	690	731
268	2	753	726	734
269	3	1092	762	736
270	4	1431	799	739
271	5	1769	835	742
272	6	2108	871	745
273	0	2447	908	747
274	1	2785	944	750
275	2	3124	980	753
276	3	3462	16	756
277	4	3801	53	758
278	5	4140	89	761
279	6	4478	125	764
280	0	4817	162	767
281	1	5156	198	769
282	2	5494	234	772
283	3	5833	271	775
284	4	6171	307	778
285	5	6510	343	780
286	6	6849	379	783
287	0	7187	416	786
288	1	7526	452	788
289	2	7865	488	791
290	3	8203	525	794
291	4	8542	561	797
292	5	8881	597	799
293	6	9219	633	802
294	0	9558	670	805
295	1	9896	706	808
296	2	235	742	810
297	3	574	779	813
298	4	912	815	816
299	5	1251	851	819
300	6	1590	887	821
301	0	1928	924	824

No. of days.	(w.)	(a.)	(b.)	(c.)
302	1	2267	960	827
303	2	2605	996	830
304	3	2944	33	832
305	4	3283	69	835
306	5	3621	105	838
307	6	3960	142	840
308	0	4299	178	843
309	1	4637	214	846
310	2	4976	250	849
311	3	5315	287	851
312	4	5653	323	854
313	5	5992	359	857
314	6	6330	396	860
315	0	6669	432	862
316	1	7008	468	865
317	2	7346	504	868
318	3	7685	541	871
319	4	8024	577	873
320	5	8362	613	876
321	6	8701	650	879
322	0	9039	686	882
323	1	9378	722	884
324	2	9717	758	887
325	3	55	795	890
326	4	394	831	893
327	5	733	867	895
328	6	1071	904	898
329	0	1410	940	901
330	1	1749	976	903
331	2	2087	13	906
332	3	2426	49	909
333	4	2764	85	912
334	5	3103	121	914
335	6	3442	158	917
336	0	3780	194	920
337	1	4119	230	923
338	2	4458	267	925
339	3	4796	303	928
340	4	5135	339	931
341	5	5473	375	934
342	6	5812	412	936
343	0	6151	448	939

No. of days.	(w.)	(a.)	(b.)	(c.)
344	1	6489	484	942
345	2	6828	521	945
346	3	7167	557	947
347	4	7505	593	950
348	5	7844	629	953
349	6	8183	666	955
350	0	8521	702	958
351	1	8860	738	961
352	2	9198	775	964
353	3	9537	811	966
354	4	9876	847	969
355	5	214	884	972
356	6	553	920	975
357	0	892	956	977
358	1	1230	992	980
359	2	1569	29	983
360	3	1907	65	986
361	4	2246	101	988
362	5	2585	138	991
363	6	2923	174	994
364	0	3262	210	997
365	1	3601	246	999
366	2	3939	283	2
367	3	4278	319	5
368	4	4617	355	8
369	5	4955	392	10
370	6	5294	428	13
371	0	5632	464	16
372	1	5971	500	18
373	2	6310	537	21
374	3	6648	573	24
375	4	6987	609	27
376	5	7326	646	29
377	6	7664	682	32
378	0	8003	718	35
379	1	8342	755	38
380	2	8680	791	40
381	3	9019	827	43
382	4	9357	863	46
383	5	9696	900	49
384	6	35	936	51
385	0	373	972	54

TABLE V.

(*A*) (*B*) (*C*) FOR HOURS AND MINUTES.

(*Prof. Jacobi's Ind. Ant., Table* 8).

Hours.	(*a.*)	(*b.*)	(*c.*)	Minutes.	(*a.*)	(*b.*)	(*c.*)	Minutes.	(*a.*)	(*b.*)	(*c.*)
1	14	2	0	1	0	0	0	31	7	1	0
2	28	3	0	2	0	0	0	32	8	1	0
3	42	5	0	3	1	0	0	33	8	1	0
4	56	6	0	4	1	0	0	34	8	1	0
5	71	8	1	5	1	0	0	35	8	1	0
6	85	9	1	6	1	0	0	36	8	1	0
7	99	11	1	7	2	0	0	37	9	1	0
8	113	12	1	8	2	0	0	38	9	1	0
9	127	14	1	9	2	0	0	39	9	1	0
10	141	15	1	10	2	0	0	40	9	1	0
11	155	17	1	11	3	0	0	41	10	1	0
12	169	18	1	12	3	0	0	42	10	1	0
13	183	20	1	13	3	0	0	43	10	1	0
14	198	21	2	14	3	0	0	44	10	1	0
15	212	23	2	15	4	0	0	45	11	1	0
16	226	24	2	16	4	0	0	46	11	1	0
17	240	26	2	17	4	0	0	47	11	1	0
18	254	27	2	18	4	0	0	48	11	1	0
19	268	29	2	19	4	0	0	49	12	1	0
20	282	30	2	20	5	1	0	50	12	1	0
21	296	32	2	21	5	1	0	51	12	1	0
22	310	33	3	22	5	1	0	52	12	1	0
23	325	35	3	23	5	1	0	53	12	1	0
24	339	36	3	24	6	1	0	54	13	1	0
—	—	—	—	25	6	1	0	55	13	1	0
—	—	—	—	26	6	1	0	56	13	1	0
—	—	—	—	27	6	1	0	57	13	1	0
—	—	—	—	28	7	1	0	58	14	1	0
—	—	—	—	29	7	1	0	59	14	1	0
—	—	—	—	30	7	1	0	60	14	2	0

TABLE VI.

LUNAR EQUATION.

(*Arts.* 107,108).

ARGUMENT (*b*).

N.B. The equation in col. 2 corresponds to either of the arguments in cols. 1 and 3.

*(This is Prof. Jacobi's **Ind. Ant.**, Vol. XVII., Table 9, re-arranged.)*

Argu.	Equ.	Argu.
1	2	3
0	140	500
10	149	490
20	158	480
30	166	470
40	175	460
50	184	450
60	192	440
70	200	430
80	208	420
90	215	410
100	223	400
110	230	390
120	236	380
130	242	370
140	248	360
150	253	350
160	258	340
170	263	330
180	267	320
190	270	310
200	273	300
210	276	290
220	277	280
230	279	270
240	280	260
250	280	250

Argu.	Equ.	Argu.
1	2	3
500	140	1000
510	131	990
520	122	980
530	114	970
540	105	960
550	96	950
560	88	940
570	80	930
580	72	920
590	65	910
600	57	900
610	50	890
620	44	880
630	38	870
640	32	860
650	27	850
660	22	840
670	17	830
680	13	820
690	10	810
700	7	800
710	4	790
720	3	780
730	1	770
740	0	760
750	0	750

TABLE VII.

SOLAR EQUATION.

(*Arts.* 107,108).

ARGUMENT (*c*).

N.B. The equation in col. 2 corresponds to either of the arguments in cols. 1 and 3.

*(This is Prof. Jacobi's **Ind. Ant.**, Vol. XVII., Table 10, re-arranged.)*

Argu.	Equ.	Argu.
1	2	3
0	60	500
10	57	490
20	53	480
30	49	470
40	45	460
50	41	450
60	38	440
70	34	430
80	31	420
90	28	410
100	25	400
110	22	390
120	19	380
130	16	370
140	14	360
150	11	350
160	9	340
170	7	330
180	6	320
190	4	310
200	3	300
210	2	290
220	1	280
230	0	270
240	0	260
250	0	250

Argu.	Equ.	Argu.
1	2	3
500	60	1000
510	64	990
520	68	980
530	72	970
540	76	960
550	79	950
560	83	940
570	86	930
580	90	920
590	93	910
600	96	900
610	99	890
620	102	880
630	105	870
640	107	860
650	109	850
660	112	840
670	113	830
680	115	820
690	117	810
700	118	800
710	119	790
720	120	780
730	120	770
740	121	760
750	121	750

AUXILIARY TABLE TO TABLES VI. AND VII.

Difference in equation.	LAST FIGURE OF ARGUMENT.								
	9	8	7	6	5	4	3	2	1
	ADD OR SUBTRACT.								
9	8	7	6	5	4 or 5	4	3	2	1
8	7	6	6	5	4	3	2	2	1
7	6	6	5	4	3 or 4	3	2	1	1
6	5	5	4	4	3	2	2	1	1
5	4 or 5	4	3 or 4	3	2 or 3	2	1 or 2	1	0 or 1
4	4	3	3	2	2	2	1	1	0
3	3	2	2	2	1 or 2	1	1	1	0
2	2	2	1	1	1	1	1	0	0
1	1	1	1	1	0 or 1	0	0	0	0

Note the difference in the (Tables VI., VII.) equation-figures for the nearest figures of the argument. Take this difference in the left-hand column of this Table, and run the eye to the right till it reaches the figure standing under the last figure of the given argument. The result is to be added to or subtracted from the equation-figure for the lower of the two argument figures, according as the scale is increasing or decreasing.

Thus; Table VI., argument 334. Difference between equations for 330 and 340 is (263 — 258) 5, decreasing. The figure in the Auxiliary Table opposite 5 and under 4 is 2. The proper equation therefore is 263 — 2 or 261.

Argument 837. Difference between 830 and 840 is (22 — 17) 5, increasing. The figure opposite 5 and under 7 is 3 or 4. The equation therefore is 17 + 3 = 20, or 17 + 4 = 21.

TABLE VIII.

INDICES OF TITHIS, NAKSHATRAS, AND YOGAS; AND THE KARANAS OF TITHIS.

TITHI AND KARAṆA.					NAKSHATRA.					YOGA.		
Serial number.	No. in pakshas (lunar fortnights).	Index (*t*)	Karaṇas. For the 1st half of the tithi.	Karaṇas. For the 2nd half of the tithi.	Serial number.	Name.	Index (*n*) (Ordinary system).	Index for the ending point of the Nakshatra according to the unequal space system of Garga.	Index for the ending point of the Nakshatra according to the unequal space system of Brahma Siddhânta.	Serial number.	Name.	Index (*y*)
1	2	3	4	5	6	7	8	9	10	11	12	13
	Śukla.											
1	1	0- 333	Kiṁstughna *	1 Bava.	1	Aśvinî	0- 370	370	366	1	Vishkambha	0- 370
2	2	333- 667	2 Bâlava	3 Kaulava.	2	Bharaṇî	370- 741	556	549	2	Prîti	370- 741
3	3	667- 1000	4 Taitila	5 Gara.	3	Kṛittikâ	741- 1111	926	915	3	Ayushmat	741- 1111
4	4	1000- 1333	6 Vaṇij	7 Vishṭi †.	4	Rohiṇî	1111- 1481	1481	1464	4	Saubhâgya	1111- 1481
5	5	1333- 1667	1 Bava	2 Bâlava.	5	Mṛigaśiras	1481- 1852	1852	1830	5	Śobhana	1481- 1852
6	6	1667- 2000	3 Kaulava	4 Taitila.	6	Ârdrâ	1852- 2222	2037	2013	6	Atigaṇḍa	1852- 2222
7	7	2000- 2333	5 Gara	6 Vaṇij.	7	Punarvasu	2222- 2593	2593	2562	7	Sukarman	2222- 2593
8	8	2333- 2667	7 Vishṭi †	1 Bava.	8	Pushya	2593- 2963	2963	2928	8	Dhṛiti	2593- 2963
9	9	2667- 3000	2 Bâlava	3 Kaulava.	9	Âśleshâ	2963- 3333	3148	3111	9	Śûla	2963- 3333
10	10	3000- 3333	4 Taitila	5 Gara.	10	Maghâ	3333- 3704	3518	3477	10	Gaṇḍa	3333- 3704
11	11	3333- 3667	6 Vaṇij	7 Vishṭi.	11	Pûrva Phalgunî	3704- 4074	3888	3843	11	Vṛiddhi	3704- 4074
12	12	3667- 4000	1 Bava	2 Bâlava.	12	Uttara Phalgunî	4074- 4444	4444	4392	12	Dhruva	4074- 4444
13	13	4000- 4333	3 Kaulava	4 Taitila.	13	Hasta	4444- 4815	4815	4758	13	Vyâghâta	4444- 4815
14	14	4333- 4667	5 Gara	6 Vaṇij.	14	Chitrâ	4815- 5185	5185	5124	14	Harshaṇa	4815- 5185
15	15	4667- 5000	7 Vishṭi	1 Bava.	15	Svâti	5185- 5556	5370	5307	15	Vajra	5185- 5556
	Kṛish.											
16	1	5000- 5333	2 Bâlava	3 Kaulava.	16	Viśâkhâ	5556- 5926	5926	5856	16	Siddhi §	5556- 5926
17	2	5333- 5667	4 Taitila	5 Gara.	17	Anurâdhâ	5926- 6296	6296	6222	17	Vyatîpâta	5926- 6296
18	3	5667- 6000	6 Vaṇij	7 Vishṭi.	18	Jyeshṭhâ	6296- 6667	6481	6405	18	Varîyas	6296- 6667
19	4	6000- 6333	1 Bava	2 Bâlava.	19	Mûla	6667- 7037	6852	6771	19	Parigha	6667- 7037
20	5	6333- 6667	3 Kaulava	4 Taitila.	20	Pûrva Ashâḍhâ	7037- 7407	7222	7137	20	Śiva	7037- 7407
21	6	6667- 7000	5 Gara	6 Vaṇij.	21	Uttara Ashâḍhâ	7407- 7778	7778	7686	21	Siddha	7407- 7778
						Abhijit	(7685- 7802)		7804			
22	7	7000- 7333	7 Vishṭi	1 Bava.	22	Sravaṇa	7778- 8148	8148	8170	22	Sâdhya	7778- 8148
23	8	7333- 7667	2 Bâlava	3 Kaulava.	23	Dhanishṭhâ **	8148- 8519	8519	8536	23	Śubha	8148- 8519
24	9	7667- 8000	4 Taitila	5 Gara.	24	Śatabhishaj ††	8519- 8889	8704	8719	24	Śukla	8519- 8889
25	10	8000- 8333	6 Vaṇij	7 Vishṭi.	25	Pûrva Bhadrapadâ	8889- 9259	9074	9085	25	Brahman	8889- 9259
26	11	8333- 8667	1 Bava	2 Bâlava.	26	Uttara Bhadrapadâ	9259- 9630	9630	9634	26	Indra	9259- 9630
27	12	8667- 9000	3 Kaulava	4 Taitila.	27	Revatî	9630-10000	10000	10000	27	Vaidhṛiti	9630-10000
28	13	9000- 9333	5 Gara	6 Vaṇij.	—	—	—	—	—	—	—	—
29	14	9333- 9667	7 Vishṭi	Śakuni.	—	—	—	—	—	—	—	—
30	15	9667-10000	Chatushpada.	Nâga.	—	—	—	—	—	—	—	—

* or Kiṁtughna.

† Vishṭi is also called Bhadrâ, Kalyâṇî.

** or Śravishṭhâ.

†† or Śatatârakâ.

§ or Asṛij.

TABLE VIIIA.

LONGITUDES OF ENDING-POINTS OF TITHIS.

Tithi-Index (Lunation-parts) (*t*.)	Tithi.	Degrees.
1	2	3
333	1	12° 0′
667	2	24° 0′
1000	3	36° 0′
1333	4	48° 0′
1667	5	60° 0′
2000	6	72° 0′
2333	7	84° 0′
2667	8	96° 0′
3000	9	108° 0′
3333	10	120° 0′
3667	11	132° 0′
4000	12	144° 0′
4333	13	156° 0′
4667	14	168° 0′
5000	15	180° 0′
5333	16	192° 0′
5667	17	204° 0′
6000	18	216° 0′
6333	19	228° 0′
6667	20	240° 0′
7000	21	252° 0′
7333	22	264° 0′
7667	23	276° 0′
8000	24	288° 0′
8333	25	300° 0′
8667	26	312° 0′
9000	27	324° 0′
9333	28	336° 0′
9667	29	348° 0′
10000	30	360° 0′

For longitudes of ending-points of Nakshatras and Yogas, see text, Table Art. 38.

TABLE VIIIB.

LONGITUDES OF PARTS OF TITHIS, NAKSHATRAS AND YOGAS.

TITHI.			NAKSHATRA AND YOGA.		
Tithi-Index (Lunation parts) (*t*.)	Tithis (and decimals).	Degrees and minutes.	Nakshatra and Yoga-Index (*n* and *y*.)	Nakshatras and Yogas (and decimals).	Degrees. and minutes.
1	2	3	4	5	6
33	0.1	1° 12′	33	0.09	1° 12′
66	0.2	2° 24′	66	0.18	2° 24′
100	0.3	3° 36′	100	0.27	3° 36′
200	0.6	7° 12′	200	0.54	7° 12′
300	0.9	10° 48′	300	0.81	10° 48′
400	1.2	14° 24′	400	1.08	14° 24′
500	1.5	18° 0′	500	1.35	18° 0′
600	1.8	21° 36′	600	1.62	21° 36′
700	2 1	25° 12′	700	1.89	25° 12′
800	2.4	28° 48′	800	2.16	28° 48′
900	2.7	32° 24′	900	2.43	32° 24′
1000	3.0	36° 0′	1000	2.70	36° 0′
1100	3.3	39° 36′	1100	2.97	39° 36′
1200	3.6	43° 12′	1200	3.24	43° 12′
1300	3.9	46° 48′	1300	3.51	46° 48′
1400	4.2	50° 24′	1400	3.78	50° 24′
1500	4.5	54° 0′	1500	4.05	54° 0′
1600	4.8	57° 36′	1600	4.32	57° 36′
1700	5.1	61° 12′	1700	4.59	61° 12′
1800	5.4	64° 48′	1800	4.86	64° 48′
1900	5.7	68° 24′	1900	5.13	68° 24′
2000	6.0	72° 0′	2000	5.40	72° 0′
2100	6.3	75° 36′	2100	5.67	75° 36′
2200	6.6	79° 12′	2200	5.94	79° 12′
2300	6.9	82° 48′	2300	6.21	82° 48′
2400	7.2	86° 24′	2400	6.48	86° 24′
2500	7.5	90° 0′	2500	6.75	90° 0′
2600	7.8	93° 36′	2600	7.02	93° 36′
2700	8.1	97° 12′	2700	7.29	97° 12′
2800	8.4	100° 48′	2800	7.56	100° 48′
2900	8.7	104° 24′	2900	7.83	104° 24′
3000	9.0	108° 0′	3000	8.10	108° 0′
3100	9.3	111° 36′	3100	8.37	111° 36′
3200	9.6	115° 12′	3200	8.64	115° 12′
3300	9.9	118° 48′	3300	8.91	118° 48′
3400	10.2	122° 24′	3400	9.18	122° 24′

TABLE VIII^B. (CONTINUED.)

TITHI.			NAKSHATRA AND YOGA.		
Tithi-Index (Lunation parts) (*t.*)	Tithis (and decimals).	Degrees and minutes.	Nakshatra and Yoga-Index (*n* and *y*).	Nakshatras and Yogas (and decimals).	Degrees and minutes.
1	2	3	4	5	6
3500	10.5	126° 0′	3500	9.45	126° 0′
3600	10.8	129° 36′	3600	9.72	129° 36′
3700	11.1	133° 12′	3700	9.99	133° 12′
3800	11.4	136° 48′	3800	10.26	136° 48′
3900	11.7	140° 24′	3900	10.53	140° 24′
4000	12.0	144° 0′	4000	10.80	144° 0′
4100	12.3	147° 36′	4100	11.07	147° 36′
4200	12.6	151° 12′	4200	11.34	151° 12′
4300	12.9	154° 48′	4300	11.61	154° 48′
4400	13.2	158° 24′	4400	11.88	158° 24′
4500	13.5	162° 0′	4500	12.15	162° 0′
4600	13.8	165° 36′	4600	12.42	165° 36′
4700	14.1	169° 12′	4700	12.69	169° 12′
4800	14.4	172° 48′	4800	12.96	172° 48′
4900	14.7	176° 24′	4900	13.23	176° 24′
5000	15.0	180° 0′	5000	13.50	180° 0′
5100	15.3	183° 36′	5100	13.77	183° 36′
5200	15.6	187° 12′	5200	14.04	187° 12′
5300	15.9	190° 48′	5300	14.31	190° 48′
5400	16.2	194° 24′	5400	14.58	194° 24′
5500	16.5	198° 0′	5500	14.85	198° 0′
5600	16.8	201° 36′	5600	15.12	201° 36′
5700	17.1	205° 12′	5700	15.39	205° 12′
5800	17.4	208° 48′	5800	15.66	208° 48′
5900	17.7	212° 24′	5900	15.93	212° 24′
6000	18.0	216° 0′	6000	16.20	216° 0′
6100	18.3	219° 36′	6100	16.47	219° 36′
6200	18.6	223° 12′	6200	16.74	223° 12′
6300	18.9	226° 48′	6300	17.01	226° 48′
6400	19.2	230° 24′	6400	17.28	230° 24′
6500	19.5	234° 0′	6500	17.55	234° 0′
6600	19.8	237° 36′	6600	17.82	237° 36′
6700	20.1	241° 12′	6700	18.09	241° 12′
6800	20.4	244° 48′	6800	18.36	244° 48′
6900	20.7	248° 24′	6900	18.63	248° 24′
7000	21.0	252° 0′	7000	18.90	252° 0′
7100	21.3	255° 36′	7100	19.17	255° 36′
7200	21.6	259° 12′	7200	19.44	259° 12′

TABLE VIII^B. (CONTINUED.)

TITHI.			NAKSHATRA AND YOGA.		
Tithi-Index (Lunation parts) (*t.*)	Tithis (and decimals).	Degrees and minutes.	Nakshatra and Yoga-Index (*n* and *y*).	Nakshatras and Yogas (and decimals).	Degrees and minutes.
1	2	3	4	5	6
7300	21.9	262° 48′	7300	19.71	262° 48′
7400	22.2	266° 24′	7400	19.98	266° 24′
7500	22.5	270° 0′	7500	20.25	270° 0′
7600	22.8	273° 36′	7600	20.52	273° 36′
7700	23.1	277° 12′	7700	20.79	277° 12′
7800	23.4	280° 48′	7800	21.06	280° 48′
7900	23.7	284° 24′	7900	21.33	284° 24′
8000	24.0	288° 0′	8000	21.60	288° 0′
8100	24.3	291° 36′	8100	21.87	291° 36′
8200	24.6	295° 12′	8200	22.14	295° 12′
8300	24.9	298° 48′	8300	22.41	298° 48′
8400	25.2	302° 24′	8400	22.68	302° 24′
8500	25.5	306° 0′	8500	22.95	306° 0′
8600	25.8	309° 36′	8600	23.22	309° 36′
8700	26.1	313° 12′	8700	23.49	313° 12′
8800	26.4	316° 48′	8800	23.76	316° 48′
8900	26.7	320° 24′	8900	24.03	320° 24′
9000	27.0	324° 0′	9000	24.30	324° 0′
9100	27.3	327° 36′	9100	24.57	327° 36′
9200	27.6	331° 12′	9200	24.84	331° 12′
9300	27.9	334° 48′	9300	25.11	334° 48′
9400	28.2	338° 24′	9400	25.38	338° 24′
9500	28.5	342° 0′	9500	25.65	342° 0′
9600	28.8	345° 36′	9600	25.92	345° 36′
9700	29.1	349° 12′	9700	26.19	349° 12′
9800	29.4	352° 48′	9800	26.46	352° 48′
9900	29.7	356° 24′	9900	26.73	356° 24′
10000	30.0	360° 0′	10000	27.00	360° 0′

TABLE IX.

TABLE GIVING THE SERIAL NUMBER OF DAYS FROM THE END OF A YEAR A.D. FOR TWO CONSECUTIVE A.D. YEARS.

PART I.

Number of days reckoned from the 1st of January of the same year.

	Jan.	Feb.	March.	April.	May.	June.	July.	Aug.	Sep.	Oct.	Nov.	Dec.	
1	1	32	60	91	121	152	182	213	244	274	305	335	**1**
2	2	33	61	92	122	153	183	214	245	275	306	336	**2**
3	3	34	62	93	123	154	184	215	246	276	307	337	**3**
4	4	35	63	94	124	155	185	216	247	277	308	338	**4**
5	5	36	64	95	125	156	186	217	248	278	309	339	**5**
6	6	37	65	96	126	157	187	218	249	279	310	340	**6**
7	7	38	66	97	127	158	188	219	250	280	311	341	**7**
8	8	39	67	98	128	159	189	220	251	281	312	342	**8**
9	9	40	68	99	129	160	190	221	252	282	313	343	**9**
10	10	41	69	100	130	161	191	222	253	283	314	344	**10**
11	11	42	70	101	131	162	192	223	254	284	315	345	**11**
12	12	43	71	102	132	163	193	224	255	285	316	346	**12**
13	13	44	72	103	133	164	194	225	256	286	317	347	**13**
14	14	45	73	104	134	165	195	226	257	287	318	348	**14**
15	15	46	74	105	135	166	196	227	258	288	319	349	**15**
16	16	47	75	106	136	167	197	228	259	289	320	350	**16**
17	17	48	76	107	137	168	198	229	260	290	321	351	**17**
18	18	49	77	108	138	169	199	230	261	291	322	352	**18**
19	19	50	78	109	139	170	200	231	262	292	323	353	**19**
20	20	51	79	110	140	171	201	232	263	293	324	354	**20**
21	21	52	80	111	141	172	202	233	264	294	325	355	**21**
22	22	53	81	112	142	173	203	234	265	295	326	356	**22**
23	23	54	82	113	143	174	204	235	266	296	327	357	**23**
24	24	55	83	114	144	175	205	236	267	297	328	358	**24**
25	25	56	84	115	145	176	206	237	268	298	329	359	**25**
26	26	57	85	116	146	177	207	238	269	299	330	360	**26**
27	27	58	86	117	147	178	208	239	270	300	331	361	**27**
28	28	59	87	118	148	179	209	240	271	301	332	362	**28**
29	29	60	88	119	149	180	210	241	272	302	333	363	**29**
30	30	—	89	120	150	181	211	242	273	303	334	364	**30**
31	31	—	90	—	151	—	212	243	—	304	—	365	**31**
	Jan.	Feb.	March.	April.	May.	June.	July.	Aug.	Sep.	Oct.	Nov.	Dec.	

TABLE IX. (CONTINUED.)

TABLE GIVING THE SERIAL NUMBER OF DAYS FROM THE END OF A YEAR A.D. FOR TWO CONSECUTIVE A.D. YEARS.

PART II.

Number of days reckoned from the 1st of January of the preceding year.

	Jan.	Feb.	March.	April.	May.	June.	July.	Aug.	Sep.	Oct.	Nov.	Dec.	
1	366	397	425	456	486	517	547	578	609	639	670	700	1
2	367	398	426	457	487	518	548	579	610	640	671	701	2
3	368	399	427	458	488	519	549	580	611	641	672	702	3
4	369	400	428	459	489	520	550	581	612	642	673	703	4
5	370	401	429	460	490	521	551	582	613	643	674	704	5
6	371	402	430	461	491	522	552	583	614	644	675	705	6
7	372	403	431	462	492	523	553	584	615	645	676	706	7
8	373	404	432	463	493	524	554	585	616	646	677	707	8
9	374	405	433	464	494	525	555	586	617	647	678	708	9
10	375	406	434	465	495	526	556	587	618	648	679	709	10
11	376	407	435	466	496	527	557	588	619	649	680	710	11
12	377	408	436	467	497	528	558	589	620	650	681	711	12
13	378	409	437	468	498	529	559	590	621	651	682	712	13
14	379	410	438	469	499	530	560	591	622	652	683	713	14
15	380	411	439	470	500	531	561	592	623	653	684	714	15
16	381	412	440	471	501	532	562	593	624	654	685	715	16
17	382	413	441	472	502	533	563	594	625	655	686	716	17
18	383	414	442	473	503	534	564	595	626	656	687	717	18
19	384	415	443	474	504	535	565	596	627	657	688	718	19
20	385	416	444	475	505	536	566	597	628	658	689	719	20
21	386	417	445	476	506	537	567	598	629	659	690	720	21
22	387	418	446	477	507	538	568	599	630	660	691	721	22
23	388	419	447	478	508	539	569	600	631	661	692	722	23
24	389	420	448	479	509	540	570	601	632	662	693	723	24
25	390	421	449	480	510	541	571	602	633	663	694	724	25
26	391	422	450	481	511	542	572	603	634	664	695	725	26
27	392	423	451	482	512	543	573	604	635	665	696	726	27
28	393	424	452	483	513	544	574	605	636	666	697	727	28
29	394	425	453	484	514	545	575	606	637	667	698	728	29
30	395	—	454	485	515	546	576	607	638	668	699	729	30
31	396	—	455	—	516	—	577	608	—	669	—	730	31
	Jan.	Feb.	March.	April.	May.	June.	July.	Aug.	Sep.	Oct.	Nov.	Dec.	

TABLE X.

FOR CONVERTING TITHI-PARTS, AND INDICES OF TITHIS, NAKSHATRAS, AND YOGAS INTO TIME

[N.B. In this Table a tithi is supposed to contain .... 1,000 parts.
" " " " lunation " " " " .... 10,000 "
" " " " sidereal month " " " " .... 10,000 "
" " " " yoga chakra " " " " .... 10,000 "

Therefore:

In the case of Tithi-parts the argument shews .... 1,000ths of a tithi.
" " " " Tithi-index (t) " " " .... 10,000ths " " lunation.
" " " " Nakshatra-index (n) " " " .... 10,000ths " " sidereal month.
" " " " Yoga-index (y) " " " .... 10,000ths " " yoga-chakra].

Argument.	Time equivalent of								Argument.	Time equivalent of								Argument.	Time equivalent of							
	Tithi-parts.		Tithi-index (t).		Nakshatra-index (n).		Yoga-index (y).			Tithi-parts.		Tithi-index (t).		Nakshatra-index (n).		Yoga-index (y).			Tithi-parts.		Tithi-index (t).		Nakshatra-index (n).		Yoga-index (y).	
	H.	M.	H.	M.	H.	M.	H.	M.		H.	M.	H.	M.	H.	M.	H.	M.		H.	M.	H.	M.	H.	M.	H.	M.
1	0	1	0	4	0	4	0	4	41	0	58	2	54	2	41	2	30	81	1	55	5	44	5	19	4	57
2	0	3	0	9	0	8	0	7	42	1	0	2	59	2	45	2	34	82	1	56	5	49	5	23	5	0
3	0	4	0	13	0	12	0	11	43	1	1	3	3	2	49	2	37	83	1	58	5	53	5	27	5	4
4	0	6	0	17	0	16	0	15	44	1	2	3	7	2	53	2	41	84	1	59	5	57	5	30	5	7
5	0	7	0	21	0	20	0	18	45	1	4	3	11	2	57	2	45	85	2	0	6	1	5	34	5	11
6	0	9	0	26	0	24	0	22	46	1	5	3	16	3	1	2	48	86	2	2	6	6	5	38	5	15
7	0	10	0	30	0	28	0	26	47	1	7	3	20	3	5	2	52	87	2	3	6	10	5	42	5	18
8	0	11	0	34	0	31	0	29	48	1	8	3	24	3	9	2	56	88	2	5	6	14	5	46	5	22
9	0	13	0	38	0	35	0	33	49	1	9	3	28	3	13	2	59	89	2	6	6	18	5	50	5	26
10	0	14	0	43	0	39	0	37	50	1	11	3	33	3	17	3	3	90	2	8	6	23	5	54	5	29
11	0	16	0	47	0	43	0	40	51	1	12	3	37	3	21	3	7	91	2	9	6	27	5	58	5	33
12	0	17	0	51	0	47	0	44	52	1	14	3	41	3	25	3	10	92	2	10	6	31	6	2	5	37
13	0	18	0	55	0	51	0	48	53	1	15	3	45	3	29	3	14	93	2	12	6	35	6	6	5	40
14	0	20	1	0	0	55	0	51	54	1	17	3	50	3	32	3	18	94	2	13	6	40	6	10	5	44
15	0	21	1	4	0	59	0	55	55	1	18	3	54	3	36	3	21	95	2	15	6	44	6	14	5	48
16	0	23	1	8	1	3	0	59	56	1	19	3	58	3	40	3	25	96	2	16	6	48	6	18	5	51
17	0	24	1	12	1	7	1	2	57	1	21	4	2	3	44	3	29	97	2	17	6	52	6	22	5	55
18	0	26	1	17	1	11	1	6	58	1	22	4	7	3	48	3	32	98	2	19	6	57	6	26	5	59
19	0	27	1	21	1	15	1	10	59	1	24	4	11	3	52	3	36	99	2	20	7	1	6	29	6	2
20	0	28	1	25	1	19	1	13	60	1	25	4	15	3	56	3	40	100	2	22	7	5	6	33	6	6
21	0	30	1	29	1	23	1	17	61	1	26	4	19	4	0	3	43	200	4	43	14	10	13	7	12	12
22	0	31	1	34	1	27	1	21	62	1	28	4	24	4	4	3	47	300	7	5	21	16	19	40	18	18
23	0	33	1	38	1	30	1	24	63	1	29	4	28	4	8	3	51	400	9	27	28	21	—	—	—	—
24	0	34	1	42	1	34	1	28	64	1	31	4	32	4	12	3	54	500	11	49	35	26	—	—	—	—
25	0	35	1	46	1	38	1	32	65	1	32	4	36	4	16	3	58	600	14	10	42	31	—	—	—	—
26	0	37	1	51	1	42	1	35	66	1	34	4	41	4	20	4	2	700	16	32	49	37	—	—	—	—
27	0	38	1	55	1	46	1	39	67	1	35	4	45	4	24	4	5	800	18	54	56	42	—	—	—	—
28	0	40	1	59	1	50	1	42	68	1	36	4	49	4	28	4	9	900	21	16	63	47	—	—	—	—
29	0	41	2	3	1	54	1	46	69	1	38	4	53	4	31	4	13	1000	23	37	70	52	—	—	—	—
30	0	43	2	8	1	58	1	50	70	1	39	4	58	4	35	4	16									
31	0	44	2	12	2	2	1	53	71	1	41	5	2	4	39	4	20									
32	0	45	2	16	2	6	1	57	72	1	42	5	6	4	43	4	24									
33	0	47	2	20	2	10	2	1	73	1	43	5	10	4	47	4	27									
34	0	48	2	25	2	14	2	4	74	1	45	5	15	4	51	4	31									
35	0	50	2	29	2	18	2	8	75	1	46	5	19	4	55	4	35									
36	0	51	2	33	2	22	2	12	76	1	48	5	23	4	59	4	38									
37	0	52	2	37	2	26	2	15	77	1	49	5	27	5	3	4	42									
38	0	54	2	42	2	30	2	19	78	1	51	5	32	5	7	4	46									
39	0	55	2	46	2	33	2	23	79	1	52	5	36	5	11	4	49									
40	0	57	2	50	2	37	2	26	80	1	53	5	40	5	15	4	53									

TABLE XI.

LATITUDES AND LONGITUDES OF PRINCIPAL PLACES.

(Latitudes and longitudes in degrees and minutes; Longitudes in minutes of time, being the difference in time between Ujjain and the place in question.)

[N.B. This Table is based on the maps of the Great Trigonometrical Survey of India, but all longitudes require a correction of — 3′ 39″ to bring them to the latest corrected longitude of the Madras Observatory, namely, 80° 14′ 51″].

To convert Ujjain mean time, as found by the previous Tables, into local mean time, add to or subtract from the former the minutes of longitude of the place in question, as indicated by the sign of plus or minus in this Table.

NAME OF PLACE.	N. Latitude.	Long. E from Greenwich.	Long. from Ujjain in minutes of time.	NAME OF PLACE.	N. Latitude.	Long. E from Greenwich.	Long. from Ujjain in minutes of time.
Abû (Arbuda)	24° 36′	72° 50′	− 12	Bombay (Gt. Trig. Station)	18° 54′	72° 52′	− 12
Âgra (Fort)	27° 10′	78° 5′	+ 9	Broach (Bhṛigukachha)	21° 42′	73° 2′	− 11
Ahmadâbâd	23° 1′	72° 39′	− 13	Bundi	25° 26′	75° 42′	− 1
Ahmadnagar	19° 4′	74° 48′	− 4	Burhânpur	21° 19′	76° 18′	+ 2
Ajanta	20° 32′	75° 49′	− 0	Calcutta (Fort William)	22° 33′	88° 24′	+ 50
Âjmêr	26° 30′	74° 45′	− 4	Calingapatam (*see* Kaliṅgapatam)	—	—	—
Alîgaḍh (Allyghur. Coel)	27° 52′	78° 8′	+ 9	Cambay (Khambât, Sthambaratî)	22° 18′	72° 41′	− 13
Allahâbâd (Prayâga)	25° 26′	81° 54′	+ 24	Cawnpore (Kâhnpur, Old City)	26° 29′	80° 22′	+ 18
Amarâvatî (on the Kṛishṇâ)	16° 34′	80° 25′	+ 18	Cochin	9° 58′	76° 18′	+ 2
Amarâvatî (Amrâoti, Oomra-				Congeeveram (*see* Kâñchî)	—	—	—
wuttee, in Berar)	20° 55′	77° 49′	+ 8	Cuttack (*see* Kaṭak)	—	—	—
Amritsar	31° 37′	74° 56′	− 4	Dacca (Dhaka)	23° 43′	90° 27′	+ 58
Aṇhilvâḍ (Pâtan)	23° 51′	72° 11′	− 15	Dehli (Delhi, Old City)	28° 39′	77° 18′	+ 6
Arcot (Ârkâḍu)	12° 54′	79° 24′	+ 14	Devagiri (Daulatâbâd)	19° 57′	75° 17′	− 2
Aurangâbâd	19° 54′	75° 24′	− 2	Dhârâ (Dhar)	22° 36′	75° 22′	− 2
Ayodhyâ (*see* Oude)	—	—	—	Dhârvâḍ (Dharwar)	15° 27′	75° 5′	− 8
Bâdâmi	15° 55′	75° 45′	− 0	Dhôlpur (City)	26° 41′	77° 58′	+ 9
Balagâvi, or Balagâmve	14° 23′	75° 18′	− 2	Dhulia	20° 54′	74° 50′	− 4
Banavâsi	14° 32′	75° 5′	− 3	Dvârakâ	22° 14′	69° 2′	− 27
Bardhvân (Burdwan)	23° 14′	87° 55′	+ 48	Ellora (Vêlâpura)	20° 2′	75° 14′	− 2
Baroda (Baḍôda)	22° 18′	73° 16′	− 10	Farukhâbâd (Furruck°.)	27° 23′	79° 37′	+ 15
Bârśî	18° 13′	75° 46′	− 0	Gayâ	24° 47′	85° 4′	+ 37
Belgaum	15° 51′	74° 35′	− 5	Ghâzîpur	25° 35′	83° 39′	+ 31
Benares	25° 19′	83° 4′	+ 29	Girnâr	21° 32′	70° 36′	− 21
Bhâgalpur (Bengal)	25° 15′	87° 2′	+ 45	Goa (Gôpakapaṭṭana)	15° 30′	73° 57′	− 8
Bharatpur (Bhurtpoor)	27° 13′	77° 33′	+ 7	Gôrakhapur (Goruckpoor)	26° 45′	83° 25′	+ 30
Bhelsâ	23° 32′	77° 52′	+ 8	Gurkhâ	27° 55′	84° 30′	+ 35
Bhopâl	23° 15′	77° 28′	+ 6	Gwalior	26° 14′	78° 14′	+ 10
Bihar (Behar, in Bengal)	25° 11′	85° 35′	+ 39	Haidarâbâd (Dekhan)	17° 22′	78° 32′	+ 11
Bîjâpur (Beejapoor)	16° 50′	75° 47′	− 0	Haidarâbâd (Sindh)	25° 23′	68° 26′	− 30
Bijnagar (*see* Vijayanagar)	—	—	—	Hardâ (in Gwalior)	22° 20′	77° 9′	+ 5
Bîkânêr	28° 0′	73° 22′	− 10	Hardwâr	29° 57′	78° 14′	+ 10

TABLE XI. (CONTINUED.)

NAME OF PLACE.	N. Latitude.	Long. E from Greenwich.	Long. from Ujjain in minutes of time.	NAME OF PLACE.	N. Latitude.	Long. E from Greenwich.	Long. from Ujjain in minutes of time.
Hoshangâbâd	22° 45′	77° 47′	+ 8	Oude (Oudh, Ayôdhyâ)	26° 48′	82° 16′	+ 26
Indore	22° 43′	75° 55′	— 0	Paithân	19° 29′	75° 27′	— 2
Jabalpur (Jubbulpore)	23° 11′	80° 0′	+ 17	Paṇḍhâpûr	17° 41′	75° 24′	— 2
Jagaṇâthapurî	19° 48′	85° 53′	+ 40	Pâtan (*see* Aṇhilwaḍ)	—	—	—
Jalgaum	21° 1′	75° 38′	— 1	Patan (*see* Somnâthpaṭan)	—	—	—
Jaypur (Jeypore, in Râjputâna)	26° 55′	75° 53′	— 0	Patiâlâ	30° 19′	76° 28′	+ 3
Jhânsî	25° 28′	78° 38′	+ 11	Pâtṇa	25° 36′	85° 16′	+ 37
Jôdhpur	26° 18′	73° 5′	— 11	Peshawur	34° 0′	71° 40′	— 17
Junâgaḍh	21° 31′	70° 31′	— 21	Poona (Puṇêm)	18° 30′	73° 55′	— 8
Kaliṅgapaṭam (Calingapatam)	18° 20′	84° 11′	+ 33	Pooree (Puri, *see* Jagannâthapurî)	—	—	—
Kalyân (Bombay)	19° 15′	73° 11′	— 11	Purṇiyâ (Poorneah)	25° 48′	87° 34′	+ 47
Kalyân (Kalliannee, Nizam's				Râmeśvara (Rameshwur)	9° 17′	79° 23′	+ 14
Dominions)	17° 53′	77° 1′	+ 5	Ratnâgiri	17° 0′	73° 21′	— 10
Kanauj	27° 3′	79° 59′	+ 17	Rêvâ (Rewa, Rîwâṅ)	24° 31′	81° 21′	+ 22
Kâñchî (or Congeeveram)	12° 50′	79° 46′	+ 16	Śâgar (Saugor)	23° 50′	78° 48′	+ 12
Kaṭak (Cuttack)	20° 28′	85° 56′	+ 40	Saheṭ Maheṭ (Śrâvastî) [2]	27° 31′	82° 5′	+ 25
Khâtmâṇḍu	27° 39′	85° 19′	+ 38	Sambhalpur (Sumbulpore)	21° 28′	84° 2′	+ 33
Kôlâpur (Kolhapur)	16° 41′	74° 17′	— 6	Sâtârâ	17° 41′	74° 3′	— 7
Lâhôr (Lahore)	31° 35′	74° 23′	— 6	Seringapatam (Śrîraṅgapaṭṭana)	12° 25′	76° 44′	+ 4
Lakhnau (Lucknow)	26° 51′	80° 58′	+ 21	Shôlâpur	17° 41′	75° 58′	+ 1
Madhura (Madura, Madras Pres.)	9° 55′	78° 11′	+ 9	Sirônj	24° 6′	77° 45′	+ 8
Madras (Observatory) [1]	13° 4′	80° 18½′	+ 18	Somnâthpaṭaṇ	20° 53′	70° 28′	— 22
Maisûr (Mysore)	12° 18′	76° 43′	+ 4	Śrînagar (in Kashmîr)	34° 6′	74° 52′	— 4
Malkhêḍ (Mânyakhêṭa)	17° 12′	77° 13′	+ 6	Surat	21° 12′	72° 53′	— 12
Mâṇḍavî (in Cutch)	22° 50′	69° 25′	— 26	Tanjore (Tañjâvûr)	10° 47′	79° 12′	+ 14
Maṅgalûr (Mangalore)	12° 52′	74° 54′	— 4	Thâṇâ (Tannah)	19° 12′	73° 1′	— 11
Mathurâ (Muttra N.W.P.)	27° 30′	77° 45′	+ 8	Travancore (Tiruvaṅkâdu)	8° 14′	77° 19′	+ 6
Moṇgîr (or Muṅgêr)	25° 23′	86° 32′	+ 43	Trichinopoly	10° 49′	78° 45′	+ 12
Multân (Mooltan)	30° 12′	71° 32′	— 17	Trivandrum	8° 29′	77° 0′	+ 5
Nâgpur (Nagpore)	21° 9′	79° 10′	+ 13	Udaipur (Oodeypore)	24° 34′	73° 45′	— 8
Nâsik	20° 0′	73° 51′	— 8	Ujjain [3]	23° 11′	75° 50′	± 0
Oomrawuttee (*see* Amarâvatî	—	—	—	Vijayanagar	15° 19′	76° 32′	+ 3

[1] The longitude of the Madras Observatory, which forms the basis of the Indian Geographical surveys, has been lately corrected to 80° 14′ 51″.

[2] Sahet Mahet is not on the Survey of India map. The particulars are taken from the Imperial Gazetteer.

[3] With the correction noted in note 1 above (— 3′ 39″) the longitude of Ujjain comes to 75° 46′ 6″.

TABLE XII.

(See Arts. 53 *to* 63.*)*

Samvatsaras of the 60-year cycle of Jupiter.	Samvatsara of the twelve-year cycle of the mean-sign system.	Mean-sign of Jupiter by his mean longitude.	Samvatsaras of the 60-year cycle of Jupiter.	Samvatsara of the twelve-year cycle of the mean-sign system.	Mean-sign of Jupiter by his mean longitude.
	Corresponding to the samvatsara of the sixty-year cycle of the mean-sign system.			Corresponding to the samvatsara of the sixty-year cycle of the mean-sign system.	
1	2	3	1	2	3
1 Prabhava	5 Śrâvaṇa	11 Kumbha.	31 Hemalamba	11 Mâgha	5 Siṁha.
2 Vibhava	6 Bhâdrapada	12 Mîna.	32 Vilamba	12 Phâlguna	6 Kanyâ.
3 Śukla	7 Âśvina	1 Mesha.	33 Vikârin	1 Chaitra	7 Tulâ.
4 Pramoda	8 Kârttika	2 Vṛishabha.	34 Śârvari	2 Vaiśâkha	8 Vṛiśchika.
5 Prajâpati	9 Mârgaśîrsha	3 Mithuna.	35 Plava	3 Jyeshṭha	9 Dhanus.
6 Aṅgiras	10 Pausha	4 Karka.	36 Śubhakṛit	4 Âshâḍha	10 Makara.
7 Śrîmukha	11 Mâgha	5 Siṁha.	37 Śobhana	5 Śrâvaṇa	11 Kumbha.
8 Bhâva	12 Phâlguna	6 Kanyâ.	38 Krodhin	6 Bhâdrapada	12 Mîna.
9 Yuvan	1 Chaitra	7 Tulâ.	39 Viśvâvasu	7 Âśvina	1 Mesha.
10 Dhâtṛi	2 Vaiśâkha	8 Vṛiśchika.	40 Parâbhava	8 Kârttika	2 Vṛishabha.
11 Îśvara	3 Jyeshṭha	9 Dhanus.	41 Plavaṅga	9 Mârgaśîrsha	3 Mithuna.
12 Bahudhânya	4 Âshâḍha	10 Makara.	42 Kîlaka	10 Pausha	4 Karka.
13 Pramâthin	5 Śrâvaṇa	11 Kumbha.	43 Saumya	11 Mâgha	5 Siṁha.
14 Vikrama	6 Bhâdrapada	12 Mîna.	44 Sâdhâraṇa	12 Phâlguna	6 Kanyâ.
15 Vṛisha	7 Âśvina	1 Mesha.	45 Virodhakṛit	1 Chaitra	7 Tulâ.
16 Chitrabhânu	8 Kârttika	2 Vṛishabha.	46 Paridhâvin	2 Vaiśâkha	8 Vṛiśchika.
17 Subhânu	9 Mârgaśîrsha	3 Mithuna.	47 Pramâdin	3 Jyeshṭha	9 Dhanus.
18 Târaṇa	10 Pausha	4 Karka.	48 Ânanda	4 Âshâḍha	10 Makara.
19 Pârthiva	11 Mâgha	5 Siṁha.	49 Râkshasa	5 Śrâvaṇa	11 Kumbha.
20 Vyaya	12 Phâlguna	6 Kanyâ.	50 Anala	6 Bhâdrapada	12 Mîna.
21 Sarvajit	1 Chaitra	7 Tulâ.	51 Piṅgala	7 Âśvina	1 Mesha.
22 Sarvadhârin	2 Vaiśâkha	8 Vṛiśchika.	52 Kâlayukta	8 Kârttika	2 Vṛishabha.
23 Virodhin	3 Jyeshṭha	9 Dhanus.	53 Siddhârtin	9 Mârgaśîrsha	3 Mithuna.
24 Vikṛita	4 Âshâḍha	10 Makara.	54 Raudra	10 Pausha	4 Karka.
25 Khara	5 Śrâvaṇa	11 Kumbha.	55 Durmati	11 Mâgha	5 Siṁha.
26 Nandana	6 Bhâdrapada	12 Mîna.	56 Dundubhi	12 Phâlguna	6 Kanyâ.
27 Vijaya	7 Âśvina	1 Mesha.	57 Rudhirodgârin	1 Chaitra	7 Tulâ.
28 Jaya	8 Kârttika	2 Vṛishabha.	58 Raktâksha	2 Vaiśâkha	8 Vṛiśchika.
29 Manmatha	9 Mârgaśîrsha	3 Mithuna.	59 Krodhana	3 Jyeshṭha	9 Dhanus.
30 Durmukha	10 Pausha	4 Karka.	60 Kshaya	4 Âshâḍha	10 Makara.

N.B. i. The samvatsara and sign (cols. 2. 3.) correspond to the samvatsara in col. 1 only when the latter is taken as the samvatsara of the *mean-sign* (Northern) 60-year cycle (Table I., col. 7).

N.B. ii. Jupiter's sign by his apparent longitude is either the same, as or the next preceding, or the next succeeding his mean-sign. Thus, in Prabhava Jupiter stands in mean Kumbha, when be may have been either in apparent Makara, Kumbha, or Mîna.

TABLE XIII.

(The following Table for finding the day of the week for any date from A.D. 300 to 2300 has been supplied by Dr. Burgess.)

CALENDAR FOR THE YEARS FROM A.D. 300 TO 2300.

			Old Style.	300 1000 1700	400 1100 1800	500 1200 —	600 1300 —	700 1400 —	800 1500 —	900 1600 —
Odd Years of the Centuries.			New Style.	— — —	1500 1900 G *	1600 2000 —	— — —	1700 2100 C	— — —	1800 2200 E
0	28	56	84	GF	AG	BA	CB	DC	ED	FE
1	29	57	85	E	F	G	A	B	C	D
2	30	58	86	D	E	F	G	A	B	C
3	31	59	87	C	D	E	F	G	A	B
4	32	60	88	BA	CB	DC	ED	FE	GF	AG
5	33	61	89	G	A	B	C	D	E	F
6	34	62	90	F	G	A	B	C	D	E
7	35	63	91	E	F	G	A	B	C	D
8	36	64	92	DC	ED	FE	GF	AG	BA	CB
9	37	65	93	B	C	D	E	F	G	A
10	38	66	94	A	B	C	D	E	F	G
11	39	67	95	G	A	B	C	D	E	F
12	40	68	96	FE	GF	AG	BA	CB	DC	ED
13	41	69	97	D	E	F	G	A	B	C
14	42	70	98	C	D	E	F	G	A	B
15	43	71	99	B	C	D	E	F	G	A
16	44	72	—	AG	BA	CB	DC	ED	FE	GF
17	45	73	—	F	G	A	B	C	D	E
18	46	74	—	E	F	G	A	B	C	D
19	47	75	—	D	E	F	G	A	B	C
20	48	76	—	CB	DC	ED	FE	GF	AG	BA
21	49	77	—	A	B	C	D	E	F	G
22	50	78	—	G	A	B	C	D	E	F
23	51	79	—	F	G	A	B	C	D	E
24	52	80	—	ED	FE	GF	AG	BA	CB	DC
25	53	81	—	C	D	E	F	G	A	B
26	54	82	—	B	C	D	E	F	G	A
27	55	83	—	A	B	C	D	E	F	G

* For the years 1500, 1700, &c. (N.S.) which are not leap years, the Dominical letters are given in this line.

January..............	October..........	A	G	F	E	D	C	B
February, March.......	November........	D	C	B	A	G	F	E
April..................	July.............	G	F	E	D	C	B	A
May..		B	A	G	F	E	D	C
June..		E	D	C	B	A	G	F
August......................................		C	B	A	G	F	E	D
September............	December........	F	E	D	C	B	A	G

1	8	15	22	29	1 Sun.	2 Mon.	3 Tues.	4 Wed.	5 Thur.	6 Fri.	0 Sat.
2	9	16	23	30	2 Mon.	3 Tues.	4 Wed.	5 Thur.	6 Fri.	0 Sat.	1 Sun.
3	10	17	24	31	3 Tues.	4 Wed.	5 Thur.	6 Fri.	0 Sat.	1 Sun.	2 Mon.
4	11	18	25	—	4 Wed.	5 Thur.	6 Fri.	0 Sat.	1 Sun.	2 Mon.	3 Tues.
5	12	19	26	—	5 Thur.	6 Fri.	0 Sat.	1 Sun.	2 Mon.	3 Tues.	4 Wed.
6	13	20	27	—	6 Fri.	0 Sat.	1 Sun.	2 Mon.	3 Tues.	4 Wed.	5 Thur.
7	14	21	28	—	0 Sat.	1 Sun.	2 Mon.	3 Tues.	4 Wed.	5 Thur.	6 Fri.

Look out for the century in the head of the Table, and the odd years in the left hand columns; and in the corresponding column and line is the Dominical letter. Thus for 1893 N.S. the Dominical letter is found to be A.

In the 2nd Table find the month, and in line with it the same Dominical letter, in the same column with which are the days of the week corresponding to the days of the month on the left. Thus, for July 1893, we find, in line with July, A (in the last column), and in the column below Saturday corresponds to the 1st, 8th, 15th, &c. of the month, Sunday to 2nd, 9th, &c.

When there are two letters together it is a leap year and the first letter serves for January and February, the second for the rest of the year. Thus, for A.D. 600, the Dominical letters are CB, and 29th February is found with C to be Monday 1st March is found with B to be Tuesday.

TABLE XIV.

FOR CONVERSION OF A HINDU SOLAR DATE INTO THE CORRESPONDING DATE A.D. AND VICE VERSÂ.

[This Table is dangerous to use unless all the bases of calculation of the Hindu Date are known. When they are known, let it be borne in mind that the result, as found from the Table, though often correct, is often wrong by one day, occasionally by two days. This variation is unavoidable in an eye-table. Where absolute correctness is required, proceed by Art. 149.]

MESHÂDI YEARS. (Beginning with Mesha, or Vaiśâkha (Baiśâk.) Sittirai (Tam.)

SIMHÂDI YEARS. (Beginning with Simha, Chingam or Âvaṇi (Tinnevelly & South Malayâḷa.)

KANYÂDI YEARS. (Beginning with Kanyâ, Kanni (North Malayâḷa), or Assin (N. W. India).

Ferial numbers found from Table I.

	1	2	3	4	5	6	0
(1)	Sun.	Mon.	Tues.	Wed.	Thur.	Fri.	Sat.
(2)	Mon.	Tues.	Wed.	Thur.	Fri.	Sat.	Sun.
(3)	Tues	Wed.	Thur.	Fri.	Sat.	Sun.	Mon.
(4)	Wed.	Thur.	Fri.	Sat.	Sun.	Mon.	Tues.
(5)	Thur.	Fri.	Sat.	Sun.	Mon.	Tues.	Wed.
(6)	Fri.	Sat.	Sun.	Mon.	Tues.	Wed.	Thur.
(7)	Sat.	Sun.	Mon.	Tues.	Wed.	Thur.	Fri.
	(1)	(2)	(3)	(4)	(5)	(6)	(7)
	Mar13	Mar.—	Mar.—	Mar.—	Mar.—	Mar.—	Mar.—
	14	13	—	—	—	—	—
	15	14	13	—	—	—	—
	16	15	14	13	—	—	—
	17	16	15	14	13	—	—
	18	17	16	15	14	13	—
	19	18	17	16	15	14	13
	20	19	18	17	16	15	14
	21	20	19	18	17	16	15
	22	21	20	19	18	17	16
	23	22	21	20	19	18	17
	24	23	22	21	20	19	18
	25	24	23	22	21	20	19
	26	25	24	23	22	21	20
	27	26	25	24	23	22	21
	28	27	26	25	24	23	22
	29	28	27	26	25	24	23
	30	29	28	27	26	25	24
	31	30	29	28	27	26	25
	Apr. 1	31	30	29	28	27	26
	2	Apr. 1	31	30	29	28	27
	3	2	Apr. 1	31	30	29	28
	4	3	2	Apr. 1	31	30	29
	5	4	3	2	Apr. 1	31	30
	6	5	4	3	2	Apr. 1	31
	7	6	5	4	3	2	Apr. 1
	8	7	6	5	4	3	2
	9	8	7	6	5	4	3
	10	9	8	7	6	5	4
	11	10	9	8	7	6	5
	12	11	10	9	8	7	6
	13	12	11	10	9	8	7
	14	13	12	11	10	9	8
	15	14	13	12	11	10	9
	16	15	14	13	12	11	10
	17	16	15	14	13	12	11
	18	17	16	15	14	13	12
	19	18	17	16	15	14	13
	20	19	18	17	16	15	14
	21	20	19	18	17	16	15

Row	1. MESHA, VAIŚÂKHA ŚITTIRAI (Tam.)					2. Vṛishabha, Jyeshṭha Vaigâśi (Tam.)					3. Mithuna, Âshâḍha Âni (Tam.)					
	9. *Medam, Śittirai.*					10. *Edanam, Vaigâśi.*					11. *Midunam, Âni.*					
	8. *Medam.*					9. *Edanam.*					10. *Midunam.*					
(1)	1	8	15	22	29	—	5	12	19	26	—	2	9	16	23	30
(2)	2	9	16	23	30	—	6	13	20	27	—	3	10	17	24	31
(3)	3	10	17	24	31	—	7	14	21	28	—	4	11	18	25	32
(4)	4	11	18	25	—	1	8	15	22	29	—	5	12	19	26	—
(5)	5	12	19	26	—	2	9	16	23	30	—	6	13	20	27	—
(6)	6	13	20	27	—	3	10	17	24	31	—	7	14	21	28	—
(7)	7	14	21	28	—	4	11	18	25	—	1	8	15	22	29	—
Mar13	Mar. 13	Mar. 20	Mar. 27	Apr. 3	Apr. 10	Apr. 10	Apr 17	Apr. 24	May 1	May 8	May 8	May 15	May 22	May 29	Jun. 5	Jun. 12
14	14	21	28	4	11	11	18	25	2	9	9	16	23	30	6	13
15	15	22	29	5	12	12	19	26	3	10	10	17	24	31	7	14
16	16	23	30	6	13	13	20	27	4	11	11	18	25	Jun. 1	8	15
17	17	24	31	7	14	14	21	28	5	12	12	19	26	2	9	16
18	18	25	Apr. 1	8	15	15	22	29	6	13	13	20	27	3	10	17
19	19	26	2	9	16	16	23	30	7	14	14	21	28	4	11	18
20	20	27	3	10	17	17	24	May 1	8	15	15	22	29	5	12	19
21	21	28	4	11	18	18	25	2	9	16	16	23	30	6	13	20
22	22	29	5	12	19	19	26	3	10	17	17	24	31	7	14	21
23	23	30	6	13	20	20	27	4	11	18	18	25	Jun. 1	8	15	22
24	24	31	7	14	21	21	28	5	12	19	19	26	2	9	16	23
25	25	Apr. 1	8	15	22	22	29	6	13	20	20	27	3	10	17	24
26	26	2	9	16	23	23	30	7	14	21	21	28	4	11	18	25
27	27	3	10	17	24	24	May 1	8	15	22	22	29	5	12	19	26
28	28	4	11	18	25	25	2	9	16	23	23	30	6	13	20	27
29	29	5	12	19	26	26	3	10	17	24	24	31	7	14	21	28
30	30	6	13	20	27	27	4	11	18	25	25	Jun. 1	8	15	22	29
31	31	7	14	21	28	28	5	12	19	26	26	2	9	16	23	30
Apr. 1	Apr. 1	8	15	22	29	29	6	13	20	27	27	3	10	17	24	Jul. 1
2	2	9	16	23	30	30	7	14	21	28	28	4	11	18	25	2
3	3	10	17	24	May 1	May 1	8	15	22	29	29	5	12	19	26	3
4	4	11	18	25	2	2	9	16	23	30	30	6	13	20	27	4
5	5	12	19	26	3	3	10	17	24	31	31	7	14	21	28	5
6	6	13	20	27	4	4	11	18	25	Jun. 1	Jun. 1	8	15	22	29	6
7	7	14	21	28	5	5	12	19	26	2	2	9	16	23	30	7
8	8	15	22	29	6	6	13	20	27	3	3	10	17	24	Jul. 1	8
9	9	16	23	30	7	7	14	21	28	4	4	11	18	25	2	9
10	10	17	24	May 1	8	8	15	22	29	5	5	12	19	26	3	10
11	11	18	25	2	9	9	16	23	30	6	6	13	20	27	4	11
12	12	19	26	3	10	10	17	24	31	7	7	14	21	28	5	12
13	13	20	27	4	11	11	18	25	Jun. 1	8	8	15	22	29	6	13
14	14	21	28	5	12	12	19	26	2	9	9	16	23	30	7	14
15	15	22	29	6	13	13	20	27	3	10	10	17	24	Jul. 1	8	15
16	16	23	30	7	14	14	21	28	4	11	11	18	25	2	9	16
17	17	24	May 1	8	15	15	22	29	5	12	12	19	26	3	10	17
18	18	25	2	9	16	16	23	30	6	13	13	20	27	4	11	18
19	19	26	3	10	17	17	24	31	7	14	14	21	28	5	12	19
20	20	27	4	11	18	18	25	Jun. 1	8	15	15	22	29	6	13	20
21	21	28	5	12	19	19	26	2	9	16	16	23	30	7	14	21

Row	4. Karka, Śrâvana Âḍi (Tam.)					5. Simha, Bhâdrapada Âvaṇi (Tam.)						6. Kanyâ, Âśvina Puraṭṭâdi (Tam.)				
	12. *Karkaḍakam, Âḍi.*					1. CHINGAM, ÂVANI.						2. Kanni, Puraṭṭâdi.				
	11. *Karkaḍakam.*					12. *Chingam.*						1. KANNI.				
(1)	—	5	12	19	26	—	2	9	16	23	30	—	6	13	20	27
(2)	—	6	13	20	27	—	3	10	17	24	31	—	7	14	21	28
(3)	—	7	14	21	28	—	4	11	18	25	—	1	8	15	22	29
(4)	1	8	15	22	29	—	5	12	19	26	—	2	9	16	23	30
(5)	2	9	16	23	30	—	6	13	20	27	—	3	10	17	24	31
(6)	3	10	17	24	31	—	7	14	21	28	—	4	11	18	25	—
(7)	4	11	18	25	—	1	8	15	22	29	—	5	12	19	26	—
Mar13	Jun. 12	Jun. 19	Jun. 26	Jul. 3	Jul. 10	Jul. 10	Jul. 17	Jul. 24	Jul. 31	Aug. 7	Aug. 14	Aug. 14	Aug. 21	Aug. 28	Sep. 4	Sep. 11
14	13	20	27	4	11	11	18	25	Aug. 1	8	15	15	22	29	5	12
15	14	21	28	5	12	12	19	26	2	9	16	16	23	30	6	13
16	15	22	29	6	13	13	20	27	3	10	17	17	24	31	7	14
17	16	23	30	7	14	14	21	28	4	11	18	18	25	Sep. 1	8	15
18	17	24	Jul. 1	8	15	15	22	29	5	12	19	19	26	2	9	16
19	18	25	2	9	16	16	23	30	6	13	20	20	27	3	10	17
20	19	26	3	10	17	17	24	31	7	14	21	21	28	4	11	18
21	20	27	4	11	18	18	25	Aug. 1	8	15	22	22	29	5	12	19
22	21	28	5	12	19	19	26	2	9	16	23	23	30	6	13	20
23	22	29	6	13	20	20	27	3	10	17	24	24	31	7	14	21
24	23	30	7	14	21	21	28	4	11	18	25	25	Sep. 1	8	15	22
25	24	Jul. 1	8	15	22	22	29	5	12	19	26	26	2	9	16	23
26	25	2	9	16	23	23	30	6	13	20	27	27	3	10	17	24
27	26	3	10	17	24	24	31	7	14	21	28	28	4	11	18	25
28	27	4	11	18	25	25	Aug. 1	8	15	22	29	29	5	12	19	26
29	28	5	12	19	26	26	2	9	16	23	30	30	6	13	20	27
30	29	6	13	20	27	27	3	10	17	24	31	31	7	14	21	28
31	30	7	14	21	28	28	4	11	18	25	Sep. 1	Sep. 1	8	15	22	29
Apr. 1	Jul. 1	8	15	22	29	29	5	12	19	26	2	2	9	16	23	30
2	2	9	16	23	30	30	6	13	20	27	3	3	10	17	24	Oct. 1
3	3	10	17	24	31	31	7	14	21	28	4	4	11	18	25	2
4	4	11	18	25	Aug. 1	Aug. 1	8	15	22	29	5	5	12	19	26	3
5	5	12	19	26	2	2	9	16	23	30	6	6	13	20	27	4
6	6	13	20	27	3	3	10	17	24	31	7	7	14	21	28	5
7	7	14	21	28	4	4	11	18	25	Sep. 1	8	8	15	22	29	6
8	8	15	22	29	5	5	12	19	26	2	9	9	16	23	30	7
9	9	16	23	30	6	6	13	20	27	3	10	10	17	24	Oct. 1	8
10	10	17	24	31	7	7	14	21	28	4	11	11	18	25	2	9
11	11	18	25	Aug. 1	8	8	15	22	29	5	12	12	19	26	3	10
12	12	19	26	2	9	9	16	23	30	6	13	13	20	27	4	11
13	13	20	27	3	10	10	17	24	31	7	14	14	21	28	5	12
14	14	21	28	4	11	11	18	25	Sep. 1	8	15	15	22	29	6	13
15	15	22	29	5	12	12	19	26	2	9	16	16	23	30	7	14
16	16	23	30	6	13	13	20	27	3	10	17	17	24	Oct. 1	8	15
17	17	24	31	7	14	14	21	28	4	11	18	18	25	2	9	16
18	18	25	Aug. 1	8	15	15	22	29	5	12	19	19	26	3	10	17
19	19	26	2	9	16	16	23	30	6	13	20	20	27	4	11	18
20	20	27	3	10	17	17	24	31	7	14	21	21	28	5	12	19
21	21	28	4	11	18	18	25	Sep. 1	8	15	22	22	29	6	13	20

Row	7. Tulâ, Kârttika Aippaśi (Tam.)					8. Vṛiśchika, Mârgaśirsha, Kârttigai (Tam.)					9. Dhanus, Pausha Mârgaḷi (Tam.)				
	3. Tulâm, Aippaśi.					4. Vṛiśchikam, Kârttigai.					5. Dhanu, Mârgaḷi.				
	2. Tulâm.					3. Vṛiśchikam.					4. Dhanu.				
(1)	—	3	10	17	24	1	8	15	22	29	—	7	14	21	28
(2)	—	4	11	18	25	2	9	16	23	—	1	8	15	22	29
(3)	—	5	12	19	26	3	10	17	24	—	2	9	16	23	30
(4)	—	6	13	20	27	4	11	18	25	—	3	10	17	24	—
(5)	—	7	14	21	28	5	12	19	26	—	4	11	18	25	—
(6)	1	8	15	22	29	6	13	20	27	—	5	12	19	26	—
(7)	2	9	16	23	30	7	14	21	28	—	6	13	20	27	—
Mar13	Sep. 11	Sep. 18	Sep. 25	Oct. 2	Oct. 9	Oct. 16	Oct. 23	Oct. 30	Nov. 6	Nov. 13	Nov. 13	Nov. 20	Nov. 27	Dec. 4	Dec. 11
14	12	19	26	3	10	17	24	31	7	14	14	21	28	5	12
15	13	20	27	4	11	18	25	Nov. 1	8	15	15	22	29	6	13
16	14	21	28	5	12	19	26	2	9	16	16	23	30	7	14
17	15	22	29	6	13	20	27	3	10	17	17	24	Dec. 1	8	15
18	16	23	30	7	14	21	28	4	11	18	18	25	2	9	16
19	17	24	Oct. 1	8	15	22	29	5	12	19	19	26	3	10	17
20	18	25	2	9	16	23	30	6	13	20	20	27	4	11	18
21	19	26	3	10	17	24	31	7	14	21	21	28	5	12	19
22	20	27	4	11	18	25	Nov. 1	8	15	22	22	29	6	13	20
23	21	28	5	12	19	26	2	9	16	23	23	30	7	14	21
24	22	29	6	13	20	27	3	10	17	24	24	Dec. 1	8	15	22
25	23	30	7	14	21	28	4	11	18	25	25	2	9	16	23
26	24	Oct. 1	8	15	22	29	5	12	19	26	26	3	10	17	24
27	25	2	9	16	23	30	6	13	20	27	27	4	11	18	25
28	26	3	10	17	24	31	7	14	21	28	28	5	12	19	26
29	27	4	11	18	25	Nov. 1	8	15	22	29	29	6	13	20	27
30	28	5	12	19	26	2	9	16	23	30	30	7	14	21	28
31	29	6	13	20	27	3	10	17	24	Dec. 1	Dec. 1	8	15	22	29
Apr. 1	30	7	14	21	28	4	11	18	25	2	2	9	16	23	30
2	Oct. 1	8	15	22	29	5	12	19	26	3	3	10	17	24	31
3	2	9	16	23	30	6	13	20	27	4	4	11	18	25	Jan. 1
4	3	10	17	24	31	7	14	21	28	5	5	12	19	26	2
5	4	11	18	25	Nov. 1	8	15	22	29	6	6	13	20	27	3
6	5	12	19	26	2	9	16	23	30	7	7	14	21	28	4
7	6	13	20	27	3	10	17	24	Dec. 1	8	8	15	22	29	5
8	7	14	21	28	4	11	18	25	2	9	9	16	23	30	6
9	8	15	22	29	5	12	19	26	3	10	10	17	24	31	7
10	9	16	23	30	6	13	20	27	4	11	11	18	25	Jan. 1	8
11	10	17	24	31	7	14	21	28	5	12	12	19	26	2	9
12	11	18	25	Nov. 1	8	15	22	29	6	13	13	20	27	3	10
13	12	19	26	2	9	16	23	30	7	14	14	21	28	4	11
14	13	20	27	3	10	17	24	Dec. 1	8	15	15	22	29	5	12
15	14	21	28	4	11	18	25	2	9	16	16	23	30	6	13
16	15	22	29	5	12	19	26	3	10	17	17	24	31	7	14
17	16	23	30	6	13	20	27	4	11	18	18	25	Jan. 1	8	15
18	17	24	31	7	14	21	28	5	12	19	19	26	2	9	16
19	18	25	Nov. 1	8	15	22	29	6	13	20	20	27	3	10	17
20	19	26	2	9	16	23	30	7	14	21	21	28	4	11	18
21	20	27	3	10	17	24	Dec. 1	8	15	22	22	29	5	12	19

10. Makara, Mâgha Tai (Tam.)					11. Kumbha, Phâlguna Mâśi (Tam.)					12. Mîna, Chaitra Paṅguni (Tam.)						
6. Makaram, Tai.					7. Kumbham, Mâśi.					8. Mînam, Paṅguni.						
5. Makaram.					6. Kumbham.					7. Mînam.						
—	5	12	19	26	—	4	11	18	25	—	2	9	16	23	30	(1)
—	6	13	20	27	—	5	12	19	26	—	3	10	17	24	—	(2)
—	7	14	21	28	—	6	13	20	27	—	4	11	18	25	—	(3)
1	8	15	22	29	—	7	14	21	28	—	5	12	19	26	—	(4)
2	9	16	23	—	1	8	15	22	29	—	6	13	20	27	—	(5)
3	10	17	24	—	2	9	16	23	30	—	7	14	21	28	—	(6)
4	11	18	25	—	3	10	17	24	—	1	8	15	22	29	—	(7)
Dec. 11	Dec. 18	Dec. 25	Jan. 1	Jan. 8	Jan. 8	Jan. 15	Jan. 22	Jan. 29	Feb. 5	Feb. 5	Feb. 12	Feb. 19	Feb. 26	Mar. 5	Mar. 12	Mar13
12	19	26	2	9	9	16	23	30	6	6	13	20	27	6	13	14
13	20	27	3	10	10	17	24	31	7	7	14	21	28	7	14	15
14	21	28	4	11	11	18	25	Feb. 1	8	8	15	22	Mar. 1	8	15	16
15	22	29	5	12	12	19	26	2	9	9	16	23	2	9	16	17
16	23	30	6	13	13	20	27	3	10	10	17	24	3	10	17	18
17	24	31	7	14	14	21	28	4	11	11	18	25	4	11	18	19
18	25	Jan. 1	8	15	15	22	29	5	12	12	19	26	5	12	19	20
19	26	2	9	16	16	23	30	6	13	13	20	27	6	13	20	21
20	27	3	10	17	17	24	31	7	14	14	21	28	7	14	21	22
21	28	4	11	18	18	25	Feb. 1	8	15	15	22	Mar. 1	8	15	22	23
22	29	5	12	19	19	26	2	9	16	16	23	2	9	16	23	24
23	30	6	13	20	20	27	3	10	17	17	24	3	10	17	24	25
24	31	7	14	21	21	28	4	11	18	18	25	4	11	18	25	26
25	Jan. 1	8	15	22	22	29	5	12	19	19	26	5	12	19	26	27
26	2	9	16	23	23	30	6	13	20	20	27	6	13	20	27	28
27	3	10	17	24	24	31	7	14	21	21	28	7	14	21	28	29
28	4	11	18	25	25	Feb. 1	8	15	22	22	Mar. 1	8	15	22	29	30
29	5	12	19	26	26	2	9	16	23	23	2	9	16	23	30	31
30	6	13	20	27	27	3	10	17	24	24	3	10	17	24	31	Apr. 1
31	7	14	21	28	28	4	11	18	25	25	4	11	18	25	Apr. 1	2
Jan. 1	8	15	22	29	29	5	12	19	26	26	5	12	19	26	2	3
2	9	16	23	30	30	6	13	20	27	27	6	13	20	27	3	4
3	10	17	24	31	31	7	14	21	28	28	7	14	21	28	4	5
4	11	18	25	Feb. 1	Feb. 1	8	15	22	Mar. 1	Mar. 1	8	15	22	29	5	6
5	12	19	26	2	2	9	16	23	2	2	9	16	23	30	6	7
6	13	20	27	3	3	10	17	24	3	3	10	17	24	31	7	8
7	14	21	28	4	4	11	18	25	4	4	11	18	25	Apr. 1	8	9
8	15	22	29	5	5	12	19	26	5	5	12	19	26	2	9	10
9	16	23	30	6	6	13	20	27	6	6	13	20	27	3	10	11
10	17	24	31	7	7	14	21	28	7	7	14	21	28	4	11	12
11	18	25	Feb. 1	8	8	15	22	Mar. 1	8	8	15	22	29	5	12	13
12	19	26	2	9	9	16	23	2	9	9	16	23	30	6	13	14
13	20	27	3	10	10	17	24	3	10	10	17	24	31	7	14	15
14	21	28	4	11	11	18	25	4	11	11	18	25	Apr. 1	8	15	16
15	22	29	5	12	12	19	26	5	12	12	19	26	2	9	16	17
16	23	30	6	13	13	20	27	6	13	13	20	27	3	10	17	18
17	24	31	7	14	14	21	28	7	14	14	21	28	4	11	18	19
18	25	Feb. 1	8	15	15	22	Mar. 1	8	15	15	22	29	5	12	19	20
19	26	2	9	16	16	23	2	9	16	16	23	30	6	13	20	21

TABLE XV. (CONTINUED.)

FOR CONVERSION OF A HINDU LUNI-SOLAR DATE INTO THE CORRESPONDING DATE A.D. AND VICE-VERSÂ.

[It is not safe to use this Table unless all the bases of calculation of the given Hindu Date are known. When they are known, let it be borne in mind that the result, as found from this Table, though often correct, is often wrong by one day, occasionally by two days. This variation is unavoidable in an eye-table. Where absolute correctness is required, proceed by Art. 139.]

Amânta months of Chaitrâdi years beginning with Chaitra Śukla (Mahrâṭhi Tel. Can.), or Paggu (Tuḷu.)								1. Chaitra (Tel. Can.) 1. Paggu (Tuḷu.)					2. Vaiśâkha (Tel. Can.) 2. Beśâ (Tuḷu.)				
Pûrṇimânta months of Chaitrâdi years beginning with Chaitra Śukla (Chaitrâdi Vikrama) (Beng. Samvat.)								1. Chaitra śukla.			2. Vaiśâkha kṛishṇa.		2. Vaiśâkha śukla.			3. Jyeshṭha kṛishṇa.	
Amânta months of Kârttikâdi years beginning with Kârttika Śukla (S. Vikrama. Nevâr.)								6. *Chaitra* (S. Vikrama. Nevâr.)					7. *Vaiśâkha* (S. Vikrama. Nevâr.)				
	1	2	3	4	5	6	0	Śukla.			Kṛishṇa.		Śukla.			Kṛishṇa.	
(1)	Sun.	Mon.	Tues.	Wed.	Thur.	Fri.	Sat.	Śu. 1	8	15	7	14	—	6	13	5	12
(2)	Mon.	Tues.	Wed.	Thur.	Fri.	Sat.	Sun.	2	9	Kṛ. 1	8	30	—	7	14	6	13
(3)	Tues.	Wed.	Thur.	Fri.	Sat.	Sun.	Mon.	3	10	2	9	—	Śu. 1	8	15	7	14 or 30
(4)	Wed.	Thur.	Fri.	Sat.	Sun.	Mon.	Tues.	4	11	3	10	—	2	9	Kṛ. 1	8	—
(5)	Thur.	Fri.	Sat.	Sun.	Mon.	Tues.	Wed.	5	12	4	11	—	3	10	2	9	—
(6)	Fri.	Sat.	Sun.	Mon.	Tues.	Wed.	Thur.	6	13	5	12	—	4	11	3	10	—
(7)	Sat.	Sun.	Mon.	Tues.	Wed.	Thur.	Fri.	7	14	6	13	—	5	12	4	11	—
	(1)	(2)	(3)	(4)	(5)	(6)	(7)										
	Mar. 13	—	—	—	—	—	—	Mar. 13	Mar. 20	Mar. 27	Apr. 3	Apr. 10	Apr. 10	Apr. 17	Apr. 24	May 1	May 8
	14	Mar. 13	—	—	—	—	—	14	21	28	4	11	11	18	25	2	9
	15	14	Mar. 13	—	—	—	—	15	22	29	5	12	12	19	26	3	10
	16	15	14	Mar. 13	—	—	—	16	23	30	6	13	13	20	27	4	11
	17	16	15	14	Mar. 13	—	—	17	24	31	7	14	14	21	28	5	12
	18	17	16	15	14	Mar. 13	—	18	25	Apr. 1	8	15	15	22	29	6	13
	19	18	17	16	15	14	Mar. 13	19	26	2	9	16	16	23	30	7	14
	20	19	18	17	16	15	14	20	27	3	10	17	17	24	May 1	8	15
	21	20	19	18	17	16	15	21	28	4	11	18	18	25	2	9	16
	22	21	20	19	18	17	16	22	29	5	12	19	19	26	3	10	17
	23	22	21	20	19	18	17	23	30	6	13	20	20	27	4	11	18
	24	23	22	21	20	19	18	24	31	7	14	21	21	28	5	12	19
	25	24	23	22	21	20	19	25	Apr. 1	8	15	22	22	29	6	13	20
	26	25	24	23	22	21	20	26	2	9	16	23	23	30	7	14	21
	27	26	25	24	23	22	21	27	3	10	17	24	24	May 1	8	15	22
	28	27	26	25	24	23	22	28	4	11	18	25	25	2	9	16	23
	29	28	27	26	25	24	23	29	5	12	19	26	26	3	10	17	24
	30	29	28	27	26	25	24	30	6	13	20	27	27	4	11	18	25
	31	30	29	28	27	26	25	31	7	14	21	28	28	5	12	19	26
	Apr. 1	31	30	29	28	27	26	Apr. 1	8	15	22	29	29	6	13	20	27
	2	Apr. 1	31	30	29	28	27	2	9	16	23	30	30	7	14	21	28
	3	2	Apr. 1	31	30	29	28	3	10	17	24	May 1	May 1	8	15	22	29
	4	3	2	Apr. 1	31	30	29	4	11	18	25	2	2	9	16	23	30
	5	4	3	2	Apr. 1	31	30	5	12	19	26	3	3	10	17	24	31
	6	5	4	3	2	Apr. 1	31	6	13	20	27	4	4	11	18	25	Jun. 1
	7	6	5	4	3	2	Apr. 1	7	14	21	28	5	5	12	19	26	2
	8	7	6	5	4	3	2	8	15	22	29	6	6	13	20	27	3
	9	8	7	6	5	4	3	9	16	23	30	7	7	14	21	28	4
	10	9	8	7	6	5	4	10	17	24	May 1	8	8	15	22	29	5
	11	10	9	8	7	6	5	11	18	25	2	9	9	16	23	30	6
	12	11	10	9	8	7	6	12	19	26	3	10	10	17	24	31	7
	13	12	11	10	9	8	7	13	20	27	4	11	11	18	25	Jun. 1	8
	14	13	12	11	10	9	8	14	21	28	5	12	12	19	26	2	9
	15	14	13	12	11	10	9	15	22	29	6	13	13	20	27	3	10
	—	15	14	13	12	11	10	16	23	30	7	14	14	21	28	4	11
	—	—	15	14	13	12	11	17	24	May 1	8	15	15	22	29	5	12

3. Jyeshṭha (Tel. Can.) 3. Kârtelu (Tuḷu.)					4. Âshâḍha (Tel. Can.) 4. Âṭi (Tuḷu.)					5. Śrâvaṇa (Tel. Can.) 5. Sôṇa (Tuḷu.)						6. Bhâdrapada (Tel. Can.) 6. Nirṇâla (Tuḷu.)				
3. Jyeshṭha śukla.			4. Âshâḍha kṛishṇa.		4. Âshâḍha śukla.			5. Śrâvaṇa kṛishṇa.		5. Śrâvaṇa śukla.			6. Bhâdrapada kṛishṇa.			6. Bhâdrapada śukla.			7. Âśvina kṛishṇa.	
8. *Jyeshṭha* (S. Vikrama. Nevâr.)					9. *Âshâḍha* (S. Vikrama. Nevâr.)					10. *Śrâvaṇa.* (S. Vikrama. Nevâr.)						11. *Bhâdrapada* (S. Vikrama. Nevâr.)				
Śukla.			Kṛishṇa.		Śukla.			Kṛishṇa.		Śukla.			Kṛishṇa.			Śukla.			Kṛishṇa.	
—	5	12	4	11	—	3	10	2	9	—	2	9	Kṛ. 1	8	30	—	7	14	6	13
—	6	13	5	12	—	4	11	3	10	—	3	10	2	9	—	Śu. 1	8	15	7	14 or 30
—	7	14	6	13	—	5	12	4	11	—	4	11	3	10	—	2	9	Kṛ. 1	8	—
Śu. 1	8	15	7	14	—	6	13	5	12	—	5	12	4	11	—	3	10	2	9	—
2	9	Kṛ. 1	8	30	—	7	14	6	13	—	6	13	5	12	—	4	11	3	10	—
3	10	2	9	—	Śu. 1	8	15	7	14 or 30	—	7	14	6	13	—	5	12	4	11	—
4	11	3	10	—	2	9	Kṛ. 1	8	—	Śu. 1	8	15	7	14	—	6	13	5	12	—
May 8	May 15	May 22	May 29	Jun. 5	Jun. 5	Jun. 12	Jun. 19	Jun. 26	Jul. 3	Jul. 3	Jul. 10	Jul. 17	Jul. 24	Jul. 31	Aug. 7	Aug. 7	Aug. 14	Aug. 21	Aug. 28	Sep. 4
9	16	23	30	6	6	13	20	27	4	4	11	18	25	Aug. 1	8	8	15	22	29	5
10	17	24	31	7	7	14	21	28	5	5	12	19	26	2	9	9	16	23	30	6
11	18	25	Jun. 1	8	8	15	22	29	6	6	13	20	27	3	10	10	17	24	31	7
12	19	26	2	9	9	16	23	30	7	7	14	21	28	4	11	11	18	25	Sep. 1	8
13	20	27	3	10	10	17	24	Jul. 1	8	8	15	22	29	5	12	12	19	26	2	9
14	21	28	4	11	11	18	25	2	9	9	16	23	30	6	13	13	20	27	3	10
15	22	29	5	12	12	19	26	3	10	10	17	24	31	7	14	14	21	28	4	11
16	23	30	6	13	13	20	27	4	11	11	18	25	Aug. 1	8	15	15	22	29	5	12
17	24	31	7	14	14	21	28	5	12	12	19	26	2	9	16	16	23	30	6	13
18	25	Jun. 1	8	15	15	22	29	6	13	13	20	27	3	10	17	17	24	31	7	14
19	26	2	9	16	16	23	30	7	14	14	21	28	4	11	18	18	25	Sep. 1	8	15
20	27	3	10	17	17	24	Jul. 1	8	15	15	22	29	5	12	19	19	26	2	9	16
21	28	4	11	18	18	25	2	9	16	16	23	30	6	13	20	20	27	3	10	17
22	29	5	12	19	19	26	3	10	17	17	24	31	7	14	21	21	28	4	11	18
23	30	6	13	20	20	27	4	11	18	18	25	Aug. 1	8	15	22	22	29	5	12	19
24	31	7	14	21	21	28	5	12	19	19	26	2	9	16	23	23	30	6	13	20
25	Jun. 1	8	15	22	22	29	6	13	20	20	27	3	10	17	24	24	31	7	14	21
26	2	9	16	23	23	30	7	14	21	21	28	4	11	18	25	25	Sep. 1	8	15	22
27	3	10	17	24	24	Jul. 1	8	15	22	22	29	5	12	19	26	26	2	9	16	23
28	4	11	18	25	25	2	9	16	23	23	30	6	13	20	27	27	3	10	17	24
29	5	12	19	26	26	3	10	17	24	24	31	7	14	21	28	28	4	11	18	25
30	6	13	20	27	27	4	11	18	25	25	Aug. 1	8	15	22	29	29	5	12	19	26
31	7	14	21	28	28	5	12	19	26	26	2	9	16	23	30	30	6	13	20	27
Jun. 1	8	15	22	29	29	6	13	20	27	27	3	10	17	24	31	31	7	14	21	28
2	9	16	23	30	30	7	14	21	28	28	4	11	18	25	Sep. 1	Sep. 1	8	15	22	29
3	10	17	24	Jul. 1	Jul. 1	8	15	22	29	29	5	12	19	26	2	2	9	16	23	30
4	11	18	25	2	2	9	16	23	30	30	6	13	20	27	3	3	10	17	24	Oct. 1
5	12	19	26	3	3	10	17	24	31	31	7	14	21	28	4	4	11	18	25	2
6	13	20	27	4	4	11	18	25	Aug. 1	Aug. 1	8	15	22	29	5	5	12	19	26	3
7	14	21	28	5	5	12	19	26	2	2	9	16	23	30	6	6	13	20	27	4
8	15	22	29	6	6	13	20	27	3	3	10	17	24	31	7	7	14	21	28	5
9	16	23	30	7	7	14	21	28	4	4	11	18	25	Sep. 1	8	8	15	22	29	6
10	17	24	Jul. 1	8	8	15	22	29	5	5	12	19	26	2	9	9	16	23	30	7
11	18	25	2	9	9	16	23	30	6	6	13	20	27	3	10	10	17	24	Oct. 1	8
12	19	26	3	10	10	17	24	31	7	7	14	21	28	4	11	11	18	25	2	9

7. Âśvina (Tel. Can.) 7. Bontelu (Tuḷu.)					8. Kârttika (Tel. Can.) 8. Jârde (Tuḷu.)					9. Mârgaśîrsha (Tel. Can.) 9. Perârde (Tuḷu.)					10. Pausha (Tel. Can.) 10. Pûntelu (Tuḷu.)				
7. Âśvina śukla.			8. Kârttika kṛishṇa.		8. Kârttika śukla.			9. Mârgaśîrsha kṛishṇa.		9. Mârgaśîrsha śukla.			10. Pausha kṛishṇa.		10. Pausha śukla.			11. Mâgha kṛishṇa.	
12. *Âśvina* (S. Vikrama. Nevâr.)					1. Kârttika (S. Vikrama. Nevâr.)					2. Mârgaśîrsha (S. Vikrama. Nevâr.)					3. Pausha (S. Vikrama. Nevâr.)				
Śukla.			Kṛishṇa.		Śukla.			Kṛishṇa.		Śukla.			Kṛishṇa.		Śukla.			Kṛishṇa.	
—	6	13	5	12	—	4	11	3	10	—	3	10	2	9	Śu. 1	8	15	7	14 or 30
—	7	14	6	13	—	5	12	4	11	—	4	11	3	10	2	9	Kṛ. 1	8	—
Śu. 1	8	15	7	14	—	6	13	5	12	—	5	12	4	11	3	10	2	9	—
2	9	Kṛ. 1	8	30	—	7	14	6	13	—	6	13	5	12	4	11	3	10	—
3	10	2	9	—	Śu. 1	8	15	7	14 or 30	—	7	14	6	13	5	12	4	11	—
4	11	3	10	—	2	9	Kṛ. 1	8	—	Śu. 1	8	15	7	14	6	13	5	12	—
5	12	4	11	—	3	10	2	9	—	2	9	Kṛ. 1	8	30	7	14	6	13	—
Sep. 4	Sep. 11	Sep. 18	Sep. 25	Oct. 2	Oct. 2	Oct. 9	Oct. 16	Oct. 23	Oct. 30	Oct. 30	Nov. 6	Nov. 13	Nov. 20	Nov. 27	Dec. 4	Dec. 11	Dec. 18	Dec. 25	Jan. 1
5	12	19	26	3	3	10	17	24	31	31	7	14	21	28	5	12	19	26	2
6	13	20	27	4	4	11	18	25	Nov. 1	Nov. 1	8	15	22	29	6	13	20	27	3
7	14	21	28	5	5	12	19	26	2	2	9	16	23	30	7	14	21	28	4
8	15	22	29	6	6	13	20	27	3	3	10	17	24	Dec. 1	8	15	22	29	5
9	16	23	30	7	7	14	21	28	4	4	11	18	25	2	9	16	23	30	6
10	17	24	Oct. 1	8	8	15	22	29	5	5	12	19	26	3	10	17	24	31	7
11	18	25	2	9	9	16	23	30	6	6	13	20	27	4	11	18	25	Jan. 1	8
12	19	26	3	10	10	17	24	31	7	7	14	21	28	5	12	19	26	2	9
13	20	27	4	11	11	18	25	Nov. 1	8	8	15	22	29	6	13	20	27	3	10
14	21	28	5	12	12	19	26	2	9	9	16	23	30	7	14	21	28	4	11
15	22	29	6	13	13	20	27	3	10	10	17	24	Dec. 1	8	15	22	29	5	12
16	23	30	7	14	14	21	28	4	11	11	18	25	2	9	16	23	30	6	13
17	24	Oct. 1	8	15	15	22	29	5	12	12	19	26	3	10	17	24	31	7	14
18	25	2	9	16	16	23	30	6	13	13	20	27	4	11	18	25	Jan. 1	8	15
19	26	3	10	17	17	24	31	7	14	14	21	28	5	12	19	26	2	9	16
20	27	4	11	18	18	25	Nov. 1	8	15	15	22	29	6	13	20	27	3	10	17
21	28	5	12	19	19	26	2	9	16	16	23	30	7	14	21	28	4	11	18
22	29	6	13	20	20	27	3	10	17	17	24	Dec. 1	8	15	22	29	5	12	19
23	30	7	14	21	21	28	4	11	18	18	25	2	9	16	23	30	6	13	20
24	Oct. 1	8	15	22	22	29	5	12	19	19	26	3	10	17	24	31	7	14	21
25	2	9	16	23	23	30	6	13	20	20	27	4	11	18	25	Jan. 1	8	15	22
26	3	10	17	24	24	31	7	14	21	21	28	5	12	19	26	2	9	16	23
27	4	11	18	25	25	Nov. 1	8	15	22	22	29	6	13	20	27	3	10	17	24
28	5	12	19	26	26	2	9	16	23	23	30	7	14	21	28	4	11	18	25
29	6	13	20	27	27	3	10	17	24	24	Dec. 1	8	15	22	29	5	12	19	26
30	7	14	21	28	28	4	11	18	25	25	2	9	16	23	30	6	13	20	27
Oct. 1	8	15	22	29	29	5	12	19	26	26	3	10	17	24	31	7	14	21	28
2	9	16	23	30	30	6	13	20	27	27	4	11	18	25	Jan. 1	8	15	22	29
3	10	17	24	31	31	7	14	21	28	28	5	12	19	26	2	9	16	23	30
4	11	18	25	Nov. 1	Nov. 1	8	15	22	29	29	6	13	20	27	3	10	17	24	31
5	12	19	26	2	2	9	16	23	30	30	7	14	21	28	4	11	18	25	Feb. 1
6	13	20	27	3	3	10	17	24	Dec. 1	Dec. 1	8	15	22	29	5	12	19	26	2
7	14	21	28	4	4	11	18	25	2	2	9	16	23	30	6	13	20	27	3
8	15	22	29	5	5	12	19	26	3	3	10	17	24	31	7	14	21	28	4
9	16	23	30	6	6	13	20	27	4	4	11	18	25	Jan. 1	8	15	22	29	5

11. Mâgha (Tel. Can.) 11. Mâyi (Tuḷu.)					12. Phâlguna (Tel. Can.) 12. Suggi (Tuḷu.)					13th Month in intercalary years.				
11. Mâgha śukla.			12. Phâlguna kṛishṇa.		12. Phâlguna śukla.			1. Chaitra kṛishṇa.						
5. Mâgha (S. Vikrama. Nevâr.)					5. Phâlguna (S. Vikrama. Nevâr.)									
Śukla.			Kṛishṇa.		Śukla.			Kṛishṇa.		Śukla.			Kṛishṇa.	
—	7	14	6	13	—	5	12	4	11	—	4	11	3	10
Śu. 1	8	15	7	14	—	6	13	5	12	—	5	12	4	11
2	9	Kṛ. 1	8	30	—	7	14	6	13	—	6	13	5	12
3	10	2	9	—	Śu. 1	8	15	7	14 or 30	—	7	14	6	13
4	11	3	10	—	2	9	Kṛ. 1	8	—	Śu. 1	8	15	7	14
5	12	4	11	—	3	10	2	9	—	2	9	Kṛ. 1	8	30
6	13	5	12	—	4	11	3	10	—	3	10	2	9	—
Jan. 1	Jan. 8	Jan. 15	Jan. 22	Jan. 29	Jan. 29	Feb. 5	Feb. 12	Feb. 19	Feb. 26	Feb. 26	Mar. 5	Mar. 12	Mar. 19	Mar. 26
2	9	16	23	30	30	6	13	20	27	27	6	13	20	27
3	10	17	24	31	31	7	14	21	28	28	7	14	21	28
4	11	18	25	Feb. 1	Feb. 1	8	15	22	Mar. 1	Mar. 1	8	15	22	29
5	12	19	26	2	2	9	16	23	2	2	9	16	23	30
6	13	20	27	3	3	10	17	24	3	3	10	17	24	31
7	14	21	28	4	4	11	18	25	4	4	11	18	25	Apr. 1
8	15	22	29	5	5	12	19	26	5	5	12	19	26	2
9	16	23	30	6	6	13	20	27	6	6	13	20	27	3
10	17	24	31	7	7	14	21	28	7	7	14	21	28	4
11	18	25	Feb. 1	8	8	15	22	Mar. 1	8	8	15	22	29	5
12	19	26	2	9	9	16	23	2	9	9	16	23	30	6
13	20	27	3	10	10	17	24	3	10	10	17	24	31	7
14	21	28	4	11	11	18	25	4	11	11	18	25	Apr. 1	8
15	22	29	5	12	12	19	26	5	12	12	19	26	2	9
16	23	30	6	13	13	20	27	6	13	13	20	27	3	10
17	24	31	7	14	14	21	28	7	14	14	21	28	4	11
18	25	Feb. 1	8	15	15	22	Mar. 1	8	15	15	22	29	5	12
19	26	2	9	16	16	23	2	9	16	16	23	30	6	13
20	27	3	10	17	17	24	3	10	17	17	24	31	7	14
21	28	4	11	18	18	25	4	11	18	18	25	Apr. 1	8	15
22	29	5	12	19	19	26	5	12	19	19	26	2	9	16
23	30	6	13	20	20	27	6	13	20	20	27	3	10	17
24	31	7	14	21	21	28	7	14	21	21	28	4	11	18
25	Feb. 1	8	15	22	22	Mar. 1	8	15	22	22	29	5	12	19
26	2	9	16	23	23	2	9	16	23	23	30	6	13	20
27	3	10	17	24	24	3	10	17	24	24	31	7	14	21
28	4	11	18	25	25	4	11	18	25	25	Apr. 1	8	15	22
29	5	12	19	26	26	5	12	19	26	26	2	9	16	23
30	6	13	20	27	27	6	13	20	27	27	3	10	17	24
31	7	14	21	28	28	7	14	21	28	28	4	11	18	25
Feb. 1	8	15	22	Mar. 1	Mar. 1	8	15	22	29	29	5	12	19	26
2	9	16	23	2	2	9	16	23	30	30	6	13	20	27
3	10	17	24	3	3	10	17	24	31	31	7	14	21	28
4	11	18	25	4	4	11	18	25	Apr. 1	Apr. 1	8	15	22	29
5	12	19	26	5	5	12	19	26	2	2	9	16	23	30

TABLE XV.

FOR CONVERSION OF A HINDU LUNI-SOLAR DATE INTO THE CORRESPONDING DATE A.D. AND VICE-VERSÂ.

[It is not safe to use this Table unless all the bases of calculation of the given Hindu Date are known. When they are known, let it be borne in mind that the result, as found from this Table, though often correct, is often wrong by one day, occasionally by two days. This variation is unavoidable in an eye-table. Where absolute correctness is required, proceed by Art. 139.]

AMÂNTA MONTHS OF CHAITRÂDI YEARS beginning with Chaitra Śukla (Mahrâṭhî Tel. Can.), or Paggu (Tuḷu.)								1. Chaitra (Tel. Can.) 1. Paggu (Tuḷu.)					2. Vaiśâkha (Tel. Can.) 2. Beśâ (Tuḷu.)				
PÛRṆIMÂNTA MONTHS OF CHAITRÂDI YEARS beginning with Chaitra Śukla (Chaitrâdi Vikrama) (Beng. Samvat.)								1. Chaitra śukla.			2. Vaiśâkha kṛishṇa.		2. Vaiśâkha śukla.			3. Jyeshṭha kṛishṇa.	
AMÂNTA MONTHS OF KÂRTTIKÂDI YEARS beginning with Kârttika Śukla (S. Vikrama. Nevâr.)								6. *Chaitra* (S. Vikrama. Nevâr.)					7. *Vaiśâkha* (S. Vikrama. Nevâr.)				
	1	2	3	4	5	6	0	Śukla.			Kṛishṇa.		Śukla.			Kṛishṇa.	
(1)	Sun.	Mon.	Tues.	Wed.	Thur.	Fri.	Sat.	Śu. 1	8	15	7	14	—	6	13	5	12
(2)	Mon.	Tues.	Wed.	Thur.	Fri.	Sat.	Sun.	2	9	Kṛ. 1	8	30	—	7	14	6	13
(3)	Tues.	Wed.	Thur.	Fri.	Sat.	Sun.	Mon.	3	10	2	9	—	Śu. 1	8	15	7	14 or 30
(4)	Wed.	Thur.	Fri.	Sat.	Sun.	Mon.	Tues.	4	11	3	10	—	2	9	Kṛ. 1	8	—
(5)	Thur.	Fri.	Sat.	Sun.	Mon.	Tues.	Wed.	5	12	4	11	—	3	10	2	9	—
(6)	Fri.	Sat.	Sun.	Mon.	Tues.	Wed.	Thur.	6	13	5	12	—	4	11	3	10	—
(7)	Sat.	Sun.	Mon.	Tues.	Wed.	Thur.	Fri.	7	14	6	13	—	5	12	4	11	—
	(1)	(2)	(3)	(4)	(5)	(6)	(7)										
	Feb. 16	Feb. 15	Feb. 14	Feb. 13	Feb. 12	—	—	Feb. 16	Feb. 23	Mar. 2	Mar. 9	Mar. 16	Mar. 16	Mar. 23	Mar. 30	Apr. 6	Apr. 13
	17	16	15	14	13	Feb. 12	—	17	24	3	10	17	17	24	31	7	14
	18	17	16	15	14	13	Feb. 12	18	25	4	11	18	18	25	Apr. 1	8	15
	19	18	17	16	15	14	13	19	26	5	12	19	19	26	2	9	16
	20	19	18	17	16	15	14	20	27	6	13	20	20	27	3	10	17
	21	20	19	18	17	16	15	21	28	7	14	21	21	28	4	11	18
	22	21	20	19	18	17	16	22	Mar. 1	8	15	22	22	29	5	12	19
	23	22	21	20	19	18	17	23	2	9	16	23	23	30	6	13	20
	24	23	22	21	20	19	18	24	3	10	17	24	24	31	7	14	21
	25	24	23	22	21	20	19	25	4	11	18	25	25	Apr. 1	8	15	22
	26	25	24	23	22	21	20	26	5	12	19	26	26	2	9	16	23
	27	26	25	24	23	22	21	27	6	13	20	27	27	3	10	17	24
	28	27	26	25	24	23	22	28	7	14	21	28	28	4	11	18	25
	29 / Mar. 1	28	27	26	25	24	23	Mar. 1	8	15	22	29	29	5	12	19	26
	2	29 / Mar. 1	28	27	26	25	24	2	9	16	23	30	30	6	13	20	27
	3	2	29 / Mar. 1	28	27	26	25	3	10	17	24	31	31	7	14	21	28
	4	3	2	29 / Mar. 1	28	27	26	4	11	18	25	Apr. 1	Apr. 1	8	15	22	29
	5	4	3	2	29 / Mar. 1	28	27	5	12	19	26	2	2	9	16	23	30
	6	5	4	3	2	29 / Mar. 1	28	6	13	20	27	3	3	10	17	24	May 1
	7	6	5	4	3	2	29 / Mar. 1	7	14	21	28	4	4	11	18	25	2
	8	7	6	5	4	3	2	8	15	22	29	5	5	12	19	26	3
	9	8	7	6	5	4	3	9	16	23	30	6	6	13	20	27	4
	10	9	8	7	6	5	4	10	17	24	31	7	7	14	21	28	5
	11	10	9	8	7	6	5	11	18	25	Apr. 1	8	8	15	22	29	6
	12	11	10	9	8	7	6	12	19	26	2	9	9	16	23	30	7
	13	12	11	10	9	8	7	13	20	27	3	10	10	17	24	May 1	8
	—	13	12	11	10	9	8	14	21	28	4	11	11	18	25	2	9
	—	—	13	12	11	10	9	15	22	29	5	12	12	19	26	3	10
	—	—	—	13	12	11	10	16	23	30	6	13	13	20	27	4	11
	—	—	—	—	13	12	11	17	24	31	7	14	14	21	28	5	12
	—	—	—	—	—	13	12	18	25	Apr. 1	8	15	15	22	29	6	13
	—	—	—	—	—	—	13	19	26	2	9	16	16	23	30	7	14

3. Jyeshṭha (Tel. Can.) 3. Kârtelu (Tuḷu.)					4. Âshâḍha (Tel. Can.) 4. Âṭi (Tuḷu.)					5. Śrâvaṇa (Tel. Can.) 5. Sōna (Tuḷu.)					
3. Jyeshṭha śukla.			4. Âshâḍha kṛishṇa.		4. Âshâḍha śukla.			5. Śrâvaṇa kṛishṇa.		5. Śrâvaṇa śukla.			6. Bhâdrapada kṛishṇa.		
8. *Jyeshṭha* (S. Vikrama. Nevâr.)					9. *Âshâḍha* (S. Vikrama. Nevâr.)					10. *Śrâvaṇa.* (S. Vikrama. Nevâr.)					
Śukla.			Kṛishṇa.		Śukla.			Kṛishṇa.		Śukla.			Kṛishṇa.		
—	5	12	4	11	—	3	10	2	9	—	2	9	Kṛ. 1	8	30
—	6	13	5	12	—	4	11	3	10	—	3	10	2	9	—
—	7	14	6	13	—	5	12	4	11	—	4	11	3	10	—
Śu. 1	8	15	7	14	—	6	13	5	12	—	5	12	4	11	—
2	9	Kṛ. 1	8	30	—	7	14	6	13	—	6	13	5	12	—
3	10	2	9	—	Śu. 1	8	15	7	14 or 30	—	7	14	6	13	—
4	11	3	10	—	2	9	Kṛ. 1	8	—	Śu. 1	8	15	7	14	—
Apr. 13	Apr. 20	Apr. 27	May 4	May 11	May 11	May 18	May 25	Jun. 1	Jun. 8	Jun. 8	Jun. 15	Jun. 22	Jun. 29	Jul. 6	Jul. 13
14	21	28	5	12	12	19	26	2	9	9	16	23	30	7	14
15	22	29	6	13	13	20	27	3	10	10	17	24	Jul. 1	8	15
16	23	30	7	14	14	21	28	4	11	11	18	25	2	9	16
17	24	May 1	8	15	15	22	29	5	12	12	19	26	3	10	17
18	25	2	9	16	16	23	30	6	13	13	20	27	4	11	18
19	26	3	10	17	17	24	31	7	14	14	21	28	5	12	19
20	27	4	11	18	18	25	Jun. 1	8	15	15	22	29	6	13	20
21	28	5	12	19	19	26	2	9	16	16	23	30	7	14	21
22	29	6	13	20	20	27	3	10	17	17	24	Jul. 1	8	15	22
23	30	7	14	21	21	28	4	11	18	18	25	2	9	16	23
24	May 1	8	15	22	22	29	5	12	19	19	26	3	10	17	24
25	2	9	16	23	23	30	6	13	20	20	27	4	11	18	25
26	3	10	17	24	24	31	7	14	21	21	28	5	12	19	26
27	4	11	18	25	25	Jun. 1	8	15	22	22	29	6	13	20	27
28	5	12	19	26	26	2	9	16	23	23	30	7	14	21	28
29	6	13	20	27	27	3	10	17	24	24	Jul. 1	8	15	22	29
30	7	14	21	28	28	4	11	18	25	25	2	9	16	23	30
May 1	8	15	22	29	29	5	12	19	26	26	3	10	17	24	31
2	9	16	23	30	30	6	13	20	27	27	4	11	18	25	Aug. 1
3	10	17	24	31	31	7	14	21	28	28	5	12	19	26	2
4	11	18	25	Jun. 1	Jun. 1	8	15	22	29	29	6	13	20	27	3
5	12	19	26	2	2	9	16	23	30	30	7	14	21	28	4
6	13	20	27	3	3	10	17	24	Jul. 1	Jul. 1	8	15	22	29	5
7	14	21	28	4	4	11	18	25	2	2	9	16	23	30	6
8	15	22	29	5	5	12	19	26	3	3	10	17	24	31	7
9	16	23	30	6	6	13	20	27	4	4	11	18	25	Aug. 1	8
10	17	24	31	7	7	14	21	28	5	5	12	19	26	2	9
11	18	25	Jun. 1	8	8	15	22	29	6	6	13	20	27	3	10
12	19	26	2	9	9	16	23	30	7	7	14	21	28	4	11
13	20	27	3	10	10	17	24	Jul. 1	8	8	15	22	29	5	12
14	21	28	4	11	11	18	25	2	9	9	16	23	30	6	13

6. Bhâdrapada (Tel. Can.) 6. Nirnâla (Tuḷu.)					7. Âśvina (Tel. Can.) 7. Bontelu (Tuḷu.)					8. Kârttika (Tel. Can.) 8. Jârde (Tuḷu.)				
6. Bhâdrapada śukla.			7. Âśvina kṛishṇa.		7. Âśvina śukla.			8. Kârttika kṛishṇa.		8. Kârttika śukla.			9. Mârgaśirsha kṛishṇa.	
11. *Bhâdrapada* (S. Vikrama. Nevâr.)					12. *Âśvina* (S. Vikrama. Nevâr.)					1. KÂRTTIKA (S. Vikrama. Nevâr.)				
Śukla.			Kṛishṇa.		Śukla.			Kṛishṇa.		Śukla.			Kṛishṇa.	
—	7	14	6	13	—	6	13	5	12	—	4	11	3	10
Śu. 1	8	15	7	14 or 30	—	7	14	6	13	—	5	12	4	11
2	9	Kṛ. 1	8	—	Śu. 1	8	15	7	14	—	6	13	5	12
3	10	2	9	—	2	9	Kṛ. 1	8	30	—	7	14	6	13
4	11	3	10	—	3	10	2	9	—	Śu. 1	8	15	7	14 or 30
5	12	4	11	—	4	11	3	10	—	2	9	Kṛ. 1	8	—
6	13	5	12	—	5	12	4	11	—	3	10	2	9	—
Jul. 13	Jul. 20	Jul. 27	Aug. 3	Aug. 10	Aug. 10	Aug. 17	Aug. 24	Aug. 31	Sep. 7	Sep. 7	Sep. 14	Sep. 21	Sep. 28	Oct. 5
14	21	28	4	11	11	18	25	Sep. 1	8	8	15	22	29	6
15	22	29	5	12	12	19	26	2	9	9	16	23	30	7
16	23	30	6	13	13	20	27	3	10	10	17	24	Oct. 1	8
17	24	31	7	14	14	21	28	4	11	11	18	25	2	9
18	25	Aug. 1	8	15	15	22	29	5	12	12	19	26	3	10
19	26	2	9	16	16	23	30	6	13	13	20	27	4	11
20	27	3	10	17	17	24	31	7	14	14	21	28	5	12
21	28	4	11	18	18	25	Sep. 1	8	15	15	22	29	6	13
22	29	5	12	19	19	26	2	9	16	16	23	30	7	14
23	30	6	13	20	20	27	3	10	17	17	24	Oct. 1	8	15
24	31	7	14	21	21	28	4	11	18	18	25	2	9	16
25	Aug. 1	8	15	22	22	29	5	12	19	19	26	3	10	17
26	2	9	16	23	23	30	6	13	20	20	27	4	11	18
27	3	10	17	24	24	31	7	14	21	21	28	5	12	19
28	4	11	18	25	25	Sep. 1	8	15	22	22	29	6	13	20
29	5	12	19	26	26	2	9	16	23	23	30	7	14	21
30	6	13	20	27	27	3	10	17	24	24	Oct. 1	8	15	22
31	7	14	21	28	28	4	11	18	25	25	2	9	16	23
Aug. 1	8	15	22	29	29	5	12	19	26	26	3	10	17	24
2	9	16	23	30	30	6	13	20	27	27	4	11	18	25
3	10	17	24	31	31	7	14	21	28	28	5	12	19	26
4	11	18	25	Sep. 1	Sep. 1	8	15	22	29	29	6	13	20	27
5	12	19	26	2	2	9	16	23	30	30	7	14	21	28
6	13	20	27	3	3	10	17	24	Oct. 1	Oct. 1	8	15	22	29
7	14	21	28	4	4	11	18	25	2	2	9	16	23	30
8	15	22	29	5	5	12	19	26	3	3	10	17	24	31
9	16	23	30	6	6	13	20	27	4	4	11	18	25	Nov. 1
10	17	24	31	7	7	14	21	28	5	5	12	19	26	2
11	18	25	Sep. 1	8	8	15	22	29	6	6	13	20	27	3
12	19	26	2	9	9	16	23	30	7	7	14	21	28	4
13	20	27	3	10	10	17	24	Oct. 1	8	8	15	22	29	5

9. Mârgaśirsha (Tel. Can.) 9. Perârde (Tuḷu.)					10. Pausha (Tel. Can.) 10. Puntelu (Tuḷu.)					11. Mâgha (Tel. Can.) 11. Mâyi (Tuḷu.)				
9. Mârgaśirsha śukla.			10. Pausha kṛishṇa.		10. Pausha śukla.			11. Mâgha kṛishṇa.		11. Mâgha śukla.			12. Phâlguna kṛishṇa.	
2. Mârgaśirsha (S. Vikrama. Nevâr.)					3. Pausha (S. Vikrama. Nevâr.)					5. Mâgha (S. Vikrama. Nevâr.)				
Śukla.			Kṛishṇa.		Śukla.			Kṛishṇa.		Śukla.			Kṛishṇa.	
—	3	10	2	9	Śu. 1	8	15	7	14 or 30	—	7	14	6	13
—	4	11	3	10	2	9	Kṛ. 1	8	—	Śu. 1	8	15	7	14
—	5	12	4	11	3	10	2	9	—	2	9	Kṛ. 1	8	30
—	6	13	5	12	4	11	3	10	—	3	10	2	9	—
—	7	14	6	13	5	12	4	11	—	4	11	3	10	—
Śu. 1	8	15	7	14	6	13	5	12	—	5	12	4	11	—
2	9	Kṛ. 1	8	30	7	14	6	13	—	6	13	5	12	—
Oct. 5	Oct. 12	Oct. 19	Oct. 26	Nov. 2	Nov. 9	Nov. 16	Nov. 23	Nov. 30	Dec. 7	Dec. 7	Dec. 14	Dec. 21	Dec. 28	Jan. 4
6	13	20	27	3	10	17	24	Dec. 1	8	8	15	22	29	5
7	14	21	28	4	11	18	25	2	9	9	16	23	30	6
8	15	22	29	5	12	19	26	3	10	10	17	24	31	7
9	16	23	30	6	13	20	27	4	11	11	18	25	Jan. 1	8
10	17	24	31	7	14	21	28	5	12	12	19	26	2	9
11	18	25	Nov. 1	8	15	22	29	6	13	13	20	27	3	10
12	19	26	2	9	16	23	30	7	14	14	21	28	4	11
13	20	27	3	10	17	24	Dec. 1	8	15	15	22	29	5	12
14	21	28	4	11	18	25	2	9	16	16	23	30	6	13
15	22	29	5	12	19	26	3	10	17	17	24	31	7	14
16	23	30	6	13	20	27	4	11	18	18	25	Jan. 1	8	15
17	24	31	7	14	21	28	5	12	19	19	26	2	9	16
18	25	Nov. 1	8	15	22	29	6	13	20	20	27	3	10	17
19	26	2	9	16	23	30	7	14	21	21	28	4	11	18
20	27	3	10	17	24	Dec. 1	8	15	22	22	29	5	12	19
21	28	4	11	18	25	2	9	16	23	23	30	6	13	20
22	29	5	12	19	26	3	10	17	24	24	31	7	14	21
23	30	6	13	20	27	4	11	18	25	25	Jan. 1	8	15	22
24	31	7	14	21	28	5	12	19	26	26	2	9	16	23
25	Nov. 1	8	15	22	29	6	13	20	27	27	3	10	17	24
26	2	9	16	23	30	7	14	21	28	28	4	11	18	25
27	3	10	17	24	Dec. 1	8	15	22	29	29	5	12	19	26
28	4	11	18	25	2	9	16	23	30	30	6	13	20	27
29	5	12	19	26	3	10	17	24	31	31	7	14	21	28
30	6	13	20	27	4	11	18	25	Jan. 1	Jan. 1	8	15	22	29
31	7	14	21	28	5	12	19	26	2	2	9	16	23	30
Nov. 1	8	15	22	29	6	13	20	27	3	3	10	17	24	31
2	9	16	23	30	7	14	21	28	4	4	11	18	25	Feb. 1
3	10	17	24	Dec. 1	8	15	22	29	5	5	12	19	26	2
4	11	18	25	2	9	16	23	30	6	6	13	20	27	3
5	12	19	26	3	10	17	24	31	7	7	14	21	28	4

12. Phâlguna (Tel. Can.) 12. Suggi (Tuḷu.)					13th Month in intercalary years.				
12. Phâlguna śukla.			1. Chaitra kṛishṇa.						
5. Phâlguna (S. Vikrama. Nevâr.)									
Śukla.			Kṛishṇa.		Śukla.			Kṛishṇa.	
—	5	12	4	11	—	4	11	3	10
—	6	13	5	12	—	5	12	4	11
—	7	14	6	13	—	6	13	5	12
Śu. 1	8	15	7	14 or 30	—	7	14	6	13
2	9	Kṛ. 1	8	—	Śu. 1	8	15	7	14
3	10	2	9	—	2	9	Kṛ. 1	8	30
4	11	3	10	—	3	10	2	9	—
Jan. 4	Jan. 11	Jan. 18	Jan. 25	Feb. 1	Feb. 1	Feb. 8	Feb. 15	Feb. 22	Mar. 1
5	12	19	26	2	2	9	16	23	2
6	13	20	27	3	3	10	17	24	3
7	14	21	28	4	4	11	18	25	4
8	15	22	29	5	5	12	19	26	5
9	16	23	30	6	6	13	20	27	6
10	17	24	31	7	7	14	21	28	7
11	18	25	Feb. 1	8	8	15	22	Mar. 1	8
12	19	26	2	9	9	16	23	2	9
13	20	27	3	10	10	17	24	3	10
14	21	28	4	11	11	18	25	4	11
15	22	29	5	12	12	19	26	5	12
16	23	30	6	13	13	20	27	6	13
17	24	31	7	14	14	21	28	7	14
18	25	Feb. 1	8	15	15	22	Mar. 1	8	15
19	26	2	9	16	16	23	2	9	16
20	27	3	10	17	17	24	3	10	17
21	28	4	11	18	18	25	4	11	18
22	29	5	12	19	19	26	5	12	19
23	30	6	13	20	20	27	6	13	20
24	31	7	14	21	21	28	7	14	21
25	Feb. 1	8	15	22	22	Mar. 1	8	15	22
26	2	9	16	23	23	2	9	16	23
27	3	10	17	24	24	3	10	17	24
28	4	11	18	25	25	4	11	18	25
29	5	12	19	26	26	5	12	19	26
30	6	13	20	27	27	6	13	20	27
31	7	14	21	28	28	7	14	21	28
Feb. 1	8	15	22	Mar. 1	Mar. 1	8	15	22	29
2	9	16	23	2	2	9	16	23	30
3	10	17	24	3	3	10	17	24	31
4	11	18	25	4	4	11	18	25	Apr. 1

TABLE XV. (CONTINUED.)

FOR CONVERSION OF A HINDU LUNI-SOLAR DATE INTO THE CORRESPONDING DATE A.D. AND VICE-VERSÂ.

ey are known, let it be borne in mind that the result, as found from this Table, though often correct, is often wrong by one day, occasionally by two days. T

n.)		5. Śrâvaṇa (Tel. Can.) 5. Sôṇa (Tuḷu.)						6. Bhâdrapada (Tel. Can.) 6. Nirṇâla (Tuḷu.)					7. Âśvina (Tel. Can.) 7. Bontelu (Tuḷu.)					8. Kârttika (Tel. Can.) 8. Jârde (Tuḷu.)				
râvaṇa ṣhṇa.		5. Śrâvaṇa śukla.			6. Bhâdrapada kṛishṇa.			6. Bhâdrapada śukla.			7. Âśvina kṛishṇa.		7. Âśvina śukla.			8. Kârttika kṛishṇa.		8. Kârttika śukla.			9. Mârgaśîrsha kṛishṇa.	
)		10. *Śrâvaṇa.* (S. Vikrama. Nevâr.)						11. *Bhâdrapada* (S. Vikrama. Nevâr.)					12. *Âśvina* (S. Vikrama. Nevâr.)					1. KÂRTTIKA (S. Vikrama. Nevâr.)				
ṛishṇa.		Śukla.			Kṛishṇa.			Śukla.			Kṛishṇa.		Śukla.			Kṛishṇa.		Śukla.			Kṛishṇa.	
	9	—	2	9	**Kṛ. 1**	**8**	**30**	—	7	14	**6**	**13**	—	6	13	**5**	**12**	—	4	11	**3**	**10**
	10	—	3	10	**2**	**9**	—	Śu. 1	8	15	**7**	**14 or 30**	—	7	14	**6**	**13**	—	5	12	**4**	**11**
	11	—	4	11	**3**	**10**	—	2	9	**Kṛ. 1**	**8**	—	Śu. 1	8	15	**7**	**14**	—	6	13	**5**	**12**
	12	—	5	12	**4**	**11**	—	3	10	**2**	**9**	—	2	9	**Kṛ. 1**	**8**	**30**	—	7	14	**6**	**13**
	13	—	6	13	**5**	**12**	—	4	11	**3**	**10**	—	3	10	**2**	**9**	—	Śu. 1	8	15	**7**	**14 or 30**
	14 or 30	—	7	14	**6**	**13**	—	5	12	**4**	**11**	—	4	11	**3**	**10**	—	2	9	**Kṛ. 1**	**8**	—
	—	Śu. 1	8	15	**7**	**14**	—	6	13	**5**	**12**	—	5	12	**4**	**11**	—	3	10	**2**	**9**	—
26	Jul. 3	Jul. 3	Jul. 10	Jul. 17	Jul. 24	Jul. 31	Aug. 7	Aug. 7	Aug. 14	Aug. 21	Aug. 28	Sep. 4	Sep. 4	Sep. 11	Sep. 18	Sep. 25	Oct. 2	Oct. 2	Oct. 9	Oct. 16	Oct. 23	Oct. 3
27	4	4	11	18	25	Aug. 1	8	8	15	22	29	5	5	12	19	26	3	3	10	17	24	3
28	5	5	12	19	26	2	9	9	16	23	30	6	6	13	20	27	4	4	11	18	25	Nov.
29	6	6	13	20	27	3	10	10	17	24	31	7	7	14	21	28	5	5	12	19	26	
30	7	7	14	21	28	4	11	11	18	25	Sep. 1	8	8	15	22	29	6	6	13	20	27	
1	8	8	15	22	29	5	12	12	19	26	2	9	9	16	23	30	7	7	14	21	28	
2	9	9	16	23	30	6	13	13	20	27	3	10	10	17	24	Oct. 1	8	8	15	22	29	
3	10	10	17	24	31	7	14	14	21	28	4	11	11	18	25	2	9	9	16	23	30	
4	11	11	18	25	Aug. 1	8	15	15	22	29	5	12	12	19	26	3	10	10	17	24	31	
5	12	12	19	26	2	9	16	16	23	30	6	13	13	20	27	4	11	11	18	25	Nov. 1	
6	13	13	20	27	3	10	17	17	24	31	7	14	14	21	28	5	12	12	19	26	2	
7	14	14	21	28	4	11	18	18	25	Sep. 1	8	15	15	22	29	6	13	13	20	27	3	1
8	15	15	22	29	5	12	19	19	26	2	9	16	16	23	30	7	14	14	21	28	4	1
9	16	16	23	30	6	13	20	20	27	3	10	17	17	24	Oct. 1	8	15	15	22	29	5	1
10	17	17	24	31	7	14	21	21	28	4	11	18	18	25	2	9	16	16	23	30	6	1
11	18	18	25	Aug. 1	8	15	22	22	29	5	12	19	19	26	3	10	17	17	24	31	7	1
12	19	19	26	2	9	16	23	23	30	6	13	20	20	27	4	11	18	18	25	Nov. 1	8	1
13	20	20	27	3	10	17	24	24	31	7	14	21	21	28	5	12	19	19	26	2	9	1
14	21	21	28	4	11	18	25	25	Sep. 1	8	15	22	22	29	6	13	20	20	27	3	10	1
15	22	22	29	5	12	19	26	26	2	9	16	23	23	30	7	14	21	21	28	4	11	1
16	23	23	30	6	13	20	27	27	3	10	17	24	24	Oct. 1	8	15	22	22	29	5	12	1
17	24	24	31	7	14	21	28	28	4	11	18	25	25	2	9	16	23	23	30	6	13	2
18	25	25	Aug. 1	8	15	22	29	29	5	12	19	26	26	3	10	17	24	24	31	7	14	2
19	26	26	2	9	16	23	30	30	6	13	20	27	27	4	11	18	25	25	Nov. 1	8	15	2
20	27	27	3	10	17	24	31	31	7	14	21	28	28	5	12	19	26	26	2	9	16	2
21	28	28	4	11	18	25	Sep. 1	Sep. 1	8	15	22	29	29	6	13	20	27	27	3	10	17	2
22	29	29	5	12	19	26	2	2	9	16	23	30	30	7	14	21	28	28	4	11	18	2
23	30	30	6	13	20	27	3	3	10	17	24	Oct. 1	Oct. 1	8	15	22	29	29	5	12	19	2
24	31	31	7	14	21	28	4	4	11	18	25	2	2	9	16	23	30	30	6	13	20	2
25	Aug. 1	Aug. 1	8	15	22	29	5	5	12	19	26	3	3	10	17	24	31	31	7	14	21	2
26	2	2	9	16	23	30	6	6	13	20	27	4	4	11	18	25	Nov. 1	Nov. 1	8	15	22	2
27	3	3	10	17	24	31	7	7	14	21	28	5	5	12	19	26	2	2	9	16	23	3
28	4	4	11	18	25	Sep. 1	8	8	15	22	29	6	6	13	20	27	3	3	10	17	24	Dec.
29	5	5	12	19	26	2	9	9	16	23	30	7	7	14	21	28	4	4	11	18	25	
30	6	6	13	20	27	3	10	10	17	24	Oct. 1	8	8	15	22	29	5	5	12	19	26	
31	7	7	14	21	28	4	11	11	18	25	2	9	9	16	23	30	6	6	13	20	27	

TABLE XVI.

INITIAL DAYS OF MUHAMMADAN YEARS OF THE HIJRA.

N.B. i. *Asterisks indicate Leap-years.*
ii. *Up to Hijra 1165 inclusive, the A.D. dates are Old Style.*

Hijra year.	Commencement of the year.		Hijra year.	Commencement of the year.		Hijra year.	Commencement of the year.	
	Weekday.	Date A.D.		Weekday.	Date A.D.		Weekday.	Date A.D.
1	2	3	1	2	3	1	2	3
1	6 Fri.	16 July 622 (197)	38	0 Sat.	9 June 658 (160)	75	0 Sun.	2 May 694 (122)
*2	3 Tues.	5 July 623 (186)	39	4 Wed.	29 May 659 (149)	*76	4 Wed.	21 Apr. 695 (111)
3	1 Sun.	24 June 624* (176)	*40	1 Sun.	17 May 660* (138)	77	2 Mon.	10 Apr. 696* (101)
4	5 Thurs.	13 June 625 (164)	41	6 Fri.	7 May 661 (127)	*78	6 Fri.	30 Mar. 697 (89)
*5	2 Mon.	2 June 626 (153)	42	3 Tues.	26 Apr. 662 (116)	79	4 Wed.	20 Mar. 698 (79)
6	0 Sat.	23 May 627 (143)	*43	0 Sat.	15 Apr. 663 (105)	80	1 Sun.	9 Mar. 699 (68)
*7	4 Wed.	11 May 628* (132)	44	5 Thurs.	4 Apr. 664* (95)	*81	5 Thurs.	26 Feb. 700* (57)
8	2 Mon.	1 May 629 (121)	45	2 Mon.	24 Mar. 665 (83)	82	3 Tues.	15 Feb. 701 (46)
9	6 Fri.	20 Apr. 630 (110)	*46	6 Fri.	13 Mar. 666 (72)	83	0 Sat.	4 Feb. 702 (35)
*10	3 Tues.	9 Apr. 631 (99)	47	4 Wed.	3 Mar. 667 (62)	*84	4 Wed.	24 Jan. 703 (24)
11	1 Sun.	29 Mar. 632* (89)	*48	1 Sun.	20 Feb. 668* (51)	85	2 Mon.	14 Jan. 704* (14)
12	5 Thurs.	18 Mar. 633 (77)	49	6 Fri.	9 Feb. 669 (40)	*86	6 Fri.	2 Jan. 705 (2)
*13	2 Mon.	7 Mar. 634 (66)	50	3 Tues.	29 Jan. 670 (29)	87	4 Wed.	23 Dec. 705 (357)
14	0 Sat.	25 Feb. 635 (56)	*51	0 Sat.	18 Jan. 671 (18)	88	1 Sun.	12 Dec. 706 (346)
15	4 Wed.	14 Feb. 636* (45)	52	5 Thurs.	8 Jan. 672* (8)	*89	5 Thurs.	1 Dec. 707 (335)
*16	1 Sun.	2 Feb. 637 (33)	53	2 Mon.	27 Dec. 672* (362)	90	3 Tues.	20 Nov. 708* (325)
17	6 Fri.	23 Jan. 638 (23)	*54	6 Fri.	16 Dec. 673 (350)	91	0 Sat.	9 Nov. 709 (313)
*18	3 Tues.	12 Jan. 639 (12)	55	4 Wed.	6 Dec. 674 (340)	*92	4 Wed.	29 Oct. 710 (302)
19	1 Sun.	2 Jan. 640* (2)	*56	1 Sun.	25 Nov. 675 (329)	93	2 Mon.	19 Oct. 711 (292)
20	5 Thurs.	21 Dec. 640* (356)	57	6 Fri.	14 Nov. 676* (319)	94	6 Fri.	7 Oct. 712* (281)
*21	2 Mon.	10 Dec. 641 (344)	58	3 Tues.	3 Nov. 677 (307)	*95	3 Tues.	26 Sep. 713 (269)
22	0 Sat.	30 Nov. 642 (334)	*59	0 Sat.	23 Oct. 678 (296)	96	1 Sun.	16 Sep. 714 (259)
23	4 Wed.	19 Nov. 643 (323)	60	5 Thurs.	13 Oct. 679 (286)	*97	5 Thurs.	5 Sep. 715 (248)
*24	1 Sun.	7 Nov. 644* (312)	61	2 Mon.	1 Oct. 680* (275)	98	3 Tues.	25 Aug. 716* (238)
25	6 Fri.	28 Oct. 645 (301)	*62	6 Fri.	20 Sep. 681 (263)	99	0 Sat.	14 Aug. 717 (226)
*26	3 Tues.	17 Oct. 646 (290)	63	4 Wed.	10 Sep. 682 (253)	*100	4 Wed.	3 Aug. 718 (215)
27	1 Sun.	7 Oct. 647 (280)	64	1 Sun.	30 Aug. 683 (242)	101	2 Mon.	24 July 719 (205)
28	5 Thurs.	25 Sep. 648* (269)	*65	5 Thurs.	18 Aug. 684* (231)	102	6 Fri.	12 July 720* (194)
*29	2 Mon.	14 Sep. 649 (257)	66	3 Tues.	8 Aug. 685 (220)	*103	3 Tues.	1 July 721 (182)
30	0 Sat.	4 Sep. 650 (247)	*67	0 Sat.	28 July 686 (209)	104	1 Sun.	21 June 722 (172)
31	4 Wed.	24 Aug. 651 (236)	68	5 Thurs.	18 July 687 (199)	105	5 Thurs.	10 June 723 (161)
*32	1 Sun.	12 Aug. 652* (225)	69	2 Mon.	6 July 688* (188)	*106	2 Mon.	29 May 724* (150)
33	6 Fri.	2 Aug. 653 (214)	*70	6 Fri.	25 June 689 (176)	107	0 Sat.	19 May 725 (139)
34	3 Tues.	22 July 654 (203)	71	4 Wed.	15 June 690 (166)	*108	4 Wed.	8 May 726 (128)
*35	0 Sat.	11 July 655 (192)	72	1 Sun.	4 June 691 (155)	109	2 Mon.	28 Apr. 727 (118)
36	5 Thurs.	30 June 656* (182)	*73	5 Thurs.	23 May 692* (144)	110	6 Fri.	16 Apr. 728* (107)
*37	2 Mon.	19 June 657 (170)	74	3 Tues.	13 May 693 (133)	*111	3 Tues.	5 Apr. 729 (95)

TABLE XVI. (CONTINUED.)

INITIAL DAYS OF MUHAMMADAN YEARS OF THE HIJRA.

N.B. i. *Asterisks indicate Leap-years.*

ii. *Up to Hijra* 1165 *inclusive, the A.D. dates are Old Style.*

Hijra year.	Commencement of the year.		Hijra year.	Commencement of the year.		Hijra year.	Commencement of the year.	
	Weekday.	Date A.D.		Weekday.	Date A.D.		Weekday.	Date A.D.
1	2	3	1	2	3	1	2	3
112	1 Sun.	26 Mar. 730 (85)	*149	1 Sun.	16 Feb. 766 (47)	186	2 Mon.	10 Jan. 802 (10)
113	5 Thurs.	15 Mar. 731 (74)	150	6 Fri.	6 Feb. 767 (37)	*187	6 Fri.	30 Dec. 802 (364)
*114	2 Mon.	3 Mar. 732* (63)	151	3 Tues.	26 Jan. 768* (26)	188	4 Wed.	20 Dec. 803 (354)
115	0 Sat.	21 Feb. 733 (52)	*152	0 Sat.	14 Jan. 769 (14)	189	1 Sun.	8 Dec. 804* (343)
*116	4 Wed.	10 Feb. 734 (41)	153	5 Thurs.	4 Jan. 770 (4)	*190	5 Thurs.	27 Nov. 805 (331)
117	2 Mon.	31 Jan. 735 (31)	154	2 Mon.	24 Dec. 770 (358)	191	3 Tues.	17 Nov. 806 (321)
118	6 Fri.	20 Jan. 736* (20)	*155	6 Fri.	13 Dec. 771 (347)	192	0 Sat.	6 Nov. 807 (310)
*119	3 Tues.	8 Jan. 737 (8)	156	4 Wed.	2 Dec. 772* (337)	*193	4 Wed.	25 Oct. 808* (299)
120	1 Sun.	29 Dec. 737 (363)	*157	1 Sun.	21 Nov. 773 (325)	194	2 Mon.	15 Oct. 809 (288)
121	5 Thurs.	18 Dec. 738 (352)	158	6 Fri.	11 Nov. 774 (315)	195	6 Fri.	4 Oct. 810 (277)
*122	2 Mon.	7 Dec. 739 (341)	159	3 Tues.	31 Oct. 775 (304)	*196	3 Tues.	23 Sep. 811 (266)
123	0 Sat.	26 Nov. 740* (331)	*160	0 Sat.	19 Oct. 776* (293)	197	1 Sun.	12 Sep. 812* (256)
124	4 Wed.	15 Nov. 741 (319)	161	5 Thurs.	9 Oct. 777 (282)	*198	5 Thurs.	1 Sep. 813 (244)
*125	1 Sun.	4 Nov. 742 (308)	162	2 Mon.	28 Sep. 778 (271)	199	3 Tues.	22 Aug. 814 (234)
126	6 Fri.	25 Oct. 743 (298)	*163	6 Fri.	17 Sep. 779 (260)	200	0 Sat.	11 Aug. 815 (223)
*127	3 Tues.	13 Oct. 744* (287)	164	4 Wed.	6 Sep. 780* (250)	*201	4 Wed.	30 July 816* (212)
128	1 Sun.	3 Oct. 745 (276)	165	1 Sun.	26 Aug. 781 (238)	202	2 Mon.	20 July 817 (201)
129	5 Thurs.	22 Sep. 746 (265)	*166	5 Thurs.	15 Aug. 782 (227)	203	6 Fri.	9 July 818 (190)
*130	2 Mon.	11 Sep. 747 (254)	167	3 Tues.	5 Aug. 783 (217)	*204	3 Tues.	28 June 819 (179)
131	0 Sat.	31 Aug. 748* (244)	*168	0 Sat.	24 July 784* (206)	205	1 Sun.	17 June 820* (169)
132	4 Wed.	20 Aug. 749 (232)	169	5 Thurs.	14 July 785 (195)	*206	5 Thurs.	6 June 821 (157)
*133	1 Sun.	9 Aug. 750 (221)	170	2 Mon.	3 July 786 (184)	207	3 Tues.	27 May 822 (147)
134	6 Fri.	30 July 751 (211)	*171	6 Fri.	22 June 787 (173)	208	0 Sat.	16 May 823 (136)
135	3 Tues.	18 July 752* (200)	172	4 Wed.	11 June 788* (163)	*209	4 Wed.	4 May 824* (125)
*136	0 Sat.	7 July 753 (188)	173	1 Sun.	31 May 789 (151)	210	2 Mon.	24 Apr. 825 (114)
137	5 Thurs.	27 June 754 (178)	*174	5 Thurs.	20 May 790 (140)	211	6 Fri.	13 Apr. 826 (103)
*138	2 Mon.	16 June 755 (167)	175	3 Tues.	10 May 791 (130)	*212	3 Tues.	2 Apr. 827 (92)
139	0 Sat.	5 June 756* (157)	*176	0 Sat.	28 Apr. 792* (119)	213	1 Sun.	22 Mar. 828* (82)
140	4 Wed.	25 May 757 (145)	177	5 Thurs.	18 Apr. 793 (108)	214	5 Thurs.	11 Mar. 829 (70)
*141	1 Sun.	14 May 758 (134)	178	2 Mon.	7 Apr. 794 (97)	*215	2 Mon.	28 Feb. 830 (59)
142	6 Fri.	4 May 759 (124)	*179	6 Fri.	27 Mar. 795 (86)	216	0 Sat.	18 Feb. 831 (49)
143	3 Tues.	22 Apr. 760* (113)	180	4 Wed.	16 Mar. 796* (76)	*217	4 Wed.	7 Feb. 832* (38)
*144	0 Sat.	11 Apr. 761 (101)	181	1 Sun.	5 Mar. 797 (64)	218	2 Mon	27 Jan. 833 (27)
145	5 Thurs.	1 Apr. 762 (91)	*182	5 Thurs.	22 Feb. 798 (53)	219	6 Fri.	16 Jan. 834 (16)
*146	2 Mon.	21 Mar. 763 (80)	183	3 Tues.	12 Feb. 799 (43)	*220	3 Tues.	5 Jan. 835 (5)
147	0 Sat.	10 Mar. 764* (70)	184	0 Sat.	1 Feb. 800* (32)	221	1 Sun.	26 Dec. 835 (360)
148	4 Wed.	27 Feb. 765 (58)	*185	4 Wed.	20 Jan. 801 (20)	222	5 Thurs.	14 Dec. 836* (349)

TABLE XVI. (CONTINUED.)

INITIAL DAYS OF MUHAMMADAN YEARS OF THE HIJRA.

N.B. i. *Asterisks indicate Leap-years.*
ii. *Up to Hijra* 1165 *inclusive, the A.D. dates are Old Style.*

Hijra year.	Commencement of the year.		Hijra year.	Commencement of the year.		Hijra year.	Commencement of the year.	
	Weekday.	Date A.D.		Weekday.	Date A.D.		Weekday.	Date A.D.
1	2	3	1	2	3	1	2	3
*223	2 Mon.	3 Dec. 837 (337)	260	3 Tues.	27 Oct. 873 (300)	297	4 Wed.	20 Sep. 909 (263)
224	0 Sat.	23 Nov. 838 (327)	*261	0 Sat.	16 Oct. 874 (289)	298	1 Sun.	9 Sep. 910 (252)
225	4 Wed.	12 Nov. 839 (316)	262	5 Thurs.	6 Oct. 875 (279)	*299	5 Thurs.	29 Aug. 911 (241)
*226	1 Sun.	31 Oct. 840* (305)	263	2 Mon.	24 Sep. 876* (268)	300	3 Tues.	18 Aug. 912* (231)
227	6 Fri.	21 Oct. 841 (294)	*264	6 Fri.	13 Sep. 877 (256)	301	0 Sat.	7 Aug. 913 (219)
*228	3 Tues.	10 Oct. 842 (283)	265	4 Wed.	3 Sep. 878 (246)	*302	4 Wed.	27 July 914 (208)
229	1 Sun.	30 Sep. 843 (273)	*266	1 Sun.	23 Aug. 879 (235)	303	2 Mon.	17 July 915 (198)
230	5 Thurs.	18 Sep. 844* (262)	267	6 Fri.	12 Aug. 880* (225)	304	6 Fri.	5 July 916* (187)
*231	2 Mon.	7 Sep. 845 (250)	268	3 Tues.	1 Aug. 881 (213)	*305	3 Tues.	24 June 917 (175)
232	0 Sat.	28 Aug. 846 (240)	*269	0 Sat.	21 July 882 (202)	306	1 Sun.	14 June 918 (165)
233	4 Wed.	17 Aug. 847 (229)	270	5 Thurs.	11 July 883 (192)	*307	5 Thurs.	3 June 919 (154)
*234	1 Sun.	5 Aug. 848* (218)	271	2 Mon.	29 June 884* (181)	308	3 Tues.	23 May 920* (144)
235	6 Fri.	26 July 849 (207)	*272	6 Fri.	18 June 885 (169)	309	0 Sat.	12 May 921 (132)
*236	3 Tues.	15 July 850 (196)	273	4 Wed.	8 June 886 (159)	*310	4 Wed.	1 May 922 (121)
237	1 Sun.	5 July 851 (186)	274	1 Sun.	28 May 887 (148)	311	2 Mon.	21 Apr. 923 (111)
238	5 Thurs.	23 June 852* (175)	*275	5 Thurs.	16 May 888* (137)	312	6 Fri.	9 Apr. 924* (100)
*239	2 Mon.	12 June 853 (163)	276	3 Tues.	6 May 889 (126)	*313	3 Tues.	29 Mar. 925 (88)
240	0 Sat.	2 June 854 (153)	*277	0 Sat.	25 Apr. 890 (115)	314	1 Sun.	19 Mar. 926 (78)
241	4 Wed.	22 May 855 (142)	278	5 Thurs.	15 Apr. 891 (105)	315	5 Thurs.	8 Mar. 927 (67)
*242	1 Sun.	10 May 856* (131)	279	2 Mon.	3 Apr. 892* (94)	*316	2 Mon.	25 Feb. 928* (56)
243	6 Fri.	30 Apr. 857 (120)	*280	6 Fri.	23 Mar. 893 (82)	317	0 Sat.	14 Feb. 929 (45)
244	3 Tues.	19 Apr. 858 (109)	281	4 Wed.	13 Mar. 894 (72)	*318	4 Wed.	3 Feb. 930 (34)
*245	0 Sat.	8 Apr. 859 (98)	282	1 Sun.	2 Mar. 895 (61)	319	2 Mon.	24 Jan. 931 (24)
246	5 Thurs.	28 Mar. 860* (88)	*283	5 Thurs.	19 Feb. 896* (50)	320	6 Fri.	13 Jan. 932* (13)
*247	2 Mon.	17 Mar. 861 (76)	284	3 Tues.	8 Feb. 897 (39)	*321	3 Tues.	1 Jan. 933 (1)
248	0 Sat.	7 Mar. 862 (66)	285	0 Sat.	28 Jan. 898 (28)	322	1 Sun.	22 Dec. 933 (356)
249	4 Wed.	24 Feb. 863 (55)	*286	4 Wed.	17 Jan. 899 (17)	323	5 Thurs.	11 Dec. 934 (345)
*250	1 Sun.	13 Feb. 864* (44)	287	2 Mon.	7 Jan. 900* (7)	*324	2 Mon.	30 Nov. 935 (334)
251	6 Fri.	2 Feb. 865 (33)	*288	6 Fri.	26 Dec. 900* (361)	325	0 Sat.	19 Nov. 936* (324)
252	3 Tues.	22 Jan. 866 (22)	289	4 Wed.	16 Dec. 901 (350)	*326	4 Wed.	8 Nov. 937 (312)
*253	0 Sat.	11 Jan. 867 (11)	290	1 Sun.	5 Dec. 902 (339)	327	2 Mon.	29 Oct. 938 (302)
254	5 Thurs.	1 Jan. 868* (1)	*291	5 Thurs.	24 Nov. 903 (328)	328	6 Fri.	18 Oct. 939 (291)
255	2 Mon.	20 Dec. 868* (355)	292	3 Tues.	13 Nov. 904* (318)	*329	3 Tues.	6 Oct. 940* (280)
*256	6 Fri.	9 Dec. 869 (343)	293	0 Sat.	2 Nov. 905 (306)	330	1 Sun.	26 Sep. 941 (269)
257	4 Wed.	29 Nov. 870 (333)	*294	4 Wed.	22 Oct. 906 (295)	331	5 Thurs.	15 Sep. 942 (258)
*258	1 Sun.	18 Nov. 871 (322)	295	2 Mon.	12 Oct. 907 (285)	*332	2 Mon.	4 Sep. 943 (247)
259	6 Fri.	7 Nov. 872* (312)	*296	6 Fri.	30 Sep. 908* (274)	333	0 Sat.	24 Aug. 944* (237)

TABLE XVI. (CONTINUED.)

INITIAL DAYS OF MUHAMMADAN YEARS OF THE HIJRA.

N.B. i. *Asterisks indicate Leap-years.*

ii. *Up to Hijra* 1165 *inclusive, the A.D. dates are Old Style.*

Hijra year.	Commencement of the year.		Hijra year.	Commencement of the year.		Hijra year.	Commencement of the year.	
	Weekday.	Date A.D.		Weekday.	Date A.D.		Weekday.	Date A.D.
1	2	3	1	2	3	1	2	3
334	4 Wed.	13 Aug. 945 (225)	371	5 Thurs.	7 July 981 (188)	*408	5 Thurs.	30 May 1017 (150)
*335	1 Sun.	2 Aug. 946 (214)	372	2 Mon.	26 June 982 (177)	409	3 Tues.	20 May 1018 (140)
336	6 Fri.	23 July 947 (204)	*373	6 Fri.	15 June 983 (166)	410	0 Sat.	9 May 1019 (129)
*337	3 Tues.	11 July 948* (193)	374	4 Wed.	4 June 984* (156)	*411	4 Wed.	27 Apr. 1020* (118)
338	1 Sun.	1 July 949 (182)	375	1 Sun.	24 May 985 (144)	412	2 Mon.	17 Apr. 1021 (107)
339	5 Thurs.	20 June 950 (171)	*376	5 Thurs.	13 May 986 (133)	413	6 Fri.	6 Apr. 1022 (96)
*340	2 Mon.	9 June 951 (160)	377	3 Tues.	3 May 987 (123)	*414	3 Tues.	26 Mar. 1023 (85)
341	0 Sat.	29 May 952* (150)	*378	0 Sat.	21 Apr. 988* (112)	415	1 Sun.	15 Mar. 1024* (75)
342	4 Wed.	18 May 953 (138)	379	5 Thurs.	11 Apr. 989 (101)	*416	5 Thurs.	4 Mar. 1025 (63)
*343	1 Sun.	7 May 954 (127)	380	2 Mon.	31 Mar. 990 (90)	417	3 Tues.	22 Feb. 1026 (53)
344	6 Fri.	27 Apr. 955 (117)	*381	6 Fri.	20 Mar 991 (79)	418	0 Sat.	11 Feb. 1027 (42)
345	3 Tues.	15 Apr. 956* (106)	382	4 Wed.	9 Mar. 992* (69)	*419	4 Wed.	31 Jan. 1028* (31)
*346	0 Sat.	4 Apr. 957 (94)	383	1 Sun.	26 Feb. 993 (57)	420	2 Mon.	20 Jan. 1029 (20)
347	5 Thurs.	25 Mar. 958 (84)	*384	5 Thurs.	15 Feb. 994 (46)	421	6 Fri.	9 Jan. 1030 (9)
*348	2 Mon.	14 Mar. 959 (73)	385	3 Tues.	5 Feb. 995 (36)	*422	3 Tues.	29 Dec. 1030 (363)
349	0 Sat.	3 Mar. 960* (63)	*386	0 Sat.	25 Jan. 996* (25)	423	1 Sun.	19 Dec. 1031 (353)
350	4 Wed.	20 Feb. 961 (51)	387	5 Thurs	14 Jan. 997 (14)	424	5 Thurs.	7 Dec. 1032* (342)
*351	1 Sun.	9 Feb. 962 (40)	388	2 Mon.	3 Jan. 998 (3)	*425	2 Mon.	26 Nov. 1033 (330)
352	6 Fri.	30 Jan. 963 (30)	*389	6 Fri.	23 Dec. 998 (357)	426	0 Sat.	16 Nov. 1034 (320)
353	3 Tues.	19 Jan. 964* (19)	390	4 Wed.	13 Dec. 999 (347)	*427	4 Wed.	5 Nov. 1035 (309)
*354	0 Sat.	7 Jan. 965 (7)	391	1 Sun.	1 Dec. 1000* (336)	428	2 Mon.	25 Oct. 1036* (299)
355	5 Thurs.	28 Dec. 965 (362)	*392	5 Thurs.	20 Nov. 1001 (324)	429	6 Fri.	14 Oct. 1037 (287)
*356	2 Mon.	17 Dec. 966 (351)	393	3 Tues.	10 Nov. 1002 (314)	*430	3 Tues.	3 Oct. 1038 (276)
357	0 Sat.	7 Dec. 967 (341)	394	0 Sat.	30 Oct. 1003 (303)	431	1 Sun.	23 Sep. 1039 (266)
358	4 Wed.	25 Nov. 968* (330)	*395	4 Wed.	18 Oct. 1004* (292)	432	5 Thurs.	11 Sep. 1040* (255)
*359	1 Sun.	14 Nov. 969 (318)	396	2 Mon.	8 Oct. 1005 (281)	*433	2 Mon.	31 Aug. 1041 (243)
360	6 Fri.	4 Nov. 970 (308)	*397	6 Fri.	27 Sep. 1006 (270)	434	0 Sat.	21 Aug. 1042 (233)
361	3 Tues.	24 Oct. 971 (297)	398	4 Wed.	17 Sep. 1007 (260)	435	4 Wed.	10 Aug. 1043 (222)
*362	0 Sat.	12 Oct. 972* (286)	399	1 Sun.	5 Sep. 1008* (249)	*436	1 Sun.	29 July 1044* (211)
363	5 Thurs.	2 Oct. 973 (275)	*400	5 Thurs.	25 Aug. 1009 (237)	437	6 Fri.	19 July 1045 (200)
364	2 Mon.	21 Sep. 974 (264)	401	3 Tues.	15 Aug. 1010 (227)	*438	3 Tues.	8 July 1046 (189)
*365	6 Fri.	10 Sep. 975 (253)	402	0 Sat	4 Aug. 1011 (216)	439	1 Sun.	28 June 1047 (179)
366	4 Wed.	30 Aug. 976* (243)	*403	4 Wed.	23 July 1012* (205)	440	5 Thurs.	16 June 1048* (168)
*367	1 Sun.	19 Aug. 977 (231)	404	2 Mon.	13 July 1013 (194)	*441	2 Mon.	5 June 1049 (156)
368	6 Fri.	9 Aug. 978 (221)	405	6 Fri.	2 July 1014 (183)	442	0 Sat.	26 May 1050 (146)
369	3 Tues.	29 July 979 (210)	*406	3 Tues.	21 June 1015 (172)	443	4 Wed.	15 May 1051 (135)
*370	0 Sat.	17 July 980* (199)	407	1 Sun.	10 June 1016* (162)	*444	1 Sun.	3 May 1052* (124)

TABLE XVI. (CONTINUED.)

INITIAL DAYS OF MUHAMMADAN YEARS OF THE HIJRA.

N.B. i. *Asterisks indicate Leap-years.*

ii. *Up to Hijra* 1165 *inclusive, the A.D. dates are Old Style.*

Hijra year.	Commencement of the year.		Hijra year.	Commencement of the year.		Hijra year.	Commencement of the year.	
	Weekday.	Date A.D.		Weekday.	Date A.D.		Weekday.	Date A.D.
1	2	3	1	2	3	1	2	3
445	6 Fri.	23 Apr. 1053 (113)	*482	6 Fri.	16 Mar. 1089 (75)	519	0 Sat.	7 Feb. 1125 (38)
*446	3 Tues.	12 Apr. 1054 (102)	483	4 Wed.	6 Mar. 1090 (65)	*520	4 Wed.	27 Jan. 1126 (27)
447	1 Sun.	2 Apr. 1055 (92)	484	1 Sun.	23 Feb. 1091 (54)	521	2 Mon.	17 Jan. 1127 (17)
448	5 Thurs.	21 Mar. 1056* (81)	*485	5 Thurs.	12 Feb. 1092* (43)	522	6 Fri.	6 Jan. 1128* (6)
*449	2 Mon.	10 Mar. 1057 (69)	486	3 Tues.	1 Feb. 1093 (32)	*523	3 Tues.	25 Dec. 1128* (360)
450	0 Sat.	28 Feb. 1058 (59)	*487	0 Sat.	21 Jan. 1094 (21)	524	1 Sun.	15 Dec. 1129 (349)
451	4 Wed.	17 Feb. 1059 (48)	488	5 Thurs.	11 Jan. 1095 (11)	525	5 Thurs.	4 Dec. 1130 (338)
*452	1 Sun.	6 Feb. 1060* (37)	489	2 Mon.	31 Dec. 1095 (365)	*526	2 Mon.	23 Nov. 1131 (327)
453	6 Fri.	26 Jan. 1061 (26)	*490	6 Fri.	19 Dec. 1096* (354)	527	0 Sat.	12 Nov. 1132* (317)
454	3 Tues.	15 Jan. 1062 (15)	491	4 Wed.	9 Dec. 1097 (343)	*528	4 Wed.	1 Nov. 1133 (305)
*455	0 Sat.	4 Jan. 1063 (4)	492	1 Sun.	28 Nov. 1098 (332)	529	2 Mon.	22 Oct. 1134 (295)
456	5 Thurs.	25 Dec. 1063 (359)	*493	5 Thurs.	17 Nov. 1099 (321)	530	6 Fri.	11 Oct. 1135 (284)
*457	2 Mon.	13 Dec. 1064* (348)	494	3 Tues.	6 Nov. 1100* (311)	*531	3 Tues.	29 Sep. 1136* (273)
458	0 Sat.	3 Dec. 1065 (337)	495	0 Sat.	26 Oct. 1101 (299)	532	1 Sun.	19 Sep. 1137 (262)
459	4 Wed.	22 Nov. 1066 (326)	*496	4 Wed.	15 Oct. 1102 (288)	533	5 Thurs.	8 Sep. 1138 (251)
*460	1 Sun.	11 Nov. 1067 (315)	497	2 Mon.	5 Oct. 1103 (278)	*534	2 Mon.	28 Aug. 1139 (240)
461	6 Fri.	31 Oct. 1068* (305)	*498	6 Fri.	23 Sep. 1104* (267)	535	0 Sat.	17 Aug. 1140* (230)
462	3 Tues.	20 Oct. 1069 (293)	499	4 Wed.	13 Sep. 1105 (256)	*536	4 Wed.	6 Aug. 1141 (218)
*463	0 Sat.	9 Oct. 1070 (282)	500	1 Sun.	2 Sep. 1106 (245)	537	2 Mon.	27 July 1142 (208)
464	5 Thurs.	29 Sep. 1071 (272)	*501	5 Thurs.	22 Aug. 1107 (234)	538	6 Fri.	16 July 1143 (197)
465	2 Mon.	17 Sep. 1072* (261)	502	3 Tues.	11 Aug. 1108* (224)	*539	3 Tues.	4 July 1144* (186)
*466	6 Fri	6 Sep. 1073 (249)	503	0 Sat.	31 July 1109 (212)	540	1 Sun.	24 June 1145 (175)
467	4 Wed.	27 Aug. 1074 (239)	*504	4 Wed.	20 July 1110 (201)	541	5 Thurs.	13 June 1146 (164)
*468	1 Sun.	16 Aug. 1075 (228)	505	2 Mon.	10 July 1111 (191)	*542	2 Mon.	2 June 1147 (153)
469	6 Fri.	5 Aug. 1076* (218)	*506	6 Fri.	28 June 1112* (180)	543	0 Sat.	22 May 1148* (143)
470	3 Tues.	25 July 1077 (206)	507	4 Wed.	18 June 1113 (169)	544	4 Wed.	11 May 1149 (131)
*471	0 Sat.	14 July 1078 (195)	508	1 Sun.	7 June 1114 (158)	*545	1 Sun.	30 Apr. 1150 (120)
472	5 Thurs.	4 July 1079 (185)	*509	5 Thurs.	27 May 1115 (147)	546	6 Fri.	20 Apr. 1151 (110)
473	2 Mon.	22 June 1080* (174)	510	3 Tues.	16 May 1116 (137)	*547	3 Tues.	8 Apr. 1152* (99)
*474	6 Fri.	11 June 1081 (162)	511	0 Sat.	5 May 1117 (125)	548	1 Sun.	29 Mar. 1153 (88)
475	4 Wed.	1 June 1082 (152)	*512	4 Wed.	24 Apr. 1118 (114)	549	5 Thurs.	18 Mar. 1154 (77)
*476	1 Sun.	21 May 1083 (141)	513	2 Mon.	14 Apr. 1119 (104)	*550	2 Mon.	7 Mar. 1155 (66)
477	6 Fri.	10 May 1084* (131)	514	6 Fri.	2 Apr. 1120* (93)	551	0 Sat.	25 Feb. 1156* (56)
478	3 Tues.	29 Apr. 1085 (119)	*515	3 Tues.	22 Mar. 1121 (81)	552	4 Wed.	13 Feb. 1157 (44)
*479	0 Sat.	18 Apr. 1086 (108)	516	1 Sun.	12 Mar. 1122 (71)	*553	1 Sun.	2 Feb. 1158 (33)
480	5 Thurs.	8 Apr. 1087 (98)	*517	5 Thurs.	1 Mar. 1123 (60)	554	6 Fri.	23 Jan. 1159 (23)
481	2 Mon.	27 Mar. 1088* (87)	518	3 Tues.	19 Feb. 1124* (50)	555	3 Tues.	12 Jan. 1160* (12)

TABLE XVI. (CONTINUED.)

INITIAL DAYS OF MUHAMMADAN YEARS OF THE HIJRA.

N.B. i. *Asterisks indicate Leap-years.*

ii. *Up to Hijra* 1165 *inclusive, the A.D. dates are Old Style.*

Hijra year.	Commencement of the year.		Hijra year.	Commencement of the year.		Hijra year.	Commencement of the year.	
	Weekday.	Date A.D.		Weekday.	Date A.D.		Weekday.	Date A.D.
1	2	3	1	2	3	1	2	3
*556	0 Sat.	31 Dec. 1160* (366)	593	1 Sun.	24 Nov. 1196* (329)	630	2 Mon.	18 Oct. 1232* (292)
557	5 Thurs.	21 Dec. 1161 (355)	*594	5 Thurs.	13 Nov. 1197 (317)	631	6 Fri.	7 Oct. 1233 (280)
*558	2 Mon.	10 Dec. 1162 (344)	595	3 Tues.	3 Nov. 1198 (307)	*632	3 Tues.	26 Sep. 1234 (269)
559	0 Sat.	30 Nov. 1163 (334)	*596	0 Sat.	23 Oct. 1199 (296)	633	1 Sun.	16 Sep. 1235 (259)
560	4 Wed.	18 Nov. 1164* (323)	597	5 Thurs.	12 Oct. 1200* (286)	634	5 Thurs.	4 Sep. 1236* (248)
*561	1 Sun.	7 Nov. 1165 (311)	598	2 Mon.	1 Oct. 1201 (274)	*635	2 Mon.	24 Aug. 1237 (236)
562	6 Fri.	28 Oct. 1166 (301)	*599	6 Fri.	20 Sep. 1202 (263)	636	0 Sat.	14 Aug. 1238 (226)
563	3 Tues.	17 Oct. 1167 (290)	600	4 Wed.	10 Sep. 1203 (253)	*637	4 Wed.	3 Aug. 1239 (215)
*564	0 Sat.	5 Oct. 1168* (279)	601	1 Sun.	29 Aug. 1204* (242)	638	2 Mon.	23 July 1240* (205)
565	5 Thurs.	25 Sep. 1169 (268)	*602	5 Thurs.	18 Aug. 1205 (230)	639	6 Fri.	12 July 1241 (193)
*566	2 Mon.	14 Sep. 1170 (257)	603	3 Tues.	8 Aug. 1206 (220)	*640	3 Tues.	1 July 1242 (182)
567	0 Sat.	4 Sep. 1171 (247)	604	0 Sat.	28 July 1207 (209)	641	1 Sun.	21 June 1243 (172)
568	4 Wed.	23 Aug. 1172* (236)	*605	4 Wed.	16 July 1208* (198)	642	5 Thurs.	9 June 1244* (161)
*569	1 Sun.	12 Aug. 1173 (224)	606	2 Mon.	6 July 1209 (187)	*643	2 Mon.	29 May 1245 (149)
570	6 Fri.	2 Aug. 1174 (214)	*607	6 Fri.	25 June 1210 (176)	644	0 Sat.	19 May 1246 (139)
571	3 Tues.	22 July 1175 (203)	608	4 Wed.	15 June 1211 (166)	645	4 Wed.	8 May 1247 (128)
*572	0 Sat.	10 July 1176* (192)	609	1 Sun.	3 June 1212* (155)	*646	1 Sun.	26 Apr. 1248* (117)
573	5 Thurs.	30 June 1177 (181)	*610	5 Thurs.	23 May 1213 (143)	647	6 Fri.	16 Apr. 1249 (106)
574	2 Mon.	19 June 1178 (170)	611	3 Tues.	13 May 1214 (133)	*648	3 Tues.	5 Apr. 1250 (95)
*575	6 Fri.	8 June 1179 (159)	612	0 Sat.	2 May 1215 (122)	649	1 Sun.	26 Mar. 1251 (85)
576	4 Wed.	28 May 1180* (149)	*613	4 Wed.	20 Apr. 1216* (111)	650	5 Thurs.	14 Mar. 1252* (74)
*577	1 Sun.	17 May 1181 (137)	614	2 Mon.	10 Apr. 1217 (100)	*651	2 Mon.	3 Mar. 1253 (62)
578	6 Fri.	7 May 1182 (127)	615	6 Fri.	30 Mar. 1218 (89)	652	0 Sat.	21 Feb. 1254 (52)
579	3 Tues.	26 Apr. 1183 (116)	*616	3 Tues.	19 Mar. 1219 (78)	653	4 Wed.	10 Feb. 1255 (41)
*580	0 Sat.	14 Apr. 1184* (105)	617	1 Sun.	8 Mar. 1220* (68)	*654	1 Sun.	30 Jan. 1256* (30)
581	5 Thurs.	4 Apr. 1185, (94)	*618	5 Thurs.	25 Feb. 1221 (56)	655	6 Fri.	19 Jan. 1257 (19)
582	2 Mon.	24 Mar. 1186 (83)	619	3 Tues.	15 Feb. 1222 (46)	*656	3 Tues.	8 Jan. 1258 (8)
*583	6 Fri.	13 Mar. 1187 (72)	620	0 Sat.	4 Feb. 1223 (35)	657	1 Sun.	29 Dec. 1258 (363)
584	4 Wed.	2 Mar. 1188* (62)	*621	4 Wed.	24 Jan. 1224* (24)	658	5 Thurs.	18 Dec. 1259 (352)
585	1 Sun.	19 Feb. 1189 (50)	622	2 Mon.	13 Jan. 1225 (13)	*659	2 Mon.	6 Dec. 1260* (341)
*586	5 Thurs.	8 Feb. 1190 (39)	623	6 Fri.	2 Jan. 1226 (2)	660	0 Sat.	26 Nov. 1261 (330)
587	3 Tues.	29 Jan. 1191 (29)	*624	3 Tues.	22 Dec. 1226 (356)	661	4 Wed.	15 Nov. 1262 (319)
*588	0 Sat.	18 Jan. 1192* (18)	625	1 Sun.	12 Dec. 1227 (346)	*662	1 Sun.	4 Nov. 1263 (308)
589	5 Thurs.	7 Jan. 1193 (7)	*626	5 Thurs.	30 Nov. 1228* (335)	663	6 Fri.	24 Oct. 1264* (298)
590	2 Mon.	27 Dec. 1193 (361)	627	3 Tues.	20 Nov. 1229 (324)	664	3 Tues.	13 Oct. 1265 (286)
*591	6 Fri.	16 Dec. 1194 (350)	628	0 Sat.	9 Nov. 1230 (313)	*665	0 Sat.	2 Oct. 1266 (275)
592	4 Wed.	6 Dec. 1195 (340)	*629	4 Wed.	29 Oct. 1231 (302)	666	5 Thurs.	22 Sep. 1267 (265)

TABLE XVI. (CONTINUED.)

INITIAL DAYS OF MUHAMMADAN YEARS OF THE HIJRA.

N.B. i. *Asterisks indicate Leap-years.*
ii. *Up to Hijra* 1165 *inclusive, the A.D. dates are Old Style.*

Hijra year.	Commencement of the year.		Hijra year.	Commencement of the year.		Hijra year.	Commencement of the year.	
	Weekday.	Date A.D.		Weekday.	Date A.D.		Weekday.	Date A.D.
1	2	3	1	2	3	1	2	3
*667	2 Mon.	10 Sep. 1268* (254)	704	3 Tues.	4 Aug. 1304* (217)	*741	3 Tues.	27 June 1340* (179)
668	0 Sat.	31 Aug. 1269 (243)	705	0 Sat.	24 July 1305 (205)	742	1 Sun.	17 June 1341 (168)
669	4 Wed.	20 Aug. 1270 (232)	*706	4 Wed.	13 July 1306 (194)	743	5 Thurs.	6 June 1342 (157)
*670	1 Sun.	9 Aug. 1271 (221)	707	2 Mon.	3 July 1307 (184)	*744	2 Mon.	26 May 1343 (146)
671	6 Fri.	29 July 1272* (211)	*708	6 Fri.	21 June 1308* (173)	745	0 Sat.	15 May 1344* (136)
672	3 Tues.	18 July 1273 (199)	709	4 Wed.	11 June 1309 (162)	*746	4 Wed.	4 May 1345 (124)
*673	0 Sat.	7 July 1274 (188)	710	1 Sun.	31 May 1310 (151)	747	2 Mon.	24 Apr. 1346 (114)
674	5 Thurs.	27 June 1275 (178)	*711	5 Thurs.	20 May 1311 (140)	748	6 Fri.	13 Apr. 1347 (103)
675	2 Mon.	15 June 1276* (167)	712	3 Tues.	9 May 1312* (130)	*749	3 Tues.	1 Apr. 1348* (92)
*676	6 Fri.	4 June 1277 (155)	713	0 Sat.	28 Apr. 1313 (118)	750	1 Sun.	22 Mar. 1349 (81)
677	4 Wed.	25 May 1278 (145)	*714	4 Wed.	17 Apr. 1314 (107)	751	5 Thurs.	11 Mar. 1350 (70)
*678	1 Sun.	14 May 1279 (134)	715	2 Mon.	7 Apr. 1315 (97)	*752	2 Mon.	28 Feb. 1351 (59)
679	6 Fri.	3 May 1280* (124)	*716	6 Fri.	26 Mar. 1316* (86)	753	0 Sat.	18 Feb. 1352* (49)
680	3 Tues.	22 Apr. 1281 (112)	717	4 Wed.	16 Mar. 1317 (75)	754	4 Wed.	6 Feb. 1353 (37)
*681	0 Sat.	11 Apr. 1282 (101)	718	1 Sun.	5 Mar. 1318 (64)	*755	1 Sun.	26 Jan. 1354 (26)
682	5 Thurs.	1 Apr. 1283 (91)	*719	5 Thurs.	22 Feb. 1319 (53)	756	6 Fri.	16 Jan. 1355 (16)
683	2 Mon.	20 Mar. 1284* (80)	720	3 Tues.	12 Feb. 1320* (43)	*757	3 Tues.	5 Jan. 1356* (5)
*684	6 Fri.	9 Mar. 1285 (68)	721	0 Sat.	31 Jan. 1321 (31)	758	1 Sun.	25 Dec. 1356* (360)
685	4 Wed.	27 Feb. 1286 (58)	*722	4 Wed.	20 Jan. 1322 (20)	759	5 Thurs.	14 Dec. 1357 (348)
*686	1 Sun.	16 Feb. 1287 (47)	723	2 Mon.	10 Jan. 1323 (10)	*760	2 Mon.	3 Dec. 1358 (337)
687	6 Fri.	6 Feb. 1288* (37)	724	6 Fri.	30 Dec. 1323 (364)	761	0 Sat.	23 Nov. 1359 (327)
688	3 Tues.	25 Jan. 1289 (25)	*725	3 Tues.	18 Dec. 1324* (353)	762	4 Wed.	11 Nov. 1360* (316)
*689	0 Sat.	14 Jan. 1290 (14)	726	1 Sun.	8 Dec. 1325 (342)	*763	1 Sun.	31 Oct. 1361 (304)
690	5 Thurs.	4 Jan. 1291 (4)	*727	5 Thurs.	27 Nov. 1326 (331)	764	6 Fri.	21 Oct. 1362 (294)
691	2 Mon.	24 Dec. 1291 (358)	728	3 Tues.	17 Nov. 1327 (321)	765	3 Tues.	10 Oct. 1363 (283)
*692	6 Fri.	12 Dec. 1292* (347)	729	0 Sat.	5 Nov. 1328* (310)	*766	0 Sat.	28 Sep. 1364* (272)
693	4 Wed.	2 Dec. 1293 (336)	*730	4 Wed.	25 Oct. 1329 (298)	767	5 Thurs.	18 Sep. 1365 (261)
694	1 Sun.	21 Nov. 1294 (325)	731	2 Mon.	15 Oct. 1330 (288)	*768	2 Mon.	7 Sep. 1366 (250)
*695	5 Thurs.	10 Nov. 1295 (314)	732	6 Fri.	4 Oct. 1331 (277)	769	0 Sat.	28 Aug. 1367 (240)
696	3 Tues.	30 Oct. 1296* (304)	*733	3 Tues.	22 Sep. 1332* (266)	770	4 Wed.	16 Aug. 1368* (229)
*697	0 Sat.	19 Oct. 1297 (292)	734	1 Sun.	12 Sep. 1333 (255)	*771	1 Sun.	5 Aug. 1369 (217)
698	5 Thurs.	9 Oct. 1298 (282)	735	5 Thurs.	1 Sep. 1334 (244)	772	6 Fri.	26 July 1370 (207)
699	2 Mon.	28 Sep. 1299 (271)	*736	2 Mon.	21 Aug. 1335 (233)	773	3 Tues.	15 July 1371 (196)
*700	6 Fri.	16 Sep. 1300* (260)	737	0 Sat.	10 Aug. 1336* (223)	*774	0 Sat.	3 July 1372* (185)
701	4 Wed.	6 Sep. 1301 (249)	*738	4 Wed.	30 July 1337 (211)	775	5 Thurs.	23 June 1373 (174)
702	1 Sun.	26 Aug. 1302 (238)	739	2 Mon.	20 July 1338 (201)	*776	2 Mon.	12 June 1374 (163)
*703	5 Thurs.	15 Aug. 1303 (227)	740	6 Fri.	9 July 1339 (190)	777	0 Sat.	2 June 1375 (153)

TABLE XVI. (CONTINUED.)

INITIAL DAYS OF MUHAMMADAN YEARS OF THE HIJRA.

N.B. i. *Asterisks indicate Leap-years.*

ii. *Up to Hijra* 1165 *inclusive, the A.D. dates are Old Style.*

Hijra year.	Commencement of the year.		Hijra year.	Commencement of the year.		Hijra year.	Commencement of the year.	
	Weekday.	Date A.D.		Weekday.	Date A.D.		Weekday.	Date A.D.
1	2	3	1	2	3	1	2	3
778	4 Wed.	21 May 1376* (142)	*815	4 Wed.	13 Apr. 1412* (104)	852	5 Thurs.	7 Mar. 1448* (67)
*779	1 Sun.	10 May 1377 (130)	816	2 Mon.	3 Apr. 1413 (93)	*853	2 Mon.	24 Feb. 1449 (55)
780	6 Fri.	30 Apr. 1378 (120)	*817	6 Fri.	23 Mar. 1414 (82)	854	0 Sat.	14 Feb. 1450 (45)
781	3 Tues.	19 Apr. 1379 (109)	818	4 Wed.	13 Mar. 1415 (72)	855	4 Wed.	3 Feb. 1451 (34)
*782	0 Sat.	7 Apr. 1380* (98)	819	1 Sun.	1 Mar. 1416* (61)	*856	1 Sun.	23 Jan. 1452* (23)
783	5 Thurs.	28 Mar. 1381 (87)	*820	5 Thurs.	18 Feb. 1417 (49)	857	6 Fri.	12 Jan. 1453 (12)
784	2 Mon.	17 Mar. 1382 (76)	821	3 Tues.	8 Feb. 1418 (39)	*858	3 Tues.	1 Jan. 1454 (1)
*785	6 Fri.	6 Mar. 1383 (65)	822	0 Sat.	28 Jan. 1419 (28)	859	1 Sun.	22 Dec. 1454 (356)
786	4 Wed.	24 Feb. 1384* (55)	*823	4 Wed.	17 Jan. 1420* (17)	860	5 Thurs.	11 Dec. 1455 (345)
*787	1 Sun.	12 Feb. 1385 (43)	824	2 Mon.	6 Jan. 1421 (6)	*861	2 Mon.	29 Nov. 1456* (334)
788	6 Fri.	2 Feb. 1386 (33)	825	6 Fri.	26 Dec. 1421 (360)	862	0 Sat.	19 Nov. 1457 (323)
789	3 Tues.	22 Jan. 1387 (22)	*826	3 Tues.	15 Dec. 1422 (349)	863	4 Wed.	8 Nov. 1458 (312)
*790	0 Sat.	11 Jan. 1388* (11)	827	1 Sun.	5 Dec. 1423 (339)	*864	1 Sun.	28 Oct. 1459 (301)
791	5 Thurs.	31 Dec. 1388* (366)	*828	5 Thurs.	23 Nov. 1424* (328)	865	6 Fri.	17 Oct. 1460* (291)
792	2 Mon.	20 Dec. 1389 (354)	829	3 Tues.	13 Nov. 1425 (317)	*866	3 Tues.	6 Oct. 1461 (279)
*793	6 Fri.	9 Dec. 1390 (343)	830	0 Sat.	2 Nov. 1426 (306)	867	1 Sun.	26 Sep. 1462 (269)
794	4 Wed.	29 Nov. 1391 (333)	*831	4 Wed.	22 Oct. 1427 (295)	868	5 Thurs.	15 Sep. 1463 (258)
795	1 Sun.	17 Nov. 1392* (322)	832	2 Mon.	11 Oct. 1428* (285)	*869	2 Mon.	3 Sep. 1464* (247)
*796	5 Thurs.	6 Nov. 1393 (310)	833	6 Fri.	30 Sep. 1429 (273)	870	0 Sat.	24 Aug. 1465 (236)
797	3 Tues.	27 Oct. 1394 (300)	*834	3 Tues.	19 Sep. 1430 (262)	871	4 Wed.	13 Aug. 1466 (225)
*798	0 Sat.	16 Oct. 1395 (289)	835	1 Sun.	9 Sep. 1431 (252)	*872	1 Sun.	2 Aug. 1467 (214)
799	5 Thurs.	5 Oct. 1396* (279)	*836	5 Thurs.	28 Aug. 1432* (241)	873	6 Fri.	22 July 1468* (204)
800	2 Mon.	24 Sep. 1397 (267)	837	3 Tues.	18 Aug. 1433 (230)	874	3 Tues.	11 July 1469 (192)
*801	6 Fri.	13 Sep. 1398 (256)	838	0 Sat.	7 Aug. 1434 (219)	*875	0 Sat.	30 June 1470 (181)
802	4 Wed.	3 Sep. 1399 (246)	*839	4 Wed.	27 July 1435 (208)	876	5 Thurs.	20 June 1471 (171)
803	1 Sun.	22 Aug. 1400* (235)	840	2 Mon.	16 July 1436* (198)	*877	2 Mon.	8 June 1472* (160)
*804	5 Thurs.	11 Aug. 1401 (223)	841	6 Fri.	5 July 1437 (186)	878	0 Sat.	29 May 1473 (149)
805	3 Tues.	1 Aug. 1402 (213)	*842	3 Tues.	24 June 1438 (175)	879	4 Wed.	18 May 1474 (138)
*806	0 Sat.	21 July 1403 (202)	843	1 Sun.	14 June 1439 (165)	*880	1 Sun.	7 May 1475 (127)
807	5 Thurs.	10 July 1404* (192)	844	5 Thurs.	2 June 1440* (154)	881	6 Fri.	26 Apr. 1476* (117)
808	2 Mon.	29 June 1405 (180)	*845	2 Mon.	22 May 1441 (142)	882	3 Tues.	15 Apr. 1477 (105)
*809	6 Fri.	18 June 1406 (169)	846	0 Sat.	12 May 1442 (132)	*883	0 Sat.	4 Apr. 1478 (94)
810	4 Wed.	8 June 1407 (159)	*847	4 Wed.	1 May 1443 (121)	884	5 Thurs.	25 Mar. 1479 (84)
811	1 Sun.	27 May 1408* (148)	848	2 Mon.	20 Apr. 1444* (111)	885	2 Mon.	13 Mar. 1480* (73)
*812	5 Thurs.	16 May 1409 (136)	849	6 Thurs.	9 Apr. 1445 (99)	*886	6 Fri.	2 Mar. 1481 (61)
813	3 Tues.	6 May 1410 (126)	*850	3 Tues.	29 Mar. 1446 (88)	887	4 Wed.	20 Feb. 1482 (51)
814	0 Sat.	25 Apr. 1411 (115)	851	1 Sun.	19 Mar. 1447 (78)	*888	1 Sun.	9 Feb. 1483 (40)

TABLE XVI. (CONTINUED.)

INITIAL DAYS OF MUHAMMADAN YEARS OF THE HIJRA.

N.B. i. *Asterisks indicate Leap-years.*
ii. *Up to Hijra* 1165 *inclusive, the A.D. dates are Old Style.*

Hijra year.	Commencement of the year.		Hijra year.	Commencement of the year.		Hijra year.	Commencement of the year.	
	Weekday.	Date A.D.		Weekday.	Date A.D.		Weekday.	Date A.D.
1	2	3	1	2	3	1	2	3
889	6 Fri.	30 Jan. 1484* (30)	*926	6 Fri.	23 Dec. 1519 (357)	963	0 Sat.	16 Nov. 1555 (320)
890	3 Tues.	18 Jan. 1485 (18)	927	4 Wed.	12 Dec. 1520* (347)	964	4 Wed.	4 Nov. 1556* (309)
*891	0 Sat.	7 Jan. 1486 (7)	928	1 Sun.	1 Dec. 1521 (335)	*965	1 Sun.	24 Oct. 1557 (297)
892	5 Thurs.	28 Dec. 1486 (362)	*929	5 Thurs.	20 Nov. 1522 (324)	966	6 Fri.	14 Oct. 1558 (287)
893	2 Mon.	17 Dec. 1487 (351)	930	3 Tues.	10 Nov. 1523 (314)	*967	3 Tues.	3 Oct. 1559 (276)
*894	6 Fri.	5 Dec. 1488* (340)	931	0 Sat.	29 Oct. 1524* (303)	968	1 Sun.	22 Sep. 1560* (266)
895	4 Wed.	25 Nov. 1489 (329)	*932	4 Wed.	18 Oct. 1525 (291)	969	5 Thurs.	11 Sep. 1561 (254)
*896	1 Sun.	14 Nov. 1490 (318)	933	2 Mon.	8 Oct. 1526 (281)	*970	2 Mon.	31 Aug. 1562 (243)
897	6 Fri.	4 Nov. 1491 (308)	934	6 Fri.	27 Sep. 1527 (270)	971	0 Sat.	21 Aug. 1563 (233)
898	3 Tues.	23 Oct. 1492* (297)	*935	3 Tues.	15 Sep. 1528* (259)	972	4 Wed.	9 Aug. 1564* (222)
*899	0 Sat.	12 Oct. 1493 (285)	936	1 Sun.	5 Sep. 1529 (248)	*973	1 Sun.	29 July 1565 (210)
900	5 Thurs.	2 Oct. 1494 (275)	*937	5 Thurs.	25 Aug. 1530 (237)	974	6 Fri.	19 July 1566 (200)
901	2 Mon.	21 Sep. 1495 (264)	938	3 Tues.	15 Aug. 1531 (227)	975	3 Tues.	8 July 1567 (189)
*902	6 Fri.	9 Sep. 1496* (253)	939	0 Sat.	3 Aug. 1532* (216)	*976	0 Sat.	26 June 1568* (178)
903	4 Wed.	30 Aug. 1497 (242)	*940	4 Wed.	23 July 1533 (204)	977	5 Thurs.	16 Juue 1569 (167)
904	1 Sun.	19 Aug. 1498 (231)	941	2 Mon.	13 July 1534 (194)	*978	2 Mon.	5 June 1570 (156)
*905	5 Thurs.	8 Aug. 1499 (220)	942	6 Fri.	2 July 1535 (183)	979	0 Sat.	26 May 1571 (146)
906	3 Tues.	28 July 1500* (210)	*943	3 Tues.	20 June 1536* (172)	980	4 Wed.	14 May 1572* (135)
*907	0 Sat.	17 July 1501 (198)	944	1 Sun.	10 June 1537 (161)	*981	1 Sun.	3 May 1573 (123)
908	5 Thurs.	7 July 1502 (188)	945	5 Thurs.	30 May 1538 (150)	982	6 Fri.	23 Apr. 1574 (113)
909	2 Mon.	26 June 1503 (177)	*946	2 Mon.	19 May 1539 (139)	983	3 Tues.	12 Apr. 1575 (102)
*910	6 Fri.	14 June 1504* (166)	947	0 Sat.	8 May 1540* (129)	*984	0 Sat.	31 Mar. 1576* (91)
911	4 Wed.	4 June 1505 (155)	*948	4 Wed.	27 Apr. 1541 (117)	985	5 Thurs.	21 Mar. 1577 (80)
912	1 Sun.	24 May 1506 (144)	949	2 Mon.	17 Apr. 1542 (107)	*986	2 Mon.	10 Mar. 1578 (69)
*913	5 Thurs.	13 May 1507 (133)	950	6 Fri.	6 Apr. 1543 (96)	987	0 Sat.	28 Feb. 1579 (59)
914	3 Tues.	2 May 1508* (123)	*951	3 Tues.	25 Mar. 1544* (85)	988	4 Wed.	17 Feb. 1580* (48)
915	0 Sat.	21 Apr. 1509 (111)	952	1 Sun.	15 Mar. 1545 (74)	*989	1 Sun.	5 Feb. 1581 (36)
*916	4 Wed.	10 Apr. 1510 (100)	953	5 Thurs.	4 Mar. 1546 (63)	990	6 Fri.	26 Jan. 1582[1] 26)
917	2 Mon.	31 Mar. 1511 (90)	*954	2 Mon.	21 Feb. 1547 (52)	991	3 Tues.	15 Jan. 1583 (15)
*918	6 Fri.	19 Mar. 1512* (79)	955	0 Sat.	11 Feb. 1548* (42)	*992	0 Sat.	4 Jan. 1584* (4)
919	4 Wed.	9 Mar. 1513 (68)	*956	4 Wed.	30 Jan. 1549 (30)	993	5 Thurs.	24 Dec. 1584* (359)
920	1 Sun.	26 Feb. 1514 (57)	957	2 Mon.	20 Jan. 1550 (20)	994	2 Mon.	13 Dec. 1585 (347)
*921	5 Thurs.	15 Feb. 1515 (46)	958	6 Fri.	9 Jan. 1551 (9)	*995	6 Fri.	2 Dec. 1586 (336)
922	3 Tues.	5 Feb. 1516* (36)	*959	3 Tues.	29 Dec. 1551 (363)	996	4 Wed.	22 Nov. 1587 (326)
923	0 Sat.	24 Jan. 1517 (24)	960	1 Sun.	18 Dec. 1552* (353)	*997	1 Sun.	10 Nov. 1588* (315)
*924	4 Wed.	13 Jan. 1518 (13)	961	5 Thurs.	7 Dec. 1553 (341)	998	6 Fri.	31 Oct. 1589 (304)
925	2 Mon.	3 Jan. 1519 (3)	*962	2 Mon.	26 Nov. 1554 (330)	999	3 Tues.	20 Oct. 1590 (293)

[1]) In the Roman Catholic countries of Europe the New Style was introduced from October 5th 1582 A.D. and the year 1700 was ordered to be a common, not a Leap-year. Dates in the above Table are however for English reckoning, where the New Style was not introduced till Sept. 3rd 1752 A.D. For the initial dates of the Hijra years, therefore, in the former countries, add 10 days to the date given in the Table from Hijra 991 to Hijra 1111 inclusive, and 11 days from Hijra 1112 to Hijra 1165 inclusive.

TABLE XVI. (CONTINUED.)

INITIAL DAYS OF MUHAMMADAN YEARS OF THE HIJRA.

N.B. i. *Asterisks indicate Leap-years.*
ii. *Up to Hijra 1165 inclusive, the A.D. dates are Old Style.*

Hijra year.	Commencement of the year.		Hijra year.	Commencement of the year.		Hijra year.	Commencement of the year.	
	Weekday.	Date A.D.		Weekday.	Date A.D.		Weekday.	Date A.D.
1	2	3	1	2	3	1	2	3
*1000	0 Sat.	9 Oct. 1591 (282)	1037	1 Sun.	2 Sep. 1627 (245)	*1074	1 Sun.	26 July 1663 (207)
1001	5 Thurs.	28 Sep. 1592* (272)	*1038	5 Thurs.	21 Aug. 1628* (234)	1075	6 Fri.	15 July 1664* (197)
1002	2 Mon.	17 Sep. 1593 (260)	1039	3 Tues.	11 Aug. 1629 (223)	*1076	3 Tues.	4 July 1665 (185)
*1003	6 Fri.	6 Sep. 1594 (249)	1040	0 Sat.	31 July 1630 (212)	1077	1 Sun.	24 June 1666 (175)
1004	4 Wed.	27 Aug. 1595 (239)	*1041	4 Wed.	20 July 1631 (201)	1778	5 Thurs.	13 June 1667 (164)
1005	1 Sun.	15 Aug. 1596* (228)	1042	2 Mon.	9 July 1632* (191)	*1079	2 Mon.	1 June 1668* (153)
*1006	5 Thurs.	4 Aug. 1597 (216)	1043	6 Fri.	28 June 1633 (179)	1080	0 Sat.	22 May 1669 (142)
1007	3 Tues.	25 July 1598 (206)	*1044	3 Tues.	17 June 1634 (168)	1081	4 Wed.	11 May 1670 (131)
*1008	0 Sat.	14 July 1599 (195)	1045	1 Sun.	7 June 1635 (158)	*1082	1 Sun.	30 Apr. 1671 (120)
1009	5 Thurs.	3 July 1600* (185)	*1046	5 Thurs.	26 May 1636* (147)	1083	6 Fri.	19 Apr. 1672* (110)
1010	2 Mon.	22 June 1601 (173)	1047	3 Tues.	16 May 1637 (136)	1084	3 Tues.	8 Apr. 1673 (98)
*1011	6 Fri.	11 June 1602 (162)	1048	0 Sat.	5 May 1638 (125)	*1085	0 Sat.	28 Mar. 1674 (87)
1012	4 Wed.	1 June 1603 (152)	*1049	4 Wed.	24 Apr. 1639 (114)	1086	5 Thurs.	18 Mar. 1675 (77)
1013	1 Sun.	20 May 1604* (141)	1050	2 Mon.	13 Apr. 1640* (104)	*1087	2 Mon.	6 Mar. 1676* (66)
*1014	5 Thurs.	9 May 1605 (129)	1051	6 Fri.	2 Apr. 1641 (92)	1088	0 Sat.	24 Feb. 1677 (55)
1015	3 Tues.	29 Apr. 1606 (119)	*1052	3 Tues.	22 Mar. 1642 (81)	1089	4 Wed.	13 Feb. 1678 (44)
*1016	0 Sat.	18 Apr. 1607 (108)	1053	1 Sun.	12 Mar. 1643 (71)	*1090	1 Sun.	2 Feb. 1679 (33)
1017	5 Thurs.	7 Apr. 1608* (98)	1054	5 Thurs.	29 Feb. 1644* (60)	1091	6 Fri.	23 Jan. 1680* (23)
1018	2 Mon.	27 Mar. 1609 (86)	*1055	2 Mon.	17 Feb. 1645 (48)	1092	3 Tues.	11 Jan. 1681 (11)
*1019	6 Fri.	16 Mar. 1610 (75)	1056	0 Sat.	7 Feb. 1646 (38)	*1093	0 Sat.	31 Dec. 1681 (365)
1020	4 Wed.	6 Mar. 1611 (65)	*1057	4 Wed.	27 Jan. 1647 (27)	1094	5 Thurs.	21 Dec. 1682 (355)
1021	1 Sun.	23 Feb. 1612* (54)	1058	2 Mon.	17 Jan. 1648* (17)	1095	2 Mon.	10 Dec. 1683 (344)
*1022	5 Thurs.	11 Feb. 1613 (42)	1059	6 Fri.	5 Jan. 1649 (5)	*1096	6 Fri.	28 Nov. 1684* (333)
1023	3 Tues.	1 Feb. 1614 (32)	*1060	3 Tues.	25 Dec. 1649 (359)	1097	4 Wed.	18 Nov. 1685 (322)
1024	0 Sat.	21 Jan. 1615 (21)	1061	1 Sun.	15 Dec. 1650 (349)	*1098	1 Sun.	7 Nov. 1686 (311)
*1025	4 Wed.	10 Jan. 1616* (10)	1062	5 Thurs.	4 Dec. 1651 (338)	1099	6 Fri.	28 Oct. 1687 (301)
1026	2 Mon.	30 Dec. 1616* (365)	*1063	2 Mon.	22 Nov. 1652* (327)	1100	3 Tues.	16 Oct. 1688* (290)
*1027	6 Fri.	19 Dec. 1617 (353)	1064	0 Sat.	12 Nov. 1653 (316)	*1101	0 Sat.	5 Oct. 1689 (278)
1028	4 Wed.	9 Dec. 1618 (343)	1065	4 Wed.	1 Nov. 1654 (305)	1102	5 Thurs.	25 Sep. 1690 (268)
1029	1 Sun.	28 Nov. 1619 (332)	*1066	1 Sun.	21 Oct. 1655 (294)	1103	2 Mon.	14 Sep. 1691 (257)
*1030	5 Thurs.	16 Nov. 1620* (321)	1067	6 Fri.	10 Oct. 1656* (284)	*1104	6 Fri.	2 Sep. 1692* (246)
1031	3 Tues.	6 Nov. 1621 (310)	*1068	3 Tues.	29 Sep. 1657 (272)	1105	4 Wed.	23 Aug. 1693 (235)
1032	0 Sat.	26 Oct. 1622 (299)	1069	1 Sun.	19 Sep. 1658 (262)	*1106	1 Sun.	12 Aug. 1694 (224)
*1033	4 Wed.	15 Oct. 1623 (288)	1070	5 Thurs.	8 Sep. 1659 (251)	1107	6 Fri.	2 Aug. 1695 (214)
1034	2 Mon.	4 Oct. 1624* (278)	*1071	2 Mon.	27 Aug. 1660* (240)	1108	3 Tues.	21 July 1696* (203)
1035	6 Fri.	23 Sep. 1625 (266)	1072	0 Sat.	17 Aug. 1661 (229)	*1109	0 Sat.	10 July 1697 (191)
*1036	3 Tues.	12 Sep. 1626 (255)	1073	4 Wed.	6 Aug. 1662 (218)	1110	5 Thurs.	30 June 1698 (181)

TABLE XVI. (CONTINUED.)

INITIAL DAYS OF MUHAMMADAN YEARS OF THE HIJRA.

N.B. i. *Asterisks indicate Leap-years.*
ii. *Up to Hijra* 1165 *inclusive, the A.D. dates are Old Style.*

Hijra year.	Commencement of the year.		Hijra year.	Commencement of the year.		Hijra year.	Commencement of the year.	
	Weekday.	Date A.D.		Weekday.	Date A.D.		Weekday.	Date A.D.
1	2	3	1	2	3	1	2	3
1111	2 Mon.	19 June 1699 (170)	1148	3 Tues.	13 May 1735 (133)	1185	3 Tues.	16 Apr. 1771 (106)
*1112	6 Fri.	7 June 1700* (159)	1149	0 Sat.	1 May 1736* (122)	*1186	0 Sat.	4 Apr. 1772* (95)
1113	4 Wed.	28 May 1701 (148)	*1150	4 Wed.	20 Apr. 1737 (110)	1187	5 Thurs.	25 Mar. 1773 (84)
1114	1 Sun.	17 May 1702 (137)	1151	2 Mon.	10 Apr. 1738 (100)	*1188	2 Mon.	14 Mar. 1774 (73)
*1115	5 Thurs.	6 May 1703 (126)	1152	6 Fri.	30 Mar. 1739 (89)	1189	0 Sat.	4 Mar. 1775 (63)
1116	3 Tues.	25 Apr. 1704* (116)	*1153	3 Tues.	18 Mar. 1740* (78)	1190	4 Wed.	21 Feb. 1776* (52)
*1117	0 Sat.	14 Apr. 1705 (104)	1154	1 Sun.	8 Mar. 1741 (67)	*1191	1 Sun.	9 Feb. 1777 (40)
1118	5 Thurs.	4 Apr. 1706 (94)	1155	5 Thurs.	25 Feb. 1742 (56)	1192	6 Fri.	30 Jan. 1778 (30)
1119	2 Mon.	24 Mar. 1707 (83)	*1156	2 Mon.	14 Feb. 1743 (45)	1193	3 Tues.	19 Jan. 1779 (19)
*1120	6 Fri.	12 Mar. 1708* (72)	1157	0 Sat.	4 Feb. 1744* (35)	*1194	0 Sat.	8 Jan. 1780* (8)
1121	4 Wed.	2 Mar. 1709 (61)	*1158	4 Wed.	23 Jan. 1745 (23)	1195	5 Thurs.	28 Dec. 1780* (363)
1122	1 Sun.	19 Feb. 1710 (50)	1159	2 Mon.	13 Jan. 1746 (13)	*1196	2 Mon.	17 Dec. 1781 (351)
*1123	5 Thurs.	8 Feb. 1711 (39)	1160	6 Fri.	2 Jan. 1747 (2)	1197	0 Sat.	7 Dec. 1782 (341)
1124	3 Tues.	29 Jan. 1712* (29)	*1161	3 Tues.	22 Dec. 1747 (356)	1198	4 Wed.	26 Nov. 1783 (330)
1125	0 Sat.	17 Jan. 1713 (17)	1162	1 Sun.	11 Dec. 1748* (346)	*1199	1 Sun.	14 Nov. 1784* (319)
*1126	4 Wed.	6 Jan. 1714 (6)	1163	5 Thurs.	30 Nov. 1749 (334)	1200	6 Fri.	4 Nov. 1785 (308)
1127	2 Mon.	27 Dec. 1714 (361)	*1164	2 Mon.	19 Nov. 1750 (323)	1201	3 Tues.	24 Oct. 1786 (297)
*1128	6 Fri.	16 Dec. 1715 (350)	1165	0 Sat.	9 Nov. 1751† (313)	*1202	0 Sat.	13 Oct. 1787 (286)
1129	4 Wed.	5 Dec. 1716* (340)	*1166	4 Wed.	8 Nov. 1752* (313)	1203	5 Thurs.	2 Oct. 1788* (276)
1130	1 Sun.	24 Nov. 1717 (328)	1167	2 Mon.	29 Oct. 1753 (302)	1204	2 Mon.	21 Sep. 1789 (264)
*1131	5 Thurs.	13 Nov. 1718 (317)	1168	6 Fri.	18 Oct. 1754 (291)	*1205	6 Fri.	10 Sep. 1790 (253)
1132	3 Tues.	3 Nov. 1719 (307)	*1169	3 Tues.	7 Oct. 1755 (280)	1206	4 Wed.	31 Aug. 1791 (243)
1133	0 Sat.	22 Oct. 1720* (296)	1170	1 Sun.	26 Sep. 1756* (270)	*1207	1 Sun.	19 Aug. 1792* (232)
*1134	4 Wed.	11 Oct. 1721 (284)	1171	5 Thurs.	15 Sep. 1757 (258)	1208	6 Fri.	9 Aug. 1793 (221)
1135	2 Mon.	1 Oct. 1722 (274)	*1172	2 Mon.	4 Sep. 1758 (247)	1209	3 Tues.	29 July 1794 (210)
*1136	6 Fri.	20 Sep. 1723 (263)	1173	0 Sat.	25 Aug. 1759 (237)	*1210	0 Sat.	18 July 1795 (199)
1137	4 Wed.	9 Sep. 1724* (253)	1174	4 Wed.	13 Aug. 1760* (226)	1211	5 Thurs.	7 July 1796* (189)
1138	1 Sun.	29 Aug. 1725 (241)	*1175	1 Sun.	2 Aug. 1761 (214)	1212	2 Mon.	26 June 1797 (177)
*1139	5 Thurs.	18 Aug. 1726 (230)	1176	6 Fri.	23 July 1762 (204)	*1213	6 Fri.	15 June 1798 (166)
1140	3 Tues.	8 Aug. 1727 (220)	*1177	3 Tues.	12 July 1763 (193)	1214	4 Wed.	5 June 1799 (156)
1141	0 Sat.	27 July 1728* (209)	1178	1 Sun.	1 July 1764* (183)	1215	1 Sun.	25 May 1800 (145)
*1142	4 Wed.	16 July 1729 (197)	1179	5 Thurs.	20 June 1765 (171)	*1216	5 Thurs.	14 May 1801 (134)
1143	2 Mon.	6 July 1730 (187)	*1180	2 Mon.	9 June 1766 (160)	1217	3 Tues.	4 May 1802 (124)
1144	6 Fri.	25 June 1731 (176)	1181	0 Sat.	30 May 1767 (150)	*1218	0 Sat.	23 Apr. 1803 (113)
*1145	3 Tues.	13 June 1732* (165)	1182	4 Wed.	18 May 1768* (139)	1219	5 Thurs.	12 Apr. 1804* (103)
1146	1 Sun.	3 June 1733 (154)	*1183	1 Sun.	7 May 1769 (127)	1220	2 Mon.	1 Apr. 1805 (91)
*1147	5 Thurs.	23 May 1734 (143)	1184	6 Fri.	27 Apr. 1770 (117)	*1221	6 Fri.	21 Mar. 1806 (80)

† The New Style was introduced into England from 3rd September, 1752. The 9th November, 1751, is therefore an Old Style date, and the 8th November, 1752, is a New Style one (see above, *Note* 2. p. 11, *Note* 1, p. 88).

TABLE XVI. (CONTINUED.)

INITIAL DAYS OF MUHAMMADAN YEARS OF THE HIJRA.

N.B. i. *Asterisks indicate Leap-years.*

ii. *Up to Hijra* 1165 *inclusive, the A.D. dates are Old Style.*

Hijra year.	Commencement of the year.		Hijra year.	Commencement of the year.		Hijra year.	Commencement of the year.	
	Weekday.	Date A.D.		Weekday.	Date A.D.		Weekday.	Date A.D.
1	2	3	1	2	3	1	2	3
1222	4 Wed.	11 Mar. 1807 (70)	1255	1 Sun.	17 Mar. 1839 (76)	1288	5 Thurs.	23 Mar. 1871 (82)
1223	1 Sun.	28 Feb. 1808* (59)	*1256	5 Thurs.	5 Mar. 1840* (65)	*1289	2 Mon.	11 Mar. 1872* (71)
*1224	5 Thurs.	16 Feb. 1809 (47)	1257	3 Tues.	23 Feb. 1841 (54)	1290	0 Sat.	1 Mar. 1873 (60)
1225	3 Tues.	6 Feb. 1810 (37)	1258	0 Sat.	12 Feb. 1842 (43)	1291	4 Wed.	18 Feb. 1874 (49)
*1226	0 Sat.	26 Jan. 1811 (26)	*1259	4 Wed.	1 Feb. 1843 (32)	*1292	1 Sun.	7 Feb. 1875 (38)
1227	5 Thurs.	16 Jan. 1812* (16)	1260	2 Mon.	22 Jan. 1844* (22)	1293	6 Fri.	28 Jan. 1876* (28)
1228	2 Mon.	4 Jan. 1813 (4)	1261	6 Fri.	10 Jan. 1845 (10)	1294	3 Tues.	16 Jan. 1877 (16)
*1229	6 Fri.	24 Dec. 1813 (358)	*1262	3 Tues.	30 Dec. 1845 (364)	*1295	0 Sat.	5 Jan. 1878 (5)
1230	4 Wed.	14 Dec. 1814 (348)	1263	1 Sun.	20 Dec. 1846 (354)	1296	5 Thurs.	26 Dec. 1878 (360)
1231	1 Sun.	3 Dec. 1815 (337)	1264	5 Thurs.	9 Dec. 1847 (343)	*1297	2 Mon.	15 Dec. 1879 (349)
*1232	5 Thurs.	21 Nov. 1816* (326)	*1265	2 Mon.	27 Nov. 1848* (332)	1298	0 Sat.	4 Dec. 1880* (339)
1233	3 Tues.	11 Nov. 1817 (315)	1266	0 Sat.	17 Nov. 1849 (321)	1299	4 Wed.	23 Nov. 1881 (327)
1234	0 Sat.	31 Oct. 1818 (304)	*1267	4 Wed.	6 Nov. 1850 (310)	*1300	1 Sun.	12 Nov. 1882 (316)
*1235	4 Wed.	20 Oct. 1819 (293)	1268	2 Mon.	27 Oct. 1851 (300)	1301	6 Fri.	2 Nov. 1883 (306)
1236	2 Mon.	9 Oct. 1820* (283)	1269	6 Fri.	15 Oct. 1852* (289)	1302	3 Tues.	21 Oct. 1884* (295)
*1237	6 Fri.	28 Sep. 1821 (271)	*1270	3 Tues.	4 Oct. 1853 (277)	*1303	0 Sat.	10 Oct. 1885 (283)
1238	4 Wed.	18 Sep. 1822 (261)	1271	1 Sun.	24 Sep. 1854 (267)	1304	5 Thurs.	30 Sep. 1886 (273)
1239	1 Sun.	7 Sep. 1823 (250)	1272	5 Thurs.	13 Sep. 1855 (256)	1305	2 Mon.	19 Sep. 1887 (262)
*1240	5 Thurs.	26 Aug. 1824* (239)	*1273	2 Mon.	1 Sep. 1856* (245)	*1306	6 Fri.	7 Sep. 1888* (251)
1241	3 Tues.	16 Aug. 1825 (228)	1274	0 Sat.	22 Aug. 1857 (234)	1307	4 Wed.	28 Aug. 1889 (240)
1242	0 Sat.	5 Aug. 1826 (217)	1275	4 Wed.	11 Aug. 1858 (223)	*1308	1 Sun.	17 Aug. 1890 (229)
*1243	4 Wed.	25 July 1827 (206)	*1276	1 Sun.	31 July 1859 (212)	1309	6 Fri.	7 Aug. 1891 (219)
1244	2 Mon.	14 July 1828* (196)	1277	6 Fri.	20 July 1860* (202)	1310	3 Tues.	26 July 1892* (208)
1245	6 Fri.	3 July 1829 (184)	*1278	3 Tues.	9 July 1861 (190)	*1311	0 Sat.	15 July 1893 (196)
*1246	3 Tues.	22 June 1830 (173)	1279	1 Sun.	29 June 1862 (180)	1312	5 Thurs.	5 July 1894 (186)
1247	1 Sun.	12 June 1831 (163)	1280	5 Thurs.	18 June 1863 (169)	1313	2 Mon.	24 June 1895 (175)
*1248	5 Thurs.	31 May 1832* (152)	*1281	2 Mon.	6 June 1864* (158)	*1314	6 Fri.	12 June 1896* (164)
1249	3 Tues.	21 May 1833 (141)	1282	0 Sat.	27 May 1865 (147)	1315	4 Wed.	2 June 1897 (153)
1250	0 Sat.	10 May 1834 (130)	1283	4 Wed.	16 May 1866 (136)	*1316	1 Sun.	22 May 1898 (142)
*1251	4 Wed.	29 Apr. 1835 (119)	*1284	1 Sun.	5 May 1867 (125)	1317	6 Fri.	12 May 1899 (132)
1252	2 Mon.	18 Apr. 1836* (109)	1285	6 Fri.	24 Apr. 1868* (115)	1318	3 Tues.	1 May 1900 (121)
1253	6 Fri.	7 Apr. 1837 (97)	*1286	3 Tues.	13 Apr. 1869 (103)			
*1254	3 Tues.	27 Mar. 1838 (86)	1287	1 Sun.	3 Apr. 1870 (93)			

APPENDIX.

ECLIPSES OF THE SUN IN INDIA.[1]

By Dr. Robert Schram.

A complete list of all eclipses of the sun for any part of the globe between the years 1200 B.C. and 2160 A.D. has been published by Oppolzer in his "Canon der Finsternisse", *(Denkschriften der mathematisch naturwissenschaftlichen Classe der Kais. Akademie der Wissenschaften in Wien, Vol. LII. 1887).* In this work are given for every eclipse all the data necessary for the calculation of the path of the shadow on the earth's surface, and of its beginning, greatest phase, and end for any particular place. But inasmuch as the problem is a complicated one the calculations required are also unavoidably complicated. It takes considerable time to work out by the exact formulæ the time of the greatest phase of a given eclipse for a particular place, and when, as is often the case with Indian inscriptions, we are not sure of the year in which a reported eclipse has taken place, and it is therefore necessary to calculate for a large number of eclipses, the work becomes almost impossible.

The use, however, of the exact formulæ is seldom necessary. In most cases it is sufficient to make use of a close approximation, or still better of tables based on approximate formulæ.

Such tables I have published under the title "Tafeln zur Berechnung der näheren Umstände der Sonnenfinsternisse", *(Denkschriften der mathematisch naturwissenschaftlichen Classe der Kais. Akademie der Wissenschaften in Wien, Vol. LI. 1886)* and the Tables B, C, and D, now given are based on those. That is to say, they contain extracts from those tables, somewhat modified and containing only what is of interest for the continent of India. Table A is a modified extract from Oppolzer's *Canon,* containing only eclipses visible in India and the immediate neighbourhood. All others are eliminated, and thus the work of calculation is greatly diminished, as no other eclipses need be examined to ascertain their visibility at the given place.

Oppolzer's *Canon* gives the following elements:

Date of eclipse and Greenwich mean civil time of conjunction in longitude.

L' = longitude of Sun and Moon, which is of course identical at the middle of the eclipse.

Z = Equation of time in degrees.

ε = Obliquity of the ecliptic.

P, $\log p$ — $p \sin P$ being equal to $\frac{\sin (b-b')}{\sin (\pi-\pi')}$ where b and b' denote the moon's and sun's latitude, π and π' their respective parallaxes.

Q, $\log q$ — $q \cos Q$ being the hourly motion of $p \sin P$.

$\log \Delta L$ = the hourly motion of $\frac{\cos b \sin (L-L')}{\sin (\pi-\pi')}$ where L denotes the moon's, L' the sun's longitude.

[1] I propose to publish, either in a second edition of this work, if such should be called for, or in one of the scientific periodicals, tables of lunar eclipses, compiled from Oppolzer's *Canon der Finsternisse*, and containing those visible in India during the period comprised in the present volume. [R. S.]

u'_a = radius of shadow.
f_a = angle of shadow's cone.
γ = shortest distance of shadow's centre from earth's centre.
μ = Sun's hour-angle at Greenwich at the moment of this shortest distance.
log n = hourly motion of shadow's centre.
$\left.\begin{array}{l}\log \sin \delta' \\ \log \cos \delta'\end{array}\right\}$ Sun's declination.
N' = angle of moon's orbit with declination circle ($N' = N - h$, where N is the angle of the moon's orbit with latitude circle, and $\tan h = \cos L' \cos \varepsilon$.

$$\left.\begin{array}{l} G \\ K \\ \sin g \\ \sin k \\ \cos g \\ \cos k \end{array}\right| \begin{array}{l} \sin g \sin G = \sin \delta' \sin N'. \\ \sin g \cos G = \cos N'. \\ \qquad \cos g = \cos \delta' \sin N'. \\ \sin k \sin K = \sin N'. \\ \sin k \cos K = \sin \delta' \cos N'. \\ \qquad \cos k = \cos \delta' \cos N'. \end{array}$$

With these elements the calculation of the moment of greatest phase of eclipse at a given place, whose longitude from Greenwich is λ, and whose latitude is Φ, is found by the formulæ:

$$\log \Phi_1 = 0{,}9966 \log \Phi.$$

$$m \sin M = \gamma - 0{,}9966 \cos g \sin \Phi_1 + \cos \Phi_1 \sin g \sin (G + t_0).$$

$$m \cos M = (t_0 - \lambda - \mu) \frac{n}{15} - 0{,}9966 \sin \Phi_1 \cos k + \cos \Phi_1 \sin k \cos (K + t_0).$$

$$m' \sin M' = - 0{,}2618 \cos \Phi_1 \sin g \cos (G + t_0).$$

$$m' \cos M' = n - 0{,}2618 \cos \Phi_1 \sin k \sin (K + t_0).$$

$$t_1 = t_0 - 15 \frac{m}{m'} \cos (M + M').$$

Making firstly $t_0 = \lambda + \mu$, this formulæ gives the value of t_1. This value is put in the formulæ instead of t_0 and the calculation repeated, and thus we get a closer value for t; which, again put in the place of t_0, gives a second corrected value of t. Calculation by these formulæ must be repeated as long as the new value of t differs from the former one, but, as a general rule, three or four times suffices. The last value of t is then the hour-angle of the sun at the given place for the moment of greatest phase at that place. With the last value of m we find the magnitude of the greatest phase at the given place in digits $= 6 \frac{u'_a - m}{u'_a - 0{,}2736}$.

These calculations are, as will be seen, very complicated, and for other than astronomical problems it is hardly ever necessary to attain to so great a degree of accuracy. For ordinary purposes they may be greatly simplified, as it suffices to merely fix the hour-angle to the nearest degree.

The angle N is very nearly constant, its mean value being $N = 84°3$ or $N = 95°7$ according as the moon is in the ascending or descending node. Which of these is the case is always shown by the value of P, as P is always near 0° when the moon is in the ascending, and near 180° when she is in the descending node. Taking also for ε a mean value, say $\varepsilon = 23°60$, and making the calculations separately for the cases of the ascending and descending node, we find that δ', h, N', sin g, cos g, sin k, cos k, G and K are all dependents of L', and can therefore be tabulated for single values of L', say from 10 to 10 degrees.

The second of the above formulæ

$$m \cos M = (t_0 - \lambda - \mu) \frac{n}{15} - 0{,}9966 \sin \Phi_1 \cos k + \cos \Phi_1 \sin k \cos (K + t_0)$$

will give for t the value

$$t = (\lambda + \mu) + \frac{15}{n} \times 0{,}9966 \sin \Phi_1 \cos k - \frac{15}{n} \cos \Phi_1 \sin k \cos (K + t) + \frac{15}{n} m \cos M.$$

The angle M being, at the moment of greatest phase, always sufficiently near 90° or 270°, $\frac{15}{n} m \cos M$ can be neglected; and, introducing for $\frac{15}{n}$ its mean value 27,544, and identifying Φ_1 with Φ, the value of t_0 can simply be determined by the expression

$$t = (\lambda + \mu) + 27{,}447 \sin \Phi \cos k - 27{,}544 \cos \Phi \sin k \cos (K + t)$$

instead of determining it by the whole of the above formulæ. Now in this last expression k and K are mere dependents on L′, and therefore the values of t can be tabulated for each value of L′ with the two arguments $\lambda + \mu$ and Φ. Table D is constructed on this formula, only instead of counting t in degrees and from true noon it is counted, for Indian purposes, in ghaṭikâs and their tenths from true sunrise.

The value of t for the instant of the greatest phase at the given place being found, it can be introduced into the formula

$$m \sin M = \gamma - 0{,}9966 \cos g \sin \Phi_1 + \cos \Phi_1 \sin g \sin (G + t).$$

As M is always near 90° or 270°, sin M can be considered equal to ± 1, so we have

$$\pm m = \gamma - 0{,}9966 \cos g \sin \Phi + \cos \Phi \sin g \sin (G + t)$$

where the sign ± is to be selected so that the value of m may always be positive.

The second part of the above expression

$$-0{,}9966 \cos g \sin\Phi + \cos\Phi \sin g \sin(G + t)$$

(which, for the sake of brevity, may be called by the letter Γ′) contains only values which directly depend on L′, such as cos g, sin g, G, or which, for a given value of L′, depend only on $\lambda + \mu$ and Φ, and therefore the values of Γ′ can be tabulated for each value of L′ with the two arguments $\lambda + \mu$ and Φ. This has been done in the Table B which follows, but instead of Γ′ the value $1 + \Gamma' = \Gamma$ has been tabulated to avoid negative numbers. The value of m can then be found from

$$m = \pm (\gamma + \Gamma').$$

Both Tables B and D ought to consist of two separate tables, one containing the values of L′ from 0° to 360° in the case of P being near 0°, the other containing the values of L′ from 0° to 360° for the case of P being near 180°. To avoid this division into two tables, and the trouble of having always to remember whether P is near 0° or 180°, the two tables are combined into one single one; but, whilst in the case of P being near 0° L′ is given as argument, in the case of P being near 180° the table contains, instead of L′, L′ + 400° as argument. We need therefore no longer care whether the moon is in the ascending or descending node, but simply take the argument as given in the first table.

With the value of m, found by $m = \pm (\gamma + \Gamma')$, we can find the magnitude of the greatest phase in digits $= 6 \frac{u'_a - m}{u'_a - 0{,}2736}$, which formula can also be tabulated with the arguments u'_a, and m, or with u'_a and $(\gamma + \Gamma)$. This has been done in Table C. As u'_a when abbreviated to two places of decimals has only the six values 0.53, 0.54, 0.55, 0.56, 0.57 and 0.58, every column of this Table is calculated for another value of u'_a, whilst to γ the constant 5 has been added so that all values in the first Table may be positive. Instead of giving u'_a directly, its last cipher is given as tenths to the value of $(\gamma + \Gamma)$ so that there is no need for ascertaining the value of u'_a.

Of all elements, then, given by the *Canon* we want only the following ones;—

Date of eclipse, and Greenwich mean time of conjunction in longitude.

L′ = longitude of sun and moon.
P (only indication if P is near 0° or near 180°).
u'_a = radius of shadow.
γ = shortest distance of shadow's centre from earth's centre.
μ = Sun's hour-angle at Greenwich at the moment of this shortest distance.

(There is no necessity for attempting any further explanation of all the other elements and formulæ noted above, which would be impossible without going into the whole theory of eclipses. Such an attempt is not called for in a work of this kind.)

These elements are given in Table A in the following form:—

Column 1. Date of eclipse,—year, month, and day; Old Style till 2 September, 1752 A.D., New Style from 14 September, 1752.

Column 2. Lanka time of conjunction in longitude, counted from mean sunrise in hours and minutes.

Column 3. L = longitude of sun and moon in degrees, when P is near 0°; or longitude of sun and moon plus 400°, when P is near 180°; so that numbers in this column under 360° give directly the value of this longitude, and indicate that P is near 0°, or that the moon is in the ascending node, whilst numbers over 400° must be diminished by 400 when it is desired to ascertain this longitude. At the same time these last indicate that P is near 180°, that is that the moon is in the descending node.

Column 4. μ = Sun's hour-angle at Greenwich at the moment of shortest distance of shadow's centre from earth.

Column 5. $\gamma' =$ ten times the second decimal cipher of $u'_a + 5 + \gamma$. So the tenths of the numbers of this column give the last cipher of u'_a, whose first ciphers are 0.5, and the rest of the number diminished by 5 gives the value of γ.

For instance; the line 975 II 14, 0 h 52 m, 730°, 202°, 74.66 shows that on the 14th February, A.D. 975, the conjunction took place at 0 h 52 m after mean Lanka sunrise, that the longitude of sun and moon was 330° (the moon in the descending node), $\mu = 202°$, $u'_a = 0{,}57$, and $\gamma = -0{,}34$.

Use of the Tables.

Table A gives, in the first column, the year, month, and day of all eclipses visible in any part of India, or quite close to the frontiers of India. The frontiers are purposely taken on rather too large a scale, but this is a fault on the right side. The letters appended shew the kind of eclipse; "a" stands for annular, "t" for total, "p" for partial. Eclipses of the last kind are visible only as very slight ones in India and are therefore not of much importance.[1] When the letter is in brackets the meaning is that the eclipse was only visible quite on the frontiers or even beyond them, and was without importance. When the letter is marked with an asterisk it shews that the eclipse was either total or annular in India or close to it, and is therefore one of greater importance. The second column shews, in hours and minutes counted from mean sunrise at Lanka, the time of conjunction in longitude. This column serves only as an indication as to whether the eclipse took place in the morning or afternoon; for the period of the greatest phase at any particular place may differ very sensibly from the time thus given, and must in every case be determined from Table D, if required. The third, fourth, and fifth columns, headed respectively L, μ, and γ', furnish the arguments for the following Tables B, C, and D, by which can be found the magnitude and the moment of the greatest phase of the eclipse at a particular place.

[1] But see Art. 40*a*, p. 23, paragraph 2, Professor Jacobi's remarks on eclipses mentioned in Indian inscriptions. [R. S.]

Table B (as well as Table D) consists of seventy-two different Tables, each of which is calculated for a particular value of L taken in tens of degrees. Each of these little tables is a table with a double argument, giving the value of γ''. The arguments are, vertically the latitude ϕ, and horizontally the longitude λ of the given place, the latter being stated in degrees from Greenwich and augmented by the value of μ given in Table A. The reader selects that table which is nearest to the value of L given by Table A, and determines from it, by interpolation with the arguments ϕ and $\lambda+\mu$, the value of γ''. If a greater degree of accuracy is desired, it is necessary to determine, with the arguments ϕ and $\lambda+\mu$, the value of γ'' by both tables preceding and following the given value of L, and to interpolate between the two values of γ'' so found.

The final value of γ'' is added to the value of γ' given by Table A, and this value of $\gamma' + \gamma''$ serves as argument for Table C, which gives directly the magnitude of the greatest phase at the given place in digits, or twelfths of the sun's diameter.

Table D is arranged just like Table B, and gives, with the arguments ϕ and $\lambda+\mu$, the moment of the greatest phase at the given place in ghaṭikâs and their tenths, counted from true sunrise at the given place.

The first value in each line of Tables B and D corresponds to a moment before sunrise and the last value in each line to a moment after sunset. Both values are given only for purposes of interpolation. Therefore in both cases the *greatest phase* is invisible when $\lambda + \mu$ coincides exactly with the first or last value of the line, and still more so when it is less than the first or greater than the last value. But in both cases, when the difference between $\lambda + \mu$ and the last value given does not exceed 15 degrees, it is possible that in the given place the *end* of the eclipse might have been visible after sunrise, or the *beginning* of the eclipse before sunset. As the tables give only the time for the greatest phase this question must be decided by direct calculation.

EXAMPLES.

EXAMPLE 1. Was the eclipse of the 20th June, A.D. 540, visible at Jâlna, whose latitude ϕ, is 19° 48′ N., and whose longitude, λ, is 75° 54′ E.?

Table A gives: 540 VI 20, 7 h 57 m L = 490 $\mu = 314°$ $\gamma' = 35{,}34$

Jâlna has $\phi = 20°$, and . . . . $\lambda = 76°$

$\lambda+\mu = 30°$

Table B. L = 490 gives, with $\phi = 20°$ and $\lambda + \mu = 30°$, ... $\gamma'' = 0{,}86$

$\gamma'+\gamma'' = 36{,}20$

Table C gives, with γ' $\gamma'' = 36{,}20$, the magnitude of the greatest phase as nearly 8 digits.

Table D. L = 490 gives, with $\phi = 20°$ and $\lambda+\mu = 30°$, for the moment of the greatest phase, 24.8 ghaṭikâs or 24 gh. 48 pa. after true sunrise at Jâlna.

EXAMPLE 2. Was the same eclipse visible at Multân, whose latitude ϕ is 30° 13′ N., and whose longitude, λ, is 71° 26′ E.?

Table A gives: A.D. 540 VI 20, 7 h.57 m. L = 490. $\mu = 314°$ $\gamma' = 35{,}34$

Multan has $\phi = 30°$ and . . . . $\lambda = 71°$

$\lambda + \mu = 25°$

Table B. L = 490 gives, with $\phi = 30°$ and $\lambda + \mu = 25°$. . . . $\gamma'' = 0{,}76$ (diff. between 0.80 and 0.72)

$\gamma' + \gamma'' = 36{,}10$

Table C gives, with $\gamma' + \gamma'' = 36{,}10$, the magnitude of the greatest phase as exactly 10 digits.

Table D. L = 490 gives, with $\phi = 30°$ and $\lambda + \mu = 25°$, for the moment of the greatest phase, 24,0 ghaṭikâs, or 24 gh. 0 pa. after true sunrise at Multân.

EXAMPLE 3. Was the eclipse of the 7th June, A.D. 913, visible at Trivandrum, whose latitude, ϕ, is 8° 30′ N., and longitude, λ, 76° 56′ E.?

Table A gives: 913 VI 7, 8 h.35 m.	L = 480	$\mu = 323°$	$\gamma' = 44{,}98$
Trivandrum has, $\phi = 8°$ and		$\lambda = 77°$	
		$\lambda + \mu = 40°$	
Table B. L = 480 gives, with $\phi = 8°$ and $\lambda + \mu = 40°$, ...			$\gamma'' = 1{,}02$
			$\gamma' + \gamma'' = 46{,}00$

Table C shews, with $\gamma' + \gamma'' = 46{,}00$, that the eclipse was total at Trivandrum.

Table D. L = 480 gives, with $\phi = 8°$ and $\lambda + \mu = 40$, for the moment of totality 26,2 ghaṭikâs or 26 gh. 12 pa. after true sunrise at Trivandrum.

EXAMPLE 4. Was the same eclipse visible at Lahore whose latitude, ϕ, is 31° 33′ N., and longitude, λ, 74° 16′ E.?

Table A gives: 913 VI 7, 8 h. 35 m.	L = 480	$\mu = 323°$	$\gamma' = 44{,}98$
Lahore has $\phi = 32°$ and		$\lambda = 74°$	
		$\lambda + \mu = 37°$	
Table B. L = 480 gives, with $\phi = 32°$ and $\lambda + \mu = 37°$, ...			$\gamma'' = 0{,}69$
			$\gamma' + \gamma'' = 45{,}67$

Table C gives, with $\gamma' + \gamma'' = 45{,}67$, the magnitude of the greatest phase 4,8 digits.

Table D. L = 480 gives, with $\phi = 32°$ and $\lambda + \mu = 37°$, for the moment of the greatest phase 26,9 ghaṭikâs, or 26 gh. 54 pa. after true sunrise at Lahore.

In all these examples the value of L (Table A) was divisible by 10, and therefore a special table for this value was found in Table B. When the value of L is not divisible by 10, as will mostly be the case, there is no special table exactly fitting the given value. In such a case we may take the small table in Table B for the value of L nearest to that given. Thus for instance, if L is 233 we may work by the table L = 230, or when L is 487 we may work by the Table L = 490 and proceed as before, but the result will not be very accurate. The better course is to take the value of γ'' from both the table next preceding and the table next following the given value of L, and to fix a value of γ'' between the two.[1] Thus for L = 233 we take the value of γ'' both from Table 230 and from Table 240 and fix its truer value from the two. But where the only question is whether an eclipse was visible at a given place and there is no necessity to ascertain its magnitude, the first process is sufficient.

EXAMPLE 5. Was the eclipse of the 15 January, A.D. 1032, visible at Karâchi, whose latitude, ϕ, is 24° 53′ N., and longitude, λ, 66° 57′ E.?

Table A gives 1032 I 15, 10 h.1 m.	L = 701	$\mu = 342°$	$\gamma' = 45{,}46$
Karâchi has $\phi = 25°$, and		$\lambda + 67°$	
		$\lambda + \mu = 49°$	
Table B. L = 700 gives, with $\phi = 25°$ and $\lambda + \mu = 49°$ . . . $\gamma'' = 0{,}63$; Table B. L = 710 ,, ,, ,, ,, ,, ,, . . . $\gamma'' = 0{,}69$; or[1] for L 701 . .			$\gamma'' = 0{,}64$
			$\gamma' + \gamma'' = 46{,}10$

[1] Here the auxiliary table to Tables VI. and VII. above may be used. [R. S.]

Table C gives, with $\gamma' + \gamma'' = 46,10$, the magnitude of the greatest phase as 10,0 digits.
Table D. L 700 gives, with $\phi = 25$ and $\lambda + \mu = 49°$, ... 25,7 ⎫
Table D. L 710 „ „ „ „ „ „ ..... 26,0 ⎭ or for L 701, for the moment of the greatest phase, 25,7 ghaṭikâs, or 25 gh. 42 pa. after true sunrise at Karâchi.

EXAMPLE 6. Was the same eclipse visible at Calcutta, whose latitude, ϕ, is 22° 36′ N., and longitude, λ, 88° 23′ E.?

Table A gives 1032 I 15, 10 h. 1 m. L = 701 $\mu = 342°$ $\gamma' = 45,56$
Calcutta has $\phi = 23°$, and . . . . $\lambda = 88°$

$\lambda + \mu = 70°$

$\lambda + \mu$ is *greater* than the arguments for which values are given in Table B, 700 and 710. This indicates that the greatest phase of the eclipse takes place *after sunset* and is therefore invisible. [1]

EXAMPLE. 7. Was the eclipse of the 31st. December, A.D. 1358, visible at Dhaka, whose latitude, ϕ, is 23° 45′ N., and longitude, λ, 90° 23′ E.?

Table A gives: 1358 XII 31, 1 h. 28 m. L = 288 $\mu = 213°$ $\gamma' = 45,48$
Dhaka has $\phi = 24°$, and . . . . $\lambda = 90°$

$\lambda + \mu = 303°$

Table B. L 280 gives, with $\phi = 24°$ and $\lambda + \mu$ 303°, .. $\gamma'' = 0,42$ ⎫
Table B. L 290 „ „ „ „ „ „ „ $\gamma'' = 0,35$ ⎭, or for L 288 ... $\gamma'' = 0,36$

$\gamma' + \gamma'' = 45,84$

Table C gives, with $\gamma' + \gamma'' = 45,84$, the magnitude of the greatest phase as 8,5 digits.
Table D. L 280 gives, with $\phi = 24°$ and $\lambda + \mu = 303°$, .. 0,0 ⎫
Table D. L 290 „ „ „ „ „ „ ... 0,2 ⎭, or for L 288, for the moment of the greatest phase 0,2 ghaṭikâs, or 0 gh. 12 pa. after true sunrise at Dhaka.

EXAMPLE 8. Was the same eclipse visible at Bombay whose latitude, ϕ, is 18° 57′ N., and longitude, λ, 72° 51′ E.?

Table A gives: 1358 XII 31, 1 h. 28 m. L = 288° $\mu = 213°$ $\gamma' = 45,48$
Bombay has $\phi = 19°$ . . . . $\lambda = 73°$

$\lambda + \mu = 286°$

$\lambda + \mu$ is *less* than the arguments for which there are values given in Table B 280 and B 290. This indicates that the greatest phase of the eclipse took place *before sunrise* and was therefore invisible. [2]

EXAMPLE 9. Was the eclipse of the 7th June, A.D. 1415, visible at Śrînagar, whose latitude, ϕ, is 34° 6′ N., and longitude, λ, = 74° 55′ E.?

Table A gives: 1415 VI 7, 6 h. 14 m. L = 484 $\mu = 289°$ $\gamma' = 35,58$
Srînagar has $\phi = 34°$, and . . . . $\lambda = 75°$

$\lambda + \mu = 4°$

Table B 480 gives, with $\phi = 34°$ and $\lambda + \mu = 4°$, ... $\gamma'' = 0,81$ ⎫
Table B 490 „ „ „ „ „ „ „ .... $\gamma'' = 0,82$ ⎭, or for L 484 .. $\gamma'' = 0,81$

$\gamma' + \gamma'' = 36,39$

Table C gives, with $\gamma' + \gamma'' = 36,39$, the magnitude of the greatest phase as 3,3 digits.

1 For the visibility of the *beginning* of the eclipse see page 111.
2 For the visibility of the *end* of the eclipse see page 111.

Table D 480 gives, with $\phi = 34°$ and $\lambda + \mu = 4°$, . . . 18,8 ⎫
Table D 490 „ „ „ „ „ „ „ . . . 18,9 ⎭, or for L 484, for the moment of the greatest phase 18,8 ghaṭikâs, or 18 gh. 48 pa. after true sunrise at Śrînagar.

EXAMPLE 10. Was the same eclipse visible at Madras, whose latitude, ϕ, = 13° 5′ N., and longitude, λ, 80° 17′ E.?

Table A gives: 1415 VI 7, 6 h. 14 m. L = 484 $\mu = 289°$ $\gamma' = 35{,}58$
Madras has $\phi = 13°$, and . . . . $\lambda = 80°$
$\lambda + \mu = 9°$

Table B. L 480 gives, with $\phi = 13°$ and $\lambda + \mu = 9°$, ... $\gamma'' = 1{,}15$ ⎫
Table B. L 490 „ „ „ „ „ „ „ . . . . $\gamma'' = 1{,}14$ ⎭, or for L 484 . . . $\gamma'' = 1{,}14$
$\gamma' + \gamma'' = 36{,}72$

$\gamma' + \gamma''$ is greater than the values contained in Table C.

This indicates that Madras is too much to the south to see the eclipse.

EXAMPLE 11. Was the eclipse of the 20th August, A.D. 1495, visible at Madras, whose latitude, ϕ, is 13° 5′ N., and longitude, λ, 80° 17′ E.?

Table A gives: 1495 VIII 20, 4 h. 55 m L = 155 $\mu = 269°$ $\gamma' = 54{,}62$
Madras has $\phi = 13°$ and . . . . $\lambda = 80°$
$\lambda + \mu = 349°$

Table B. L 150 gives, with $\phi = 13°$ and $\lambda + \mu = 349°$, $\gamma'' = 1{,}05$ ⎫
Table B. L 160 „ „ „ „ „ „ $\gamma'' = 1{,}01$ ⎭, or for L 155 . . . $\gamma'' = 1{,}03$
$\gamma' + \gamma'' = 55{,}65$

Table C gives, with $\gamma' + \gamma'' = 55{,}65$, the magnitude of the greatest phase as 4,4 digits.

Table D. L 150 gives, with $\phi = 13°$ and $\gamma + \mu = 349°$; . . 12,1 ⎫
Table D. L 160 „ „ „ „ „ „ . . 11,8 ⎭ or for L 155, for the greatest phase 12.0 ghaṭikâs, or 12 gh. 0 pa. after true sunrise at Madras.

EXAMPLE 12. Was the same eclipse visible at Śrînagar whose latitude, ϕ, = 34° 6′ N., and longitude, λ, 74° 55′ E.?

Table A gives: 1495 VIII 20, 4 h. 55 m. L = 155 $\mu = 269°$ $\gamma' = 54{,}62$
Śrînagar has $\phi = 34°$ . . . . $\lambda = 75°$
$\lambda + \mu = 344°$

Table B. L 150 gives, with $\phi = 34°$ and $\gamma + \mu = 344°$, $\gamma'' = 0{,}72$ ⎫
Table B. L 160 „ „ „ „ . . . . . . $\gamma'' = 0{,}69$ ⎭, or for L 155 . . $\gamma'' = 0{,}71$
$\gamma' + \gamma'' = 55{,}33$

$\gamma' + \gamma''$ is less than the values contained in Table C.

This indicates that Śrînagar is too much to the north to see the eclipse.

It was intended that these tables should be accompanied by maps shewing the centre-lines, across the continent of India, of all eclipses of the sun between A.D. 300 and 1900, but it has not been found possible to complete them in time, owing to the numerous calculations that have to be made in order that the path of the shadow may be exactly marked in each case. Such maps would plainly be of considerable value as a first approximation, and I hope to be able soon to publish them separately.

Vienna, November, 1895. R. SCHRAM.

TABLE A.

te A. D.	Lanka time of conjunction measured from sunrise.	L.	μ.	γ'.		Date A. D.	Lanka time of conjunction measured from sunrise.	L.	μ.	γ'.		Date A. D.	Lanka time of conjunction measured from sunrise.	L.	μ.	γ'.	
IV 25	6 h. 6 m.	434	288	45.46	t*	361 VIII 17	4 h. 12 m.	144	254	66.00	a	415 IX 19	2 h. 27 m.	176	230	65.85	a
II 22	7 12	733	301	76.10	p	363 I 1	23 52	682	191	75.38	a	418 VII 19	10 8	116	344	45.35	t*
VIII 7	4 19	134	259	64.72	a*	364 VI 16	11 58	85	13	45.57	t	419 XII 3	1 29	652	221	46.15	(p)
I 31	2 4	712	220	44.62	(t)	365 VI 6	0 46	75	203	56.38	(p)	421 XI 11	6 41	630	297	54.81	(a)
VII 27	6 26	123	288	75.47	a	367 X 10	5 15	597	275	54.77	t	425 III 6	7 29	347	302	55.29	a*
VI 5	4 30	74	265	44.27	t	368 IV 3	22 27	15	168	55.90	a	425 VIII 29	9 45	556	340	44.84	(t)
XI 29	23 27	649	189	75.36	(a)	370 VIII 8	0 40	535	205	65.45	a	426 VIII 19	1 43	546	217	34.14	t
XI 8	0 12	626	198	74.01	(a)	371 II 2	7 32	314	302	55.38	a*	427 VII 10	9 16	508	335	45.98	t
IX 7	4 44	564	265	44.69	t	372 VII 17	2 23	514	227	33.96	(p)	429 XII 12	3 23	262	243	45.87	t
III 2	23 49	343	185	56.06	p	373 VI 7	11 32	476	10	45.75	t	432 IV 16	10 44	427	355	34.91	t
VII 6	3 48	503	252	65.24	a*	374 XI 20	9 6	239	333	45.21	t	432 X 10	8 28	198	324	75.12	a
XII 31	6 18	281	285	55.41	a*	375 XI 10	0 38	228	205	45.87	t	433 IX 29	10 12	187	347	65.82	a*
IV 25	1 40	435	219	54.76	a	378 IX 8	10 6	166	346	75.23	a	434 II 25	4 24	738	260	66.15	(p)
X 18	6 57	206	301	45.23	t	379 VIII 28	11 27	155	3	65.94	a	435 II 14	7 8	727	298	75.46	a*
II 11	10 32	723	347	44.64	t	380 I 24	4 28	705	260	66.07	p	435 VIII 10	1 37	137	219	34.55	t
XII 22	3 18	671	246	66.03	p	381 I 12	7 52	694	310	75.39	a*	436 II 3	6 45	715	290	74.76	a
XII 11	7 37	660	310	75.37	a	381 VII 8	2 32	106	232	34.74	t	438 XII 3	2 10	652	229	45.49	t*
VI 6	4 2	74	256	34.96	t*	382 I 1	7 6	682	298	74.71	a	440 V 17	3 26	57	245	45.61	t
X 9	5 38	596	284	46.12	p	383 XI 11	7 43	630	316	46.15	p	442 IX 20	6 40	578	298	65.64	a
III 25	2 16	4	226	75.29	a	385 IV 25	22 52	36	178	65.08	a	446 I 13	7 45	295	308	54.49	a
III 13	7 29	353	301	56.01	(p)	386 IV 15	5 47	25	279	55.83	t	446 VII 10	1 30	508	217	65.32	a*
II 1	9 41	313	338	44.02	(t)	387 III 6	10 47	346	355	43.94	(p)	447 VI 29	3 48	497	250	74.55	a
VII 28	8 18	525	321	76.09	p	388 VIII 18	7 55	546	314	65.51	a*	449 V 8	2 24	448	233	45.73	t
I 22	1 47	303	218	44.70	(t)	392 VI 7	5 14	476	274	55.07	a*	454 VIII 10	1 11	138	210	45.23	t*
VII 17	10 38	514	354	65.31	a	393 V 27	8 38	466	323	74.29	(a)	455 VII 30	11 31	127	3	66.03	p
V 6	8 41	445	325	54.83	a*	393 XI 20	9 30	239	337	45.87	t	457 VI 8	1 32	78	219	64.75	a
X 19	7 4	206	301	45.89	t	395 IV 6	4 12	416	258	45.54	t*	457 XII 2	23 55	653	194	54.81	a
III 4	5 11	744	269	55.40	t*	399 VII 19	10 9	116	346	34.68	(t)	458 V 28	10 35	67	353	45.53	t
VI 6	4 38	75	263	45.64	t	400 VII 8	2 43	106	233	45.42	t*	459 V 18	1 48	57	220	36.24	(p)
IV 15	8 33	26	324	74.47	a	402 V 18	4 5	57	259	74.23	(a)	459 X 12	10 42	600	2	76.42	(p)
X 9	6 16	597	292	45.45	t*	402 XI 11	8 26	630	325	45.49	t	460 IV 7	11 11	19	3	44.44	(t)
IV 4	9 14	15	331	65.22	a*	403 V 7	5 34	46	279	65.00	a*	461 III 27	22 36	8	171	55.19	a
II 2	10 22	314	346	44.68	t*	407 II 23	23 40	336	184	55.32	a	461 IX 20	1 54	578	224	44.92	t*
VII 17	3 13	514	241	44.61	t	407 VIII 19	1 54	546	222	44.79	t*	462 III 17	2 52	358	232	75.96	a
I 11	5 9	292	265	76.14	p	408 II 13	4 44	325	258	76.09	p	464 VII 20	8 18	518	319	65.40	a*
V 28	4 15	466	261	45.68	t	409 VI 29	2 1	497	227	45.91	(t)	465 I 13	5 16	295	269	45.19	t
XI 9	0 18	228	201	45.22	t	410 VI 18	11 59	487	15	65.16	a	465 VII 9	10 14	507	346	74.63	(a)
III 26	5 11	406	274	66.23	(p)	410 XII 12	2 49	262	236	45.21	t	467 V 19	9 42	458	343	45.80	t
IX 9	2 3	166	227	64.55	a	413 X 11	0 55	199	213	74.45	a	467 XI 13	0 47	232	211	74.40	a
III 4	3 5	744	236	44.70	(t)	414 IV 6	2 59	417	238	34.85	t	468 V 8	1 58	448	225	35.04	t
VIII 28	2 59	155	238	75.28	a*	414 IX 30	0 52	187	209	75.15	a	468 XI 1	0 6	221	199	75.08	a

TABLE A.

Date A. D.	Lanka time of conjunction measured from sunrise.		L.	μ.	γ'.		Date A. D.	Lanka time of conjunction measured from sunrise.		L.	μ.	γ'.		Date A. D.	Lanka time of conjunction measured from sunrise.		L.	μ.	γ'.
469 X 21	2 h.	13 m.	209	229	65.77	*a*	519 VIII 11	6 h.	6 m.	539	284	74.86	*a**	567 VII 21	22 h.	49 m.	120	173	35.81
472 VIII 20	8	51	148	326	45.18	*t**	521 VI 20	7	36	490	311	46.02	*p*	568 VI 11	7	6	82	304	44.00
474 I 4	4	10	686	257	46.15	*p*	521 XII 15	1	9	266	213	74.38	(*a*)	569 XI 24	5	30	645	279	45.01
475 VI 19	8	14	88	319	64.67	*a*	522 VI 10	0	27	480	203	35.26	*t**	572 IX 23	3	11	582	246	75.75
475 XII 14	8	32	264	322	64.81	*a*	522 XII 4	0	14	254	199	75.06	*a*	573 III 19	7	36	1	306	35.03
479 IV 8	5	54	19	282	55.13	*a*	523 XI 23	3	9	243	242	65.74	*a*	573 IX 12	3	11	571	243	75.04
479 X 1	10	12	589	349	44.95	(*t*)	526 IX 22	8	30	181	323	55.05	*t*	574 III 9	0	14	350	193	45.74
480 IX 20	2	8	579	226	44.26	*t*	528 II 6	6	15	719	287	46.19	(*p*)	574 IX 1	5	32	560	276	64.31
481 VIII 11	7	24	539	307	56.19	(*p*)	529 VII 21	4	46	119	266	64.44	*a*	576 VII 11	22	59	511	179	35.48
484 I 14	5	57	296	278	45.86	*t*	530 I 15	10	5	698	341	64.83	*a*	577 I 5	0	33	288	200	75.04
485 XI 23	8	53	243	332	74.40	(*a*)	531 VI 30	7	40	99	307	35.95	(*t*)	577 XII 25	4	36	276	260	65.73
486 V 19	9	30	459	338	35.11	*t**	532 XI 12	23	45	633	195	65.72	(*a*)	580 X 24	9	12	214	336	54.99
486 XI 12	8	4	232	318	75.07	*a*	533 V 10	2	59	50	241	64.91	*a*	583 VIII 23	2	25	151	232	54.25
487 V 9	2	31	449	232	44.37	(*t*)	534 IV 29	6	10	40	286	75.69	*a*	584 II 17	10	37	731	349	64.88
487 XI 1	10	25	220	352	65.76	*a*	534 X 23	3	43	612	252	44.32	*t*	585 VIII 1	6	31	130	289	35.75
488 III 29	2	49	410	239	66.30	(*p*)	535 IX 13	6	21	571	294	56.34	(*p*)	586 XII 16	1	30	667	218	55.72
489 III 18	4	59	759	269	75.60	*a**	538 II 15	7	43	329	304	45.81	*t*	587 VI 11	23	13	82	184	64.66
489 IX 11	1	39	169	221	44.41	*t*	539 XII 26	9	14	277	333	74.38	*a*	588 V 31	1	30	71	216	75.44
490 III 7	5	21	748	271	74.87	*a*	540 VI 20	7	57	490	314	35.34	*t**	589 V 20	2	47	61	234	66.18
491 II 24	10	57	737	352	54.15	(*a*)	540 XII 14	8	21	265	319	75.05	*a*	589 X 15	6	21	604	297	66.44
491 VIII 21	1	50	148	219	65.91	(*a*)	541 VI 10	0	36	480	203	44.58	*t*	590 X 4	10	45	593	0	75.78
493 I 4	4	46	686	265	45.50	*t**	543 IV 20	1	27	431	219	75.80	*a*	591 IX 23	10	31	582	354	75.08
494 VI 19	0	56	88	208	45.37	*t**	543 X 14	2	49	202	241	44.33	*t*	592 III 19	8	15	1	314	4[illegible].70
496 X 22	6	55	611	303	65.70	*t**	544 IV 8	2	45	420	235	65.04	*a*	594 I 27	9	1	310	327	74.33
500 II 15	8	37	328	321	54.44	*t*	545 III 28	10	6	409	342	54.29	*t*	594 VII 23	6	35	522	293	35.55
501 VII 30	23	21	528	183	74.79	*a*	545 IX 22	0	9	181	196	65.78	*a*	595 I 16	8	33	299	319	75.03
502 VII 20	1	3	518	206	64.05	(*a*)	547 II 6	6	41	719	291	45.55	*t**	596 XII 25	0	39	277	199	46.35
503 VI 10	0	17	479	202	45.95	*t*	548 VII 20	22	55	119	176	45.15	*t*	598 V 10	23	17	452	186	65.26
505 V 19	9	57	459	343	44.44	*t*	549 XII 5	2	55	656	243	76.46	(*p*)	599 IV 30	8	19	441	319	44.48
506 XI 1	4	44	221	265	56.38	(*p*)	550 XI 24	8	17	644	323	65.72	*a**	601 III 10	7	24	752	304	45.64
508 IX 11	0	30	170	202	55.09	*t*	551 V 21	9	48	61	343	64.83	*a**	604 I 7	3	30	689	248	76.47
509 VIII 31	9	8	159	329	65.86	*a*	554 III 19	8	28	0	321	44.34	*t*	604 XII 26	10	7	678	346	55.72
512 I 5	1	39	686	216	64.82	*a*	555 III 8	23	31	350	184	45.07	*t*	605 VI 22	5	52	92	284	64.58
512 VI 29	8	11	98	316	45.30	*t**	559 VI 21	7	54	490	312	44.66	*t*	606 VI 11	7	52	82	312	75.35
513 VI 19	0	11	88	195	36.02	*p*	560 XII 3	7	0	254	297	56.36	(*p*)	608 IV 20	7	19	32	307	44.17
514 V 10	9	24	50	338	44.23	*t*	561 IV 30	8	1	441	318	75.87	*a*	609 IV 9	23	24	22	185	34.92
515 X 23	3	12	611	246	44.99	*t**	562 IV 19	9	40	431	340	65.11	*a**	613 VII 23	5	52	522	281	44.87
516 IV 17	23	33	29	185	75.77	*a*	562 X 14	0	52	203	210	55.00	*a**	616 V 21	6	3	462	287	65.34
517 IV 7	0	1	19	190	76.50	(*p*)	563 X 3	7	50	192	312	75.75	*a**	616 XI 15	2	8	236	229	64.97
518 VIII 22	5	13	550	274	65.60	*a*	566 II 6	2	35	720	228	64.86	*a*	617 XI 4	7	35	225	309	75.70
519 II 15	6	58	328	294	45.14	*t**	566 VIII 1	6	27	130	290	45.09	*t**	618 III 31	23	22	413	187	36.37

TABLE A.

Date A. D.	Lanka time of conjunction measured from sunrise.	*L.*	*μ.*	*γ'.*		Date A. D.	Lanka time of conjunction measured from sunrise.	*L.*	*μ.*	*γ'.*		Date A. D.	Lanka time of conjunction measured from sunrise.	*L.*	*μ.*	*γ'.*	
618 X 24	7 h. 21 m.	213	304	76.39	(*p*)	663 V 12	22 h. 21 m.	54	171	34.72	(*t*)	714 VIII 14	23 h. 4 m.	144	180	74.86	*a*
620 III 10	2 10	752	224	64.96	*a*	665 IV 21	3 1	33	237	56.28	(*p*)	715 VIII 4	1 57	134	221	65.61	*a*
620 IX 2	5 48	162	282	44.93	*t**	667 VIII 25	4 25	554	260	55.05	*t**	716 VII 23	12 2	123	10	46.32	(*p*)
623 XII 27	8 9	678	315	45.02	*t*	670 VI 23	2 20	493	231	55 58	*a*	719 V 23	23 57	65	192	56.07	*p*
624 XII 15	23 58	668	192	44.35	*t*	670 XII 18	3 46	270	250	64.97	*a*	721 IX 26	3 55	586	256	55.18	*t**
626 X 26	2 18	615	235	75.83	*a*	671 XII 7	7 58	258	313	75.68	*a**	724 VII 24	23 13	525	183	55.80	*a*
627 IV 21	7 8	33	302	34.86	*t**	672 VI 1	5 36	473	277	34.05	(*t*)	725 I 19	5 0	303	266	64.94	*a*
627 X 15	1 42	604	223	75.14	*a**	672 XI 25	7 13	247	301	86.36	*p*	725 VII 14	11 19	514	3	45.01	*t*
628 IV 9	23 54	23	191	45.60	*t*	674 IV 12	0 13	424	198	65.12	*a*	726 I 8	8 17	292	313	75.66	*a*
628 X 3	4 39	593	265	64.43	*a*	674 X 5	6 28	195	294	44.83	*t*	726 VII 4	4 3	504	253	34.27	*t*
630 VIII 13	22 3	543	166	35.67	*t*	678 I 28	10 25	712	346	45.04	*t*	726 XII 28	7 28	280	300	76 33	(*p*)
631 II 7	0 17	321	194	74.99	*a*	678 VII 24	9 38	123	337	75.01	*a**	727 V 25	12 9	466	21	46.09	(*p*)
632 I 27	5 47	310	275	55.69	*a**	679 VII 13	12 4	113	12	65.76	*a*	728 XI 6	8 19	228	323	44.79	*t*
633 VI 12	9 42	483	344	76.21	(*p*)	680 XI 27	2 17	649	233	85.87	*a*	729 X 27	0 17	217	201	45.46	*t*
634 XI 26	10 40	247	356	64.97	(*a*)	681 V 23	5 52	64	284	34.65	*t*	732 VIII 25	6 0	155	285	74.80	*a*
637 III 31	23 7	414	182	45.74	*t*	681 XI 16	1 28	637	220	75.19	*a**	733 VIII 14	9 7	144	329	65.55	*a**
637 IX 24	1 32	183	222	54.13	(*a*)	682 V 12	22 27	54	171	45.40	*t*	734 XII 30	2 29	682	232	85.89	*a*
638 III 21	9 41	403	338	65.00	*a**	682 XI 5	5 10	626	274	64.49	(*a*)	735 VI 25	4 17	96	260	34.43	*t*
639 IX 3	6 14	162	287	35.59	*t*	686 II 28	6 8	343	281	55.61	*t*	735 XII 19	1 54	671	223	75.20	*a**
641 I 17	3 12	700	241	55.73	*a**	688 VII 3	9 12	504	334	55.66	*a*	737 X 28	7 17	619	311	46.54	(*p*)
642 XII 27	8 50	679	324	44.35	(*t*)	692 IV 22	7 15	435	304	65.19	*a**	740 IV 1	5 25	15	273	45.47	*t**
643 VI 21	22 36	92	171	65.93	*a*	693 IV 11	9 48	424	339	74.43	*a*	742 VIII 5	6 25	535	292	55.86	*a*
643 XI 17	7 15	638	310	66.48	(*p*)	693 X 5	7 6	195	302	45.50	*t**	746 V 25	3 39	466	251	65.43	*a*
644 XI 5	10 14	626	354	75.85	*a**	695 II 19	4 13	733	255	55.78	*t**	747 V 14	5 32	456	277	74.66	*a*
645 X 25	9 30	615	341	75.16	*a*	697 I 28	11 4	712	354	44.37	*t*	747 XI 7	9 1	228	332	45.45	*t**
646 IV 21	7 32	33	306	45.54	*t*	698 XII 8	10 23	660	353	85.87	(*a*)	749 III 23	4 11	406	258	45.89	*t*
648 II 29	7 38	343	307	74.24	*a*	699 XI 27	9 34	648	340	75.19	*a*	753 I 9	10 28	693	351	85.90	(*a*)
648 VIII 24	5 57	553	285	35.72	*t*	700 V 23	5 47	65	281	45.33	(*t*)	753 XII 29	10 3	682	344	75.21	*a*
649 II 17	7 58	332	310	74.96	*a**	702 IV 2	4 52	15	269	74.07	*a*	754 VI 25	3 31	96	247	45.10	*t**
650 VIII 3	5 38	533	275	64.21	(*a*)	702 IX 26	6 21	586	294	45.84	*t*	756 X 28	7 51	619	318	45.91	*t*
651 I 27	2 48	310	229	46.32	*p*	703 III 22	6 16	4	287	64.83	*a*	757 IV 23	3 30	36	249	64.63	*a*
651 XII 18	7 30	269	308	44.29	*t*	704 IX 4	3 3	565	239	64.38	*a*	758 X 7	1 35	597	219	74.50	*a*
653 VI 1	6 5	473	286	44.71	*t**	705 II 28	4 4	343	249	46.24	*p*	759 IV 2	4 14	15	254	36.11	(*p*)
653 XI 25	23 48	247	191	75.68	(*a*)	705 VII 25	11 40	525	12	76.53	(*p*)	760 II 21	11 5	336	359	44.20	(*t*)
655 IV 12	6 46	424	298	45.80	*t*	706 I 19	9 46	303	339	44.27	*t*	761 VIII 5	2 25	535	230	45.14	*t**
658 IX 3	5 51	163	279	46.29	*p*	707 VII 4	3 56	504	252	44.94	*t**	762 I 30	0 4	314	189	75.63	*a*
659 VII 25	1 57	124	224	64.33	*a*	707 XII 29	0 14	281	194	75.67	*a*	763 I 18	23 27	303	178	76.31	(*p*)
660 I 18	1 45	701	217	45.03	*t*	709 V 14	4 57	456	272	46.01	(*p*)	764 VI 4	10 17	477	351	65.51	*a**
660 VII 13	3 5	113	239	75.09	*a**	710 X 26	23 35	217	192	44.80	*t*	764 XI 28	2 0	250	227	44.78	*t*
661 VII 2	5 18	102	271	65.84	*a*	712 X 5	6 3	195	285	56.20	*p*	766 XI 7	7 13	229	303	56.17	*p*
662 V 23	5 31	64	281	43.97	(*p*)	714 II 19	3 27	734	242	45.09	*t**	767 IV 3	11 56	417	15	45.94	(*t*)

TABLE A.

Date A. D.	Lanka time of conjunction measured from sunrise.	L.	μ.	γ'.		Date A. D.	Lanka time of conjunction measured from sunrise.	L.	μ.	γ'.		Date A. D.	Lanka time of conjunction measured from sunrise.	L.	μ.	γ'.	
768 III 23	4 h. 2 m.	406	254	35.20	t*	815 IX 7	1 h. 59 m.	568	226	45.29	t	861 III 15	7 h. 50 m.	759	313	76.08	(p)
769 IX 4	23 55	166	192	65.44	a	816 III 2	22 42	347	170	75.53	(a)	862 III 4	9 21	748	332	65.34	a*
770 VIII 25	10 53	155	354	46.14	p	817 II 19	22 41	336	167	76.23	(p)	862 VIII 28	23 40	159	190	54.71	t
772 VII 5	10 45	106	355	45.03	t	818 VII 7	6 1	508	286	65.77	a	863 VIII 18	6 23	149	288	65.47	a*
772 XII 28	23 44	682	187	64.52	a	818 XII 31	4 41	284	263	44.77	(t)	864 VIII 6	7 20	138	300	76.22	(p)
775 V 4	10 25	46	353	64.56	(a)	819 VI 26	7 4	497	300	75.01	a*	866 VI 16	9 5	88	331	44.97	t*
775 X 29	4 27	619	265	65.25	a*	820 XII 9	8 57	262	326	66.17	p	866 XII 11	1 25	664	215	74.58	a
779 II 21	5 11	336	268	64.88	a	821 V 5	10 39	448	358	46.11	(p)	867 VI 6	1 57	78	222	35.71	t
779 VIII 16	10 8	546	346	45.20	t	822 IV 25	3 31	438	249	35.37	t*	869 X 9	2 49	600	241	45.39	t*
780 II 10	7 45	325	305	75.61	a	823 X 7	23 22	198	187	65.33	a	873 II 1	6 56	317	295	44.74	t
780 VIII 5	2 57	536	236	34.47	t	824 IX 26	11 2	187	359	46.01	p	873 VII 28	2 35	529	233	75.26	a*
781 VI 26	9 28	498	339	56.33	(p)	826 VIII 7	8 40	138	324	54.82	t	874 VII 17	6 9	518	284	54.50	a
782 XII 9	10 54	262	359	44.78	(t)	829 VI 5	6 58	78	301	54.33	a	876 V 27	2 12	470	230	35.58	t
783 XI 29	2 41	251	235	45 45	t*	829 XI 30	5 41	653	282	65.27	a	877 XI 9	0 12	231	200	65.28	a
786 IV 3	11 58	417	14	35.25	(t)	831 V 15	10 57	57	357	35.86	t	878 V 6	4 22	449	258	64.02	(a)
786 IX 27	3 46	187	254	74.66	a	833 III 25	3 53	8	252	64.74	a	880 IX 8	7 20	170	306	54.66	(t)
787 III 24	4 20	407	256	44.52	t	833 IX 17	10 7	578	348	45.33	t	883 VII 8	3 42	109	251	54.10	(a)
787 IX 16	7 34	176	308	65.39	a*	834 III 14	5 55	358	279	75.49	a*	884 I 2	7 1	686	298	65.28	a
789 I 31	2 8	716	225	75.93	a	834 IX 7	2 42	568	234	44.63	(t)*	884 XII 21	9 31	675	335	74.58	a
789 VII 27	2 55	127	239	34.22	t	835 III 3	6 12	346	280	76.19	(p)	885 VI 16	9 24	89	334	35.64	t
790 I 20	2 12	704	224	75.23	a*	836 VII 17	12 39	518	25	65.85	(a)	888 IV 15	2 40	30	234	75.30	a*
791 I 9	8 14	693	313	54.52	(a)	837 XII 31	5 16	284	270	45.44	t*	888 X 9	3 33	601	250	44.72	t
791 VII 6	2 57	106	236	65.75	a	840 V 5	11 9	449	4	35.43	t*	889 IV 4	3 54	19	249	66 03	p
792 XI 19	1 17	641	218	45.93	t	840 X 29	2 57	220	243	74.59	a	890 VIII 19	8 58	550	331	76.07	p
794 V 4	3 49	47	252	45.27	t*	841 IV 25	3 22	439	245	44.69	t	891 VIII 8	9 18	539	334	75.34	a*
796 IX 6	4 53	567	271	56.02	p	841 X 18	7 31	209	310	65.30	a	892 II 2	7 19	318	299	45.41	t*
800 VI 25	23 27	498	188	65.69	a	843 III 5	0 38	748	204	76.03	p	894 VI 7	9 40	480	341	35.65	t
801 VI 15	0 42	487	205	74.92	a	843 VIII 29	2 16	159	231	44.05	(t)	894 XII 1	3 14	254	246	74.56	(a)
802 VI 4	3 3	476	238	64.16	a	844 II 22	1 45	737	217	65.30	a*	895 V 28	1 23	470	216	44.90	t
802 XI 29	0 21	251	198	56.17	(p)	845 II 10	9 20	726	329	54.57	t	895 XI 20	8 42	243	327	65.27	a*
803 IV 25	3 10	438	245	46.05	(p)	845 VIII 6	23 23	138	182	65.53	a	897 IV 5	21 46	420	164	76.19	(p)
806 IX 16	2 50	177	235	46.05	(p)	846 XII 22	3 42	675	251	55.94	t	898 III 26	0 11	410	197	65.43	a
807 II 11	9 47	727	340	75.96	(a)	848 VI 5	1 47	78	221	45.05	t*	899 III 15	9 28	759	333	54.67	t
808 I 31	10 10	715	343	75.25	a*	850 X 9	4 50	600	273	56.11	p	901 I 23	5 46	708	279	55.97	t
808 VII 27	1 18	127	213	44.89	t*	851 IV 5	11 6	19	1	64.68	(a)	902 VII 7	23 49	109	191	44.82	t
809 VII 16	9 42	117	337	65.68	a	853 IX 7	1 31	568	215	53.92	(p)	904 XI 10	6 4	633	291	56.14	p
810 XI 30	10 5	652	349	45.93	(t)	854 II 1	7 23	317	303	54.05	t	905 V 7	7 52	51	315	64.47	a
812 V 14	11 10	57	2	45.20	t*	856 VII 5	23 16	508	181	64.42	(a)	906 IV 26	9 20	40	334	75.22	a*
812 XI 8	1 11	630	214	74.55	a	856 XII 31	2 5	285	220	66.17	p	907 X 10	1 34	601	218	54.01	(a)
813 V 4	3 24	47	244	35.93	t	859 V 6	10 48	449	357	44.76	t	908 III 5	8 9	350	316	43.98	(p)
814 III 25	11 4	8	1	44.07	(t)	860 X 8	3 52	209	253	45.96	t	911 II 2	3 10	318	234	66.15	p

TABLE A.

Date A. D.	Lanka time of conjunction measured from sunrise.	*L.*	μ.	γ'.		Date A. D.	Lanka time of conjunction measured from sunrise.	*L.*	μ.	γ'.		Date A. D.	Lanka time of conjunction measured from sunrise.	*L.*	μ.	γ'.	
913 VI 7	8 h. 35 m.	480	323	44.98	t*	960 V 28	4 h. 45 m.	71	267	74.97	a*	1005 I 13	2 h. 14 m.	299	222	45.90	t
914 XI 20	5 58	243	284	45.93	t	961 V 17	7 27	61	305	65.73	a	1007 V 19	6 55	463	299	45.03	t*
916 IV 5	7 26	420	307	65.48	a	965 III 6	3 0	351	233	66.07	p	1012 VIII 20	5 32	152	274	55.95	t
916 IX 29	23 0	192	183	54.58	(a)	967 VII 10	6 2	512	284	55.21	t*	1014 I 4	1 12	690	211	45.45	t*
917 IX 19	4 0	181	255	75.32	a*	968 XII 22	8 34	277	319	45.92	t	1014 VI 29	23 58	103	194	74.71	(a)
918 IX 8	4 7	170	254	76.04	(p)	970 V 8	4 38	452	267	55.68	a	1015 VI 19	3 46	92	249	55.48	a
920 I 23	23 34	709	185	65.30	(a)	970 XI 1	23 21	225	190	64.52	a	1019 IV 8	1 20	23	212	65.93	a
920 VII 18	7 17	120	303	44.75	t	971 X 22	2 49	214	239	75.22	a*	1021 VIII 11	3 44	543	250	55.42	t
921 I 12	1 34	697	213	74.60	(a)	972 IV 16	8 23	431	318	34.17	(t)	1024 VI 9	1 27	483	219	55.91	a
921 VII 8	0 23	110	198	35.49	t*	972 X 10	2 19	202	229	75.92	a	1024 XII 4	0 24	258	203	64.49	a
923 XI 11	4 47	633	270	45.43	t*	974 II 24	23 24	742	183	65.38	(a)	1025 XI 23	2 36	247	235	75.18	a*
927 III 6	8 14	350	316	44.66	t	974 VIII 20	6 18	152	289	44.57	t	1026 V 19	7 15	463	303	34.37	t
927 VIII 29	23 9	560	183	75.46	a	975 II 14	0 52	730	202	74.66	a	1026 XI 12	1 50	235	222	75.86	a
928 II 24	0 7	340	191	45.37	t	975 VIII 9	23 17	141	182	35.30	t	1027 XI 1	5 37	224	278	66.50	(p)
928 VIII 18	3 34	550	246	54.70	a*	977 XII 13	7 25	667	307	45.44	t*	1028 IX 21	6 27	184	294	44.44	(t)
930 VI 29	0 34	501	204	35.80	t	978 VI 8	11 9	82	2	74.88	a	1029 IX 10	23 2	173	181	45.15	(t)
931 XII 12	1 53	265	222	55.26	a*	978 XII 2	23 2	656	180	44.77	(t)	1032 I 15	10 1	701	342	45.46	t*
935 IV 6	0 58	420	208	44.77	t	980 V 17	0 14	61	195	46.37	(p)	1032 VII 10	6 26	113	291	74.62	a
935 IX 30	11 29	192	8	75.28	(a)	981 IV 7	8 20	22	320	34.52	t	1033 I 4	1 29	690	213	44.78	t
936 IX 18	11 20	180	3	75.99	a	982 III 28	0 11	12	195	45.25	t	1033 VI 29	10 37	102	351	55.40	a*
937 II 13	22 37	731	172	56.01	(p)	982 IX 20	2 22	582	231	54.85	a*	1034 VI 18	22 0	92	161	46.13	p
938 II 3	7 39	720	306	65.32	a*	984 VII 30	23 9	533	183	36.01	(t)	1035 V 10	7 25	54	308	34.32	t
939 I 23	9 27	708	331	74.61	a	986 I 13	3 41	299	245	55.25	t	1036 IV 28	22 56	44	179	45.07	t
939 VII 19	7 57	120	311	35.42	t*	988 V 18	11 35	462	11	55.76	a	1036 X 22	2 38	615	237	54.93	a*
940 VII 7	23 54	110	189	46.19	(p)	988 XI 12	7 39	236	313	64.51	(a)	1039 VIII 22	11 7	554	2	55.48	t
942 V 17	22 21	61	170	75.06	a	989 V 7	23 32	452	188	44.96	t	1040 II 15	4 54	332	263	55.20	t
942 XI 11	5 26	634	278	44.77	t	989 XI 1	10 39	225	357	75.21	(a)	1042 VI 20	8 25	494	323	55.98	a
943 V 7	0 40	50	203	65.81	a*	990 X 21	10 1	213	345	75.89	a	1042 XII 15	8 47	269	327	64.49	a
944 IX 20	6 21	582	295	76.23	p	991 III 18	22 47	403	177	56.12	p	1043 VI 9	21 39	483	160	45.18	t
945 IX 9	6 19	571	292	75.52	a*	992 III 7	7 1	752	298	65.42	a*	1043 XII 4	10 39	258	355	85.18	a
946 III 6	8 17	351	315	45.34	t	993 II 24	8 21	741	315	74.70	a	1044 XI 22	9 53	247	342	75.85	a
948 VII 9	8 2	511	316	35.87	t	993 VIII 20	7 5	152	299	35.24	t*	1045 IV 19	21 32	435	161	56.29	(p)
949 VI 28	22 53	501	177	45.13	t	995 I 4	1 32	689	218	56.14	p	1046 IV 9	4 50	425	268	65.58	a
949 XII 22	10 30	276	350	55.26	a	996 XII 13	7 53	668	312	44.78	t	1047 III 29	5 54	414	281	74.84	a
950 VI 18	7 21	491	302	64.33	a	998 X 23	5 0	615	277	76.33	(p)	1047 IX 22	7 11	184	304	45.11	t
952 IV 26	21 39	441	161	55.61	(a)	999 X 12	4 50	604	272	75.63	a	1048 III 17	7 12	403	298	64.12	(a)
953 IV 16	8 34	431	323	44.83	t*	1000 IV 7	7 54	23	312	45.20	t*	1049 II 5	3 17	723	242	46.17	p
955 II 25	6 49	741	296	56.04	p	1000 IX 30	10 18	593	351	54.89	(a)	1051 I 15	10 12	701	343	44.79	t
958 VII 19	7 13	121	298	46.13	p	1001 IX 19	22 57	582	178	44.18	(t)	1052 XI 24	4 41	648	271	86.37	p
958 XII 13	8 6	667	319	56.14	(p)	1002 VIII 11	6 48	543	298	46.07	p	1053 XI 13	4 41	637	270	75.68	a*
959 VI 9	3 42	82	252	64.21	a	1004 VII 20	3 18	522	241	64.58	a	1054 V 10	6 16	55	289	45.00	t*

TABLE A.

Date A. D.	Lanka time of conjunction measured from sunrise.	L.	μ.	γ'.		Date A. D.	Lanka time of conjunction measured from sunrise.	L.	μ.	γ'.		Date A. D.	Lanka time of conjunction measured from sunrise.	L.	μ.	γ'.	
1054 XI 2	11 h. 0 m.	626	3	54.95	(a)	1107 XII 16	5 h. 22 m.	671	276	75.69	a*	1161 I 28	4 h. 34 m.	715	263	76.43	(p)
1055 X 23	0 9	615	198	44.26	(t)	1108 VI 11	3 46	86	252	44.77	t	1162 I 17	6 8	704	284	65.71	a*
1056 IX 12	6 24	575	295	46.23	(p)	1109 V 31	11 41	75	8	65.57	a	1162 VII 14	0 58	117	209	54.53	t
1058 VIII 21	23 48	554	190	74.79	a	1109 XI 24	2 21	648	230	44.30	(t)	1163 VII 3	7 25	107	303	65.31	a*
1059 II 15	4 8	332	250	45 86	t	1110 X 15	7 3	608	307	46.32	p	1164 VI 21	8 29	96	318	76.08	(p)
1059 VIII 11	0 16	543	194	74.04	(a)	1113 III 19	4 58	5	265	35.75	t	1164 XI 16	8 39	641	330	56.37	p
1061 VI 20	5 0	494	270	35.26	t*	1115 VII 23	3 23	525	245	35.47	t	1166 V 1	11 53	47	14	44.87	(t)
1064 IV 19	11 47	435	13	65.65	(a)	1118 V 22	7 54	467	316	65.89	a	1167 IV 21	4 40	37	263	35.60	t
1064 X 12	23 15	206	188	44.39	t	1118 XI 15	1 18	239	218	44.35	(t)	1168 IX 3	11 39	567	13	56.41	p
1066 IX 22	4 44	185	265	55.82	a	1119 V 11	8 43	456	326	75.13	a*	1169 VIII 24	2 32	557	234	35.65	t
1068 II 6	3 25	723	242	45.48	t*	1120 X 24	4 58	218	270	65.75	a*	1172 I 27	1 32	314	209	56.42	p
1069 VII 21	0 31	123	200	55.24	a*	1122 III 10	4 37	756	262	45.57	t*	1173 VI 12	4 4	487	256	65.39	a
1070 VII 10	12 40	112	20	45.98	t	1123 VIII 22	22 17	155	168	55.05	(t)	1174 VI 1	8 22	477	319	54.61	a
1073 V 9	22 17	55	167	65.73	a	1124 VIII 11	11 16	145	0	45.78	t*	1174 XI 26	6 0	251	284	65.73	a*
1074 IV 29	0 20	44	196	76.50	(p)	1126 VI 22	10 51	96	357	54.69	(t)	1176 IV 11	4 37	428	265	35.71	t
1075 III 19	10 59	4	359	64.37	(a)	1129 IV 20	8 55	36	331	54.21	a	1178 III 21	4 47	407	262	64.21	(a)
1075 IX 13	2 12	575	230	55.59	a	1129 X 15	1 42	608	225	65.69	a	1178 IX 13	10 59	177	359	45.62	t*
1076 IX 1	6 51	565	297	74.85	a	1130 X 4	4 47	597	269	74.98	a*	1180 VII 24	8 5	128	315	54.46	(t)
1079 VII 1	12 24	504	20	35.33	t	1131 IX 23	4 32	586	262	74.27	(a)	1181 I 16	23 19	704	180	54.99	(t)
1079 XII 26	2 47	280	234	85.16	a	1133 VIII 2	11 0	536	359	35.54	t*	1183 V 23	6 9	68	290	54.00	(p)
1080 VI 20	5 41	494	278	34.59	t	1134 I 27	2 34	314	228	75.12	a	1183 XI 17	2 9	641	231	65.74	a
1080 XII 14	2 11	269	224	75.83	a	1134 VII 23	4 12	526	255	34.80	t*	1184 XI 5	3 54	630	256	75.06	a*
1081 XII 3	6 56	258	295	66.47	(p)	1135 I 16	2 35	302	227	75.81	a*	1185 V 1	12 22	47	19	35.53	(t)
1083 X 13	23 52	206	196	45.06	t	1137 XI 15	1 41	240	222	45.02	t*	1185 X 25	3 25	619	247	74.37	a
1086 VIII 12	2 27	145	232	74.39	a	1140 IX 12	23 45	177	194	74.22	a	1187 IX 4	10 30	568	354	35.70	t*
1087 II 6	3 21	723	240	44.81	t	1141 III 10	4 3	756	252	44.90	t	1188 II 29	1 20	347	211	75.04	a
1087 VIII 1	7 39	134	307	55.17	t*	1141 IX 2	5 50	166	282	54.99	t*	1188 VIII 24	3 18	558	244	44.99	t*
1089 VI 11	5 50	86	284	34.11	t	1143 VIII 12	11 52	145	8	36.41	(p)	1189 II 17	2 22	336	224	75.74	a*
1090 XI 24	4 4	648	257	54.96	a	1144 XII 26	6 3	682	283	54.97	t	1190 VII 4	9 47	508	343	66.23	p
1091 V 21	5 1	65	269	65.65	a	1145 VI 22	0 51	96	205	65.40	a*	1191 VI 23	10 30	498	353	65.48	a*
1093 IX 23	9 55	586	347	65.63	a*	1146 VI 11	2 7	86	223	76.17	(p)	1191 XII 18	4 0	273	254	55.01	t
1094 III 19	5 8	4	269	45.09	t*	1147 X 26	9 46	619	346	65.71	a*	1193 VI 1	3 8	477	239	43.95	(p)
1097 I 16	9 40	303	337	74.47	a	1148 IV 20	4 20	36	260	44.93	t*	1195 IV 12	3 23	428	245	45.04	t
1098 I 5	10 47	292	353	85.15	a	1151 II 18	9 36	336	336	74.40	a	1195 X 5	5 28	198	280	54.88	t
1100 V 11	1 18	456	217	65.80	a	1152 II 7	10 18	325	344	75.10	a*	1197 IX 13	11 42	177	8	46.27	(p)
1101 IV 30	2 10	445	228	75.05	a*	1153 I 26	10 37	314	347	75.79	(a)	1198 II 7	22 20	726	167	65.74	(a)
1101 X 24	8 23	217	324	45.04	t	1153 VII 23	2 35	526	229	44.09	t	1199 I 28	7 51	715	308	55.00	t
1102 IV 19	4 43	435	263	64.30	(a)	1155 VI 1	21 38	477	160	65.30	a	1201 XI 27	10 26	653	355	75.75	(a)
1103 III 10	4 7	755	257	46.24	(p)	1155 XI 26	10 26	251	353	45.01	t	1202 V 23	2 48	68	238	34.72	t
1106 VIII 1	3 38	134	245	45.84	t	1156 V 21	1 30	466	216	54.53	a	1202 XI 16	11 49	641	14	85.07	(a)
1106 XII 27	4 47	682	268	86.40	p	1160 IX 2	2 56	166	237	45.67	t	1205 III 22	8 7	9	317	74.27	a

TABLE A.

te A. D.	Lanka time of conjunction measured from sunrise.	$L.$	$\mu.$	$\gamma'.$		Date A. D.	Lanka time of conjunction measured from sunrise.	$L.$	$\mu.$	$\gamma'.$		Date A. D.	Lanka time of conjunction measured from sunrise.	$L.$	$\mu.$	$\gamma'.$	
06 III 11	8 h. 38 m.	358	321	74.99	*a**	1253 III 1	8 h. 51 m.	748	324	45.07	*t**	1300 VIII 15	9 h. 47 m.	550	341	55.14	*t*
06 IX 4	11 12	568	3	45.04	*t*	1255 I 10	4 0	697	255	56.41	(*p*)	1301 VIII 4	23 38	540	186	44.39	*t*
07 II 28	10 4	346	340	65.71	(*a*)	1256 VI 24	1 1	99	210	34.50	*t*	1302 VI 26	9 15	501	335	36.20	*p*
07 VIII 25	0 43	558	203	54.28	*t*	1258 VI 3	9 53	79	340	46.03	(*p*)	1303 VI 15	22 40	491	175	55.48	*t*
1 XII 7	1 40	262	216	76.45	(*p*)	1260 IV 12	5 40	30	280	74.82	*a*	1303 XII 9	8 22	265	321	54.81	*t*
3 IV 22	10 52	439	358	45.10	*t**	1260 X 6	11 38	601	12	45.15	(*t*)	1304 VI 4	5 5	481	270	64.70	*a**
4 X 5	3 28	199	248	45.56	*t**	1261 IV 1	8 26	19	319	65.56	*a*	1304 XI 27	22 48	254	177	45.49	(*t*)
6 II 19	6 16	737	287	65.76	*a**	1261 IX 25	23 44	590	191	54.41	*a*	1307 IV 3	8 49	421	326	45.19	*t**
7 VIII 4	3 19	138	243	75.08	*a**	1262 VIII 16	12 10	550	21	76.54	(*p*)	1310 VII 26	23 31	131	187	34.29	(*t*)
8 I 28	7 23	716	299	44.33	(*t*)	1265 I 18	23 55	307	187	65.71	*a*	1312 VII 5	7 19	111	301	45.81	*t*
8 VII 24	3 53	127	249	75.83	*a**	1266 I 8	1 51	295	215	86.44	(*p*)	1314 V 15	1 38	61	221	74.59	*a*
0 VI 2	10 12	78	349	34.65	*t*	1267 V 25	8 36	470	325	55.32	*t**	1315 V 4	5 51	51	282	55.36	*a**
1 V 23	3 29	68	246	35.39	*t**	1268 XI 6	5 11	232	274	45.50	*t**	1315 X 28	23 47	623	193	64.48	*a*
3 IX 26	2 49	589	241	45.78	*t*	1270 III 23	5 24	410	276	55.87	*a*	1317 IX 6	10 2	571	348	65.98	*a*
6 II 28	2 15	347	221	56.34	*p*	1271 IX 6	0 1	170	196	74.88	*a*	1319 II 20	23 59	340	189	65.66	*a*
7 I 19	6 31	306	290	44.33	*t*	1272 III 1	8 55	749	323	44.40	*t*	1319 VIII 16	7 20	550	302	44.46	(*t*)
7 VII 14	23 32	518	188	65.64	*a*	1272 VIII 25	0 11	159	195	75.61	*a*	1320 II 10	1 22	329	207	76.39	*p*
8 VII 3	5 4	508	269	54.85	*t**	1274 VII 5	8 28	110	321	34.43	*t*	1321 VI 26	5 39	502	280	55.56	*t*
8 XII 28	7 18	284	300	65.73	*a**	1275 VI 25	1 51	100	221	35.17	*t**	1322 XII 9	7 41	265	309	45.48	*t**
0 V 14	3 34	460	251	35.90	*t*	1277 X 28	4 17	622	264	45.85	*t*	1324 IV 24	3 31	442	251	56.03	*p*
2 IV 22	2 16	439	227	64.38	(*a*)	1280 IV 1	1 57	19	220	46.21	*p*	1325 X 7	21 55	202	167	74.75	(*a*)
3 X 5	4 13	199	257	46.21	(*p*)	1281 II 20	8 20	339	317	44.27	*t*	1326 IV 3	9 17	421	332	34.52	*t*
4 VIII 26	5 47	159	283	54.26	(*a*)	1282 II 9	23 7	329	177	54.96	(*t*)	1328 VIII 6	7 11	141	303	34.23	(*t*)
5 II 19	0 38	737	200	45.04	*t*	1282 VIII 5	2 25	539	230	55.07	*t**	1329 VII 27	0 18	131	197	34.96	*t**
5 VIII 15	10 6	149	345	75.00	*a*	1283 I 30	8 5	318	309	65.70	*a*	1331 XI 30	6 38	656	297	45.87	*t**
6 VIII 3	10 31	138	349	75.75	*a**	1284 VI 15	1 53	491	225	36.12	(*p*)	1332 V 25	8 9	72	318	64.50	*a*
7 XII 19	3 3	675	241	75.77	*a**	1285 XI 27	23 40	254	191	54.81	*t*	1334 V 4	0 42	51	203	46.02	*p*
8 XII 8	3 50	664	252	85.09	*a*	1287 XI 7	5 49	232	282	46.17	*p*	1335 III 25	9 0	12	330	44.16	*t*
9 VI 3	10 58	79	358	35.32	*t**	1289 III 23	0 56	410	207	45.14	*t*	1336 IX 6	0 57	571	210	55.25	*t*
9 XI 27	3 29	652	247	74.41	(*a*)	1289 IX 16	7 11	181	304	74.83	*a*	1337 III 3	7 42	351	305	65.62	*a*
0 V 23	2 40	69	232	46.10	*p*	1290 IX 5	7 15	170	302	75.55	*a**	1339 VII 7	12 37	512	24	55.64	*t*
1 X 6	11 11	600	7	45.81	(*t*)	1291 VIII 25	11 59	159	11	56.26	*p*	1339 XII 31	1 49	287	220	54.80	*t*
2 IX 26	3 22	590	248	45.12	*t**	1292 I 21	3 39	708	248	75.80	*a**	1341 XII 9	8 8	266	314	46.15	*p*
3 III 22	1 6	8	208	65.62	*a**	1293 I 9	3 53	697	250	85.12	*a*	1342 V 5	10 44	452	359	56.09	(*p*)
5 VII 25	6 10	529	287	65.72	*a*	1293 VII 5	9 18	110	332	35.10	*t*	1343 IV 25	0 14	442	199	45.30	*t**
6 I 19	6 9	307	283	54.99	*t*	1293 XII 29	4 7	686	252	74.44	*a*	1343 X 19	5 30	213	281	74.72	*a*
7 VII 4	1 8	508	208	44.18	(*t*)	1294 VI 25	0 12	100	194	45.88	*t*	1344 X 7	5 26	202	278	75.42	*a**
8 V 24	11 4	470	3	35.97	*t*	1296 X 28	4 30	623	266	45.19	*t**	1345 IX 26	10 58	191	358	56.11	*p*
9 V 14	1 27	460	218	55.24	*t**	1297 IV 22	22 48	40	176	65.43	*a*	1346 II 22	3 17	741	243	75.87	*a*
9 XI 6	6 27	231	295	54.82	*t*	1299 VIII 27	2 50	561	239	65.93	(*a*)	1347 II 11	3 19	730	241	75.17	*a*
0 V 3	9 8	449	331	64.45	*a*	1300 II 21	7 25	340	302	54.94	*t**	1347 VIII 7	7 54	142	312	44.89	*t*

TABLE A.

Date A. D.	Lanka time of conjunction measured from sunrise.	L.	μ.	γ'.		Date A. D.	Lanka time of conjunction measured from sunrise.	L.	μ.	γ'.		Date A. D.	Lanka time of conjunction measured from sunrise.	L.	μ.	γ'.	
1348 VII 26	21 h. 38 m.	131	155	55.67	(*t*)	1391 IV 5	5 h. 50 m.	23	280	65.48	*a*	1447 IX 10	7 h. 29 m.	576	311	66.05	
1350 XI 30	6 26	656	293	55.22	*t*	1393 VIII 8	9 42	544	341	55.87	*a*	1448 III 5	4 45	354	264	44.71	
1354 III 25	7 22	12	304	54.82	*t**	1394 II 1	3 42	321	246	44.78	(*t*)	1448 VIII 29	10 1	565	346	75.33	
1354 IX 17	8 46	582	328	55.29	*t*	1397 V 26	22 48	473	178	35.51	*t*	1451 XII 23	5 0	280	269	84.64	
1355 IX 6	23 7	572	181	44.56	(*t*)	1398 XI 9	5 1	235	272	75.35	*a**	1452 XII 11	5 35	269	277	75.33	
1358 I 10	10 30	299	349	54.80	*t*	1400 III 26	1 29	414	218	76.00	*a*	1453 VI 7	5 3	485	268	44.20	
1358 VII 7	0 36	512	202	64.95	*a**	1401 III 15	1 36	403	217	75.28	*a*	1454 IV 27	22 14	446	172	76.20	
1358 XII 31	1 28	288	213	45.48	*t*	1401 IX 8	7 14	174	305	44.73	*t*	1455 IV 16	22 38	435	175	75.46	
1359 VI 26	1 21	501	211	64.19	(*a*)	1402 III 4	4 8	752	252	64.55	(*a*)	1456 IV 5	2 40	424	233	64.70	
1361 V 5	7 49	452	313	35.37	*t*	1405 I 1	8 36	690	321	55.23	*t**	1459 II 3	10 17	723	345	55.26	
1362 IV 25	0 54	442	208	34.63	(*t*)	1406 VI 16	6 15	93	286	35.72	*t*	1460 VII 18	4 31	124	259	35.50	
1364 III 4	10 51	752	357	75.90	(*a*)	1407 VI 5	23 27	83	183	36.43	(*p*)	1461 VII 7	21 50	114	157	36.22	
1365 II 21	10 53	741	355	75.20	*a*	1408 IV 26	5 55	44	285	54.65	*t*	1461 XII 2	1 14	659	217	66.16	
1366 VIII 7	4 52	142	264	55.60	*t*	1408 X 19	9 9	615	336	55.38	*t*	1462 V 29	3 20	76	246	54.42	
1367 VII 27	11 17	131	358	66.41	(*p*)	1409 X 8	23 47	604	194	44.67	*t*	1462 XI 21	10 44	648	359	55.41	
1367 XII 22	0 25	678	202	45.88	(*t*)	1412 II 12	12 10	332	13	44.76	(*t*)	1463 V 18	9 10	65	332	65.19	
1369 VI 5	2 46	82	235	55.13	*t**	1413 II 1	3 48	321	246	45.45	*t**	1463 XI 11	1 35	637	220	44.73	
1369 XI 30	0 37	656	204	64.51	*a*	1415 VI 7	6 14	484	289	35.58	*t*	1464 V 6	9 57	55	342	75.95	
1371 X 9	8 38	604	330	66.09	*p*	1416 V 26	23 37	474	189	34.84	*t*	1467 III 6	5 14	354	269	45.37	
1373 III 24	22 37	12	171	65.54	*a*	1419 III 26	8 45	414	325	75.34	*a**	1469 VII 9	4 35	515	263	35.80	
1373 IX 17	7 12	582	303	44.60	(*t*)	1420 IX 8	3 4	174	240	55.43	*a**	1470 VI 28	21 53	505	162	35.06	
1374 III 13	23 40	1	183	76.28	*p*	1421 VIII 28	7 50	163	309	76.21	(*p*)	1473 IV 27	5 24	446	278	75.53	
1375 II 1	8 42	321	323	64.05	(*a*)	1422 I 23	2 54	712	236	45.90	*t*	1474 IV 16	9 57	435	343	54.76	
1375 VII 29	2 37	533	234	55.79	*a*	1423 VII 7	23 46	113	190	54.89	*t*	1474 X 11	2 15	207	231	65.32	
1376 VII 17	7 8	522	300	65.04	*a**	1424 I 2	1 40	690	215	74.52	(*a*)	1475 IX 30	5 27	195	276	76.07	
1377 I 10	10 19	299	345	45.47	*t*	1425 XI 10	8 29	637	330	66.15	*p*	1476 II 25	4 36	745	262	45.96	
1377 VII 6	7 48	512	308	64.28	(*a*)	1428 X 9	0 25	605	201	44.00	*t*	1478 VII 29	12 4	135	13	35.43	
1377 XII 31	1 44	288	215	46.15	*p*	1429 III 5	8 40	354	324	63.98	(*p*)	1479 XII 13	9 37	670	342	66.16	
1378 V 27	1 1	473	213	56.23	(*p*)	1430 VIII 19	9	554	242	75.27	*a**	1480 VI 8	10 18	86	350	54.34	
1380 V 5	8 34	453	323	34.70	*t*	1431 VIII 8	5 37	543	246	64.52	*a*	1481 XI 21	10 23	649	352	44.73	
1381 X 18	3 7	213	242	56.05	*p*	1432 II 2	3 44	322	243	56.14	*p*	1482 XI 11	1 58	638	225	44.05	
1383 VIII 28	23 21	163	185	44.78	*t*	1434 VI 7	7 4	484	300	34.91	*t**	1484 IX 20	0 12	586	201	75.44	
1384 VIII 17	12 10	153	15	55.54	*t*	1435 XI 20	4 19	246	259	56.00	*p*	1485 IX 9	0 37	575	204	74.71	
1386 I 1	9 18	690	334	45.88	*t*	1437 IX 29	23 21	195	188	44.65	*t*	1486 III 6	4 40	355	259	56.07	
1386 VI 27	3 37	103	250	64.25	*a*	1438 IX 19	10 40	185	355	65.39	*a*	1487 VII 20	12 7	526	16	35.87	
1386 XII 21	23 54	679	192	55.23	*a*	1441 I 23	1 49	712	218	55.25	*t**	1488 VII 9	5 19	516	273	35.13	
1387 VI 16	9 43	92	340	55.05	*t**	1441 VII 18	6 53	124	296	54.81	*t**	1489 XII 22	6 15	280	284	55.98	
1387 XII 11	8 59	668	328	64.51	(*a*)	1442 I 12	9 56	701	338	74.52	*a*	1491 V 8	12 5	456	18	65.60	
1388 VI 4	22 53	82	176	45.80	*t*	1444 XI 10	2 6	637	230	55.41	*t**	1491 XI 2	0 23	228	205	54.58	
1389 IV 26	8 29	44	325	33.99	*t*	1445 V 7	2 31	55	232	65.27	*a**	1492 X 21	10 13	218	350	65.30	
1390 X 9	0 52	604	212	55.36	*t*	1446 IV 26	3 20	44	242	76.03	*p*	1493 IV 16	5 19	435	272	44.09	

TABLE A.

Date A. D.	Lanka time of conjunction measured from sunrise.	L.	μ.	γ'.		Date A. D.	Lanka time of conjunction measured from sunrise.	L.	μ.	γ'.		Date A. D.	Lanka time of conjunction measured from sunrise.	L.	μ.	γ'.	
95 II 25	2 h. 49 m.	745	234	55.31	*t**	1545 VI 9	7 h. 48 m.	487	313	65.85	*a*	1595 IX 23	11 h. 14 m.	590	8	46.19	(*p*)
95 VIII 20	4 55	155	269	54.62	*t*	1545 XII 4	2 12	262	229	54.56	(*t*)	1596 IX 12	3 4	579	243	45.51	*t*
96 II 14	10 4	734	340	74.57	*a*	1546 XI 23	10 40	251	356	75.26	(*a*)	1597 III 7	22 27	357	168	65.19	*a*
97 VII 29	12 53	135	23	36.09	(*p*)	1547 V 19	3 57	467	252	44.29	*t*	1599 II 15	0 55	336	201	46.54	(*p*)
98 XII 13	4 11	671	258	55.42	*t**	1549 III 29	2 27	418	231	55.43	*t**	1600 VI 30	11 35	508	8	45.28	*t*
99 VI 8	22 14	86	167	65.02	*a*	1549 IX 21	4 11	188	261	54.48	*t*	1600 XII 25	11 30	284	4	75.24	(*a*)
00 V 27	22 58	75	177	75.79	*a*	1550 III 18	8 53	407	325	74.68	*a*	1601 VI 20	2 11	498	225	34.51	*t*
01 X 12	6 17	608	295	66.17	*p*	1551 VIII 31	12 3	167	13	45.92	(*t*)	1603 V 1	0 41	450	207	55.61	*t**
02 IV 7	4 46	26	267	44.58	*t*	1553 I 14	6 25	704	288	45.43	*t**	1604 IV 19	6 12	439	287	74.85	*a**
02 X 1	7 30	597	311	75.49	*a**	1555 VI 18	23 22	96	181	56.26	*p*	1605 IV 8	6 39	428	291	74.11	(*a*)
03 III 27	21 32	16	156	35.29	(*t*)	1555 XI 14	6 6	641	292	76.24	(*p*)	1607 II 16	8 9	737	314	45.47	*t**
03 IX 20	7 55	586	315	74.76	(*a*)	1556 V 9	3 49	58	254	34.39	*t*	1608 II 6	0 8	727	192	44.78	*t*
6 I 24	4 53	314	265	74.61	(*a*)	1556 XI 2	6 16	630	294	75.58	*a**	1609 XII 16	6 31	675	295	76.28	*p*
6 VII 20	12 45	526	24	45.21	*t*	1557 X 22	6 52	619	301	74.87	(*a*)	1610 VI 11	2 18	89	230	34.18	(*t*)
7 I 13	6 23	302	286	65.31	*a**	1558 IV 18	11 50	38	10	55.90	(*t*)	1610 XII 5	6 2	663	287	85.62	*a**
7 VII 10	2 13	516	224	54.43	*t*	1560 II 26	3 57	347	252	74.53	(*a*)	1611 XI 24	7 7	652	303	74.92	*a*
9 XI 12	8 56	240	332	54.57	(*t*)	1560 VIII 21	11 28	558	7	45.40	*t*	1612 V 20	9 45	69	339	55.70	*t*
0 V 8	0 17	456	199	54.89	*t*	1561 II 14	6 44	336	291	65.25	*a**	1614 IX 23	11 1	590	4	45.55	*t*
3 III 7	10 51	756	356	55.34	(*t*)	1561 VIII 10	23 32	547	185	54.64	*a*	1615 III 19	6 8	8	284	65.15	*a**
4 VIII 20	3 28	156	245	35.31	*t**	1563 XII 15	10 52	273	358	54.55	(*t*)	1616 IX 1	0 58	569	207	74.05	*a*
6 I 4	2 26	693	231	66.16	*p*	1564 VI 8	21 27	487	156	55.12	*t*	1617 VII 22	10 19	529	351	66.17	*p*
7 VI 19	4 40	97	264	64.[illegible]4	*a**	1567 IV 9	10 1	429	346	55.48	*a*	1619 VII 1	9 37	509	336	34.59	(*t*)
7 XII 13	4 7	671	255	44.74	(*t*)	1568 IX 21	3 28	188	248	45.16	*t**	1621 V 11	7 49	460	314	55.68	*a*
3 VI 8	5 24	86	273	65.70	*a**	1570 II 5	3 23	726	244	66.18	*p*	1622 X 24	4 38	221	267	45.08	*t*
IV 7	5 29	27	276	35.24	*t**	1571 VII 22	0 4	128	195	74.68	*a*	1624 III 9	3 30	759	248	56.25	(*p*)
3 VIII 11	3 23	547	247	35.99	(*t*)	1572 I 15	6 43	705	291	44.76	*t**	1626 II 16	8 43	738	321	44.80	*t*
I 12	23 33	302	181	55.97	(*t*)	1572 VII 10	0 49	117	204	65.44	*a*	1627 VIII 1	3 30	138	243	55.94	(*a*)
V 30	1 16	477	216	65.76	*a*	1575 V 10	4 38	58	264	35.06	*t**	1629 VI 11	3 0	90	239	34.84	*t**
V 18	7 22	466	305	54.97	*t**	1578 III 8	11 22	358	4	74.49	(*a*)	1630 XI 23	23 50	652	192	54.24	*t*
XI 12	2 27	240	233	65.27	*a**	1579 VIII 22	6 46	558	295	54.70	*a*	1631 V 20	23 46	69	187	66.45	(*p*)
XI 1	4 17	228	259	75.99	*a*	1580 II 15	1 3	336	204	45.92	*t**	1631 X 15	3 55	612	260	46.25	(*p*)
III 29	5 7	418	273	46.07	(*p*)	1582 VI 20	4 30	498	262	55.20	*t**	1632 IV 9	8 50	30	329	74.33	*t*
VIII 30	11 20	166	4	35.25	*t*	1582 XII 15	3 13	273	241	75.25	*a*	1633 IX 23	5 5	590	273	64.86	*a**
VIII 20	4 14	156	255	45.97	(*t*)	1583 XII 4	4 2	262	253	85.95	*a*	1634 III 19	1 37	8	215	45.82	*t*
VI 30	11 7	107	0	64.85	*a*	1587 IX 22	4 1	188	255	45.84	*t*	1636 VII 22	1 57	529	223	45.43	*t*
VI 18	11 51	96	9	65.61	*a**	1589 II 4	23 39	726	186	45.45	*t*	1637 I 16	3 54	307	248	75.23	*a*
X 11	23 4	608	183	74.84	(*a*)	1589 VIII 1	6 38	138	294	74.60	*a*	1638 I 5	4 6	295	250	85.93	*a*
IV 7	4 16	27	256	55.95	*t*	1590 VII 21	7 24	128	303	65.35	*a**	1641 X 24	4 51	221	269	45.76	*t**
VIII 21	11 10	557	4	36.05	*p*	1593 V 20	12 9	69	17	34.99	(*t*)	1643 III 10	0 46	759	205	45.52	*t**
VIII 11	3 49	547	251	45.34	*t*	1593 XI 12	22 55	641	181	74.91	(*a*)	1643 IX 3	2 56	170	241	74.39	*a*
I 24	8 8	314	310	55.96	*t*	1594 V 10	2 33	59	231	55.77	*t*	1644 VIII 22	3 50	159	251	65.13	*a**

TABLE A.

Date A. D.	Lanka time of conjunction measured from sunrise.	L.	μ.	γ'.	
1645 VIII 11	10 h. 47 m.	149	353	55.87	*t*
1647 VI 22	10 23	100	350	34.77	(*t*)
1647 XII 15	23 43	674	189	74.93	*a*
1648 VI 10	23 53	90	190	55.55	*t**
1650 X 15	3 19	612	249	55.61	*t*
1652 III 29	9 34	19	335	45.77	(*t*)
1653 III 19	1 55	9	218	36.45	(*p*)
1654 II 7	5 35	329	276	54.50	*a*
1654 VIII 2	9 16	540	333	45.49	*t**
1655 I 27	11 58	318	9	75.22	(*a*)
1655 VII 23	0 35	529	201	34.74	*t**
1657 VI 1	21 46	481	163	55.84	*a*
1658 V 22	2 15	471	229	65.08	*a**
1659 V 11	2 51	460	236	74.32	*a*
1661 III 20	8 54	410	328	45.56	*t*
1662 III 10	1 28	760	214	44.86	*t*
1662 IX 2	10 55	170	359	65.07	*a*
1664 I 18	6 51	708	297	76.31	(*p*)
1665 I 6	6 8	697	285	85.64	*a**
1665 XII 26	8 4	685	313	64.94	*a*
1666 VI 22	6 52	100	295	55.47	*t*
1667 VI 11	12 55	90	24	66.29	*p*
1669 IV 20	4 30	40	262	54.98	*t**
1671 VIII 24	7 12	561	306	66.37	(*p*)
1673 VIII 2	8 10	540	315	34.80	*t*
1674 VII 23	1 21	530	211	34.07	*t*
1675 VI 13	4 38	492	266	55.92	(*a*)
1676 VI 1	8 44	481	326	65.17	*a**
1676 XI 25	6 46	254	298	45.05	*t*
1677 V 21	9 25	470	334	64.41	*a*
1680 III 20	9 38	411	337	44.89	*t**
1681 IX 2	1 45	170	219	55.75	*t*
1683 VII 14	1 7	121	210	44.62	*t*
1685 XI 16	5 46	645	287	46.30	*p*
1686 V 12	5 16	61	276	64.12	*a*
1687 V 1	11 46	51	12	54.92	*a*
1687 X 26	4 27	623	265	64.95	*a*
1688 IV 20	1 8	41	210	45.66	*t**
1690 VIII 24	0 16	561	200	45.62	*t*
1691 II 18	3 45	340	246	75.17	*a*
1692 II 7	3 42	329	243	75.88	*a*

Date A. D.	Lanka time of conjunction measured from sunrise.	L.	μ.	γ'.	
1693 VI 23	11 h. 27 m.	502	8	56.00	*p*
1695 XI 26	6 35	255	293	55.73	*t**
1697 IV 11	0 47	432	208	35.65	*t**
1697 X 5	0 29	202	207	74.24	*a*
1698 IX 24	1 36	191	221	64.97	*a**
1699 III 21	8 2	411	311	54.19	*a*
1699 IX 13	9 27	181	336	55.70	*t**
1701 VII 24	8 32	132	322	44.55	*t*
1702 I 17	0 43	708	201	64.95	*a*
1703 I 6	10 37	697	349	54.26	(*t*)
1704 XI 16	4 32	645	267	55.67	*t**
1706 V 1	8 46	51	325	45.60	*t*
1707 IV 21	1 46	41	218	36.31	(*p*)
1708 III 11	5 50	2	281	54.41	*a*
1708 IX 3	7 58	572	316	45.67	*t**
1709 II 28	11 24	351	2	75.14	(*a*)
1709 VIII 23	23 38	561	189	34.93	*t*
1711 XII 28	8 57	287	328	44.36	*t*
1712 VI 22	21 35	502	158	75.34	(*a*)
1712 XII 17	0 31	277	201	45.04	*t*
1715 IV 22	8 35	442	325	35.71	*t*
1716 IV 11	1 34	432	218	44.99	*t*
1716 X 4	9 11	202	336	64.93	*a*
1718 IX 13	7 51	181	310	46.33	(*p*)
1719 II 8	5 50	730	280	75.68	*a**
1720 I 28	8 58	719	325	64.96	*a**
1720 VII 24	3 46	132	248	55.24	*a**
1721 VII 13	8 24	121	316	66.04	*p*
1723 V 23	2 7	72	227	54.78	*t*
1727 IX 4	7 32	572	308	34.98	*t*
1728 VIII 24	0 12	562	195	44.25	*t*
1730 VII 4	3 59	512	254	75.43	*a*
1730 XII 28	9 23	288	333	45.03	*t**
1731 VI 23	4 55	502	266	64.66	*a**
1731 XII 17	23 59	277	191	55.72	*t*
1734 IV 22	9 21	443	335	45.05	*t**
1735 X 5	1 22	202	216	55.62	*t*
1737 VIII 14	23 31	153	188	44.41	*t*
1738 VIII 4	10 47	142	354	55.17	*a*
1739 XII 19	8 15	678	320	46.32	(*p*)
1741 VI 2	9 15	82	334	44.70	*t*

Date A. D.	Lanka time of conjunction measured from sunrise.	L.	μ.	γ'.
1741 XI 27	4 h. 43 m.	656	267	75.00
1742 V 22	23 50	72	191	35.46
1744 IX 24	23 48	593	196	45.75
1745 III 22	2 15	12	227	75.05
1746 III 11	2 16	1	224	75.78
1747 VIII 26	7 52	533	314	66.25
1748 VII 14	10 25	523	350	75.52
1749 XII 28	8 42	288	321	55.72
1751 V 13	23 52	463	195	35.84
New Style.				
1752 XI 6	0 52	224	211	64.8
1753 V 3	6 52	443	296	54.3
1753 X 26	9 32	213	339	55.5
1755 IX 6	7 8	163	303	44.3
1756 III 1	1 12	741	209	65.0
1758 XII 30	6 17	679	289	55.6
1760 VI 13	7 17	83	302	35.3
1761 VI 3	0 38	73	201	36.1
1762 IV 24	4 39	34	266	54.2
1762 X 17	7 57	604	319	45.7
1763 IV 13	9 25	23	335	75.0
1763 X 6	23 42	593	193	45.0
1764 IV 1	9 31	12	334	75.7
1766 II 9	11 8	321	359	44.3
1767 I 30	3 2	310	236	45.0
1768 VII 14	0 55	512	204	54.0
1769 I 8	1 47	288	215	76.4
1769 VI 4	7 24	474	308	35.9
1770 V 25	0 33	464	204	45.1
1770 XI 17	8 55	235	332	64.8
1772 X 26	8 37	214	324	46.2
1773 III 23	4 32	403	263	75.7
1774 III 12	9 10	752	329	65.0
1774 IX 6	1 2	163	210	65.0
1775 VIII 26	4 14	153	255	75.8
1776 I 21	1 55	701	223	46.
1777 VII 4	23 30	103	187	44.
1781 X 17	7 59	604	318	45.
1782 X 6	23 54	594	194	44.
1784 VIII 15	23 28	544	187	75.
1785 II 9	11 46	321	7	45.

TABLE A.

te A. D.	Lanka time of conjunction measured from sunrise.	*L.*	μ.	γ'.		Date A. D.	Lanka time of conjunction measured from sunrise.	*L.*	μ.	γ'.		Date A. D.	Lanka time of conjunction measured from sunrise.	*L.*	μ.	γ'.	
5 VIII 5	0 h. 43 m.	533	203	64.92	*a**	1817 XI 9	0 h. 57 m	626	213	45.15	*t**	1856 IV 5	4 h. 57 m.	16	270	44.21	(*t*)
6 I 30	1 58	310	218	55.71	*t**	1818 V 5	6 27	44	290	75.54	*a*	1856 IX 29	2 53	586	242	75.94	(*a*)
8 VI 4	8 1	474	316	45.25	*t**	1819 IX 19	11 51	576	17	66.53	(*p*)	1857 IX 18	4 38	575	266	65.19	*a**
9 XI 17	2 19	235	231	55.55	*t**	1821 III 4	4 55	343	265	44.97	*t*	1858 III 15	11 17	355	359	55.65	(*a*)
1 IV 3	11 50	414	13	75.82	(*a*)	1823 II 11	2 24	322	222	76.46	(*p*)	1861 I 11	2 32	291	280	64.82	(*a*)
1 IX 27	22 39	185	178	44.25	(*t*)	1824 VI 26	22 47	495	176	45.40	*t*	1861 VII 8	1 17	506	212	54.78	*a*
2 IX 16	8 18	174	320	64.98	*a*	1824 XII 20	9 44	269	341	64.83	*a*	1862 XII 21	4 8	269	254	46.16	*p*
3 III 12	5 11	752	268	44.35	(*t*)	1825 VI 16	11 28	485	5	54.62	(*t*)	1864 V 5	23 18	446	185	55.26	*t*
3 IX 5	11 2	163	358	75.74	*a**	1827 IV 26	2 5	435	228	65.93	*a*	1867 III 6	8 42	745	324	65.77	*a*
4 VIII 25	11 31	152	2	66.46	(*p*)	1828 IV 14	8 22	424	320	55.15	*t**	1868 VIII 18	4 16	145	257	34.95	*t**
5 I 20	23 26	701	185	55.71	(*a*)	1828 X 8	23 11	196	185	64.89	*a*	1871 VI 18	1 34	86	219	74.54	*a*
5 VII 16	6 40	114	294	44.47	*t*	1829 IX 28	1 0	185	209	75.62	*a*	1871 XII 12	3 6	660	243	45.19	*t**
I 10	5 20	690	172	75.02	*a*	1830 II 23	3 56	734	253	46.37	(*p*)	1872 VI 6	2 28	76	230	65.31	*a**
VII 4	22 9	104	265	35.24	*t*	1832 VII 27	13 6	124	29	35.09	(*t*)	1874 X 10	10 6	597	352	75.99	*a*
XI 8	0 40	626	210	45.83	(*t*)	1833 VII 17	6 21	114	286	35.83	*t*	1875 IV 6	5 40	16	279	44.87	*t**
V 4	23 17	44	184	74.87	(*a*)	1835 XI 20	9 35	637	342	45.17	*t*	1875 IX 29	11 59	586	17	65.24	(*a*)
IV 23	23 36	34	187	75.61	*a*	1836 XI 9	0 39	627	206	54.47	*t*	1877 III 15	1 58	355	217	76.39	*p*
IV 13	3 27	23	242	66.32	(*p*)	1840 III 4	3 10	344	237	55.67	*t**	1879 I 22	10 56	302	356	64.82	(*a*)
VIII 28	6 8	554	288	75.76	*a*	1840 VIII 27	5 49	554	279	54.38	(*t*)	1879 VII 19	8 10	516	314	54.86	*a*
VIII 17	7 29	543	305	65.00	*a**	1842 VII 8	6 7	506	286	45.47	*t*	1881 V 27	22 40	467	178	66.14	*p*
II 11	10 29	322	346	55.71	(*t*)	1843 XII 21	4 14	269	257	55.52	*t**	1882 V 17	6 38	456	295	55.33	*t**
VI 26	22 22	495	172	36.05	*p*	1845 V 6	9 1	446	333	66.00	(*a*)	1887 VIII 19	4 43	146	262	45.63	*t*
XII 10	1 22	257	217	64.84	*a*	1846 X 20	6 48	207	300	64.85	*a*	1889 VI 28	7 58	97	314	74.46	*a*
VI 6	4 28	475	260	54.54	*t*	1847 IV 15	5 26	425	274	44.47	*t*	1890 VI 17	9 2	86	329	65.22	*a**
XI 29	10 53	246	359	55.54	(*t*)	1847 X 9	8 12	195	318	75.58	*a**	1890 XII 12	2 15	660	228	54.50	*t*
XI 18	1 46	236	221	46.19	(*p*)	1848 IX 27	8 40	184	323	76.28	*p*	1894 IV 6	3 5	16	238	55.57	*t**
IV 4	0 45	414	205	55.10	*a*	1849 II 23	0 34	734	201	65.75	*a**	1894 IX 29	4 47	586	267	44.54	*t*
II 1	7 55	712	311	65.72	*a**	1849 VIII 18	4 37	145	264	44.26	*t*	1895 VIII 20	12 0	547	17	36.39	(*p*)
VII 17	5 37	114	276	35.16	*t**	1850 II 12	5 33	723	274	75.05	*a*	1896 VIII 9	4 6	537	256	45.70	*t*
VII 6	22 57	104	175	35.91	*t*	1852 XII 11	2 36	659	237	45.86	*t*	1898 I 22	6 28	302	287	45.51	*t**
XI 19	9 13	637	338	45.84	*t**	1855 V 16	1 17	55	211	56.12	*p*	1900 XI 22	6 21	240	293	74.77	(*a*)
V 16	6 0	55	286	74.79	*a**												

TABLE B.

$\lambda + \mu$.	260°	270°	280°	290°	300°	310°	320°	330°	340°	350°	0°	10°	20°	30°	40°	50°	60°	70°	80°	90°	100°
L. = 0° ϕ = 40°		0.08	0.07	0.08	0.10	0.13	0.18	0.25	0.33	0.43	0.53	0.61	0.69	0.74	0.78	0.81	0.82	0.82			
30°			0.14	0.14	0.16	0.19	0.24	0.32	0.41	0.53	0.65	0.75	0.84	0.90	0.95	0.98	0.99	0.99			
20°			0.24	0.24	0.25	0.28	0.34	0.41	0.51	0.63	0.77	0.89	0.99	1.07	1.12	1.15	1.16	1.16			
10°				0.37	0.38	0.40	0.44	0.51	0.62	0.73	0.88	1.02	1.13	1.23	1.28	1.31	1.33	1.33			
0°				0.51	0.51	0.53	0.57	0.64	0.74	0.85	1.00	1.15	1.26	1.36	1.43	1.47	1.49	1.49			
L. = 10° ϕ = 40°		0.06	0.06	0.08	0.11	0.15	0.21	0.28	0.36	0.46	0.55	0.64	0.72	0.76	0.80	0.81	0.82	0.81			
30°			0.14	0.15	0.18	0.22	0.28	0.36	0.45	0.57	0.68	0.78	0.87	0.93	0.97	0.99	0.99	0.98			
20°			0.25	0.26	0.27	0.31	0.37	0.45	0.55	0.67	0.81	0.93	1.03	1.10	1.14	1.16	1.16	1.15			
10°			0.37	0.37	0.39	0.42	0.48	0.55	0.66	0.78	0.93	1.06	1.17	1.25	1.30	1.33	1.33	1.32			
1°				0.51	0.52	0.55	0.60	0.68	0.78	0.90	1.04	1.19	1.31	1.39	1.45	1.48	1.49	1.48			
L. = 20° ϕ = 40°		0.07	0.08	0.10	0.14	0.18	0.25	0.32	0.41	0.50	0.59	0.67	0.74	0.78	0.81	0.81	0.81	0.79	0.76		
30°		0.15	0.16	0.17	0.21	0.25	0.32	0.40	0.50	0.61	0.72	0.82	0.90	0.95	0.98	0.99	0.98	0.96			
20°			0.25	0.27	0.30	0.34	0.41	0.50	0.60	0.72	0.85	0.96	1.06	1.12	1.15	1.16	1.16	1.14			
10°				0.38	0.40	0.44	0.51	0.60	0.70	0.83	0.97	1.09	1.20	1.27	1.31	1.32	1.32	1.30			
0°				0.52	0.54	0.58	0.64	0.72	0.82	0.95	1.09	1.22	1.34	1.42	1.46	1.48	1.48	1.46			
L. = 30° ϕ = 40°		0.08	0.09	0.12	0.16	0.21	0.27	0.35	0.44	0.54	0.63	0.69	0.75	0.79	0.80	0.80	0.79	0.77	0.73		
30°		0.15	0.16	0.19	0.23	0.29	0.36	0.44	0.54	0.65	0.75	0.85	0.92	0.96	0.98	0.98	0.97	0.94	0.89		
20°			0.26	0.29	0.33	0.38	0.44	0.53	0.65	0.77	0.89	1.00	1.08	1.14	1.15	1.15	1.15	1.11			
10°			0.39	0.41	0.44	0.49	0.56	0.65	0.77	0.88	1.02	1.14	1.24	1.29	1.32	1.32	1.30	1.28			
0°				0.54	0.57	0.63	0.69	0.77	0.88	1.01	1.15	1.28	1.38	1.44	1.48	1.48	1.46	1.43			
L. = 40° ϕ = 40°	0.08	0.09	0.11	0.15	0.19	0.24	0.32	0.40	0.48	0.57	0.65	0.71	0.76	0.79	0.79	0.78	0.75	0.72	0.69		
30°		0.17	0.19	0.23	0.27	0.32	0.40	0.48	0.59	0.69	0.80	0.88	0.94	0.96	0.97	0.95	0.92	0.89	0.84		
20°			0.29	0.32	0.37	0.43	0.50	0.59	0.69	0.82	0.93	1.04	1.10	1.14	1.15	1.13	1.10	1.06			
10°			0.40	0.44	0.48	0.53	0.62	0.70	0.81	0.94	1.06	1.18	1.27	1.30	1.31	1.29	1.27	1.22			
0°				0.58	0.61	0.67	0.74	0.82	0.93	1.07	1.19	1.32	1.41	1.45	1.48	1.47	1.43	1.39			
L. = 50° ϕ = 40°	0.09	0.11	0.14	0.17	0.22	0.29	0.35	0.43	0.51	0.60	0.68	0.73	0.77	0.78	0.78	0.76	0.72	0.69	0.64	0.59	
30°		0.19	0.21	0.25	0.30	0.37	0.44	0.53	0.63	0.73	0.82	0.90	0.94	0.96	0.95	0.93	0.89	0.84	0.79		
20°			0.32	0.35	0.40	0.47	0.54	0.64	0.74	0.85	0.97	1.06	1.12	1.14	1.13	1.10	1.06	1.01			
10°			0.44	0.47	0.52	0.58	0.67	0.77	0.87	0.98	1.11	1.21	1.28	1.30	1.30	1.27	1.22	1.17			
0°				0.61	0.66	0.71	0.80	0.89	1.00	1.12	1.24	1.35	1.43	1.46	1.45	1.43	1.39	1.33			
L. = 60° ϕ = 40°	0.11	0.14	0.17	0.21	0.26	0.33	0.40	0.48	0.55	0.63	0.70	0.75	0.78	0.78	0.75	0.73	0.69	0.64	0.59	0.54	
30°		0.22	0.25	0.30	0.36	0.42	0.50	0.58	0.68	0.77	0.86	0.92	0.95	0.95	0.93	0.89	0.84	0.79	0.73		
20°			0.35	0.40	0.45	0.52	0.60	0.69	0.80	0.91	1.01	1.08	1.10	1.11	1.09	1.05	1.00	0.94	0.88		
10°			0.49	0.52	0.57	0.65	0.73	0.82	0.94	1.06	1.16	1.24	1.29	1.30	1.27	1.24	1.18	1.11			
0°				0.66	0.72	0.79	0.87	0.96	1.07	1.18	1.30	1.39	1.44	1.45	1.44	1.39	1.34	1.27			
L. = 70° ϕ = 40°	0.15	0.17	0.21	0.25	0.32	0.38	0.44	0.52	0.59	0.65	0.72	0.75	0.77	0.76	0.73	0.69	0.65	0.59	0.54	0.49	
30°		0.25	0.29	0.34	0.40	0.47	0.54	0.63	0.71	0.79	0.87	0.92	0.93	0.92	0.89	0.84	0.79	0.73	0.67		
20°			0.40	0.45	0.51	0.57	0.66	0.75	0.85	0.94	1.03	1.09	1.11	1.09	1.05	1.00	0.94	0.89	0.82		
10°				0.58	0.64	0.71	0.79	0.88	0.98	1.09	1.19	1.26	1.28	1.26	1.22	1.16	1.10	1.04			
0°				0.72	0.78	0.84	0.93	1.02	1.13	1.24	1.34	1.41	1.44	1.42	1.38	1.33	1.27	1.20			

TABLE B.

$\lambda + \mu$.	260°	270°	280°	290°	300°	310°	320°	330°	340°	350°	0°	10°	20°	30°	40°	50°	60°	70°	80°	90°	100°
L. = 80° ϕ = 40°	0.17	0.21	0.26	0.30	0.36	0.42	0.49	0.55	0.62	0.68	0.72	0.74	0.74	0.72	0.68	0.64	0.59	0.53	0.49	0.43	
30°		0.29	0.33	0.39	0.45	0.52	0.59	0.67	0.75	0.82	0.88	0.91	0.91	0.88	0.83	0.78	0.72	0.66	0.60		
20°			0.45	0.51	0.57	0.64	0.71	0.81	0.90	0.99	1.05	1.09	1.08	1.05	1.00	0.94	0.87	0.81	0.75		
10°				0.63	0.70	0.76	0.86	0.95	1.04	1.14	1.22	1.26	1.25	1.22	1.16	1.10	1.03	0.96			
0°				0.78	0.85	0.92	1.01	1.10	1.20	1.30	1.38	1.42	1.42	1.38	1.33	1.27	1.20	1.13			
L. = 90° ϕ = 40°	0.21	0.25	0.29	0.35	0.40	0.46	0.52	0.58	0.65	0.69	0.72	0.73	0.72	0.68	0.63	0.58	0.53	0.48	0.43	0.38	0.33
30°		0.34	0.39	0.45	0.51	0.57	0.65	0.72	0.80	0.85	0.89	0.90	0.88	0.84	0.78	0.72	0.66	0.60	0.55	0.49	
20°			0.51	0.56	0.62	0.70	0.77	0.86	0.94	1.01	1.06	1.07	1.05	1.00	0.94	0.86	0.80	0.73	0.67		
10°				0.71	0.77	0.85	0.93	1.02	1.10	1.18	1.23	1.25	1.23	1.17	1.10	1.03	0.96	0.89			
0°				0.85	0.92	0.99	1.08	1.16	1.25	1.34	1.39	1.41	1.39	1.34	1.27	1.19	1.12	1.05			
L. = 100° ϕ = 40°	0.25	0.29	0.34	0.38	0.44	0.50	0.55	0.61	0.66	0.69	0.71	0.70	0.68	0.64	0.58	0.53	0.47	0.42	0.37	0.32	0.28
30°		0.39	0.44	0.49	0.56	0.62	0.69	0.76	0.82	0.87	0.89	0.88	0.84	0.79	0.73	0.67	0.60	0.54	0.48	0.44	
20°			0.57	0.63	0.69	0.77	0.84	0.91	0.98	1.03	1.06	1.06	1.01	0.95	0.89	0.81	0.74	0.68	0.62		
10°				0.77	0.83	0.90	0.99	1.07	1.14	1.20	1.23	1.22	1.17	1.11	1.04	0.96	0.89	0.82			
0°				0.92	0.98	1.05	1.14	1.22	1.30	1.36	1.39	1.38	1.33	1.26	1.19	1.11	1.04	0.97			
L. = 110° ϕ = 40°		0.34	0.39	0.44	0.49	0.54	0.59	0.63	0.67	0.70	0.70	0.68	0.64	0.59	0.54	0.49	0.43	0.38	0.32	0.27	0.24
30°		0.45	0.50	0.56	0.61	0.67	0.73	0.78	0.83	0.86	0.87	0.84	0.79	0.73	0.67	0.61	0.54	0.48	0.43	0.39	
20°			0.64	0.70	0.76	0.82	0.89	0.95	1.00	1.04	1.04	1.01	0.95	0.89	0.81	0.74	0.67	0.62	0.56		
10°				0.84	0.91	0.97	1.04	1.11	1.17	1.21	1.21	1.18	1.12	1.05	0.96	0.88	0.82	0.75			
0°				1.00	1.07	1.13	1.20	1.28	1.34	1.37	1.38	1.34	1.28	1.20	1.12	1.04	0.98	0.91			
L. = 120° ϕ = 40°		0.39	0.43	0.48	0.52	0.57	0.61	0.65	0.68	0.68	0.67	0.64	0.59	0.54	0.49	0.43	0.37	0.32	0.28	0.24	0.21
30°			0.55	0.60	0.66	0.71	0.76	0.80	0.84	0.85	0.84	0.79	0.74	0.67	0.61	0.54	0.48	0.43	0.38	0.34	
20°			0.70	0.75	0.81	0.86	0.92	0.97	1.01	1.02	1.00	0.95	0.89	0.82	0.75	0.67	0.61	0.55	0.51		
10°				0.91	0.97	1.02	1.08	1.14	1.18	1.19	1.17	1.12	1.04	0.96	0.89	0.82	0.75	0.69			
0°				1.07	1.13	1.19	1.25	1.31	1.35	1.36	1.34	1.29	1.20	1.12	1.04	0.97	0.91	0.85			
L. = 130° ϕ = 40°		0.44	0.48	0.52	0.56	0.60	0.63	0.66	0.67	0.67	0.65	0.60	0.55	0.49	0.43	0.37	0.33	0.28	0.24	0.21	
30°			0.62	0.66	0.71	0.75	0.79	0.82	0.84	0.83	0.81	0.75	0.69	0.62	0.55	0.48	0.43	0.38	0.34	0.31	
20°			0.76	0.81	0.86	0.91	0.95	0.99	1.01	1.00	0.97	0.90	0.83	0.75	0.67	0.61	0.55	0.50	0.46		
10°				0.97	1.02	1.07	1.11	1.16	1.18	1.17	1.13	1.06	0.97	0.89	0.81	0.74	0.68	0.63			
0°				1.14	1.19	1.24	1.28	1.32	1.35	1.34	1.29	1.22	1.13	1.05	0.97	0.88	0.84	0.79			
L. = 140° ϕ = 40°			0.52	0.55	0.58	0.61	0.64	0.65	0.65	0.64	0.60	0.56	0.50	0.43	0.38	0.33	0.28	0.24	0.21	0.18	
30°			0.65	0.69	0.73	0.77	0.80	0.82	0.82	0.80	0.76	0.70	0.62	0.55	0.49	0.43	0.38	0.34	0.30		
20°				0.86	0.90	0.94	0.97	0.99	1.00	0.97	0.92	0.85	0.77	0.69	0.62	0.56	0.51	0.46	0.43		
10°				1.02	1.07	1.10	1.14	1.16	1.17	1.14	1.08	1.00	0.92	0.84	0.77	0.71	0.65	0.61			
0°				1.19	1.24	1.27	1.31	1.33	1.33	1.30	1.24	1.16	1.07	0.99	0.91	0.85	0.79	0.75			
L. = 150° ϕ = 40°			0.55	0.58	0.61	0.63	0.64	0.64	0.63	0.61	0.56	0.51	0.45	0.39	0.33	0.28	0.24	0.21	0.18	0.17	
30°			0.70	0.73	0.76	0.79	0.80	0.81	0.80	0.77	0.72	0.65	0.57	0.50	0.44	0.39	0.35	0.31	0.29		
20°				0.89	0.92	0.96	0.97	0.98	0.97	0.93	0.87	0.79	0.70	0.62	0.55	0.50	0.46	0.43	0.40		
10°				1.07	1.10	1.13	1.15	1.16	1.15	1.10	1.03	0.94	0.85	0.77	0.70	0.65	0.60	0.57			
0°				1.24	1.28	1.30	1.32	1.33	1.31	1.26	1.19	1.09	1.00	0.92	0.86	0.80	0.76	0.73			

TABLE B.

λ + μ.	260°	270°	280°	290°	300°	310°	320°	330°	340°	350°	0°	10°	20°	30°	40°	50°	60°	70°	80°	90°	100°
L. = 160° φ = 40°			0.58	0.60	0.62	0.63	0.64	0.63	0.61	0.57	0.52	0.46	0.40	0.34	0.29	0.25	0.22	0.19	0.17	0.16	
30°				0.76	0.78	0.79	0.80	0.79	0.77	0.72	0.66	0.59	0.52	0.45	0.39	0.34	0.31	0.28	0.27		
20°				0.92	0.95	0.96	0.97	0.96	0.93	0.88	0.81	0.73	0.64	0.57	0.51	0.46	0.43	0.40	0.39		
10°				1.10	1.13	1.14	1.15	1.14	1.11	1.05	0.97	0.88	0.79	0.71	0.65	0.60	0.57	0.55			
0°				1.27	1.30	1.31	1.32	1.31	1.27	1.21	1.13	1.03	0.94	0.86	0.81	0.76	0.73	0.71			
L. = 170° φ = 40°				0.62	0.63	0.63	0.62	0.60	0.57	0.52	0.47	0.39	0.33	0.29	0.24	0.21	0.18	0.16	0.15		
30°				0.78	0.79	0.79	0.79	0.77	0.73	0.67	0.61	0.53	0.46	0.40	0.34	0.31	0.28	0.27	0.26		
20°				0.95	0.96	0.97	0.96	0.94	0.90	0.83	0.76	0.67	0.59	0.52	0.47	0.43	0.41	0.40			
10°				1.12	1.13	1.14	1.13	1.11	1.06	0.99	0.91	0.82	0.73	0.66	0.61	0.57	0.54	0.53			
0°				1.30	1.30	1.31	1.30	1.27	1.22	1.15	1.06	0.97	0.88	0.81	0.76	0.72	0.70	0.69			
L. = 180° φ = 40°				0.63	0.63	0.62	0.60	0.57	0.54	0.49	0.42	0.36	0.30	0.25	0.21	0.18	0.17	0.16	0.16		
30°				0.79	0.79	0.79	0.77	0.73	0.69	0.63	0.56	0.48	0.41	0.35	0.31	0.28	0.27	0.26	0.26		
20°				0.96	0.96	0.96	0.94	0.90	0.85	0.78	0.70	0.61	0.53	0.47	0.43	0.40	0.39	0.38			
10°				1.14	1.14	1.13	1.11	1.07	1.02	0.94	0.85	0.76	0.67	0.61	0.57	0.55	0.53	0.53			
0°				1.31	1.31	1.30	1.28	1.24	1.18	1.09	1.00	0.91	0.82	0.77	0.73	0.71	0.69	0.69			
L. = 190° φ = 40°				0.63	0.62	0.60	0.57	0.54	0.49	0.44	0.38	0.31	0.26	0.21	0.18	0.16	0.15	0.15	0.16		
30°				0.79	0.78	0.77	0.74	0.70	0.65	0.58	0.51	0.43	0.37	0.32	0.28	0.26	0.26	0.26			
20°				0.97	0.96	0.94	0.91	0.87	0.81	0.73	0.65	0.56	0.49	0.44	0.41	0.39	0.39	0.40			
10°				1.14	1.13	1.11	1.08	1.03	0.97	0.88	0.79	0.70	0.62	0.57	0.54	0.53	0.53	0.54			
0°				1.31	1.30	1.28	1.24	1.19	1.12	1.03	0.94	0.85	0.78	0.73	0.70	0.69	0.69	0.70			
L. = 200° φ = 40°					0.60	0.58	0.54	0.50	0.45	0.39	0.33	0.27	0.22	0.18	0.16	0.15	0.16	0.17			
30°					0.77	0.74	0.70	0.66	0.60	0.52	0.45	0.38	0.32	0.28	0.26	0.26	0.26	0.28			
20°				0.96	0.94	0.91	0.87	0.82	0.75	0.66	0.58	0.50	0.44	0.40	0.38	0.38	0.39	0.41			
10°				1.14	1.11	1.08	1.04	0.98	0.91	0.82	0.73	0.65	0.58	0.54	0.53	0.53	0.55	0.57			
0°				1.30	1.28	1.25	1.20	1.14	1.07	0.98	0.88	0.80	0.73	0.70	0.69	0.69	0.71	0.73			
L. = 210° φ = 40°					0.58	0.55	0.50	0.46	0.40	0.34	0.28	0.22	0.18	0.15	0.15	0.15	0.17	0.19			
30°					0.74	0.71	0.66	0.61	0.54	0.47	0.40	0.33	0.29	0.26	0.25	0.26	0.28	0.31			
20°					0.91	0.87	0.82	0.76	0.69	0.61	0.52	0.45	0.40	0.38	0.37	0.38	0.41	0.44			
10°				1.11	1.08	1.04	0.99	0.93	0.85	0.76	0.67	0.60	0.55	0.52	0.52	0.54	0.57	0.60			
0°				1.28	1.25	1.20	1.15	1.08	1.00	0.91	0.82	0.75	0.70	0.68	0.69	0.71	0.73	0.77			
L. = 220° φ = 40°					0.55	0.51	0.46	0.41	0.34	0.28	0.23	0.18	0.15	0.14	0.15	0.16	0.19	0.22			
30°					0.71	0.66	0.61	0.55	0.48	0.40	0.34	0.28	0.25	0.24	0.25	0.27	0.30	0.34			
20°					0.88	0.83	0.77	0.70	0.63	0.55	0.47	0.41	0.38	0.37	0.38	0.41	0.45	0.49			
10°					1.05	1.00	0.94	0.86	0.78	0.70	0.61	0.54	0.51	0.51	0.53	0.56	0.60	0.64			
0°				1.25	1.21	1.16	1.10	1.02	0.93	0.85	0.76	0.70	0.67	0.67	0.69	0.73	0.77	0.81			
L. = 230° φ = 40°					0.51	0.47	0.42	0.35	0.29	0.24	0.19	0.16	0.14	0.14	0.16	0.19	0.22				
30°					0.67	0.62	0.56	0.49	0.42	0.35	0.30	0.25	0.24	0.24	0.27	0.30	0.35				
20°					0.83	0.78	0.71	0.64	0.56	0.48	0.41	0.37	0.35	0.37	0.40	0.44	0.49				
10°					0.99	0.94	0.87	0.79	0.71	0.62	0.55	0.50	0.49	0.51	0.54	0.59	0.64	0.69			
0°				1.21	1.16	1.10	1.02	0.95	0.86	0.78	0.70	0.66	0.65	0.67	0.71	0.75	0.81	0.86			

TABLE B.

$\lambda + \mu$.	260°	270°	280°	290°	300°	310°	320°	330°	340°	350°	0°	10°	20°	30°	40°	50°	60°	70°	80°	90°	100°
L. = 240° ϕ = 40°					0.46	0.41	0.35	0.29	0.24	0.19	0.15	0.13	0.13	0.15	0.18	0.22	0.26				
30°					0.61	0.55	0.49	0.43	0.35	0.30	0.25	0.22	0.23	0.25	0.29	0.34	0.39				
20°					0.78	0.72	0.65	0.57	0.49	0.43	0.37	0.34	0.35	0.38	0.43	0.49	0.54				
10°					0.94	0.87	0.81	0.73	0.64	0.57	0.51	0.48	0.49	0.53	0.58	0.64	0.70	0.76			
0°				1.16	1.10	1.04	0.96	0.88	0.79	0.72	0.66	0.64	0.65	0.69	0.74	0.80	0.86	0.93			
L. = 250° ϕ = 40°						0.35	0.29	0.24	0.18	0.14	0.13	0.12	0.14	0.18	0.22	0.27	0.32				
30°					0.55	0.49	0.42	0.36	0.29	0.24	0.22	0.22	0.24	0.28	0.34	0.40	0.45				
20°					0.71	0.65	0.57	0.50	0.43	0.37	0.34	0.34	0.37	0.42	0.48	0.55	0.61				
10°					0.87	0.81	0.73	0.65	0.57	0.50	0.47	0.48	0.51	0.57	0.64	0.71	0.77				
0°				1.09	1.03	0.97	0.89	0.81	0.73	0.66	0.63	0.63	0.67	0.73	0.80	0.87	0.94	1.00			
L. = 260° ϕ = 40°					0.34	0.29	0.23	0.18	0.13	0.11	0.10	0.12	0.17	0.22	0.27	0.32					
30°					0.48	0.42	0.35	0.29	0.24	0.21	0.20	0.23	0.28	0.33	0.40	0.47	0.53				
20°					0.64	0.57	0.50	0.43	0.37	0.33	0.32	0.35	0.40	0.47	0.54	0.62	0.69				
10°					0.80	0.72	0.65	0.58	0.52	0.47	0.45	0.49	0.55	0.62	0.70	0.78	0.85				
0°				1.02	0.96	0.88	0.81	0.73	0.67	0.62	0.60	0.63	0.70	0.78	0.86	0.93	1.01	1.08			
L. = 270° ϕ = 40°					0.28	0.23	0.18	0.14	0.11	0.10	0.11	0.15	0.21	0.27	0.33	0.40					
30°					0.41	0.36	0.29	0.24	0.21	0.19	0.21	0.26	0.32	0.39	0.47	0.54	0.61				
20°					0.56	0.49	0.42	0.37	0.32	0.30	0.32	0.37	0.45	0.53	0.61	0.69	0.76				
10°				0.80	0.72	0.65	0.58	0.52	0.47	0.44	0.46	0.51	0.59	0.68	0.76	0.85	0.93				
0°				0.95	0.88	0.81	0.74	0.67	0.62	0.59	0.61	0.66	0.74	0.83	0.92	1.01	1.08	1.15			
L. = 280° ϕ = 40°					0.23	0.18	0.13	0.11	0.10	0.10	0.14	0.19	0.26	0.33	0.40	0.46					
30°					0.35	0.29	0.24	0.20	0.18	0.18	0.23	0.29	0.38	0.46	0.53	0.60	0.67				
20°					0.49	0.43	0.37	0.31	0.29	0.30	0.35	0.42	0.51	0.60	0.68	0.76	0.83				
10°				0.71	0.65	0.57	0.51	0.46	0.42	0.43	0.48	0.55	0.65	0.75	0.84	0.92	1.00				
0°				0.87	0.81	0.74	0.67	0.62	0.58	0.58	0.63	0.71	0.81	0.91	1.00	1.09	1.16	1.22			
L. = 290° ϕ = 40°					0.17	0.13	0.11	0.09	0.10	0.13	0.18	0.26	0.33	0.40	0.47	0.53					
30°					0.28	0.23	0.19	0.17	0.18	0.21	0.27	0.35	0.44	0.53	0.61	0.68	0.74				
20°					0.42	0.37	0.32	0.29	0.28	0.32	0.39	0.48	0.58	0.68	0.77	0.84	0.91				
10°				0.63	0.57	0.51	0.45	0.42	0.41	0.45	0.51	0.62	0.72	0.83	0.92	1.00	1.07				
0°				0.79	0.72	0.66	0.61	0.57	0.56	0.58	0.65	0.76	0.86	0.97	1.07	1.15	1.23	1.28			
L. = 300° ϕ = 40°					0.13	0.10	0.08	0.09	0.11	0.16	0.23	0.30	0.39	0.46	0.53	0.59					
30°				0.29	0.24	0.20	0.18	0.17	0.19	0.25	0.33	0.42	0.52	0.60	0.68	0.75	0.81				
20°				0.41	0.36	0.31	0.28	0.27	0.29	0.34	0.43	0.54	0.65	0.75	0.83	0.91	0.97				
10°				0.57	0.51	0.46	0.42	0.41	0.42	0.47	0.57	0.68	0.80	0.90	0.99	1.07	1.13				
0°				0.73	0.67	0.61	0.57	0.55	0.56	0.61	0.70	0.82	0.94	1.05	1.14	1.22	1.29	1.35			
L. = 310° ϕ = 40°				0.13	0.10	0.08	0.08	0.10	0.14	0.20	0.28	0.36	0.45	0.52	0.59	0.65					
30°				0.23	0.19	0.16	0.16	0.17	0.22	0.29	0.38	0.48	0.58	0.67	0.74	0.81	0.86				
20°				0.36	0.32	0.28	0.27	0.27	0.32	0.40	0.50	0.61	0.73	0.83	0.91	0.97	1.03				
10°				0.51	0.46	0.42	0.40	0.40	0.44	0.52	0.62	0.75	0.87	0.98	1.06	1.13	1.19	1.23			
0°				0.67	0.61	0.57	0.55	0.54	0.57	0.65	0.75	0.88	1.00	1.11	1.20	1.29	1.34	1.39			

TABLE B.

λ + μ.	260°	270°	280°	290°	300°	310°	320°	330°	340°	350°	0°	10°	20°	30°	40°	50°	60°	70°	80°	90°	100°
L. = 320° φ = 40°				0.10	0.08	0.07	0.09	0.12	0.17	0.24	0.33	0.42	0.50	0.58	0.64	0.69	0.73				
30°				0.19	0.17	0.15	0.16	0.19	0.25	0.34	0.44	0.54	0.64	0.72	0.80	0.86	0.90				
20°				0.32	0.29	0.26	0.26	0.29	0.35	0.44	0.55	0.68	0.79	0.87	0.96	1.03	1.07				
10°				0.46	0.42	0.39	0.38	0.40	0.46	0.56	0.67	0.81	0.93	1.03	1.12	1.19	1.24	1.28			
0°				0.62	0.57	0.54	0.53	0.54	0.59	0.68	0.80	0.93	1.06	1.18	1.27	1.33	1.39	1.43			
L. = 330° φ = 40°				0.08	0.07	0.08	0.10	0.15	0.21	0.29	0.38	0.47	0.56	0.63	0.69	0.74	0.77				
30°				0.17	0.15	0.15	0.17	0.22	0.29	0.39	0.50	0.60	0.70	0.79	0.85	0.90	0.94				
20°				0.28	0.26	0.25	0.27	0.31	0.39	0.49	0.62	0.74	0.85	0.95	1.02	1.07	1.11				
10°				0.42	0.39	0.38	0.39	0.42	0.49	0.60	0.74	0.87	0.99	1.10	1.17	1.23	1.28	1.30			
0°				0.57	0.54	0.52	0.52	0.56	0.62	0.72	0.86	0.99	1.12	1.23	1.32	1.38	1.43	1.46			
L. = 340° φ = 40°			0.08	0.07	0.07	0.09	0.13	0.18	0.26	0.34	0.44	0.53	0.61	0.68	0.73	0.78	0.80				
30°			0.17	0.15	0.15	0.16	0.20	0.26	0.34	0.44	0.55	0.66	0.76	0.84	0.90	0.95	0.97				
20°				0.26	0.25	0.26	0.29	0.34	0.43	0.54	0.68	0.80	0.90	1.00	1.06	1.11	1.14	1.16			
10°				0.39	0.37	0.37	0.39	0.44	0.53	0.65	0.79	0.93	1.04	1.15	1.22	1.27	1.30	1.32			
0°				0.53	0.51	0.51	0.53	0.57	0.66	0.77	0.90	1.04	1.18	1.28	1.36	1.41	1.45	1.47			
L. = 350° φ = 40°			0.06	0.06	0.08	0.10	0.15	0.21	0.29	0.39	0.48	0.57	0.65	0.72	0.76	0.79	0.81	0.81			
30°			0.15	0.14	0.15	0.17	0.22	0.29	0.36	0.48	0.60	0.71	0.80	0.88	0.93	0.96	0.98	0.99			
20°			0.26	0.25	0.25	0.26	0.31	0.38	0.46	0.59	0.72	0.84	0.95	1.04	1.09	1.13	1.15	1.16			
10°				0.37	0.37	0.38	0.42	0.49	0.57	0.70	0.84	0.98	1.09	1.19	1.25	1.29	1.32	1.33			
0°				0.52	0.51	0.52	0.55	0.61	0.70	0.82	0.96	1.10	1.23	1.33	1.40	1.45	1.48	1.49			
L. = 360° φ = 40°		0.08	0.07	0.08	0.10	0.13	0.18	0.25	0.33	0.43	0.53	0.61	0.69	0.74	0.78	0.81	0.82	0.82			
30°			0.14	0.14	0.16	0.19	0.24	0.32	0.41	0.53	0.65	0.75	0.84	0.90	0.95	0.98	0.99	0.99			
20°			0.24	0.24	0.25	0.28	0.34	0.41	0.51	0.63	0.77	0.89	0.99	1.07	1.12	1.15	1.16	1.16			
10°				0.37	0.38	0.40	0.44	0.51	0.62	0.73	0.88	1.02	1.13	1.23	1.28	1.31	1.33	1.33			
0°				0.51	0.51	0.53	0.57	0.64	0.74	0.85	1.00	1.15	1.26	1.36	1.43	1.47	1.49	1.49			
L. = 400° φ = 40°			0.15	0.15	0.16	0.18	0.21	0.25	0.30	0.36	0.42	0.48	0.54	0.57	0.60	0.62	0.62	0.62			
30°			0.26	0.26	0.26	0.28	0.31	0.35	0.41	0.48	0.56	0.63	0.69	0.73	0.76	0.78	0.79	0.79			
20°				0.39	0.39	0.41	0.44	0.48	0.54	0.62	0.70	0.79	0.86	0.90	0.94	0.96	0.97	0.97			
10°				0.53	0.53	0.54	0.57	0.61	0.68	0.76	0.85	0.94	1.02	1.07	1.11	1.13	1.14	1.14			
0°				0.69	0.69	0.70	0.72	0.76	0.82	0.91	1.00	1.09	1.18	1.23	1.27	1.29	1.31	1.31			
L. = 410° φ = 40°			0.15	0.16	0.18	0.21	0.24	0.29	0.34	0.40	0.47	0.53	0.57	0.60	0.62	0.63	0.63	0.62			
30°			0.26	0.26	0.28	0.30	0.34	0.40	0.45	0.53	0.60	0.67	0.73	0.77	0.79	0.79	0.79	0.78			
20°				0.39	0.41	0.43	0.47	0.52	0.59	0.67	0.76	0.83	0.90	0.94	0.96	0.97	0.96	0.95			
10°				0.53	0.54	0.57	0.60	0.66	0.73	0.82	0.91	0.99	1.06	1.11	1.13	1.14	1.13	1.12			
0°				0.69	0.70	0.72	0.76	0.81	0.88	0.97	1.06	1.15	1.22	1.27	1.30	1.31	1.31	1.30			
L. = 420° φ = 40°		0.16	0.17	0.19	0.21	0.25	0.29	0.34	0.40	0.46	0.52	0.57	0.61	0.63	0.64	0.63	0.62	0.60	0.58		
30°			0.27	0.28	0.31	0.34	0.39	0.45	0.52	0.59	0.66	0.72	0.77	0.80	0.80	0.80	0.78	0.76			
20°			0.39	0.40	0.43	0.46	0.51	0.57	0.65	0.73	0.81	0.88	0.94	0.97	0.97	0.97	0.95	0.92			
10°				0.54	0.56	0.60	0.65	0.71	0.78	0.87	0.97	1.05	1.11	1.14	1.14	1.14	1.12	1.09			
0°				0.70	0.72	0.75	0.80	0.86	0.93	1.02	1.12	1.20	1.27	1.30	1.31	1.31	1.29	1.27			

TABLE B.

$\lambda + \mu$.	260°	270°	280°	290°	300°	310°	320°	330°	340°	350°	0°	10°	20°	30°	40°	50°	60°	70°	80°	90°	100°
L. = 430° ϕ = 40°		0.16	0.18	0.20	0.24	0.28	0.33	0.39	0.44	0.51	0.56	0.60	0.63	0.64	0.64	0.63	0.61	0.58	0.55		
30°			0.28	0.30	0.34	0.38	0.43	0.50	0.57	0.64	0.71	0.76	0.80	0.81	0.80	0.79	0.76	0.73	0.70		
20°			0.40	0.42	0.46	0.50	0.55	0.62	0.70	0.78	0.86	0.92	0.97	0.98	0.97	0.95	0.92	0.89			
10°				0.56	0.59	0.64	0.69	0.77	0.85	0.93	1.02	1.09	1.14	1.15	1.14	1.12	1.09	1.06			
0°				0.72	0.75	0.80	0.85	0.92	1.00	1.09	1.18	1.25	1.30	1.32	1.31	1.29	1.27	1.23			
L. = 440° ϕ = 40°		0.19	0.21	0.24	0.28	0.33	0.39	0.44	0.50	0.56	0.61	0.64	0.66	0.66	0.64	0.62	0.59	0.56	0.52		
30°			0.30	0.34	0.38	0.43	0.49	0.55	0.62	0.70	0.76	0.80	0.82	0.81	0.80	0.77	0.74	0.70	0.65		
20°			0.42	0.46	0.50	0.55	0.61	0.68	0.76	0.85	0.91	0.97	0.99	0.98	0.97	0.93	0.90	0.85			
10°				0.60	0.64	0.69	0.75	0.83	0.91	1.00	1.08	1.14	1.16	1.16	1.14	1.10	1.06	1.02			
0°				0.75	0.79	0.84	0.90	0.98	1.07	1.15	1.24	1.30	1.33	1.33	1.31	1.27	1.23	1.19			
L. = 450° ϕ = 40°		0.21	0.24	0.28	0.32	0.37	0.43	0.48	0.54	0.60	0.64	0.67	0.67	0.66	0.63	0.60	0.56	0.52	0.48	0.44	
30°		0.30	0.33	0.37	0.42	0.48	0.54	0.61	0.68	0.74	0.80	0.83	0.83	0.82	0.78	0.74	0.70	0.65	0.61		
20°			0.46	0.50	0.55	0.61	0.67	0.75	0.82	0.90	0.96	1.00	1.00	0.99	0.95	0.91	0.86	0.81	0.76		
10°				0.64	0.69	0.75	0.82	0.89	0.97	1.06	1.13	1.17	1.18	1.16	1.12	1.08	1.02	0.97			
0°				0.79	0.84	0.90	0.98	1.05	1.14	1.22	1.30	1.34	1.35	1.33	1.29	1.25	1.19	1.14			
L. = 460° ϕ = 40°	0.21	0.24	0.28	0.32	0.37	0.42	0.48	0.53	0.59	0.64	0.67	0.68	0.68	0.65	0.62	0.58	0.53	0.48	0.43	0.39	
30°		0.34	0.37	0.42	0.47	0.54	0.60	0.67	0.73	0.79	0.84	0.85	0.84	0.81	0.77	0.72	0.66	0.61	0.55		
20°			0.50	0.55	0.60	0.66	0.74	0.81	0.89	0.96	1.01	1.03	1.01	0.98	0.93	0.87	0.81	0.75	0.70		
10°				0.69	0.75	0.81	0.89	0.96	1.05	1.12	1.18	1.20	1.19	1.15	1.09	1.04	0.98	0.91			
0°				0.84	0.90	0.96	1.04	1.12	1.21	1.28	1.34	1.36	1.35	1.31	1.26	1.20	1.14	1.07			
L. = 470° ϕ = 40°	0.24	0.28	0.32	0.37	0.43	0.48	0.53	0.58	0.64	0.68	0.70	0.69	0.67	0.64	0.59	0.54	0.48	0.43	0.39	0.34	
30°		0.39	0.44	0.49	0.55	0.61	0.67	0.73	0.79	0.84	0.87	0.86	0.84	0.79	0.73	0.67	0.61	0.56	0.50	0.45	
20°			0.56	0.62	0.68	0.74	0.81	0.88	0.95	1.01	1.05	1.03	1.01	0.95	0.88	0.82	0.76	0.70	0.64		
10°				0.75	0.81	0.88	0.96	1.03	1.11	1.18	1.21	1.20	1.17	1.11	1.04	0.97	0.91	0.84			
0°				0.91	0.97	1.03	1.11	1.19	1.27	1.34	1.37	1.37	1.33	1.27	1.20	1.13	1.06	1.00			
L. = 480° ϕ = 40°	0.29	0.33	0.38	0.43	0.48	0.53	0.59	0.64	0.68	0.71	0.71	0.70	0.66	0.61	0.55	0.50	0.44	0.39	0.34	0.29	0.26
30°		0.44	0.49	0.55	0.61	0.67	0.73	0.79	0.85	0.88	0.89	0.87	0.82	0.76	0.69	0.62	0.57	0.50	0.44	0.40	
20°			0.61	0.67	0.74	0.81	0.88	0.95	1.01	1.05	1.06	1.03	0.98	0.91	0.84	0.76	0.69	0.62	0.57		
10°				0.82	0.89	0.96	1.04	1.11	1.17	1.22	1.23	1.20	1.14	1.07	0.99	0.92	0.84	0.77			
0°				0.98	1.04	1.12	1.19	1.27	1.33	1.38	1.40	1.37	1.30	1.22	1.14	1.07	0.99	0.92			
L. = 490° ϕ = 40°	0.33	0.38	0.43	0.48	0.54	0.58	0.64	0.68	0.72	0.73	0.72	0.70	0.65	0.58	0.52	0.46	0.40	0.35	0.29	0.25	0.21
30°		0.49	0.55	0.61	0.66	0.73	0.78	0.84	0.88	0.91	0.90	0.86	0.80	0.72	0.65	0.57	0.51	0.45	0.39	0.34	
20°			0.68	0.74	0.81	0.87	0.95	1.00	1.06	1.08	1.07	1.02	0.95	0.86	0.78	0.70	0.63	0.57	0.52		
10°				0.89	0.96	1.03	1.10	1.17	1.22	1.25	1.23	1.18	1.10	1.01	0.93	0.84	0.76	0.71			
0°				1.05	1.12	1.19	1.26	1.33	1.38	1.41	1.39	1.34	1.26	1.17	1.08	0.99	0.92	0.85			
L. = 500° ϕ = 40°		0.43	0.48	0.53	0.58	0.63	0.68	0.72	0.74	0.74	0.72	0.68	0.62	0.55	0.48	0.41	0.35	0.29	0.25	0.20	0.17
30°			0.61	0.67	0.72	0.78	0.84	0.88	0.91	0.92	0.89	0.83	0.76	0.68	0.60	0.52	0.46	0.40	0.34	0.30	
20°			0.75	0.81	0.87	0.94	1.00	1.05	1.08	1.09	1.05	0.99	0.90	0.81	0.71	0.64	0.57	0.51	0.45		
10°				0.96	1.03	1.10	1.16	1.22	1.25	1.26	1.22	1.14	1.04	0.95	0.86	0.77	0.70	0.63			
0°				1.13	1.19	1.26	1.33	1.38	1.42	1.43	1.37	1.29	1.19	1.09	1.00	0.91	0.84	0.78			

TABLE B.

$\lambda + \mu$.	260°	270°	280°	290°	300°	310°	320°	330°	340°	350°	0°	10°	20°	30°	40°	50°	60°	70°	80°	90°	100°
L. = 510° ϕ = 40°		0.49	0.54	0.59	0.65	0.69	0.73	0.76	0.77	0.75	0.72	0.67	0.59	0.52	0.44	0.38	0.32	0.26	0.21	0.17	0.14
30°			0.67	0.73	0.79	0.84	0.89	0.92	0.94	0.92	0.88	0.80	0.72	0.63	0.54	0.47	0.41	0.35	0.30	0.26	
20°			0.82	0.88	0.94	1.00	1.05	1.09	1.11	1.09	1.03	0.95	0.85	0.75	0.66	0.57	0.50	0.45	0.40		
10°				1.05	1.11	1.17	1.23	1.26	1.28	1.26	1.19	1.10	0.99	0.88	0.79	0.71	0.64	0.58			
0°				1.21	1.28	1.34	1.39	1.43	1.44	1.42	1.35	1.24	1.14	1.03	0.93	0.85	0.77	0.72			
L. = 520° ϕ = 40°		0.54	0.59	0.64	0.69	0.73	0.76	0.78	0.78	0.76	0.70	0.63	0.56	0.49	0.40	0.33	0.27	0.21	0.17	0.14	0.11
30°			0.73	0.79	0.84	0.89	0.93	0.95	0.95	0.92	0.86	0.77	C.68	0.58	0.50	0.42	0.36	0.30	0.26	0.22	
20°			0.88	0.94	1.00	1.05	1.10	1.12	1.11	1.08	1.01	0.91	0.80	0.70	0.60	0.52	0.45	0.40	0.36		
10°				1.11	1.17	1.22	1.27	1.29	1.29	1.24	1.16	1.05	0.94	0.82	0.72	0.64	0.57	0.52	0.48		
0°				1.27	1.33	1.39	1.43	1.45	1.44	1.39	1.30	L.18	1.06	0.95	0.86	0.78	0.71	0.65			
L. = 530° ϕ = 40°		0.59	0.64	0.69	0.73	0.76	0.78	0.79	0.77	0.74	0.68	0.60	0.52	0.43	0.35	0.29	0.22	0.17	0.14	0.11	0.09
30°			0.79	0.84	0.89	0.93	0.96	0.96	0.95	0.90	0.83	0.73	0.63	0.54	0.44	0.37	0.30	0.26	0.22	0.19	
20°				1.00	1.06	1.10	1.13	1.13	1.12	1.07	0.97	0.86	0.74	0.64	0.54	0.47	0.40	0.35	0.31		
10°				1.17	1.23	1.27	1.30	1.31	1.28	1.22	1.12	0.99	0.87	0.76	0.67	0.59	0.52	0.48	0.44		
0°				1.33	1.39	1.43	1.45	1.46	1.43	1.35	1.25	1.12	1.00	0.89	0.80	0.71	0.66	0.61			
L. = 540° ϕ = 40°			0.69	0.73	0.76	0.78	0.80	0.79	0.77	0.72	0.65	0.58	0.49	0.40	0.32	0.25	0.20	0.16	0.12	0.10	0.09
30°			0.84	0.89	0.93	0.95	0.97	0.96	0.94	0.88	0.79	0.69	0.59	0.48	0.40	0.32	0.27	0.22	0.18	0.16	
20°				1.05	1.10	1.12	1.44	1.13	1.10	1.03	0.93	0.81	0.69	0.58	0.49	0.42	0.36	0.32	0.28		
10°				1.22	1.27	1.30	1.32	1.31	1.26	1.19	1.07	0.94	0.82	0.70	0.61	0.54	0.48	0.43	0.41		
0°				1.38	1.43	1.46	1.47	1.46	1.41	1.32	1.20	1.07	0.94	0.82	0.73	0.67	0.61	0.57			
L. = 550° ϕ = 40°			0.73	0.77	0.80	0.81	0.81	0.80	0.76	0.70	0.63	0.54	0.45	0.36	0.28	0.22	0.16	0.13	0.10	0.08	
30°				0.89	0.93	0.96	0.98	0.97	0.92	0.86	0.76	0.65	0.55	0.44	0.36	0.29	0.23	0.19	0.17	0.15	
20°				1.10	1.13	1.16	1.16	1.14	1.08	1.00	0.89	0.77	0.65	0.53	0.44	0.38	0.33	0.29	0.26		
10°				1.27	1.30	1.32	1.32	1.29	1.24	1.14	1.02	0.89	0.76	0.65	0.56	0.49	0.44	0.41	0.39		
0°				1.43	1.46	1.48	1.48	1.44	1.38	1.28	1.14	1.01	0.88	0.77	0.68	0.62	0.57	0.54			
L. = 560° ϕ = 40°			0.76	0.79	0.80	0.81	0.80	0.78	0.74	0.67	0.59	0.50	0.41	0.32	0.25	0.18	0.13	0.10	0.08	0.07	
30°				0.95	0.97	0.98	0.97	0.95	0.90	0.81	0.72	0.60	0.49	0.39	0.31	0.24	0.20	0.17	0.15	0.14	
20°				1.13	1.15	1.16	1.15	1.12	1.06	0.96	0.84	0.72	0.59	0.49	0.40	0.34	0.29	0.26	0.25		
10°				1.30	1.32	1.33	1.31	1.28	1.20	1.09	0.97	0.83	0.70	0.60	0.51	0.44	0.41	0.38			
0°				1.47	1.49	1.49	1.47	1.43	1.34	1.23	1.10	0.96	0.82	0.72	0.64	0.59	0.55	0.53			
L. = 570° ϕ = 40°				0.81	0.82	0.82	0.80	0.77	0.72	0.64	0.55	0.46	0.37	0.28	0.21	0.16	0.11	0.08	0.07	0.07	
30°				0.98	0.99	0.99	0.97	0.93	0.87	0.79	0.68	0.57	0.46	0.36	0.28	0.22	0.18	0.15	0.14		
20°				1.15	1.16	1.16	1.15	1.10	1.03	0.93	0.81	0.68	0.56	0.45	0.37	0.31	0.27	0.26	0.25		
10°				1.32	1.33	1.33	1.30	1.25	1.17	1.06	0.93	0.78	0.66	0.55	0.47	0.42	0.39	0.37	0.37		
0°				1.48	1.49	1.48	1.45	1.39	1.30	1.18	1.04	0.90	0.77	0.67	0.60	0.55	0.52	0.51			
L. = 580° ϕ = 40°				0.82	0.82	0.81	0.78	0.74	0.69	0.61	0.53	0.43	0.33	0.25	0.18	0.13	0.10	0.08	0.07	0.08	
30°				0.99	0.99	0.98	0.95	0.90	0.84	0.75	0.65	0.53	0.41	0.32	0.24	0.19	0.16	0.14	0.14		
20°				1.16	1.16	1.15	1.12	1.07	0.99	0.89	0.77	0.63	0.51	0.41	0.34	0.28	0.25	0.24	0.24		
10°				1.33	1.33	1.31	1.28	1.23	1.13	1.02	0.88	0.73	0.62	0.51	0.44	0.40	0.38	0.37			
0°				1.49	1.49	1.47	1.43	1.36	1.26	1.15	1.00	0.85	0.74	0.64	0.57	0.53	0.51	0.51			

TABLE B.

$\lambda + \mu$.	260°	270°	280°	290°	300°	310°	320°	330°	340°	350°	0°	10°	20°	30°	40°	50°	60°	70°	80°	90°	100°
L. = 590° ϕ = 40°				0.82	0.81	0.79	0.76	0.72	0.65	0.58	0.49	0.39	0.29	0.22	0.15	0.10	0.08	0.07	0.07		
30°				0.99	0.98	0.96	0.93	0.88	0.80	0.71	0.60	0.48	0.37	0.29	0.22	0.18	0.15	0.14	0.15		
20°				1.16	1.15	1.13	1.10	1.04	0.95	0.84	0.72	0.59	0.47	0.37	0.31	0.26	0.25	0.25	0.26		
10°				1.33	1.32	1.29	1.25	1.19	1.09	0.97	0.84	0.70	0.57	0.48	0.42	0.38	0.37	0.37			
0°				1.49	1.48	1.45	1.40	1.32	1.22	1.10	0.96	0.81	0.69	0.61	0.55	0.52	0.51	0.52			
L. = 600° ϕ = 40°					0.80	0.77	0.73	0.68	0.61	0.53	0.44	0.34	0.26	0.18	0.13	0.09	0.07	0.07	0.08		
30°					0.97	0.94	0.89	0.83	0.75	0.65	0.55	0.44	0.34	0.25	0.19	0.16	0.14	0.14	0.17		
20°				1.16	1.14	1.11	1.06	0.99	0.90	0.79	0.67	0.54	0.43	0.34	0.28	0.25	0.25	0.25			
10°				1.32	1.30	1.27	1.22	1.14	1.05	0.92	0.79	0.65	0.52	0.44	0.40	0.37	0.37	0.39			
0°				1.48	1.46	1.42	1.36	1.28	1.18	1.05	0.91	0.78	0.66	0.58	0.54	0.52	0.52	0.54			
L. = 610° ϕ = 40°					0.78	0.75	0.69	0.63	0.57	0.48	0.39	0.30	0.22	0.16	0.11	0.08	0.08	0.08			
30°					0.94	0.91	0.86	0.79	0.71	0.61	0.50	0.39	0.29	0.23	0.18	0.15	0.15	0.17			
20°					1.11	1.08	1.02	0.94	0.85	0.74	0.62	0.50	0.39	0.30	0.27	0.26	0.26	0.28			
10°				1.30	1.28	1.23	1.17	1.10	0.99	0.87	0.75	0.60	0.49	0.42	0.39	0.38	0.39	0.42			
0°				1.46	1.43	1.37	1.31	1.23	1.12	0.99	0.85	0.72	0.62	0.56	0.52	0.52	0.54	0.57			
L. = 620° ϕ = 40°					0.73	0.70	0.65	0.58	0.51	0.42	0.34	0.25	0.18	0.12	0.09	0.08	0.08	0.10			
30°					0.90	0.86	0.80	0.72	0.64	0.54	0.44	0.34	0.25	0.19	0.16	0.15	0.17	0.19			
20°					1.07	1.03	0.96	0.88	0.79	0.67	0.55	0.44	0.34	0.28	0.25	0.25	0.28	0.33			
10°				1.28	1.24	1.20	1.12	1.04	0.94	0.81	0.67	0.56	0.46	0.41	0.39	0.40	0.43	0.48			
0°				1.42	1.39	1.33	1.26	1.18	1.07	0.93	0.81	0.68	0.59	0.55	0.52	0.53	0.57	0.61			
L. = 630° ϕ = 40°						0.65	0.59	0.52	0.45	0.36	0.27	0.20	0.14	0.10	0.08	0.08	0.10	0.13			
30°					0.87	0.81	0.75	0.67	0.59	0.48	0.38	0.30	0.22	0.18	0.16	0.17	0.19	0.23			
20°					1.03	0.97	0.91	0.83	0.73	0.63	0.50	0.39	0.32	0.27	0.26	0.28	0.31	0.36			
10°				1.24	1.20	1.14	1.06	0.98	0.87	0.75	0.62	0.51	0.44	0.40	0.40	0.42	0.46	0.51			
0°				1.39	1.34	1.29	1.20	1.11	1.00	0.88	0.76	0.65	0.57	0.54	0.55	0.57	0.61	0.67			
L. = 640° ϕ = 40°						0.59	0.53	0.46	0.39	0.31	0.23	0.16	0.11	0.09	0.08	0.10	0.13				
30°					0.81	0.76	0.69	0.61	0.52	0.42	0.33	0.25	0.19	0.17	0.18	0.20	0.24	0.29			
20°					0.97	0.91	0.83	0.75	0.65	0.54	0.44	0.35	0.29	0.27	0.28	0.31	0.37	0.42			
10°					1.13	1.07	0.99	0.90	0.80	0.68	0.57	0.48	0.42	0.40	0.42	0.46	0.51	0.57			
0°				1.34	1.28	1.21	1.13	1.04	0.93	0.82	0.70	0.61	0.56	0.55	0.56	0.61	0.66	0.73			
L. = 650° ϕ = 40°						0.54	0.47	0.40	0.33	0.26	0.18	0.13	0.10	0.09	0.11	0.13	0.17				
30°					0.75	0.69	0.62	0.54	0.45	0.36	0.28	0.22	0.19	0.18	0.20	0.24	0.29				
20°					0.91	0.84	0.77	0.68	0.58	0.48	0.39	0.31	0.28	0.29	0.31	0.36	0.42				
10°					1.06	1.00	0.92	0.83	0.72	0.62	0.52	0.45	0.41	0.42	0.46	0.51	0.58	0.64			
0°				1.28	1.22	1.16	1.07	0.98	0.87	0.76	0.66	0.59	0.56	0.58	0.62	0.67	0.73	0.80			
L. = 660° ϕ = 40°						0.46	0.40	0.33	0.26	0.19	0.15	0.11	0.09	0.11	0.13	0.17	0.22				
30°					0.68	0.61	0.54	0.47	0.39	0.30	0.24	0.19	0.19	0.21	0.25	0.30	0.35				
20°					0.83	0.77	0.68	0.60	0.51	0.42	0.35	0.30	0.29	0.31	0.37	0.43	0.49				
10°					1.00	0.92	0.84	0.75	0.65	0.56	0.47	0.43	0.42	0.46	0.51	0.57	0.65	0.71			
0°				1.22	1.15	1.08	0.99	0.90	0.80	0.70	0.62	0.58	0.58	0.62	0.67	0.73	0.80	0.87			

TABLE B.

λ + μ.	260°	270°	280°	290°	300°	310°	320°	330°	340°	350°	0°	10°	20°	30°	40°	50°	60°	70°	80°	90°	100°
L. = 670° φ = 40°						0.39	0.33	0.27	0.21	0.15	0.11	0.10	0.11	0.14	0.18	0.23	0.28				
30°					0.61	0.54	0.47	0.39	0.32	0.26	0.21	0.20	0.21	0.25	0.29	0.36	0.42				
20°					0.77	0.69	0.61	0.53	0.46	0.38	0.32	0.30	0.32	0.37	0.43	0.50	0.57				
10°					0.93	0.85	0.76	0.68	0.59	0.51	0.46	0.44	0.46	0.52	0.58	0.65	0.72	0.79			
0°				1.15	1.08	1.01	0.92	0.84	0.75	0.66	0.61	0.59	0.61	0.66	0.73	0.81	0.88	0.95			
L. = 680° φ = 40°						0.33	0.27	0.22	0.17	0.13	0.11	0.12	0.14	0.18	0.23	0.29	0.34				
30°					0.53	0.47	0.40	0.33	0.28	0.23	0.20	0.21	0.25	0.29	0.35	0.42	0.48				
20°					0.69	0.62	0.54	0.47	0.40	0.35	0.32	0.32	0.37	0.43	0.49	0.57	0.63				
10°					0.86	0.79	0.71	0.62	0.55	0.49	0.46	0.47	0.51	0.58	0.65	0.73	0.80				
0°				1.08	1.02	0.95	0.86	0.78	0.70	0.64	0.61	0.62	0.67	0.74	0.81	0.89	0.96	1.03			
L. = 690° φ = 40°					0.32	0.27	0.22	0.18	0.14	0.12	0.12	0.14	0.18	0.24	0.29	0.35					
30°					0.46	0.40	0.34	0.29	0.24	0.21	0.22	0.25	0.29	0.36	0.42	0.49	0.55				
20°					0.62	0.55	0.48	0.42	0.37	0.34	0.34	0.37	0.43	0.51	0.58	0.64	0.71				
10°					0.77	0.71	0.64	0.56	0.51	0.47	0.47	0.50	0.57	0.65	0.73	0.80	0.86				
0°				1.00	0.93	0.87	0.80	0.72	0.66	0.63	0.62	0.66	0.72	0.80	0.88	0.96	1.02	1.09			
L. = 700° φ = 40°					0.27	0.22	0.18	0.15	0.13	0.13	0.15	0.19	0.24	0.29	0.35	0.41	0.46				
30°					0.40	0.35	0.30	0.25	0.22	0.22	0.25	0.29	0.35	0.42	0.49	0.55	0.61				
20°					0.55	0.49	0.43	0.38	0.35	0.34	0.37	0.42	0.49	0.57	0.64	0.71	0.77				
10°				0.77	0.71	0.65	0.59	0.53	0.50	0.49	0.51	0.56	0.64	0.73	0.80	0.87	0.94				
0°				0.93	0.87	0.81	0.75	0.69	0.65	0.64	0.66	0.71	0.80	0.88	0.96	1.03	1.09	1.15			
L. = 710° φ = 40°					0.22	0.19	0.16	0.14	0.14	0.15	0.19	0.24	0.30	0.35	0.41	0.46	0.51				
30°					0.34	0.30	0.27	0.24	0.23	0.25	0.29	0.34	0.42	0.48	0.55	0.61	0.66				
20°					0.49	0.44	0.40	0.37	0.35	0.37	0.41	0.48	0.58	0.64	0.71	0.78	0.83				
10°				0.70	0.65	0.59	0.55	0.51	0.49	0.50	0.56	0.62	0.71	0.80	0.87	0.94	1.00				
0°				0.86	0.81	0.76	0.72	0.68	0.65	0.66	0.71	0.78	0.87	0.95	1.03	1.12	1.16	1.21			
L. = 720° φ = 40°				0.22	0.19	0.17	0.15	0.15	0.16	0.19	0.24	0.29	0.35	0.41	0.46	0.51	0.55				
30°				0.34	0.30	0.27	0.25	0.24	0.25	0.28	0.34	0.40	0.47	0.55	0.61	0.66	0.70				
20°				0.48	0.44	0.41	0.37	0.36	0.37	0.40	0.46	0.54	0.62	0.69	0.77	0.82	0.87				
10°				0.65	0.61	0.57	0.53	0.51	0.52	0.55	0.61	0.69	0.78	0.86	0.94	0.99	1.05				
0°				0.81	0.76	0.73	0.69	0.67	0.67	0.70	0.76	0.84	0.93	1.01	1.09	1.15	1.21	1.25			
L. = 730° φ = 40°				0.18	0.16	0.15	0.14	0.16	0.18	0.22	0.28	0.34	0.40	0.45	0.50	0.54	0.58				
30°				0.30	0.28	0.26	0.25	0.25	0.28	0.33	0.39	0.47	0.54	0.60	0.66	0.70	0.74				
20°				0.44	0.41	0.38	0.37	0.38	0.40	0.45	0.52	0.61	0.69	0.76	0.82	0.87	0.91				
10°				0.59	0.56	0.52	0.51	0.51	0.54	0.58	0.66	0.75	0.84	0.92	0.98	1.04	1.07	1.11			
0°				0.76	0.72	0.70	0.68	0.67	0.69	0.74	0.81	0.91	1.00	1.08	1.14	1.20	1.24	1.27			
L. = 740° φ = 40°				0.17	0.15	0.15	0.16	0.18	0.22	0.27	0.33	0.39	0.45	0.50	0.54	0.58	0.60				
30°				0.28	0.26	0.26	0.26	0.28	0.32	0.38	0.45	0.52	0.60	0.65	0.70	0.74	0.77				
20°				0.40	0.38	0.37	0.37	0.39	0.43	0.50	0.58	0.66	0.75	0.81	0.87	0.90	0.93	0.96			
10°				0.56	0.54	0.52	0.52	0.53	0.58	0.64	0.72	0.81	0.90	0.97	1.03	1.07	1.10	1.13			
0°				0.73	0.70	0.69	0.68	0.69	0.73	0.79	0.87	0.97	1.06	1.14	1.19	1.24	1.27	1.29			

TABLE B.

$\lambda + \mu$.	260°	270°	280°	290°	300°	310°	320°	330°	340°	350°	0°	10°	20°	30°	40°	50°	60°	70°	80°	90°	100°
L. = 750° ϕ = 40°			0.16	0.15	0.15	0.16	0.18	0.21	0.26	0.31	0.39	0.44	0.49	0.54	0.57	0.60	0.62	0.63			
30°				0.26	0.26	0.26	0.28	0.32	0.37	0.43	0.51	0.58	0.65	0.70	0.74	0.77	0.78	0.79			
20°				0.39	0.39	0.39	0.41	0.44	0.49	0.56	0.65	0.73	0.81	0.87	0.91	0.94	0.96	0.97			
10°				0.54	0.53	0.53	0.54	0.57	0.62	0.70	0.79	0.88	0.97	1.03	1.08	1.11	1.13	1.14			
0°				0.70	0.70	0.69	0.70	0.73	0.78	0.85	0.94	1.03	1.12	1.19	1.24	1.28	1.30	1.31			
L. = 760° ϕ = 40°			0.15	0.15	0.16	0.18	0.21	0.25	0.30	0.36	0.42	0.48	0.54	0.57	0.60	0.62	0.62	0.62			
30°			0.26	0.26	0.26	0.28	0.31	0.35	0.41	0.48	0.56	0.63	0.69	0.73	0.76	0.78	0.79	0.79			
20°				0.39	0.39	0.41	0.44	0.48	0.54	0.62	0.70	0.79	0.86	0.90	0.94	0.96	0.97	0.97			
10°				0.53	0.53	0.54	0.57	0.61	0.68	0.76	0.85	0.94	1.02	1.07	1.11	1.13	1.14	1.14			
0°				0.69	0.69	0.70	0.72	0.76	0.82	0.91	1.00	1.09	1.18	1.23	1.27	1.29	1.31	1.31			

TABLE C.

$\gamma'+\gamma''$.	Magnitude of greatest phase in Digits.	$\gamma'+\gamma''$.	Magnitude of greatest phase in Digits.	$\gamma'+\gamma''$.	Magnitude of greatest phase in Digits.	$\gamma'+\gamma''$.	Magnitude of greatest phase in Digits.	$\gamma'+\gamma''$.	Magnitude of greatest phase in Digits.	$\gamma'+\gamma''$.	Magnitude of greatest phase in Digits.
35.47	0	45.46	0	55.45	0	65.44	0	75.43	0	85.42	0
35.51	1	45.50	1	55.50	1	65.49	1	75.48	1	85.47	1
35.56	2	45.55	2	55.54	2	65.54	2	75.53	2	85.52	2
35.60	3	45.59	3	55.59	3	65.58	3	75.58	3	85.57	3
35.64	4	45.64	4	55.63	4	65.63	4	75.63	4	85.62	4
35.68	5	45.68	5	55.68	5	65.68	5	75.68	5	85.68	5
35.73	6 Northern line.	45.73	6 Northern line.	55.73	6 Northern line.	65.73	6 Northern line.	75.73	6 Northern line.	85.73	6 Northern line.
35.77	7	45.77	7	55.77	7	65 77	7	75.78	7	85.78	7
35.81	8	45.82	8	55.82	8	65.82	8	75.83	8	85.83	8
35.85	9	45.86	9	55.86	9	65.87	9	75.87	9	85.88	9
35.90	10	45.90	10	55.91	10	65.92	10	75.92	10	85.93	10
35.94	11	45.95	11	55.96	11	65.97	11	75.97	11	85.98	11
35.98	12	45.99	12	56.00	12	—	—	—	—	—	—
36.00	Total.	46.00	Total.	56.00	Total.	66.00	Annular.	76.00	Annular.	86.00	Annular.
36.02	12	46.01	12	56.00	12	—	—	—	—	—	—
36.06	11	46.05	11	56.04	11	66.03	11	76.03	11	86.02	11
36.10	10	46.10	10	56.09	10	66.08	10	76.08	10	86.07	10
36.15	9	46.14	9	56.14	9	66.13	9	76.13	9	86.12	9
36.19	8	46.18	8	56.18	8	66.18	8	76.17	8	86.17	8
36.23	7	46.23	7	56.23	7	66.23	7	76.22	7	86.22	7
36.27	6 Southern line.	46.27	6 Southern line.	56.27	6 Southern line.	66.27	6 Southern line.	76.27	6 Southern line.	86.27	6 Southern line.
36.32	5	46.32	5	56.32	5	66.32	5	76.32	5	86.32	5
36.36	4	46.36	4	56.37	4	66.37	4	76.37	4	86.38	4
36.40	3	46.41	3	56.41	3	66.42	3	76.42	3	86.43	3
36.44	2	46.45	2	56.46	2	66.46	2	76.47	2	86.48	2
36.49	1	46.50	1	56.50	1	66.51	1	76.52	1	86.53	1
36.53	0	46.54	0	56.55	0	66.56	0	76.57	0	86.58	0

TABLE D.

$\lambda + \mu$.	260°	270°	280°	290°	300°	310°	320°	330°	340°	350°	0°	10°	20°	30°	40°	50°	60°	70°	80°	90°	100°
L. = 0° ϕ = 40°		58.3	0.0	1.7	3.5	5.5	7.7	9.8	12.2	14.7	17.2	19.5	21.8	23.8	25.8	27.8	29.5	31.2			
30°			59.3	1.0	2.8	4.7	6.8	9.2	11.5	14.2	16.8	19.3	21.7	23.8	26.0	27.8	29.7	31.3			
20°			58.7	0.3	2.2	4.0	6.0	8.3	10.8	13.5	16.3	19.0	21.5	23.8	25.8	27.7	29.5	31.2			
10°				59.8	1.5	3.3	5.3	7.7	10.2	12.8	15.7	18.5	21.0	23.5	25.7	27.5	29.3	31.0			
0°				59.3	1.0	2.8	4.8	7.0	9.5	12.2	15.0	17.8	20.5	23.0	25.2	27.2	29.0	30.7			
L. = 10° ϕ = 40°		59.0	0.5	2.2	4.0	8.0	6.0	10.2	12.5	15.0	17.3	19.8	22.2	24.3	26.3	28.2	30.0	31.7			
30°			59.7	1.3	3.0	5.0	7.0	9.3	11.7	14.3	16.8	19.3	21.8	24.2	26.2	28.2	29.8	31.5			
20°			59.0	0.7	2.3	4.3	6.3	8.5	11.0	13.7	16.3	19.0	21.7	24.0	26.0	28.0	29.8	31.5			
10°			58.3	0.0	1.7	3.5	5.5	7.7	10.0	12.7	15.5	18.3	21.0	23.5	25.7	27.7	29.5	31.2			
0°				59.3	1.0	2.8	4.7	6.8	9.3	11.8	14.7	17.5	20.3	22.8	25.0	27.2	29.0	30.7			
L. = 20° ϕ = 40°		59.3	0.8	2.5	4.3	6.3	8.3	10.5	12.8	15.2	17.7	20.2	22.5	24.7	26.7	28.7	30.5	32.2	33.8		
30°		58.5	0.0	1.7	3.5	5.3	7.3	9.7	12.0	14.5	17.2	19.7	22.2	24.5	26.7	28.7	30.3	32.2			
20°			59.2	0.7	2.5	4.3	6.3	8.5	10.8	13.5	16.3	19.0	21.7	24.0	26.2	28.2	30.0	31.7			
10°				59.8	1.5	3.3	5.3	7.5	9.8	12.5	15.3	18.2	20.8	23.3	25.7	27.7	29.5	31.2			
0°				59.3	1.0	2.7	4.7	6.7	9.0	11.7	14.5	17.3	20.2	22.7	25.0	27.2	29.0	30.7			
L. = 30° ϕ = 40°		59.8	1.5	3.2	4.8	6.7	8.7	10.8	13.2	15.7	18.2	20.5	23.0	25.2	27.3	29.3	31.0	32.7	34.3		
30°		58.8	0.3	2.0	3.7	5.5	7.5	9.7	12.0	14.5	17.2	19.8	22.3	24.7	26.8	28.8	30.7	32.3	34.0		
20°			59.3	0.8	2.5	4.3	6.3	8.5	10.8	13.3	16.2	19.0	21.7	24.2	26.3	28.3	30.2	31.8			
10°			58.5	0.0	1.7	3.5	5.3	7.5	9.8	12.3	15.2	18.2	20.8	23.5	25.8	27.8	29.7	31.3			
0°				59.3	1.0	2.7	4.5	6.5	8.8	11.5	14.2	17.2	20.0	22.7	25.0	27.2	29.0	30.7			
L = 40° ϕ = 40°	58.8	0.3	1.8	3.5	5.2	7.0	9.0	11.2	13.5	15.8	18.3	20.8	23.3	25.5	27.7	29.7	31.5	33.2	34.8		
30°		59.0	0.5	2.2	3.8	5.7	7.5	9.7	12.0	14.7	17.3	20.0	22.5	25.0	27.2	29.2	31.0	32.7	34.3		
20°			59.5	1.0	2.7	4.5	6.3	8.5	10.8	13.5	16.3	19.2	21.8	24.3	26.7	28.7	30.5	32.2			
10°			58.3	59.8	1.5	3.2	5.2	7.2	9.7	12.2	15.0	18.0	20.8	23.5	25.8	27.8	29.7	31.5			
0°				59.2	0.8	2.5	4.3	6.3	8.7	11.3	14.0	17.2	20.0	22.7	25.2	27.2	29.2	30.8			
L. = 50° ϕ = 40°	59.2	0.5	2.2	3.7	5.5	7.3	9.2	11.3	13.7	16.2	18.7	21.2	23.7	26.0	28.0	30.0	32.0	33.7	35.3	36.8	
30°		59.2	0.7	2.2	3.8	5.7	7.7	9.8	12.2	14.7	17.3	20.2	22.7	25.2	27.3	29.5	31.3	33.0	34.7		
20°			59.5	1.0	2.7	4.5	6.3	8.5	10.8	13.5	16.3	19.2	22.0	24.5	26.8	28.8	30.7	32.5			
10°			58.5	0.0	1.5	3.3	5.2	7.2	9.5	12.2	15.0	18.0	21.0	23.7	25.8	28.0	30.0	31.7			
0°				59.2	0.7	2.3	4.3	6.3	8.7	11.2	14.0	17.0	20.0	22.5	25.2	27.3	29.2	31.0			
L. = 60° ϕ = 40°	59.2	0.7	2.2	3.8	5.5	7.3	9.3	11.5	13.7	16.2	18.7	21.3	23.8	26.2	28.3	30.3	32.2	33.8	35.5	37.0	
30°		59.2	0.7	2.2	3.8	5.7	7.7	9.7	12.2	14.7	17.3	20.2	22.8	25.3	27.5	29.5	31.5	33.2	34.8		
20°			59.5	1.0	2.7	4.5	6.3	8.5	10.8	13.5	16.3	19.3	22.0	24.7	27.0	28.8	30.8	32.5	34.2		
10°			58.3	59.8	1.3	3.2	5.0	7.2	9.5	12.2	15.0	18.0	21.0	23.7	26.0	28.2	30.0	31.7			
0°				59.0	0.7	2.3	4.2	6.2	8.5	11.2	14.2	17.2	20.2	22.8	25.3	27.3	29.3	31.0			
L. = 70° ϕ = 40°	59.3	0.7	2.2	3.8	5.7	7.5	9.3	11.5	13.8	16.3	18.8	21.5	24.0	26.3	28.5	30.5	32.3	34.2	35.7	37.3	
30°		59.3	0.8	2.3	4.0	5.8	7.7	9.8	12.2	14.7	17.7	20.3	23.0	25.5	27.8	29.8	31.7	33.3	35.0		
20°			59.5	1.0	2.7	4.3	6.3	8.5	10.8	13.5	16.5	19.3	22.2	24.8	27.2	29.2	31.0	32.7	34.3		
10°				59.8	1.5	3.2	5.2	7.2	9.5	12.3	15.2	18.3	21.3	23.8	26.2	28.3	30.2	31.8			
0°				59.0	0.5	2.2	4.2	6.2	8.7	11.2	14.2	17.3	20.5	23.2	25.5	27.5	29.3	31.2			

TABLE D.

$\lambda + \mu$.	260°	270°	280°	290°	300°	310°	320°	330°	340°	350°	0°	10°	20°	30°	40°	50°	60°	70°	80°	90°	100°
L. = 80° ϕ = 40°	59.3	0.7	2.2	3.8	5.5	7.3	9.3	11.5	13.8	16.3	19.0	21.5	24.0	26.3	28.5	30.5	32.3	34.2	35.7	37.3	
30°		59.2	0.5	2.2	3.5	5.5	7.5	9.7	12.0	14.7	17.5	20.3	23.0	25.5	27.7	29.7	31.5	33.3	34.8		
20°			59.3	0.8	2.5	4.3	6.2	8.3	10.7	13.5	16.3	19.3	22.2	24.8	27.0	29.2	31.0	32.7	34.2		
10°				59.7	1.3	3.0	5.0	7.2	9.5	12.3	15.3	18.5	21.3	24.0	26.3	28.3	30.2	32.0			
0°				58.8	0.5	2.2	4.2	6.2	8.5	11.3	14.3	17.5	20.5	23.2	25.5	27.7	29.5	31.2			
L. = 90° ϕ = 40°	59.2	0.7	2.2	3.8	5.5	7.3	9.3	11.5	13.8	16.3	18.8	21.5	24.0	26.3	28.5	30.5	32.3	34.2	35.7	37.2	38.7
30°		59.0	0.5	2.2	3.8	5.5	7.5	9.7	12.2	14.8	17.5	20.3	23.2	25.5	27.8	29.8	31.7	33.3	34.8	36.3	
20°			59.2	0.7	2.3	4.2	6.0	8.2	10.7	13.5	16.5	19.5	22.2	24.8	27.0	29.2	30.8	32.7	34.2		
10°				59.7	1.2	3.0	5.0	7.2	9.7	12.3	15.5	18.7	21.5	24.2	26.3	28.3	30.2	31.8			
0°				58.8	0.5	2.2	4.2	6.3	8.7	11.5	14.7	17.8	20.8	23.5	25.7	27.7	29.5	31.2			
L. = 100° ϕ = 40°	58.8	0.3	1.8	3.3	5.2	7.0	8.8	11.0	13.3	16.0	18.5	21.2	23.7	26.0	28.2	30.2	32.0	33.8	35.3	36.8	38.3
30°		58.7	0.2	1.7	3.5	5.2	7.2	9.5	11.8	14.5	17.3	20.2	22.8	25.3	27.5	29.5	31.3	33.0	34.7	36.0	
20°			59.0	0.5	2.2	4.0	6.0	8.2	10.8	13.5	16.5	19.5	22.3	24.7	27.0	29.0	30.8	32.5	34.0		
10°				59.5	1.2	3.0	5.0	7.2	9.7	12.5	15.7	18.7	21.8	24.2	26.3	28.3	30.2	31.7			
0°				58.8	0.3	2.3	4.2	6.3	8.8	11.8	15.0	18.2	21.0	23.5	25.8	27.8	29.7	31.2			
L. = 110° ϕ = 40°		59.8	1.3	3.0	4.7	6.5	8.5	10.7	13.2	15.7	18.3	20.8	23.3	25.7	27.8	29.8	31.7	33.3	35.0	36.5	38.0
30°		58.5	0.0	1.7	3.3	5.2	7.2	9.3	11.8	14.5	17.3	20.2	22.8	25.2	27.3	29.3	31.2	32.8	34.3	35.8	
20°			59.0	0.5	2.2	4.0	6.0	8.2	10.8	13.5	16.5	19.5	22.2	24.7	27.0	29.0	30.7	32.3	33.8		
10°				59.5	1.2	2.8	5.0	7.2	9.7	12.7	15.7	18.8	21.8	24.2	26.2	28.2	30.2	31.8			
0°				58.8	0.5	2.2	4.2	6.5	9.0	12.0	15.2	18.3	21.3	23.8	25.8	27.8	29.5	31.2			
L. = 120° ϕ = 40°		59.3	0.8	2.5	4.2	6.0	8.0	10.2	12.5	15.0	17.7	20.3	22.8	25.2	27.3	29.3	31.2	32.8	34.5	36.0	37.3
30°			59.5	1.2	2.8	4.7	6.7	8.8	11.3	14.0	16.8	19.7	22.3	24.7	26.8	28.8	30.7	32.3	34.0	35.3	
20°			58.7	0.2	1.8	3.7	5.7	8.0	10.5	13.3	16.3	19.3	22.0	24.5	26.7	28.7	30.5	32.2	33.7		
10°				59.3	1.0	2.8	4.8	7.0	9.7	12.5	15.7	18.8	21.5	24.0	26.2	28.2	29.8	31.5			
0°				58.8	0.5	2.3	4.3	6.7	9.2	12.2	15.3	18.5	21.3	23.7	25.8	27.8	29.5	31.2			
L. = 130° ϕ = 40°		59.0	0.5	2.0	3.8	5.7	7.7	9.8	12.2	14.7	17.2	19.8	22.3	24.7	26.8	28.8	30.7	32.3	34.0	35.5	
30°			59.3	0.8	2.5	4.3	6.3	8.7	11.0	13.7	16.5	19.3	22.0	24.3	26.5	28.5	30.3	32.0	33.7	35.0	
20°			58.5	0.0	1.7	3.5	5.5	7.8	10.3	13.2	16.2	19.0	21.8	24.2	26.5	28.3	30.2	31.8	33.3		
10°				59.3	1.0	2.8	4.8	7.2	9.7	12.7	15.7	18.7	21.5	24.0	26.2	28.0	29.8	31.5			
0°				58.8	0.5	2.3	4.3	6.8	9.3	12.3	15.5	18.5	21.3	23.7	25.8	27.8	29.5	31.2			
L. = 140° ϕ = 40°			59.8	1.5	3.2	5.0	7.0	9.2	11.5	13.8	16.5	19.0	21.5	24.0	26.0	28.0	30.0	31.7	33.3	34.8	
30°			58.8	0.5	2.2	4.0	6.0	8.2	10.5	13.2	16.0	18.8	21.5	24.0	26.0	28.0	29.8	31.5	33.2		
20°				59.8	1.5	3.3	5.3	7.5	10.0	12.8	15.8	18.8	21.5	24.0	26.2	28.2	29.8	31.5	33.0		
10°				59.2	0.8	2.7	4.7	6.8	9.5	12.3	15.5	18.5	21.3	23.7	25.8	27.8	29.5	31.2			
0°				58.8	0.5	2.3	4.5	6.7	9.3	12.3	15.5	18.5	21.3	23.7	25.8	27.7	29.5	31.2			
L. = 150° ϕ = 40°			59.2	0.8	2.5	4.3	6.3	8.5	10.8	13.2	15.8	18.3	20.8	23.2	25.3	27.3	29.2	31.0	32.7	34.2	
30°			58.5	0.2	1.8	3.5	5.5	7.7	10.2	12.8	15.5	18.3	21.0	23.3	25.5	27.5	29.3	31.2	32.7		
20°				59.5	1.2	3.0	5.0	7.2	9.7	12.5	15.3	18.3	21.0	23.5	25.7	27.7	29.5	31.2	32.7		
10°				59.2	0.8	2.7	4.7	6.8	9.5	12.3	15.3	18.3	21.2	23.7	25.8	27.7	29.5	31.2			
0°				58.8	0.7	2.5	4.5	6.8	9.5	12.3	15.3	18.5	21.2	23.7	25.8	27.7	29.5	31.2			

TABLE D.

λ + μ.	260°	270°	280°	290°	300°	310°	320°	330°	340°	350°	0°	10°	20°	30°	40°	50°	60°	70°	80°	90°	100°
L. = 160° φ = 40°			58.5	0.2	1.8	3.7	5.7	7.7	10.0	12.5	15.2	17.7	20.0	22.3	24.5	26.5	28.5	30.2	31.8	3.33	
30°				59.7	1.3	3.2	5.2	7.3	9.7	12.3	15.0	17.8	20.3	22.8	25.0	27.0	29.0	30.7	32.2		
20°				59.3	1.0	2.7	4.7	7.0	9.3	12.2	15.0	18.0	20.7	23.2	25.3	27.3	29.2	30.8	32.3		
10°				59.0	0.7	2.5	4.5	6.7	9.2	12.0	15.0	18.0	20.8	23.3	25.5	27.5	29.3	31.0			
0°				59.0	0.7	2.5	4.5	6.8	9.3	12.2	15.3	18.3	21.0	23.5	25.7	27.7	29.3	31.0			
L. = 170° φ = 40°				59.7	1.3	3.2	5.0	7.0	9.3	11.7	14.3	16.8	19.3	21.7	24.0	26.0	27.8	29.7	31.3		
30°				59.2	0.8	2.7	4.7	6.7	9.0	11.7	14.3	17.2	19.8	22.2	24.5	26.5	28.3	30.2	31.7		
20°				59.2	0.8	2.5	4.5	6.7	9.2	11.8	14.7	17.5	20.3	22.8	25.2	27.2	29.0	30.7			
10°				59.0	0.7	2.5	4.3	6.7	9.2	11.8	14.8	17.8	20.7	23.2	25.5	27.5	29.2	30.8			
0°				59.0	0.7	2.5	4.5	6.8	9.3	12.2	15.2	18.2	21.0	23.5	25.7	27.7	29.3	31.0			
L. = 180° φ = 40°				59.2	0.8	2.5	4.5	6.5	8.7	11.2	13.7	16.2	18.7	21.2	23.3	25.3	27.3	29.2	30.8		
30°				58.8	0.5	2.3	4.2	6.3	8.7	11.2	13.8	16.5	19.3	21.8	24.0	26.0	28.0	29.8	31.3		
20°				58.8	0.5	2.2	4.2	6.3	8.7	11.3	14.2	17.0	19.8	22.5	24.7	26.7	28.5	30.3			
10°				58.8	0.5	2.2	4.2	6.3	8.8	11.7	14.5	17.5	20.3	23.0	25.2	27.2	29.0	30.7			
0°				59.0	0.7	2.5	4.5	6.7	9.2	12.0	15.0	18.0	20.8	23.3	25.5	27.5	29.3	31.0			
L. = 190° φ = 40°				58.7	0.3	2.0	3.8	6.0	8.2	10.5	13.0	15.7	18.2	20.5	22.8	24.8	26.8	28.7	30.3		
30°				58.5	0.2	2.0	3.8	6.0	8.2	10.7	13.3	16.2	18.8	21.3	23.7	25.8	27.7	29.5			
20°				58.5	0.2	1.8	3.8	5.8	8.2	10.8	13.7	16.7	19.3	22.0	24.3	26.3	28.2	30.0			
10°				58.7	0.3	2.0	4.0	6.2	8.5	11.3	14.2	17.2	20.0	22.7	25.0	27.0	28.8	30.5			
0°				59.0	0.7	2.3	4.3	6.5	9.0	11.8	14.8	17.8	20.7	23.2	25.5	27.5	29.3	31.0			
L. = 200° φ = 40°					59.8	1.7	3.5	5.5	7.7	10.0	12.5	15.0	17.7	20.0	22.3	24.5	26.3	28.2			
30°					59.7	1.5	3.3	5.3	7.7	10.2	12.8	15.7	18.3	20.8	23.2	25.3	27.2	29.0			
20°				58.3	0.0	1.7	3.5	5.7	8.0	10.7	13.5	16.3	19.2	21.8	24.2	26.2	28.0	29.8			
10°				58.7	0.3	2.0	4.0	6.0	8.5	11.2	14.2	17.2	20.0	22.7	25.0	27.0	28.8	30.7			
0°				59.0	0.7	2.3	4.3	6.5	9.0	11.7	14.7	17.8	20.7	23.2	25.5	27.5	29.3	31.0			
L. = 210° φ = 40°					59.2	1.0	2.8	4.8	7.0	9.3	11.8	14.5	17.0	19.5	21.8	23.8	25.8	27.7			
30°					59.3	1.2	3.0	5.0	7.3	9.8	12.5	15.3	18.0	20.7	23.0	25.0	27.0	28.8			
20°					59.8	1.5	3.3	5.5	7.8	10.3	13.2	16.2	19.0	21.7	24.0	26.2	28.0	29.8			
10°				58.5	0.2	1.8	3.7	5.8	8.2	10.8	13.8	17.0	19.8	22.5	24.8	27.0	28.8	30.5			
0°				58.8	0.5	2.3	4.2	6.3	8.8	11.5	14.7	17.7	20.5	23.2	25.5	27.5	29.3	31.2			
L. = 220° φ = 40°					58.8	0.5	2.3	4.3	6.7	9.0	11.5	14.2	16.7	19.2	21.5	23.5	25.5	27.3			
30°					59.2	0.8	2.7	4.8	7.2	9.7	12.3	15.2	17.8	20.5	22.8	24.8	26.8	28.5			
20°					59.5	1.2	3.0	5.2	7.5	10.2	13.0	16.0	18.8	21.5	23.8	26.0	27.8	29.5			
10°					0.0	1.8	3.7	5.8	8.2	11.0	13.8	17.0	20.0	22.7	25.0	27.0	28.8	30.5			
0°				0.5	2.2	4.0	5.8	8.0	10.0	13.2	16.2	19.0	22.3	25.0	27.3	29.3	31.2	32.8			
L. = 230° φ = 40°					58.3	0.2	2.0	4.2	6.3	8.7	11.3	13.8	16.5	18.8	21.2	23.3	25.2				
30°					58.8	0.7	2.5	4.7	6.8	9.5	12.2	15.0	17.7	20.3	22.7	24.7	26.7				
20°					59.3	1.0	3.0	5.0	7.5	10.0	13.0	16.0	18.8	21.5	23.8	25.8	27.8				
10°					59.8	1.7	3.5	5.7	8.0	10.8	13.8	17.0	19.8	22.5	24.8	26.8	28.8	30.5			
0°				58.8	0.5	2.2	4.2	6.3	8.7	11.5	14.5	17.7	20.7	23.2	25.7	27.7	29.5	31.2			

TABLE D.

λ + μ.	260°	270°	280°	290°	300°	310°	320°	330°	340°	350°	0°	10°	20°	30°	40°	50°	60°	70°	80°	90°	100°
L. = 240° φ = 40°					58.2	0.0	1.8	4.0	6.2	8.7	11.3	13.8	16.5	18.8	21.2	23.2	25.0				
30°					58.8	0.5	2.5	4.7	7.0	9.5	12.3	15.2	17.8	20.3	22.7	24.8	26.7				
20°					59.2	1.0	2.8	5.0	7.5	10.2	13.0	16.0	19.0	21.5	23.8	25.8	27.7				
10°					0.0	1.8	3.7	5.7	8.2	11.0	14.0	17.2	20.2	22.7	25.0	27.0	28.8	30.5			
0°				58.8	0.5	2.2	4.2	6.3	8.7	11.5	14.7	17.8	20.8	23.3	25.7	27.7	29.5	31.2			
L. = 250° φ = 40°						59.8	1.8	4.0	6.3	8.8	11.3	14.0	16.5	18.8	21.2	23.2	25.0				
30°					58.7	0.3	2.3	4.5	7.0	9.5	12.3	15.2	17.8	20.3	22.7	24.7	26.5				
20°					59.2	0.8	2.8	5.0	7.5	10.2	13.2	16.3	19.0	21.5	23.8	25.8	27.7				
10°					59.8	1.5	3.5	5.7	8.2	11.0	14.2	17.3	20.2	22.7	25.0	27.0	28.8				
0°				58.8	0.5	2.2	4.2	6.3	8.8	11.7	14.8	18.0	21.0	23.5	25.8	27.8	29.5	31.2			
L. = 260° φ = 40°					58.2	0.0	2.0	4.2	6.5	9.0	11.7	14.3	16.8	19.2	21.2	23.2					
30°					58.8	0.7	2.7	4.8	7.3	10.0	12.8	15.7	18.3	20.7	22.8	24.8	26.7				
20°					59.2	1.0	3.0	5.3	7.8	10.7	13.7	16.7	19.3	21.8	24.0	26.0	27.8				
10°					59.8	1.7	3.7	5.8	8.5	11.3	14.5	17.5	20.3	22.8	25.2	27.2	28.8				
0°				58.8	0.3	2.2	4.2	6.5	9.0	11.8	15.0	18.2	21.2	23.7	25.8	27.8	29.7	31.2			
L. = 270° φ = 40°					58.2	0.0	2.2	4.3	6.7	9.3	12.0	14.5	17.0	19.3	21.3	23.3					
30°					58.8	0.7	2.8	5.0	7.5	10.3	13.2	15.8	18.5	20.8	23.0	24.8	26.7				
20°					59.3	1.2	3.3	5.7	8.2	11.0	14.0	17.0	19.7	22.0	24.3	26.2	28.0				
10°				58.2	0.0	1.8	3.8	6.0	8.7	11.7	14.8	17.8	20.7	23.0	25.2	27.2	28.8				
0°				58.8	0.5	2.3	4.3	6.5	9.2	12.2	15.3	18.5	21.3	23.7	25.8	27.8	29.5	31.2			
L. = 280° φ = 40°					58.7	0.7	2.7	5.0	7.5	10.0	12.7	15.2	17.5	19.8	21.8	23.7					
30°					59.2	1.2	3.3	5.7	8.2	11.0	13.8	16.5	19.0	21.3	23.3	25.2	27.0				
20°					59.5	1.5	3.5	6.0	8.5	11.5	14.5	17.3	20.0	22.3	24.3	26.3	28.0				
10°				58.3	0.0	2.0	4.0	6.3	9.0	12.0	15.2	18.2	20.8	23.2	25.3	27.2	29.0				
0°				58.8	0.5	2.3	4.5	6.8	9.5	12.5	15.7	18.7	21.5	23.8	25.8	27.8	29.5	31.2			
L. = 290° φ = 40°					59.3	1.3	3.3	5.5	8.0	10.8	13.3	15.8	18.0	20.3	22.3	24.0					
30°					59.5	1.5	3.7	6.0	8.7	11.3	14.2	16.8	19.3	21.5	23.5	25.3	27.0				
20°					59.7	1.7	3.8	6.3	8.8	11.8	14.8	17.7	20.2	22.5	24.5	26.3	28.0				
10°				58.5	0.2	2.2	4.2	6.7	9.3	12.3	15.5	18.3	21.0	23.3	25.3	27.2	28.8				
0°				58.8	0.7	2.5	4.5	6.8	9.5	12.7	15.8	18.8	21.3	23.8	25.8	27.8	29.5	31.0			
L. = 300° φ = 40°					59.7	1.8	4.0	6.3	8.8	11.3	13.8	16.3	18.7	20.7	22.7	24.5					
30°				58.2	0.0	2.0	4.2	6.7	9.3	12.0	14.8	17.3	19.8	22.0	24.0	25.8	27.5				
20°				58.3	0.2	2.2	4.3	6.7	9.5	12.3	15.2	18.0	20.5	22.7	24.7	26.5	28.2				
10°				58.7	0.5	2.5	4.7	7.0	9.8	12.7	15.8	18.7	21.2	23.5	25.5	27.3	29.0				
0°				59.0	0.7	2.7	4.7	7.2	9.8	12.8	15.8	18.8	21.5	23.8	25.8	27.7	29.3	31.0			
L. = 310° φ = 40°				58.5	0.3	2.3	4.7	7.0	9.3	12.0	14.5	16.8	19.2	21.2	23.2	25.0					
30°				58.7	0.5	2.5	4.7	7.2	9.8	12.5	15.2	17.7	20.2	22.2	24.2	26.0	27.7				
20°				58.7	0.5	2.5	4.8	7.2	9.8	12.7	15.7	18.3	20.7	23.0	25.0	26.7	28.3				
10°				58.8	0.7	2.7	4.8	7.3	10.0	13.0	15.8	18.7	21.2	23.5	25.5	27.3	29.0	30.5			
0°				59.0	0.8	2.7	4.8	7.5	10.0	13.0	16.0	18.8	21.3	23.7	25.7	27.7	29.3	30.8			

TABLE D.

$\lambda + \mu$.	260°	270°	280°	290°	300°	310°	320°	330°	340°	350°	0°	10°	20°	30°	40°	50°	60°	70°	80°	90°	100°
L. = 320° ϕ = 40°				59.2	1.2	3.2	5.3	7.7	10.2	12.7	15.2	17.5	19.7	21.8	23.7	25.5	27.2				
30°				59.2	1.0	3.0	5.3	7.7	10.3	13.0	15.7	18.2	20.5	22.5	24.5	26.3	28.0				
20°				59.0	0.8	2.8	5.0	7.5	10.2	13.2	15.8	18.5	20.8	23.2	25.0	26.8	28.5				
10°				59.2	1.0	2.8	5.0	7.5	10.2	13.2	16.0	18.8	21.3	23.7	25.7	27.5	29.2	30.7			
0°				59.2	0.8	2.8	4.8	7.3	10.0	12.8	16.0	18.7	21.3	23.7	25.7	27.5	29.2	30.8			
L. = 330° ϕ = 40°				59.8	1.8	3.8	6.0	8.3	10.7	13.2	15.7	18.0	20.3	22.3	24.2	26.0	27.8				
30°				59.7	1.5	3.5	5.7	8.2	10.7	13.3	16.0	18.5	20.8	23.0	24.8	26.7	28.3				
20°				59.5	1.3	3.3	5.5	7.8	10.5	13.3	16.2	18.8	21.2	23.3	25.3	27.2	28.8				
10°				59.3	1.0	3.0	5.2	7.5	10.2	13.0	16.0	18.7	21.2	23.5	25.5	27.3	29.0	30.7			
0°				59.3	1.0	2.8	5.0	7.3	10.0	12.8	15.8	18.5	21.2	23.5	25.5	27.3	29.0	30.7			
L. = 340° ϕ = 40°			59.0	0.7	2.5	4.5	6.7	9.0	11.5	13.8	16.3	18.7	21.0	23.0	25.0	26.8	28.5				
30°			58.3	0.2	2.0	4.0	6.2	8.5	11.0	13.7	16.2	18.7	21.2	23.2	25.2	27.0	28.7				
20°				59.8	1.7	3.5	5.7	8.0	10.7	13.3	16.2	18.8	21.3	23.5	25.5	27.3	29.0	30.7			
10°				59.5	1.3	3.2	5.3	7.7	10 3	13.2	16.0	18.7	21.3	23.7	25.7	27.5	29.2	30.8			
0°				59.3	1.0	2.8	5.0	7.3	9.8	12.7	15.5	18.3	21.0	23.3	25.3	27.3	29.0	30.7			
L. = 350° ϕ = 40°			59.5	1.2	3.2	5.0	7.2	9.5	11.8	14.3	16.8	19.2	21.3	23.5	25.5	27.3	29.0	30.7			
30°			59.0	0.7	2.5	4.5	6.7	8.8	11.3	14.0	16.7	19.2	21.5	23.7	25.7	27.5	29.2	30.8			
20°			58.3	0.0	1.8	3.7	5.8	8.2	10.7	13.5	16.2	18.8	21.3	23.5	25.7	27.5	29.2	30.8			
10°				59.7	1.3	3.2	5.3	7.7	10.2	13.0	15.8	18.5	21.0	23.3	25.5	27.3	29.2	30.8			
0°				59.3	1.0	2.8	5.0	7.2	9.7	12.5	15.3	18.2	20.7	23.2	25.3	27.2	29.0	30.7			
L. = 360° ϕ = 40°		58.3	0.0	1.7	3.5	5.5	7.7	9.8	12.2	14.7	17.2	19.5	21.8	23.8	25.8	27.8	29.5	31.2			
30°			59.3	1.0	2.8	4.7	6.8	9.2	11.5	14.2	16.8	19.3	21.7	23.8	26.0	27.8	29.7	31.3			
20°			58.7	0.3	2.2	4.0	6.0	8.3	10.8	13.5	16.3	19.0	21.5	23.8	25.8	27.7	29.5	31.2			
10°				59.8	1.5	3.3	5.3	7.7	10.2	12.8	15.7	18.5	21.0	23.5	25.7	27.5	29.3	31.0			
0°				59.3	1.0	2.8	4.8	7.0	9.5	12.2	15.0	17.8	20.5	23.0	25.2	27.2	29.0	30.7			
L. = 400° ϕ = 40°			59.2	0.8	2.7	4.7	6.7	8.8	11.3	13.8	16.3	18.8	21.3	23.5	25.5	27.5	29.2	30.8			
30°			58.7	0.2	2.0	4.0	6.0	8.2	10.7	13.5	16.2	18.8	21.3	23.7	25.8	27.7	29.5	31.2			
20°				59.7	1.5	3.3	5.3	7.5	10.2	13.0	15.8	18.7	21.3	23.7	25.8	27.8	29.5	31.2			
10°				59.3	1.0	2.8	4.8	7.0	9.7	12.5	15.5	18.3	21.2	23.7	25.8	27.8	29.5	31.2			
0°				59.0	0.7	2.5	4.5	6.7	9.2	12.0	15.0	18.0	20.8	23.3	25.5	27.5	29.3	31.0			
L. = 410° ϕ = 40°			59.7	1.3	3.2	5.0	7.0	9.3	11.7	14.2	16.7	19.3	21.7	24.0	26.0	27.8	29.7	31.3			
30°			59.5	0.5	2.3	4.2	6.2	8.5	10.8	13.5	16.3	19.0	21.7	24.0	26.0	28.0	29.8	31.5			
20°				0.0	1.7	3.5	5.5	7.8	10.3	13.2	16.0	18.8	21.5	24.0	26.2	28.2	29.8	31.5			
10°				59.5	1.2	2.8	4.8	7.2	9.7	12.5	15.5	18.5	21.2	23.7	26.0	27.8	29.7	31.3			
0°				59.0	0.7	2.3	4.3	6.5	9.0	11.8	14.8	17.8	20.7	23.2	25.5	27.5	29.3	31.0			
L. = 420° ϕ = 40°		58.7	0.2	1.8	3.5	5.5	7.5	9.7	12.0	14.3	16.8	19.5	22.0	24.3	26.3	28.3	30.2	31.8	33.5		
30°			59.5	1.0	2.7	4.7	6.7	8.8	11.3	13.8	16.7	19.3	22.0	24.3	26.5	28.5	30.3	32.0			
20°			58.7	0.2	1.8	3.7	5.7	7.8	10.3	13.0	16.0	18.8	21.7	24.0	26.3	28.3	30.0	31.7			
10°				59.3	1.0	2.8	4.8	7.0	9.5	12.3	15.3	18.3	21.2	23.7	25.8	27.8	29.7	31.3			
0°				59.0	0.7	2.3	4.3	6.5	9.0	11.7	14.7	17.8	20.7	23.2	25.5	27.5	29.3	31.0			

TABLE D.

λ + μ.	260°	270°	280°	290°	300°	310°	320°	330°	340°	350°	0°	10°	20°	30°	40°	50°	60°	70°	80°	90°	100°
L. = 430° φ = 40°		59.2	0.7	2.3	4.2	6.0	8.0	10.2	12.5	15.0	17.5	20.2	22.5	24.8	27.0	29.0	30.8	32.5	34.2		
30°			59.7	1.2	3.0	4.8	6.8	9.0	11.3	14.0	16.8	19.5	22.2	24.7	26.8	28.8	30.5	32.2	33.8		
20°			58.7	0.2	1.8	3.7	5.7	7.8	10.3	13.0	16.0	18.8	21.7	24.2	26.3	28.3	30.2	31.8			
10°				59.5	1.2	3.0	4.8	7.0	9.5	12.3	15.3	18.3	21.2	23.8	26.0	28.0	29.8	31.5			
0°				58.8	0.5	2.3	4.2	6.3	8.8	11.5	14.7	17.7	20.5	23.2	25.5	27.5	29.3	31.2			
L. = 440° φ = 40°		59.5	1.0	2.7	4.3	6.3	8.3	10.3	12.8	15.3	17.8	20.5	22.8	25.2	27.3	29.3	31.2	32.8	34.5		
30°			59.8	1.5	3.2	5.0	7.0	9.0	11.5	14.2	17.0	19.8	22.5	24.8	27.0	29.0	30.8	32.5	34.2		
20°			59.0	0.5	2.2	3.8	5.8	8.0	10.5	13.2	16.2	19.2	22.0	24.5	26.7	28.7	30.5	32.2			
10°				59.5	1.2	2.8	4.8	7.0	9.3	12.2	15.2	18.3	21.2	23.8	26.0	28.0	29.8	31.5			
0°				58.8	0.5	2.3	4.2	6.3	8.7	11.5	14.5	17.7	20.7	23.3	25.5	27.7	29.5	31.2			
L. = 450° φ = 40°		59.8	1.3	3.0	4.7	6.5	8.5	10.7	13.0	15.5	18.2	20.7	23.2	25.5	27.7	29.7	31.5	33.3	34.8	36.3	
30°		58.7	0.0	1.7	3.3	5.2	7.2	9.3	11.7	14.3	17.2	20.0	22.7	25.0	27.3	29.3	31.2	32.8	34.3		
20°			59.0	0.5	2.2	4.0	5.8	8.2	10.5	13.3	16.2	19.2	22.0	24.5	26.8	28.8	30.7	32.3	33.8		
10°				59.5	1.2	3.0	4.8	7.0	9.5	12.3	15.3	18.3	21.3	23.8	26.2	28.2	30.0	31.7			
0°				58.8	0.5	2.2	4.2	6.3	8.7	11.5	14.5	17.7	20.7	23.2	25.7	27.7	29.5	31.2			
L. = 460° φ = 40°	58.7	0.0	1.5	3.2	4.8	6.7	8.7	10.8	13.2	15.7	18.3	21.0	23.5	25.8	28.0	30.0	31.8	33.5	35.2	36.7	
30°		58.7	0.0	1.7	3.3	5.2	7.2	9.3	11.7	14.3	17.2	20.0	22.7	25.2	27.3	29.3	31.2	32.8	34.5		
20°			59.0	0.5	2.2	4.0	6.0	8.2	10.7	13.3	16.3	19.3	22.2	24.7	27.0	29.0	30.8	32.5	34.0		
10°				59.5	1.2	2.8	4.8	7.0	9.5	12.2	15.3	18.5	21.3	24.0	26.2	28.2	30.0	31.7			
0°				58.8	0.5	2.2	4.2	6.3	8.7	11.5	14.7	17.8	20.8	23.3	25.7	27.7	29.5	31.2			
L. = 470° φ = 40°	58.7	0.2	1.7	3.3	5.0	6.8	8.8	11.0	12.3	15.8	18.3	21.0	23.5	26.0	28.2	30.2	32.0	33.7	35.3	36.8	
30°		58.8	0.3	1.8	3.5	5.3	7.3	9.5	11.8	14.5	17.3	20.2	22.8	25.3	27.5	29.5	31.3	33.0	34.7	36.2	
20°			59.2	0.7	2.3	4.0	6.0	8.3	10.7	13.5	16.5	19.5	22.3	24.8	27.0	29.0	30.8	32.5	34.0		
10°				59.5	1.2	3.0	5.0	7.2	9.7	12.5	15.7	18.7	21.7	24.2	26.3	28.5	30.2	31.8			
0°				58.8	0.5	2.2	4.2	6.3	8.8	11.7	14.8	18.0	21.0	23.5	25.8	27.8	29.5	31.2			
L. = 480° φ = 40°	58.7	0.2	1.7	3.2	5.0	6.8	8.8	11.0	13.3	15.8	18.5	21.0	23.7	26.0	28.2	30.0	31.8	33.7	35.2	36.7	38.2
30°		58.7	0.0	1.7	3.3	5.2	7.2	9.3	11.8	14.5	17.3	20.2	22.8	25.2	27.5	29.5	31.2	33.0	34.5	36.0	
20°			59.0	0.5	2.2	4.0	6.0	8.2	10.7	13.5	16.5	19.5	22.3	24.8	27.0	29.0	30.8	32.5	34.0		
10°				59.5	1.2	3.0	5.0	7.2	9.7	12.7	15.7	18.8	21.8	24.2	26.3	28.3	30.2	31.8			
0°				58.8	0.3	2.2	4.2	6.5	9.0	11.8	15.0	18.2	21.2	23.7	25.8	27.8	29.7	31.2			
L. = 490° φ = 40°	58.7	0.2	1.7	3.2	5.0	6.8	8.8	11.0	13.3	15.8	18.5	21.0	23.5	25.8	28.0	30.0	31.8	33.5	35.2	36.7	38.2
30°		58.7	0.2	1.5	3.3	5.2	7.2	9.5	11.8	14.7	17.5	20.2	22.8	25.3	27.5	29.5	31.2	32.8	34.5	36.0	
20°			58.8	0.3	2.2	3.8	6.0	8.2	10.8	13.5	16.5	19.5	22.3	24.8	27.0	28.8	30.7	32.3	33.8		
10°				59.5	1.2	3.0	5.0	7.2	9.8	12.7	15.8	19.0	21.7	24.2	26.3	28.3	30.2	31.7			
0°				58.8	0.5	2.3	4.3	6.5	9.2	12.2	15.3	18.5	21.3	23.7	25.8	27.8	29.5	31.2			
L. = 500° φ = 40°		59.7	1.3	2.8	4.7	6.5	8.5	10.7	13.0	15.5	18.0	20.7	23.2	25.5	27.7	29.7	31.5	33.2	34.8	36.3	37.7
30°			59.8	1.3	3.2	5.0	7.0	9.2	11.7	14.3	17.2	20.0	22.7	25.0	27.2	29.2	30.8	32.5	34.2	35.5	
20°			58.8	0.3	2.0	3.8	6.0	8.2	10.8	13.7	16.7	19.5	22.3	24.7	26.8	28.7	30.5	32.2	33.7		
10°				59.3	1.2	3.0	5.0	7.3	10.0	12.8	16.0	19.0	21.8	24.2	26.3	28.3	30.0	31.7			
0°				58.8	0.5	2.3	4.5	6.8	9.5	12.5	15.7	18.7	21.5	23.8	25.8	27.8	29.5	31.2			

TABLE D.

$\lambda + \mu$.	260°	270°	280°	290°	300°	310°	320°	330°	340°	350°	0°	10°	20°	30°	40°	50°	60°	70°	80°	90°	100°
L. = 510° ϕ = 40°		59.3	1.0	2.5	4.3	6.2	8.2	10.3	12.7	15.2	17.8	20.3	22.8	25.2	27.3	29.2	31.0	32.7	34.3	36.0	37.3
30°			59.7	1.3	3.0	4.8	6.8	9.2	11.7	14.3	17.0	20.0	22.5	24.8	27.0	28.8	30.7	32.3	33.8	35.3	
20°			58.7	0.3	2.0	3.8	5.8	8.2	10.8	13.7	16.5	19.5	22.2	24.5	26.7	28.7	30.3	32.0	33.5		
10°				59.5	1.2	3.0	5.2	7.5	10.0	13.0	16.2	19.0	21.8	24.2	26.2	28.2	29.8	31.5			
0°				58.8	0.7	2.5	4.5	6.8	9.5	12.7	15.8	18.8	21.3	23.8	25.8	27.8	29.5	31.0			
L. = 520° ϕ = 40°		59.0	0.5	2.2	3.8	5.7	7.7	9.8	12.2	14.7	17.3	19.8	22.3	24.5	26.7	28.7	30.5	32.2	33.8	35.3	36.8
30°			59.2	0.8	2.5	4.5	6.5	8.7	11.2	13.8	16.7	19.3	21.8	24.3	26.3	28.3	30.2	31.8	33.3	34.8	
20°			58.5	0.2	1.8	3.8	5.7	8.0	10.7	13.3	16.3	19.2	21.8	24.2	26.3	28.2	30.0	31.7	33.2		
10°				59.8	1.0	2.8	5.0	7.3	10.0	13.0	16.0	18.8	21.5	23.8	25.0	27.8	29.7	31.2	32.7		
0°				59.0	0.7	2.7	4.7	7.2	9.8	12.8	15.8	18.8	21.5	23.8	25.8	27.7	29.3	31.0			
L. = 530° ϕ = 40°		58.5	0.0	1.7	3.3	5.3	7.3	9.3	11.7	14.2	16.7	19.2	21.7	24.0	26.2	28.0	29.8	31.7	33.2	34.8	36.2
30°			59.0	0.7	2.3	4.2	6.3	8.5	11.0	13.5	16.3	19.0	21.5	23.8	26.0	28.0	29.8	31.5	33.0	34.5	
20°				59.8	1.7	3.5	5.5	7.8	10.3	13.2	16.0	18.8	21.5	23.8	26.0	27.8	29.7	31.3	32.8		
10°				59.3	1.0	3.0	5.2	7.3	10.0	13.0	16.0	18.8	21.5	23.8	25.8	27.7	29.5	31.0	32.5		
0°				59.0	0.8	2.7	4.8	7.5	10.0	13.0	16.0	18.8	21.3	23.7	25.7	27.7	29.3	30.8			
L. = 540° ϕ = 40°			59.5	1.2	2.8	4.7	6.7	8.8	11.0	13.5	16.0	18.5	20.8	23.2	25.3	27.3	29.2	30.8	32.5	34.0	35.5
30°			58.7	0.3	2.0	3.8	5.8	8.0	10.5	13.0	15.7	18.3	21.0	23.3	25.5	27.3	29.2	30.8	32.5	34.0	
20°				59.8	1.5	3.3	5.3	7.7	10.2	12.8	15.7	18.5	21.2	23.5	25.7	27.5	29.3	31.0	32.5		
10°				59.2	1.0	2.8	4.8	7.2	9.8	12.7	15.7	18.5	21.0	23.5	25.5	27.5	29.2	30.8	32.3		
0°				59.2	0.8	2.8	4.8	7.3	10.0	12.8	16.0	18.7	21.3	23.7	25.7	27.5	29.2	30.8			
L. = 550° ϕ = 40°			59.0	0.7	2.3	4.0	6.0	8.2	10.3	12.8	15.2	17.7	20.2	22.5	24.7	26.7	28.5	30.2	31.8	33.5	
30°			58.3	0.0	1.7	3.5	5.5	7.7	10.0	12.5	15.2	17.8	20.3	22.7	24.8	26.8	28.7	30.3	32.0	33.5	
20°				59.5	1.2	3.0	5.0	7.2	9.7	12.3	15.2	18.0	20.5	22.8	25.0	27.0	28.8	30.5	32.0		
10°				59.3	1.0	2.8	4.8	7.2	9.8	12.5	15.5	18.3	20.8	23.2	25.3	27.2	29.0	30.7	32.2		
0°				59.3	1.0	2.8	5.0	7.3	10.0	12.8	15.8	18.5	21.2	23.5	25.5	27.3	29.0	30.7			
L. = 560° ϕ = 40°			58.2	59.8	1.5	3.3	5.3	7.3	9.5	11.8	14.3	16.8	19.2	21.5	23.7	25.7	27.7	29.5	31.2	32.7	
30°				59.5	1.3	3.0	5.0	7.2	9.5	12.0	14.5	17.2	19.7	22.0	24.3	26.3	28.2	30.0	31.7	33.2	
20°				59.3	1.0	2.8	4.8	7.0	9.3	12.0	14.7	17.5	20.2	22.5	24.7	26.7	28.5	30.3	31.8		
10°				59.2	0.8	2.7	4.7	7.0	9.5	12.2	15.0	17.8	20.5	22.8	25.0	27.0	28.8	30.5			
0°				59.3	1.0	2.8	5.0	7.3	9.8	12.7	15.5	18.3	21.0	23.3	25.3	27.3	29.0	30.7			
L. = 570° ϕ = 40°				59.3	1.0	2.8	4.7	6.7	8.8	11.2	13.7	16.0	18.5	20.8	23.0	25.0	27.0	28.8	30.5	32.0	
30°				59.2	0.8	2.5	4.5	6.5	8.8	11.3	13.8	16.3	19.0	21.3	23.7	25.7	27.7	29.3	31.0		
20°				59.2	0.8	2.7	4.7	6.7	9.0	11.7	14.3	17.0	19.7	22.2	24.3	26.3	28.3	30.0	31.7		
10°				59.2	0.8	2.7	4.7	6.8	9.3	12.0	14.8	17.7	20.3	22.7	24.8	26.8	28.7	30.3	32.0		
0°				59.3	1.0	2.8	5.0	7.2	9.7	12.5	15.3	18.2	20.7	23.2	25.3	27.2	29.0	30.7			
L. = 580° ϕ = 40°				58.8	0.5	2.2	4.2	6.2	8.2	10.5	12.8	15.3	17.8	20.2	22.3	24.5	26.5	28.3	30.0	31.7	
30°				58.7	0.3	2.2	4.0	6.2	8.3	10.7	13.2	15.8	18.5	20.8	23.2	25.3	27.2	29.0	30.7		
20°				58.8	0.5	2.3	4.2	6.2	8.5	11.0	13.7	16.5	19.2	21.7	24.0	26.0	27.8	29.7	31.3		
10°				59.0	0.7	2.5	4.3	6.5	9.0	11.5	14.3	17.2	19.8	22.3	24.7	26.7	28.5	30.2			
0°				59.3	1.0	2.8	4.8	7.0	9.5	12.2	15.0	17.8	20.5	23.0	25.2	27.2	29.0	30.7			

TABLE D.

λ + μ.	260°	270°	280°	290°	300°	310°	320°	330°	340°	350°	0°	10°	20°	30°	40°	50°	60°	70°	80°	90°	100°
L. = 590° φ = 40°				58.3	0.0	1.7	3.5	5.5	7.7	9.8	12.2	14.7	17.2	19.5	21.8	24.0	25.8	27.8	29.5		
30°				58.5	0.2	1.8	3.7	5:7	7.8	10.2	12.7	15.3	18.0	20.5	22.7	24.8	26.8	28.7	30.3		
20°				58.5	0.2	1.8	3.7	5.8	8.0	10.5	13.2	15.8	18.7	21.2	23.5	25.7	27.5	29.3	31.0		
10°				58.8	0.5	2.3	4.2	6.3	8.7	11.2	13.8	16.7	19.5	22.0	24.3	26.5	28.3	30.0			
0°				59.3	1.0	2.8	4.7	6.8	9.3	11.8	14.7	17.5	20.3	22.7	25.0	27.2	29.0	30.7			
L. = 600° φ = 40°					59.5	1.2	3.0	5.0	7.0	9.3	11.7	14.2	16.5	19.0	21.3	23.5	25.5	27.3	29.0		
30°					59.7	1.3	3.2	5.2	7.2	9.7	12.2	14.7	17.3	19.8	22.2	24.3	26.3	28.2	30.0		
20°				58.3	0.0	1.7	3.5	5.5	7.7	10.2	12.8	15.7	18.3	21.0	23.3	25.5	27.3	29.2			
10°				58.8	0.5	2.2	4.0	6.0	8.3	11.0	13.7	16.5	19.3	22.0	24.3	26.5	28.3	30.2			
0°				59.3	1.0	2.7	4.7	6.7	9.0	11.7	14.5	17.3	20.2	22.7	25.0	27.2	29.0	30.7			
L. = 610° φ = 40°					58.8	0.7	2.5	4.3	6.3	8.7	11.0	13.5	16.0	18.3	20.7	22.8	24.8	26.8			
30°					59.3	1.0	2.8	4.7	6.8	9.2	11.7	14.3	17.0	19.5	22.0	24.2	26.2	28.0			
20°					59.8	1.5	3.3	5.3	7.5	9.8	12.5	15.3	18.2	20.8	23.2	25.3	27.3	29.2			
10°				58.7	0.3	2.0	3.8	5.8	8.2	10.7	13.3	16.3	19.2	21.8	24.2	26.3	28.3	30.0			
0°				59.3	1.0	2.7	4.5	6.5	8.8	11.5	14.2	17.2	20.0	22.7	25.0	27.2	29.0	30.7			
L. = 620° φ = 40°					58.5	0.2	2.0	3.8	6.0	8.2	10.5	13.0	15.5	18.0	20.3	22.5	24.5	26.5			
30°					59.0	0.7	2.5	4.5	6.5	8.8	11.3	14.0	16.7	19.3	21.7	24.0	26.0	27.8			
20°					59.5	1.2	3.0	4.8	7.2	9.5	12.2	14.8	17.8	20.5	23.0	25.2	27.2	29.0			
10°				58.7	0.2	1.8	3.7	5.7	8.0	10.5	13.3	16.2	19.2	21.8	24.3	26.5	28.3	30.2			
0°				59.2	0.8	2.5	4.3	6.3	8.7	11.3	14.0	17.2	20.0	22.7	25.2	27.2	29.2	30.8			
L. = 630° φ = 40°						59.7	1.5	3.5	5.5	7.8	10.2	12.7	15.3	17.7	20.0	22.3	24.3	26.2			
30°					58.7	0.3	2.2	4.2	6.2	8.7	11.2	13.8	16.5	19.2	21.7	23.8	25.8	27.7			
20°					59.3	1.0	2.7	4.7	7.0	9.3	12.0	15.0	17.8	20.5	22.8	25.2	27.2	29.0			
10°				58.5	0.0	1.7	3.5	5.5	7.8	10.3	13.2	16.0	19.0	21.7	24.2	26.3	28.3	30.2			
0°				59.2	0.7	2.3	4.3	6.3	8.7	11.2	14.0	17.0	20.0	22.5	25.2	27.3	29.2	31.0			
L. = 640° φ = 40°						59.5	1.3	3.3	5.3	7.7	10.2	12.7	15.2	17.7	20.0	22.2	24.3				
30°					58.5	0.2	2.0	4.0	6.2	8.7	11.2	14.0	16.7	19.3	21.8	24.0	26.0	27.8			
20°					59.2	0.8	2.7	4.7	6.8	9.3	12.2	15.0	17.8	20.7	23.0	25.2	27.2	29.0			
10°					0.0	1.7	3.5	5.5	7.8	10.3	13.2	16.3	19.2	22.0	24.3	26.5	28.5	30.3			
0°				59.0	0.7	2.3	4.2	6.2	8.5	11.2	14.2	17.2	20.2	22.8	25.3	27.3	29.3	31.0			
L. = 650° φ = 40°						59.3	1.2	3.2	5.3	7.7	10.2	12.7	15.3	17.8	20.2	22.2	24.2				
30°					58.3	0.0	1.8	3.8	6.0	8.5	11.2	14.0	16.7	19.3	21.7	23.8	25.8				
20°					59.0	0.7	2.5	4.5	6.8	9.3	12.2	15.2	18.2	20.7	23.2	25.3	27.3				
10°					59.8	1.5	3.3	5.3	7.7	10.3	13.2	16.3	19.3	22.0	24.5	26.5	28.5	30.2			
0°				59.0	0.5	2.2	4.2	6.2	8.7	11.2	14.2	17.3	20.5	23.2	25.5	27.5	29.3	31.2			
L. = 660° φ = 40°						59.3	1.2	3.2	5.5	7.8	10.3	13.0	15.5	18.0	20.3	22.3	24.3				
30°					58.3	0.2	2.0	4.0	6.3	8.8	11.5	14.3	17.2	19.7	22.0	24.2	26.2				
20°					59.0	0.7	2.7	4.7	7.0	9.7	12.5	15.5	18.5	21.0	23.5	25.5	27.5				
10°					59.7	1.5	3.3	5.5	7.8	10.5	13.5	16.7	19.7	22.3	24.7	26.7	28.7	30.3			
0°				58.8	0.5	2.2	4.2	6.3	8.5	11.3	14.3	17.5	20.5	23.2	25.5	27.7	29.5	31.2			

TABLE D.

λ + μ.	260°	270°	280°	290°	300°	310°	320°	330°	340°	350°	0°	10°	20°	30°	40°	50°	60°	70°	80°	90°	100°
L. = 670° φ = 40°						59.3	1.3	3.3	5.7	8.2	10.7	13.3	16.0	18.3	20.5	22.7	24.5				
30°					58.3	0.2	2.0	4.2	6.5	9.2	11.8	14.7	17.5	20.0	22.2	24.3	26.2				
20°					59.0	0.8	2.7	5.0	7.3	10.0	13.0	16.0	18.8	21.3	23.7	25.8	27.7				
10°					59.8	1.5	3.5	5.7	8.0	10.8	13.8	17.0	20.0	22.7	24.8	26.8	28.7	30.5			
0°				58.8	0.5	2.2	4.2	6.3	8.7	11.5	14.7	17.8	20.8	23.5	25.7	27.7	29.5	31.2			
L. = 680° φ = 40°						59.8	1.8	3.8	6.2	8.7	11.3	14.0	16.5	18.8	21.0	23.0	24.8				
30°					58.7	0.5	2.5	4.7	7.0	9.7	12.5	15.3	18.0	20.5	22.7	24.7	26.5				
20°					59.2	1.0	3.0	5.2	7.7	10.3	13.3	16.3	19.2	21.7	24.0	26.0	27.8				
10°					59.8	1.5	3.5	5.8	8.3	11.2	14.2	17.3	20.2	22.8	25.0	27.0	28.8				
0°				58.8	0.3	2.2	4.2	6.3	8.8	11.8	15.0	18.2	21.0	23.5	25.8	27.8	29.7	31.2			
L. = 690° φ = 40°					58.3	0.2	2.2	4.5	6.8	9.3	12.0	14.5	17.0	19.3	21.5	23.5					
30°					58.8	0.7	2.7	5.0	7.5	10.2	13.0	15.8	18.3	20.8	23.0	25.0	26.7				
20°					59.3	1.2	3.2	5.5	8.0	10.7	13.8	16.8	19.5	22.0	24.2	26.2	27.8				
10°					59.8	1.7	3.7	6.0	8.5	11.3	14.5	17.7	20.5	23.0	25.2	27.2	28.8				
0°				58.8	0.5	2.2	4.2	6.5	9.0	12.0	15.2	18.3	21.2	23.7	25.8	27.8	29.5	31.2			
L. = 700° φ = 40°					59.0	0.8	2.8	5.2	7.5	10.2	12.7	15.3	17.8	20.0	22.2	24.0	25.8				
30°					59.3	1.2	3.3	5.7	8.2	10.8	13.7	16.5	19.0	21.3	23.5	25.5	27.2				
20°					59.7	1.5	3.5	5.8	8.3	11.3	14.3	17.2	19.8	22.3	24.5	26.3	28.2				
10°				58.5	0.2	2.0	4.0	6.3	8.8	11.8	15.0	18.0	20.8	23.3	25.3	27.2	29.0				
0°				58.8	0.5	2.3	4.3	6.7	9.2	12.2	15.3	18.5	21.3	23.7	25.8	27.8	29.5	31.2			
L. = 710° φ = 40°					59.5	1.3	3.5	5.8	8.2	10.8	13.3	16.0	18.3	20.5	22.7	24.5	26.3				
30°					59.7	1.7	3.7	6.0	8.7	11.3	14.2	16.8	19.5	21.7	23.8	25.7	27.5				
20°					59.8	1.8	3.8	6.2	8.8	11.7	14.7	17.7	20.2	22.7	24.7	26.7	28.3				
10°				58.5	0.2	2.2	4.2	6.5	9.2	12 0	15.2	18.2	21.0	23.3	25.5	27.3	29.2				
0°				58.8	0.5	2.3	4.3	6.8	9.3	12.3	15.5	18.5	21.3	23.7	25.8	27.8	29.5	31.2			
L. = 720° φ = 40°				58.3	0.2	2.2	4.2	6.5	9.0	11.5	14.2	16.7	19.0	21.3	23.3	25.2	26.8				
30°				58.5	0.2	2.2	4.2	6.5	9.2	11.8	14.7	17.3	19.8	22.2	24.3	26.2	27.8				
20°				58.5	0.2	2.0	4.2	6.5	9.2	12.0	15.0	17.8	20.5	22.8	25.0	26.8	28.5				
10°				58.8	0.5	2.3	4.3	6.7	9.3	12.3	15.5	18.3	21.2	23.5	25.7	27.5	29.3				
0°				58.8	0.5	2.3	4.5	6.7	9.3	12.3	15.5	18.5	21.3	23.7	25.8	27.7	29.5	31.2			
L. = 730° φ = 40°				59.0	0.8	2.8	4.8	7.2	9.7	12.2	14.8	17.3	19.7	21.8	23.8	25.7	27.5				
30°				58.8	0.7	2.7	4.7	7.0	9.7	12.3	15.2	17.8	20.3	22.7	24.7	26.5	28.3				
20°				58.8	0.7	2.5	4.7	7.0	9.7	12.5	15.5	18.3	20.8	23.2	25.3	27.2	28.8				
10°				58.8	0.5	2.3	4.5	6.8	9.5	12.3	15.5	18.5	21.2	23.5	25.7	27.5	29.2	30.8			
0°				58.8	0.7	2.5	4.5	6.8	9.5	12.3	15.3	18.5	21.2	23.7	25.8	27.7	29.5	31.2			
L. = 740° φ = 40°				59.8	1.7	3.5	5.7	8.0	10.3	13.0	15.5	18.0	20.3	22.5	24.5	26.3	28.2				
30°				59.3	1.2	3.0	5.2	7.5	10.0	12.7	15.5	18.2	20.7	23.0	25.0	26.8	28.7				
20°				59.2	1.0	2.8	4.8	7.2	9.8	12.7	15.5	18.3	21.0	23.3	25.5	27.3	29.0	30.7			
10°				59.0	0.8	2.7	4.7	7.0	9.7	12.5	15.5	18.5	21.2	23.7	25.7	27.7	29.3	31.0			
0°				59.0	0.7	2.5	4.5	6.8	9.3	12.2	15.3	18.3	21.0	23.5	25.7	27.7	29.3	31.0			

TABLE D.

λ + μ.	260°	270°	280°	290°	300°	310°	320°	330°	340°	350°	0°	10°	20°	30°	40°	50°	60°	70°	80°	90°	100°
L. = 750° φ = 40°			58.7	0.3	2.2	4.2	6.2	8.5	19.8	13.3	16.0	18.5	20.8	23.0	25.2	27.0	28.7	30.3			
30°				59.8	1.7	3.5	5.7	8.0	10.5	13.2	16.0	18.7	21.2	23.3	25.5	27.3	29.2	30.8			
20°				59.3	1.2	3.0	5.0	7.3	10.0	12.7	15.7	18.5	21.2	23.5	25.5	27.5	29.2	30.8			
10°				59.2	0.8	2.7	4.7	7.0	9.7	12.5	15.5	18.3	21.2	23.5	25.7	27.7	29.3	31.0			
0°				59.0	0.7	2 5	4.5	6.8	9.3	12.2	15.2	18.2	21.0	23.5	25.7	27.7	29.3	31.0			
L. = 760° φ = 40°			59.2	0.8	2.7	4.7	6.7	8.8	11.3	13.8	16.3	18.8	21.3	23.5	25.5	27.5	29.2	30.8			
30°			58.7	0.2	2.0	4.0	6.0	8.2	10.7	13.5	16.2	18.8	21.3	23.7	25.8	27.7	29.5	31.2			
20°				59.7	1.5	3.3	5.3	7.5	10.2	13.0	15.8	18.7	21.3	23.7	25.8	27.8	29.5	31.2			
10°				59.3	1.0	2.8	4.8	7.0	9.7	12.5	15.5	18.3	21.2	23.7	25.8	27.8	29.5	31.2			
0°				59.0	0.7	2.5	4.5	6.7	9.2	12.0	15.0	18.0	20.8	23.3	25.5	27.5	29.3	31.0			

ADDITIONS AND CORRECTIONS.

Art. 23, p. 9.

A better description of the saṅkrântis may be given thus. The sâyana Mesha saṅkrânti, also called a Vishuva saṅkrânti, marks the vernal equinox, or the moment of the sun's passing the first point of Aries. The sâyana Karka saṅkrânti, three solar months later, is also called the dakshiṇâyana (southward-going) saṅkrânti. It is the point of the summer solstice, and marks the moment when the sun turns southward. The sâyana Tulâ saṅkrânti, three solar months later, also called a Vishuva saṅkrânti, marks the autumnal equinox or the moment of the sun's passing the first point of Libra. The sâyana Makara saṅkrânti, three solar months later still, is also called the uttarâyana (northward-going) saṅkrânti. It is the other solstitial point, the moment when the sun turns northward. The *nirayana* (or sidereal) Mesha and Tulâ saṅkrântis are also called Vishuva saṅkrântis, and the *nirayana* Karka and Makara saṅkrântis are also, though erroneously, called dakshiṇâyana and uttarâyana saṅkrântis.

Art. 90, p. 52.

Line 6. After "we proceed thus" *add*;—"The interval of time between the initial point of the luni-solar year (*Table I., Cols. 19, 20*) and the initial point of the solar year by the *Sûrya Siddhânta* (*Table I., Cols. 13, 14, and 15a, or 17a*[1]) can be easily found.

Line 9. After "Art. 151" *add*;—"or according to the process in Example 1, Art. 148."

Line 16. After "intercalations and suppressions" *add*;—We will give an example. In Professor Chhatre's Table, Kârttika is intercalary in Śaka 551 expired, A.D. 629—30 (see *Ind. Ant., XXIII.* p. 106); while in our Table Âśvina is the intercalary month for that year. Let us work for Âśvina. First we want the tithi-index (t) for the moments of the Kanyâ and Tulâ saṅkrântis. In the given year we have (*Table I., Col.* 19) the initial point of the luni-solar year at sunrise on 1st March, A.D. 629, (=60), and (*Cols. 13, 17*) the initial point of the solar year by the *Ârya-Siddhânta* (= 17 h. 32 m. after sunrise on March 19th of the same year). By the Table given below (p. 151) we find that the initial moment of the solar year by the *Sûrya Siddhânta* was 15 minutes later than that by the *Ârya Siddhânta*. Thus we have the interval between the initial points of the luni-solar and solar years, according to the *Sûrya Siddhânta*, as 18 days, 17 hours, and 47 minutes. Adding this to the collective duration up to the moment of the Kanyâ and Tulâ saṅkrântis (*Table III., Col. 9*), *i.e.*, 156 days, 11 hours and 52 minutes, and 186 days, 22 hours and 27 minutes respectively, we get 175 days, 5 hours, 39 minutes, and 205 days, 16 hours, 14 minutes.

We work for these moments according to the usual rules (Method C, p. 77).

	a.	*b.*	*c.*
For the beginning of the luni-solar year (*Table I., Cols. 23, 24, 25*)	9994	692	228
For 175 days (*Table IV.*)	9261	351	479
For 5 hours (*Table V.*)	71	8	1
For 39 minutes (*Do.*)	9	1	0
	9335	52	708

[1] Our a, b, c, (*Table I., Cols.* 23, 24, 25) are calculated by the *Sûrya Siddhânta*, and therefore we give the rule for the *Sûrya Siddhânta*. The time of the Mesha saṅkrântis by the *Ârya Siddhânta* from A.D. 1101 to 1900 is given in Table I. That for years from A.D. 300 to 1100 can be obtained from the Table on p. 151.

	a.	b.	c.
over	9335	52	708
Equation for *b* (52) (*Table VI.*)	186		
Do. for *c* (708) (*Table VII.*)	119		
	9640		

Again	*a.*	*b.*	*c.*
For the beginning of the luni-solar year	9994	692	228
For 205 days	9420	440	561
For 16 hours	226	24	2
For 14 minutes	3	0	0
	9643	156	791
Equation for (*b*)	256		
Do. for (*c*)	119		
	18		

This proves that the moon was waning at the Kanyâ saṅkrânti, and waxing at the Tulâ saṅkrânti, and therefore Âśvina was intercalary (*see Art. 45*). This being so, Kârttika could not have been intercalary.

The above constitutes an easy method of working out all the intercalations and suppressions of months. To still further simplify matters we give a Table shewing the saṅkrântis whose moments it is necessary to fix in order to establish these intercalations and suppressions. Equation *c* is always the same at the moment of the saṅkrântis and we give its figure here to save further reference.

Months.	Saṅkrântis to be fixed	Equation *c*.
1.	2.	3.
1. Chaitra	Mîna . . . . . Mesha	3
2. Vaiśâkha	Mesha . . . . Vṛishabha . . .	1
3. Jyeshṭha	Vṛishabha. . . Mithuna	15
4. Âshâḍha	Mithuna . . . Karka	42
5. Śrâvaṇa	Karka . . . . Siṁha	75
6. Bhâdrapada	Siṁha . . . . Kanyâ	103
7. Âśvina	Kanyâ . . . . Tulâ	119
8. Kârttika	Tulâ . . . . . Vṛiśchika . . .	119
9. Mârgaśîrsha	Vṛiśchika . . . Dhanus	104
10. Pausha	Dhanus . . . Makara	78
11. Mâgha	Makara . . . . Kumbha	47
12. Phâlguna	Kumbha . . . Mîna	20

Art. 96, Table, p. 55.

Instead of this Table the following may be used. It shews the difference in time between the Mesha-saṅkrântis as calculated by the *Present Sûrya* and *First Ârya Siddhântas*, and will save the trouble of making any calculation according to the Table in the text. But if great accuracy is required the latter will yield results correct up to 24 seconds, while the new Table gives it in minutes.

TABLE

Shewing time-difference in minutes between the moments of the Mesha saṅkrânti as calculated by the Present Sûrya and First Ârya Siddhântas.

[The sign — shews that the Mesha saṅkranti according to the Sûrya Siddhânta took place before, the sign + that it took place after, that according to the Ârya Siddhânta].

Years A.D.	Diff. in minutes.	Years A.D.	Diff. in minutes.	Years A.D.	Diff. in minutes.	Years A.D.	Diff. in minutes.
	—		+		+		+
300—8	21	501—9	1	703—11	23	904—12	45
309—17	20	510—19	2	712—20	24	913—21	46
318—27	19	520—28	3	721—29	25	922—30	47
328—36	18	529—37	4	730—38	26	931—39	48
337—45	17	538—46	5	739—47	27	940—48	49
346—54	16	547—55	6	748—56	28	949—58	50
355—63	15	556—64	7	757—66	29	959—67	51
364—72	14	565—73	8	767—75	30	968—76	52
373—81	13	574—83	9	776—84	31	977—85	53
382—91	12	584—92	10	785—93	32	986—94	54
392—400	11	593—601	11	794—802	33	995—1003	55
401—9	10	602—10	12	803—11	34	1004—13	56
410—18	9	611—19	13	812—20	35	1014—22	57
419—27	8	620—28	14	821—30	36	1023—31	58
428—36	7	629—38	15	831—39	37	1032—40	59
437—45	6	639—47	16	840—48	38	1041—49	60
446—55	5	648—56	17	849—57	39	1050—58	61
456—64	4	657—65	18	858—66	40	1059—67	62
465—73	3	666—74	19	867—75	41	1068—77	63
474—82	2	675—83	20	876—84	42	1078—86	64
483—91	1	684—92	21	885—94	43	1087—95	65
492—500	0	693—702	22	895—903	44	1096—1104	66

Art. 102, pp. 56, 57.

From the initial figures for the *w. a. b. c.* of luni-solar Kali 3402, A.D. 300—1, given in the first entry in Table I., and the figures given in the Table annexed to this article (which gives the increase in *w. a. b. c.* for the different year-lengths) it is easy to calculate with exactness the initial *w. a. b. c.* for subsequent luni-solar years. Thus—

					(Our entries in Table I.)			
	w.	*a.*	*b.*	*c.*	*w.*	*a.*	*b.*	*c.*
For *Kali* 3402	6	9981·41	895·17	255·93	6	9981	895	256
355 days	5	214·34	883·51	971·91				
For *Kali* 3403	4	195·75	778·68	227·84	4	196	779	228
384 days	5	34·66	935·97	51·31				
For *Kali* 3404	3	230·41	714·65	279·15	3	230	715	279
etc.	etc.	etc.	etc.	etc.	etc.	etc.	etc.	etc.

To ascertain how many days there were in each year it is only necessary to use col. 19 of Table I. with Table IX. Kali 3403 began 26th February. Table IX. gives the figure 57 on left-hand side, and 422 on the right-hand side, the former being entered in our Table I.

But since A.D. 300 was a leap-year we must take, not 422, but 423, as the proper figure. Kali 3402 began 8th March (68). 423—68 = 355, and this in days was the length of Kali 3402. Similarly (17th March) 441 – (26 February) 57 = 384, and this was the length of Kali 3403; and so on.

It may be interesting to note that in every century there are on an average one year of 385 days, four years of 383 days, twenty-three years of 355 days, thirty-two years of 384 days, and forty years of 354 days.

P. 98.

To end of Art. 160, add the following;—"160(a). To find the tropical (sâyana) as well as the sidereal (nirayana) saṅkrânti. Find the time of the nirayana saṅkrânti (*see Art. 23*) required, by adding to the time of the Mesha saṅkrânti for the year (*Table I., Cols. 13 to 17a*) the collective duration of the nirayana saṅkrânti as given in col. 5 of Table III., under head "saṅkrântis." Then, roughly, the sâyana saṅkrânti took place as many ghaṭikâs before or after the nirayana one as there are years between Śaka 445 current, and the year next following or next preceding the given year, respectively.

"For more accurate purposes, however, the following calculation must be made. Find the number of years intervening between Śaka 445 current, or Śaka 422 current in the case of the *Sûrya Siddhânta*, and the given year. Multiply that number by $\frac{1}{60}$, or $\frac{3}{200}$ in the case of the *Sûrya Siddhânta*. Take the product as in ayanâmśas, or the amount of precession in degrees. Multiply the length of the solar month (*Art. 24*) in which the sâyana saṅkrânti occurs (as shewn in the preceding paragraph) by these ayanâmśas and divide by 30. Take the result as days; and by so many days will the sâyana saṅkrânti take place before or after the nirayana saṅkrânti of the same name, according as the given year is after or before Śaka 445 (or Śaka 422). This will be found sufficiently accurate, though it is liable to a maximum error (in A.D. 1900) of 15 ghaṭikâs. The maximum error by the first rule is one day in A.D. 1900. The smaller the distance of the given date from Śaka 445 (or 422) the smaller will be the error. For absolute accuracy special Tables would have to be constructed, and it seems hardly necessary to do this.

The following example will shew the method of work.

Wanted the moment of occurrence of the nirayana Makara saṅkrânti and of the sâyana Makara (or uttarâyana) saṅkrânti in the year Śaka 1000, current.

		d.	*w.*	*h.*	*m.*
Moment of Mesha saṅkrânti *(Table I.)*	March 23	(82)	5	14	52
Add collect. duration to beginning of Makara *(Table III.)*		275	2	15	43
Then the moment of the nirayana Makara saṅkrânti is		358	1	6	35

(One day being added because the hours exceed 24.)
358 = December 24th. 1 = Sunday.

The nirayana Makara saṅkrânti, therefore, occurred on Sunday, December 24th, at 6 h. 35 m. after sunrise. Now for the sâyana Makara saṅkrânti. By the Table given above we find that in the given year the sâyana saṅkrânti took place 9 days, 6 hours before the nirayana saṅkrânti; for A.D. 1000—445 = 555 ghaṭikâs = 9 days 15 gh. = 9 days, 6 hours, and it took place in nirayana Dhanus.

		d.	*w.*	*h.*	*m.*
Moment of nirayana Makara saṅk:	24 Dec. =	358	1	6	35
Deduct	9	9	2	6	0
	15 Dec.	349	6	0	35

This shews that the sâyana Makara saṅkrânti took place on Friday, Dec. 15th, at 35 minutes after sunrise.

(2) For more accurate time we work thus. 1000—445 = 555. Multiplying by $\frac{1}{60}$ we have $9\frac{15}{60}$, or 9° 15′ in ayanâmśas. The length of the month Dhanus is 29 d. 8 h. 24 m. 48 s. *(Table. p. 10).*

$$\frac{29 \text{ d. } 8 \text{ h. } 24 \text{ m. } 48 \text{ s.} \times 9^1/_4}{30} = \overset{d.}{9} \quad \overset{h.}{1} \quad \overset{m.}{11} \quad \overset{s.}{39}$$

We take 11 m. 39 s. as = 12 m., and deduct 9 d. 1 h. 12 m. from the moment of the nirayana Makara saṅkrânti, which we have above.

	d.	*w.*	*h.*	*m.*
24 Dec.	358	1	6	35
9	9	2	1	12
15 Dec.	349	6	5	23

This shews that the sâyana Makara saṅkrânti took place on Dec. 15th at 5 h. 23 m. after sunrise, the day being Friday.[1]

"The following Table may be found useful. It may be appended to Table VIII. and called "Table VIII. C".

[1] Actual calculation by the Arya Siddhânta proves that the sâyana saṅkrânti in question took place only 1 minute after the time so found. [S. B. D.]

Table of Râśis (signs).

[The moments of the saṅkrântis are indicated by the first of the two entries in cols. 2 and 3. Thus the moment of the Siṁha saṅkrânti is shewn by *s.* = 3333, degrees = 120°.]

Râśis (signs.)	S. (See Arts. 133 and 156.)	Degrees.	Nakshatras forming the Râśis.
1	2	3	4
1. Mesha	0—833	0°—30°	1. Aśvinî; 2. Bharaṇî; 3. First quarter of Kṛittikâ.
2. Vṛishabha	833—1667	30°—60°	3. Last three quarters of Kṛittikâ; 4. Rohinî; 5. First half of Mṛigaśiras.
3. Mithuna	1667—2500	60°—90°	5. Latter half of Mṛigaśiras; 6. Ârdrâ; 7. First three quarters of Punarvasu.
4. Karka	2500—3333	90°—120°	7. Last quarter of Punarvasu; 8. Pushya; 9. Aśleshâ.
5. Siṁha	3333—4167	120°—150°	10. Maghâ; 11. Pûrva-Phalgunî; 12. First quarter of Uttara-Phalgunî.
6. Kanyâ	4167—5000	150°—180°	12. Last three quarters of Uttara-Phalgunî; 13. Hasta; 14. First half of Chitrâ.
7. Tulâ	5000 - 5833	180°—210°	14. Second half of Chitrâ; 15. Svâti; 16. First three quarters of Viśâkhâ.
8. Vṛiśchikâ	5833—6667	210°—240°	16. Last quarter of Viśâkhâ; 17. Anurâdhâ; 18 Jyeshṭhâ.
9. Dhanus	6667—7500	240°—270°	19. Mulâ; 20. Pûrva-Ashâḍhâ; 21. First quarter of Uttara-Ashâḍhâ.
10. Makara	7500—8333	270°—300°	21. Last three quarters of Uttara-Ashâḍhâ; 22. Śravaṇa; 23. First half of Dhanishṭhâ (or Śravishṭhâ.)
11. Kumbha	8333—9167	300°—330°	24. Second half of Dhanishṭhâ (or Śravishṭhâ); 24. Śatatâraka (or Satabhishaj), 25. First three quarters of Pûrva Bhadrapadâ.
12. Mîna	9167—10000	330°—360°	25. Last quarter of Pûrva Bhadrapadâ; 25. Uttara-Bhadrapadâ; 27. Revatî.

"160(*b*). The following is a summary of points to be remembered in calculating and verifying dates. The list, however, is not exhaustive.

A. A luni-solar date may be interpreted as follows:—

(I.) With reference to current and expired years, and to amânta and pûrṇimânta months.

(A) When the year of the given era is Chaitrâdi.

(*a*) For dates in bright fortnights, two possible cases; (i.) expired year, (ii.) current year.

(*b*) For dates in dark fortnights, four possible cases; viz., expired year, or current year, according to both the pûrṇimânta and amânta system of months.

(B) When the year is both Chaitrâdi and non-Chaitrâdi.

(*a*) For dates in bright fortnights, three possible cases; viz., (1) Chaitrâdi year current, (2) Chaitrâdi year expired = non-Chaitrâdi year current, (3) non-Chaitrâdi year expired.

(*b*) Dates in dark fortnights, six possible cases; viz., the same three years according to both the pûrṇimânta and amânta system of months.

For months which are common to Chaitrâdi and non-Chaitrâdi years, the cases will be as in (A).

(II.) With reference to the tithi.

All the above cases, supposing the tithi was current, (1) at the given time as well as at sunrise of the given day, (2) for the given time of the day, but not at its sunrise.

B. A solar date may be interpreted as follows:—

(I.) With reference to current and expired years.

(A) When the year of the given era is Meshâdi, two possible cases; (*a*) expired year, (*b*) current year.

(B) When the year of the given era is both Meshâdi and non-Meshâdi, three possible cases; (*a*) Meshâdi year current, (*b*) Meshâdi year expired = non-Meshâdi year current, (*c*) non-Meshâdi year expired.

(II.) With reference to the civil beginning of the month, all the cases in Art. 28.

C. When the era of a date is not known, all known possible eras should be tried.

D. (*a*) According to Hindu Astronomy a tithi of a bright or dark fortnight of a month never stands at sunrise on the same week-day more than once in three consecutive years. For instance, if Chaitra śukla pratipadâ stands at sunrise on a Sunday in one year, it cannot stand at sunrise on Sunday in the year next preceding or next following.

(*b*) It can only, in one very rare case, end on the same week-day in two consecutive years, and that is when there are thirteen lunar months between the first and second. There are only seven instances [1] of it in the 1600 years from A.D. 300 to 1900.

(*c*) It cannot end on the same week-day more than twice in three consecutive years.

(*d*) But a tithi can be connected with the same week-day for two consecutive years if there is a confusion of systems in the naming of the civil day, naming, that is, not only by the tithi current at sunrise, but also by the tithi current during any time of that day. Even this, however, can only take place when there are thirteen lunar months between the two. If, for instance, Chaitra śukla 1st be current during, though not at sunrise on, a Sunday in one year; next year, if an added month intervenes, it may stand at sunrise on a Sunday, and consequently it may be connected with a Sunday in both these (consecutive) years.

(*e*) A tithi of an amânta month of one year may end on the same week-day as it did in the pûrṇimânta month of the same name during the preceding year.

(*f*) The interval between the week-days connected with a tithi in two consecutive years, when there are 12 months between them, is generally four, and sometimes five; but when thirteen lunar months intervene, the interval is generally one of six week-days. For instance, if Chaitra śukla 1st ends on Sunday (= 1) in one year, it ends next year generally on (1 + 4 = 5 =) Thursday. and sometimes on (1 + 5 = 6 =) Friday, provided there is no added month between the two. If there is an added month it will probably end on (1 + 6 = 0 =) Saturday.

(*g*) According to Hindu Astronomy the minimum length of a lunar month is 29 days, 20 ghaṭikâs, and the maximum 29 days and 43 ghaṭikâs. Hence the interval between the week-days of a tithi in two consecutive months is generally one or two. If, for instance, Chaitra śukla pratipadâ falls on a Sunday, then Vaiśâkha śukla pratipadâ may end on Monday or Tuesday. But by the existence of the two systems of naming a civil day from the tithi current at its sunrise, as well as by that current at any time in the day, this interval may sometimes be increased to three, and we may find Vaiśâkha śukla pratipadâ, in the above example, connected with a Wednesday.

E. (*a*) A saṅkrânti cannot occur on the same week-day for at least the four years preceding and four following.

(*b*) See Art. 119, par. 3.

160 (*c*) *To find the apparent longitude of Jupiter. (See Art. 63, p. 37, and Table XII.)*

I. To find, first, the mean longitude of Jupiter and the sun.

(i.) Find the mean longitude of Jupiter at the time of the Mesha saṅkrânti by the following Table W. That of the sun is 0° at that moment.

(ii.) Add the śodhya (Art. 26, p. 11, Art. 90, p. 52) given in the following Table Y to

[1] They are A.D. 440—1; 776—7; 838—9, 857—8; 1183—4; 1264—5; 1581—2.

the time of the apparent Mesha saṅkrânti (as given in Table I., cols. 13 to 17, or 17*a*). The sum is the moment of the mean Mesha saṅkrânti. Find the interval in days, ghaṭikâs, and palas between this and the given time (for which Jupiter's place is to be calculated). Calculate the mean motion of Jupiter during the interval by Table Y below, and add it to the mean longitude at the moment of mean Mesha saṅkrânti. The sum is the mean place of Jupiter at the given moment. The motion of the sun during the interval (Table Y) is the sun's mean place at the given moment.

II. To find, secondly, the apparent longitude.

(i.) Subtract the sun's mean longitude from that of Jupiter. Call the remainder the "first commutation". If it be more than six signs, subtract it from twelve signs, and use the remainder. With this argument find the parallax by Table Z below. Parallax is *minus* when the commutation is not more than six signs, *plus* when it is more than six. Apply half the parallax to the mean longitude of Jupiter, and subtract from the sum the longitude of Jupiter's aphelion, as given at the bottom of Table Z below. The remainder is the anomaly. (If this is more than six signs, subtract it from twelve signs, as before, and use the remainder.) With this argument find the equation of the centre[1] by Table Z. This is minus or plus according as the anomaly is 0 to 6, or 6 to 12 signs. Apply it to the mean longitude of Jupiter, and the result is the heliocentric longitude.

(ii.) Apply the equation of the centre (plus or minus) to the first commutation; the sum is the "second commutation". If it is more than six signs, use, as before, the difference between it and twelve signs. With this second commutation as argument find the parallax as before. Apply it (whole) to Jupiter's heliocentric longitude, and the result is Jupiter's apparent longitude.

Example. We have a date in an inscription.—"In the year opposite Kollam year 389, Jupiter being in Kumbha, and the sun 18 days old in Mîna, Thursday, 10th lunar day of Pushya."[2]

Calculating by our method "C" in the Text, we find that the date corresponds to Śaka 1138 current, Chaitra śukla daśamî (10th), Pushya nakshatra, the 18th day of the solar month Mîna of Kollam 390 of our Tables, or March 12th, A.D. 1215.[3]

To find the place of Jupiter on the given day.

					gh.	*pa.*
Apparent Mesha saṅk. in Śaka 1137 (*Table I., Cols. 13—15*)	25 Mar.	(84)	Tues.	(3)	3	32
Add śodhya (*Table Y*)	2	2		2	8	51
	27 Mar.	(86)	Tues.	(5)	12	23
The given date is Śaka 1138	12 Mar.	(436)				
		(350)				

350, then, is the interval from mean Mesha saṅkrânti to 12 gh. 23 pa. on the given day. The interval between Śaka 1 current and Śaka 1137 current is 1136 years.

[1] Neglecting the minutes and seconds of anomaly, the equation may be taken for degrees. Thus, if the anomaly is 149° 7′ 49″, the equation may be taken for 149°. If it were 149° 31′ 12″, take the equation for 150°. And so in the case of commutation. For greater accuracy the equation and parallax may be found by proportion.

[2] *Indian Antiquary*, XXIV., p. 307, date No. XI.

[3] The year 389 in the original seems to be the expired year. There are instances in which the word "opposite" is so used and I am inclined to think that the word used for "opposite" is used to denote "expired" (*gata*). The phrase "18 days old" is used to shew the 18th day of the solar month. [S. B. D.)

		JUPITER.				SUN.			
		Sign	°	′	″	Sign	°	′	″
Śaka 1 *(Table W)*		0	9	0	29				
Years	1000	3	22	0	0				
„	100	5	5	12	0				
„	30	6	10	33	36				
„	6	6	2	6	43				
At mean Mesha saṅk:		9	18	52	48				
Days *(Table Y)*	300		24	55	44	9	25	40	51
„	50		4	9	17	1	19	16	48
Mean long: on the given day		10	17	57	49	11	14	57	39
Deduct Sun's mean longitude from that of Jupiter		11	14	57	39				
		11	3	0	10	= first commutation.			

(Note that there are 30 degrees to a sign, and only 12 signs.)

As this is more than six signs we deduct it from 12 signs. Remainder, signs 0, 26° 59′ 50″. Call this 27°.

Parallax for 27° *(see Table Z)* = 4° 20′.

	Sign	°	′	″
Mean longitude of Jupiter *(above)*	10	17	57	49
Add half the parallax		2	10	
	10	20	7	49
Subtract longitude of Jupiter's aphelion *(bottom of Table Z)*	6	0	0	0
Anomaly	4	20	7	49

4 signs, 20 degrees = 140 degrees. Equation of centre for argument 140° = *(Table Z)* 3° 25′. Deducting this from Jupiter's mean longitude found above (10s. 17° 57′ 49″) we have 10s. 14° 32′ 49″ = Jupiter's heliocentric longitude; and deducting it from the first commutation (11s. 3° 0′ 10″) we have, as second commutation, 10s. 29° 35′ 10″. Remainder from 12 signs, 1s. 0° 24′ 50″. Parallax for 1 sign, or 30°, *(Table Z)* = 4° 49′. Applying this (adding because the commutation is over 6 signs) to the heliocentric longitude of Jupiter we have (10s. 14° 32′ 49″ + 4° 49′ =) 10s. 19° 21′ 49″ as the apparent (true) longitude of Jupiter.

From this we know that Jupiter was in the 11th sign, Kumbha, on the given date.

TABLE W.

[For finding the mean place of Jupiter. Argument = number of years between Śaka 1 and the given Śaka year.]

Constant. (Mean longitude at mean Mesha Saṅkrânti in Śaka 1 current.)	Signs	°	′	″
Sûrya Siddhânta	0	7	56	54
First Arya Do.	0	9	0	29
Sûrya Siddhânta with bîja	0	5	49	4

No. of years.	Sûrya Siddhânta				First Arya Siddhânta				Sûrya Siddhânta with bîja			
	Signs	Degrees	Mins.	Secs.	S.	°	′	″	S.	°	′	″
1	1	0	21	6	1	0	21	7	1	0	21	4
2	2	0	42	12	2	0	42	14	2	0	42	7
3	3	1	3	18	3	1	3	22	3	1	3	11
4	4	1	24	24	4	1	24	29	4	1	24	14
5	5	1	45	30	5	1	45	36	5	1	45	18
6	6	2	6	36	6	2	6	43	6	2	6	22
7	7	2	27	42	7	2	27	50	7	2	27	25
8	8	2	48	48	8	2	48	59	8	2	48	29
9	9	3	9	54	9	3	10	5	9	3	9	32
10	10	3	31	0	10	3	31	12	10	3	30	36
20	8	7	2	0	8	7	2	24	8	7	1	12
30	6	10	33	0	6	10	23	36	6	10	31	48
40	4	14	4	0	4	14	4	48	4	14	2	24
50	2	17	35	0	2	17	36	0	2	17	33	0
60	0	21	6	0	0	21	7	12	0	21	3	36
70	10	14	37	0	10	24	38	24	10	24	34	12
80	8	28	8	0	8	28	9	36	8	28	4	48
90	7	1	39	0	7	1	40	48	7	1	35	24
100	5	5	10	0	5	5	12	0	5	5	6	0
200	10	10	20	0	10	10	24	0	10	10	12	0
300	3	15	30	0	3	15	36	0	3	15	18	0
400	8	20	40	0	8	20	48	0	8	20	24	0
500	1	25	50	0	1	26	0	0	1	25	30	0
600	7	1	0	0	7	1	12	0	7	0	36	0
700	0	6	10	0	0	6	24	0	0	5	42	0
800	5	11	20	0	5	11	36	0	5	10	48	0
900	10	16	30	0	10	16	48	0	10	15	54	0
1000	3	21	40	0	3	22	0	0	3	21	0	0
2000	7	13	20	0	7	14	0	0	7	12	0	0
3000	11	5	0	0	11	6	0	0	11	3	0	0

TABLE V.

[Mean motion of Jupiter and Sun. Argument = number of days (ghaṭikâs and palas) between mean Mesha saṅkrânti and the given moment.]

(This is applicable to all the Siddhántas).

No. of days.	Jupiter.				Sun.			
	s.	°	′	″	s.	°	′	″
1	0	0	4	59	0	0	59	8
2	0	0	9	58	0	1	58	16
3	0	0	14	57	0	2	57	25
4	0	0	19	57	0	3	56	33
5	0	0	24	56	0	4	55	41
6	0	0	29	55	0	5	54	49
7	0	0	34	54	0	6	53	57
8	0	0	39	53	0	7	53	5
9	0	0	44	52	0	8	52	14
10	0	0	49	51	0	9	51	22
20	0	1	39	43	0	19	42	43
30	0	2	29	34	0	29	34	5
40	0	3	19	26	1	9	25	27
50	0	4	9	17	1	19	16	48
60	0	4	59	7	1	29	8	10
70	0	5	49	0	2	8	59	32
80	0	6	38	52	2	18	50	54
90	0	7	28	43	2	28	42	15
100	0	8	18	35	3	8	33	37
200	0	16	37	9	6	17	7	14
300	0	24	55	44	9	25	40	51

		d.	*gh.*	*pa.*
Śodhya =	Sûrya Siddhânta	2	10	14
	Ârya Siddhânta	2	8	51

Motion for ghaṭikâs = as many minutes and seconds as there are degrees and minutes for the same number of days. Motion for palas = as many seconds as there are degrees for the same number of days.

Example. The motion of Jupiter in four ghaṭikâs is $19\frac{57''}{60}$, or (say) 20 seconds. The motion of the Sun in five palas is $4\frac{55''}{60}$, or (say) 5 seconds.

TABLE Z.

[For Equation of centre, Argument = Jupiter's anomaly.

For Parallax, Argument = commutation.]

Argument in degrees.	Parallax.		Equation of centre.		Argument in degrees.	Parallax.		Equation of centre.		Argument in degrees.	Parallax.		Equation of centre.	
	°	′	°	′		°	′	°	′		°	′	°	′
1	0	10	0	5	25	4	2	2	7	49	7	33	3	45
2	0	19	0	10	26	4	11	2	11	50	7	41	3	48
3	0	29	0	15	27	4	20	2	15	51	7	48	3	52
4	0	38	0	21	28	4	30	2	20	52	7	56	3	56
5	0	48	0	26	29	4	39	2	24	53	8	4	3	59
6	0	58	0	31	30	4	49	2	29	54	8	12	4	2
7	1	8	0	37	31	4	59	2	33	55	8	20	4	5
8	1	18	0	42	32	5	7	2	38	56	8	27	4	8
9	1	27	0	47	33	5	17	2	42	57	8	34	4	11
10	1	37	0	52	34	5	26	2	47	58	8	41	4	14
11	1	47	0	57	35	5	34	2	51	59	8	48	4	17
12	1	57	1	2	36	5	43	2	55	60	8	55	4	20
13	2	7	1	7	37	5	52	2	58	61	9	1	4	22
14	2	16	1	12	38	6	1	3	4	62	9	8	4	25
15	2	26	1	17	39	6	9	3	8	63	9	14	4	27
16	2	36	1	22	40	6	18	3	12	64	9	21	4	30
17	2	46	1	27	41	6	26	3	16	65	9	28	4	32
18	2	55	1	32	42	6	35	3	20	66	9	34	4	35
19	3	4	1	37	43	6	44	3	23	67	9	40	4	37
20	3	14	1	42	44	6	52	3	27	68	9	45	4	39
21	3	24	1	47	45	7	0	3	31	69	9	49	4	41
22	3	33	1	52	46	7	8	3	35	70	9	54	4	43
23	3	42	1	57	47	7	17	3	38	71	9	59	4	45
24	3	52	2	1	48	7	25	3	42	72	10	4	4	47

Longitude of the Aphelion of Jupiter, by Sûrya Siddhânta = 5 signs 21 degrees
„ „ „ „ „ „ „ Ârya Siddhânta = 6 „ 0 „

Argument in degrees.	Parallax.		Equation of centre.		Argument in degrees.	Parallax.		Equation of centre.		Argument in degrees.	Parallax.		Equation of centre.	
	°	′	°	′		°	′	°	′		°	′	°	′
73	10	9	4	49	109	11	25	4	54	145	7	41	3	4
74	10	14	4	51	110	11	24	4	52	146	7	31	3	0
75	10	19	4	52	111	11	22	4	50	147	7	19	2	55
76	10	24	4	54	112	11	19	4	49	148	7	8	2	50
77	10	28	4	55	113	11	16	4	47	149	6	57	2	46
78	10	33	4	56	114	11	13	4	45	150	6	46	2	41
79	10	37	4	57	115	11	10	4	43	151	6	34	2	36
80	10	41	4	59	116	11	6	4	41	152	6	23	2	31
81	10	46	5	0	117	11	2	4	38	153	6	11	2	27
82	10	50	5	1	118	10	59	4	36	154	5	59	2	22
83	10	54	5	1	119	10	55	4	34	155	5	47	2	17
84	10	58	5	2	120	10	51	4	31	156	5	34	2	12
85	11	1	5	3	121	10	46	4	29	157	5	21	2	7
86	11	4	5	4	122	10	41	4	26	158	5	8	2	2
87	11	7	5	4	123	10	36	4	23	159	4	55	1	57
88	11	10	5	5	124	10	31	4	21	160	4	42	1	51
89	11	13	5	5	125	10	25	4	18	161	4	29	1	46
90	11	16	5	5	126	10	19	4	15	162	4	16	1	41
91	11	19	5	6	127	10	13	4	12	163	4	2	1	35
92	11	22	5	6	128	10	7	4	9	164	3	48	1	30
93	11	25	5	6	129	10	1	4	6	165	3	34	1	24
94	11	27	5	6	130	9	54	4	3	166	3	20	1	19
95	11	28	5	6	131	9	47	3	59	167	3	6	1	13
96	11	29	5	5	132	9	39	3	55	168	2	52	1	8
97	11	30	5	5	133	9	32	3	52	169	2	38	1	2
98	11	30	5	4	134	9	25	3	49	170	2	24	0	57
99	11	30	5	4	135	9	17	3	45	171	2	10	0	51
100	11	31	5	3	136	9	9	3	41	172	1	55	0	45
101	11	31	5	3	137	9	0	3	37	173	1	41	0	40
102	11	31	5	2	138	8	51	3	33	174	1	27	0	34
103	11	30	5	1	139	8	41	3	29	175	1	13	0	29
104	11	30	5	0	140	8	32	3	25	176	0	59	0	24
105	11	29	4	59	141	8	22	3	21	177	0	44	0	18
106	11	28	4	58	142	8	12	3	17	178	0	29	0	12
107	11	27	4	57	143	8	2	3	13	179	0	15	0	6
108	11	26	4	55	144	7	52	3	8	180	0	0	0	0

INDEX.